THE SUPERMAN CHRONICLES

VOLUME ONE

SUPERMAN CREATED BY JERRY SIEGEL & JOE SHUSTER

All stories written by Jerry Siegel and illustrated by Joe Shuster.

** SUPERMAN #1 reprinted Superman stories from ACTION COMICS #1-4. Since they are shown earlier in this volume, they are not repeated here. Only the original material from SUPERMAN #1 is represented.

* These stories were originally untitled and are titled here for reader convenience.

Dan DiDio SENIOR VP- EXECUTIVE EDITOR ☆ Anton Kawasaki EDITOR-COLLECTED EDITION ☆ Robbin Brosterman SENIOR ART DIRECTOR
Louis Prandi ART DIRECTOR ☆ Paul Levitz PRESIDENT & PUBLISHER ☆ Georg Brewer VP-DESIGN & DC DIRECT CREATIVE
Richard Bruning SENIOR VP-CREATIVE DIRECTOR ☆ Patrick Caldon EXECUTIVE VP-FINANCE & OPERATIONS ☆ Chris Caramalis VP-FINANCE
John Cunningham VP-MARKETING ☆ Terri Cunningham VP-MANAGING EDITOR ☆ Stephanie Fierman SENIOR VP-SALES & MARKETING
Alison Gill VP-MANUFACTURING ☆ Rich Johnson VP-BOOK TRADE SALES ☆ Hank Kanalz VP-GENERAL MANAGER, WILDSTORM
Lillian Laserson SENIOR VP & GENERAL COUNSEL ☆ Jim Lee EDITORIAL DIRECTOR-WILDSTORM ☆ Paula Lowitt SENIOR VP-BUSINESS & LEGAL AFFAIRS
David McKillips VP-ADVERTISING & CUSTOM PUBLISHING ☆ John Nee VP-BUSINESS DEVELOPMENT ☆ Gregory Noveck SENIOR VP-CREATIVE AFFAIRS
Cheryl Rubin SENIOR VP-BRAND MANAGEMENT ☆ Jeff Trojan VP-BUSINESS DEVELOPMENT, DC DIRECT ☆ Bob Wayne VP-SALES

DC Comics, 1700 Broadway, New York, NY 10019

A Warner Bros. Entertainment Company
Printed by World Color Press, Inc., Dubuque, IA, USA. 5/5/10
Second Printing.
ISBN-13: 978-1-4012-0764-9
Cover art by Joe Shuster

Black and white reconstruction by Rick Keene and Pure Imagination.
Color reconstruction by Bob Le Rose and Daniel Vozzo.

SUSTAINABLE
FORESTRY
INITIATIVE

Certified Fiber Sourcing
www.sfiprogram.org

Fiber used in this product line meets the
sourcing requirements of the SFI program
www.sfiprogram.org PWC-SFICOC-260

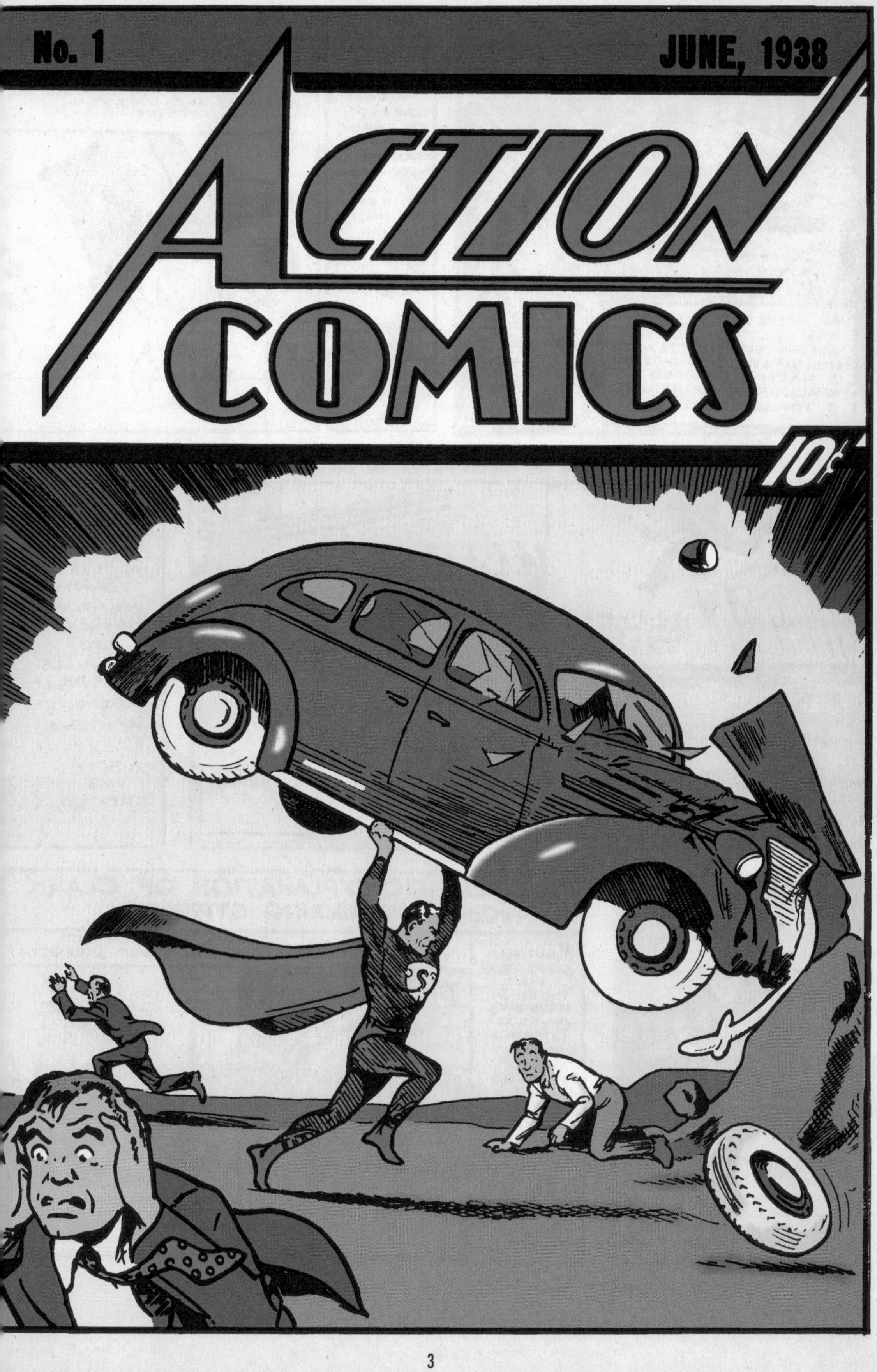
No. 1
JUNE, 1938
ACTION
COMICS
10¢

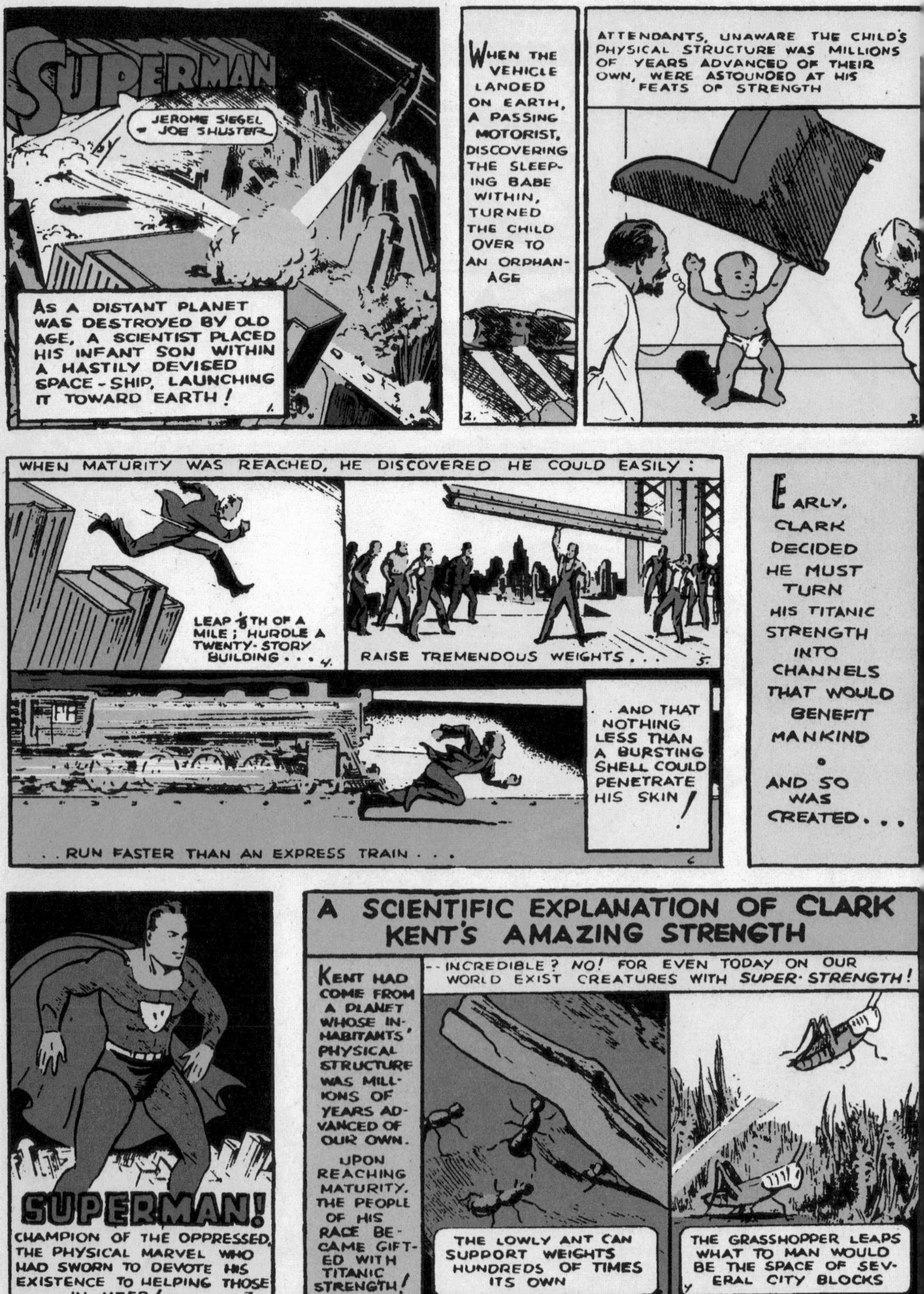
SUPERMAN
by JEROME SIEGEL - JOE SHUSTER
AS A DISTANT PLANET WAS DESTROYED BY OLD AGE, A SCIENTIST PLACED HIS INFANT SON WITHIN A HASTILY DEVISED SPACE-SHIP, LAUNCHING IT TOWARD EARTH!
WHEN THE VEHICLE LANDED ON EARTH, A PASSING MOTORIST, DISCOVERING THE SLEEPING BABE WITHIN, TURNED THE CHILD OVER TO AN ORPHANAGE
ATTENDANTS, UNAWARE THE CHILD'S PHYSICAL STRUCTURE WAS MILLIONS OF YEARS ADVANCED OF THEIR OWN, WERE ASTOUNDED AT HIS FEATS OF STRENGTH
WHEN MATURITY WAS REACHED, HE DISCOVERED HE COULD EASILY:
LEAP 1/8TH OF A MILE; HURDLE A TWENTY-STORY BUILDING . . .
RAISE TREMENDOUS WEIGHTS . . .
. . RUN FASTER THAN AN EXPRESS TRAIN . . .
. . AND THAT NOTHING LESS THAN A BURSTING SHELL COULD PENETRATE HIS SKIN!
EARLY, CLARK DECIDED HE MUST TURN HIS TITANIC STRENGTH INTO CHANNELS THAT WOULD BENEFIT MANKIND
AND SO WAS CREATED . . .
SUPERMAN!
CHAMPION OF THE OPPRESSED, THE PHYSICAL MARVEL WHO HAD SWORN TO DEVOTE HIS EXISTENCE TO HELPING THOSE IN NEED!
A SCIENTIFIC EXPLANATION OF CLARK KENT'S AMAZING STRENGTH
KENT HAD COME FROM A PLANET WHOSE INHABITANTS' PHYSICAL STRUCTURE WAS MILLIONS OF YEARS ADVANCED OF OUR OWN.
UPON REACHING MATURITY, THE PEOPLE OF HIS RACE BECAME GIFTED WITH TITANIC STRENGTH!
-- INCREDIBLE? NO! FOR EVEN TODAY ON OUR WORLD EXIST CREATURES WITH SUPER-STRENGTH!
THE LOWLY ANT CAN SUPPORT WEIGHTS HUNDREDS OF TIMES ITS OWN
THE GRASSHOPPER LEAPS WHAT TO MAN WOULD BE THE SPACE OF SEVERAL CITY BLOCKS

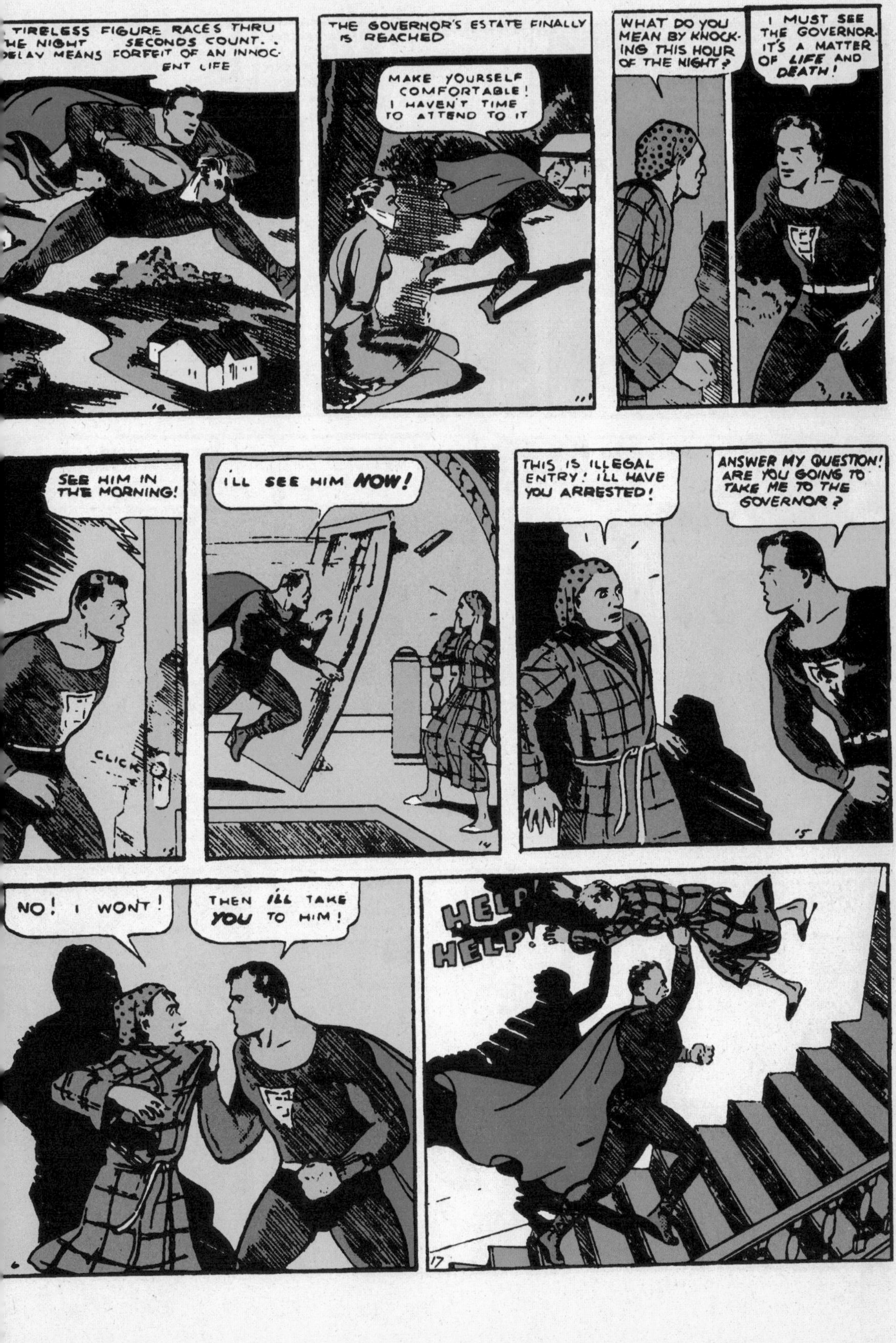
TIRELESS FIGURE RACES THRU THE NIGHT SECONDS COUNT. . DELAY MEANS FORFEIT OF AN INNOCENT LIFE
THE GOVERNOR'S ESTATE FINALLY IS REACHED
MAKE YOURSELF COMFORTABLE! I HAVEN'T TIME TO ATTEND TO IT
WHAT DO YOU MEAN BY KNOCKING THIS HOUR OF THE NIGHT?
I MUST SEE THE GOVERNOR. IT'S A MATTER OF LIFE AND DEATH!
SEE HIM IN THE MORNING!
CLICK
I'LL SEE HIM NOW!
THIS IS ILLEGAL ENTRY! I'LL HAVE YOU ARRESTED!
ANSWER MY QUESTION! ARE YOU GOING TO TAKE ME TO THE GOVERNOR?
NO! I WONT!
THEN I'LL TAKE YOU TO HIM!
HELP! HELP!

YES, THIS IS THE GOVERNOR'S SLEEPING ROOM. — DON'T THINK YOU'RE GOING TO GET AWAY WITH THIS OUTRAGE!

IT'S LOCKED!

YES! AND MADE OF STEEL! TRY AND KNOCK THIS DOOR DOWN!'

IT WAS YOUR IDEA!

WHAT'S THE MEANING OF THIS?

EVELYN CURRY IS TO BE ELECTROCUTED IN 15 MINUTES FOR MURDER. I HAVE PROOF HERE OF HER INNOCENCE— A SIGNED CONFESSION!

BELIEVING THE GOVERNOR MENACED BY A MADMAN, THE BUTLER PRODUCES A CONCEALED WEAPON!

REACH FOR THE CEILING, QUICK!

PUT THAT TOY AWAY!

I WARN YOU! TAKE ANOTHER STEP AND I SHOOT!

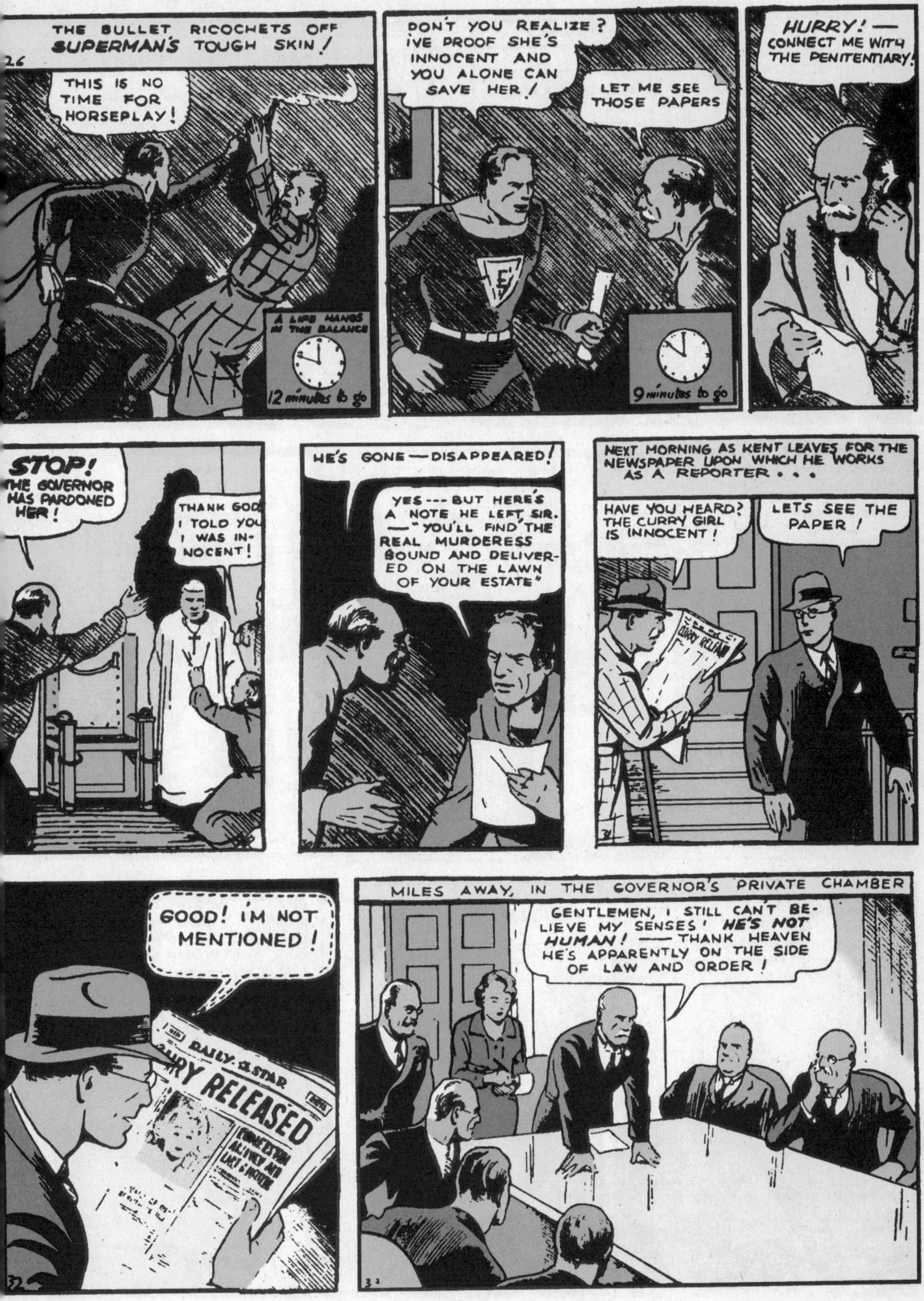
THE BULLET RICOCHETS OFF SUPERMAN'S TOUGH SKIN!
THIS IS NO TIME FOR HORSEPLAY!
A LIFE HANGS IN THE BALANCE
12 minutes to go
DON'T YOU REALIZE? I'VE PROOF SHE'S INNOCENT AND YOU ALONE CAN SAVE HER!
LET ME SEE THOSE PAPERS
9 minutes to go
HURRY! — CONNECT ME WITH THE PENITENTIARY!
STOP! THE GOVERNOR HAS PARDONED HER!
THANK GOD! I TOLD YOU I WAS INNOCENT!
HE'S GONE — DISAPPEARED!
YES --- BUT HERE'S A NOTE HE LEFT, SIR. — "YOU'LL FIND THE REAL MURDERESS BOUND AND DELIVERED ON THE LAWN OF YOUR ESTATE"
NEXT MORNING AS KENT LEAVES FOR THE NEWSPAPER UPON WHICH HE WORKS AS A REPORTER . . .
HAVE YOU HEARD? THE CURRY GIRL IS INNOCENT!
LETS SEE THE PAPER!
GOOD! I'M NOT MENTIONED!
DAILY STAR
RY RELEASED
MILES AWAY, IN THE GOVERNOR'S PRIVATE CHAMBER
GENTLEMEN, I STILL CAN'T BELIEVE MY SENSES! HE'S NOT HUMAN! — THANK HEAVEN HE'S APPARENTLY ON THE SIDE OF LAW AND ORDER!

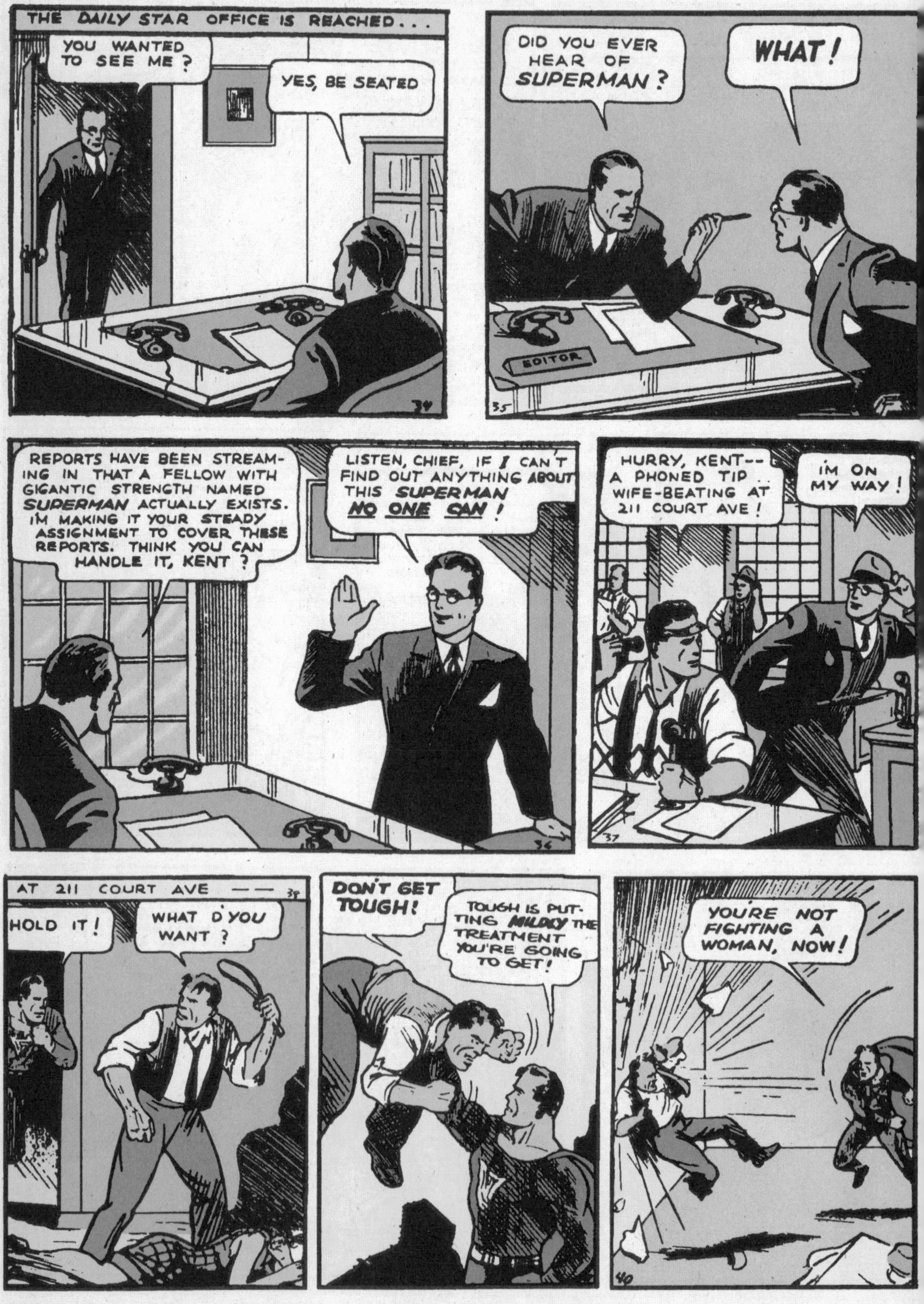
THE DAILY STAR OFFICE IS REACHED...
YOU WANTED TO SEE ME?
YES, BE SEATED
DID YOU EVER HEAR OF SUPERMAN?
WHAT!
EDITOR
REPORTS HAVE BEEN STREAMING IN THAT A FELLOW WITH GIGANTIC STRENGTH NAMED SUPERMAN ACTUALLY EXISTS. I'M MAKING IT YOUR STEADY ASSIGNMENT TO COVER THESE REPORTS. THINK YOU CAN HANDLE IT, KENT?
LISTEN, CHIEF, IF I CAN'T FIND OUT ANYTHING ABOUT THIS SUPERMAN NO ONE CAN!
HURRY, KENT-- A PHONED TIP.. WIFE-BEATING AT 211 COURT AVE!
I'M ON MY WAY!
AT 211 COURT AVE --
HOLD IT!
WHAT D'YOU WANT?
DON'T GET TOUGH!
TOUGH IS PUTTING MILDLY THE TREATMENT YOU'RE GOING TO GET!
YOU'RE NOT FIGHTING A WOMAN, NOW!

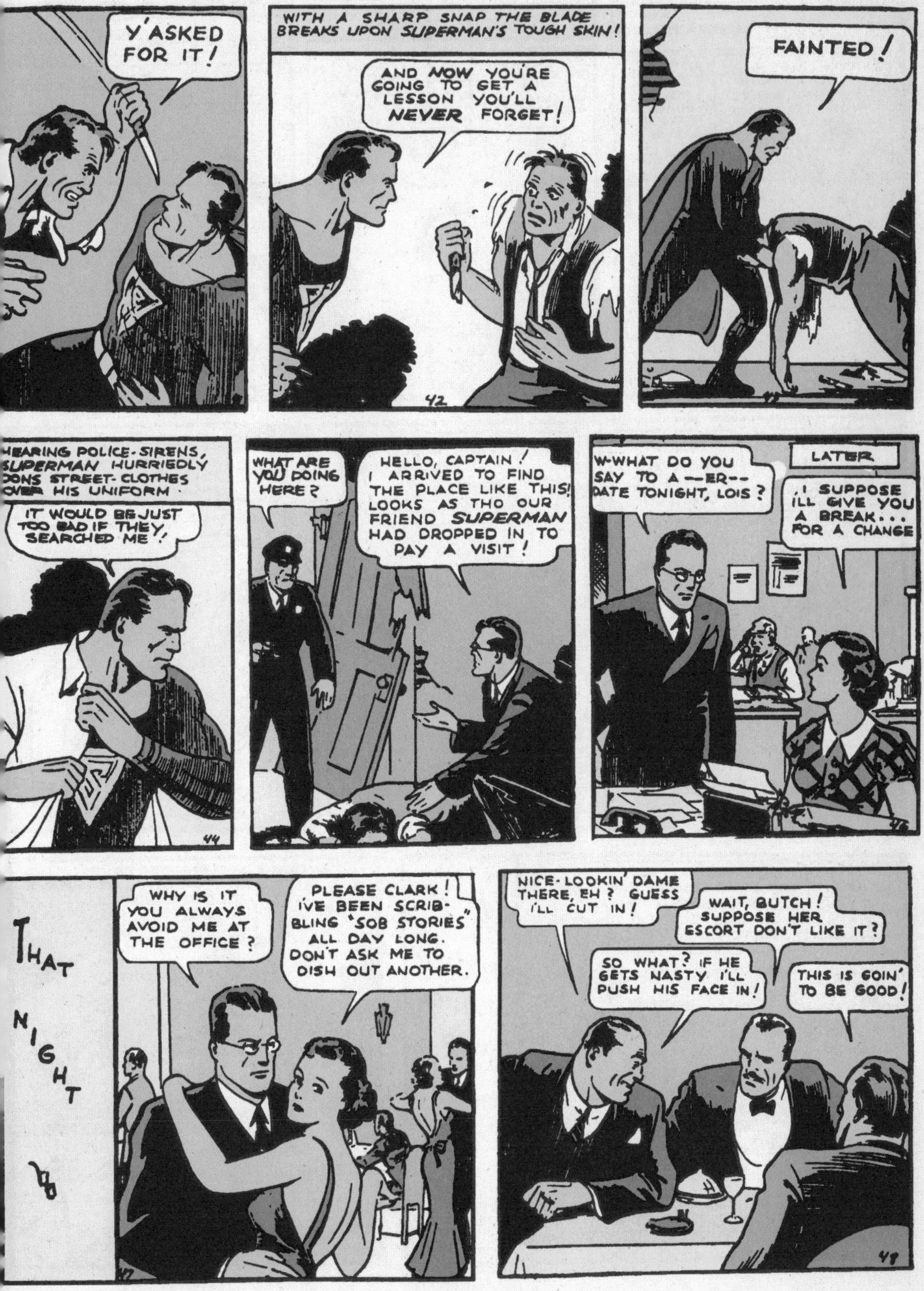
Y'ASKED FOR IT!
WITH A SHARP SNAP THE BLADE BREAKS UPON SUPERMAN'S TOUGH SKIN!
AND NOW YOU'RE GOING TO GET A LESSON YOU'LL NEVER FORGET!
FAINTED!
HEARING POLICE-SIRENS, SUPERMAN HURRIEDLY DONS STREET-CLOTHES OVER HIS UNIFORM.
IT WOULD BE JUST TOO BAD IF THEY SEARCHED ME!
WHAT ARE YOU DOING HERE?
HELLO, CAPTAIN! I ARRIVED TO FIND THE PLACE LIKE THIS! LOOKS AS THO OUR FRIEND SUPERMAN HAD DROPPED IN TO PAY A VISIT!
W-WHAT DO YOU SAY TO A --ER-- DATE TONIGHT, LOIS?
LATER
I SUPPOSE I'LL GIVE YOU A BREAK... FOR A CHANGE
THAT NIGHT
WHY IS IT YOU ALWAYS AVOID ME AT THE OFFICE?
PLEASE CLARK! I'VE BEEN SCRIBBLING "SOB STORIES" ALL DAY LONG. DON'T ASK ME TO DISH OUT ANOTHER.
NICE-LOOKIN' DAME THERE, EH? GUESS I'LL CUT IN!
WAIT, BUTCH! SUPPOSE HER ESCORT DON'T LIKE IT?
SO WHAT? IF HE GETS NASTY I'LL PUSH HIS FACE IN!
THIS IS GOIN' TO BE GOOD!

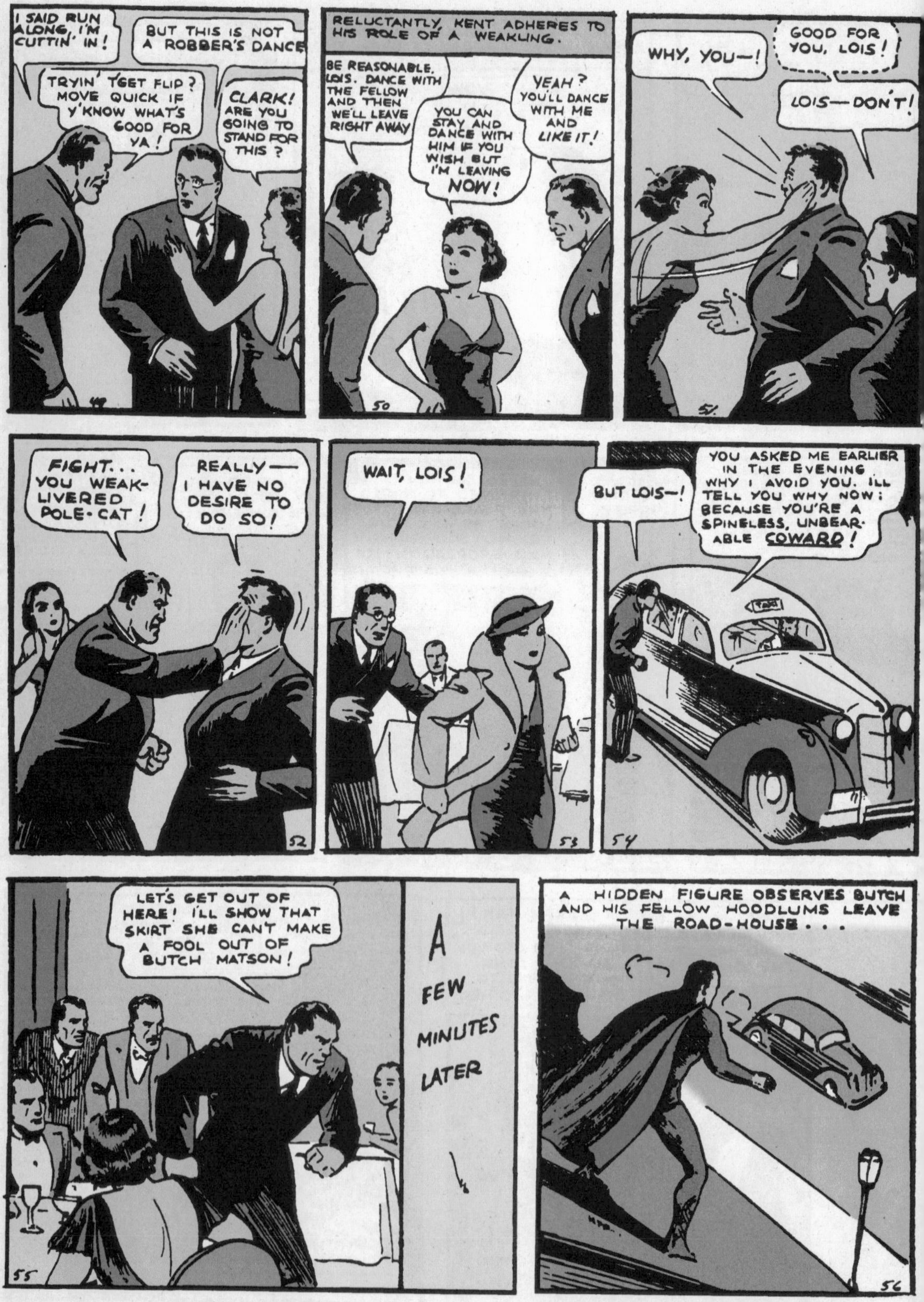
I SAID RUN ALONG, I'M CUTTIN' IN!
BUT THIS IS NOT A ROBBER'S DANCE
TRYIN' T'GET FLIP? MOVE QUICK IF Y'KNOW WHAT'S GOOD FOR YA!
CLARK! ARE YOU GOING TO STAND FOR THIS?
RELUCTANTLY, KENT ADHERES TO HIS ROLE OF A WEAKLING.
BE REASONABLE, LOIS. DANCE WITH THE FELLOW AND THEN WE'LL LEAVE RIGHT AWAY
YOU CAN STAY AND DANCE WITH HIM IF YOU WISH BUT I'M LEAVING NOW!
YEAH? YOU'LL DANCE WITH ME AND LIKE IT!
WHY, YOU—!
GOOD FOR YOU, LOIS!
LOIS—DON'T!
FIGHT... YOU WEAK-LIVERED POLE-CAT!
REALLY— I HAVE NO DESIRE TO DO SO!
WAIT, LOIS!
BUT LOIS—!
YOU ASKED ME EARLIER IN THE EVENING WHY I AVOID YOU. I'LL TELL YOU WHY NOW: BECAUSE YOU'RE A SPINELESS, UNBEARABLE COWARD!
TAXI
LET'S GET OUT OF HERE! I'LL SHOW THAT SKIRT SHE CAN'T MAKE A FOOL OUT OF BUTCH MATSON!
A FEW MINUTES LATER
A HIDDEN FIGURE OBSERVES BUTCH AND HIS FELLOW HOODLUMS LEAVE THE ROAD-HOUSE...

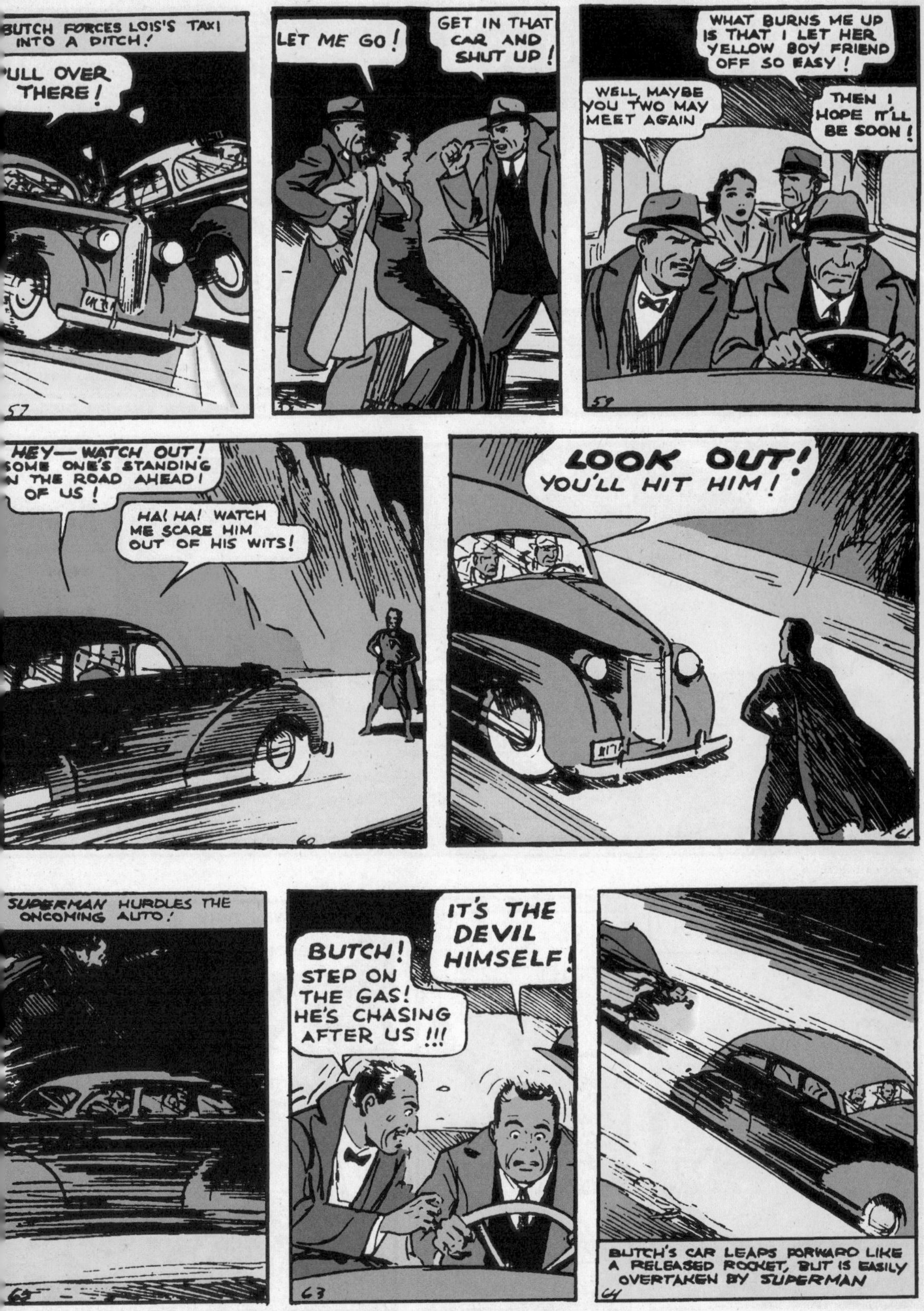
BUTCH FORCES LOIS'S TAXI INTO A DITCH!
ULL OVER THERE!
LET ME GO!
GET IN THAT CAR AND SHUT UP!
WHAT BURNS ME UP IS THAT I LET HER YELLOW BOY FRIEND OFF SO EASY!
WELL, MAYBE YOU TWO MAY MEET AGAIN
THEN I HOPE IT'LL BE SOON!
HEY—WATCH OUT! OME ONE'S STANDING N THE ROAD AHEAD! OF US!
HA! HA! WATCH ME SCARE HIM OUT OF HIS WITS!
LOOK OUT! YOU'LL HIT HIM!
SUPERMAN HURDLES THE ONCOMING AUTO!
BUTCH! STEP ON THE GAS! HE'S CHASING AFTER US !!!
IT'S THE DEVIL HIMSELF!
BUTCH'S CAR LEAPS FORWARD LIKE A RELEASED ROCKET, BUT IS EASILY OVERTAKEN BY SUPERMAN

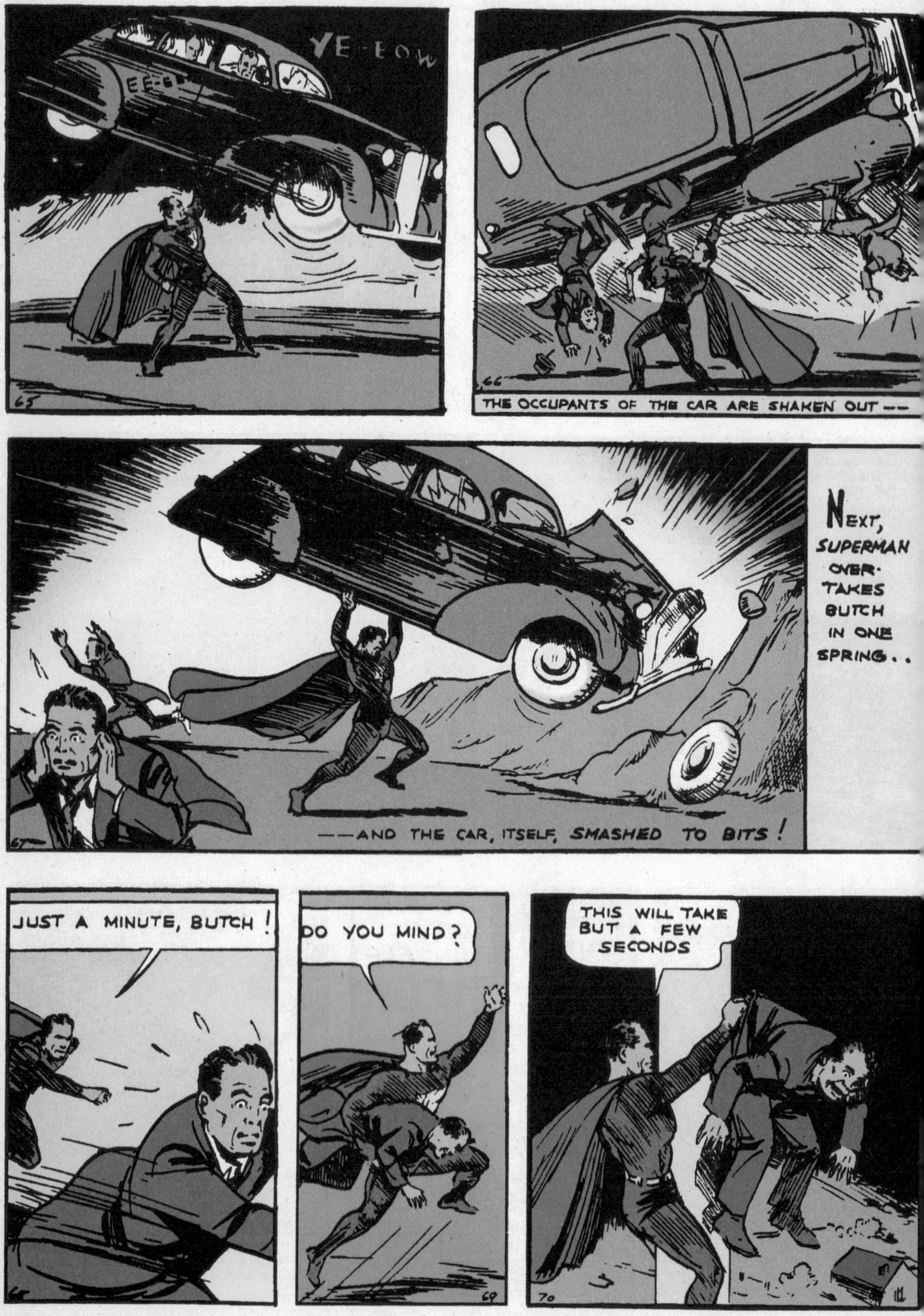
YE-EOW
THE OCCUPANTS OF THE CAR ARE SHAKEN OUT ——
——AND THE CAR, ITSELF, SMASHED TO BITS!
NEXT, SUPERMAN OVER-TAKES BUTCH IN ONE SPRING..
JUST A MINUTE, BUTCH!
DO YOU MIND?
THIS WILL TAKE BUT A FEW SECONDS

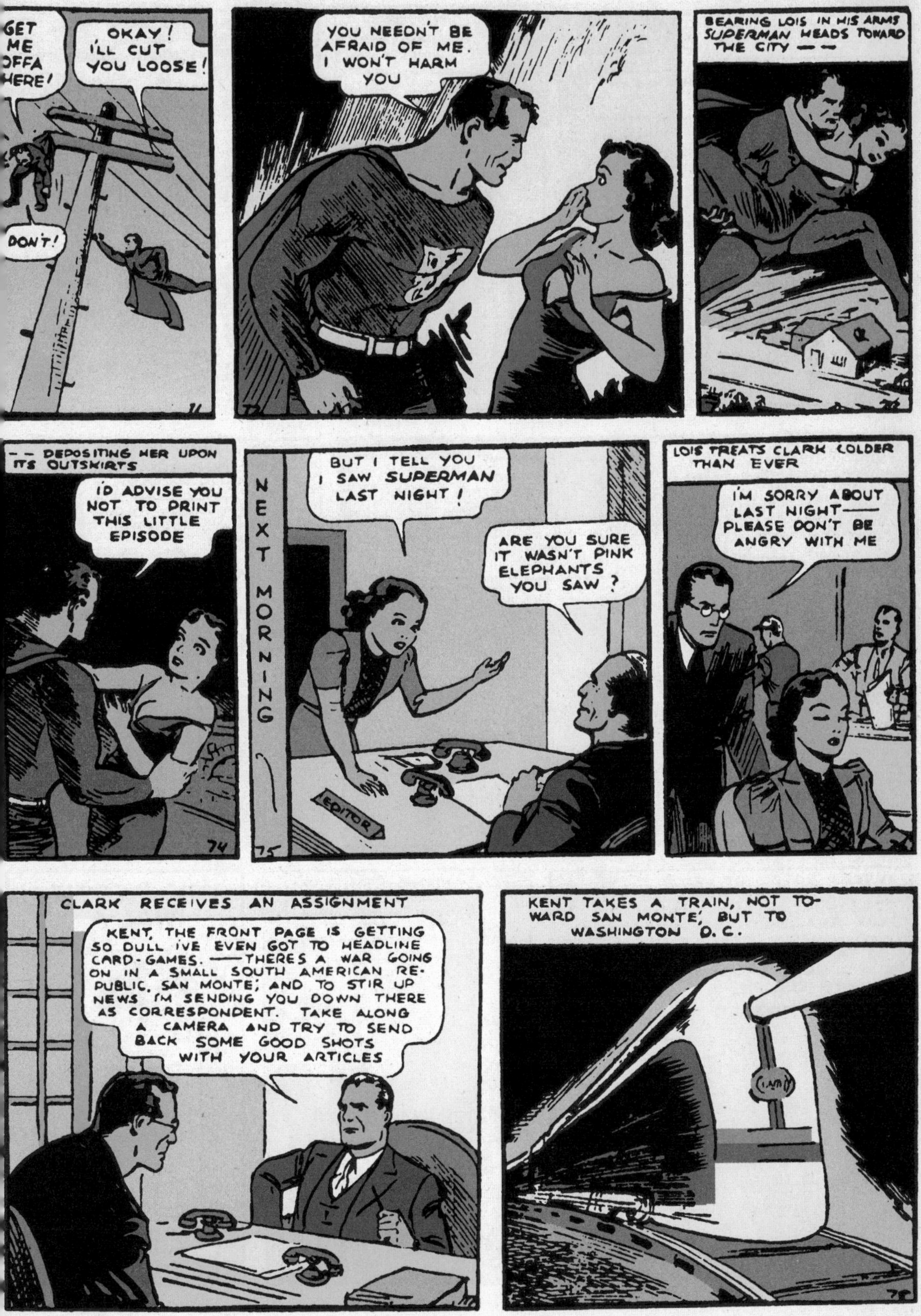
GET ME OFFA HERE!
OKAY! I'LL CUT YOU LOOSE!
DON'T!
YOU NEEDN'T BE AFRAID OF ME. I WON'T HARM YOU
BEARING LOIS IN HIS ARMS SUPERMAN HEADS TOWARD THE CITY — —
— — DEPOSITING HER UPON ITS OUTSKIRTS
I'D ADVISE YOU NOT TO PRINT THIS LITTLE EPISODE
NEXT MORNING
BUT I TELL YOU I SAW SUPERMAN LAST NIGHT!
ARE YOU SURE IT WASN'T PINK ELEPHANTS YOU SAW?
EDITOR
LOIS TREATS CLARK COLDER THAN EVER
I'M SORRY ABOUT LAST NIGHT—— PLEASE DON'T BE ANGRY WITH ME
CLARK RECEIVES AN ASSIGNMENT
KENT, THE FRONT PAGE IS GETTING SO DULL I'VE EVEN GOT TO HEADLINE CARD-GAMES. ——THERES A WAR GOING ON IN A SMALL SOUTH AMERICAN REPUBLIC, SAN MONTE; AND TO STIR UP NEWS I'M SENDING YOU DOWN THERE AS CORRESPONDENT. TAKE ALONG A CAMERA AND TRY TO SEND BACK SOME GOOD SHOTS WITH YOUR ARTICLES
KENT TAKES A TRAIN, NOT TOWARD SAN MONTE, BUT TO WASHINGTON D.C.

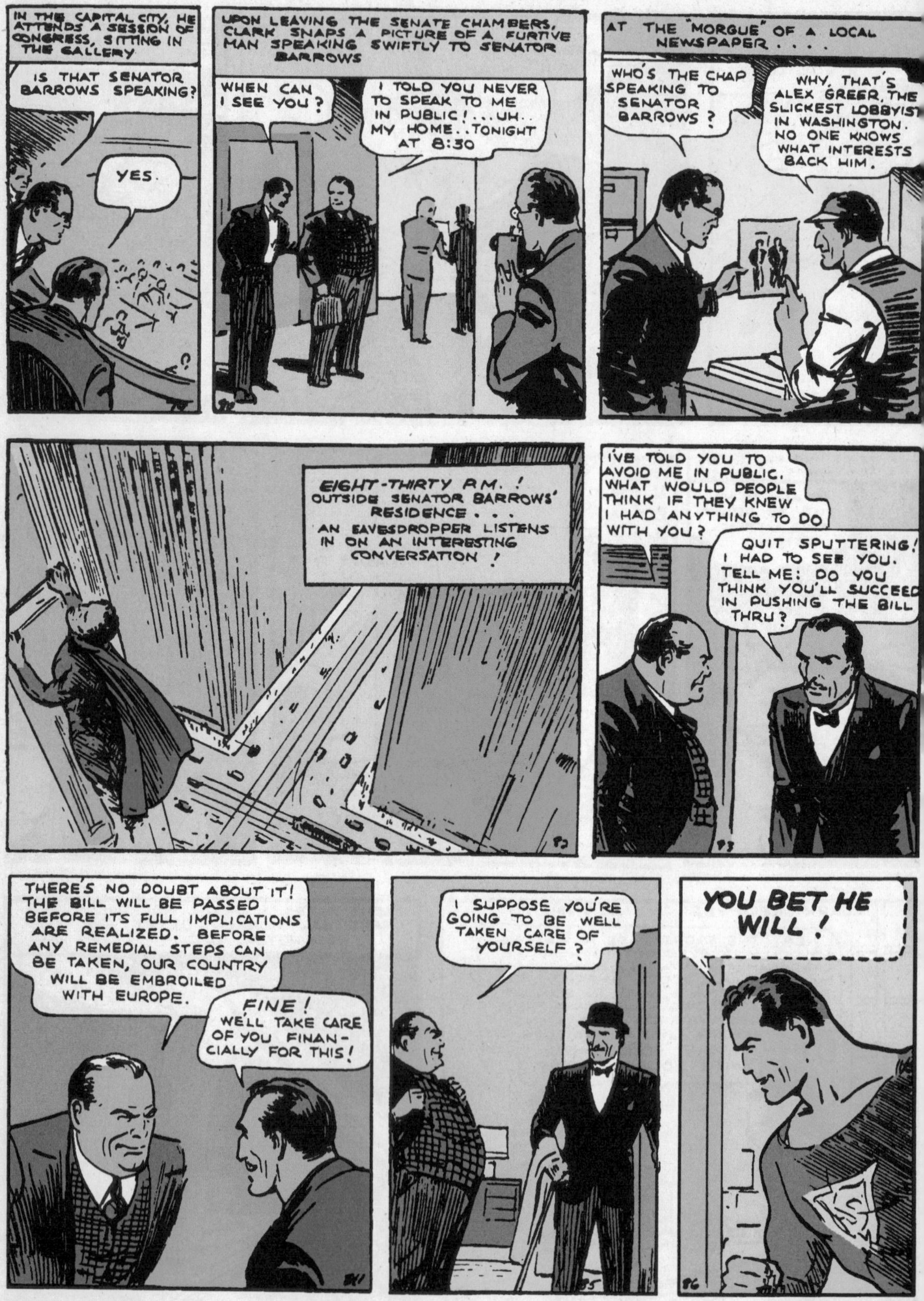

IN THE CAPITAL CITY, HE ATTENDS A SESSION OF CONGRESS, SITTING IN THE GALLERY
IS THAT SENATOR BARROWS SPEAKING?
YES.
UPON LEAVING THE SENATE CHAMBERS, CLARK SNAPS A PICTURE OF A FURTIVE MAN SPEAKING SWIFTLY TO SENATOR BARROWS
WHEN CAN I SEE YOU?
I TOLD YOU NEVER TO SPEAK TO ME IN PUBLIC!...UH.. MY HOME..TONIGHT AT 8:30
AT THE "MORGUE" OF A LOCAL NEWSPAPER....
WHO'S THE CHAP SPEAKING TO SENATOR BARROWS?
WHY, THAT'S ALEX GREER, THE SLICKEST LOBBYIST IN WASHINGTON. NO ONE KNOWS WHAT INTERESTS BACK HIM.
EIGHT-THIRTY P.M.! OUTSIDE SENATOR BARROWS' RESIDENCE... AN EAVESDROPPER LISTENS IN ON AN INTERESTING CONVERSATION!
I'VE TOLD YOU TO AVOID ME IN PUBLIC. WHAT WOULD PEOPLE THINK IF THEY KNEW I HAD ANYTHING TO DO WITH YOU?
QUIT SPUTTERING! I HAD TO SEE YOU. TELL ME: DO YOU THINK YOU'LL SUCCEED IN PUSHING THE BILL THRU?
THERE'S NO DOUBT ABOUT IT! THE BILL WILL BE PASSED BEFORE ITS FULL IMPLICATIONS ARE REALIZED. BEFORE ANY REMEDIAL STEPS CAN BE TAKEN, OUR COUNTRY WILL BE EMBROILED WITH EUROPE.
FINE! WE'LL TAKE CARE OF YOU FINANCIALLY FOR THIS!
I SUPPOSE YOU'RE GOING TO BE WELL TAKEN CARE OF YOURSELF?
YOU BET HE WILL!

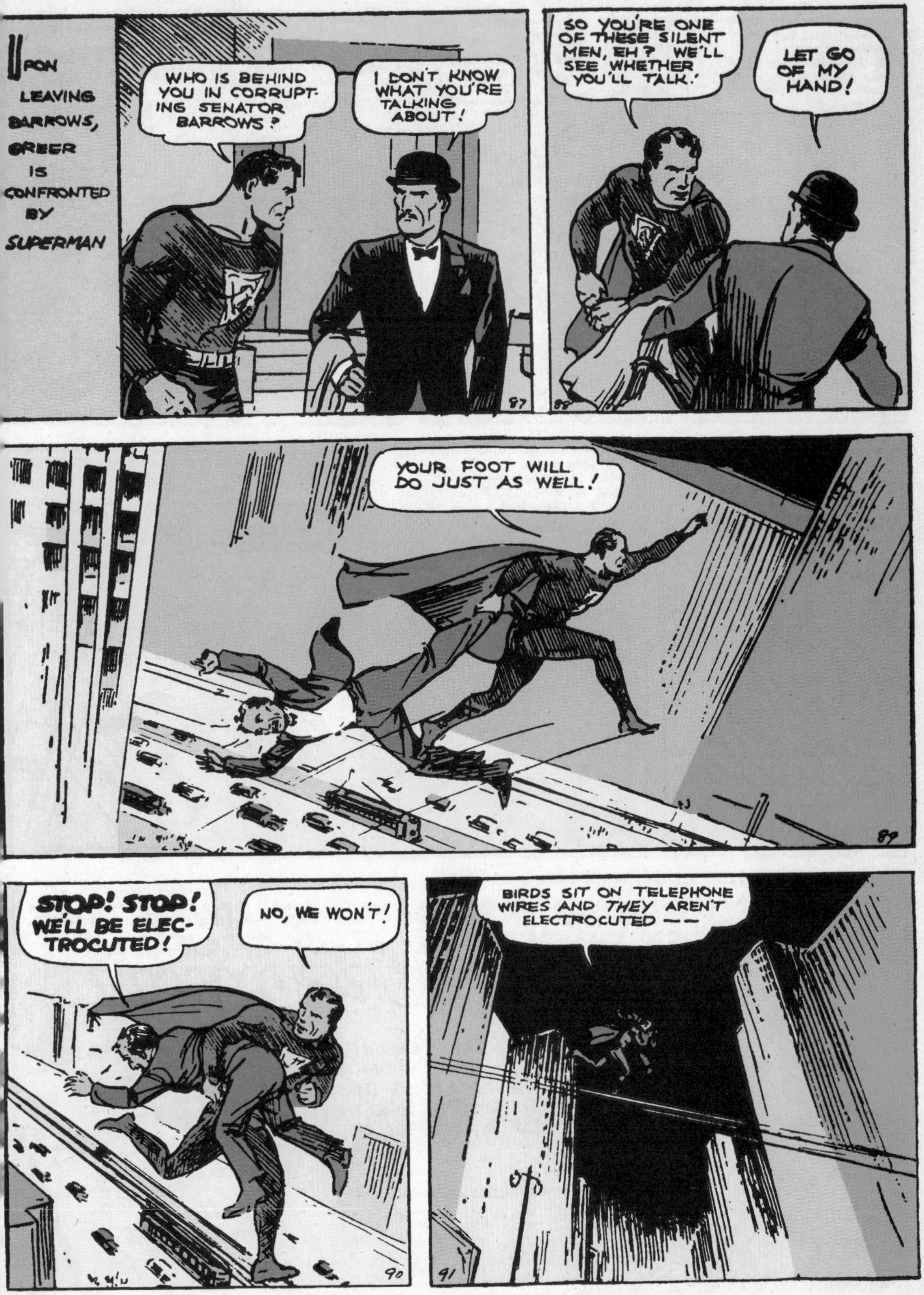
UPON LEAVING BARROWS, GREER IS CONFRONTED BY SUPERMAN
WHO IS BEHIND YOU IN CORRUPTING SENATOR BARROWS?
I DON'T KNOW WHAT YOU'RE TALKING ABOUT!
87
SO YOU'RE ONE OF THESE SILENT MEN, EH? WE'LL SEE WHETHER YOU'LL TALK.'
LET GO OF MY HAND!
88
YOUR FOOT WILL DO JUST AS WELL!
89
STOP! STOP! WE'LL BE ELECTROCUTED!
NO, WE WON'T!
90
BIRDS SIT ON TELEPHONE WIRES AND THEY AREN'T ELECTROCUTED --
91

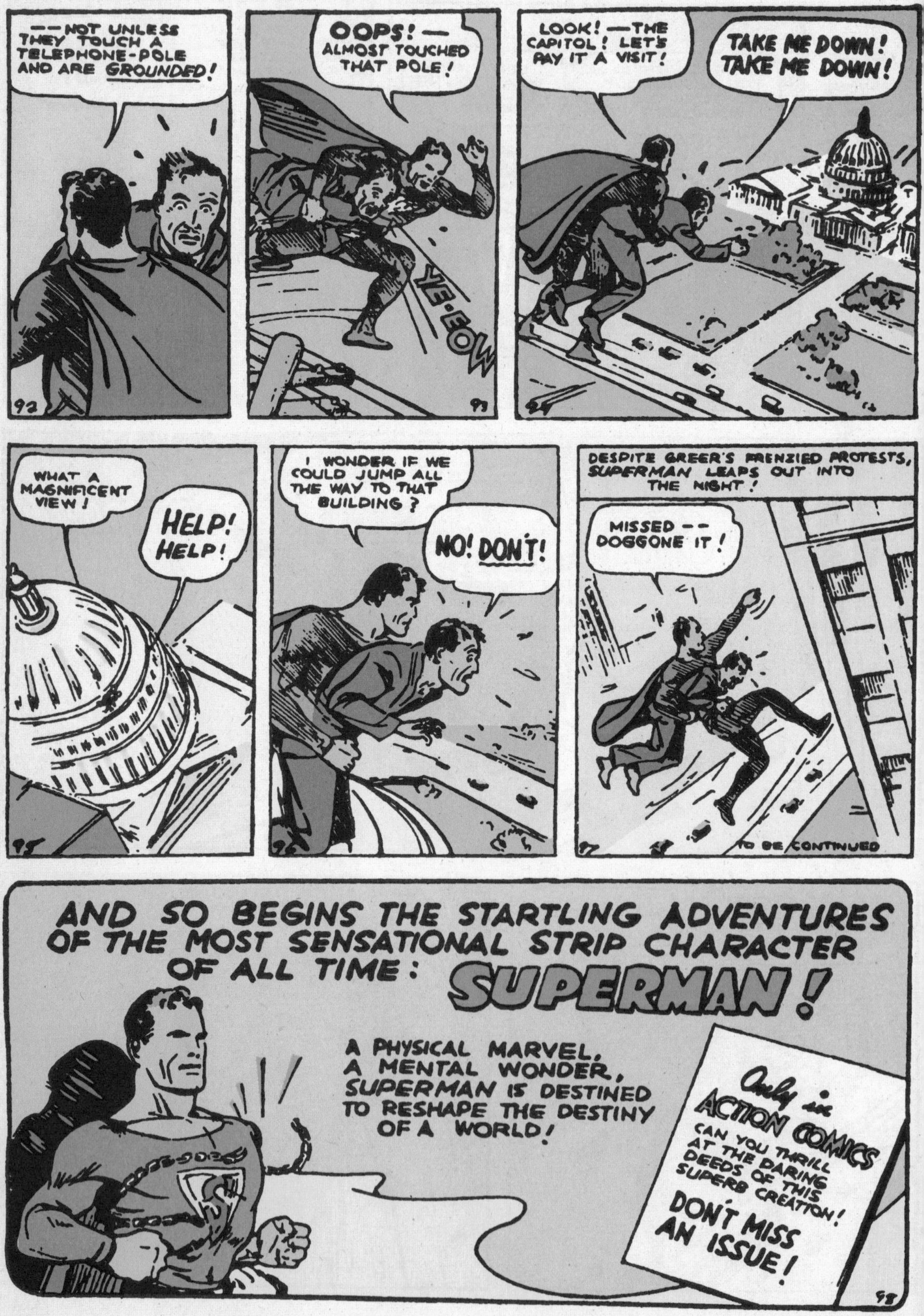
--NOT UNLESS THEY TOUCH A TELEPHONE-POLE AND ARE GROUNDED!
OOPS!— ALMOST TOUCHED THAT POLE!
YE-EOW
LOOK!—THE CAPITOL! LET'S PAY IT A VISIT!
TAKE ME DOWN! TAKE ME DOWN!
WHAT A MAGNIFICENT VIEW!
HELP! HELP!
I WONDER IF WE COULD JUMP ALL THE WAY TO THAT BUILDING?
NO! DON'T!
DESPITE GREER'S FRENZIED PROTESTS, SUPERMAN LEAPS OUT INTO THE NIGHT!
MISSED -- DOGGONE IT!
TO BE CONTINUED
AND SO BEGINS THE STARTLING ADVENTURES OF THE MOST SENSATIONAL STRIP CHARACTER OF ALL TIME: SUPERMAN!
A PHYSICAL MARVEL, A MENTAL WONDER, SUPERMAN IS DESTINED TO RESHAPE THE DESTINY OF A WORLD!
Only in ACTION COMICS
CAN YOU THRILL AT THE DARING DEEDS OF THIS SUPERB CREATION!
DON'T MISS AN ISSUE!

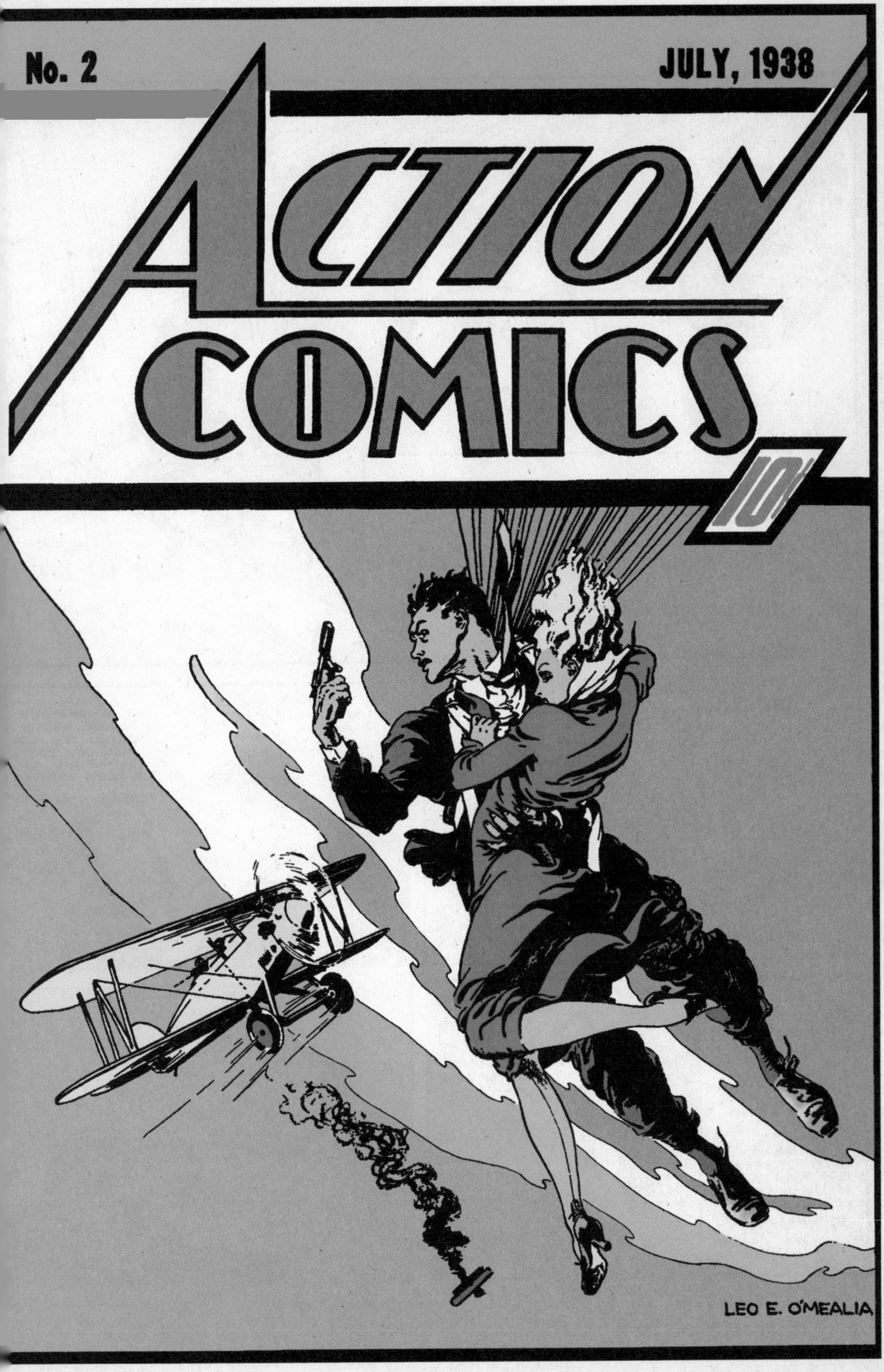

No. 2
JULY, 1938
ACTION
COMICS
10¢
LEO E. O'MEALIA

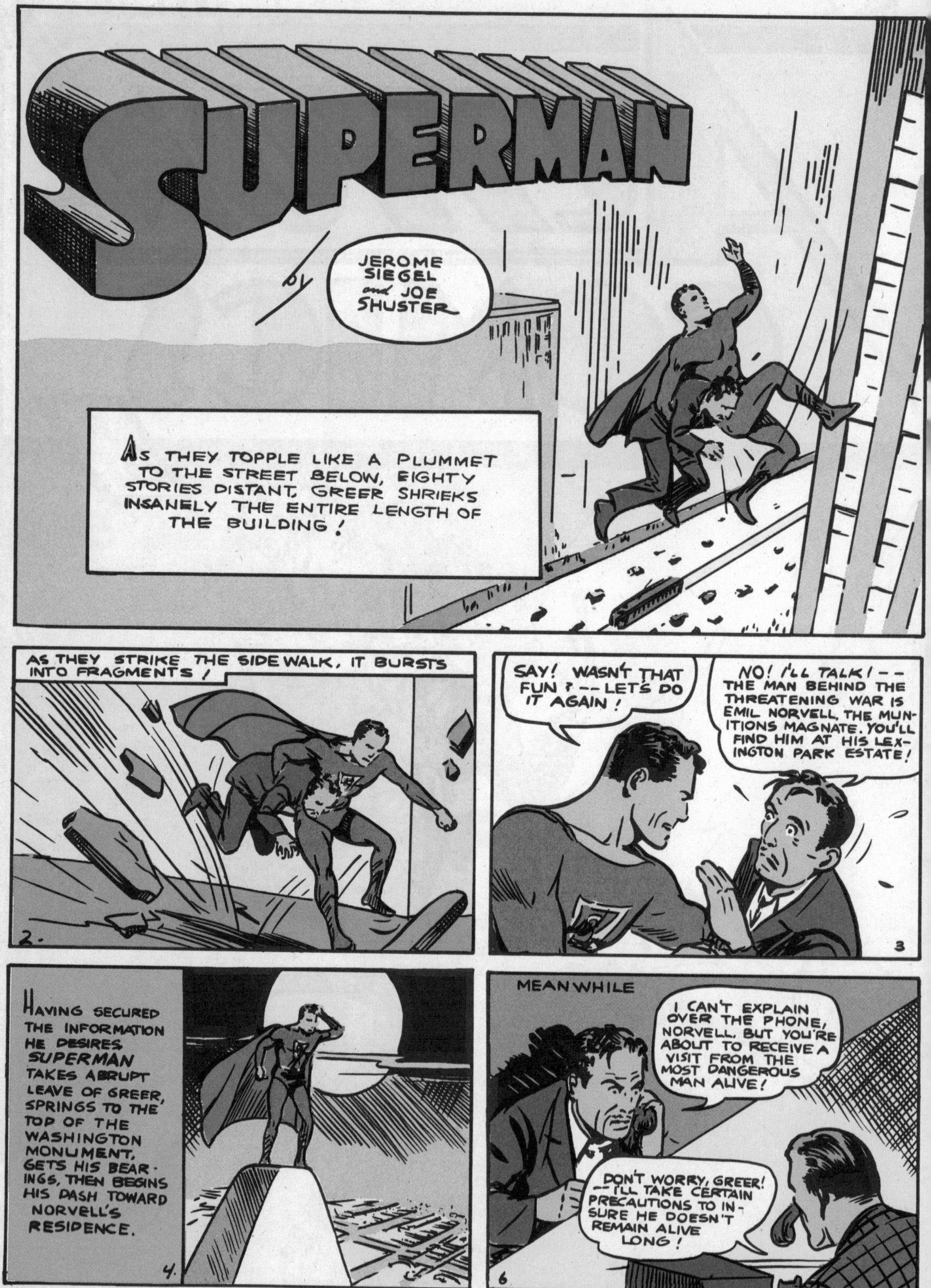
SUPERMAN
by
JEROME SIEGEL and JOE SHUSTER
AS THEY TOPPLE LIKE A PLUMMET TO THE STREET BELOW, EIGHTY STORIES DISTANT, GREER SHRIEKS INSANELY THE ENTIRE LENGTH OF THE BUILDING!
AS THEY STRIKE THE SIDEWALK, IT BURSTS INTO FRAGMENTS!
2.
SAY! WASN'T THAT FUN? -- LET'S DO IT AGAIN!
NO! I'LL TALK! -- THE MAN BEHIND THE THREATENING WAR IS EMIL NORVELL, THE MUNITIONS MAGNATE. YOU'LL FIND HIM AT HIS LEXINGTON PARK ESTATE!
3
HAVING SECURED THE INFORMATION HE DESIRES, SUPERMAN TAKES ABRUPT LEAVE OF GREER, SPRINGS TO THE TOP OF THE WASHINGTON MONUMENT, GETS HIS BEARINGS, THEN BEGINS HIS DASH TOWARD NORVELL'S RESIDENCE.
4.
MEANWHILE
I CAN'T EXPLAIN OVER THE PHONE, NORVELL, BUT YOU'RE ABOUT TO RECEIVE A VISIT FROM THE MOST DANGEROUS MAN ALIVE!
DON'T WORRY, GREER! -- I'LL TAKE CERTAIN PRECAUTIONS TO INSURE HE DOESN'T REMAIN ALIVE LONG!
6

FIVE MINUTES ELAPSE -- THEN . . . . . . SUPERMAN STEPS THRU THE WINDOW OF EMIL NORVELL'S STUDY AND CALMLY CONFRONTS HIM . . .

WHETHER YOU LIKE IT OR NOT, NORVELL, YOU'RE COMING WITH ME!

SORRY, BUT I HAVE OTHER PLANS!

7

AS HE SPEAKS, THE MUNITIONS MANUFACTURER SURREPTITIOUSLY REACHES BEHIND HIM TO PRESS A BUTTON ON HIS DESK.

8

WHAT ARE YOU HOLDING BEHIND YOU? -- GIVE IT TO ME!

ALL RIGHT BOYS! — HE ASKED FOR IT! LET HIM HAVE IT!!

9

INSTANTLY SEVERAL PANELS ABOUT THE ROOM SLIDE ASIDE AND OUT STEP A NUMBER OF ARMED GUARDS! NEXT MOMENT SUPERMAN IS THE CENTER OF A DEAFENING MACHINE-GUN BARRAGE!

10

UNHARMED BY THE RAIN OF MACHINE-GUN BULLETS, SUPERMAN STREAKS TOWARD HIS WOULD-BE MURDERERS!

GOOD HEAVENS! HE WON'T DIE!

GLAD I CAN'T SAY THE SAME FOR YOU!

11

A MOMENT LATER A DOZEN BODIES FLY HEADLONG OUT THE WINDOW INTO THE NIGHT, THE MACHINE-GUNS WRAPPED FIRMLY ABOUT THEIR NECKS!

12

YOU SEE HOW EFFORTLESSLY I CRUSH THIS BAR OF IRON IN MY HAND? -- THAT BAR COULD JUST AS EASILY BE YOUR NECK! . . . NOW, FOR THE LAST TIME: ARE YOU COMING WITH ME?

YES! YES! IMMEDIATELY!

13

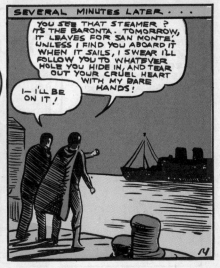

SEVERAL MINUTES LATER . . .

YOU SEE THAT STEAMER? IT'S THE BARONTA. TOMORROW, IT LEAVES FOR SAN MONTE: UNLESS I FIND YOU ABOARD IT WHEN IT SAILS, I SWEAR I'LL FOLLOW YOU TO WHATEVER HOLE YOU HIDE IN, AND TEAR OUT YOUR CRUEL HEART WITH MY BARE HANDS!

I— I'LL BE ON IT!

14

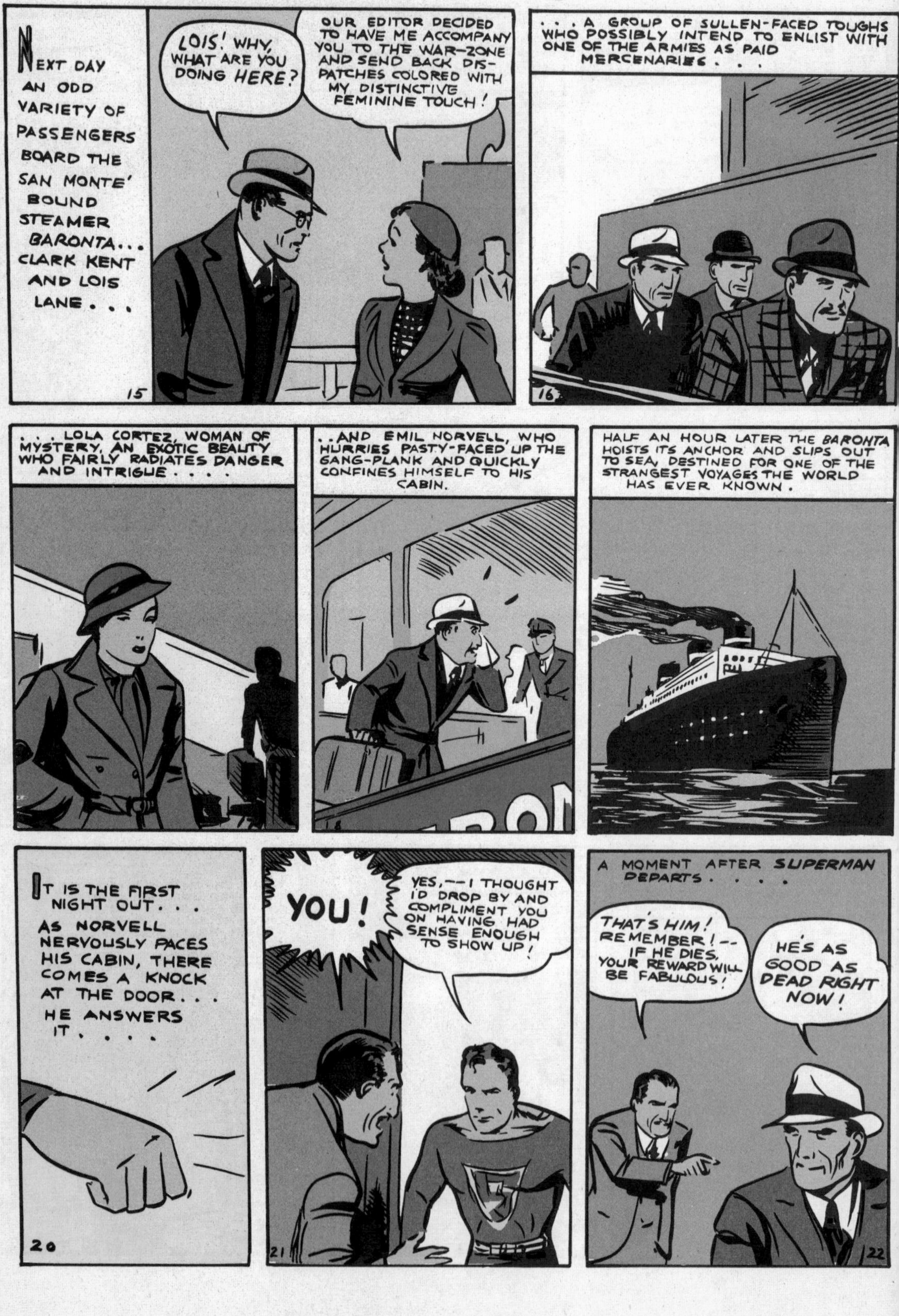
NEXT DAY AN ODD VARIETY OF PASSENGERS BOARD THE SAN MONTE' BOUND STEAMER BARONTA... CLARK KENT AND LOIS LANE . . .
LOIS! WHY, WHAT ARE YOU DOING HERE?
OUR EDITOR DECIDED TO HAVE ME ACCOMPANY YOU TO THE WAR-ZONE AND SEND BACK DIS-PATCHES COLORED WITH MY DISTINCTIVE FEMININE TOUCH!
15
. . . A GROUP OF SULLEN-FACED TOUGHS WHO POSSIBLY INTEND TO ENLIST WITH ONE OF THE ARMIES AS PAID MERCENARIES . . .
16
. . . LOLA CORTEZ, WOMAN OF MYSTERY, AN EXOTIC BEAUTY WHO FAIRLY RADIATES DANGER AND INTRIGUE . . .
..AND EMIL NORVELL, WHO HURRIES PASTY-FACED UP THE GANG-PLANK AND QUICKLY CONFINES HIMSELF TO HIS CABIN.
HALF AN HOUR LATER THE BARONTA HOISTS ITS ANCHOR AND SLIPS OUT TO SEA, DESTINED FOR ONE OF THE STRANGEST VOYAGES THE WORLD HAS EVER KNOWN.
IT IS THE FIRST NIGHT OUT. . . AS NORVELL NERVOUSLY PACES HIS CABIN, THERE COMES A KNOCK AT THE DOOR. . . HE ANSWERS IT . . .
20
YOU!
YES,--I THOUGHT I'D DROP BY AND COMPLIMENT YOU ON HAVING HAD SENSE ENOUGH TO SHOW UP!
21
A MOMENT AFTER SUPERMAN DEPARTS . . .
THAT'S HIM! REMEMBER!-- IF HE DIES, YOUR REWARD WILL BE FABULOUS!
HE'S AS GOOD AS DEAD RIGHT NOW!
22

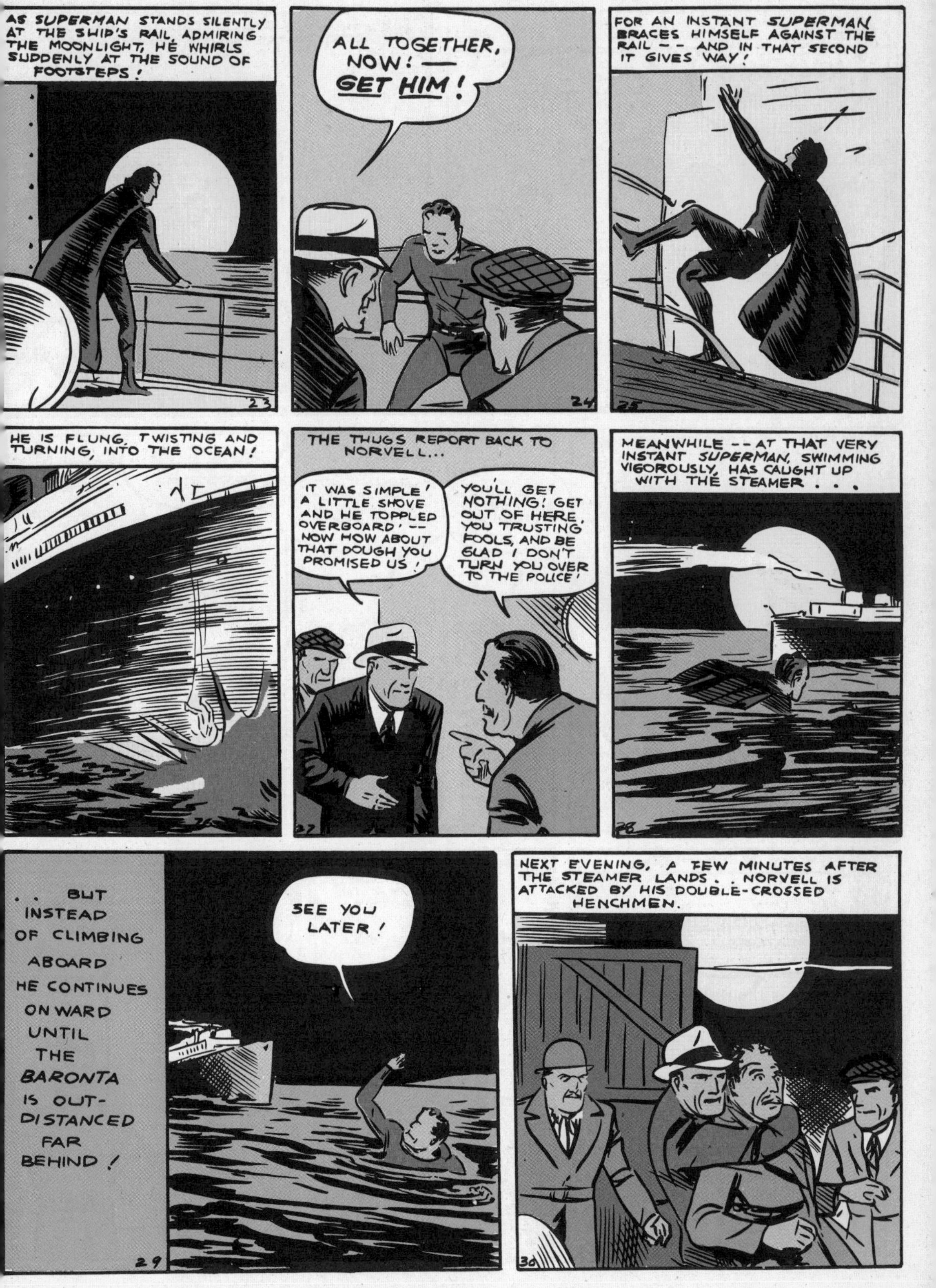
AS SUPERMAN STANDS SILENTLY AT THE SHIP'S RAIL, ADMIRING THE MOONLIGHT, HE WHIRLS SUDDENLY AT THE SOUND OF FOOTSTEPS!
ALL TOGETHER, NOW! — GET HIM!
FOR AN INSTANT SUPERMAN BRACES HIMSELF AGAINST THE RAIL -- AND IN THAT SECOND IT GIVES WAY!
HE IS FLUNG, TWISTING AND TURNING, INTO THE OCEAN!
THE THUGS REPORT BACK TO NORVELL...
IT WAS SIMPLE! A LITTLE SHOVE AND HE TOPPLED OVERBOARD! -- NOW HOW ABOUT THAT DOUGH YOU PROMISED US!
YOU'LL GET NOTHING! GET OUT OF HERE, YOU TRUSTING FOOLS, AND BE GLAD I DON'T TURN YOU OVER TO THE POLICE!
MEANWHILE -- AT THAT VERY INSTANT SUPERMAN, SWIMMING VIGOROUSLY, HAS CAUGHT UP WITH THE STEAMER . . .
. . BUT INSTEAD OF CLIMBING ABOARD HE CONTINUES ONWARD UNTIL THE BARONTA IS OUT-DISTANCED FAR BEHIND!
SEE YOU LATER!
NEXT EVENING, A FEW MINUTES AFTER THE STEAMER LANDS . . NORVELL IS ATTACKED BY HIS DOUBLE-CROSSED HENCHMEN.

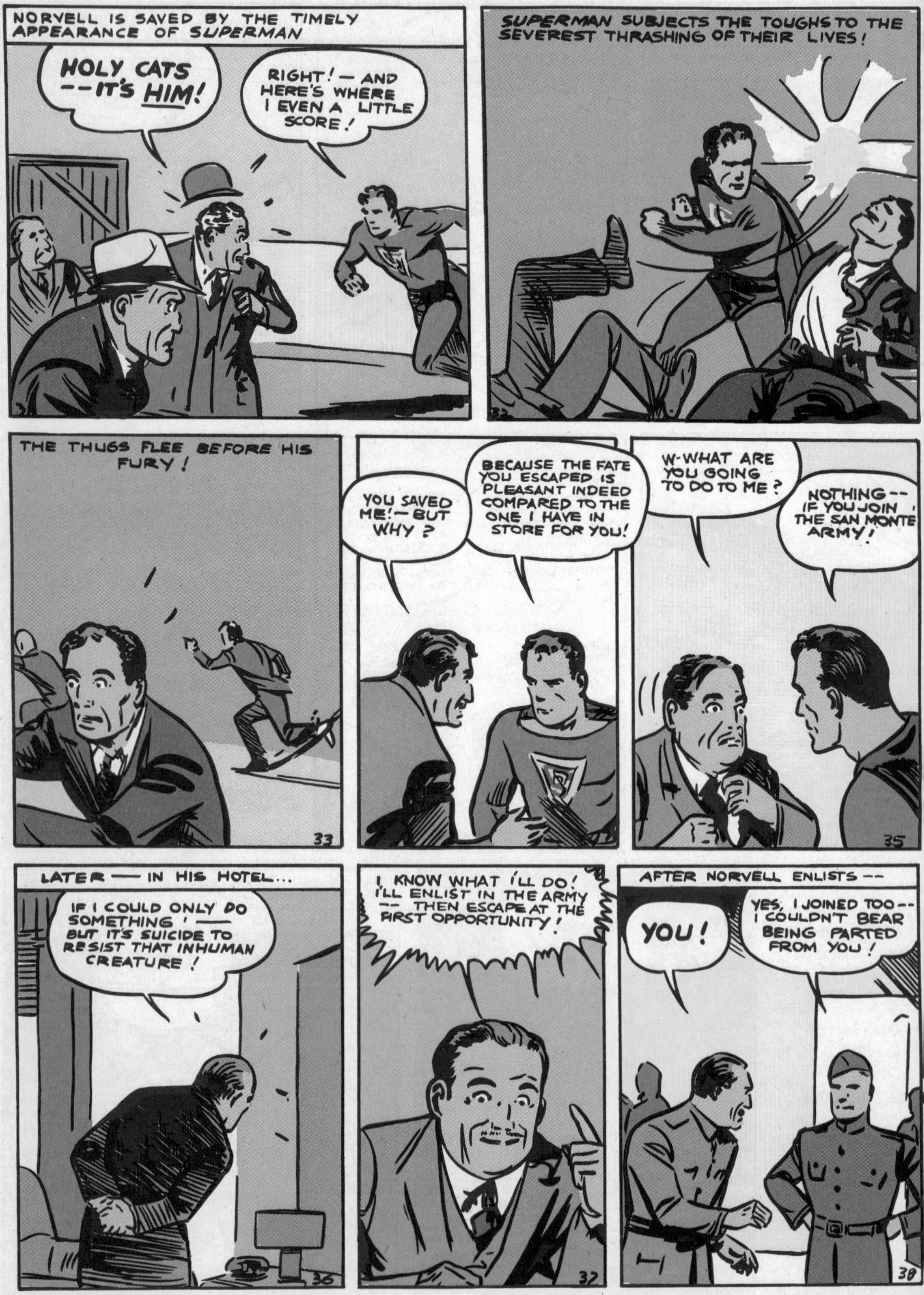
NORVELL IS SAVED BY THE TIMELY APPEARANCE OF SUPERMAN
HOLY CATS --IT'S HIM!
RIGHT! — AND HERE'S WHERE I EVEN A LITTLE SCORE!
SUPERMAN SUBJECTS THE TOUGHS TO THE SEVEREST THRASHING OF THEIR LIVES!
THE THUGS FLEE BEFORE HIS FURY!
YOU SAVED ME! — BUT WHY?
BECAUSE THE FATE YOU ESCAPED IS PLEASANT INDEED COMPARED TO THE ONE I HAVE IN STORE FOR YOU!
W-WHAT ARE YOU GOING TO DO TO ME?
NOTHING -- IF YOU JOIN THE SAN MONTE ARMY!
LATER — IN HIS HOTEL...
IF I COULD ONLY DO SOMETHING! — BUT IT'S SUICIDE TO RESIST THAT INHUMAN CREATURE!
I KNOW WHAT I'LL DO! I'LL ENLIST IN THE ARMY -- THEN ESCAPE AT THE FIRST OPPORTUNITY!
AFTER NORVELL ENLISTS --
YOU!
YES, I JOINED TOO -- I COULDN'T BEAR BEING PARTED FROM YOU!

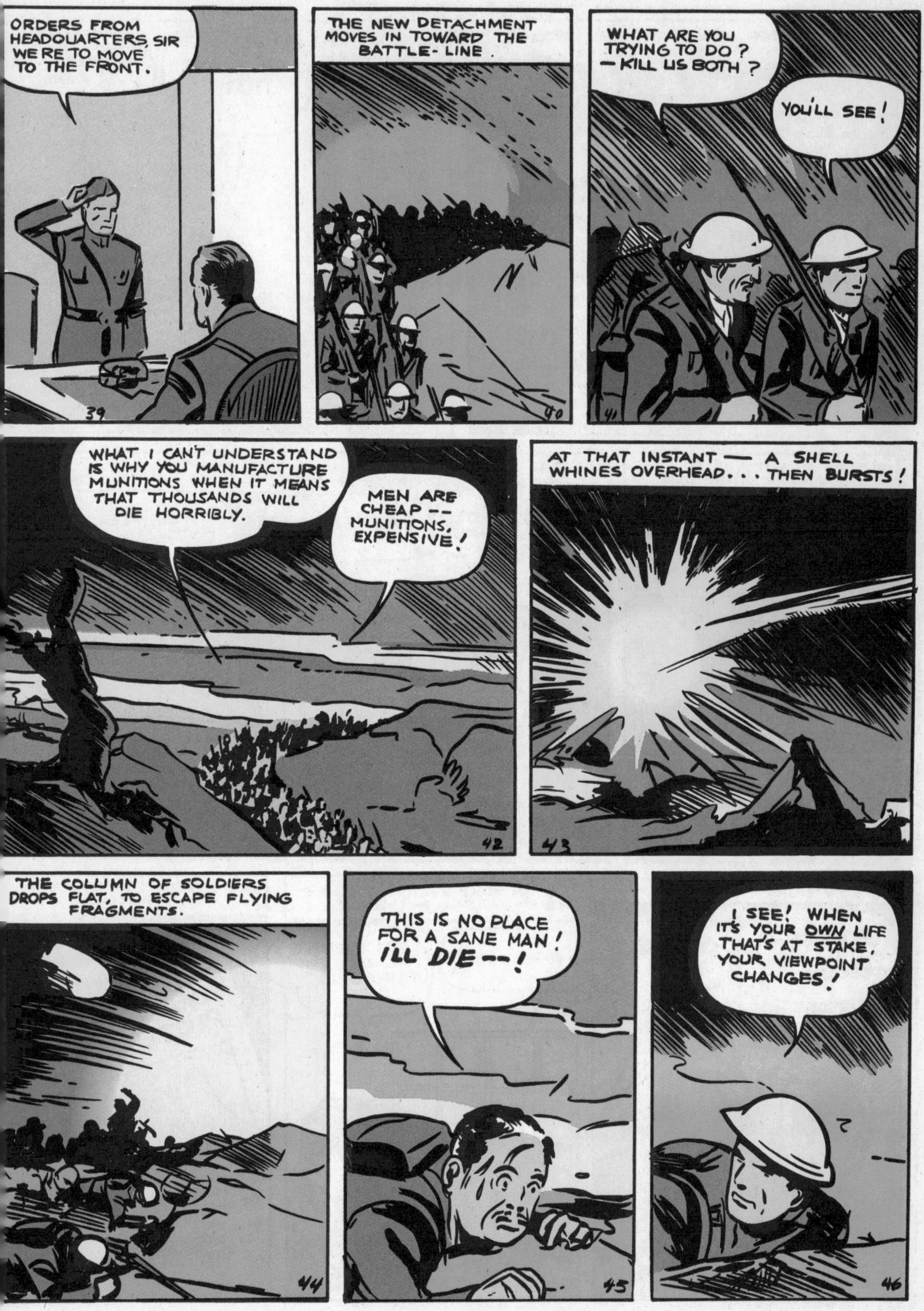
ORDERS FROM HEADQUARTERS, SIR WE'RE TO MOVE TO THE FRONT.
THE NEW DETACHMENT MOVES IN TOWARD THE BATTLE-LINE.
WHAT ARE YOU TRYING TO DO? —KILL US BOTH?
YOU'LL SEE!
WHAT I CAN'T UNDERSTAND IS WHY YOU MANUFACTURE MUNITIONS WHEN IT MEANS THAT THOUSANDS WILL DIE HORRIBLY.
MEN ARE CHEAP -- MUNITIONS, EXPENSIVE!
AT THAT INSTANT — A SHELL WHINES OVERHEAD... THEN BURSTS!
THE COLUMN OF SOLDIERS DROPS FLAT, TO ESCAPE FLYING FRAGMENTS.
THIS IS NO PLACE FOR A SANE MAN! I'LL DIE--!
I SEE! WHEN IT'S YOUR OWN LIFE THAT'S AT STAKE, YOUR VIEWPOINT CHANGES!

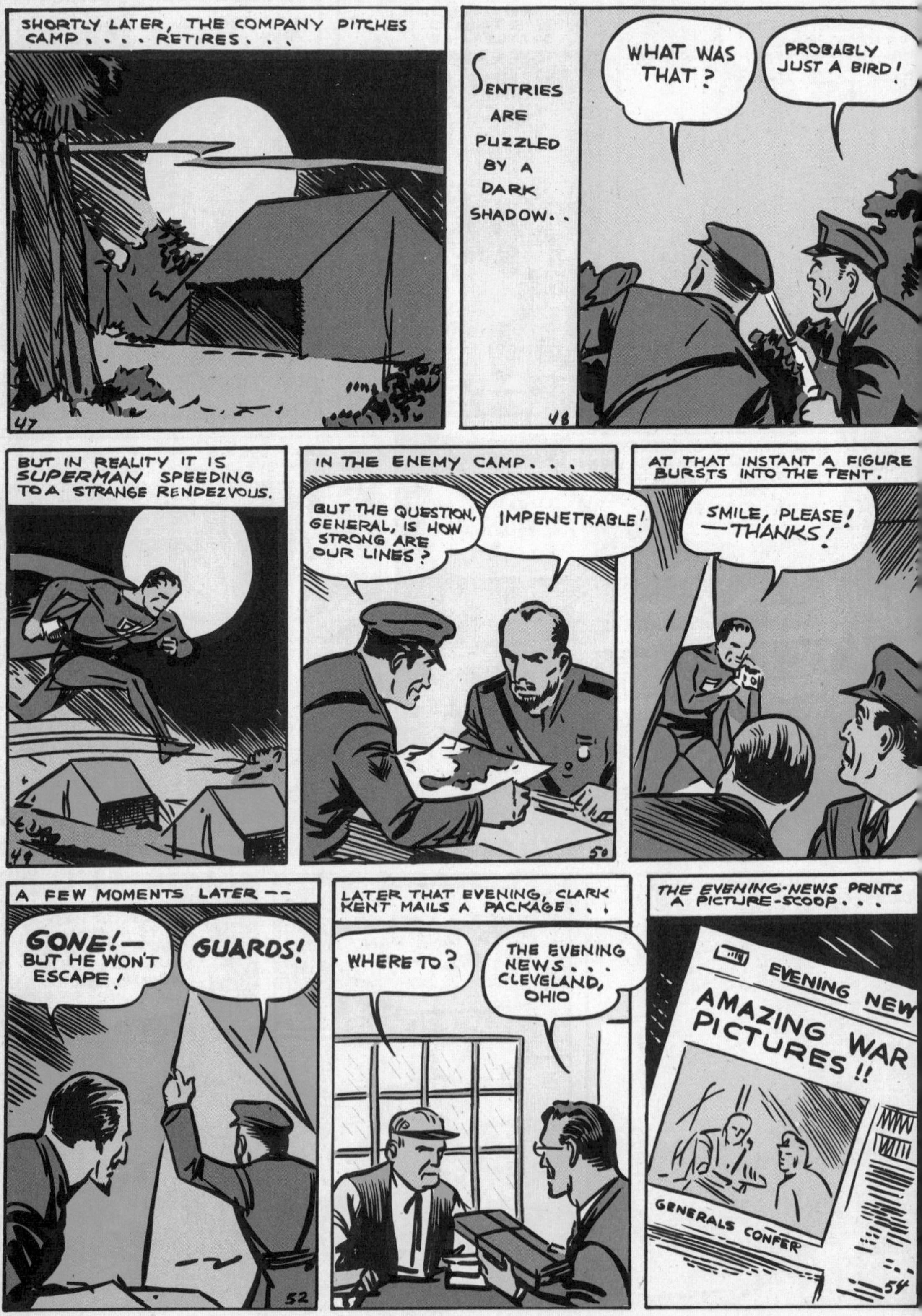
SHORTLY LATER, THE COMPANY PITCHES CAMP . . . . RETIRES . . .
SENTRIES ARE PUZZLED BY A DARK SHADOW. .
WHAT WAS THAT ?
PROBABLY JUST A BIRD !
BUT IN REALITY IT IS SUPERMAN SPEEDING TO A STRANGE RENDEZVOUS.
IN THE ENEMY CAMP . . .
BUT THE QUESTION, GENERAL, IS HOW STRONG ARE OUR LINES ?
IMPENETRABLE !
AT THAT INSTANT A FIGURE BURSTS INTO THE TENT.
SMILE, PLEASE! —THANKS !
A FEW MOMENTS LATER --
GONE!— BUT HE WON'T ESCAPE !
GUARDS!
LATER THAT EVENING, CLARK KENT MAILS A PACKAGE . . .
WHERE TO ?
THE EVENING NEWS . . . CLEVELAND, OHIO
THE EVENING-NEWS PRINTS A PICTURE-SCOOP . . .
EVENING NEW
AMAZING WAR PICTURES !!
GENERALS CONFER

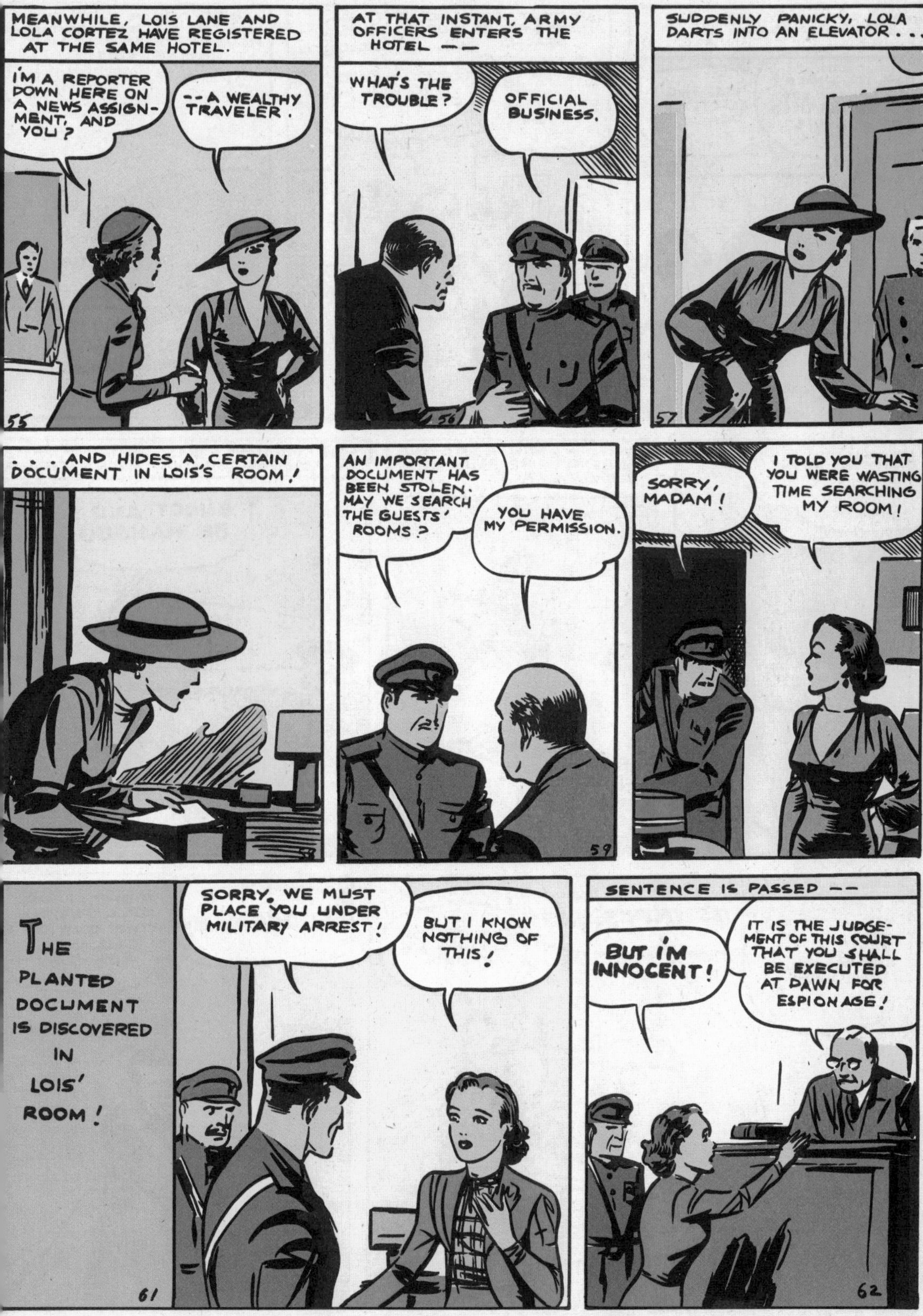
MEANWHILE, LOIS LANE AND LOLA CORTEZ HAVE REGISTERED AT THE SAME HOTEL.
I'M A REPORTER DOWN HERE ON A NEWS ASSIGNMENT, AND YOU?
-- A WEALTHY TRAVELER.
55
AT THAT INSTANT, ARMY OFFICERS ENTERS THE HOTEL --
WHAT'S THE TROUBLE?
OFFICIAL BUSINESS.
56
SUDDENLY PANICKY, LOLA DARTS INTO AN ELEVATOR . . .
57
. . . AND HIDES A CERTAIN DOCUMENT IN LOIS'S ROOM!
58
AN IMPORTANT DOCUMENT HAS BEEN STOLEN. MAY WE SEARCH THE GUESTS' ROOMS?
YOU HAVE MY PERMISSION.
59
SORRY, MADAM!
I TOLD YOU THAT YOU WERE WASTING TIME SEARCHING MY ROOM!
THE PLANTED DOCUMENT IS DISCOVERED IN LOIS' ROOM!
SORRY, WE MUST PLACE YOU UNDER MILITARY ARREST!
BUT I KNOW NOTHING OF THIS!
61
SENTENCE IS PASSED --
BUT I'M INNOCENT!
IT IS THE JUDGEMENT OF THIS COURT THAT YOU SHALL BE EXECUTED AT DAWN FOR ESPIONAGE!
62

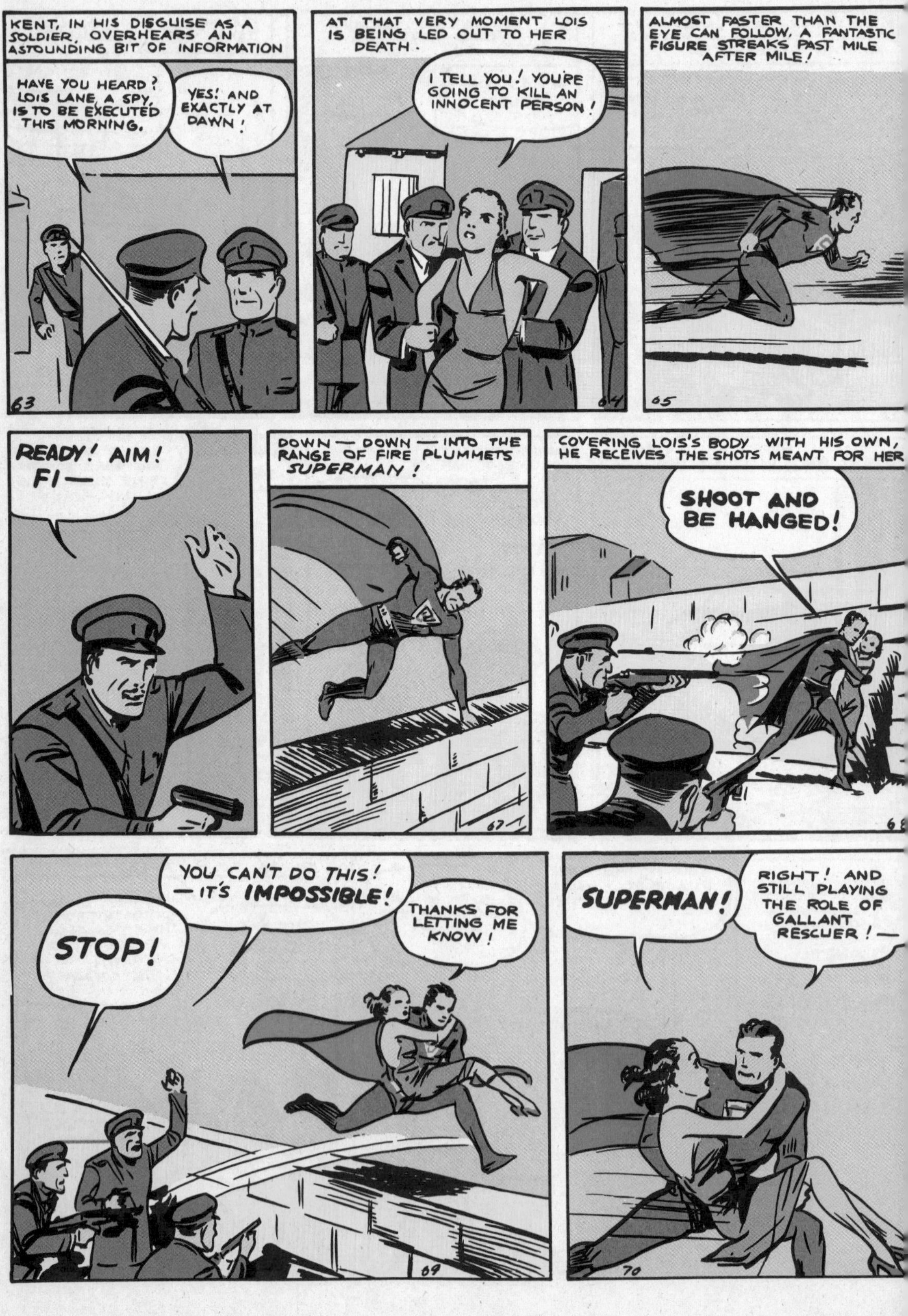
KENT, IN HIS DISGUISE AS A SOLDIER, OVERHEARS AN ASTOUNDING BIT OF INFORMATION
HAVE YOU HEARD? LOIS LANE, A SPY, IS TO BE EXECUTED THIS MORNING.
YES! AND EXACTLY AT DAWN!
63
AT THAT VERY MOMENT LOIS IS BEING LED OUT TO HER DEATH.
I TELL YOU! YOU'RE GOING TO KILL AN INNOCENT PERSON!
64
ALMOST FASTER THAN THE EYE CAN FOLLOW, A FANTASTIC FIGURE STREAKS PAST MILE AFTER MILE!
65
READY! AIM! FI—
DOWN — DOWN — INTO THE RANGE OF FIRE PLUMMETS SUPERMAN!
67
COVERING LOIS'S BODY WITH HIS OWN, HE RECEIVES THE SHOTS MEANT FOR HER
SHOOT AND BE HANGED!
STOP!
YOU CAN'T DO THIS! — IT'S IMPOSSIBLE!
THANKS FOR LETTING ME KNOW!
69
SUPERMAN!
RIGHT! AND STILL PLAYING THE ROLE OF GALLANT RESCUER! —
70

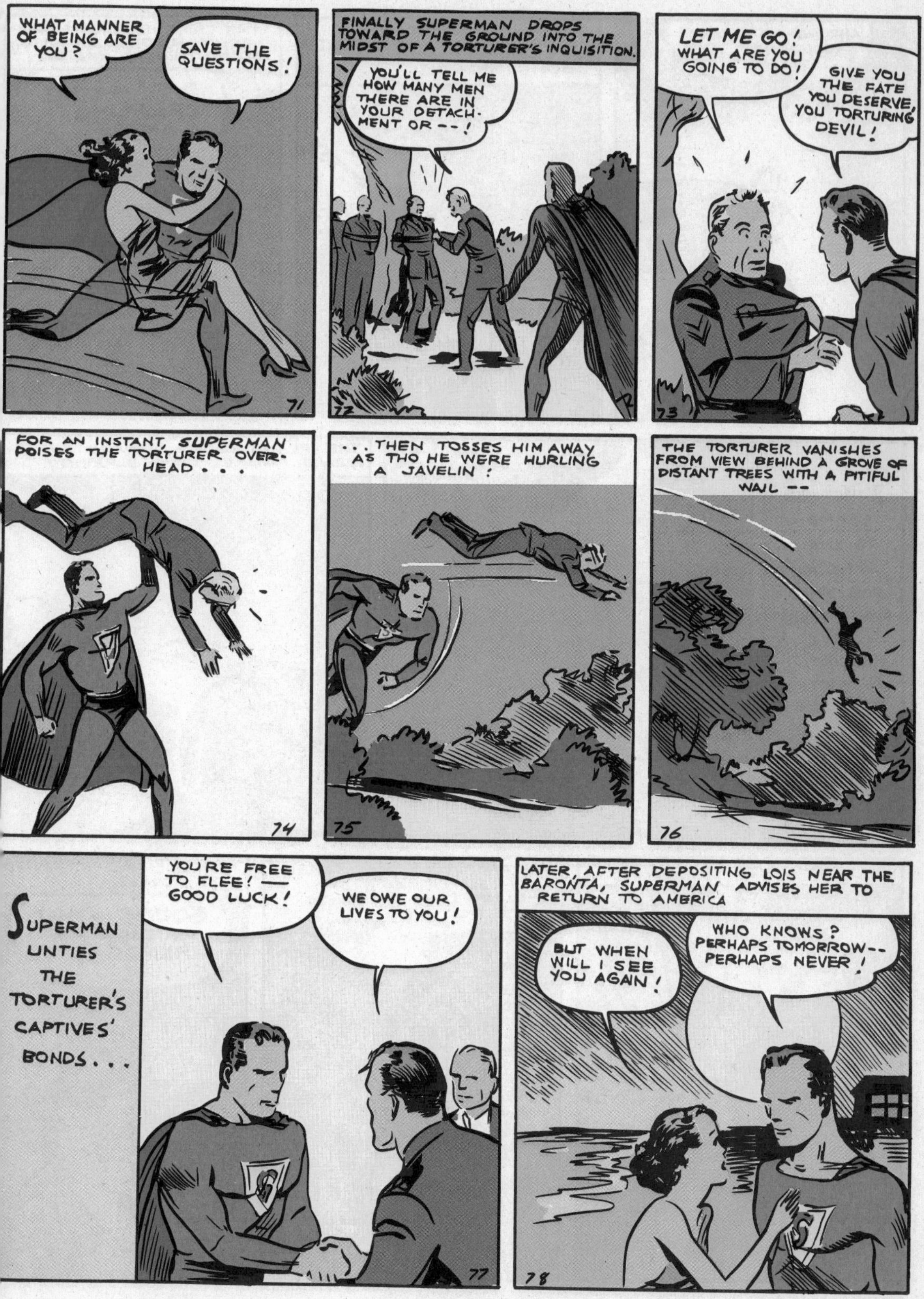
WHAT MANNER OF BEING ARE YOU?
SAVE THE QUESTIONS!
71
FINALLY SUPERMAN DROPS TOWARD THE GROUND INTO THE MIDST OF A TORTURER'S INQUISITION.
YOU'LL TELL ME HOW MANY MEN THERE ARE IN YOUR DETACHMENT OR --!
72
LET ME GO! WHAT ARE YOU GOING TO DO!
GIVE YOU THE FATE YOU DESERVE, YOU TORTURING DEVIL!
73
FOR AN INSTANT, SUPERMAN POISES THE TORTURER OVERHEAD . . .
74
. . . THEN TOSSES HIM AWAY AS THO HE WERE HURLING A JAVELIN!
75
THE TORTURER VANISHES FROM VIEW BEHIND A GROVE OF DISTANT TREES WITH A PITIFUL WAIL --
76
SUPERMAN UNTIES THE TORTURER'S CAPTIVES' BONDS . . .
YOU'RE FREE TO FLEE! — GOOD LUCK!
WE OWE OUR LIVES TO YOU!
77
LATER, AFTER DEPOSITING LOIS NEAR THE BARONTA, SUPERMAN ADVISES HER TO RETURN TO AMERICA
BUT WHEN WILL I SEE YOU AGAIN!
WHO KNOWS? PERHAPS TOMORROW-- PERHAPS NEVER!
78

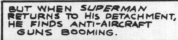

AND NOW TO ATTEND TO NORVELL!

79

BUT WHEN *SUPERMAN* RETURNS TO HIS DETACHMENT, HE FINDS ANTI-AIRCRAFT GUNS BOOMING.

80

THE CAMP IS BEING MERCILESSLY RIDDLED BY A BLOOD-THIRSTY AVIATOR!

DIE! -- LIKE CRAWLING ANTS!

81

*S*UPERMAN LEAPS TO THE ATTACK! FOR THE FIRST TIME IN ALL HISTORY, A MAN BATTLES AN AIRPLANE SINGLE-HANDED!

82

THE PLANE ZOOMS TOWARD *SUPERMAN'S* FIGURE, GUNS BLAZING!

83

-- INTO A HEAD-ON CRASH!

84

ITS PROPELLER SHATTERED UPON *SUPERMAN'S* SKIN, THE AIRPLANE FALLS TO ITS DOOM!

85

NORVELL HAD WITNESSED THE CRASH.

GOOD! -- THAT FINISHES MY NEMESIS!

86

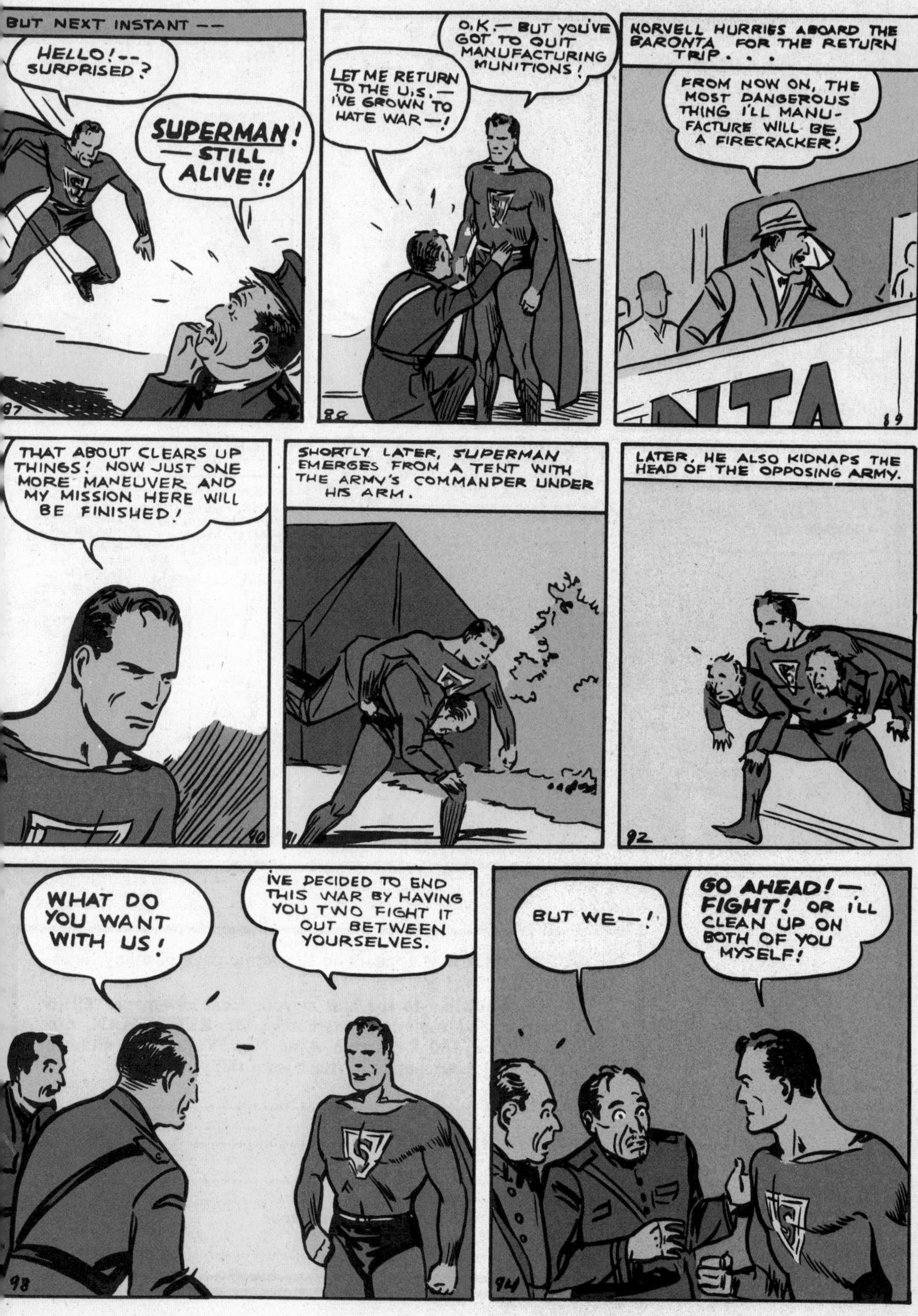
BUT NEXT INSTANT --
HELLO! -- SURPRISED?
SUPERMAN! — STILL ALIVE!!
O.K. — BUT YOU'VE GOT TO QUIT MANUFACTURING MUNITIONS!
LET ME RETURN TO THE U.S. — I'VE GROWN TO HATE WAR —!
NORVELL HURRIES ABOARD THE BARONTA FOR THE RETURN TRIP. . .
FROM NOW ON, THE MOST DANGEROUS THING I'LL MANUFACTURE WILL BE A FIRECRACKER!
THAT ABOUT CLEARS UP THINGS! NOW JUST ONE MORE MANEUVER AND MY MISSION HERE WILL BE FINISHED!
SHORTLY LATER, SUPERMAN EMERGES FROM A TENT WITH THE ARMY'S COMMANDER UNDER HIS ARM.
LATER, HE ALSO KIDNAPS THE HEAD OF THE OPPOSING ARMY.
WHAT DO YOU WANT WITH US!
I'VE DECIDED TO END THIS WAR BY HAVING YOU TWO FIGHT IT OUT BETWEEN YOURSELVES.
BUT WE—!
GO AHEAD! — FIGHT! OR I'LL CLEAN UP ON BOTH OF YOU MYSELF!

BUT WHY SHOULD WE FIGHT?

WE'RE NOT ANGRY AT EACH OTHER!

95

THEN WHY ARE YOUR ARMIES BATTLING?

96

I DON'T KNOW! CAN YOU TELL ME?

NO, CAN YOU?

97

GENTLEMEN, IT'S OBVIOUS YOU'VE BEEN FIGHTING ONLY TO PROMOTE THE SALE OF MUNITIONS! — WHY NOT SHAKE HANDS AND MAKE UP?

98

AND SO, DUE TO THE CONCILIATORY EFFORTS OF SUPERMAN, THE WAR IS HALTED.

99

WHEN KENT REPORTS BACK TO HIS EDITOR . .

SINCE YOU'VE BEEN GONE, THERE'S BEEN NO SUPERMAN NEWS. MAYBE HE'S RETIRED FOR GOOD!

SOMEHOW, CHIEF, I'VE A HUNCH HE'LL MAKE HIS APPEARANCE AGAIN—SOON!

100

THE END

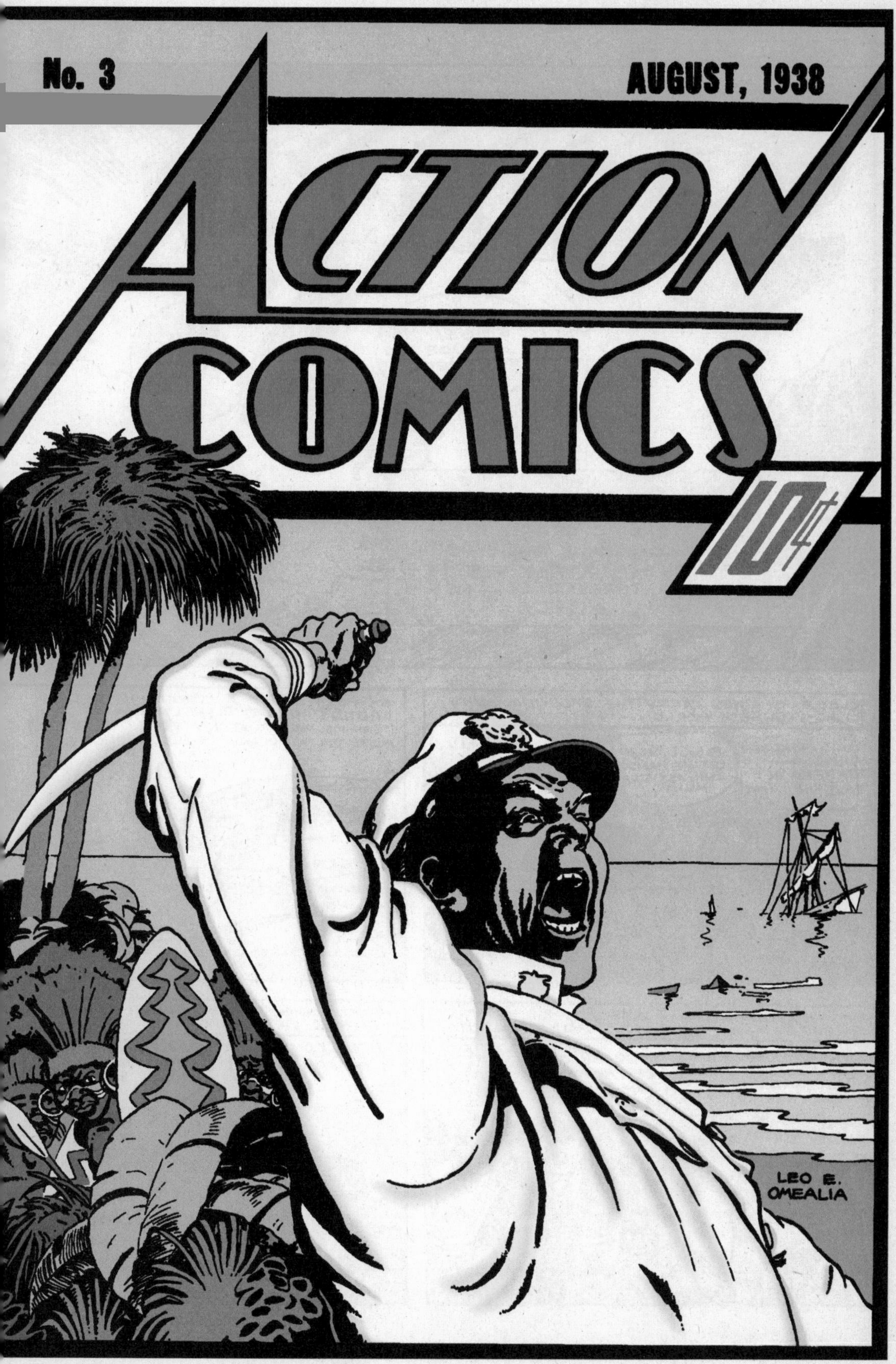
No. 3
AUGUST, 1938
ACTION COMICS
10¢
LEO E. OMEALIA

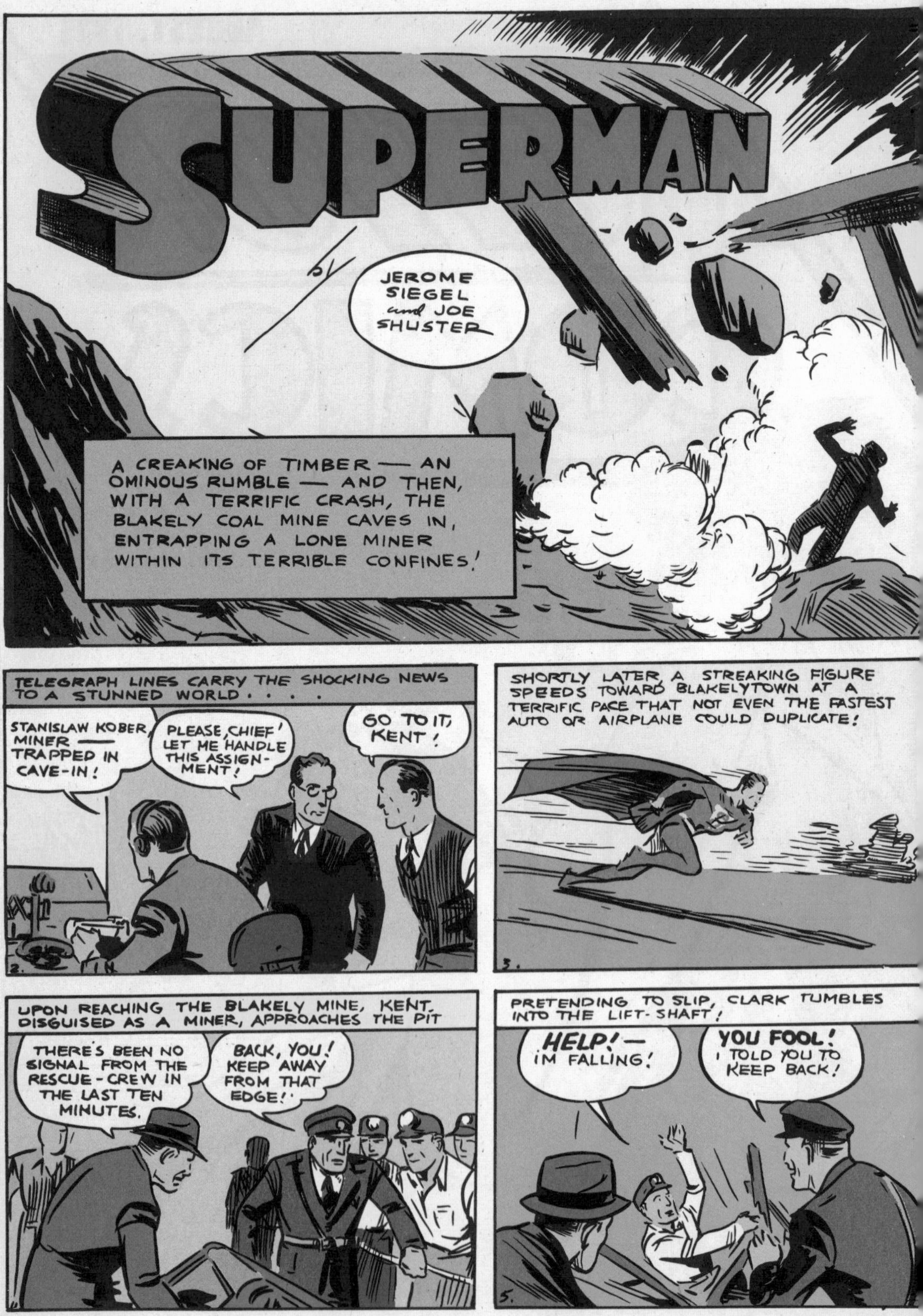
SUPERMAN
by
JEROME SIEGEL and JOE SHUSTER
A CREAKING OF TIMBER — AN OMINOUS RUMBLE — AND THEN, WITH A TERRIFIC CRASH, THE BLAKELY COAL MINE CAVES IN, ENTRAPPING A LONE MINER WITHIN ITS TERRIBLE CONFINES!
TELEGRAPH LINES CARRY THE SHOCKING NEWS TO A STUNNED WORLD . . . .
STANISLAW KOBER, MINER — TRAPPED IN CAVE-IN!
PLEASE, CHIEF! LET ME HANDLE THIS ASSIGNMENT!
GO TO IT, KENT!
SHORTLY LATER A STREAKING FIGURE SPEEDS TOWARD BLAKELYTOWN AT A TERRIFIC PACE THAT NOT EVEN THE FASTEST AUTO OR AIRPLANE COULD DUPLICATE!
UPON REACHING THE BLAKELY MINE, KENT, DISGUISED AS A MINER, APPROACHES THE PIT
THERE'S BEEN NO SIGNAL FROM THE RESCUE-CREW IN THE LAST TEN MINUTES.
BACK, YOU! KEEP AWAY FROM THAT EDGE!
PRETENDING TO SLIP, CLARK TUMBLES INTO THE LIFT-SHAFT!
HELP! — I'M FALLING!
YOU FOOL! I TOLD YOU TO KEEP BACK!

DOWN PLUNGES *SUPERMAN* IN A FALL WHICH WOULD HAVE MEANT DEATH FOR AN ORDINARY MAN!

AS *SUPERMAN* STRIKES THE BOTTOM OF THE SHAFT, HE DETECTS --

GAS! — POISON GAS!

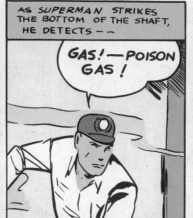

HIS PHYSICAL STRUCTURE UNAFFECTED BY THE GAS, *SUPERMAN* CONTINUES ALONG THE MINE'S BOTTOM --

-- UNTIL HE STUMBLES UPON A DOZEN UNCONSCIOUS FIGURES.

THE RESCUE-PARTY! I'D BETTER GET THEM OUT OF HERE *BEFORE* THE GAS FINISHES ITS DEADLY WORK!

A TRIFLE UNCEREMONIOUS -- BUT THE OCCASION DEMANDS IT!

PLACING THE MEN ON THE LIFT, *SUPERMAN* JERKS THE SIGNAL CORD, AND THE ELEVATOR BEGINS ITS UPWARD JOURNEY.

THAT'S THAT! — AND NOW TO *REALLY* GET TO WORK!

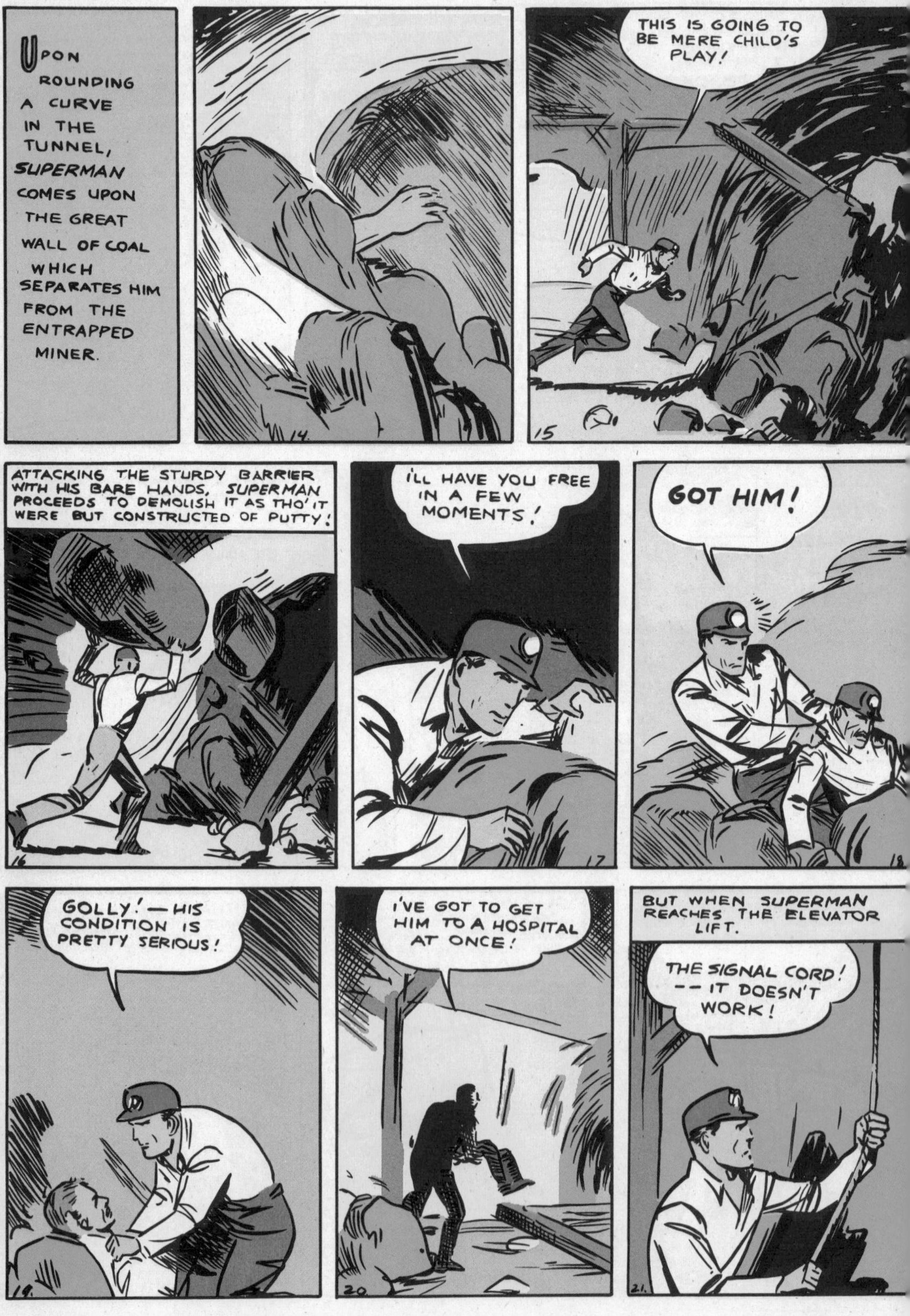
UPON ROUNDING A CURVE IN THE TUNNEL, SUPERMAN COMES UPON THE GREAT WALL OF COAL WHICH SEPARATES HIM FROM THE ENTRAPPED MINER.
THIS IS GOING TO BE MERE CHILD'S PLAY!
ATTACKING THE STURDY BARRIER WITH HIS BARE HANDS, SUPERMAN PROCEEDS TO DEMOLISH IT AS THO' IT WERE BUT CONSTRUCTED OF PUTTY!
I'LL HAVE YOU FREE IN A FEW MOMENTS!
GOT HIM!
GOLLY!—HIS CONDITION IS PRETTY SERIOUS!
I'VE GOT TO GET HIM TO A HOSPITAL AT ONCE!
BUT WHEN SUPERMAN REACHES THE ELEVATOR LIFT.
THE SIGNAL CORD! -- IT DOESN'T WORK!

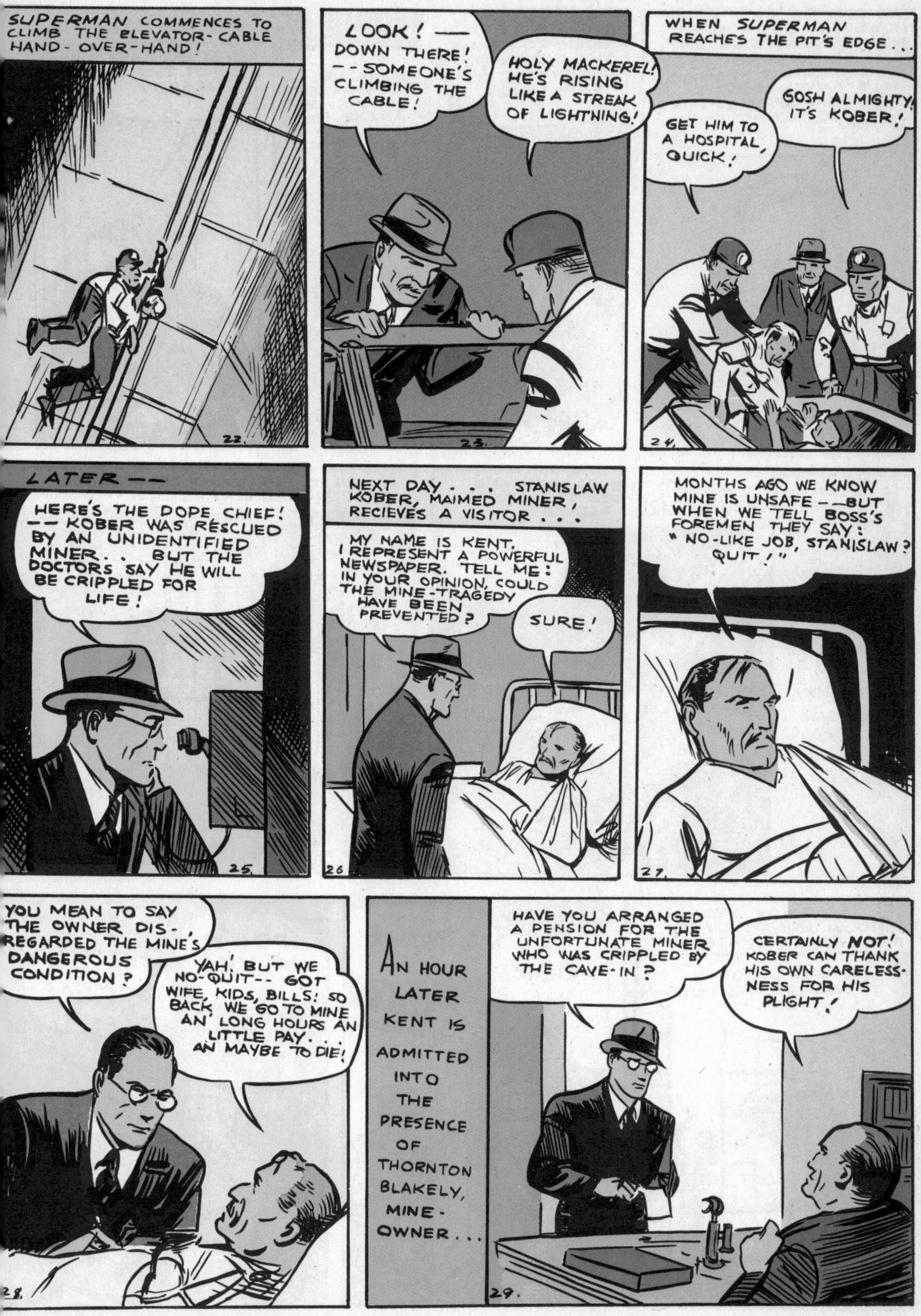
SUPERMAN COMMENCES TO CLIMB THE ELEVATOR-CABLE HAND-OVER-HAND!
22.
LOOK! — DOWN THERE! --SOMEONE'S CLIMBING THE CABLE!
HOLY MACKEREL! HE'S RISING LIKE A STREAK OF LIGHTNING!
23.
WHEN SUPERMAN REACHES THE PIT'S EDGE...
GOSH ALMIGHTY! IT'S KOBER!
GET HIM TO A HOSPITAL, QUICK!
24.
LATER--
HERE'S THE DOPE CHIEF! --KOBER WAS RESCUED BY AN UNIDENTIFIED MINER.. BUT THE DOCTORS SAY HE WILL BE CRIPPLED FOR LIFE!
25.
NEXT DAY... STANISLAW KOBER, MAIMED MINER, RECIEVES A VISITOR...
MY NAME IS KENT. I REPRESENT A POWERFUL NEWSPAPER. TELL ME: IN YOUR OPINION, COULD THE MINE-TRAGEDY HAVE BEEN PREVENTED?
SURE!
26
MONTHS AGO WE KNOW MINE IS UNSAFE --BUT WHEN WE TELL BOSS'S FOREMEN THEY SAY: "NO-LIKE JOB, STANISLAW? QUIT!"
27.
YOU MEAN TO SAY THE OWNER DIS-REGARDED THE MINE'S DANGEROUS CONDITION?
YAH! BUT WE NO-QUIT-- GOT WIFE, KIDS, BILLS! SO BACK WE GO TO MINE AN' LONG HOURS AN LITTLE PAY.. AN MAYBE TO DIE!
28.
AN HOUR LATER KENT IS ADMITTED INTO THE PRESENCE OF THORNTON BLAKELY, MINE-OWNER...
HAVE YOU ARRANGED A PENSION FOR THE UNFORTUNATE MINER WHO WAS CRIPPLED BY THE CAVE-IN?
CERTAINLY NOT! KOBER CAN THANK HIS OWN CARELESS-NESS FOR HIS PLIGHT!
29.

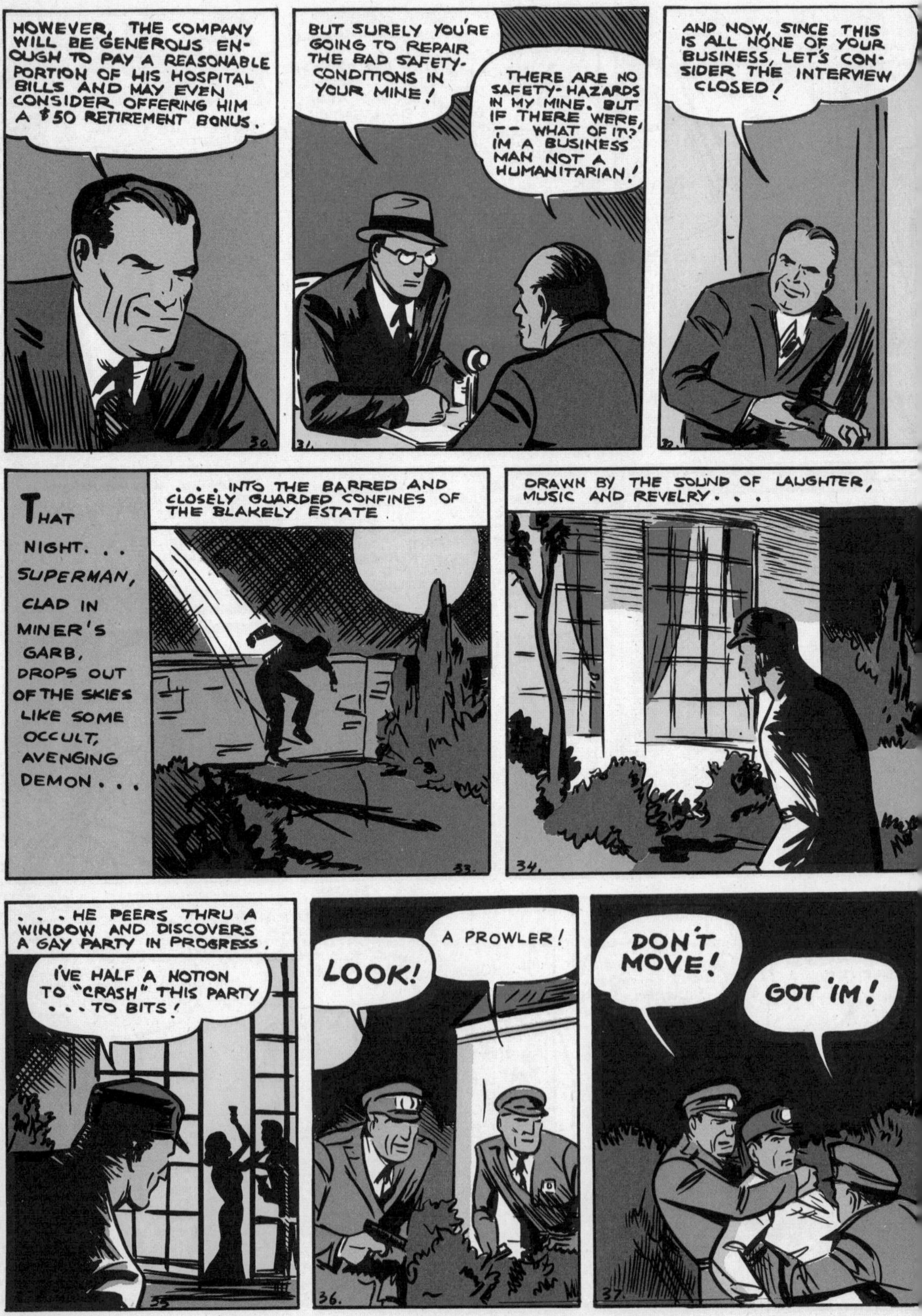

HOWEVER, THE COMPANY WILL BE GENEROUS ENOUGH TO PAY A REASONABLE PORTION OF HIS HOSPITAL BILLS AND MAY EVEN CONSIDER OFFERING HIM A $50 RETIREMENT BONUS.
BUT SURELY YOU'RE GOING TO REPAIR THE BAD SAFETY-CONDITIONS IN YOUR MINE!
THERE ARE NO SAFETY-HAZARDS IN MY MINE. BUT IF THERE WERE, -- WHAT OF IT? I'M A BUSINESS MAN NOT A HUMANITARIAN!
AND NOW, SINCE THIS IS ALL NONE OF YOUR BUSINESS, LET'S CONSIDER THE INTERVIEW CLOSED!
THAT NIGHT... SUPERMAN, CLAD IN MINER'S GARB, DROPS OUT OF THE SKIES LIKE SOME OCCULT, AVENGING DEMON...
...INTO THE BARRED AND CLOSELY GUARDED CONFINES OF THE BLAKELY ESTATE.
DRAWN BY THE SOUND OF LAUGHTER, MUSIC AND REVELRY...
...HE PEERS THRU A WINDOW AND DISCOVERS A GAY PARTY IN PROGRESS.
I'VE HALF A NOTION TO "CRASH" THIS PARTY ...TO BITS!
LOOK!
A PROWLER!
DON'T MOVE!
GOT 'IM!

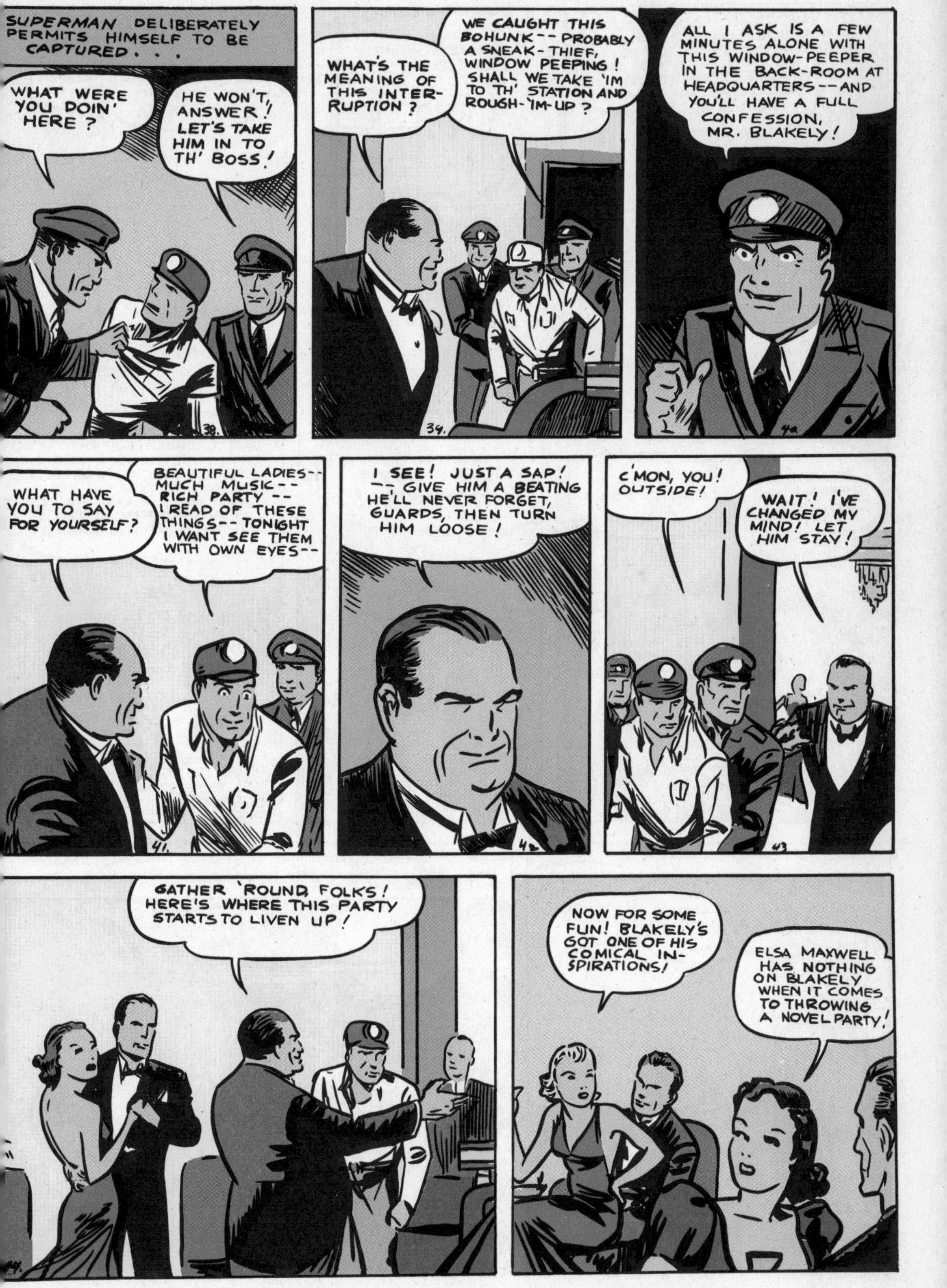
SUPERMAN DELIBERATELY PERMITS HIMSELF TO BE CAPTURED . . .
WHAT WERE YOU DOIN' HERE ?
HE WON'T ANSWER! LET'S TAKE HIM IN TO TH' BOSS!
WHAT'S THE MEANING OF THIS INTERRUPTION ?
WE CAUGHT THIS BOHUNK -- PROBABLY A SNEAK-THIEF, WINDOW PEEPING! SHALL WE TAKE 'IM TO TH' STATION AND ROUGH-'IM-UP ?
ALL I ASK IS A FEW MINUTES ALONE WITH THIS WINDOW-PEEPER IN THE BACK-ROOM AT HEADQUARTERS -- AND YOU'LL HAVE A FULL CONFESSION, MR. BLAKELY!
WHAT HAVE YOU TO SAY FOR YOURSELF?
BEAUTIFUL LADIES-- MUCH MUSIC-- RICH PARTY -- I READ OF THESE THINGS-- TONIGHT I WANT SEE THEM WITH OWN EYES--
I SEE! JUST A SAP! -- GIVE HIM A BEATING HE'LL NEVER FORGET, GUARDS, THEN TURN HIM LOOSE!
C'MON, YOU! OUTSIDE!
WAIT! I'VE CHANGED MY MIND! LET HIM STAY!
GATHER 'ROUND, FOLKS! HERE'S WHERE THIS PARTY STARTS TO LIVEN UP!
NOW FOR SOME FUN! BLAKELY'S GOT ONE OF HIS COMICAL INSPIRATIONS!
ELSA MAXWELL HAS NOTHING ON BLAKELY WHEN IT COMES TO THROWING A NOVEL PARTY!

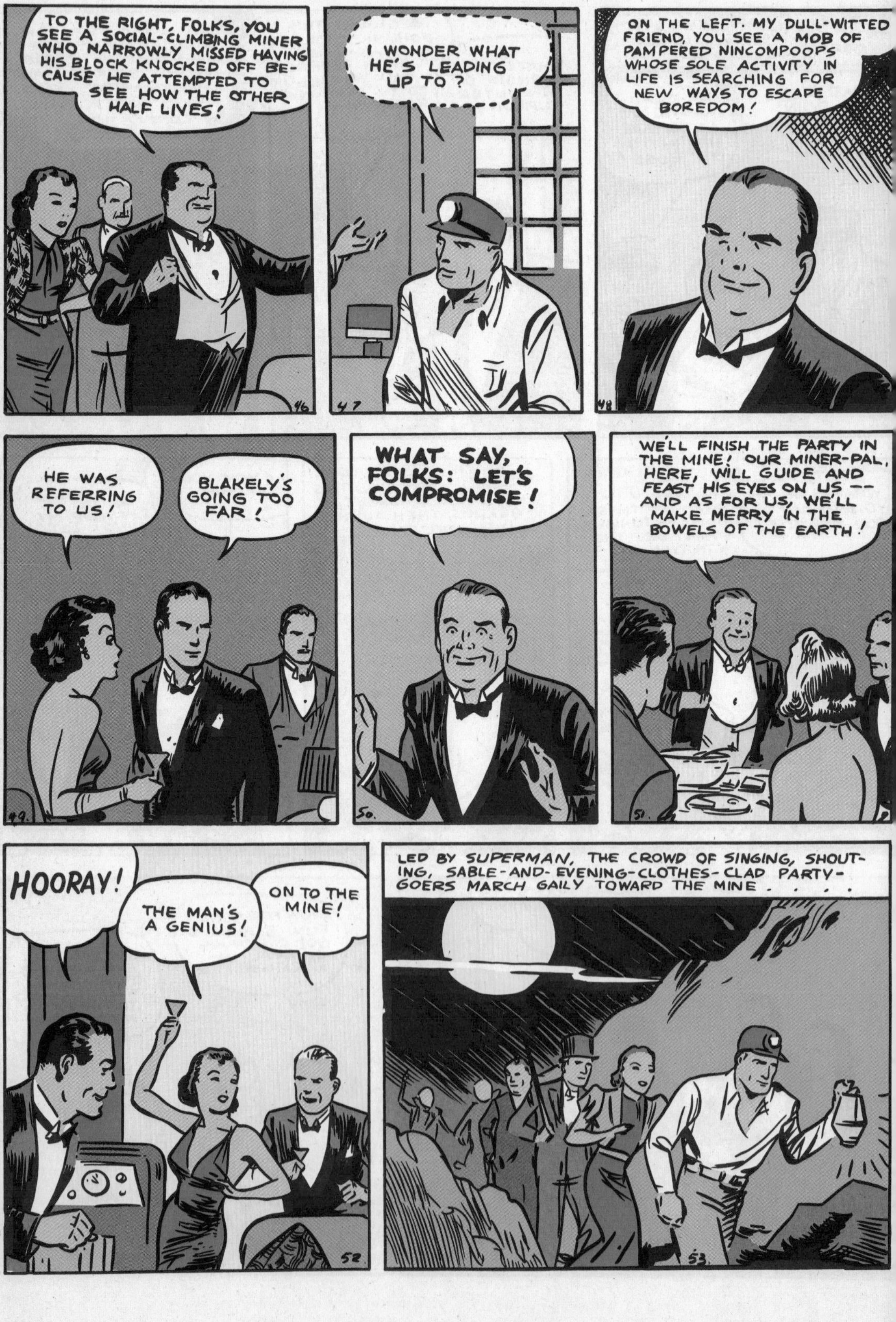
TO THE RIGHT, FOLKS, YOU SEE A SOCIAL-CLIMBING MINER WHO NARROWLY MISSED HAVING HIS BLOCK KNOCKED OFF BE-CAUSE HE ATTEMPTED TO SEE HOW THE OTHER HALF LIVES!
I WONDER WHAT HE'S LEADING UP TO?
ON THE LEFT. MY DULL-WITTED FRIEND, YOU SEE A MOB OF PAMPERED NINCOMPOOPS WHOSE SOLE ACTIVITY IN LIFE IS SEARCHING FOR NEW WAYS TO ESCAPE BOREDOM!
HE WAS REFERRING TO US!
BLAKELY'S GOING TOO FAR!
WHAT SAY, FOLKS: LET'S COMPROMISE!
WE'LL FINISH THE PARTY IN THE MINE! OUR MINER-PAL, HERE, WILL GUIDE AND FEAST HIS EYES ON US -- AND AS FOR US, WE'LL MAKE MERRY IN THE BOWELS OF THE EARTH!
HOORAY!
THE MAN'S A GENIUS!
ON TO THE MINE!
LED BY SUPERMAN, THE CROWD OF SINGING, SHOUT-ING, SABLE-AND-EVENING-CLOTHES-CLAD PARTY-GOERS MARCH GAILY TOWARD THE MINE . . . .

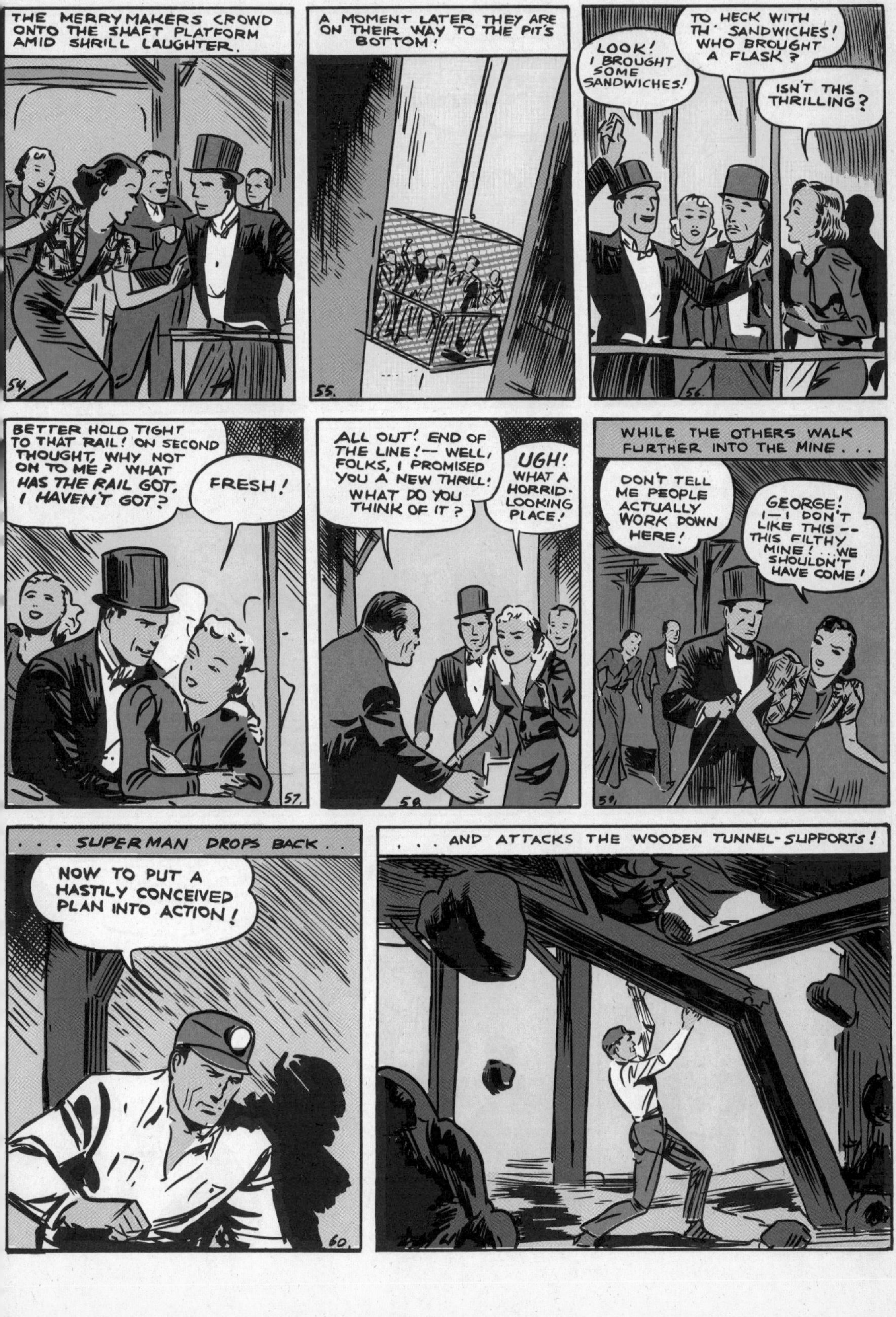
THE MERRYMAKERS CROWD ONTO THE SHAFT PLATFORM AMID SHRILL LAUGHTER.
A MOMENT LATER THEY ARE ON THEIR WAY TO THE PIT'S BOTTOM!
LOOK! I BROUGHT SOME SANDWICHES!
TO HECK WITH TH' SANDWICHES! WHO BROUGHT A FLASK?
ISN'T THIS THRILLING?
BETTER HOLD TIGHT TO THAT RAIL! ON SECOND THOUGHT, WHY NOT ON TO ME? WHAT HAS THE RAIL GOT, I HAVEN'T GOT?
FRESH!
ALL OUT! END OF THE LINE!-- WELL, FOLKS, I PROMISED YOU A NEW THRILL! WHAT DO YOU THINK OF IT?
UGH! WHAT A HORRID-LOOKING PLACE!
WHILE THE OTHERS WALK FURTHER INTO THE MINE . . .
DON'T TELL ME PEOPLE ACTUALLY WORK DOWN HERE!
GEORGE! I-I DON'T LIKE THIS -- THIS FILTHY MINE! ...WE SHOULDN'T HAVE COME!
. . . SUPERMAN DROPS BACK . .
NOW TO PUT A HASTILY CONCEIVED PLAN INTO ACTION!
. . . AND ATTACKS THE WOODEN TUNNEL-SUPPORTS!

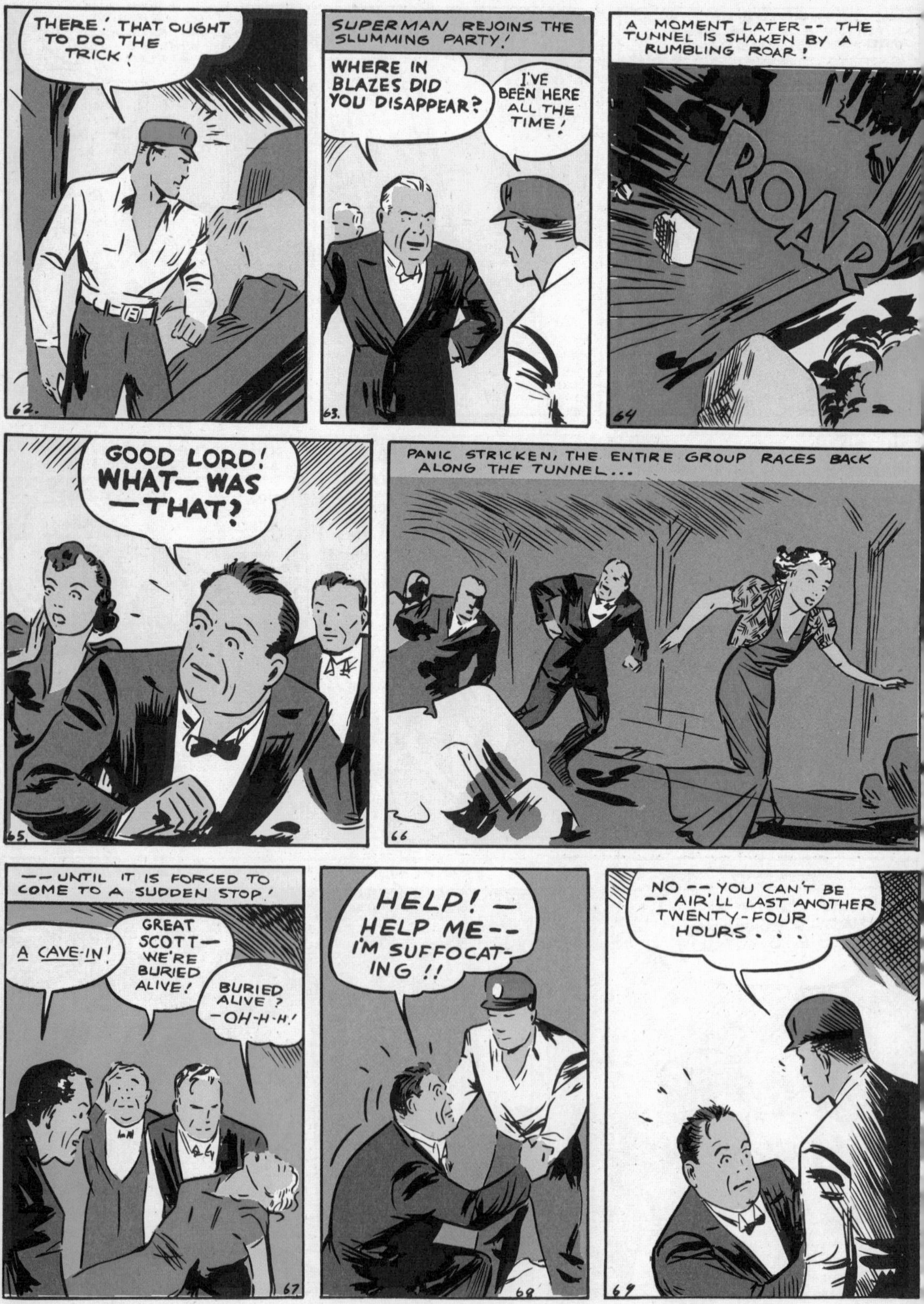

THERE! THAT OUGHT TO DO THE TRICK!
62.
SUPERMAN REJOINS THE SLUMMING PARTY!
WHERE IN BLAZES DID YOU DISAPPEAR?
I'VE BEEN HERE ALL THE TIME!
63.
A MOMENT LATER -- THE TUNNEL IS SHAKEN BY A RUMBLING ROAR!
ROAR
64
GOOD LORD! WHAT— WAS —THAT?
65.
PANIC STRICKEN, THE ENTIRE GROUP RACES BACK ALONG THE TUNNEL...
66
-- UNTIL IT IS FORCED TO COME TO A SUDDEN STOP!
A CAVE-IN!
GREAT SCOTT— WE'RE BURIED ALIVE!
BURIED ALIVE? —OH-H-H!
67
HELP! — HELP ME -- I'M SUFFOCAT-ING!!
68
NO -- YOU CAN'T BE -- AIR'LL LAST ANOTHER TWENTY-FOUR HOURS...
69

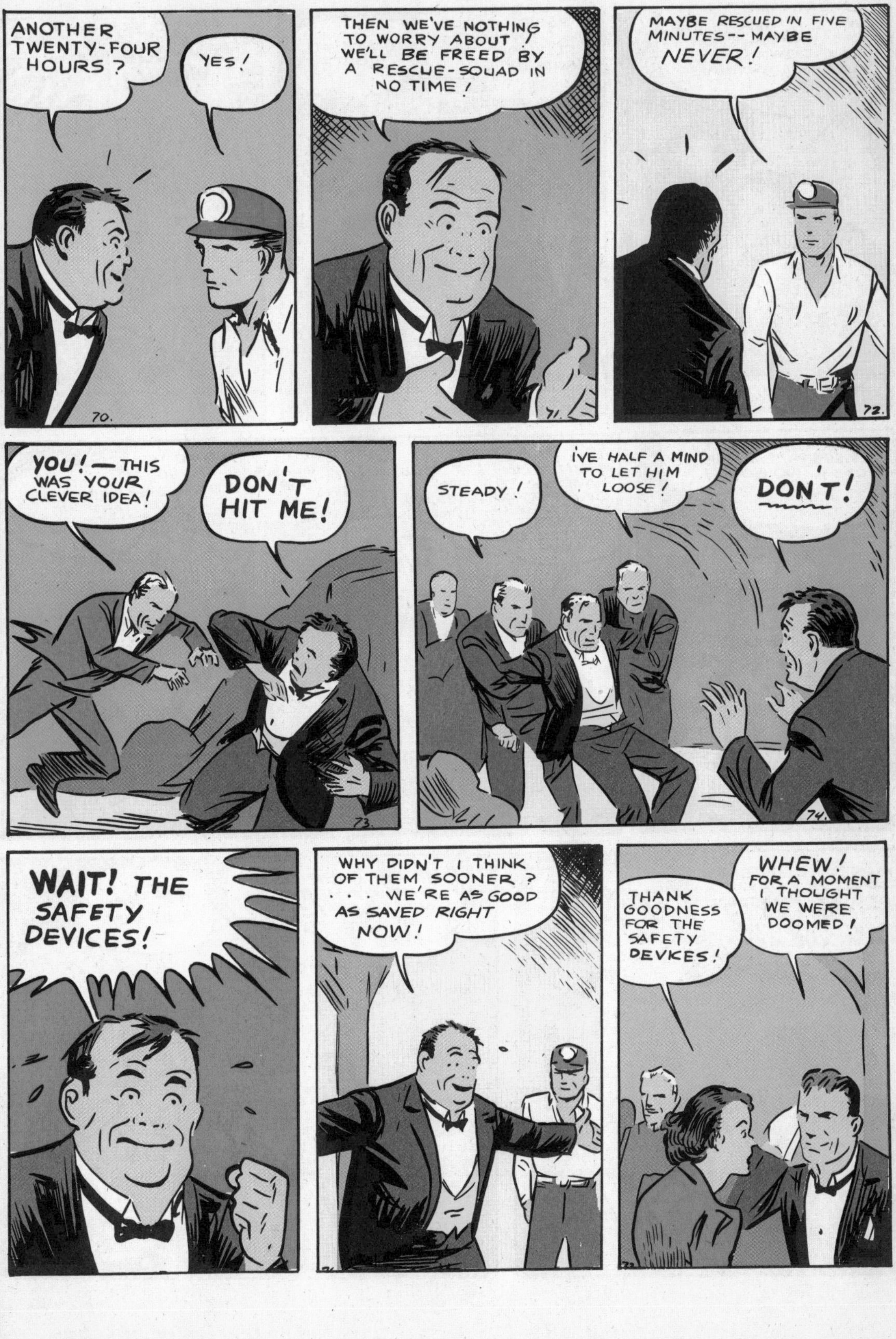
ANOTHER TWENTY-FOUR HOURS?
YES!
70.
THEN WE'VE NOTHING TO WORRY ABOUT! WE'LL BE FREED BY A RESCUE-SQUAD IN NO TIME!
71.
MAYBE RESCUED IN FIVE MINUTES-- MAYBE NEVER!
72.
YOU!—THIS WAS YOUR CLEVER IDEA!
DON'T HIT ME!
73.
STEADY!
I'VE HALF A MIND TO LET HIM LOOSE!
DON'T!
74.
WAIT! THE SAFETY DEVICES!
WHY DIDN'T I THINK OF THEM SOONER? . . . WE'RE AS GOOD AS SAVED RIGHT NOW!
THANK GOODNESS FOR THE SAFETY DEVKES!
WHEW! FOR A MOMENT I THOUGHT WE WERE DOOMED!

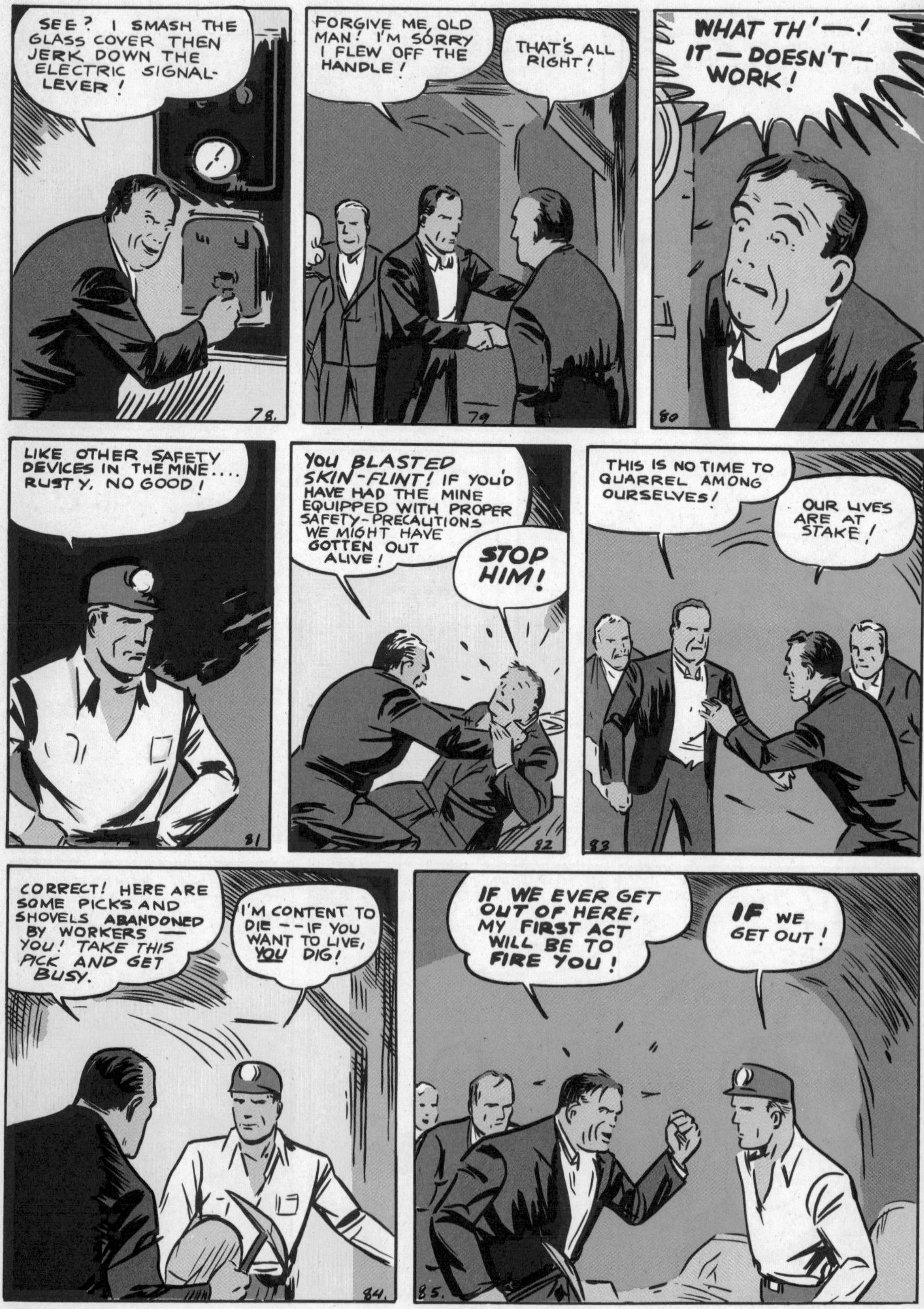
SEE? I SMASH THE GLASS COVER THEN JERK DOWN THE ELECTRIC SIGNAL-LEVER!
78.
FORGIVE ME, OLD MAN! I'M SORRY I FLEW OFF THE HANDLE!
THAT'S ALL RIGHT!
79
WHAT TH'—! IT—DOESN'T—WORK!
80
LIKE OTHER SAFETY DEVICES IN THE MINE.... RUSTY, NO GOOD!
81
YOU BLASTED SKIN-FLINT! IF YOU'D HAVE HAD THE MINE EQUIPPED WITH PROPER SAFETY-PRECAUTIONS WE MIGHT HAVE GOTTEN OUT ALIVE!
STOP HIM!
82
THIS IS NO TIME TO QUARREL AMONG OURSELVES!
OUR LIVES ARE AT STAKE!
83
CORRECT! HERE ARE SOME PICKS AND SHOVELS ABANDONED BY WORKERS — YOU! TAKE THIS PICK AND GET BUSY.
I'M CONTENT TO DIE --IF YOU WANT TO LIVE, YOU DIG!
84.
IF WE EVER GET OUT OF HERE, MY FIRST ACT WILL BE TO FIRE YOU!
IF WE GET OUT!
85.

KNEE-DEEP IN STAGNANT WATER, STRUGGLING WITH UNWIELDY TOOLS, SLIPPING, FREQUENTLY FALLING, THE ENTRAPPED PLEASURE-SEEKERS SEEK DESPERATELY, BUT VAINLY, TO BATTER DOWN THE HUGE BARRIER OF COAL!

HURRY! WHILE THE AIR SUPPLY LASTS!

WE'VE GOT TO GET OUT-- WE'VE GOT TO!

I'M WINDED! I—I CAN'T KEEP THIS UP!

THINK OF THE MINERS! THEY HAVE TO DO THIS 14 LONG HOURS EACH DAY!

MEANWHILE -- A RESCUE-PARTY WORKS FRANTICALLY ON THE OTHER SIDE OF THE BARRIER!

IT'S NO USE! WE'LL NEVER GET OUT OF HERE! WE'LL ALL DIE!

OH, IF I ONLY HAD THIS ALL TO DO OVER AGAIN! — I NEVER KNEW — REALLY KNEW — WHAT THE MEN DOWN HERE HAVE TO FACE!

THAT'S ALL I'VE BEEN WAITING TO HEAR!

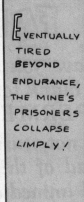

EVENTUALLY TIRED BEYOND ENDURANCE, THE MINE'S PRISONERS COLLAPSE LIMPLY!

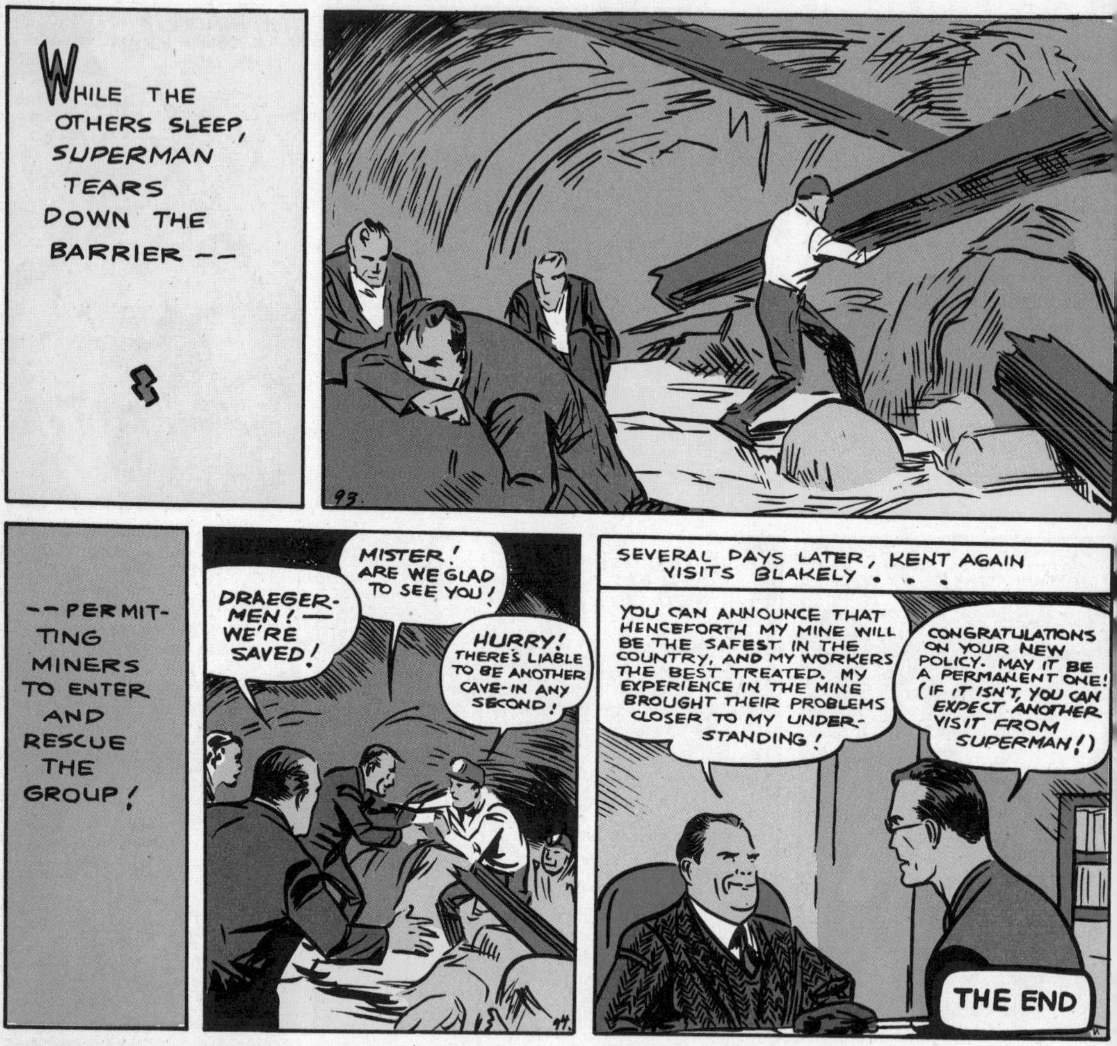
WHILE THE OTHERS SLEEP, SUPERMAN TEARS DOWN THE BARRIER --
&
93.
-- PERMITTING MINERS TO ENTER AND RESCUE THE GROUP!
DRAEGERMEN! — WE'RE SAVED!
MISTER! ARE WE GLAD TO SEE YOU!
HURRY! THERE'S LIABLE TO BE ANOTHER CAVE-IN ANY SECOND!
94.
SEVERAL DAYS LATER, KENT AGAIN VISITS BLAKELY . . .
YOU CAN ANNOUNCE THAT HENCEFORTH MY MINE WILL BE THE SAFEST IN THE COUNTRY, AND MY WORKERS THE BEST TREATED. MY EXPERIENCE IN THE MINE BROUGHT THEIR PROBLEMS CLOSER TO MY UNDERSTANDING!
CONGRATULATIONS ON YOUR NEW POLICY. MAY IT BE A PERMANENT ONE! (IF IT ISN'T, YOU CAN EXPECT ANOTHER VISIT FROM SUPERMAN!)
THE END

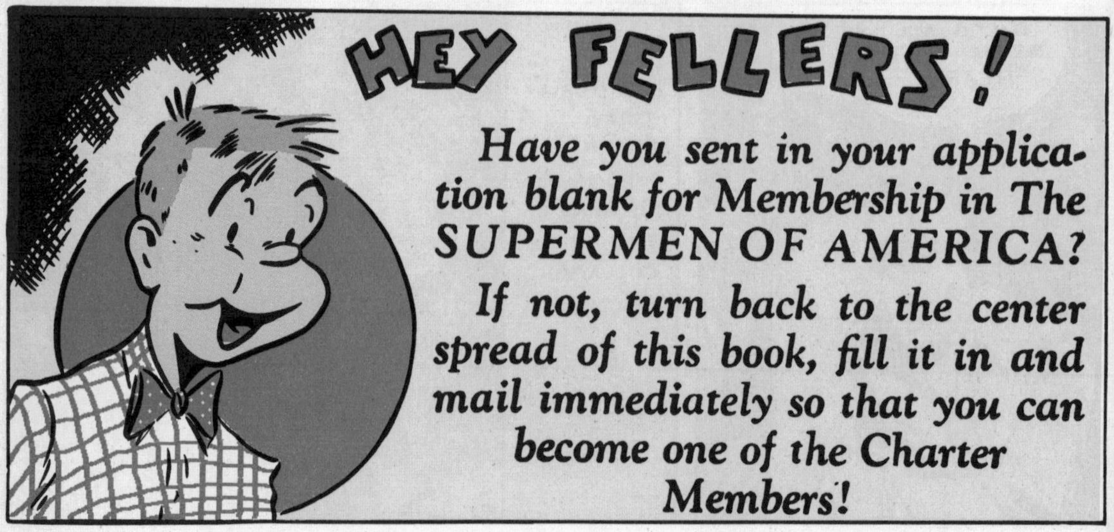
HEY FELLERS!
Have you sent in your application blank for Membership in The SUPERMEN OF AMERICA?
If not, turn back to the center spread of this book, fill it in and mail immediately so that you can become one of the Charter Members!

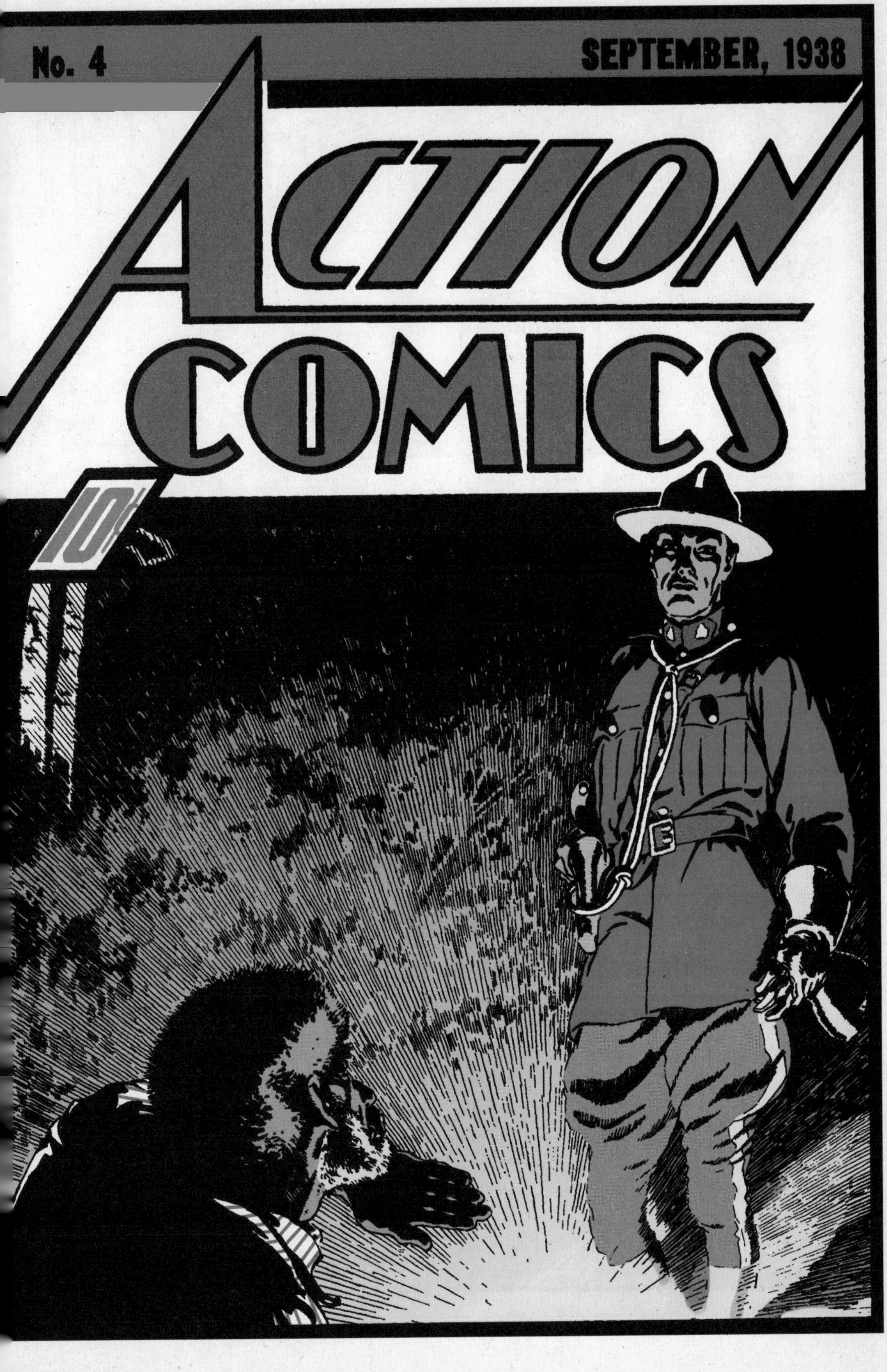
No. 4
SEPTEMBER, 1938
ACTION COMICS
10¢

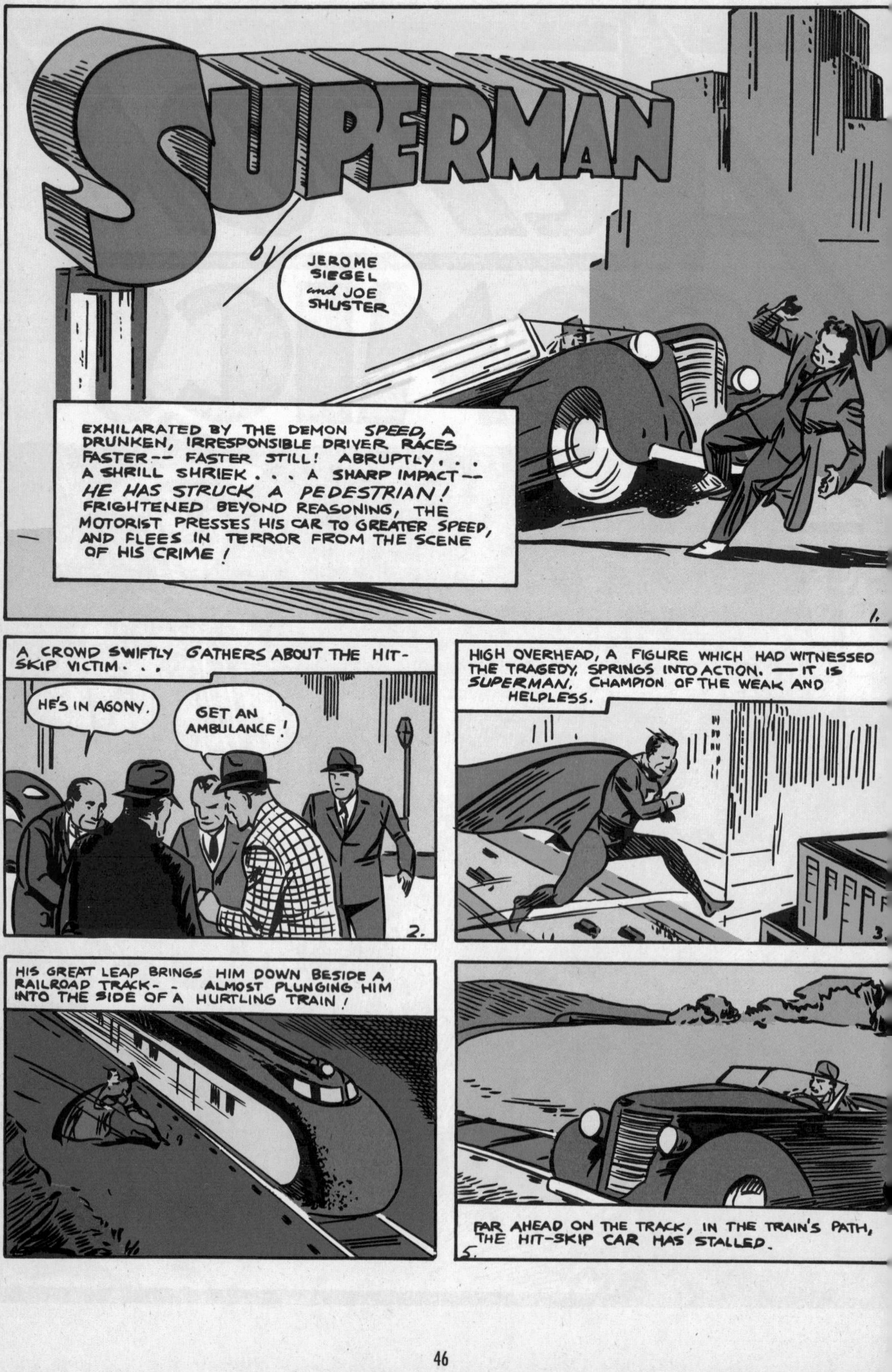
SUPERMAN
by
JEROME SIEGEL and JOE SHUSTER
EXHILARATED BY THE DEMON SPEED, A DRUNKEN, IRRESPONSIBLE DRIVER RACES FASTER-- FASTER STILL! ABRUPTLY. . . A SHRILL SHRIEK . . . A SHARP IMPACT-- HE HAS STRUCK A PEDESTRIAN! FRIGHTENED BEYOND REASONING, THE MOTORIST PRESSES HIS CAR TO GREATER SPEED, AND FLEES IN TERROR FROM THE SCENE OF HIS CRIME!
A CROWD SWIFTLY GATHERS ABOUT THE HIT-SKIP VICTIM. . .
HE'S IN AGONY.
GET AN AMBULANCE!
HIGH OVERHEAD, A FIGURE WHICH HAD WITNESSED THE TRAGEDY, SPRINGS INTO ACTION. — IT IS SUPERMAN, CHAMPION OF THE WEAK AND HELPLESS.
HIS GREAT LEAP BRINGS HIM DOWN BESIDE A RAILROAD TRACK- - ALMOST PLUNGING HIM INTO THE SIDE OF A HURTLING TRAIN!
FAR AHEAD ON THE TRACK, IN THE TRAIN'S PATH, THE HIT-SKIP CAR HAS STALLED.

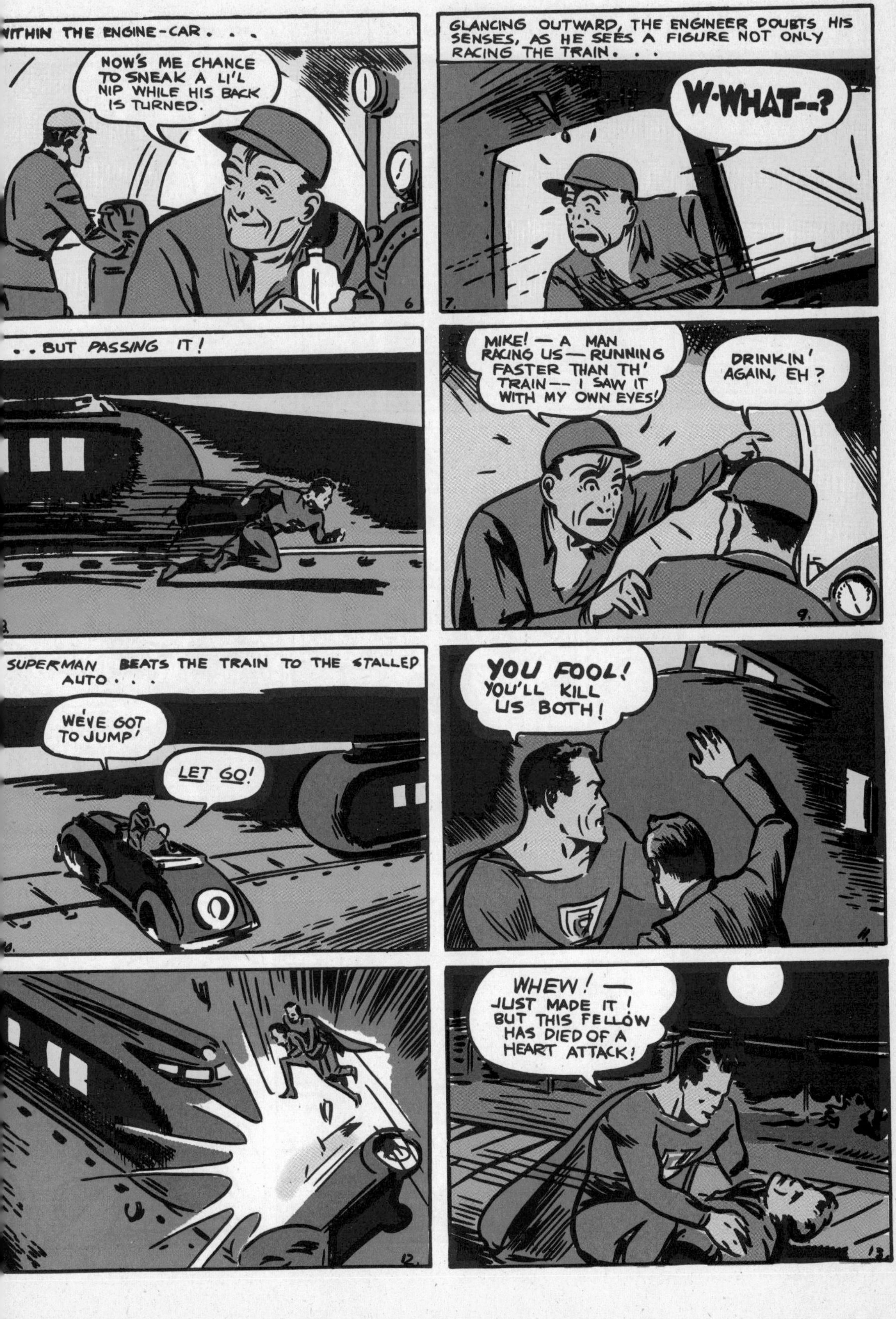
WITHIN THE ENGINE-CAR . . .
NOW'S ME CHANCE TO SNEAK A LI'L NIP WHILE HIS BACK IS TURNED.
GLANCING OUTWARD, THE ENGINEER DOUBTS HIS SENSES, AS HE SEES A FIGURE NOT ONLY RACING THE TRAIN. . .
W-WHAT--?
. . BUT PASSING IT!
MIKE! — A MAN RACING US — RUNNING FASTER THAN TH' TRAIN -- I SAW IT WITH MY OWN EYES!
DRINKIN' AGAIN, EH?
SUPERMAN BEATS THE TRAIN TO THE STALLED AUTO . . .
WE'VE GOT TO JUMP'
LET GO!
YOU FOOL! YOU'LL KILL US BOTH!
WHEW! — JUST MADE IT! BUT THIS FELLOW HAS DIED OF A HEART ATTACK!

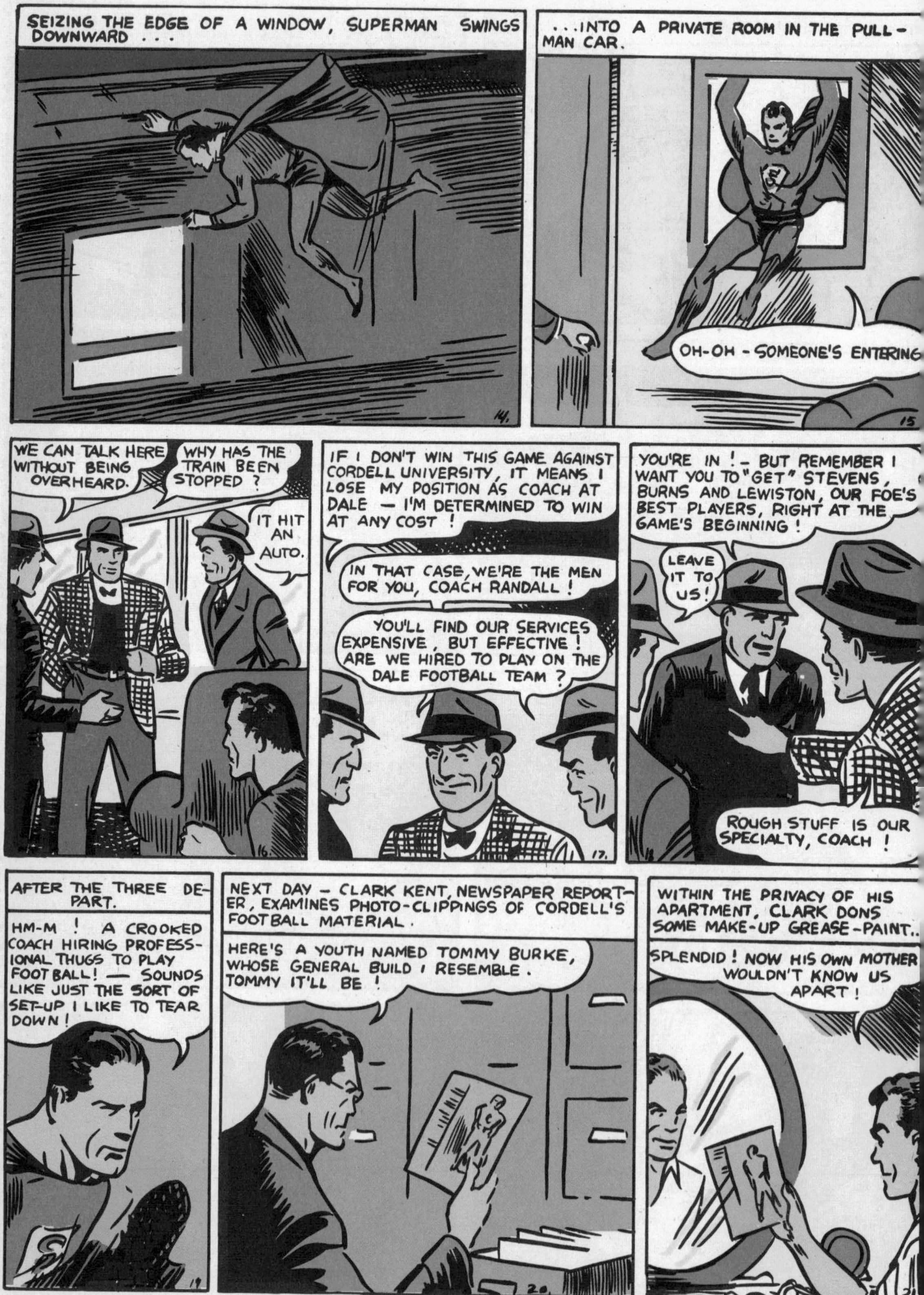
SEIZING THE EDGE OF A WINDOW, SUPERMAN SWINGS DOWNWARD . . .
. . . INTO A PRIVATE ROOM IN THE PULL-MAN CAR.
OH-OH - SOMEONE'S ENTERING
WE CAN TALK HERE WITHOUT BEING OVERHEARD.
WHY HAS THE TRAIN BEEN STOPPED ?
IT HIT AN AUTO.
IF I DON'T WIN THIS GAME AGAINST CORDELL UNIVERSITY, IT MEANS I LOSE MY POSITION AS COACH AT DALE — I'M DETERMINED TO WIN AT ANY COST !
IN THAT CASE, WE'RE THE MEN FOR YOU, COACH RANDALL !
YOU'LL FIND OUR SERVICES EXPENSIVE , BUT EFFECTIVE ! ARE WE HIRED TO PLAY ON THE DALE FOOTBALL TEAM ?
YOU'RE IN ! – BUT REMEMBER I WANT YOU TO "GET" STEVENS, BURNS AND LEWISTON, OUR FOE'S BEST PLAYERS, RIGHT AT THE GAME'S BEGINNING !
LEAVE IT TO US !
ROUGH STUFF IS OUR SPECIALTY, COACH !
AFTER THE THREE DE-PART.
HM-M ! A CROOKED COACH HIRING PROFESS-IONAL THUGS TO PLAY FOOTBALL! — SOUNDS LIKE JUST THE SORT OF SET-UP I LIKE TO TEAR DOWN !
NEXT DAY – CLARK KENT, NEWSPAPER REPORT-ER, EXAMINES PHOTO-CLIPPINGS OF CORDELL'S FOOTBALL MATERIAL .
HERE'S A YOUTH NAMED TOMMY BURKE, WHOSE GENERAL BUILD I RESEMBLE . TOMMY IT'LL BE !
WITHIN THE PRIVACY OF HIS APARTMENT, CLARK DONS SOME MAKE-UP GREASE-PAINT. .
SPLENDID ! NOW HIS OWN MOTHER WOULDN'T KNOW US APART !

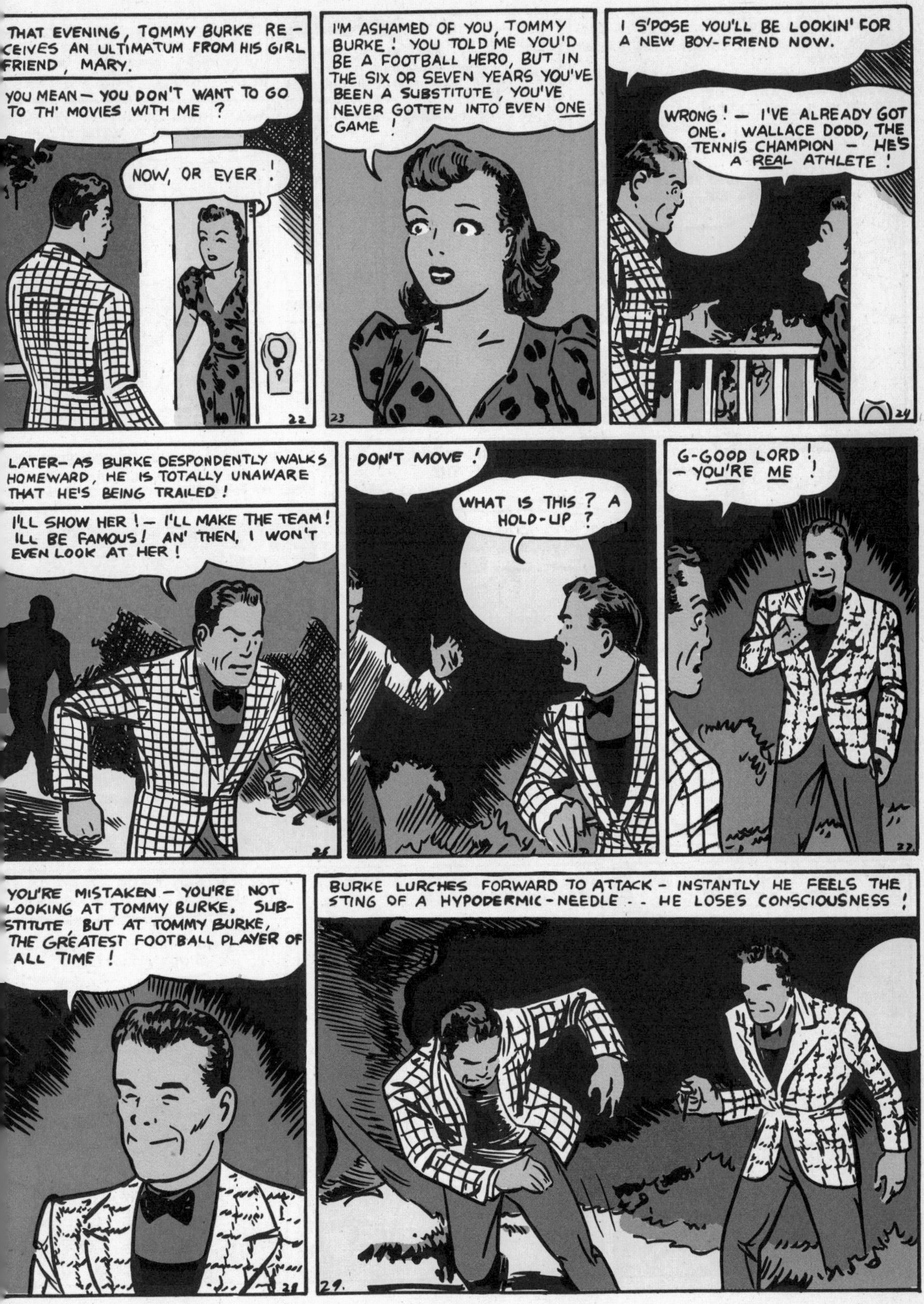

THAT EVENING, TOMMY BURKE RECEIVES AN ULTIMATUM FROM HIS GIRL FRIEND, MARY.
YOU MEAN — YOU DON'T WANT TO GO TO TH' MOVIES WITH ME ?
NOW, OR EVER !
I'M ASHAMED OF YOU, TOMMY BURKE ! YOU TOLD ME YOU'D BE A FOOTBALL HERO, BUT IN THE SIX OR SEVEN YEARS YOU'VE BEEN A SUBSTITUTE, YOU'VE NEVER GOTTEN INTO EVEN ONE GAME !
I S'POSE YOU'LL BE LOOKIN' FOR A NEW BOY-FRIEND NOW.
WRONG ! — I'VE ALREADY GOT ONE. WALLACE DODD, THE TENNIS CHAMPION — HE'S A REAL ATHLETE !
LATER — AS BURKE DESPONDENTLY WALKS HOMEWARD, HE IS TOTALLY UNAWARE THAT HE'S BEING TRAILED !
I'LL SHOW HER ! — I'LL MAKE THE TEAM ! I'LL BE FAMOUS ! AN' THEN, I WON'T EVEN LOOK AT HER !
DON'T MOVE !
WHAT IS THIS ? A HOLD-UP ?
G-GOOD LORD ! — YOU'RE ME !
YOU'RE MISTAKEN — YOU'RE NOT LOOKING AT TOMMY BURKE, SUBSTITUTE, BUT AT TOMMY BURKE, THE GREATEST FOOTBALL PLAYER OF ALL TIME !
BURKE LURCHES FORWARD TO ATTACK — INSTANTLY HE FEELS THE STING OF A HYPODERMIC-NEEDLE - - HE LOSES CONSCIOUSNESS !

BURKE REGAINS CONSCIOUSNESS TO DISCOVER HIMSELF A PRISONER IN HIS OWN APARTMENT.

W-WHAT HAVE YOU DONE TO ME? I CAN'T MOVE!

YOU NEEDN'T WORRY YOU'RE JUST RENDERED PASSIVE BY A DRUG.

30

BUT WHAT'S TH' BIG IDEA?

MERELY THIS: I'M GOING TO TAKE YOUR PLACE IN LIFE FOR A FEW DAYS — SO LONG, FOR NOW!

31

DISGUISED AS BURKE, SUPERMAN REPORTS TO THE LOCKER-ROOM OF CORDELL UNIVERSITY, PREPARATORY TO FOOTBALL PRACTICE.

WELL, HERE GOES! — WONDER IF I'LL GET AWAY WITH IT?

LOCKER ROOM

32

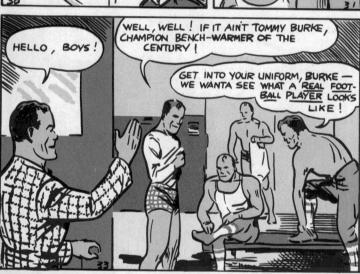

HELLO, BOYS!

WELL, WELL! IF IT AIN'T TOMMY BURKE, CHAMPION BENCH-WARMER OF THE CENTURY!

GET INTO YOUR UNIFORM, BURKE — WE WANTA SEE WHAT A REAL FOOTBALL PLAYER LOOKS LIKE!

33

I DON'T KNOW IN WHICH LOCKER BURKE KEEPS HIS STUFF — I'LL JUST CHOOSE ONE AT RANDOM... THIS ONE WILL DO.

34

SAY! — WHAT TH' BLAZES YOU DOIN' IN MY LOCKER?

SORRY-- MY MISTAKE.

35

I'LL GIVE YOU SOMETHING TO BE REALLY SORRY ABOUT!

36

DON'T STAND THERE GRINNING! PUT UP YOUR HANDS AND FIGHT!

BUT IT'S MORE FUN TO SIMPLY WATCH!

37

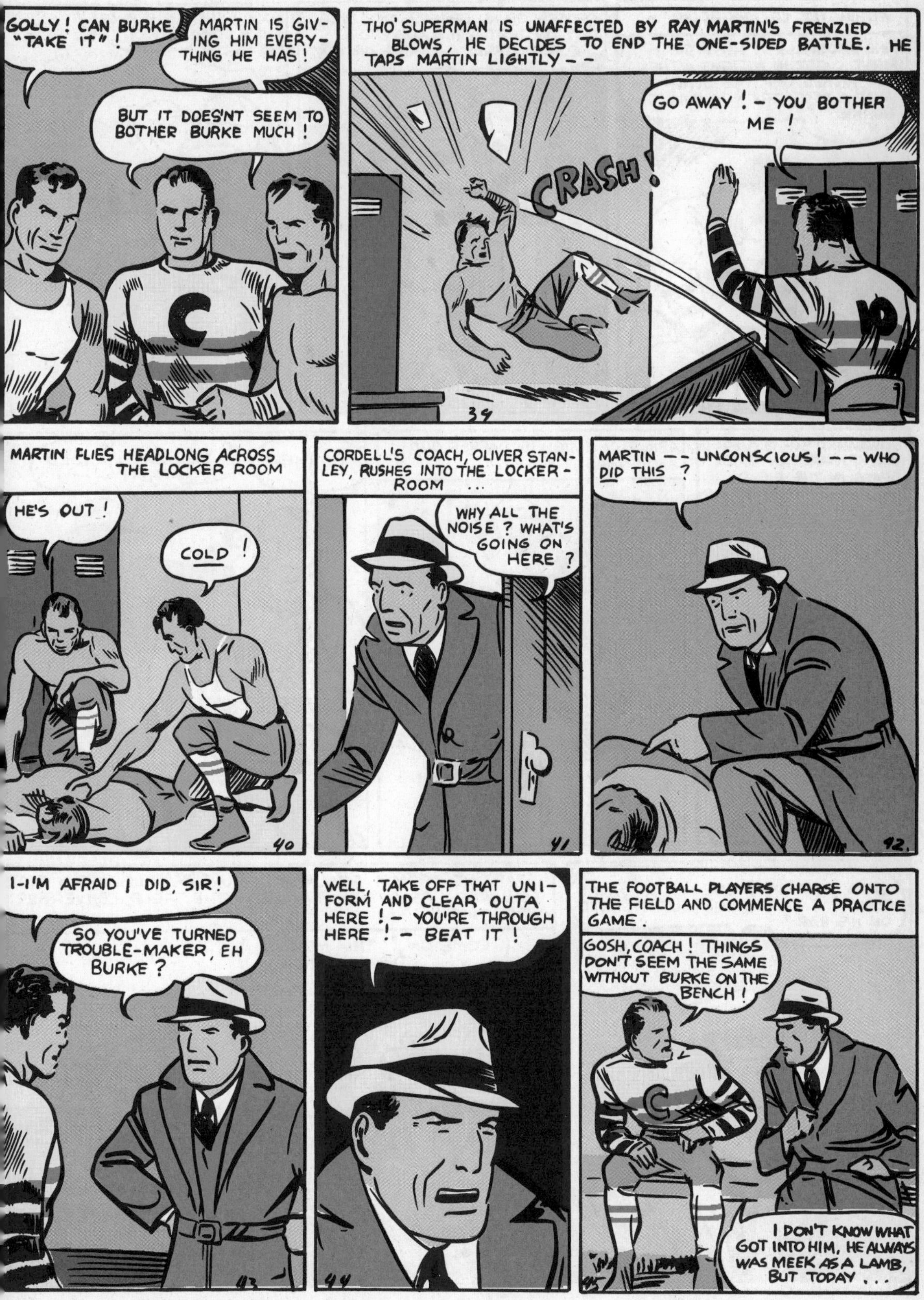
GOLLY! CAN BURKE "TAKE IT"!
MARTIN IS GIVING HIM EVERYTHING HE HAS!
BUT IT DOES'NT SEEM TO BOTHER BURKE MUCH!
THO' SUPERMAN IS UNAFFECTED BY RAY MARTIN'S FRENZIED BLOWS, HE DECIDES TO END THE ONE-SIDED BATTLE. HE TAPS MARTIN LIGHTLY - -
GO AWAY! - YOU BOTHER ME!
CRASH!
MARTIN FLIES HEADLONG ACROSS THE LOCKER ROOM
HE'S OUT!
COLD!
CORDELL'S COACH, OLIVER STANLEY, RUSHES INTO THE LOCKER-ROOM ...
WHY ALL THE NOISE? WHAT'S GOING ON HERE?
MARTIN -- UNCONSCIOUS! -- WHO DID THIS?
I-I'M AFRAID I DID, SIR!
SO YOU'VE TURNED TROUBLE-MAKER, EH BURKE?
WELL, TAKE OFF THAT UNIFORM AND CLEAR OUTA HERE! - YOU'RE THROUGH HERE! - BEAT IT!
THE FOOTBALL PLAYERS CHARGE ONTO THE FIELD AND COMMENCE A PRACTICE GAME.
GOSH, COACH! THINGS DON'T SEEM THE SAME WITHOUT BURKE ON THE BENCH!
I DON'T KNOW WHAT GOT INTO HIM, HE ALWAYS WAS MEEK AS A LAMB, BUT TODAY...

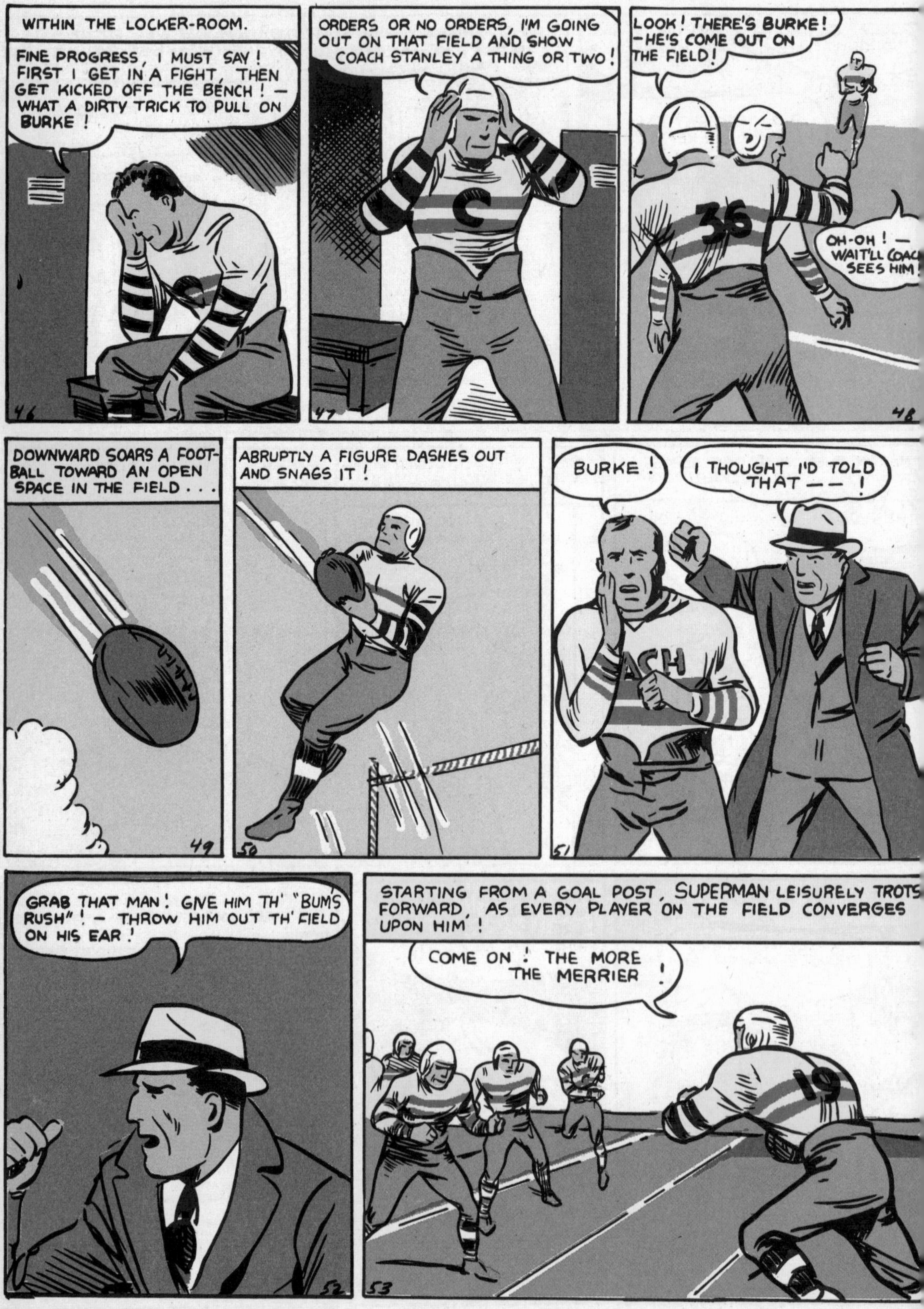
WITHIN THE LOCKER-ROOM.
FINE PROGRESS, I MUST SAY! FIRST I GET IN A FIGHT, THEN GET KICKED OFF THE BENCH! — WHAT A DIRTY TRICK TO PULL ON BURKE!
ORDERS OR NO ORDERS, I'M GOING OUT ON THAT FIELD AND SHOW COACH STANLEY A THING OR TWO!
LOOK! THERE'S BURKE! —HE'S COME OUT ON THE FIELD!
36
OH-OH! — WAIT'LL COACH SEES HIM!
DOWNWARD SOARS A FOOTBALL TOWARD AN OPEN SPACE IN THE FIELD . . .
ABRUPTLY A FIGURE DASHES OUT AND SNAGS IT!
BURKE!
I THOUGHT I'D TOLD THAT — — !
GRAB THAT MAN! GIVE HIM TH' "BUM'S RUSH"! — THROW HIM OUT TH' FIELD ON HIS EAR!
STARTING FROM A GOAL POST, SUPERMAN LEISURELY TROTS FORWARD, AS EVERY PLAYER ON THE FIELD CONVERGES UPON HIM!
COME ON! THE MORE THE MERRIER!
19

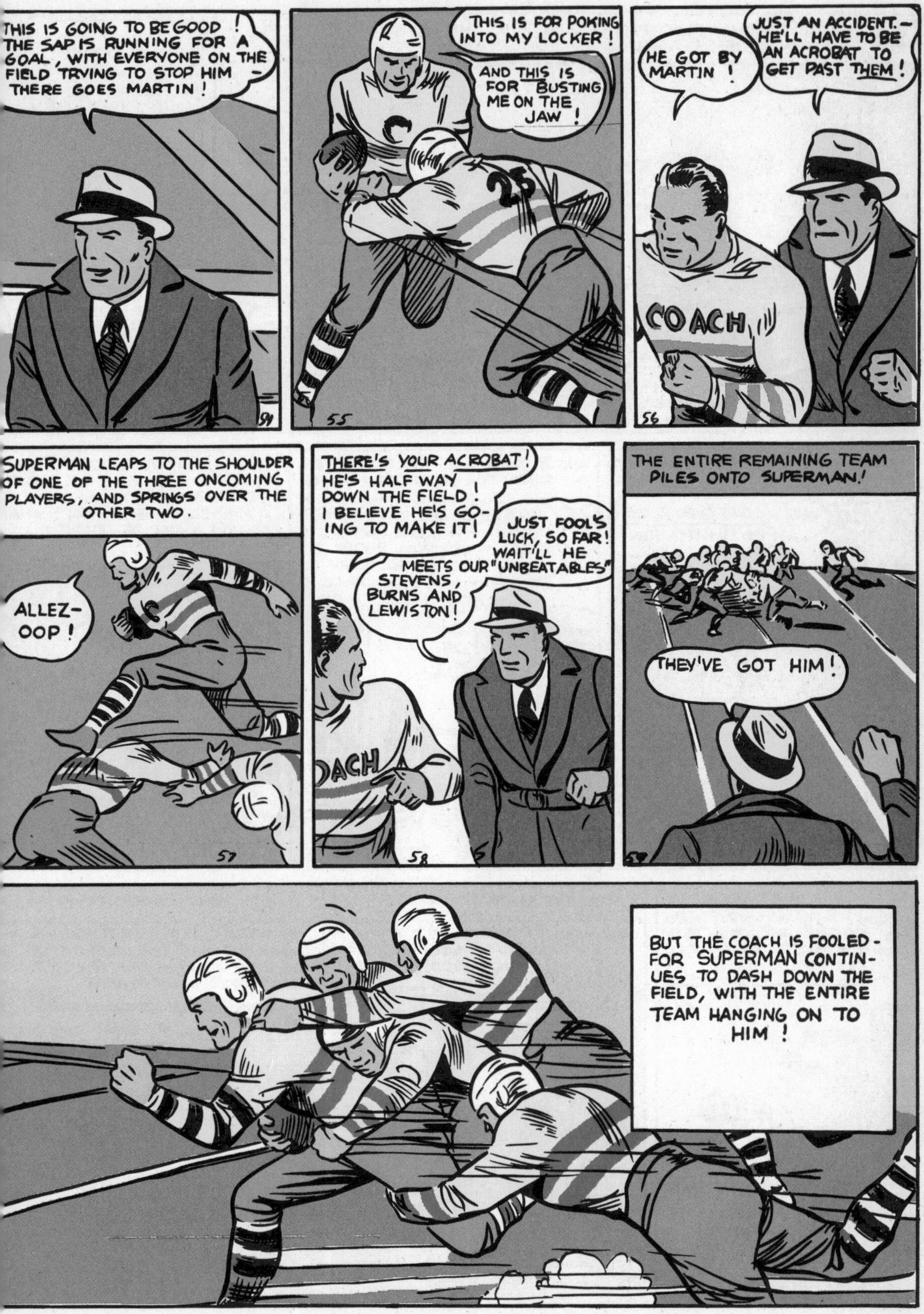

THIS IS GOING TO BE GOOD! THE SAP IS RUNNING FOR A GOAL, WITH EVERYONE ON THE FIELD TRYING TO STOP HIM — THERE GOES MARTIN!
THIS IS FOR POKING INTO MY LOCKER!
AND THIS IS FOR BUSTING ME ON THE JAW!
HE GOT BY MARTIN!
JUST AN ACCIDENT.— HE'LL HAVE TO BE AN ACROBAT TO GET PAST THEM!
COACH
SUPERMAN LEAPS TO THE SHOULDER OF ONE OF THE THREE ONCOMING PLAYERS, AND SPRINGS OVER THE OTHER TWO.
ALLEZ-OOP!
THERE'S YOUR ACROBAT! HE'S HALF WAY DOWN THE FIELD! I BELIEVE HE'S GOING TO MAKE IT!
JUST FOOL'S LUCK, SO FAR! WAIT'LL HE MEETS OUR "UNBEATABLES" STEVENS, BURNS AND LEWISTON!
THE ENTIRE REMAINING TEAM PILES ONTO SUPERMAN!
THEY'VE GOT HIM!
BUT THE COACH IS FOOLED- FOR SUPERMAN CONTINUES TO DASH DOWN THE FIELD, WITH THE ENTIRE TEAM HANGING ON TO HIM!

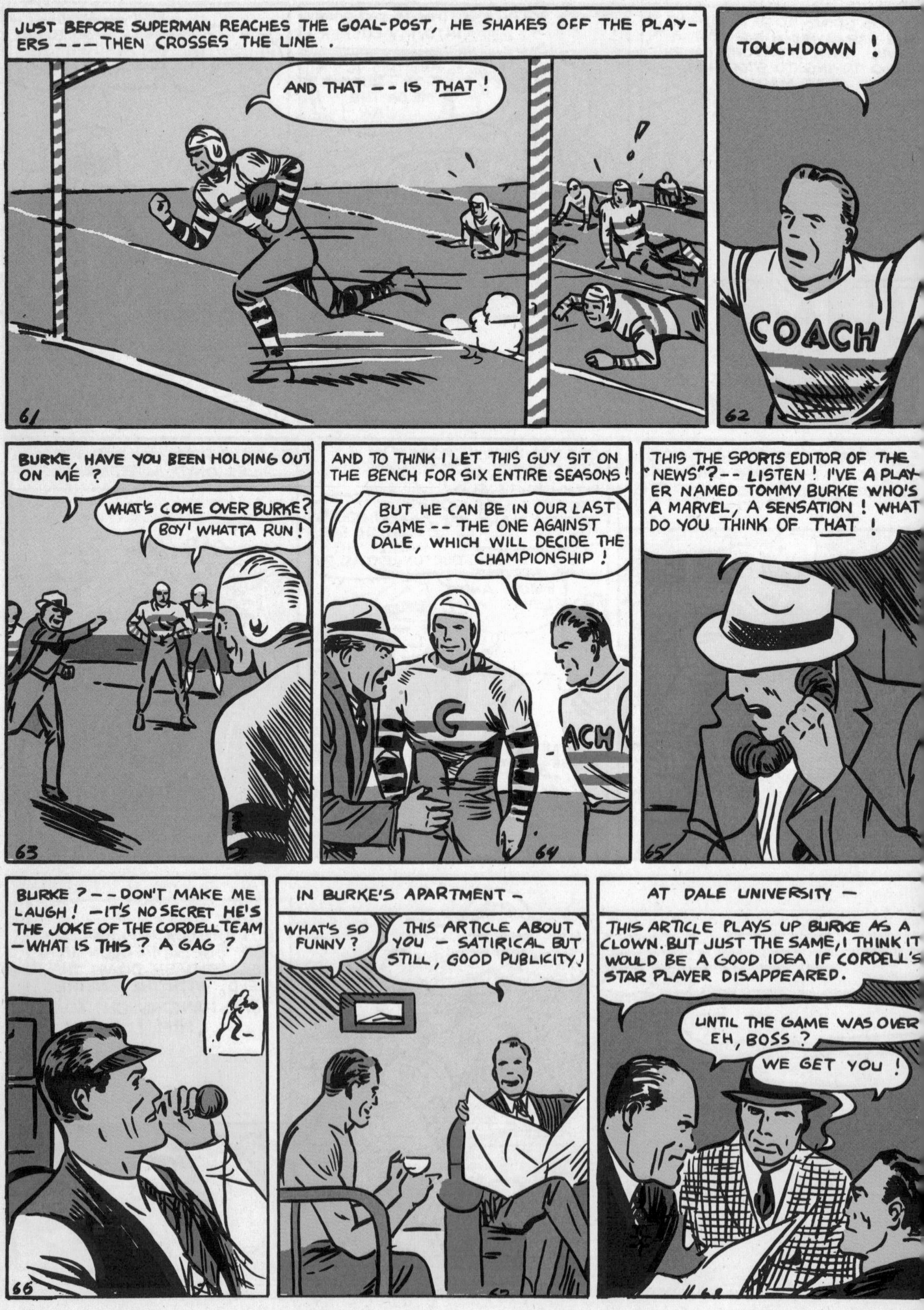
JUST BEFORE SUPERMAN REACHES THE GOAL-POST, HE SHAKES OFF THE PLAYERS --- THEN CROSSES THE LINE.
AND THAT -- IS THAT!
TOUCHDOWN!
COACH
BURKE, HAVE YOU BEEN HOLDING OUT ON ME?
WHAT'S COME OVER BURKE?
BOY! WHATTA RUN!
AND TO THINK I LET THIS GUY SIT ON THE BENCH FOR SIX ENTIRE SEASONS!
BUT HE CAN BE IN OUR LAST GAME -- THE ONE AGAINST DALE, WHICH WILL DECIDE THE CHAMPIONSHIP!
THIS THE SPORTS EDITOR OF THE "NEWS"? -- LISTEN! I'VE A PLAYER NAMED TOMMY BURKE WHO'S A MARVEL, A SENSATION! WHAT DO YOU THINK OF THAT!
BURKE? -- DON'T MAKE ME LAUGH! — IT'S NO SECRET HE'S THE JOKE OF THE CORDELL TEAM — WHAT IS THIS? A GAG?
IN BURKE'S APARTMENT —
WHAT'S SO FUNNY?
THIS ARTICLE ABOUT YOU — SATIRICAL BUT STILL, GOOD PUBLICITY!
AT DALE UNIVERSITY —
THIS ARTICLE PLAYS UP BURKE AS A CLOWN. BUT JUST THE SAME, I THINK IT WOULD BE A GOOD IDEA IF CORDELL'S STAR PLAYER DISAPPEARED.
UNTIL THE GAME WAS OVER EH, BOSS?
WE GET YOU!

DURING THE FOLLOWING DAYS, THE CORDELL TEAM PRACTICES STEADILY FOR THE BIG GAME.

I STILL DON'T GET IT! HOW IN THE WORLD CAN A PLAYER BECOME SO GOOD OVERNIGHT?

IF YOU KNEW, YOU'D BE THE GREATEST COACH IN THE WORLD!

TOMORROW'S THE GAME WITH DALE! NOW REMEMBER -- EARLY TO BED, NO SMOKING, NO DRINKING! - PLEASANT DREAMS!

THAT EVENING --

BURKE IS ASLEEP IN THAT A-PARTMENT, - YOU KNOW WHAT TO DO.

LATER -

HE'S COMPLETELY TIED!

STRANGE HE DIDN'T STRUGGLE AT ALL!

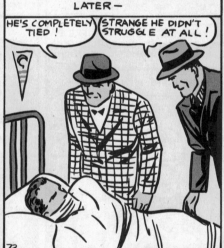

THE TWO THUGS ARE UNAWARE BURKE IS UNDER THE INFLUENCE OF A SLEEP-INDUCING DRUG OR THAT SUPERMAN IS OB-SERVING THEM FROM THE MOLD-ING OVERHEAD!

WHEN THE KIDNAPPERS DRIVE OFF, SUPERMAN RACES IN PURSUIT, EASILY KEEPING THEIR AUTO IN SIGHT!

BURKE IS BROUGHT INTO A DESERTED HOUSE!

W-WHERE AM I?

WHERE YOU WON'T BE ABLE TO GET INTO TOMORROW'S GAME.

BUT YOU DON'T WANT ME - I'M JUST A' SUB-STITUTE AND BESIDES-

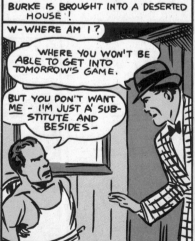

ARE YOU TOMMY BURKE?

YES, BUT IT ISN'T ME WHO--

THAT'S ALL WE WANTA KNOW - THIS GAG'ILL QUIET YOU DOWN.

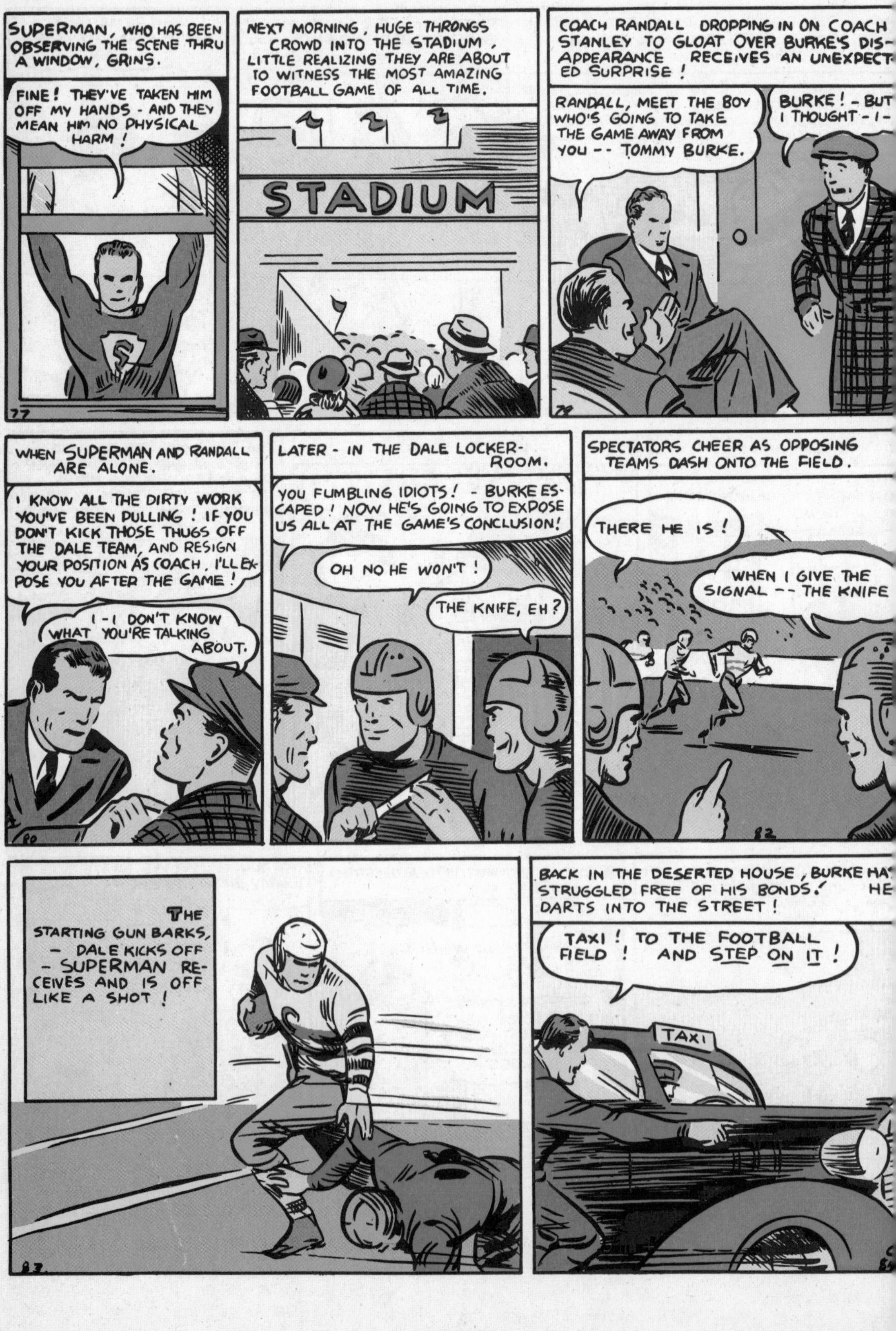
SUPERMAN, WHO HAS BEEN OBSERVING THE SCENE THRU A WINDOW, GRINS.
FINE! THEY'VE TAKEN HIM OFF MY HANDS - AND THEY MEAN HIM NO PHYSICAL HARM!
77
NEXT MORNING, HUGE THRONGS CROWD INTO THE STADIUM, LITTLE REALIZING THEY ARE ABOUT TO WITNESS THE MOST AMAZING FOOTBALL GAME OF ALL TIME.
STADIUM
COACH RANDALL DROPPING IN ON COACH STANLEY TO GLOAT OVER BURKE'S DISAPPEARANCE RECEIVES AN UNEXPECTED SURPRISE!
RANDALL, MEET THE BOY WHO'S GOING TO TAKE THE GAME AWAY FROM YOU -- TOMMY BURKE.
BURKE! - BUT I THOUGHT - I -
WHEN SUPERMAN AND RANDALL ARE ALONE.
I KNOW ALL THE DIRTY WORK YOU'VE BEEN PULLING! IF YOU DON'T KICK THOSE THUGS OFF THE DALE TEAM, AND RESIGN YOUR POSITION AS COACH, I'LL EXPOSE YOU AFTER THE GAME!
I-I DON'T KNOW WHAT YOU'RE TALKING ABOUT.
80
LATER - IN THE DALE LOCKER-ROOM.
YOU FUMBLING IDIOTS! - BURKE ESCAPED! NOW HE'S GOING TO EXPOSE US ALL AT THE GAME'S CONCLUSION!
OH NO HE WON'T!
THE KNIFE, EH?
SPECTATORS CHEER AS OPPOSING TEAMS DASH ONTO THE FIELD.
THERE HE IS!
WHEN I GIVE THE SIGNAL -- THE KNIFE
82
THE STARTING GUN BARKS, - DALE KICKS OFF - SUPERMAN RECEIVES AND IS OFF LIKE A SHOT!
83
BACK IN THE DESERTED HOUSE, BURKE HA STRUGGLED FREE OF HIS BONDS! HE DARTS INTO THE STREET!
TAXI! TO THE FOOTBALL FIELD! AND STEP ON IT!
TAXI

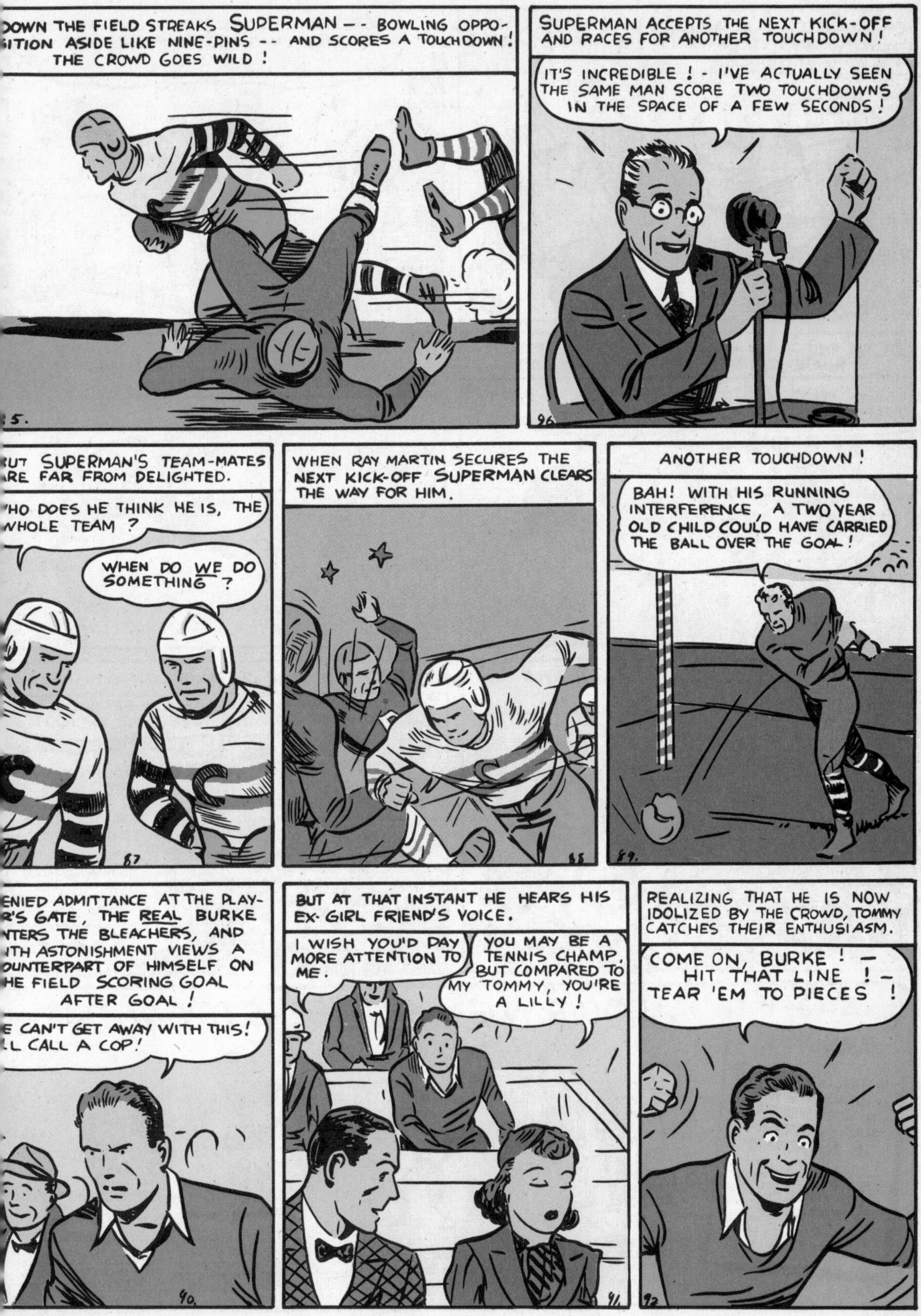

DOWN THE FIELD STREAKS SUPERMAN -- BOWLING OPPO-
SITION ASIDE LIKE NINE-PINS -- AND SCORES A TOUCHDOWN!
THE CROWD GOES WILD!
SUPERMAN ACCEPTS THE NEXT KICK-OFF AND RACES FOR ANOTHER TOUCHDOWN!
IT'S INCREDIBLE! - I'VE ACTUALLY SEEN THE SAME MAN SCORE TWO TOUCHDOWNS IN THE SPACE OF A FEW SECONDS!
UT SUPERMAN'S TEAM-MATES
RE FAR FROM DELIGHTED.
HO DOES HE THINK HE IS, THE HOLE TEAM?
WHEN DO WE DO SOMETHING?
WHEN RAY MARTIN SECURES THE NEXT KICK-OFF SUPERMAN CLEARS THE WAY FOR HIM.
ANOTHER TOUCHDOWN!
BAH! WITH HIS RUNNING INTERFERENCE, A TWO YEAR OLD CHILD COULD HAVE CARRIED THE BALL OVER THE GOAL!
ENIED ADMITTANCE AT THE PLAY-
R'S GATE, THE REAL BURKE
NTERS THE BLEACHERS, AND
ITH ASTONISHMENT VIEWS A
OUNTERPART OF HIMSELF ON
HE FIELD SCORING GOAL
AFTER GOAL!
E CAN'T GET AWAY WITH THIS!
LL CALL A COP!
BUT AT THAT INSTANT HE HEARS HIS EX-GIRL FRIEND'S VOICE.
I WISH YOU'D PAY MORE ATTENTION TO ME.
YOU MAY BE A TENNIS CHAMP, BUT COMPARED TO MY TOMMY, YOU'RE A LILLY!
REALIZING THAT HE IS NOW IDOLIZED BY THE CROWD, TOMMY CATCHES THEIR ENTHUSIASM.
COME ON, BURKE! — HIT THAT LINE! — TEAR 'EM TO PIECES!

ON THE FIELD — AS A POCKET-KNIFE SNAPS UPON SUPERMAN'S TOUGH SKIN, HE ATTENDS TO HIS TWO ATTACKERS.

HERE — TAKE THIS NOTE — MY RESIGNATION — TO DALE UNIVERSITY'S PRESIDENT.

AT THE END OF THE HALF, SUPERMAN MEETS BURKE OUTSIDE THE LOCKER-ROOM.

QUICK! WE'VE GOT TO EXCHANGE CLOTHES!

I GET IT! I'M TO CARRY ON, NOW!

AS THE SECOND HALF COMMENCES, THE BALL BOUNCES NEAR BURKE — HE CHASES IT ABOUT — AWKWARDLY — DESPERATELY — —

WHEN HE FINALLY SNAGS IT, EVERY PLAYER ON THE FIELD PILES ONTO HIM.

LATER — WHEN HE REGAINS CONSCIOUSNESS..

TOMMY, YOU WERE WONDERFUL — SPLENDID! BUT YOU MUST PROMISE YOU'LL GIVE UP FOOTBALL! IT'S TOO BRUTAL!

GIVE UP FOOT-BALL YOU DON'T KNOW WHAT YOU ASK! BUT FOR YOU, I'LL DO IT!

AND HOW!

THE END

"ACQUIRING SUPER-STRENGTH"

WARNING:

WHEN EXERCISING IT IS ALWAYS WELL TO REMEMBER THAT OVERSTRAIN IS DANGEROUS.

BE MODERATE IN YOUR EXERTIONS!

YOU MAY FIND LIFTING A HEAVY ARM-CHAIR A DIFFICULT TASK.

HOWEVER, IF YOU LIFT SMALLER WEIGHTS REGULARLY...

...AND GRAD-UALLY INCREASE THE WEIGHT OF THESE OBJECTS...

YOU'LL SOON FIND LIFTING A MERE ARMCHAIR A CINCH!

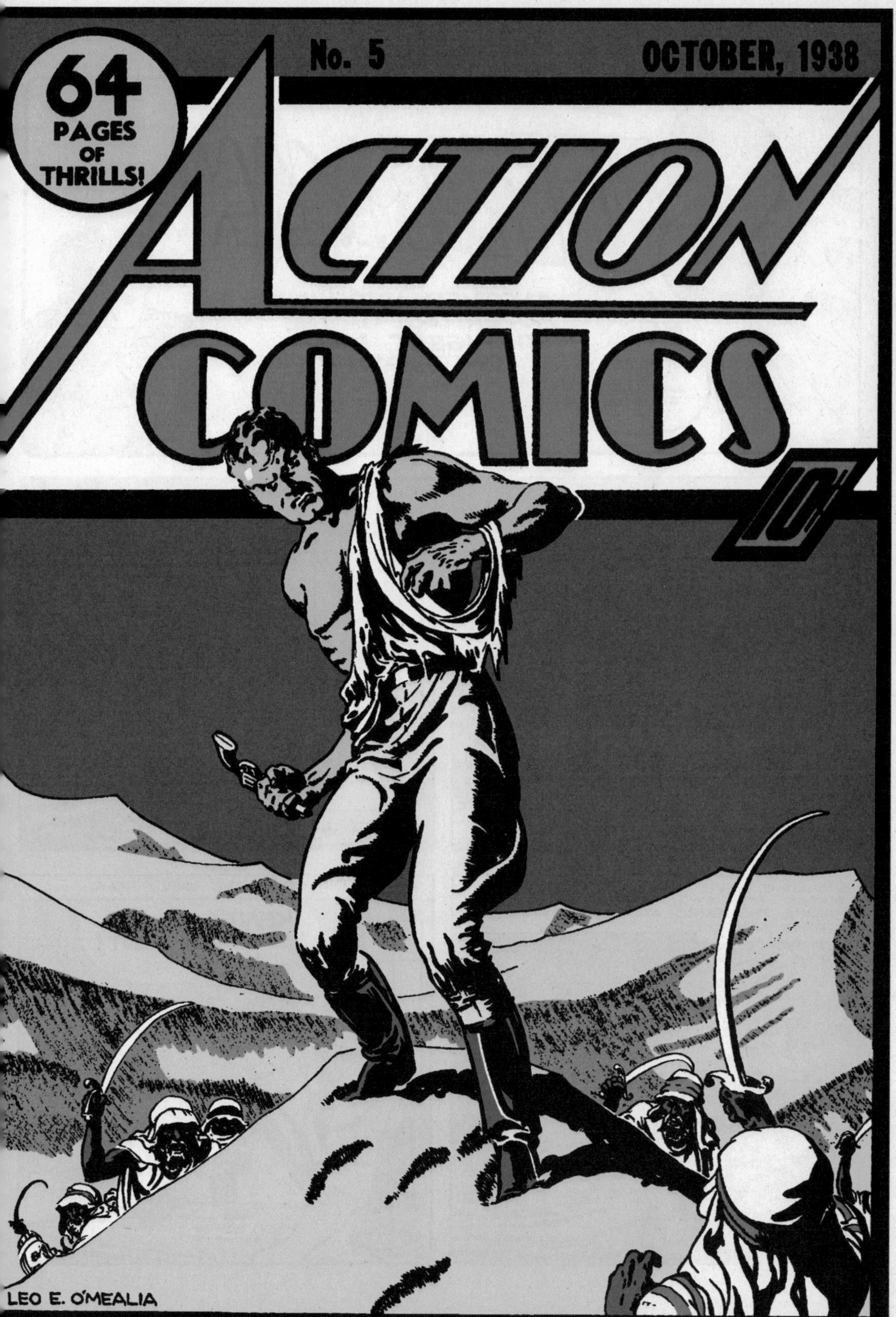

64 PAGES OF THRILLS!
No. 5
OCTOBER, 1938
ACTION COMICS
10¢
LEO E. O'MEALIA

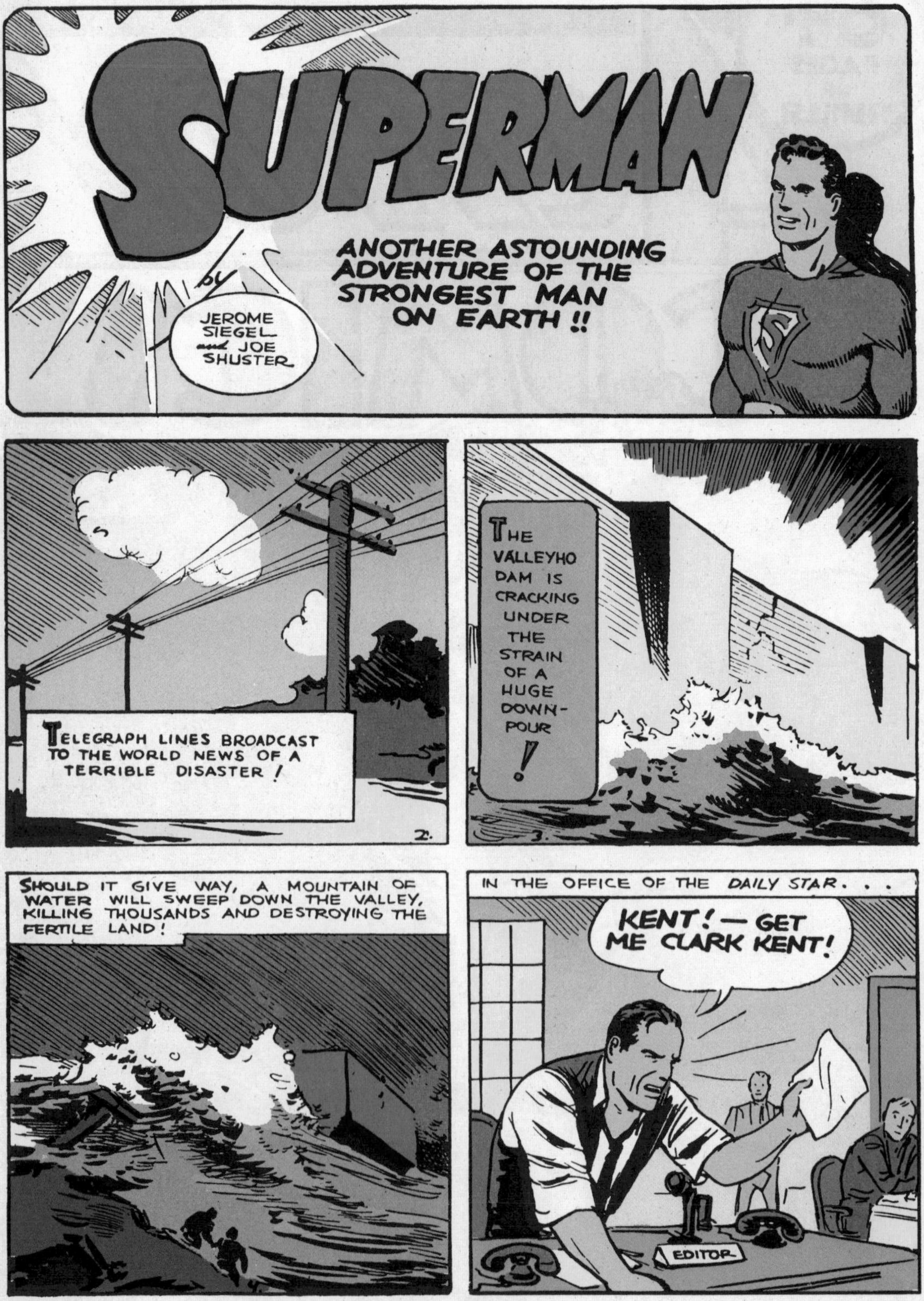
SUPERMAN
by
JEROME SIEGEL and JOE SHUSTER
ANOTHER ASTOUNDING ADVENTURE OF THE STRONGEST MAN ON EARTH !!
TELEGRAPH LINES BROADCAST TO THE WORLD NEWS OF A TERRIBLE DISASTER !
2.
THE VALLEYHO DAM IS CRACKING UNDER THE STRAIN OF A HUGE DOWN-POUR !
3.
SHOULD IT GIVE WAY, A MOUNTAIN OF WATER WILL SWEEP DOWN THE VALLEY, KILLING THOUSANDS AND DESTROYING THE FERTILE LAND !
IN THE OFFICE OF THE DAILY STAR. . .
KENT! — GET ME CLARK KENT!
EDITOR

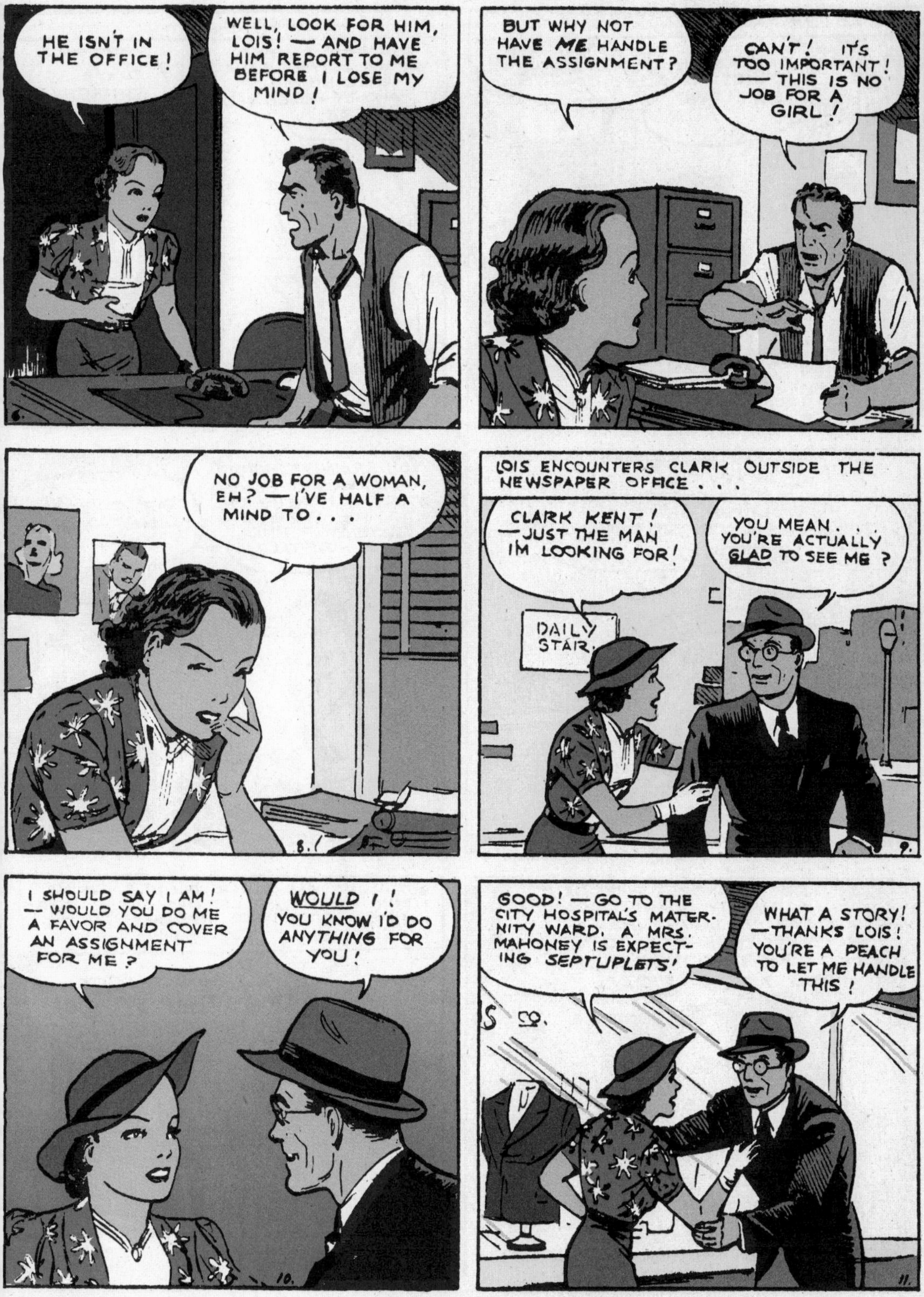

HE ISN'T IN THE OFFICE!
WELL, LOOK FOR HIM, LOIS! — AND HAVE HIM REPORT TO ME BEFORE I LOSE MY MIND!
6.
BUT WHY NOT HAVE *ME* HANDLE THE ASSIGNMENT?
CAN'T! IT'S TOO IMPORTANT! — THIS IS NO JOB FOR A GIRL!
NO JOB FOR A WOMAN, EH? — I'VE HALF A MIND TO . . .
8.
LOIS ENCOUNTERS CLARK OUTSIDE THE NEWSPAPER OFFICE . . .
CLARK KENT! —JUST THE MAN I'M LOOKING FOR!
YOU MEAN . . . YOU'RE ACTUALLY GLAD TO SEE ME?
DAILY STAR
9.
I SHOULD SAY I AM! — WOULD YOU DO ME A FAVOR AND COVER AN ASSIGNMENT FOR ME?
WOULD I! YOU KNOW I'D DO *ANYTHING* FOR YOU!
10.
GOOD! — GO TO THE CITY HOSPITAL'S MATERNITY WARD. A MRS. MAHONEY IS EXPECTING *SEPTUPLETS!*
WHAT A STORY! —THANKS LOIS! YOU'RE A PEACH TO LET ME HANDLE THIS!
S CO.
11.

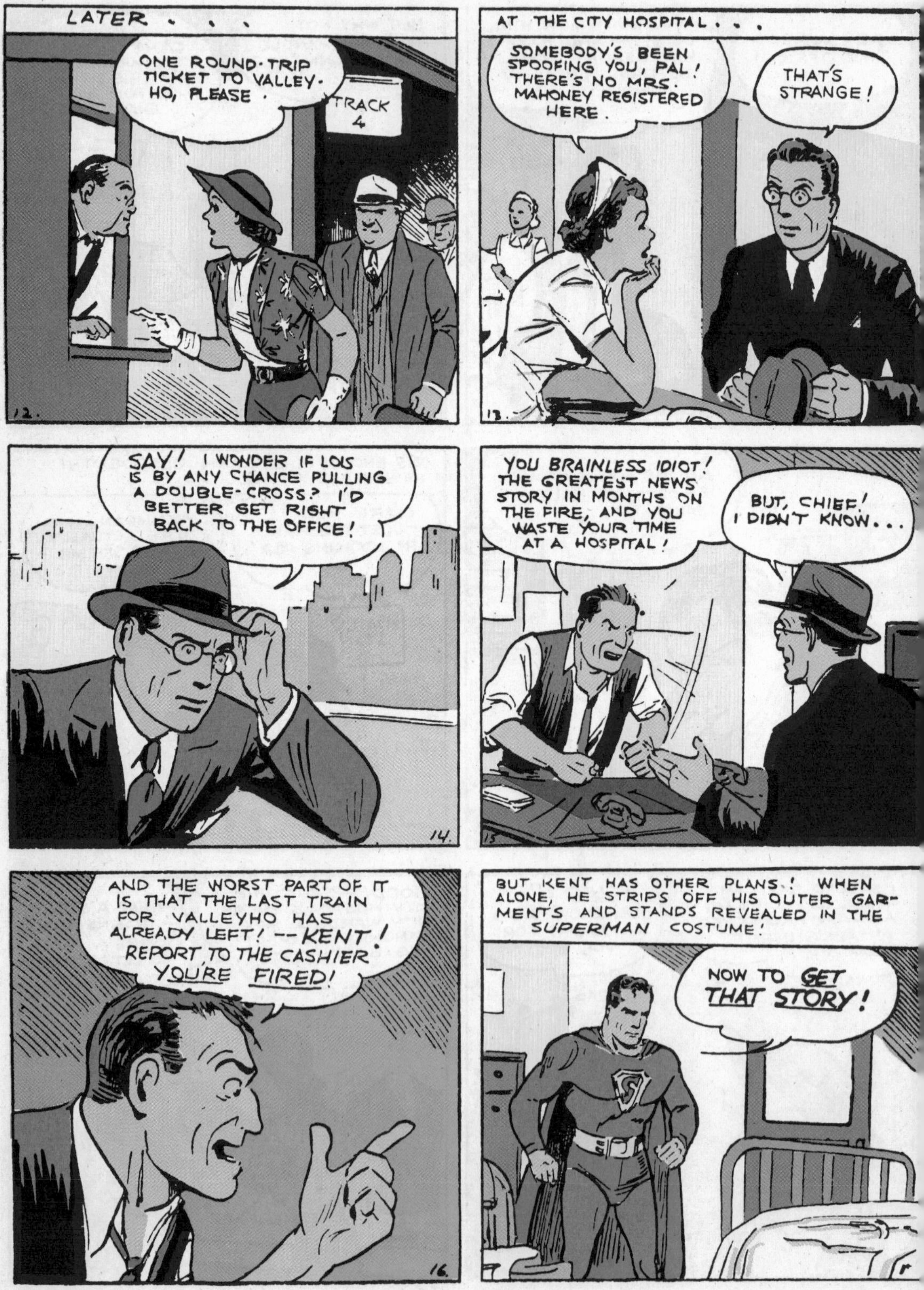
LATER . . .
ONE ROUND-TRIP TICKET TO VALLEY-HO, PLEASE .
TRACK 4
12.
AT THE CITY HOSPITAL . . .
SOMEBODY'S BEEN SPOOFING YOU, PAL! THERE'S NO MRS. MAHONEY REGISTERED HERE.
THAT'S STRANGE!
13.
SAY! I WONDER IF LOIS IS BY ANY CHANCE PULLING A DOUBLE-CROSS? I'D BETTER GET RIGHT BACK TO THE OFFICE!
14.
YOU BRAINLESS IDIOT! THE GREATEST NEWS STORY IN MONTHS ON THE FIRE, AND YOU WASTE YOUR TIME AT A HOSPITAL!
BUT, CHIEF! I DIDN'T KNOW...
15
AND THE WORST PART OF IT IS THAT THE LAST TRAIN FOR VALLEYHO HAS ALREADY LEFT! --KENT! REPORT TO THE CASHIER YOU'RE FIRED!
16.
BUT KENT HAS OTHER PLANS! WHEN ALONE, HE STRIPS OFF HIS OUTER GARMENTS AND STANDS REVEALED IN THE SUPERMAN COSTUME!
NOW TO GET THAT STORY!

FROM ATOP THE GREAT *DAILY STAR* BUILDING, A WEIRD FIGURE LEAPS OUT INTO THE NIGHT!

HUGE DISTANCES ARE SWIFTLY COVERED BY IT WITH GIANT LEAPS . . .

19.

LOOKS LIKE THE TRAIN HEADED FOR VALLEYHO! WELL . . .

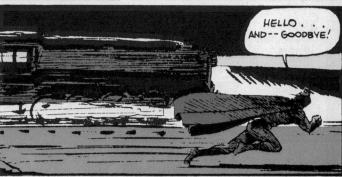

HELLO . . . . AND -- GOODBYE!

IT'S FAR OUTDISTANCED! -- IF LOIS THINKS SHE'S GOING TO SCOOP ME, SHE'S BADLY MISTAKEN!

22

WITH THE SPEED OF LIGHT, HE REACHES THE RAILROAD TRESTLE . . .

WHAT TH' -- !

A TORRENT HAS LOOSENED THE BRIDGE'S SUPPORTS, CAUSING THE TRACKS TO TILT -- MAKING A WRECK INEVITABLE!

THE WARNING WHISTLE OF THE APPROACHING TRAIN IS HEARD!

WITHOUT A MOMENTS HESITATION THE CLOAKED FIGURE MOUNTS A PEAK OF THE ROCKS AND DIVES FORWARD . . .

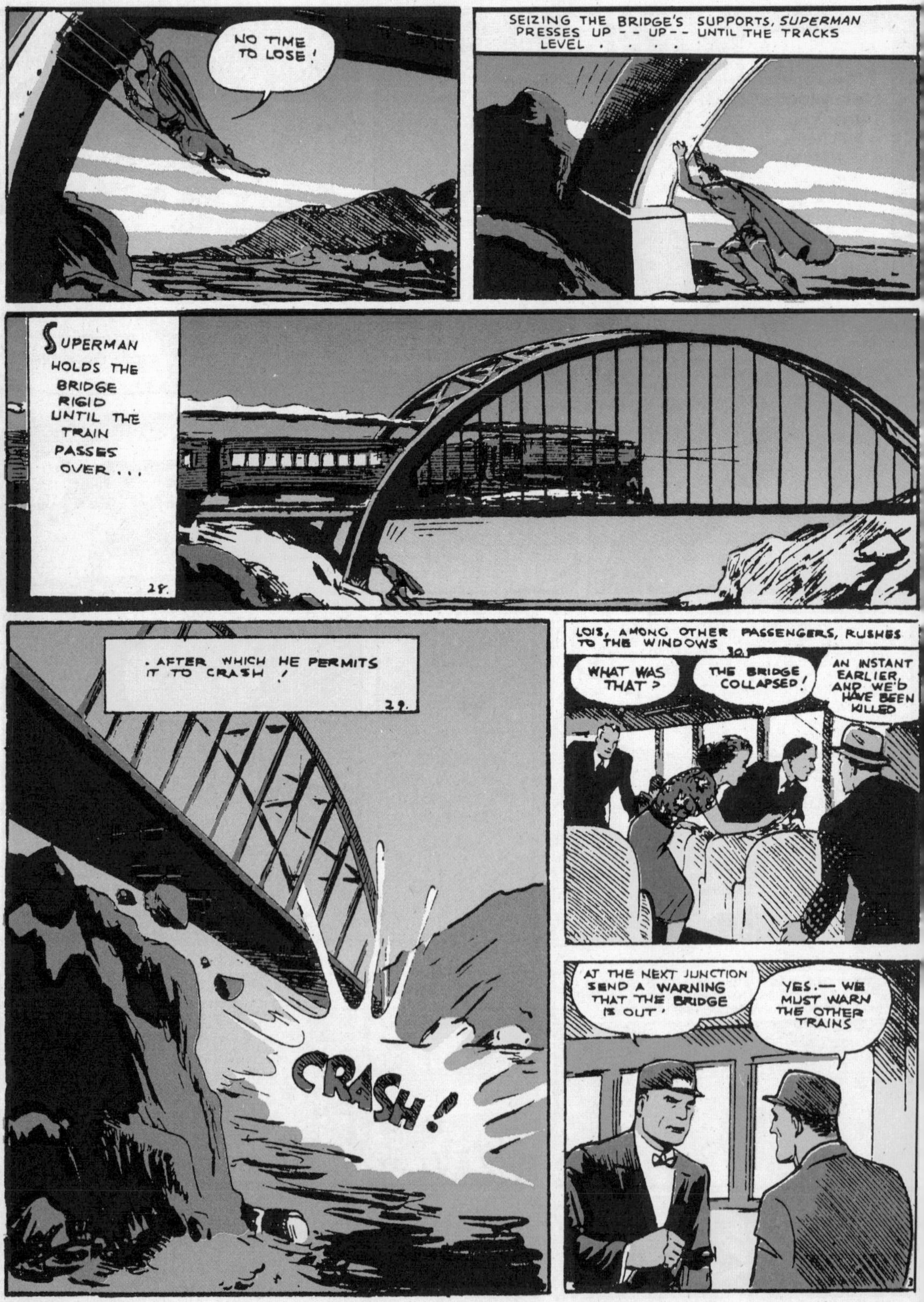

NO TIME TO LOSE!
SEIZING THE BRIDGE'S SUPPORTS, SUPERMAN PRESSES UP -- UP -- UNTIL THE TRACKS LEVEL . . . .
SUPERMAN HOLDS THE BRIDGE RIGID UNTIL THE TRAIN PASSES OVER . . .
28.
. AFTER WHICH HE PERMITS IT TO CRASH!
29.
CRASH!
LOIS, AMONG OTHER PASSENGERS, RUSHES TO THE WINDOWS
30.
WHAT WAS THAT?
THE BRIDGE COLLAPSED!
AN INSTANT EARLIER, AND WE'D HAVE BEEN KILLED
AT THE NEXT JUNCTION SEND A WARNING THAT THE BRIDGE IS OUT'
YES.— WE MUST WARN THE OTHER TRAINS

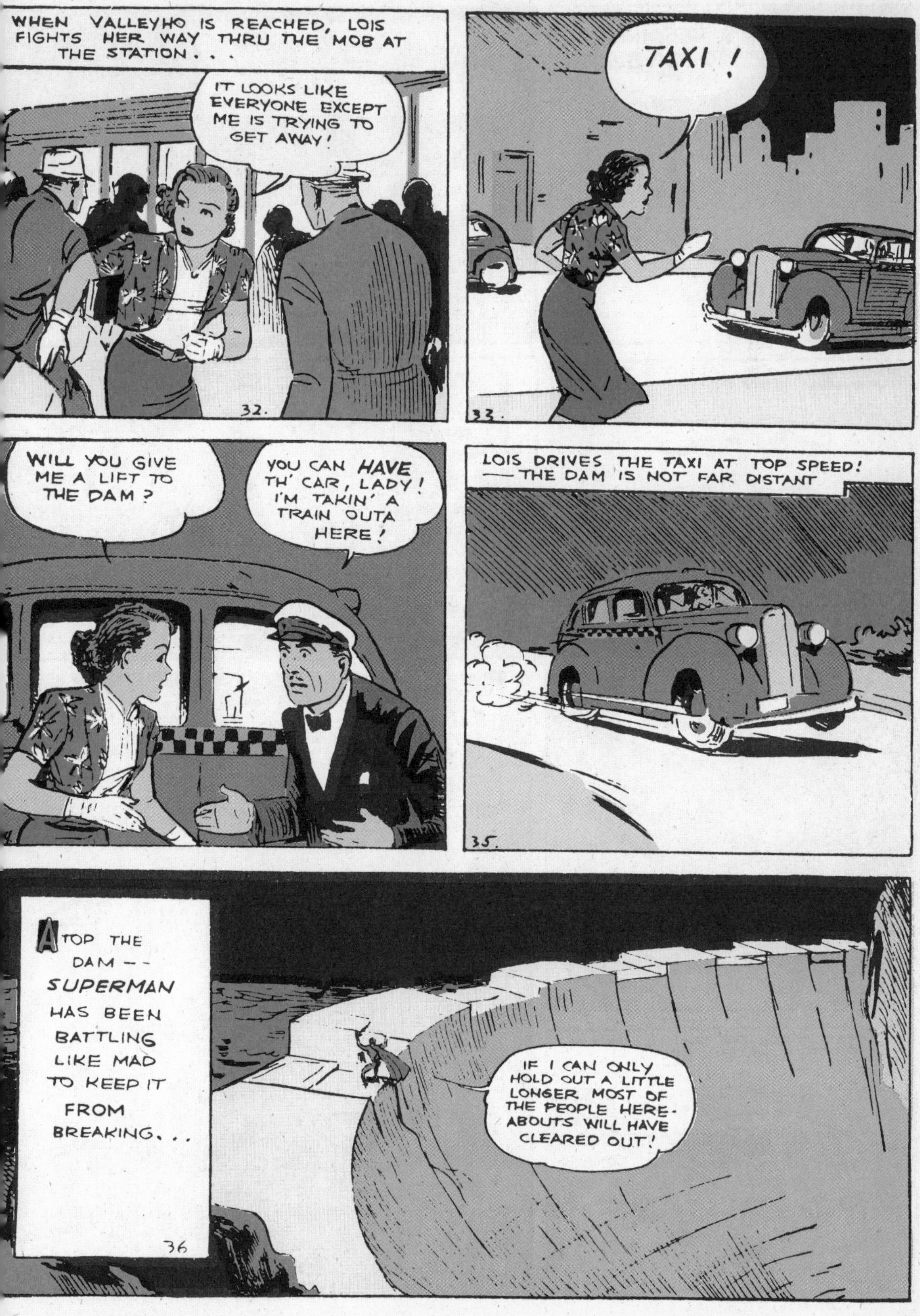
WHEN VALLEYHO IS REACHED, LOIS FIGHTS HER WAY THRU THE MOB AT THE STATION . . .
IT LOOKS LIKE EVERYONE EXCEPT ME IS TRYING TO GET AWAY!
32.
TAXI !
33.
WILL YOU GIVE ME A LIFT TO THE DAM ?
YOU CAN *HAVE* TH' CAR, LADY! I'M TAKIN' A TRAIN OUTA HERE!
LOIS DRIVES THE TAXI AT TOP SPEED! —THE DAM IS NOT FAR DISTANT
35.
ATOP THE DAM -- *SUPERMAN* HAS BEEN BATTLING LIKE MAD TO KEEP IT FROM BREAKING. . .
IF I CAN ONLY HOLD OUT A LITTLE LONGER MOST OF THE PEOPLE HERE-ABOUTS WILL HAVE CLEARED OUT!
36

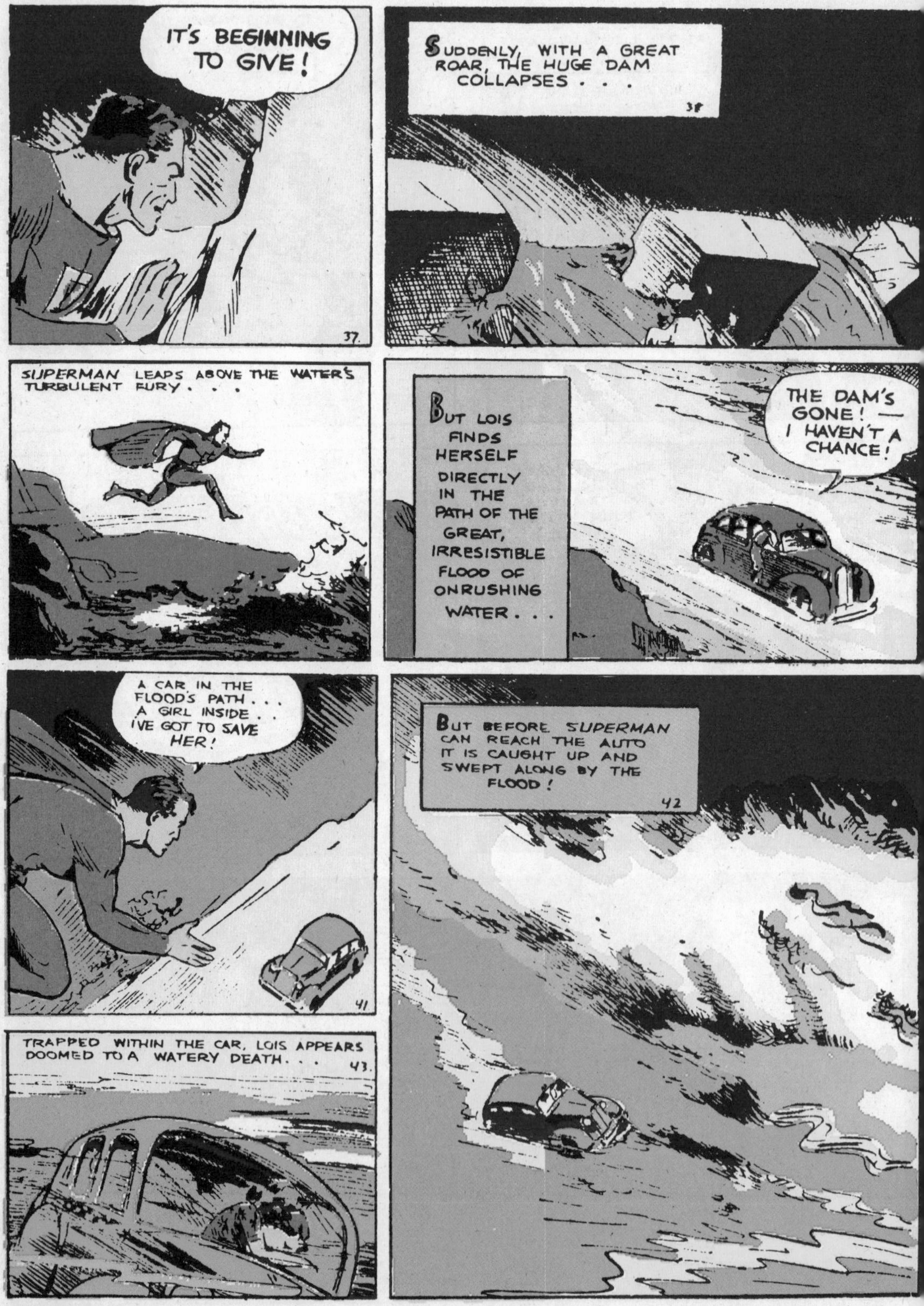
IT'S BEGINNING TO GIVE!
37.
SUDDENLY, WITH A GREAT ROAR, THE HUGE DAM COLLAPSES . . .
38
SUPERMAN LEAPS ABOVE THE WATER'S TURBULENT FURY . . .
BUT LOIS FINDS HERSELF DIRECTLY IN THE PATH OF THE GREAT, IRRESISTIBLE FLOOD OF ONRUSHING WATER . . .
THE DAM'S GONE! — I HAVEN'T A CHANCE!
A CAR IN THE FLOOD'S PATH . . . A GIRL INSIDE . . I'VE GOT TO SAVE HER!
41
BUT BEFORE SUPERMAN CAN REACH THE AUTO IT IS CAUGHT UP AND SWEPT ALONG BY THE FLOOD!
42
TRAPPED WITHIN THE CAR, LOIS APPEARS DOOMED TO A WATERY DEATH. . .
43.

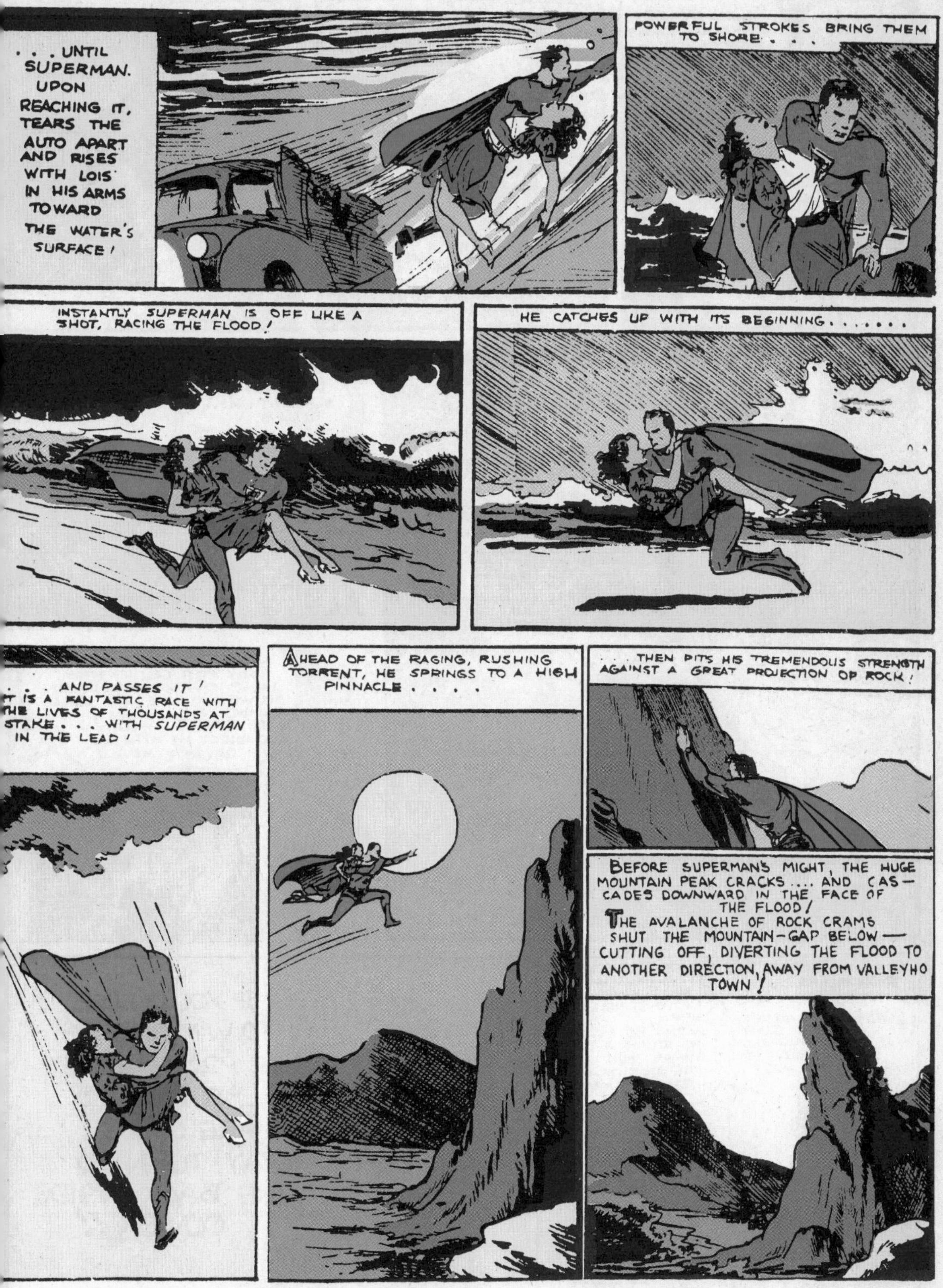
. . . UNTIL SUPERMAN. UPON REACHING IT, TEARS THE AUTO APART AND RISES WITH LOIS IN HIS ARMS TOWARD THE WATER'S SURFACE!
POWERFUL STROKES BRING THEM TO SHORE . . .
INSTANTLY SUPERMAN IS OFF LIKE A SHOT, RACING THE FLOOD!
HE CATCHES UP WITH ITS BEGINNING. . . . . .
. . . AND PASSES IT! IT IS A FANTASTIC RACE WITH THE LIVES OF THOUSANDS AT STAKE . . . WITH SUPERMAN IN THE LEAD!
AHEAD OF THE RAGING, RUSHING TORRENT, HE SPRINGS TO A HIGH PINNACLE . . . .
. . THEN PITS HIS TREMENDOUS STRENGTH AGAINST A GREAT PROJECTION OF ROCK!
BEFORE SUPERMAN'S MIGHT, THE HUGE MOUNTAIN PEAK CRACKS .... AND CAS-CADES DOWNWARD IN THE FACE OF THE FLOOD!
THE AVALANCHE OF ROCK CRAMS SHUT THE MOUNTAIN-GAP BELOW— CUTTING OFF, DIVERTING THE FLOOD TO ANOTHER DIRECTION, AWAY FROM VALLEYHO TOWN!

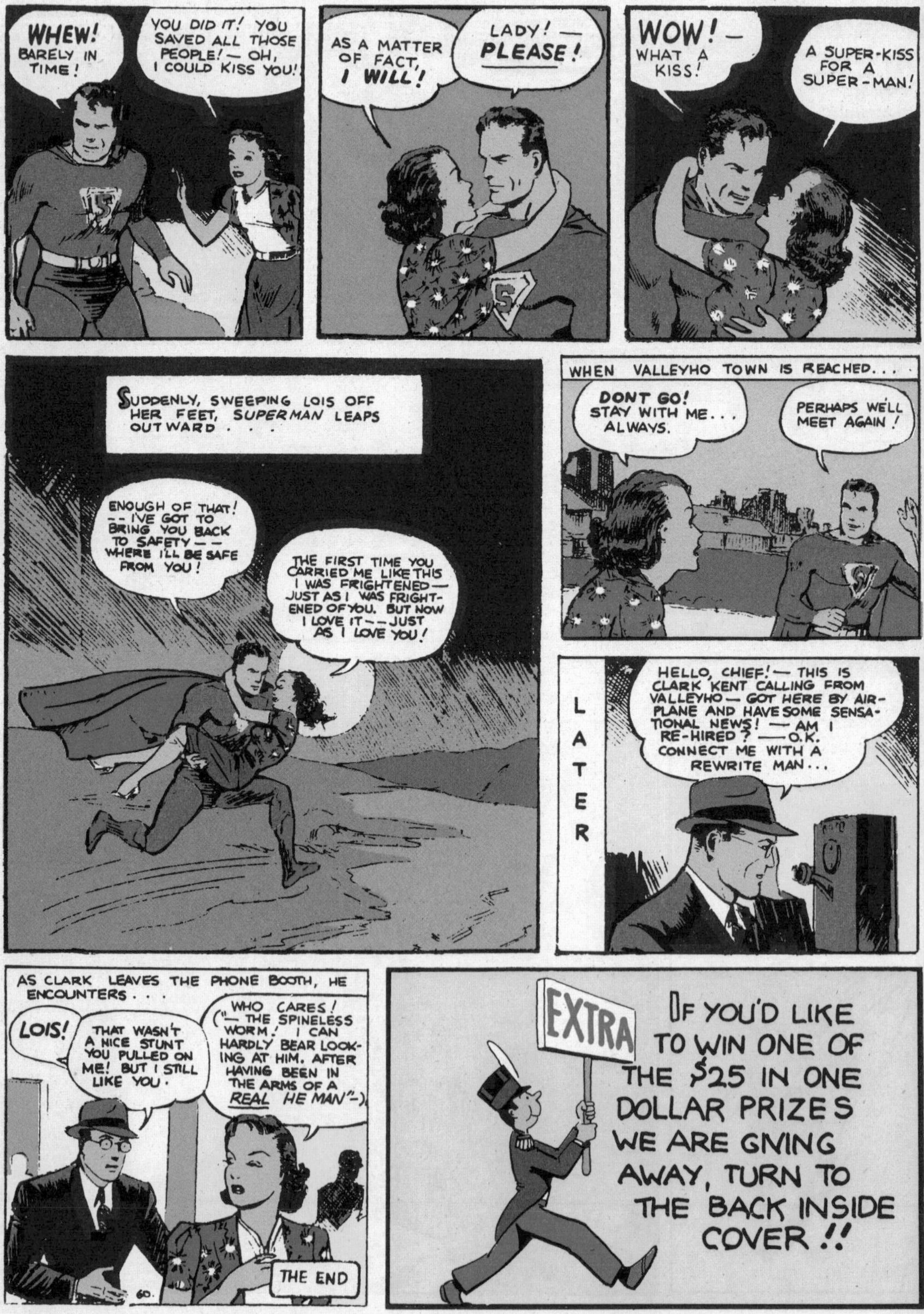
WHEW! BARELY IN TIME!
YOU DID IT! YOU SAVED ALL THOSE PEOPLE! — OH, I COULD KISS YOU!
AS A MATTER OF FACT, I WILL!
LADY! — PLEASE!
WOW! — WHAT A KISS!
A SUPER-KISS FOR A SUPER-MAN!
SUDDENLY, SWEEPING LOIS OFF HER FEET, SUPERMAN LEAPS OUTWARD . . .
ENOUGH OF THAT! -- I'VE GOT TO BRING YOU BACK TO SAFETY -- WHERE I'LL BE SAFE FROM YOU!
THE FIRST TIME YOU CARRIED ME LIKE THIS I WAS FRIGHTENED — JUST AS I WAS FRIGHTENED OF YOU. BUT NOW I LOVE IT -- JUST AS I LOVE YOU!
WHEN VALLEYHO TOWN IS REACHED . . .
DONT GO! STAY WITH ME . . . ALWAYS.
PERHAPS WE'LL MEET AGAIN!
LATER
HELLO, CHIEF! — THIS IS CLARK KENT CALLING FROM VALLEYHO — GOT HERE BY AIRPLANE AND HAVE SOME SENSATIONAL NEWS! — AM I RE-HIRED? — O.K. CONNECT ME WITH A REWRITE MAN...
AS CLARK LEAVES THE PHONE BOOTH, HE ENCOUNTERS . . .
LOIS!
THAT WASN'T A NICE STUNT YOU PULLED ON ME! BUT I STILL LIKE YOU.
("WHO CARES! — THE SPINELESS WORM! I CAN HARDLY BEAR LOOKING AT HIM. AFTER HAVING BEEN IN THE ARMS OF A REAL HE MAN"—)
THE END
EXTRA
IF YOU'D LIKE TO WIN ONE OF THE $25 IN ONE DOLLAR PRIZES WE ARE GIVING AWAY, TURN TO THE BACK INSIDE COVER!!

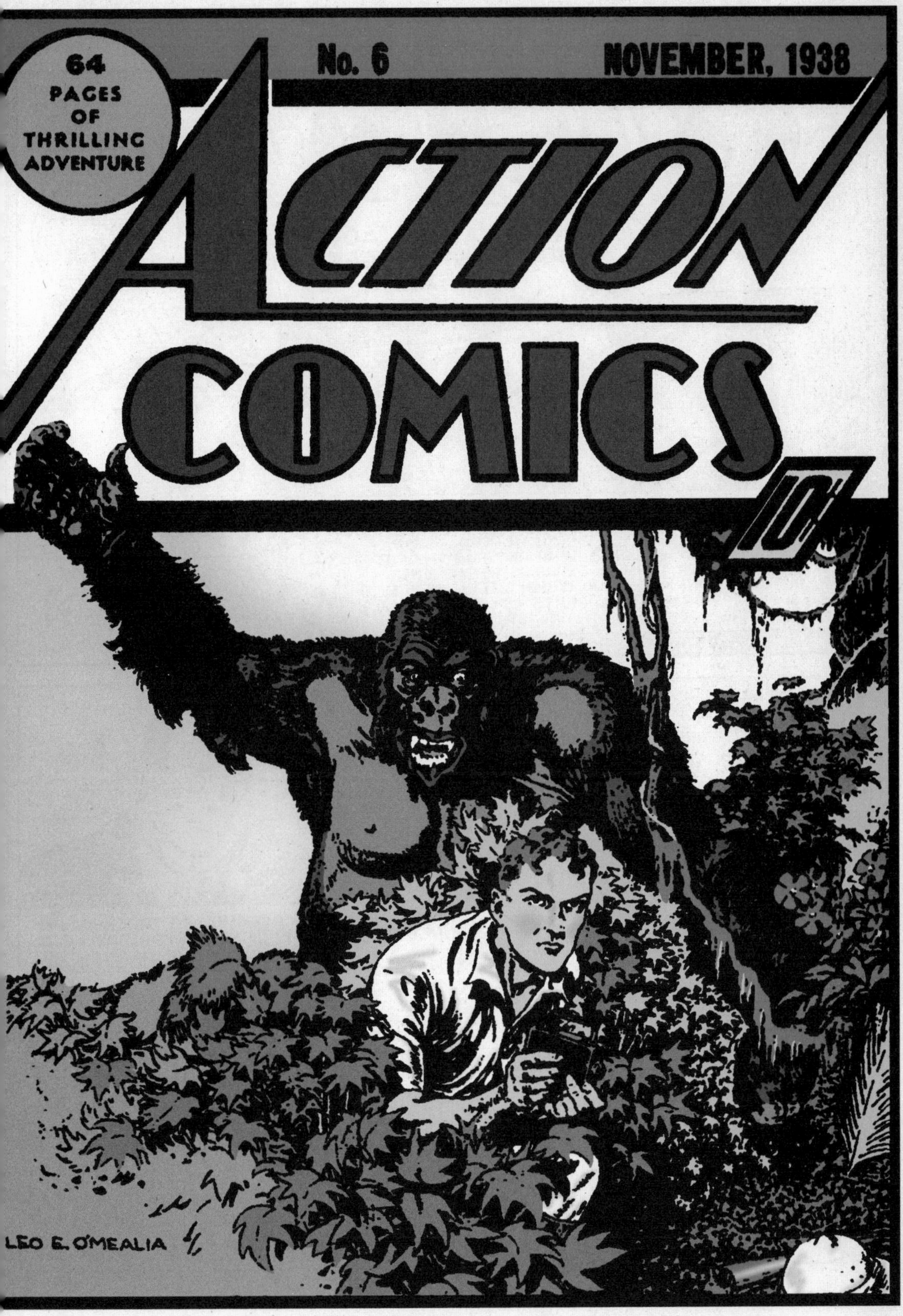
64 PAGES OF THRILLING ADVENTURE
No. 6
NOVEMBER, 1938
ACTION COMICS
10¢
LEO E. O'MEALIA

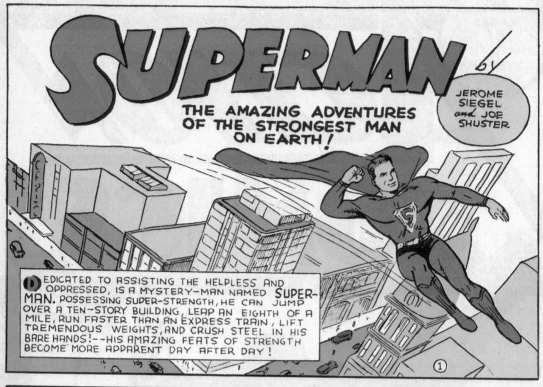

SUPERMAN BY JEROME SIEGEL and JOE SHUSTER

THE AMAZING ADVENTURES OF THE STRONGEST MAN ON EARTH!

1. DEDICATED TO ASSISTING THE HELPLESS AND OPPRESSED, IS A MYSTERY-MAN NAMED SUPERMAN. POSSESSING SUPER-STRENGTH, HE CAN JUMP OVER A TEN-STORY BUILDING, LEAP AN EIGHTH OF A MILE, RUN FASTER THAN AN EXPRESS TRAIN, LIFT TREMENDOUS WEIGHTS, AND CRUSH STEEL IN HIS BARE HANDS!--HIS AMAZING FEATS OF STRENGTH BECOME MORE APPARENT DAY AFTER DAY!

2. NEWSPAPERS HEADLINE HIS ACTIVITIES WITH EVER-INCREASING REGULARITY!

MORNING — SUPERMAN SMASHES MUNITIONS-RING

DAILY STAR — MYSTERY MAN OF STEEL RE-APPEARS

EVENING — SUPERMAN WARS ON INJUSTICES

DALD HERALD — ENTIRE TOWN SAVED BY SUPERMAN

3. ESPECIALLY ASSIGNED TO TRACK DOWN ALL SUPERMAN NEWS, IS CLARK KENT, MEEK ACE-REPORTER OF THE DAILY STAR.

4. ONE DAY, CLARK RECEIVES ASTONISHING NEWS WHEN SUMMONED BEFORE HIS EDITOR...

KENT, MEET NICK WILLIAMS, SUPERMAN'S PERSONAL MANAGER.

WHAT!

5. KENT'S HAND HAD BEEN TOYING WITH AN ASH-TRAY. UNDER HIS STARTLED, IN-CREASED GRASP, IT TWISTS INTO A SHAPE-LESS PULP. --AMAZING? NOT AT ALL! ...FOR IN REALITY, CLARK KENT IS SUPERMAN!

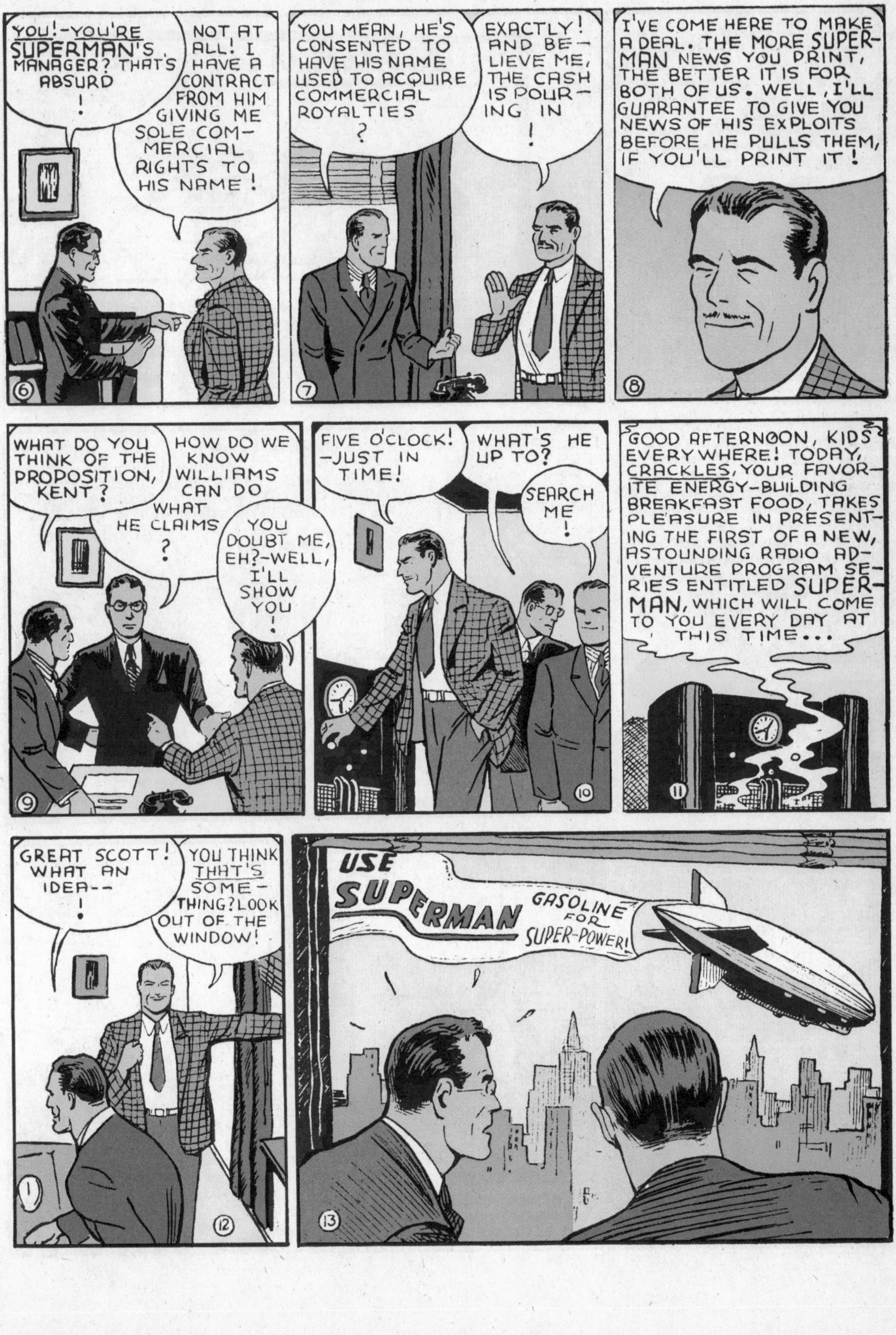

YOU!-YOU'RE SUPERMAN'S MANAGER? THAT'S ABSURD !
NOT AT ALL! I HAVE A CONTRACT FROM HIM GIVING ME SOLE COMMERCIAL RIGHTS TO HIS NAME!
YOU MEAN, HE'S CONSENTED TO HAVE HIS NAME USED TO ACQUIRE COMMERCIAL ROYALTIES ?
EXACTLY! AND BELIEVE ME, THE CASH IS POURING IN !
I'VE COME HERE TO MAKE A DEAL. THE MORE SUPERMAN NEWS YOU PRINT, THE BETTER IT IS FOR BOTH OF US. WELL, I'LL GUARANTEE TO GIVE YOU NEWS OF HIS EXPLOITS BEFORE HE PULLS THEM, IF YOU'LL PRINT IT!
WHAT DO YOU THINK OF THE PROPOSITION, KENT?
HOW DO WE KNOW WILLIAMS CAN DO WHAT HE CLAIMS ?
YOU DOUBT ME, EH?-WELL, I'LL SHOW YOU !
FIVE O'CLOCK! -JUST IN TIME!
WHAT'S HE UP TO?
SEARCH ME !
GOOD AFTERNOON, KIDS EVERYWHERE! TODAY, CRACKLES, YOUR FAVORITE ENERGY-BUILDING BREAKFAST FOOD, TAKES PLEASURE IN PRESENTING THE FIRST OF A NEW, ASTOUNDING RADIO ADVENTURE PROGRAM SERIES ENTITLED SUPERMAN, WHICH WILL COME TO YOU EVERY DAY AT THIS TIME...
GREAT SCOTT! WHAT AN IDEA-- !
YOU THINK THAT'S SOMETHING? LOOK OUT OF THE WINDOW!
USE SUPERMAN GASOLINE FOR SUPER-POWER!

GOOD LORD! —WHAT NEXT?

TAKE A GANDER AT THAT BILL—BOARD OVER YONDER!

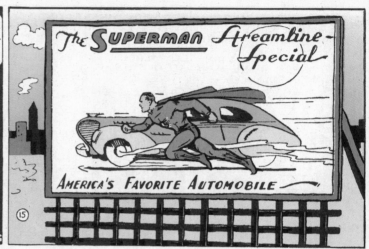

The SUPERMAN Streamline-Special

AMERICA'S FAVORITE AUTOMOBILE

I'VE ALSO LICENSED SUPERMAN BATHING-SUITS, COSTUMES, PHYSICAL DEVELOPMENT EXERCISERS, AND MOVIE RIGHTS, TO NAME A FEW.——WHY, I'VE EVEN MADE PROVISIONS FOR HIM TO APPEAR IN THE COMICS!

ALL VERY INTERESTING! BUT HOW DID SUPERMAN CONTACT YOU?

HE DROPPED IN ON ME AND SPRUNG THE PROPOSITION. I LIKED THE IDEA, AND WE EVOLVED A PARTNERSHIP.

VERY INTERESTING——IF TRUE!

YOU DOUBT ME? VERY WELL THEN! WOULD A PERSONAL INTERVIEW WITH SUPERMAN INTEREST YOU?

I SHOULD SAY IT WOULD! —IN FACT, I'D LIKE TO MEET HIM VERY MUCH!

FINE! COME TO MY OFFICE TONIGHT, AND I'LL ARRANGE YOUR FIRST INTERVIEW WITH THE STRONGEST MAN ON EARTH!

GOSH!

OUTSIDE THE EDITOR'S DOOR, AN INQUISITIVE OFFICE-BOY HAS BEEN GETTING AN EARFUL!

CAN Y'IMAGINE THAT, LOIS? CLARK KENT IS GOING TO SEE SUPERMAN TONIGHT, IN PERSON!

HE IS! —THEN SO WILL I!

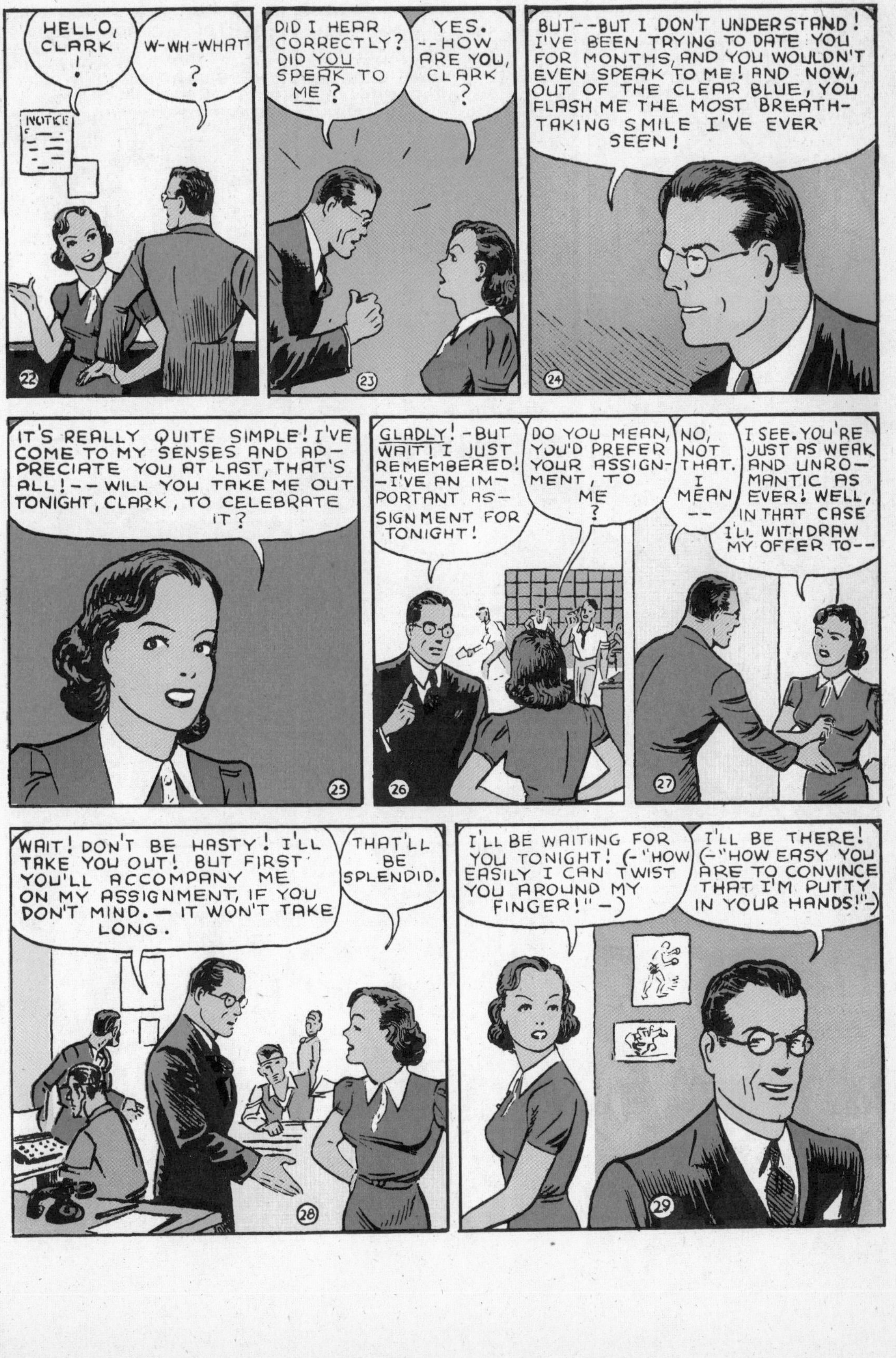
HELLO, CLARK!
W-WH-WHAT?
NOTICE
22
DID I HEAR CORRECTLY? DID YOU SPEAK TO ME?
YES. --HOW ARE YOU, CLARK?
23
BUT--BUT I DON'T UNDERSTAND! I'VE BEEN TRYING TO DATE YOU FOR MONTHS, AND YOU WOULDN'T EVEN SPEAK TO ME! AND NOW, OUT OF THE CLEAR BLUE, YOU FLASH ME THE MOST BREATH-TAKING SMILE I'VE EVER SEEN!
24
IT'S REALLY QUITE SIMPLE! I'VE COME TO MY SENSES AND AP-PRECIATE YOU AT LAST, THAT'S ALL!--WILL YOU TAKE ME OUT TONIGHT, CLARK, TO CELEBRATE IT?
25
GLADLY! -BUT WAIT! I JUST REMEMBERED! -I'VE AN IM-PORTANT AS-SIGNMENT FOR TONIGHT!
DO YOU MEAN, YOU'D PREFER YOUR ASSIGN-MENT, TO ME?
26
NO, NOT THAT. I MEAN --
I SEE. YOU'RE JUST AS WEAK AND UNRO-MANTIC AS EVER! WELL, IN THAT CASE I'LL WITHDRAW MY OFFER TO--
27
WAIT! DON'T BE HASTY! I'LL TAKE YOU OUT! BUT FIRST YOU'LL ACCOMPANY ME ON MY ASSIGNMENT, IF YOU DON'T MIND.—IT WON'T TAKE LONG.
THAT'LL BE SPLENDID.
28
I'LL BE WAITING FOR YOU TONIGHT! (-"HOW EASILY I CAN TWIST YOU AROUND MY FINGER!"—)
I'LL BE THERE! (-"HOW EASY YOU ARE TO CONVINCE THAT I'M PUTTY IN YOUR HANDS!"-)
29

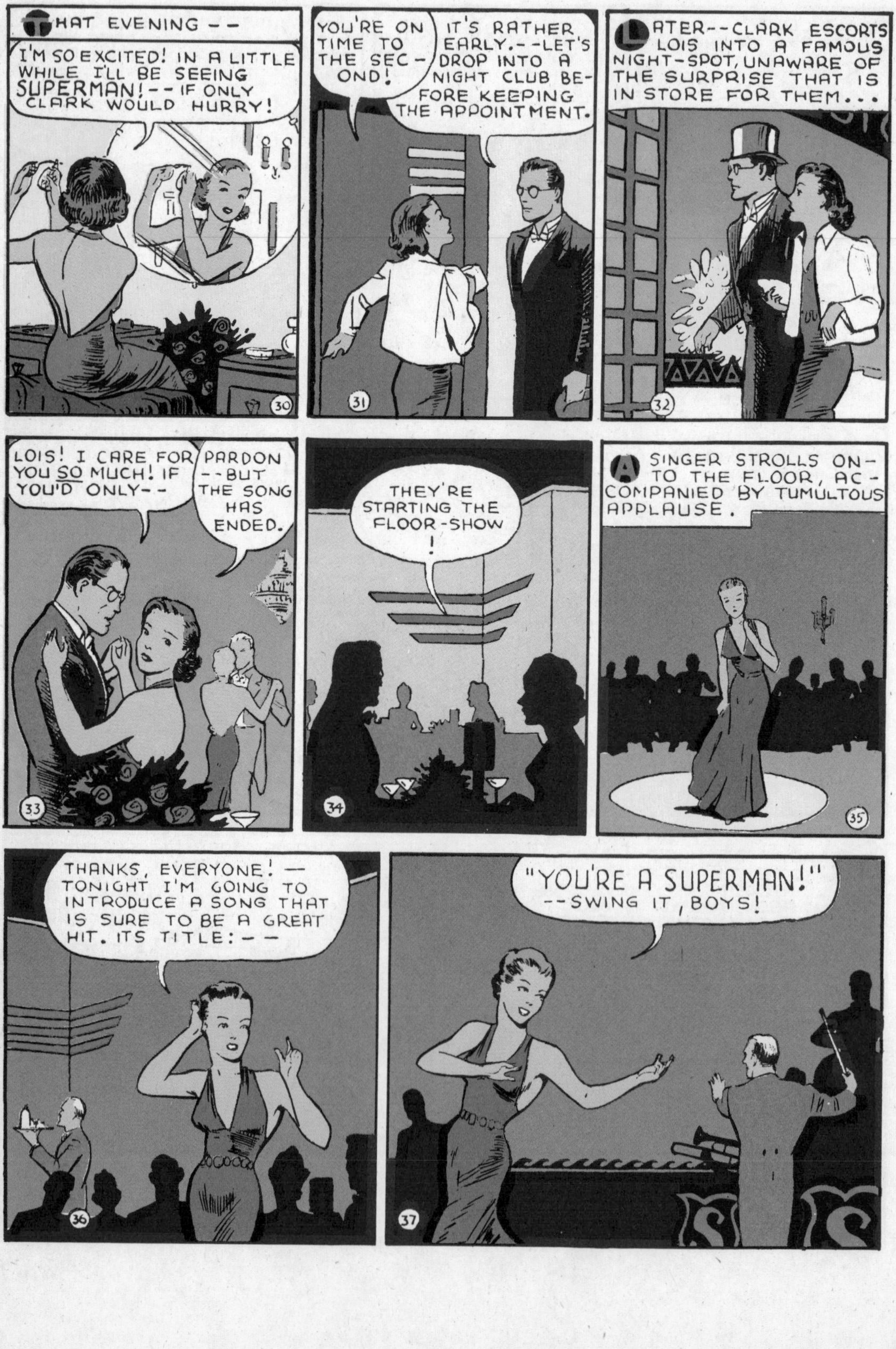
THAT EVENING --
I'M SO EXCITED! IN A LITTLE WHILE I'LL BE SEEING SUPERMAN!-- IF ONLY CLARK WOULD HURRY!
30
YOU'RE ON TIME TO THE SEC-OND!
IT'S RATHER EARLY.--LET'S DROP INTO A NIGHT CLUB BE-FORE KEEPING THE APPOINTMENT.
31
LATER--CLARK ESCORTS LOIS INTO A FAMOUS NIGHT-SPOT, UNAWARE OF THE SURPRISE THAT IS IN STORE FOR THEM...
32
LOIS! I CARE FOR YOU SO MUCH! IF YOU'D ONLY--
PARDON --BUT THE SONG HAS ENDED.
33
THEY'RE STARTING THE FLOOR-SHOW!
34
A SINGER STROLLS ON-TO THE FLOOR, AC-COMPANIED BY TUMULTOUS APPLAUSE.
35
THANKS, EVERYONE! — TONIGHT I'M GOING TO INTRODUCE A SONG THAT IS SURE TO BE A GREAT HIT. ITS TITLE:--
36
"YOU'RE A SUPERMAN!" --SWING IT, BOYS!
37

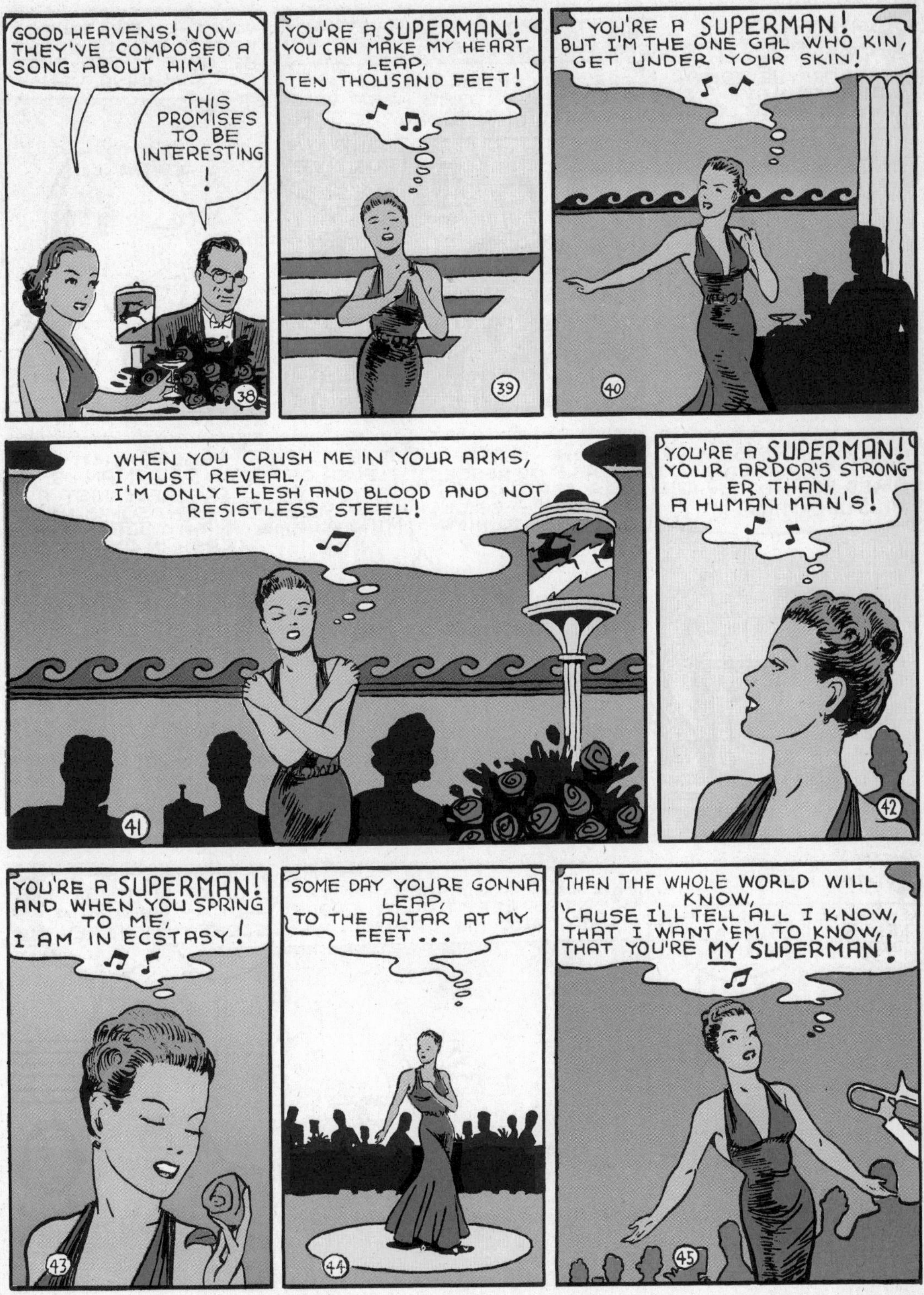
GOOD HEAVENS! NOW THEY'VE COMPOSED A SONG ABOUT HIM!
THIS PROMISES TO BE INTERESTING !
YOU'RE A SUPERMAN! YOU CAN MAKE MY HEART LEAP, TEN THOUSAND FEET!
YOU'RE A SUPERMAN! BUT I'M THE ONE GAL WHO KIN, GET UNDER YOUR SKIN!
WHEN YOU CRUSH ME IN YOUR ARMS, I MUST REVEAL, I'M ONLY FLESH AND BLOOD AND NOT RESISTLESS STEEL!
YOU'RE A SUPERMAN! YOUR ARDOR'S STRONGER THAN, A HUMAN MAN'S!
YOU'RE A SUPERMAN! AND WHEN YOU SPRING TO ME, I AM IN ECSTASY!
SOME DAY YOU'RE GONNA LEAP, TO THE ALTAR AT MY FEET...
THEN THE WHOLE WORLD WILL KNOW, 'CAUSE I'LL TELL ALL I KNOW, THAT I WANT 'EM TO KNOW, THAT YOU'RE MY SUPERMAN!

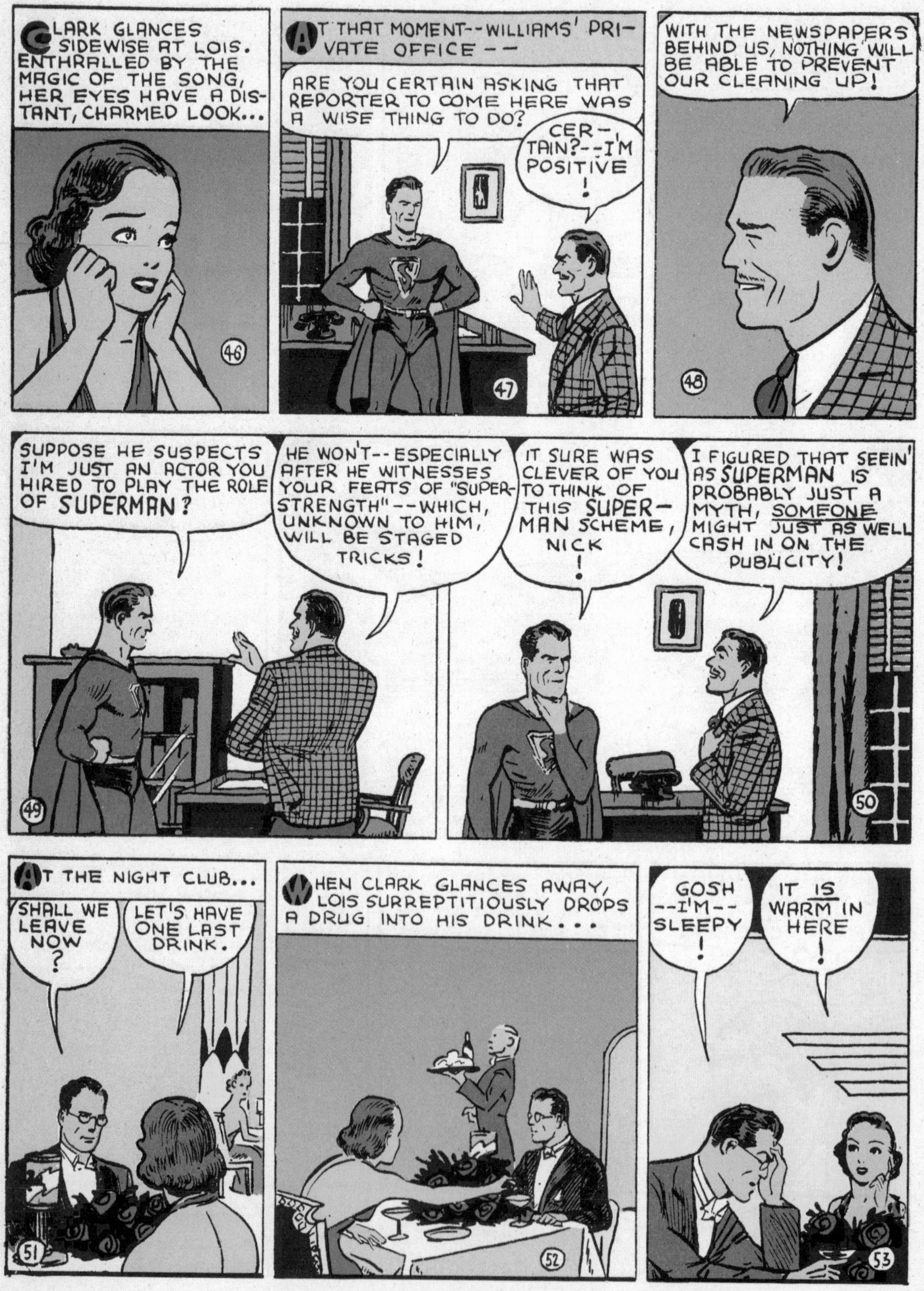
CLARK GLANCES SIDEWISE AT LOIS. ENTHRALLED BY THE MAGIC OF THE SONG, HER EYES HAVE A DISTANT, CHARMED LOOK...
46
AT THAT MOMENT--WILLIAMS' PRIVATE OFFICE --
ARE YOU CERTAIN ASKING THAT REPORTER TO COME HERE WAS A WISE THING TO DO?
CERTAIN?--I'M POSITIVE !
47
WITH THE NEWSPAPERS BEHIND US, NOTHING WILL BE ABLE TO PREVENT OUR CLEANING UP!
48
SUPPOSE HE SUSPECTS I'M JUST AN ACTOR YOU HIRED TO PLAY THE ROLE OF SUPERMAN?
HE WON'T--ESPECIALLY AFTER HE WITNESSES YOUR FEATS OF "SUPER-STRENGTH"--WHICH, UNKNOWN TO HIM, WILL BE STAGED TRICKS!
49
IT SURE WAS CLEVER OF YOU TO THINK OF THIS SUPERMAN SCHEME, NICK !
I FIGURED THAT SEEIN' AS SUPERMAN IS PROBABLY JUST A MYTH, SOMEONE MIGHT JUST AS WELL CASH IN ON THE PUBLICITY!
50
AT THE NIGHT CLUB...
SHALL WE LEAVE NOW ?
LET'S HAVE ONE LAST DRINK.
51
WHEN CLARK GLANCES AWAY, LOIS SURREPTITIOUSLY DROPS A DRUG INTO HIS DRINK...
52
GOSH --I'M-- SLEEPY !
IT IS WARM IN HERE !
53

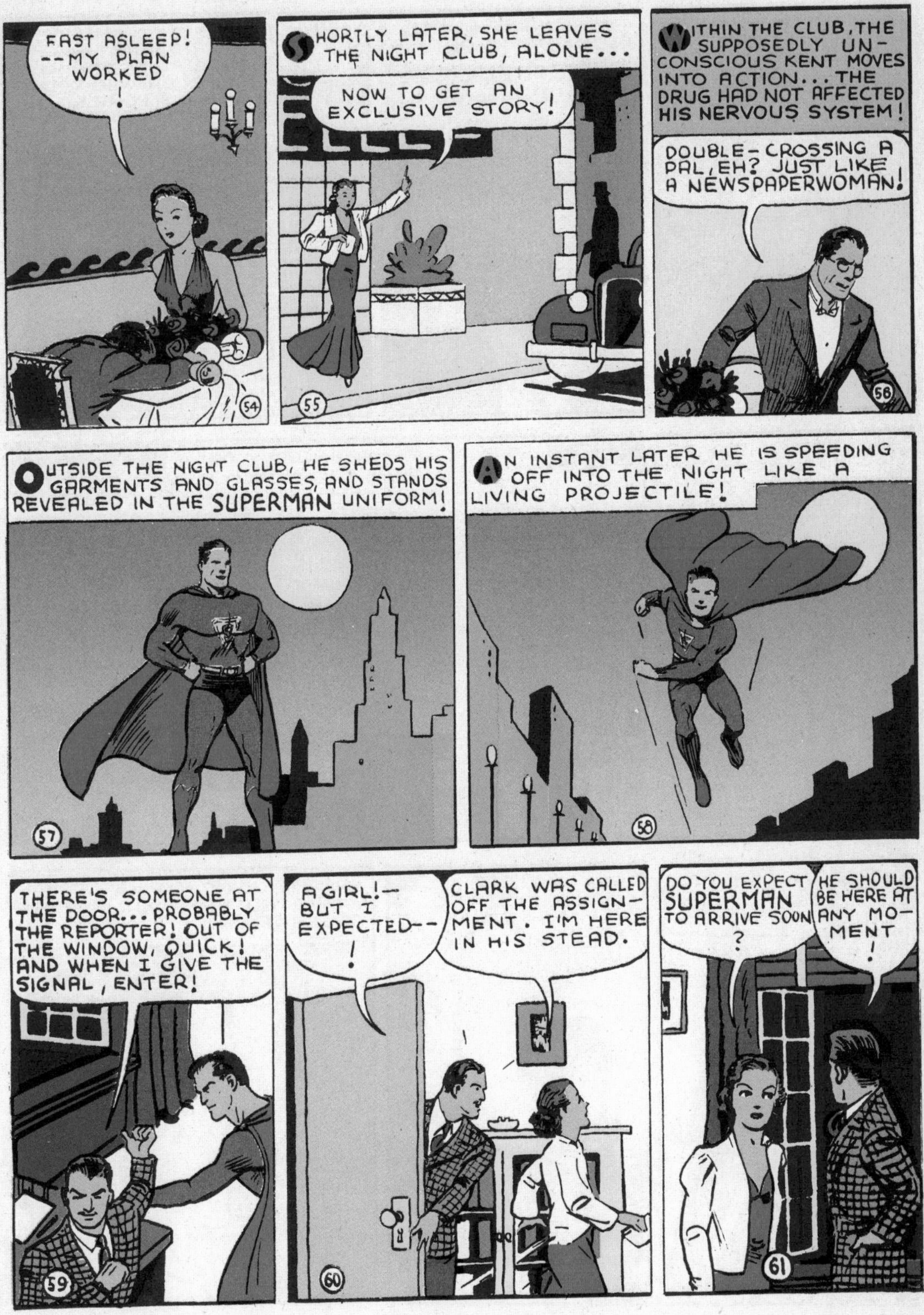
FAST ASLEEP! --MY PLAN WORKED!
SHORTLY LATER, SHE LEAVES THE NIGHT CLUB, ALONE...
NOW TO GET AN EXCLUSIVE STORY!
WITHIN THE CLUB, THE SUPPOSEDLY UN-CONSCIOUS KENT MOVES INTO ACTION... THE DRUG HAD NOT AFFECTED HIS NERVOUS SYSTEM!
DOUBLE-CROSSING A PAL, EH? JUST LIKE A NEWSPAPERWOMAN!
OUTSIDE THE NIGHT CLUB, HE SHEDS HIS GARMENTS AND GLASSES, AND STANDS REVEALED IN THE SUPERMAN UNIFORM!
AN INSTANT LATER HE IS SPEEDING OFF INTO THE NIGHT LIKE A LIVING PROJECTILE!
THERE'S SOMEONE AT THE DOOR... PROBABLY THE REPORTER! OUT OF THE WINDOW, QUICK! AND WHEN I GIVE THE SIGNAL, ENTER!
A GIRL!— BUT I EXPECTED--!
CLARK WAS CALLED OFF THE ASSIGN-MENT. I'M HERE IN HIS STEAD.
DO YOU EXPECT SUPERMAN TO ARRIVE SOON?
HE SHOULD BE HERE AT ANY MO-MENT!

PLACING HIS HAND BEHIND HIM, WILLIAMS SNAPS HIS FINGERS...

SNAP!

62

THE SIGNAL! —NOW TO GO INTO MY ACT!

63

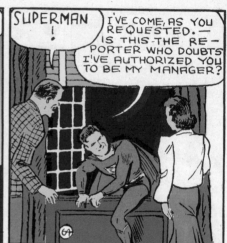

SUPERMAN!

I'VE COME, AS YOU REQUESTED.—IS THIS THE REPORTER WHO DOUBTS I'VE AUTHORIZED YOU TO BE MY MANAGER?

64

YES. BUT DEMONSTRATE SOME SUPER-STRENGTH! THAT SHOULD BANISH ANY DOUBTS THAT ARE IN HER MIND.

GLADLY!

65

BEHOLD! LIFTING A HEAVY DESK IS TO ME MERE CHILDSPLAY!

66

AND BENDING A STEEL BAR—WELL, I THINK NOTHING OF IT!

67

ARE YOU CONVINCED?

NO!

68

AND I'M GOING TO PROVE THAT YOU'RE NOTHING BUT A PAIR OF FAKERS!

69

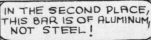
IN THE FIRST PLACE, THIS SO-CALLED "HEAVY" DESK IS CONSTRUCTED OF LIGHT, CARDBOARD!

IN THE SECOND PLACE, THIS BAR IS OF ALUMINUM, NOT STEEL!

AND FINALLY, I'VE ALREADY MET SUPERMAN PERSONALLY, AND SO I KNOW DEFINITELY THAT THIS MAN IS AN OUT-AND-OUT PHONEY!

70

71

72

AND NOW I'LL BE LEAVING YOUR UNSAVORY COMPANY !

OH, NO YOU DON'T! YOU KNOW TOO MUCH !

73

LET GO! WHAT DO YOU WANT OF ME ?

YOU'RE SMART --TOO SMART FOR YOUR OWN GOOD! AND SO WE CAN'T AFFORD TO LET YOU LEAVE HERE ALIVE !

74

HELP ME GET HER TO THE WINDOW! WE'VE GOT TO THROW HER TO HER DEATH!

BUT--BUT THAT WOULD BE MURDER!

75

IT'S EITHER HER LIFE OR OUR CHANCE OF MAKING A FORTUNE !

WE'LL CALL IT ACCIDENTAL OR A SUICIDE, EH ?

76

A MOMENT LATER--LOIS' KICKING AND SCREAMING FIGURE FALLS FROM THE WINDOW DOWNWARD TOWARD A HORRIBLE, CRUSHING DEATH!

77

SUPERMAN HAD ARRIVED IN TIME TO SEE LOIS TOSSED FROM THE WINDOW!

GOOD LORD!--THEY'RE GOING TO KILL HER!

78

UPWARD HE SPRINGS IN A GREAT, DESPERATE LEAP...

79

GOT HER!

80

AN INSTANT LATER, CRADLED IN SUPERMAN'S PROTECTIVE ARMS, LOIS DROPS SAFELY TO EARTH!

REMAIN HERE!--THERE'S SOMETHING I'VE GOT TO ATTEND TO!

81

DID YOU SEE THAT? --I THOUGHT YOU SAID THERE REALLY WASN'T A SUPERMAN!

I WAS MISTAKEN.-- LET'S GET OUTA HERE WHILE WE CAN!

82

AS SUPERMAN SPRINGS THRU THE WINDOW...

THEY'RE NO LONGER HERE!

83

QUICK! INTO THE ELEVATOR! --IT'S OUR ONLY CHANCE!

84

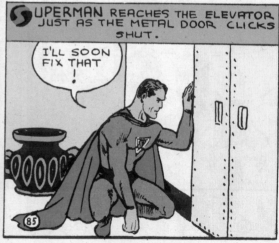

SUPERMAN REACHES THE ELEVATOR JUST AS THE METAL DOOR CLICKS SHUT.

I'LL SOON FIX THAT!

85

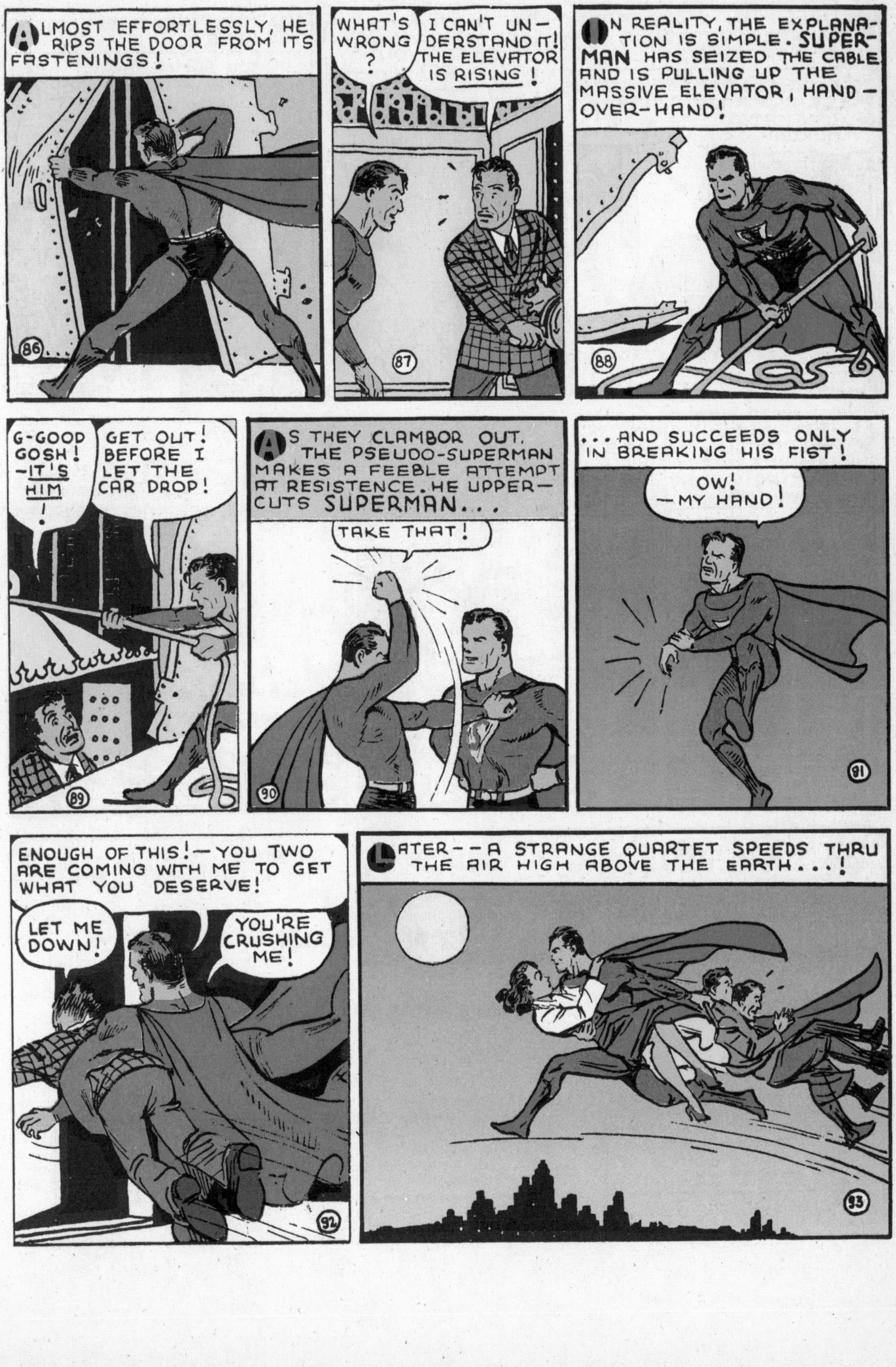
ALMOST EFFORTLESSLY, HE RIPS THE DOOR FROM ITS FASTENINGS!
86
WHAT'S WRONG ?
I CAN'T UNDERSTAND IT! THE ELEVATOR IS RISING!
87
IN REALITY, THE EXPLANATION IS SIMPLE. SUPERMAN HAS SEIZED THE CABLE AND IS PULLING UP THE MASSIVE ELEVATOR, HAND-OVER-HAND!
88
G-GOOD GOSH! -IT'S HIM !
GET OUT! BEFORE I LET THE CAR DROP!
89
AS THEY CLAMBOR OUT, THE PSEUDO-SUPERMAN MAKES A FEEBLE ATTEMPT AT RESISTENCE. HE UPPER-CUTS SUPERMAN...
TAKE THAT!
90
...AND SUCCEEDS ONLY IN BREAKING HIS FIST!
OW! —MY HAND!
91
ENOUGH OF THIS!—YOU TWO ARE COMING WITH ME TO GET WHAT YOU DESERVE!
LET ME DOWN!
YOU'RE CRUSHING ME!
92
LATER--A STRANGE QUARTET SPEEDS THRU THE AIR HIGH ABOVE THE EARTH...!
93

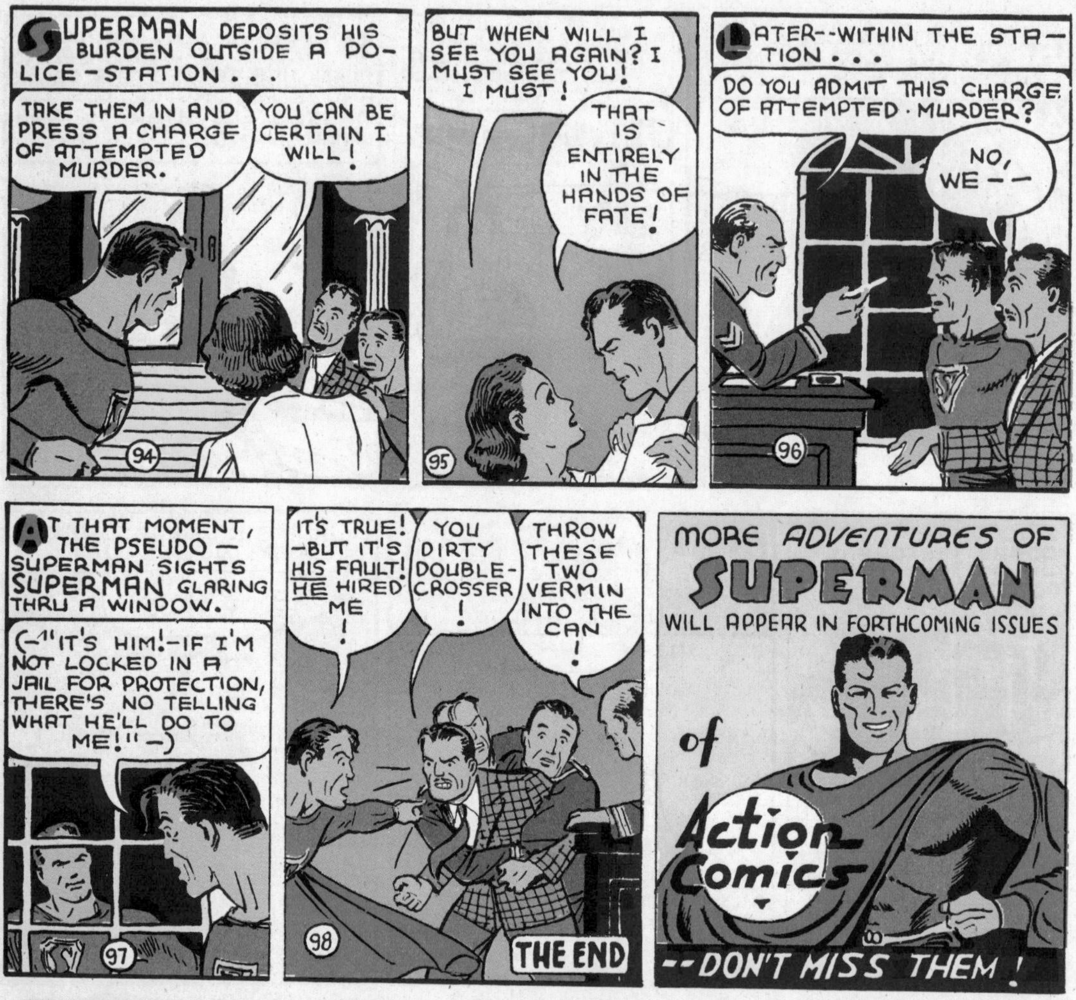
SUPERMAN DEPOSITS HIS BURDEN OUTSIDE A POLICE-STATION . . .
TAKE THEM IN AND PRESS A CHARGE OF ATTEMPTED MURDER.
YOU CAN BE CERTAIN I WILL!
94
BUT WHEN WILL I SEE YOU AGAIN? I MUST SEE YOU! I MUST!
THAT IS ENTIRELY IN THE HANDS OF FATE!
95
LATER--WITHIN THE STATION . . .
DO YOU ADMIT THIS CHARGE OF ATTEMPTED · MURDER?
NO, WE --
96
AT THAT MOMENT, THE PSEUDO — SUPERMAN SIGHTS SUPERMAN GLARING THRU A WINDOW.
(—"IT'S HIM!—IF I'M NOT LOCKED IN A JAIL FOR PROTECTION, THERE'S NO TELLING WHAT HE'LL DO TO ME!" —)
97
IT'S TRUE! —BUT IT'S HIS FAULT! HE HIRED ME!
YOU DIRTY DOUBLE-CROSSER!
THROW THESE TWO VERMIN INTO THE CAN!
98
THE END
MORE ADVENTURES OF SUPERMAN WILL APPEAR IN FORTHCOMING ISSUES of Action Comics
--DON'T MISS THEM!

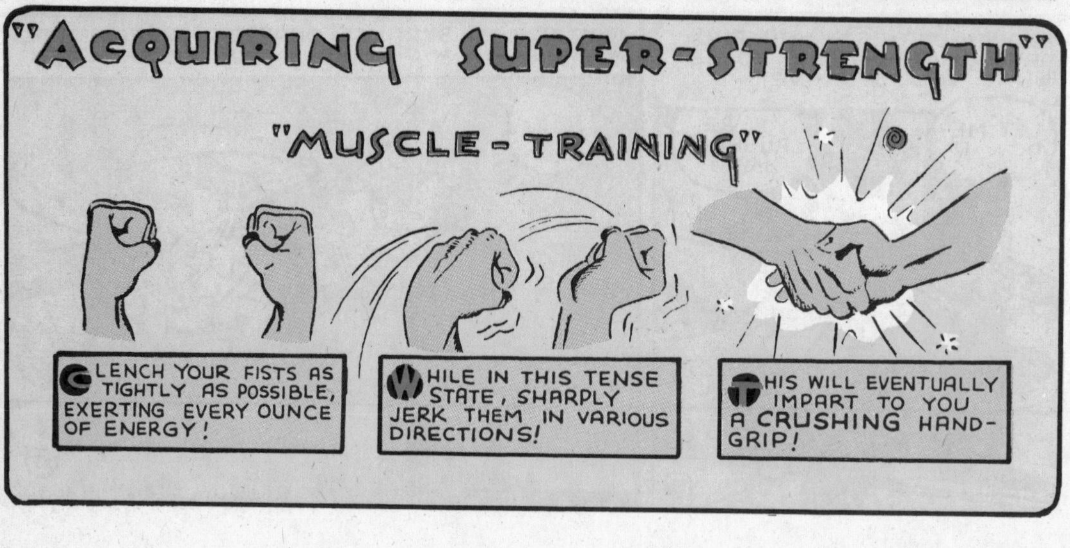
"ACQUIRING SUPER-STRENGTH"
"MUSCLE-TRAINING"
CLENCH YOUR FISTS AS TIGHTLY AS POSSIBLE, EXERTING EVERY OUNCE OF ENERGY!
WHILE IN THIS TENSE STATE, SHARPLY JERK THEM IN VARIOUS DIRECTIONS!
THIS WILL EVENTUALLY IMPART TO YOU A CRUSHING HAND-GRIP!

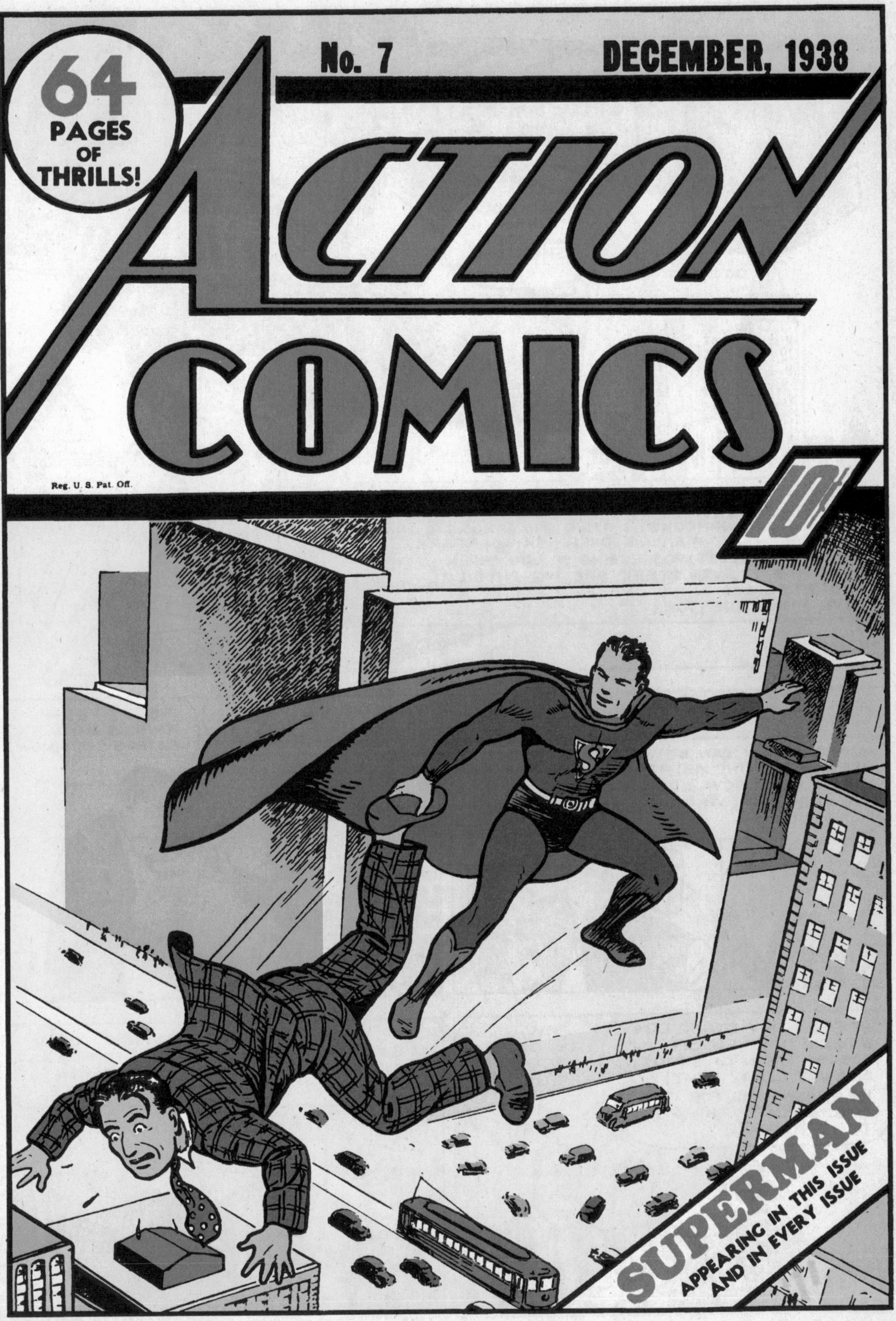
64 PAGES OF THRILLS!
No. 7
DECEMBER, 1938
ACTION COMICS
Reg. U. S. Pat. Off.
10¢
SUPERMAN
APPEARING IN THIS ISSUE
AND IN EVERY ISSUE

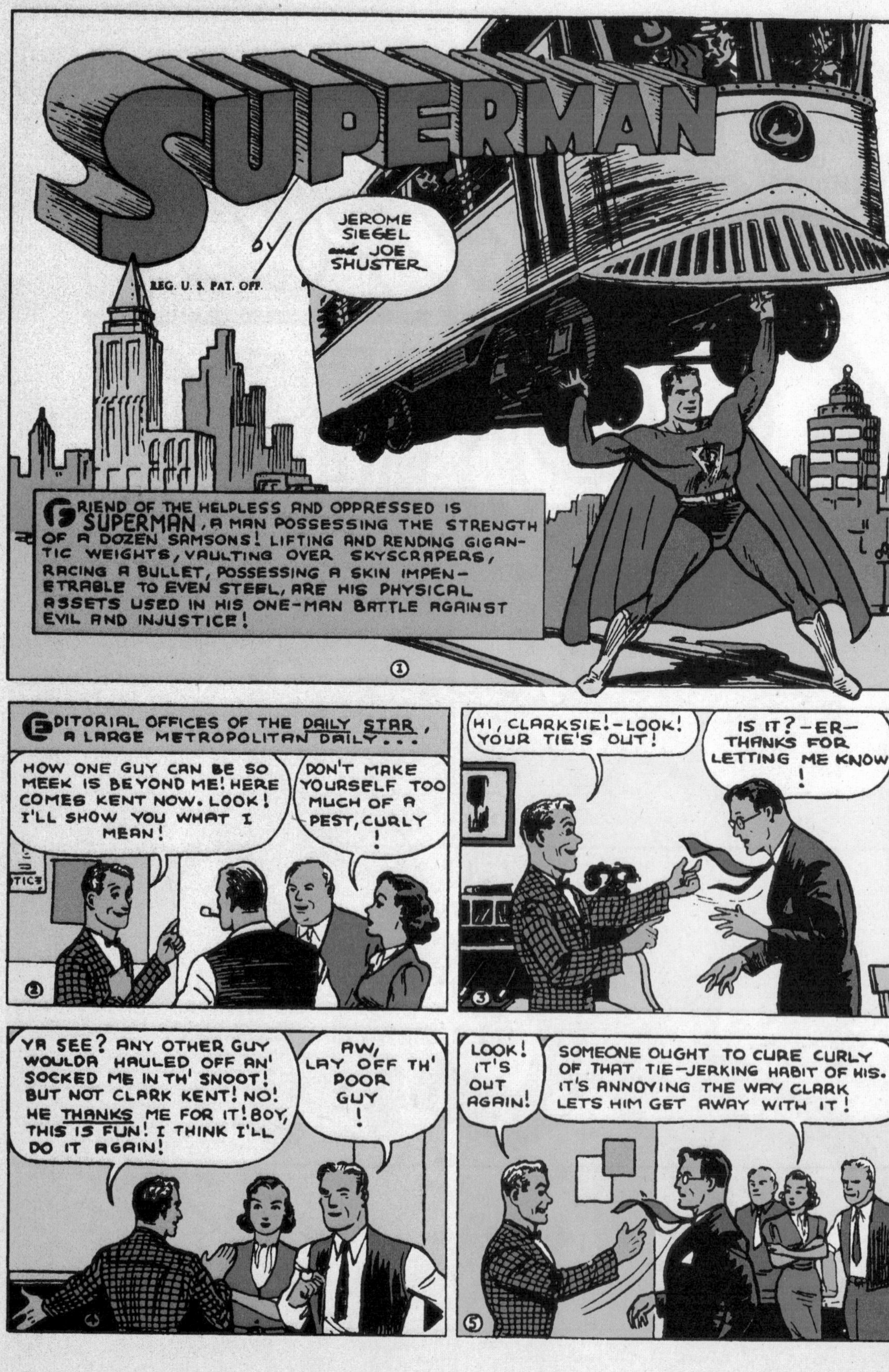
SUPERMAN
REG. U. S. PAT. OFF.
by
JEROME SIEGEL and JOE SHUSTER
FRIEND OF THE HELPLESS AND OPPRESSED IS SUPERMAN, A MAN POSSESSING THE STRENGTH OF A DOZEN SAMSONS! LIFTING AND RENDING GIGANTIC WEIGHTS, VAULTING OVER SKYSCRAPERS, RACING A BULLET, POSSESSING A SKIN IMPENETRABLE TO EVEN STEEL, ARE HIS PHYSICAL ASSETS USED IN HIS ONE-MAN BATTLE AGAINST EVIL AND INJUSTICE!
1
EDITORIAL OFFICES OF THE DAILY STAR, A LARGE METROPOLITAN DAILY...
HOW ONE GUY CAN BE SO MEEK IS BEYOND ME! HERE COMES KENT NOW. LOOK! I'LL SHOW YOU WHAT I MEAN!
DON'T MAKE YOURSELF TOO MUCH OF A PEST, CURLY!
2
HI, CLARKSIE!-LOOK! YOUR TIE'S OUT!
IS IT?-ER-THANKS FOR LETTING ME KNOW!
3
YA SEE? ANY OTHER GUY WOULDA HAULED OFF AN' SOCKED ME IN TH' SNOOT! BUT NOT CLARK KENT! NO! HE THANKS ME FOR IT! BOY, THIS IS FUN! I THINK I'LL DO IT AGAIN!
AW, LAY OFF TH' POOR GUY!
4
LOOK! IT'S OUT AGAIN!
SOMEONE OUGHT TO CURE CURLY OF THAT TIE-JERKING HABIT OF HIS. IT'S ANNOYING THE WAY CLARK LETS HIM GET AWAY WITH IT!
5

LOIS RESCUES CLARK FROM THE PESTIF-EROUS CURLY...

BOSS WANTS TO SEE YOU IN HIS OFFICE.—BETTER HURRY!

YOU CAN BE CERTAIN I WILL!

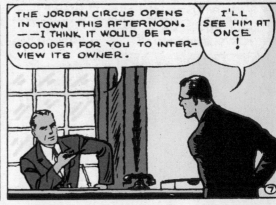

THE JORDAN CIRCUS OPENS IN TOWN THIS AFTERNOON. —I THINK IT WOULD BE A GOOD IDEA FOR YOU TO INTER-VIEW ITS OWNER.

I'LL SEE HIM AT ONCE!

AS CLARK NEARS THE OWNER'S WAGON ON THE CIRCUS-LOT, HE HEARS VOICES RAISED IN ANGER...

SOUNDS LIKE AN ARGUMENT. I'D BETTER WAIT BEFORE EN-TERING.

WITHIN THE WAGON...

YOU'LL TAKE MY OFFER--OR ELSE!

TAKE YOU IN AS A PARTNER? THE BLAZES I WOULD!

YOU'VE NO CHOICE. MY NOTES ARE COMING DUE AND YOU HAVEN'T THE MONEY TO PAY. EITHER TAKE ME IN AS A PART-NER, OR LOSE EVERY-THING.

IF I DO TAKE YOU IN, DEREK NILES -- I WILL LOSE EVERYTHING! ...INCLUDING MY SELF-RESPECT!

IF YOU EXPECT TO RAISE MONEY FROM PERFORMANCES, JORDAN, YOU'RE COMPLETELY DAFFY. PEOPLE ARE STAY-ING AWAY IN DROVES!

WE'LL SEE ABOUT THAT! NOW, GET OUT!

AS NILES ROUGHLY SHOULDERS ASIDE CLARK, HE IS COMPLETELY UNAWARE HE IS PASSING THE MAN WHO HAS DEDICATED HIS STRENGTH AND LIFE TO HELPING THOSE IN NEED OF ASSISTANCE.

PARDON ME!

CLUMSY OX!

IT'S TRUE--I'LL LOSE THE CIRCUS--MY GREATEST LOVE AND LIFE'S WORK! IF ONLY I COULD RAISE THE MONEY-- BUT NO-- I CAN'T--

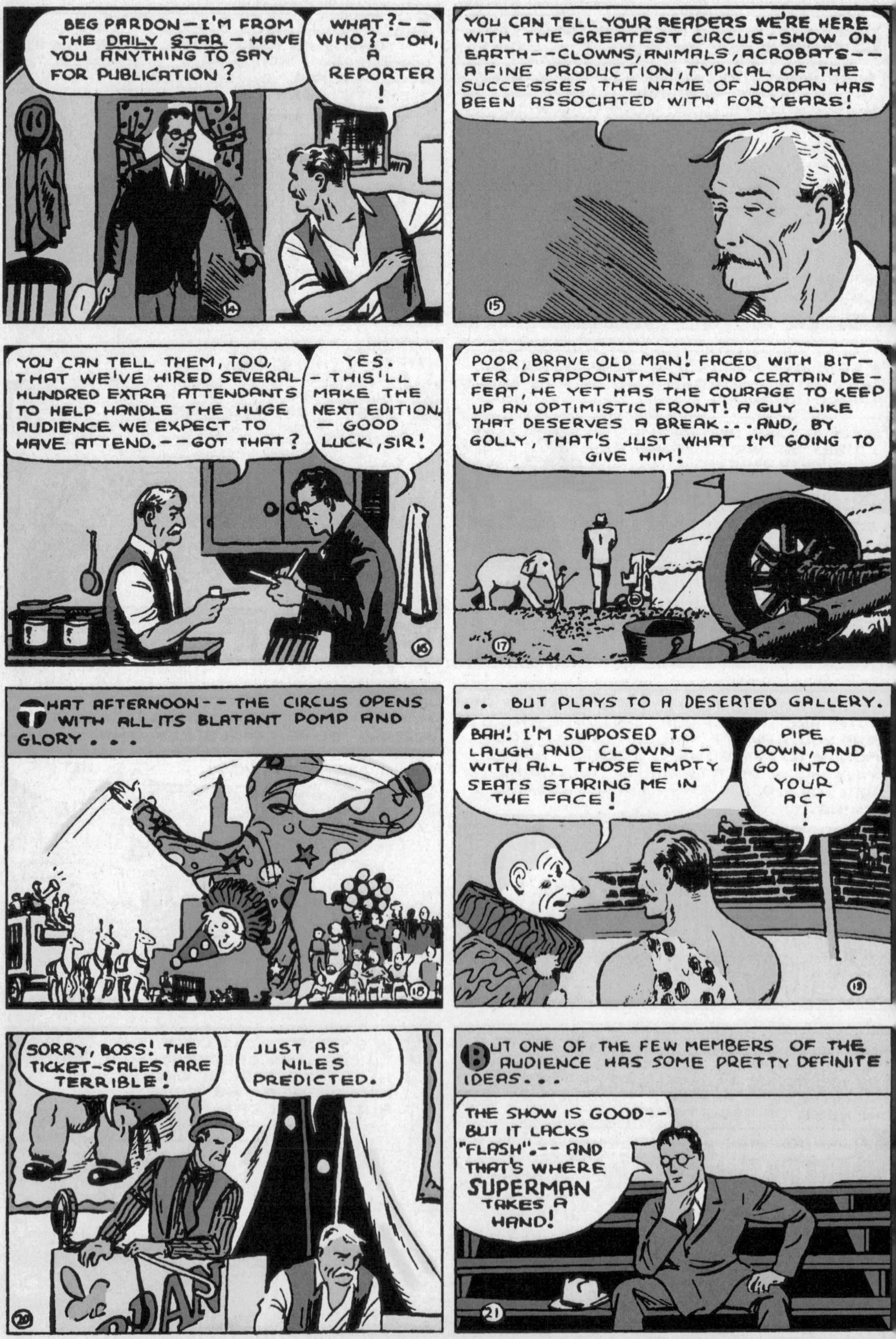

BEG PARDON—I'M FROM THE DAILY STAR—HAVE YOU ANYTHING TO SAY FOR PUBLICATION?
WHAT?--WHO?--OH, A REPORTER!
YOU CAN TELL YOUR READERS WE'RE HERE WITH THE GREATEST CIRCUS-SHOW ON EARTH--CLOWNS, ANIMALS, ACROBATS--A FINE PRODUCTION, TYPICAL OF THE SUCCESSES THE NAME OF JORDAN HAS BEEN ASSOCIATED WITH FOR YEARS!
YOU CAN TELL THEM, TOO, THAT WE'VE HIRED SEVERAL HUNDRED EXTRA ATTENDANTS TO HELP HANDLE THE HUGE AUDIENCE WE EXPECT TO HAVE ATTEND.--GOT THAT?
YES. -THIS'LL MAKE THE NEXT EDITION. —GOOD LUCK, SIR!
POOR, BRAVE OLD MAN! FACED WITH BITTER DISAPPOINTMENT AND CERTAIN DEFEAT, HE YET HAS THE COURAGE TO KEEP UP AN OPTIMISTIC FRONT! A GUY LIKE THAT DESERVES A BREAK...AND, BY GOLLY, THAT'S JUST WHAT I'M GOING TO GIVE HIM!
THAT AFTERNOON--THE CIRCUS OPENS WITH ALL ITS BLATANT POMP AND GLORY...
..BUT PLAYS TO A DESERTED GALLERY.
BAH! I'M SUPPOSED TO LAUGH AND CLOWN--WITH ALL THOSE EMPTY SEATS STARING ME IN THE FACE!
PIPE DOWN, AND GO INTO YOUR ACT!
SORRY, BOSS! THE TICKET-SALES ARE TERRIBLE!
JUST AS NILES PREDICTED.
BUT ONE OF THE FEW MEMBERS OF THE AUDIENCE HAS SOME PRETTY DEFINITE IDEAS...
THE SHOW IS GOOD--BUT IT LACKS "FLASH".--AND THAT'S WHERE SUPERMAN TAKES A HAND!

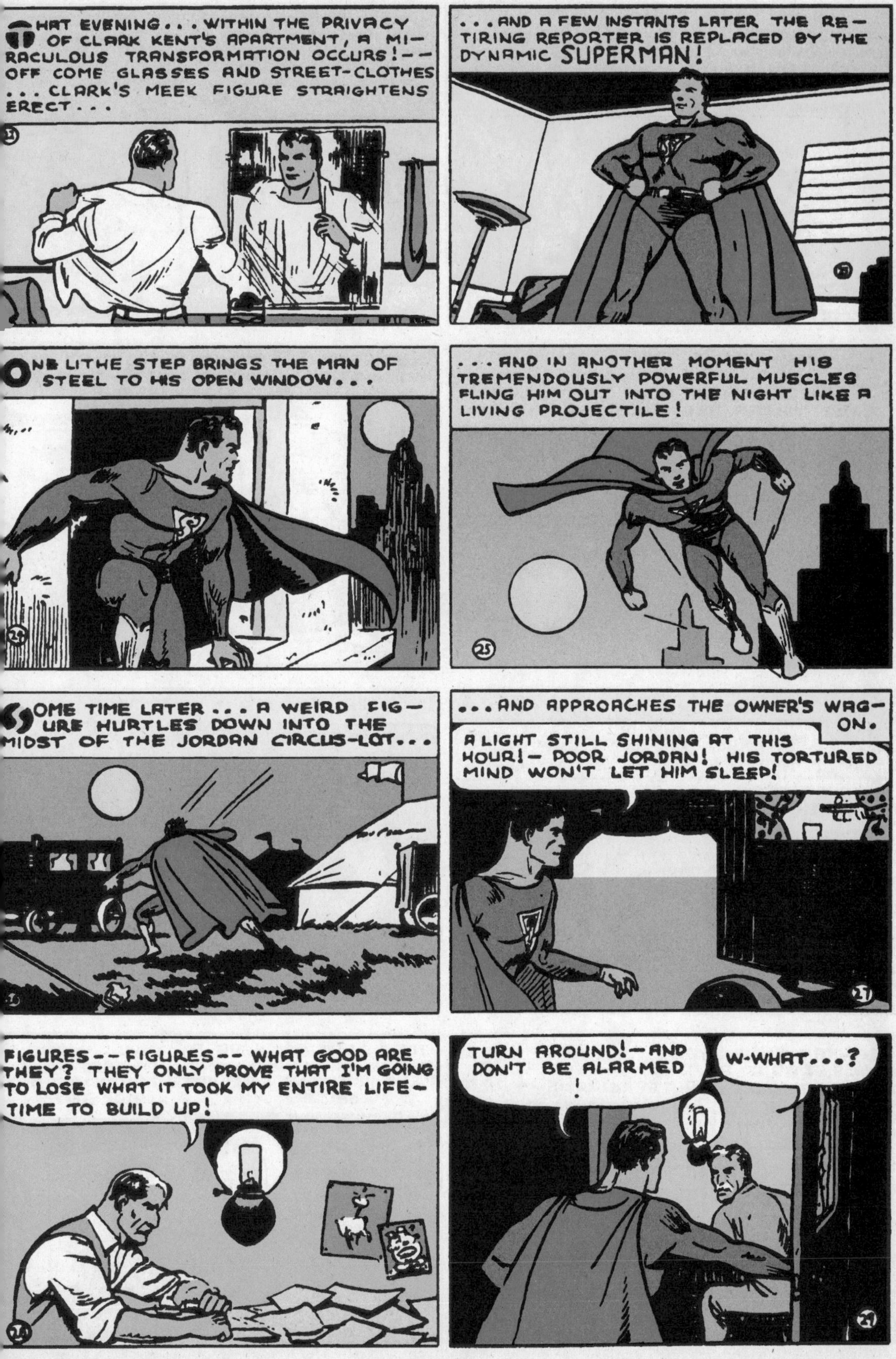
THAT EVENING... WITHIN THE PRIVACY OF CLARK KENT'S APARTMENT, A MIRACULOUS TRANSFORMATION OCCURS!-- OFF COME GLASSES AND STREET-CLOTHES ... CLARK'S MEEK FIGURE STRAIGHTENS ERECT...
...AND A FEW INSTANTS LATER THE RETIRING REPORTER IS REPLACED BY THE DYNAMIC SUPERMAN!
ONE LITHE STEP BRINGS THE MAN OF STEEL TO HIS OPEN WINDOW...
...AND IN ANOTHER MOMENT HIS TREMENDOUSLY POWERFUL MUSCLES FLING HIM OUT INTO THE NIGHT LIKE A LIVING PROJECTILE!
SOME TIME LATER... A WEIRD FIGURE HURTLES DOWN INTO THE MIDST OF THE JORDAN CIRCUS-LOT...
...AND APPROACHES THE OWNER'S WAGON.
A LIGHT STILL SHINING AT THIS HOUR!- POOR JORDAN! HIS TORTURED MIND WON'T LET HIM SLEEP!
FIGURES--FIGURES-- WHAT GOOD ARE THEY? THEY ONLY PROVE THAT I'M GOING TO LOSE WHAT IT TOOK MY ENTIRE LIFE-TIME TO BUILD UP!
TURN AROUND!-AND DON'T BE ALARMED!
W-WHAT...?

A BURGLAR! —WELL, YOU'VE COME TO THE WRONG PLACE, FELLA. YOU WON'T FIND ENOUGH IN THIS FLOP SHOW TO BUY YOU A PACKAGE OF CIGARETTES!

YOU MIS-UNDER-STAND. I — —

WHILE JORDAN SPOKE, HE HAD SLIPPED AN AUTOMATIC OUT OF A DRAWER BEHIND HIM . . .

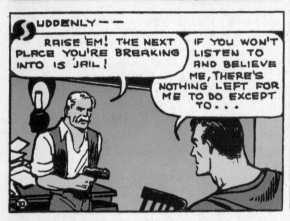

SUDDENLY — —
RAISE 'EM! THE NEXT PLACE YOU'RE BREAKING INTO IS JAIL!

IF YOU WON'T LISTEN TO AND BELIEVE ME, THERE'S NOTHING LEFT FOR ME TO DO EXCEPT TO . . .

KEEP BACK! —I WARN YOU !

LET ME HAVE THAT GUN! YOU'RE LIABLE TO HURT YOURSELF!

WITH AN INCREDIBLY SWIFT MOVEMENT FASTER THAN THE EYE CAN FOLLOW, SUPERMAN SNATCHES THE GUN OUT OF JORDAN'S HAND . . .
MUSN'T PLAY WITH DANGEROUS TOYS!

. . . THEN CRUSHES IT TO A PULP!

W-WHAT TH' —! YOU SQUEEZED IT AS THO IT WERE MADE OF PUTTY! —WHO ARE YOU? WHAT DO YOU WANT?

I WANT A JOB --WITH YOUR CIRCUS-- AS A PROFESSIONAL STRONG-MAN.

BUT I ALREADY HAVE A STRONG-MAN WHO CAN BEND IRON AND LIFT METAL BALLS.

WILL YOU PLEASE STEP OUTSIDE A MOMENT?

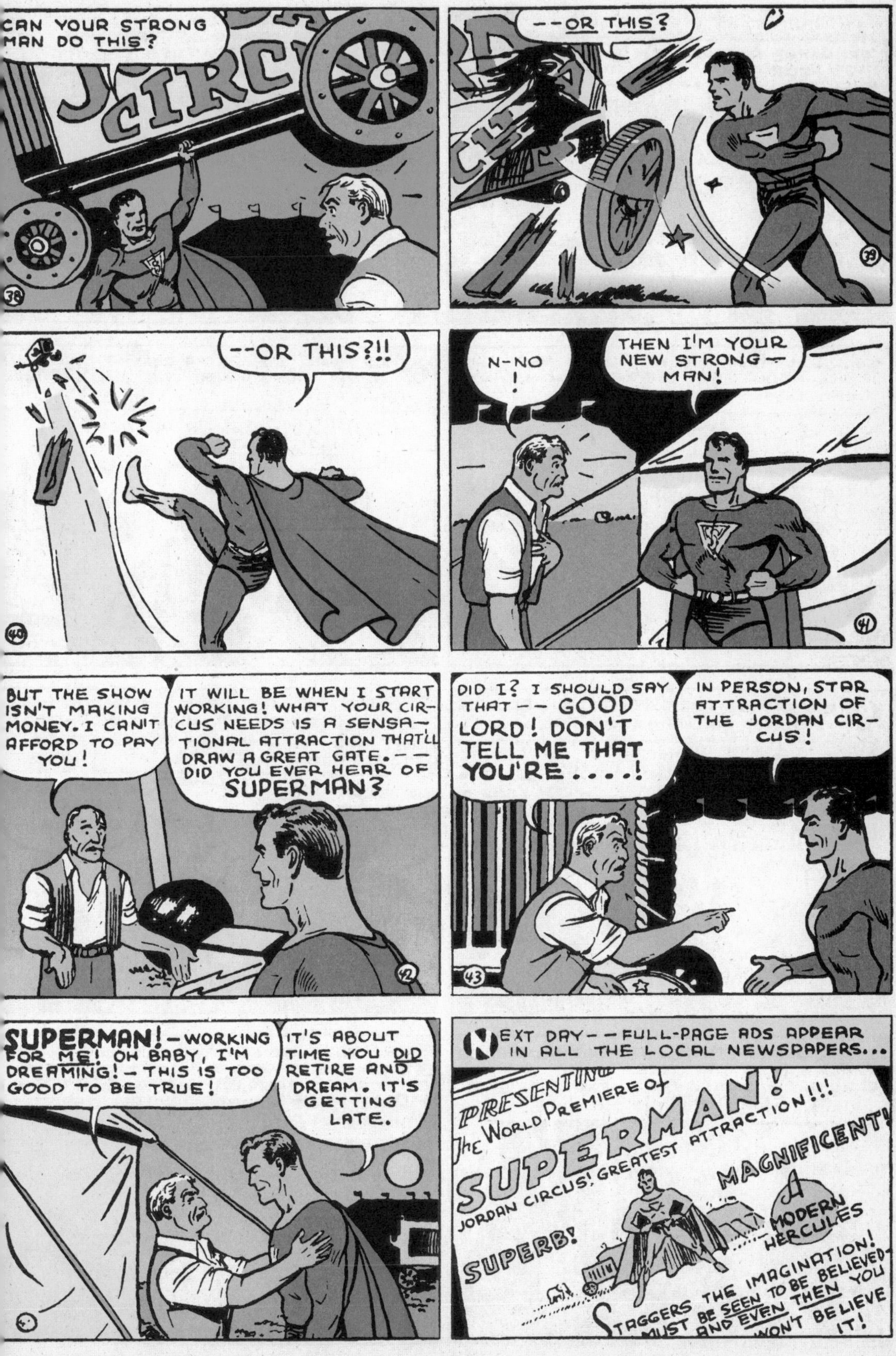
CAN YOUR STRONG MAN DO THIS?
--OR THIS?
--OR THIS?!!
N-NO!
THEN I'M YOUR NEW STRONG-MAN!
BUT THE SHOW ISN'T MAKING MONEY. I CAN'T AFFORD TO PAY YOU!
IT WILL BE WHEN I START WORKING! WHAT YOUR CIRCUS NEEDS IS A SENSATIONAL ATTRACTION THAT'LL DRAW A GREAT GATE.-- DID YOU EVER HEAR OF SUPERMAN?
DID I? I SHOULD SAY THAT-- GOOD LORD! DON'T TELL ME THAT YOU'RE....!
IN PERSON, STAR ATTRACTION OF THE JORDAN CIRCUS!
SUPERMAN!-WORKING FOR ME! OH BABY, I'M DREAMING!-THIS IS TOO GOOD TO BE TRUE!
IT'S ABOUT TIME YOU DID RETIRE AND DREAM. IT'S GETTING LATE.
NEXT DAY--FULL-PAGE ADS APPEAR IN ALL THE LOCAL NEWSPAPERS...
PRESENTING The WORLD PREMIERE of SUPERMAN!
JORDAN CIRCUS! GREATEST ATTRACTION!!!
MAGNIFICENT!
A MODERN HERCULES
SUPERB!
STAGGERS THE IMAGINATION!
MUST BE SEEN TO BE BELIEVED-AND EVEN THEN YOU WON'T BELIEVE IT!

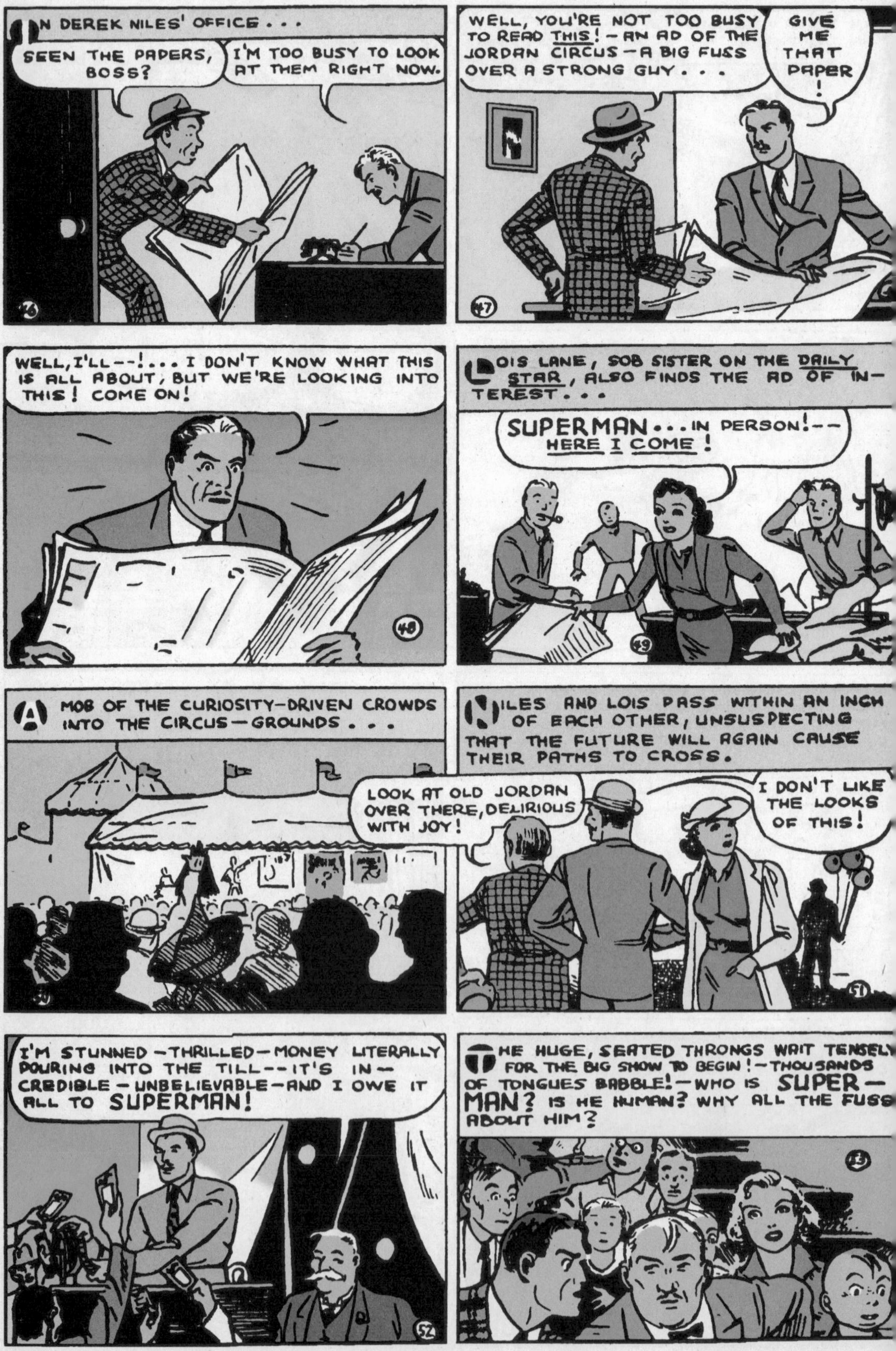
IN DEREK NILES' OFFICE . . .
SEEN THE PAPERS, BOSS?
I'M TOO BUSY TO LOOK AT THEM RIGHT NOW.
WELL, YOU'RE NOT TOO BUSY TO READ THIS! — AN AD OF THE JORDAN CIRCUS — A BIG FUSS OVER A STRONG GUY . . .
GIVE ME THAT PAPER !
WELL, I'LL — — ! . . . I DON'T KNOW WHAT THIS IS ALL ABOUT, BUT WE'RE LOOKING INTO THIS! COME ON!
LOIS LANE, SOB SISTER ON THE DAILY STAR, ALSO FINDS THE AD OF INTEREST . . .
SUPERMAN . . . IN PERSON! — — HERE I COME !
A MOB OF THE CURIOSITY-DRIVEN CROWDS INTO THE CIRCUS — GROUNDS . . .
NILES AND LOIS PASS WITHIN AN INCH OF EACH OTHER, UNSUSPECTING THAT THE FUTURE WILL AGAIN CAUSE THEIR PATHS TO CROSS.
LOOK AT OLD JORDAN OVER THERE, DELIRIOUS WITH JOY!
I DON'T LIKE THE LOOKS OF THIS!
I'M STUNNED — THRILLED — MONEY LITERALLY POURING INTO THE TILL — — IT'S IN— CREDIBLE — UNBELIEVABLE — AND I OWE IT ALL TO SUPERMAN!
THE HUGE, SEATED THRONGS WAIT TENSELY FOR THE BIG SHOW TO BEGIN! — THOUSANDS OF TONGUES BABBLE! — WHO IS SUPER— MAN? IS HE HUMAN? WHY ALL THE FUSS ABOUT HIM?

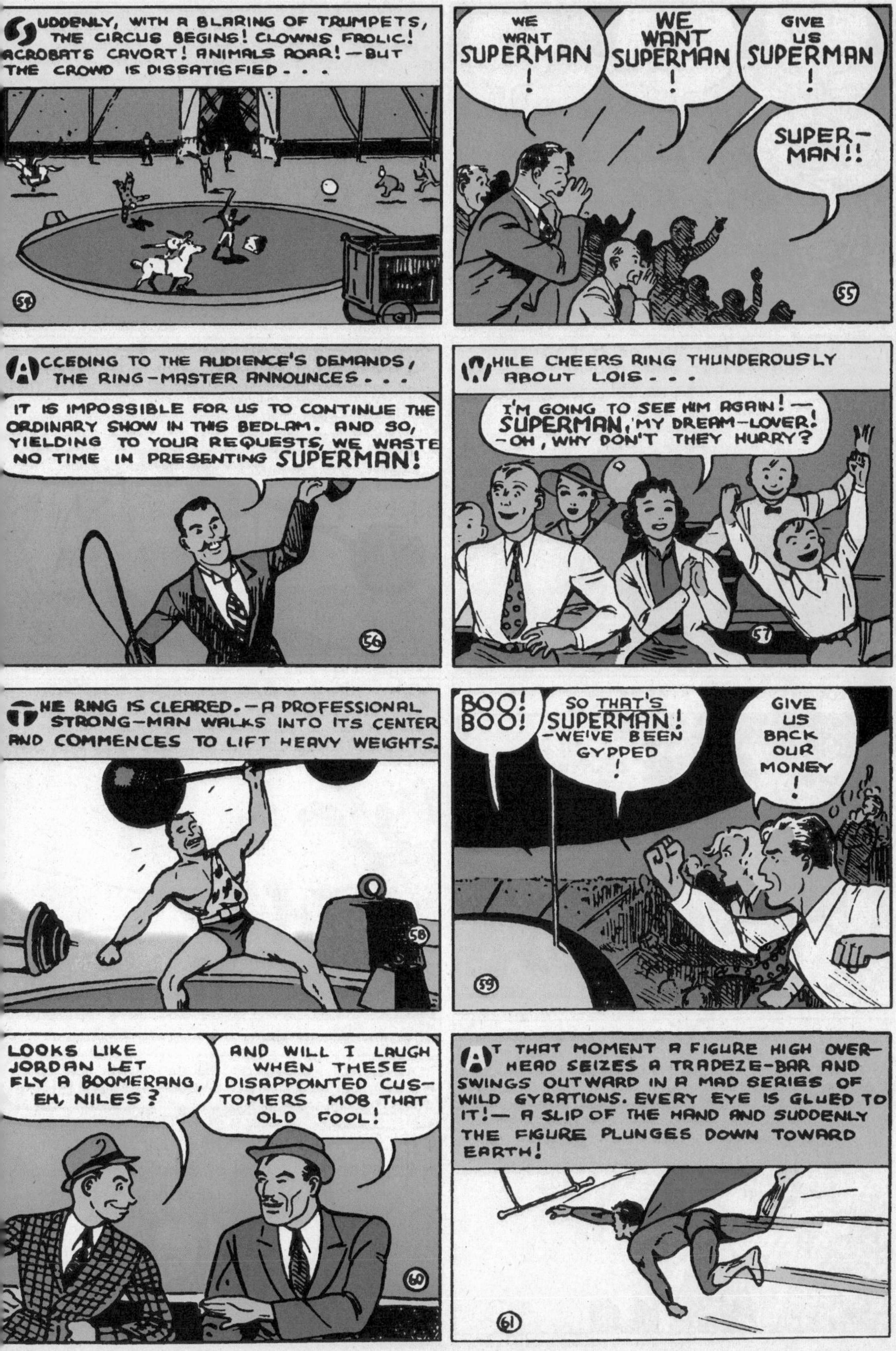
SUDDENLY, WITH A BLARING OF TRUMPETS, THE CIRCUS BEGINS! CLOWNS FROLIC! ACROBATS CAVORT! ANIMALS ROAR! — BUT THE CROWD IS DISSATISFIED . . .
54
WE WANT SUPERMAN !
WE WANT SUPERMAN !
GIVE US SUPERMAN !
SUPER-MAN!!
55
ACCEDING TO THE AUDIENCE'S DEMANDS, THE RING-MASTER ANNOUNCES . . .
IT IS IMPOSSIBLE FOR US TO CONTINUE THE ORDINARY SHOW IN THIS BEDLAM. AND SO, YIELDING TO YOUR REQUESTS, WE WASTE NO TIME IN PRESENTING SUPERMAN!
56
WHILE CHEERS RING THUNDEROUSLY ABOUT LOIS . . .
I'M GOING TO SEE HIM AGAIN! — SUPERMAN, MY DREAM-LOVER! — OH, WHY DON'T THEY HURRY?
57
THE RING IS CLEARED. — A PROFESSIONAL STRONG-MAN WALKS INTO ITS CENTER AND COMMENCES TO LIFT HEAVY WEIGHTS.
58
BOO! BOO!
SO THAT'S SUPERMAN! — WE'VE BEEN GYPPED !
GIVE US BACK OUR MONEY !
59
LOOKS LIKE JORDAN LET FLY A BOOMERANG, EH, NILES ?
AND WILL I LAUGH WHEN THESE DISAPPOINTED CUS-TOMERS MOB THAT OLD FOOL!
60
AT THAT MOMENT A FIGURE HIGH OVER-HEAD SEIZES A TRAPEZE-BAR AND SWINGS OUTWARD IN A MAD SERIES OF WILD GYRATIONS. EVERY EYE IS GLUED TO IT! — A SLIP OF THE HAND AND SUDDENLY THE FIGURE PLUNGES DOWN TOWARD EARTH!
61

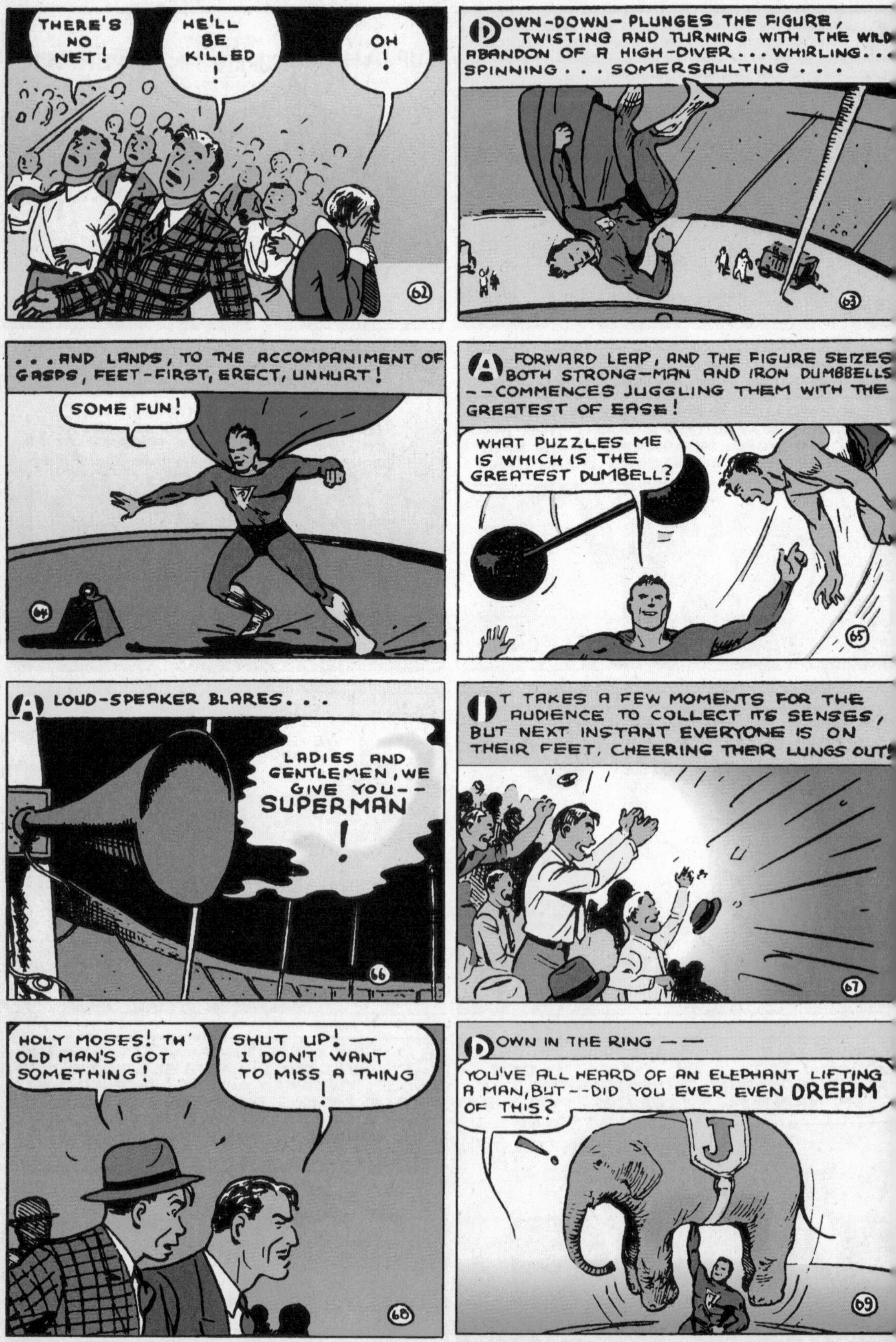

THERE'S NO NET!

HE'LL BE KILLED!

OH!

62

DOWN-DOWN-PLUNGES THE FIGURE, TWISTING AND TURNING WITH THE WILD ABANDON OF A HIGH-DIVER...WHIRLING...SPINNING...SOMERSAULTING...

63

...AND LANDS, TO THE ACCOMPANIMENT OF GASPS, FEET-FIRST, ERECT, UNHURT!

SOME FUN!

64

A FORWARD LEAP, AND THE FIGURE SEIZES BOTH STRONG-MAN AND IRON DUMBBELLS--COMMENCES JUGGLING THEM WITH THE GREATEST OF EASE!

WHAT PUZZLES ME IS WHICH IS THE GREATEST DUMBELL?

65

A LOUD-SPEAKER BLARES...

LADIES AND GENTLEMEN, WE GIVE YOU-- SUPERMAN!

66

IT TAKES A FEW MOMENTS FOR THE AUDIENCE TO COLLECT ITS SENSES, BUT NEXT INSTANT EVERYONE IS ON THEIR FEET, CHEERING THEIR LUNGS OUT!

67

HOLY MOSES! TH' OLD MAN'S GOT SOMETHING!

SHUT UP!-- I DON'T WANT TO MISS A THING!

68

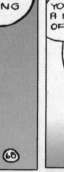

DOWN IN THE RING--

YOU'VE ALL HEARD OF AN ELEPHANT LIFTING A MAN, BUT--DID YOU EVER EVEN DREAM OF THIS?

69

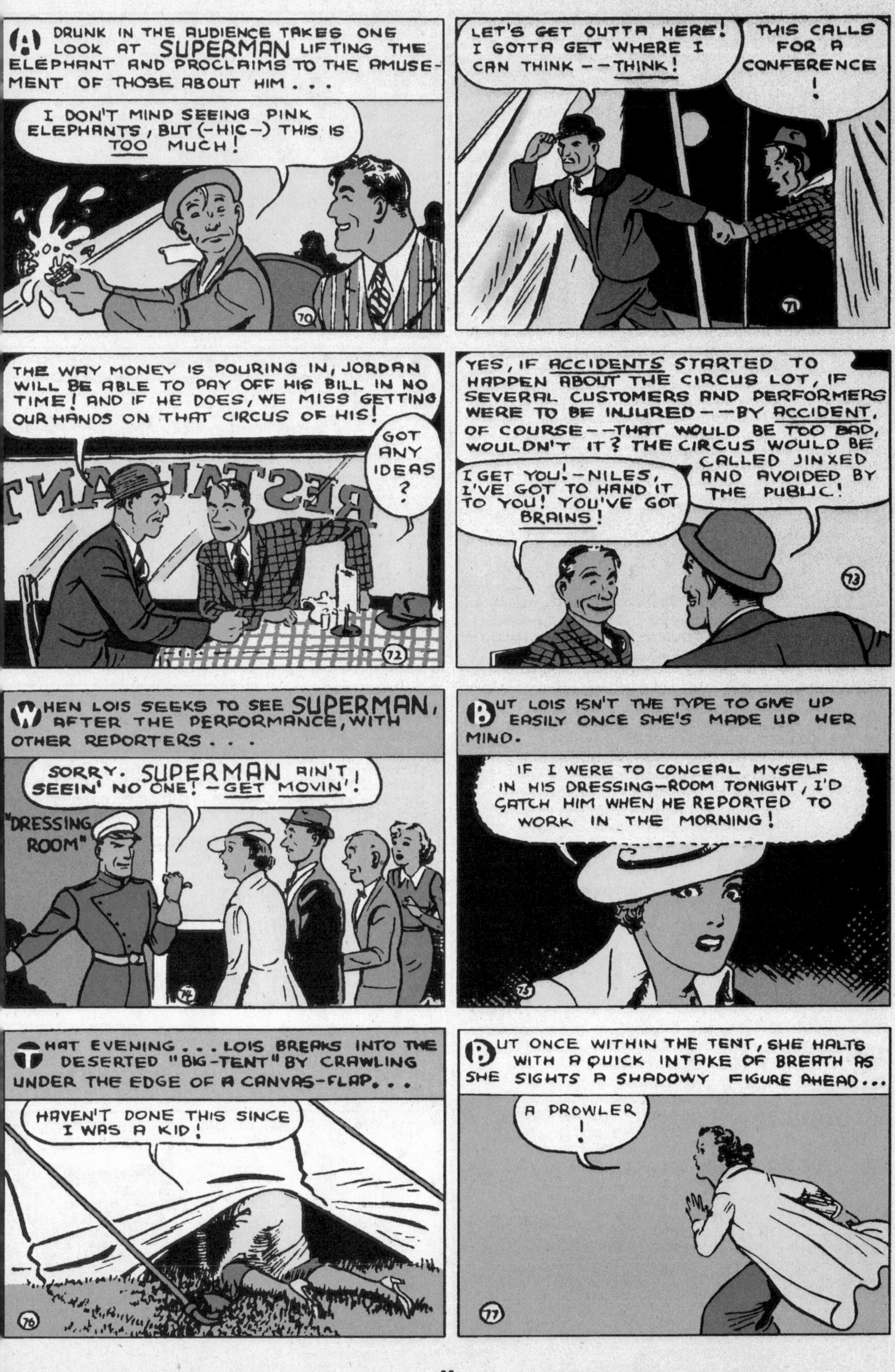
A DRUNK IN THE AUDIENCE TAKES ONE LOOK AT SUPERMAN LIFTING THE ELEPHANT AND PROCLAIMS TO THE AMUSEMENT OF THOSE ABOUT HIM . . .
I DON'T MIND SEEING PINK ELEPHANTS, BUT (-HIC-) THIS IS TOO MUCH!
70
LET'S GET OUTTA HERE! I GOTTA GET WHERE I CAN THINK --THINK!
THIS CALLS FOR A CONFERENCE !
71
THE WAY MONEY IS POURING IN, JORDAN WILL BE ABLE TO PAY OFF HIS BILL IN NO TIME! AND IF HE DOES, WE MISS GETTING OUR HANDS ON THAT CIRCUS OF HIS!
GOT ANY IDEAS ?
72
YES, IF ACCIDENTS STARTED TO HAPPEN ABOUT THE CIRCUS LOT, IF SEVERAL CUSTOMERS AND PERFORMERS WERE TO BE INJURED--BY ACCIDENT, OF COURSE--THAT WOULD BE TOO BAD, WOULDN'T IT? THE CIRCUS WOULD BE CALLED JINXED AND AVOIDED BY THE PUBLIC!
I GET YOU!-NILES, I'VE GOT TO HAND IT TO YOU! YOU'VE GOT BRAINS!
73
WHEN LOIS SEEKS TO SEE SUPERMAN, AFTER THE PERFORMANCE, WITH OTHER REPORTERS . . .
SORRY. SUPERMAN AIN'T SEEIN' NO ONE! -GET MOVIN'!
"DRESSING ROOM"
74
BUT LOIS ISN'T THE TYPE TO GIVE UP EASILY ONCE SHE'S MADE UP HER MIND.
IF I WERE TO CONCEAL MYSELF IN HIS DRESSING-ROOM TONIGHT, I'D CATCH HIM WHEN HE REPORTED TO WORK IN THE MORNING!
75
THAT EVENING . . . LOIS BREAKS INTO THE DESERTED "BIG-TENT" BY CRAWLING UNDER THE EDGE OF A CANVAS-FLAP. . .
HAVEN'T DONE THIS SINCE I WAS A KID!
76
BUT ONCE WITHIN THE TENT, SHE HALTS WITH A QUICK INTAKE OF BREATH AS SHE SIGHTS A SHADOWY FIGURE AHEAD...
A PROWLER !
77

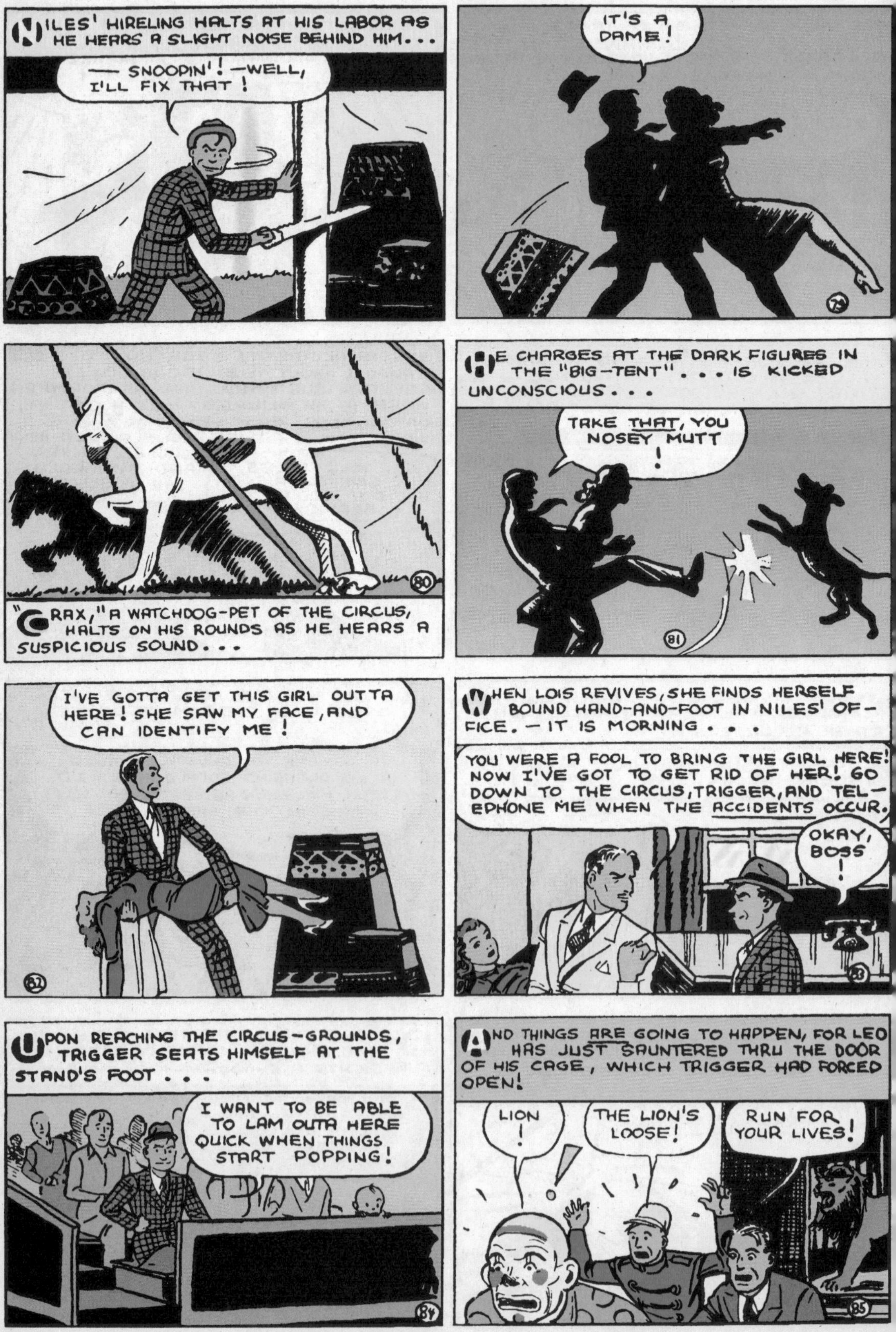
NILES' HIRELING HALTS AT HIS LABOR AS HE HEARS A SLIGHT NOISE BEHIND HIM . . .
— SNOOPIN'! —WELL, I'LL FIX THAT!
IT'S A DAME!
"CRAX," A WATCHDOG-PET OF THE CIRCUS, HALTS ON HIS ROUNDS AS HE HEARS A SUSPICIOUS SOUND . . .
HE CHARGES AT THE DARK FIGURES IN THE "BIG-TENT" . . . IS KICKED UNCONSCIOUS . . .
TAKE THAT, YOU NOSEY MUTT!
I'VE GOTTA GET THIS GIRL OUTTA HERE! SHE SAW MY FACE, AND CAN IDENTIFY ME!
WHEN LOIS REVIVES, SHE FINDS HERSELF BOUND HAND-AND-FOOT IN NILES' OF-FICE. — IT IS MORNING . . .
YOU WERE A FOOL TO BRING THE GIRL HERE! NOW I'VE GOT TO GET RID OF HER! GO DOWN TO THE CIRCUS, TRIGGER, AND TEL-EPHONE ME WHEN THE ACCIDENTS OCCUR.
OKAY, BOSS!
UPON REACHING THE CIRCUS-GROUNDS, TRIGGER SEATS HIMSELF AT THE STAND'S FOOT . . .
I WANT TO BE ABLE TO LAM OUTA HERE QUICK WHEN THINGS START POPPING!
AND THINGS ARE GOING TO HAPPEN, FOR LEO HAS JUST SAUNTERED THRU THE DOOR OF HIS CAGE, WHICH TRIGGER HAD FORCED OPEN!
LION!
THE LION'S LOOSE!
RUN FOR YOUR LIVES!

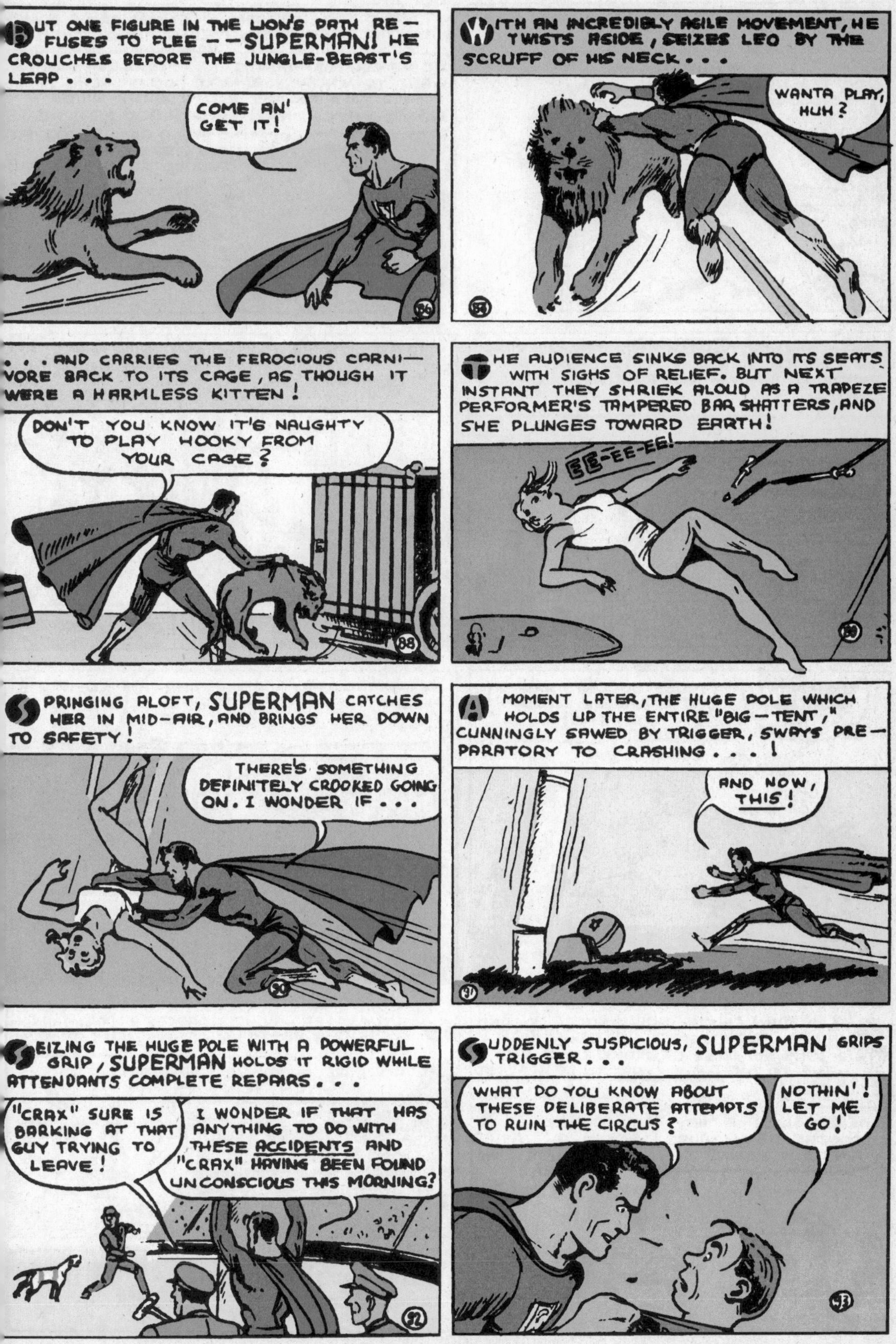
BUT ONE FIGURE IN THE LION'S PATH RE-FUSES TO FLEE --SUPERMAN! HE CROUCHES BEFORE THE JUNGLE-BEAST'S LEAP . . .
COME AN' GET IT!
WITH AN INCREDIBLY AGILE MOVEMENT, HE TWISTS ASIDE, SEIZES LEO BY THE SCRUFF OF HIS NECK . . .
WANTA PLAY, HUH?
. . . AND CARRIES THE FEROCIOUS CARNI-VORE BACK TO ITS CAGE, AS THOUGH IT WERE A HARMLESS KITTEN!
DON'T YOU KNOW IT'S NAUGHTY TO PLAY HOOKY FROM YOUR CAGE?
THE AUDIENCE SINKS BACK INTO ITS SEATS WITH SIGHS OF RELIEF. BUT NEXT INSTANT THEY SHRIEK ALOUD AS A TRAPEZE PERFORMER'S TAMPERED BAR SHATTERS, AND SHE PLUNGES TOWARD EARTH!
EE-EE-EE!
SPRINGING ALOFT, SUPERMAN CATCHES HER IN MID-AIR, AND BRINGS HER DOWN TO SAFETY!
THERE'S SOMETHING DEFINITELY CROOKED GOING ON. I WONDER IF . . .
A MOMENT LATER, THE HUGE POLE WHICH HOLDS UP THE ENTIRE "BIG-TENT," CUNNINGLY SAWED BY TRIGGER, SWAYS PRE-PARATORY TO CRASHING . . . !
AND NOW, THIS!
SEIZING THE HUGE POLE WITH A POWERFUL GRIP, SUPERMAN HOLDS IT RIGID WHILE ATTENDANTS COMPLETE REPAIRS . . .
"CRAX" SURE IS BARKING AT THAT GUY TRYING TO LEAVE!
I WONDER IF THAT HAS ANYTHING TO DO WITH THESE ACCIDENTS AND "CRAX" HAVING BEEN FOUND UNCONSCIOUS THIS MORNING?
SUDDENLY SUSPICIOUS, SUPERMAN GRIPS TRIGGER . . .
WHAT DO YOU KNOW ABOUT THESE DELIBERATE ATTEMPTS TO RUIN THE CIRCUS?
NOTHIN'! LET ME GO!

SUPERMAN TOSSES TRIGGER HIGH IN-TO THE AIR...

YAA-AA-A! — HELP! HELP ME!

24

...AND CATCHES HIM WHEN HE DROPS DOWN-WARD! HE DOES THIS SEVERAL TIMES, THEN--

NOW TELL ME WHAT I WANT TO KNOW, OR NEXT TIME I TOSS YOU UP, I WON'T CATCH YOU!

PLEASE! — DON'T DO IT AGAIN! DEREK NILES HIRED ME! HE HAS A GIRL REPORTER IN HIS OFFICE NOW...IS GOING TO FINISH HER OFF!

95

OFF SPEEDS **SUPERMAN** TOWARD NILES' OFFICE, RUNNING SO FAST HE AP-PEARS TO BE A BLURRED STREAK OF MOTION!

SUPERMAN!

HUH?

GIVE ME THAT GUN!

97

KEEP AWAY FROM ME!

THOSE BULLETS ARE AS HARMLESS TO ME AS PEAS!

96

HE FAINTED AWAY FROM SHEER FRIGHT! — WAIT! I WANT TO THANK YOU FOR SAVING MY LIFE!

SOME OTHER TIME!

99

THE JORDAN CIRCUS NOW A SUCCESS—AND NILES AND TRIGGER JAILED—**SUPER-MAN** DONS HIS GUISE OF CLARK KENT AND RETURNS TO THE DAILY STAR, TO BE GREETED BY CURLY!

WELL, WELL! — IF THAT DOGGONE TIE OF YOURS AIN'T OUT AGAIN!

YOU DESERVE A LESSON, AND BY GOLLY, YOU'RE GOING TO GET ONE!

100

SHORTLY LATER, AS CURLY PASSES A DOOR, A HAND REACHES OUT, SEIZES HIS CLOTHES, JERKS SAVAGELY...

WHY, CURLY! — YOU'RE UNDRESSED! —TCH! TCH!

101

And Don't Forget to Read:

MORE FUN COMICS

64 PAGES OF THRILLS!
No. 8
JANUARY, 1939
ACTION COMICS
Reg U.S Pat. Off.
10¢

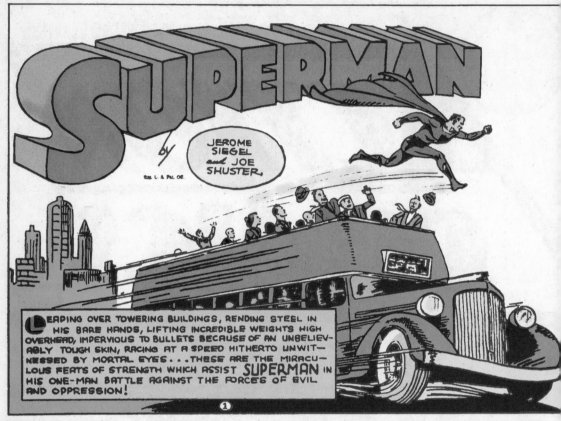

SUPERMAN

by JEROME SIEGEL and JOE SHUSTER.

Reg. U. S. Pat. Off.

LEAPING OVER TOWERING BUILDINGS, RENDING STEEL IN HIS BARE HANDS, LIFTING INCREDIBLE WEIGHTS HIGH OVERHEAD, IMPERVIOUS TO BULLETS BECAUSE OF AN UNBELIEVABLY TOUGH SKIN, RACING AT A SPEED HITHERTO UNWITNESSED BY MORTAL EYES...THESE ARE THE MIRACULOUS FEATS OF STRENGTH WHICH ASSIST SUPERMAN IN HIS ONE-MAN BATTLE AGAINST THE FORCES OF EVIL AND OPPRESSION!

1

A SESSION OF JUVENILE-COURT...

FRANKIE MARELLO...YOU ARE CHARGED WITH ASSAULT AND BATTERY. WHAT HAVE YOU TO SAY IN YOUR DEFENSE?

NOT'IN--'CEPT IF HE HAD HANDED OVER HIS DOUGH WIT' OUT SQUAWKIN' I WOULDN'TA HIT 'IM SO HARD.

2

YOU SPEAK LIKE A HARDENED CRIMINAL. IN THAT CASE, I HAVE NO COURSE BUT TO--

WAIT! WAIT, YOUR HONOR!

3

OF COURSE HE TALKS TOUGH—WHAT'S MORE HE IS TOUGH, YOUR HONOR—BUT HE'S ONLY LIKE ALL THE OTHER BOYS IN OUR NEIGHBORHOOD... HARD, RESENTFUL, UNDERPRIVILEGED. HE'S MY ONLY SON, SIR. HE MIGHT HAVE BEEN A GOOD BOY EXCEPT FOR HIS ENVIRONMENT. HE STILL MIGHT BE--IF YOU'LL BE MERCIFUL!

4

AMONG THE SPECTATORS IN THE COURT-ROOM IS CLARK KENT, ACE NEWSPAPER REPORTER...HE LISTENS INTENTLY, COMPLETELY ENGROSSED...

THE MOTHER'S RIGHT! BUT IF I KNOW THE COURT OF LAW...HER PLEA HASN'T A CHANCE!

5

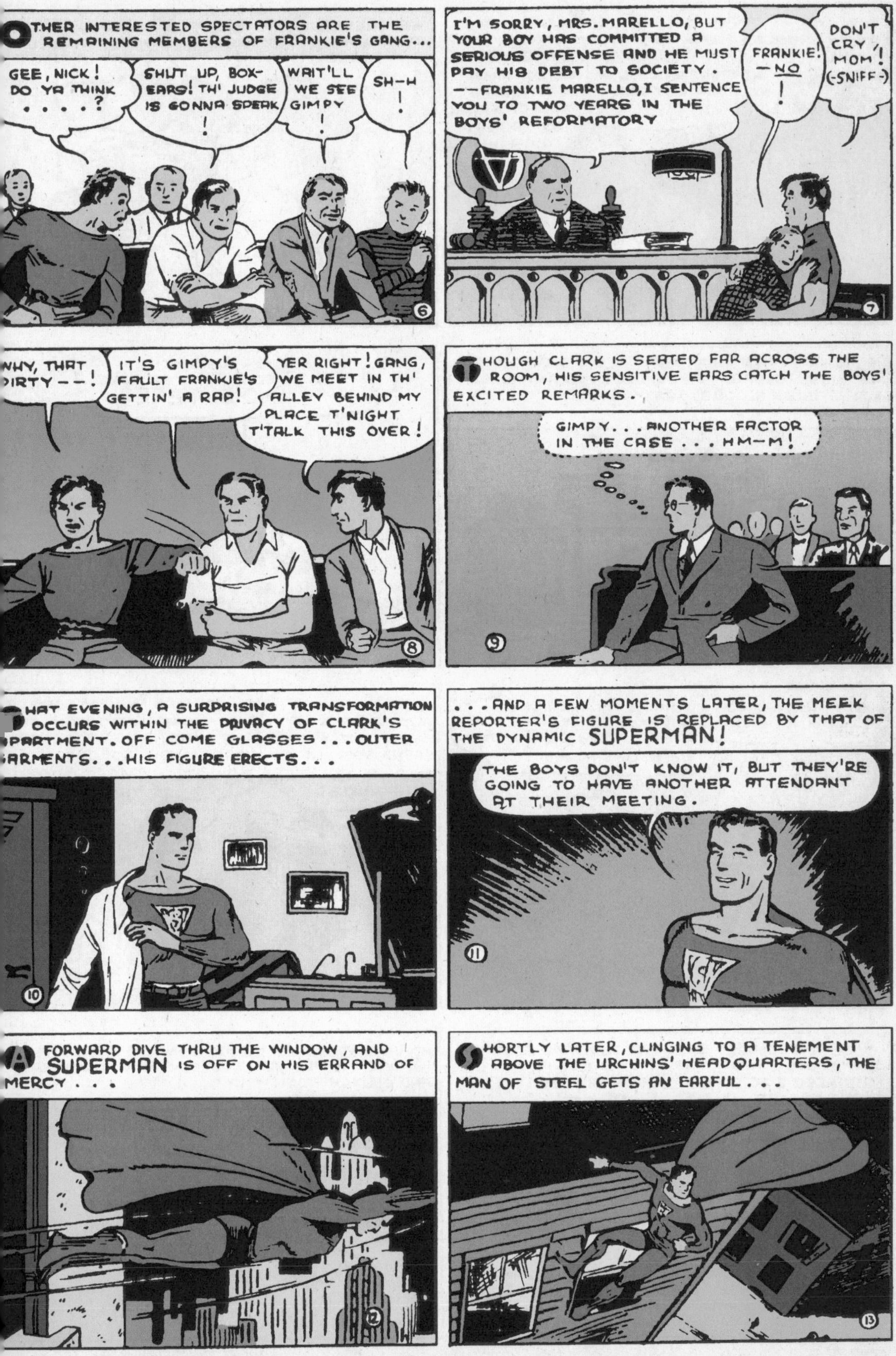
OTHER INTERESTED SPECTATORS ARE THE REMAINING MEMBERS OF FRANKIE'S GANG...
GEE, NICK! DO YA THINK ....?
SHUT UP, BOX-EARS! TH' JUDGE IS GONNA SPEAK!
WAIT'LL WE SEE GIMPY!
SH-H!
I'M SORRY, MRS. MARELLO, BUT YOUR BOY HAS COMMITTED A SERIOUS OFFENSE AND HE MUST PAY HIS DEBT TO SOCIETY. --FRANKIE MARELLO, I SENTENCE YOU TO TWO YEARS IN THE BOYS' REFORMATORY
FRANKIE! -NO!
DON'T CRY, MOM! (-SNIFF-)
WHY, THAT DIRTY--!
IT'S GIMPY'S FAULT FRANKIE'S GETTIN' A RAP!
YER RIGHT! GANG, WE MEET IN TH' ALLEY BEHIND MY PLACE T'NIGHT T'TALK THIS OVER!
THOUGH CLARK IS SEATED FAR ACROSS THE ROOM, HIS SENSITIVE EARS CATCH THE BOYS' EXCITED REMARKS.
GIMPY... ANOTHER FACTOR IN THE CASE... HM-M!
THAT EVENING, A SURPRISING TRANSFORMATION OCCURS WITHIN THE PRIVACY OF CLARK'S APARTMENT. OFF COME GLASSES... OUTER GARMENTS... HIS FIGURE ERECTS...
...AND A FEW MOMENTS LATER, THE MEEK REPORTER'S FIGURE IS REPLACED BY THAT OF THE DYNAMIC SUPERMAN!
THE BOYS DON'T KNOW IT, BUT THEY'RE GOING TO HAVE ANOTHER ATTENDANT AT THEIR MEETING.
A FORWARD DIVE THRU THE WINDOW, AND SUPERMAN IS OFF ON HIS ERRAND OF MERCY...
SHORTLY LATER, CLINGING TO A TENEMENT ABOVE THE URCHINS' HEADQUARTERS, THE MAN OF STEEL GETS AN EARFUL...

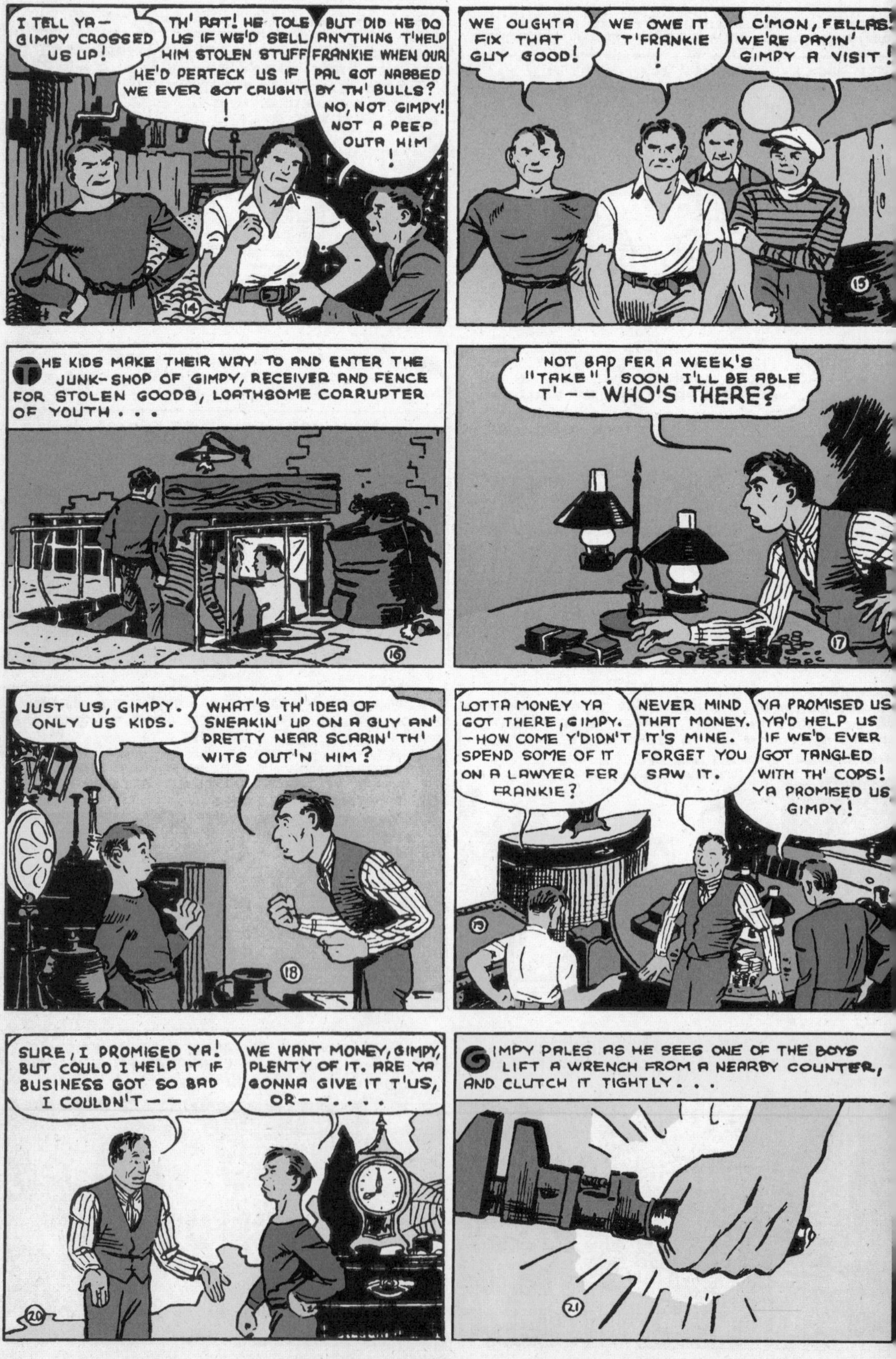
I TELL YA— GIMPY CROSSED US UP!
TH' RAT! HE TOLE US IF WE'D SELL HIM STOLEN STUFF HE'D PERTECK US IF WE EVER GOT CAUGHT!
BUT DID HE DO ANYTHING T'HELP FRANKIE WHEN OUR PAL GOT NABBED BY TH' BULLS? NO, NOT GIMPY! NOT A PEEP OUTA HIM!
WE OUGHTA FIX THAT GUY GOOD!
WE OWE IT T'FRANKIE!
C'MON, FELLAS! WE'RE PAYIN' GIMPY A VISIT!
THE KIDS MAKE THEIR WAY TO AND ENTER THE JUNK-SHOP OF GIMPY, RECEIVER AND FENCE FOR STOLEN GOODS, LOATHSOME CORRUPTER OF YOUTH . . .
NOT BAD FER A WEEK'S "TAKE"! SOON I'LL BE ABLE T'— —WHO'S THERE?
JUST US, GIMPY. ONLY US KIDS.
WHAT'S TH' IDEA OF SNEAKIN' UP ON A GUY AN' PRETTY NEAR SCARIN' TH' WITS OUT'N HIM?
LOTTA MONEY YA GOT THERE, GIMPY. —HOW COME Y'DIDN'T SPEND SOME OF IT ON A LAWYER FER FRANKIE?
NEVER MIND THAT MONEY. IT'S MINE. FORGET YOU SAW IT.
YA PROMISED US YA'D HELP US IF WE'D EVER GOT TANGLED WITH TH' COPS! YA PROMISED US GIMPY!
SURE, I PROMISED YA! BUT COULD I HELP IT IF BUSINESS GOT SO BAD I COULDN'T— —
WE WANT MONEY, GIMPY, PLENTY OF IT. ARE YA GONNA GIVE IT T'US, OR— —. . . .
GIMPY PALES AS HE SEES ONE OF THE BOYS LIFT A WRENCH FROM A NEARBY COUNTER, AND CLUTCH IT TIGHTLY . . .

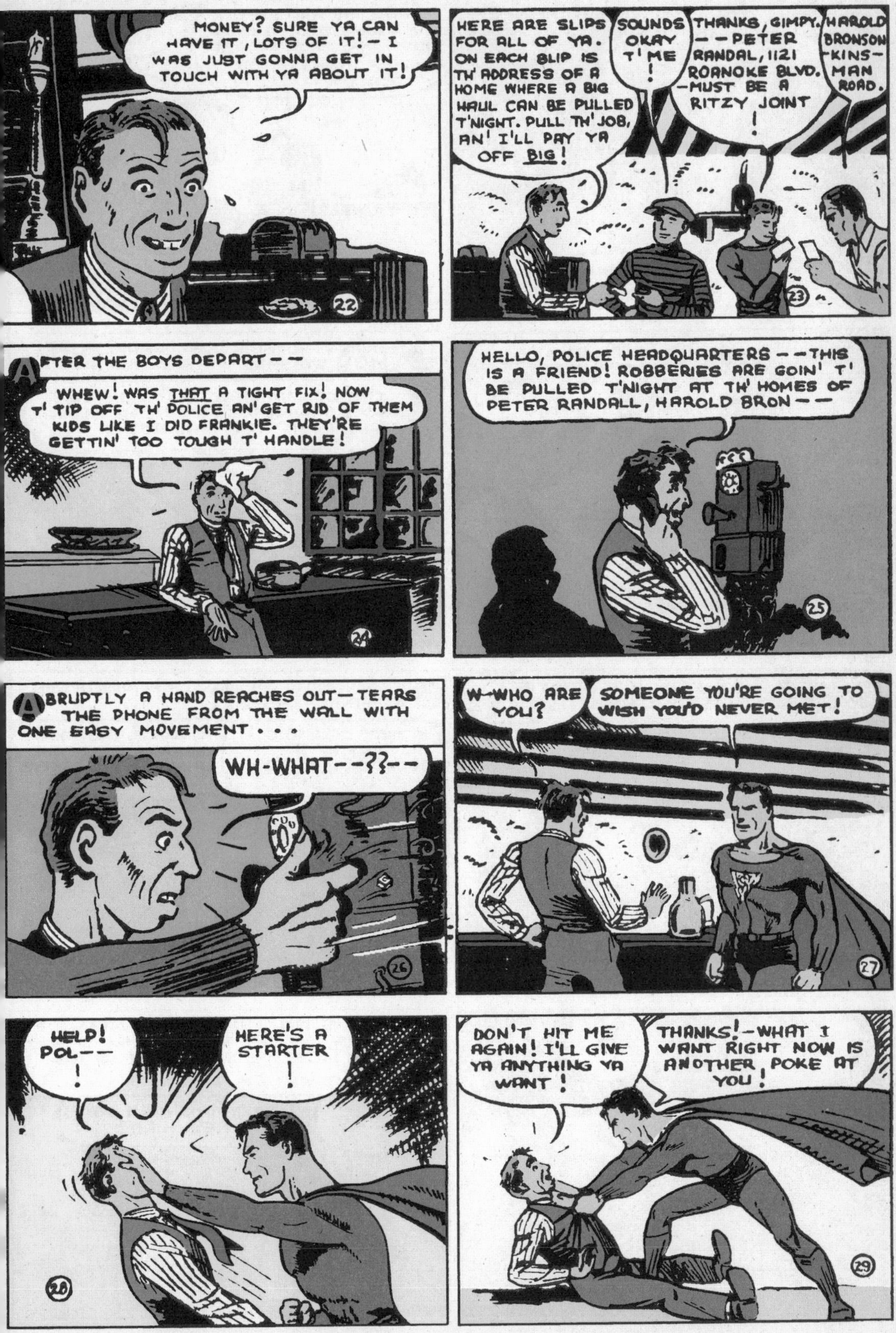

MONEY? SURE YA CAN HAVE IT, LOTS OF IT! —I WAS JUST GONNA GET IN TOUCH WITH YA ABOUT IT!
HERE ARE SLIPS FOR ALL OF YA. ON EACH SLIP IS TH' ADDRESS OF A HOME WHERE A BIG HAUL CAN BE PULLED T'NIGHT. PULL TH' JOB, AN' I'LL PAY YA OFF BIG!
SOUNDS OKAY T' ME!
THANKS, GIMPY. ——PETER RANDAL, 1121 ROANOKE BLVD. —MUST BE A RITZY JOINT!
HAROLD BRONSON —KINSMAN ROAD.
AFTER THE BOYS DEPART——
WHEW! WAS THAT A TIGHT FIX! NOW T' TIP OFF TH' POLICE AN' GET RID OF THEM KIDS LIKE I DID FRANKIE. THEY'RE GETTIN' TOO TOUGH T' HANDLE!
HELLO, POLICE HEADQUARTERS ——THIS IS A FRIEND! ROBBERIES ARE GOIN' T' BE PULLED T'NIGHT AT TH' HOMES OF PETER RANDALL, HAROLD BRON——
ABRUPTLY A HAND REACHES OUT—TEARS THE PHONE FROM THE WALL WITH ONE EASY MOVEMENT . . .
WH-WHAT——??——
W-WHO ARE YOU?
SOMEONE YOU'RE GOING TO WISH YOU'D NEVER MET!
HELP! POL——!
HERE'S A STARTER!
DON'T HIT ME AGAIN! I'LL GIVE YA ANYTHING YA WANT!
THANKS! —WHAT I WANT RIGHT NOW IS ANOTHER POKE AT YOU!

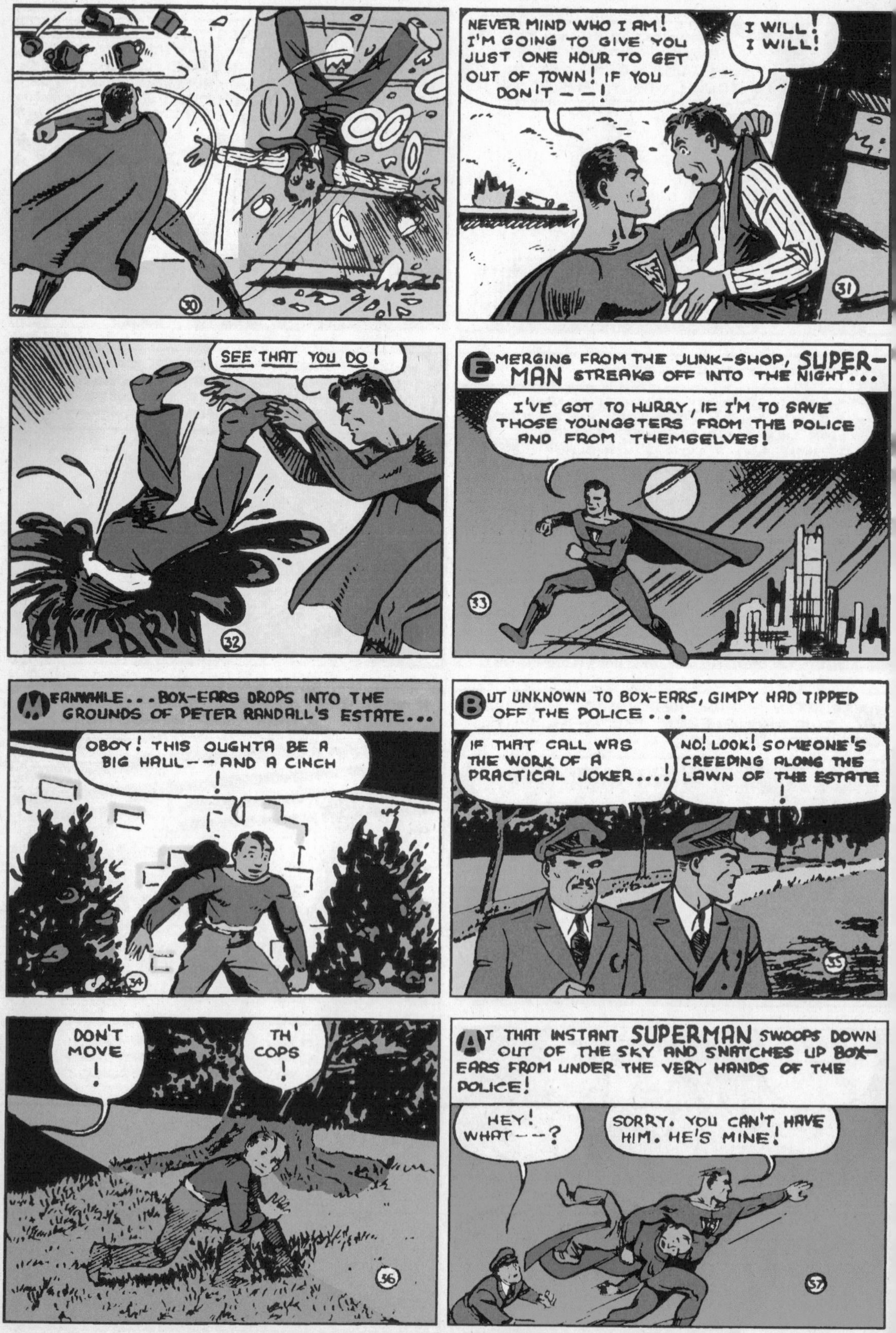

NEVER MIND WHO I AM! I'M GOING TO GIVE YOU JUST ONE HOUR TO GET OUT OF TOWN! IF YOU DON'T --!
I WILL! I WILL!
SEE THAT YOU DO!
TAR
EMERGING FROM THE JUNK-SHOP, SUPERMAN STREAKS OFF INTO THE NIGHT...
I'VE GOT TO HURRY, IF I'M TO SAVE THOSE YOUNGSTERS FROM THE POLICE AND FROM THEMSELVES!
MEANWHILE... BOX-EARS DROPS INTO THE GROUNDS OF PETER RANDALL'S ESTATE...
OBOY! THIS OUGHTA BE A BIG HAUL--AND A CINCH!
BUT UNKNOWN TO BOX-EARS, GIMPY HAD TIPPED OFF THE POLICE...
IF THAT CALL WAS THE WORK OF A PRACTICAL JOKER...!
NO! LOOK! SOMEONE'S CREEPING ALONG THE LAWN OF THE ESTATE!
DON'T MOVE!
TH' COPS!
AT THAT INSTANT SUPERMAN SWOOPS DOWN OUT OF THE SKY AND SNATCHES UP BOX-EARS FROM UNDER THE VERY HANDS OF THE POLICE!
HEY! WHAT---?
SORRY. YOU CAN'T HAVE HIM. HE'S MINE!

STOP! WE COMMAND YOU TO STOP!

AM I DREAMING?— HE--HE JUMPED OUT OF SIGHT!

HEY! LEMME GO!

NOT YET!—NOT 'TILL I'VE SAVED YOUR FRIEND NICK FROM A JAIL SENTENCE!

BUT WHEN SUPERMAN REACHES THE BRONSON RESIDENCE, IT APPEARS HE IS TOO LATE...

OUCH! LEGGO!

TH' COPS! THEY'VE GOT NICK!

SO IT SEEMS! BUT THAT CAN BE CORRECTED!

AS THE PATROL-WAGON SPEEDS ALONG THE STREETS, SUPERMAN RACES IN PURSUIT...EASILY OVERTAKING IT...

WE'RE NOT MOVING! WHAT DID YOU STOP THE CAR FOR?

BUT I DIDN'T! LOOK! MY FOOT IS PRESSING DOWN THE ACCELERATOR TO THE LIMIT!

THE EXPLANATION: SEIZING THE AUTO'S REAR-AXLE, SUPERMAN HAS RAISED THE POWER-DRIVEN WHEELS SO THAT THEY SPIN AIMLESSLY OFF THE GROUND...NATURALLY, THE WAGON IS POWERLESS TO MOVE.

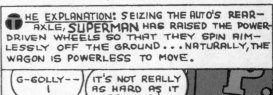

G-GOLLY--!

IT'S NOT REALLY AS HARD AS IT APPEARS!

WITH HIS FREE HAND, SUPERMAN PLUCKS NICK FREE FROM THE GRID OF HIS ASTOUNDED GUARD...

HALP! HA-ALP!

QUIET! THERE'S NOTHING TO BE AFRAID OF!

AND A MOMENT LATER HE IS STREAKING ALONG WITH TWO BEWILDERED CAPTIVES!

NOW TO GET THE OTHERS!

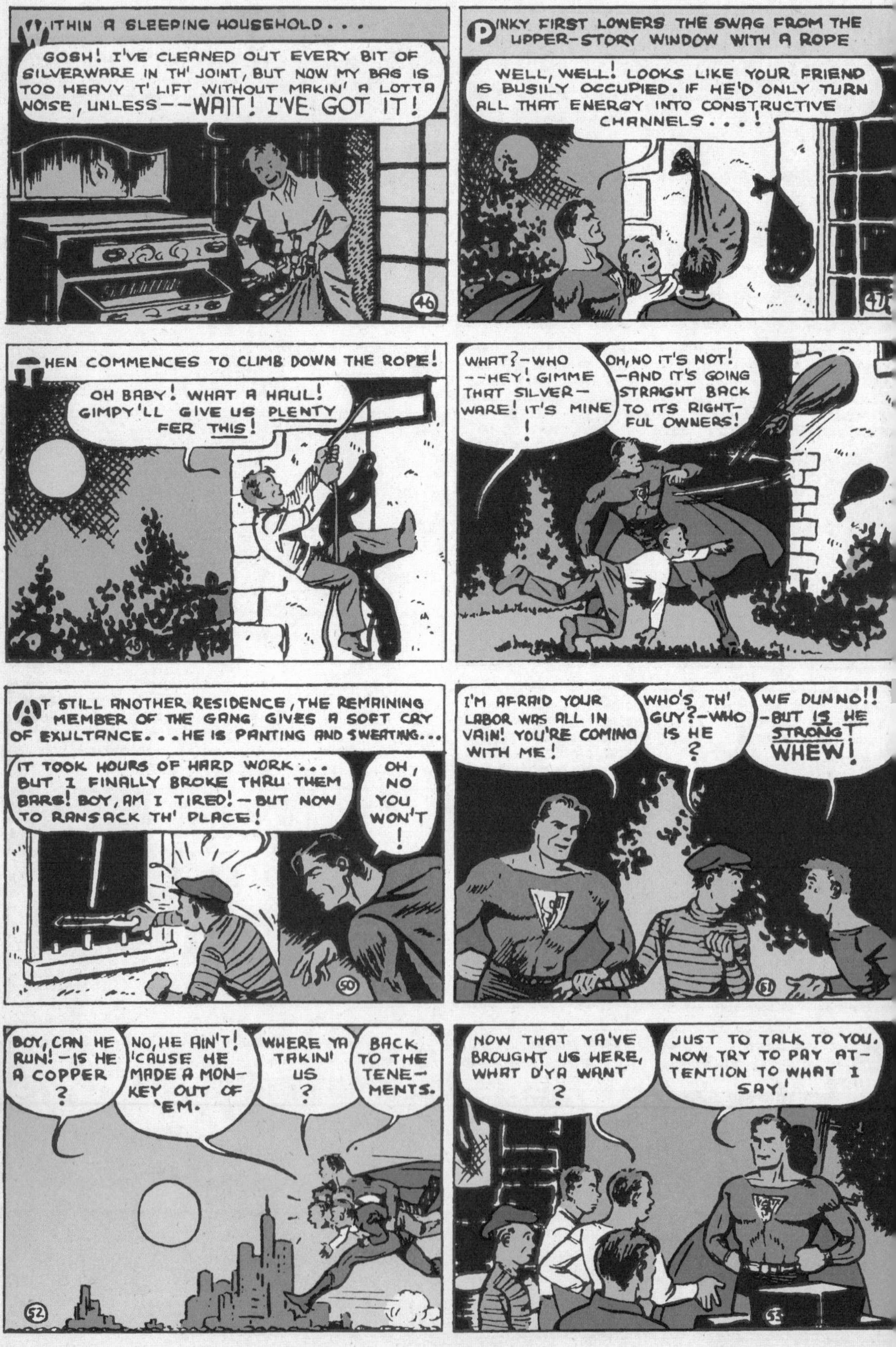
WITHIN A SLEEPING HOUSEHOLD...
GOSH! I'VE CLEANED OUT EVERY BIT OF SILVERWARE IN TH' JOINT, BUT NOW MY BAG IS TOO HEAVY T' LIFT WITHOUT MAKIN' A LOTTA NOISE, UNLESS--WAIT! I'VE GOT IT!
46
PINKY FIRST LOWERS THE SWAG FROM THE UPPER-STORY WINDOW WITH A ROPE
WELL, WELL! LOOKS LIKE YOUR FRIEND IS BUSILY OCCUPIED. IF HE'D ONLY TURN ALL THAT ENERGY INTO CONSTRUCTIVE CHANNELS...!
47
THEN COMMENCES TO CLIMB DOWN THE ROPE!
OH BABY! WHAT A HAUL! GIMPY'LL GIVE US PLENTY FER THIS!
48
WHAT?-WHO --HEY! GIMME THAT SILVER-WARE! IT'S MINE!
OH, NO IT'S NOT! -AND IT'S GOING STRAIGHT BACK TO ITS RIGHTFUL OWNERS!
AT STILL ANOTHER RESIDENCE, THE REMAINING MEMBER OF THE GANG GIVES A SOFT CRY OF EXULTANCE...HE IS PANTING AND SWEATING...
IT TOOK HOURS OF HARD WORK... BUT I FINALLY BROKE THRU THEM BARS! BOY, AM I TIRED!-BUT NOW TO RANSACK TH' PLACE!
OH, NO YOU WON'T!
50
I'M AFRAID YOUR LABOR WAS ALL IN VAIN! YOU'RE COMING WITH ME!
WHO'S TH' GUY?-WHO IS HE?
WE DUNNO!! -BUT IS HE STRONG! WHEW!
51
BOY, CAN HE RUN! -IS HE A COPPER?
NO, HE AIN'T! 'CAUSE HE MADE A MONKEY OUT OF 'EM.
WHERE YA TAKIN' US?
BACK TO THE TENEMENTS.
52
NOW THAT YA'VE BROUGHT US HERE, WHAT D'YA WANT?
JUST TO TALK TO YOU. NOW TRY TO PAY ATTENTION TO WHAT I SAY!
53

YOU'VE GOTTEN IT INTO YOUR HEADS, SOMEHOW, THAT IT'S SMART TO STEAL--THAT STOLEN MONEY IS "EASY DOUGH." BUT THAT'S NOT TRUE. NO DOUBT YOU'VE ALREADY LEARNED THAT NO MATTER HOW MUCH YOU BRING IN, GIMPY KEEPS THE LION'S SHARE.

YEAH. WE ONLY GET PEANUTS. LIKE I WAS TELLIN' PINKY TH' OTHER DAY--

SHUT UP, BOX-EARS! YER BLABBIN' TOO MUCH!

WHAT WE GET IS OUR OWN BUSINESS!

WHAT'S MORE, YOU'VE ALWAYS THE FEAR THAT THE LAW WILL MAKE YOU PAY THE PENALTY FOR YOUR CRIMES.

WELL.. SOME-TIMES I DO GET ...ER...NERVOUS...

A-SCARED OF TH' COPPERS? NOT US!

GIMPY SAYS HE'LL TAKE CARE OF US IF WE EVER GET CAUGHT.

GIMPY TAKE CARE OF YOU? HASN'T IT OCCURRED TO YOU THAT IT'S MIGHTY STRANGE THOSE POLICEMEN WERE WAITING FOR YOU AT THE PLACES TO BE ROBBED? SORT OF LIKE A TRAP, WASN'T IT?

D'YA MEAN T' SAY THAT GIMPY TIPPED OFF....!

YES. HE INTENDED TO BE-TRAY YOU TO THE POLICE JUST AS HE DID FRANKIE. AND HE WOULD HAVE SUC-CEEDED, TOO, IF I HADN'T HAP-PENED ALONG!

WHY, THAT DIRTY STOOLIE!

SO THAT'S HOW FRANKIE GOT CAUGHT!

THIS IS ONE TIME HE WON'T TALK HISSELF OUTA A TIGHT SPOT! C'MON, FELLAS!

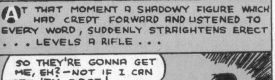

AT THAT MOMENT A SHADOWY FIGURE WHICH HAD CREPT FORWARD AND LISTENED TO EVERY WORD, SUDDENLY STRAIGHTENS ERECT ...LEVELS A RIFLE...

SO THEY'RE GONNA GET ME, EH?--NOT IF I CAN GET 'EM FIRST!

EAT LEAD, YA LITTLE RAT!

GIMPY!

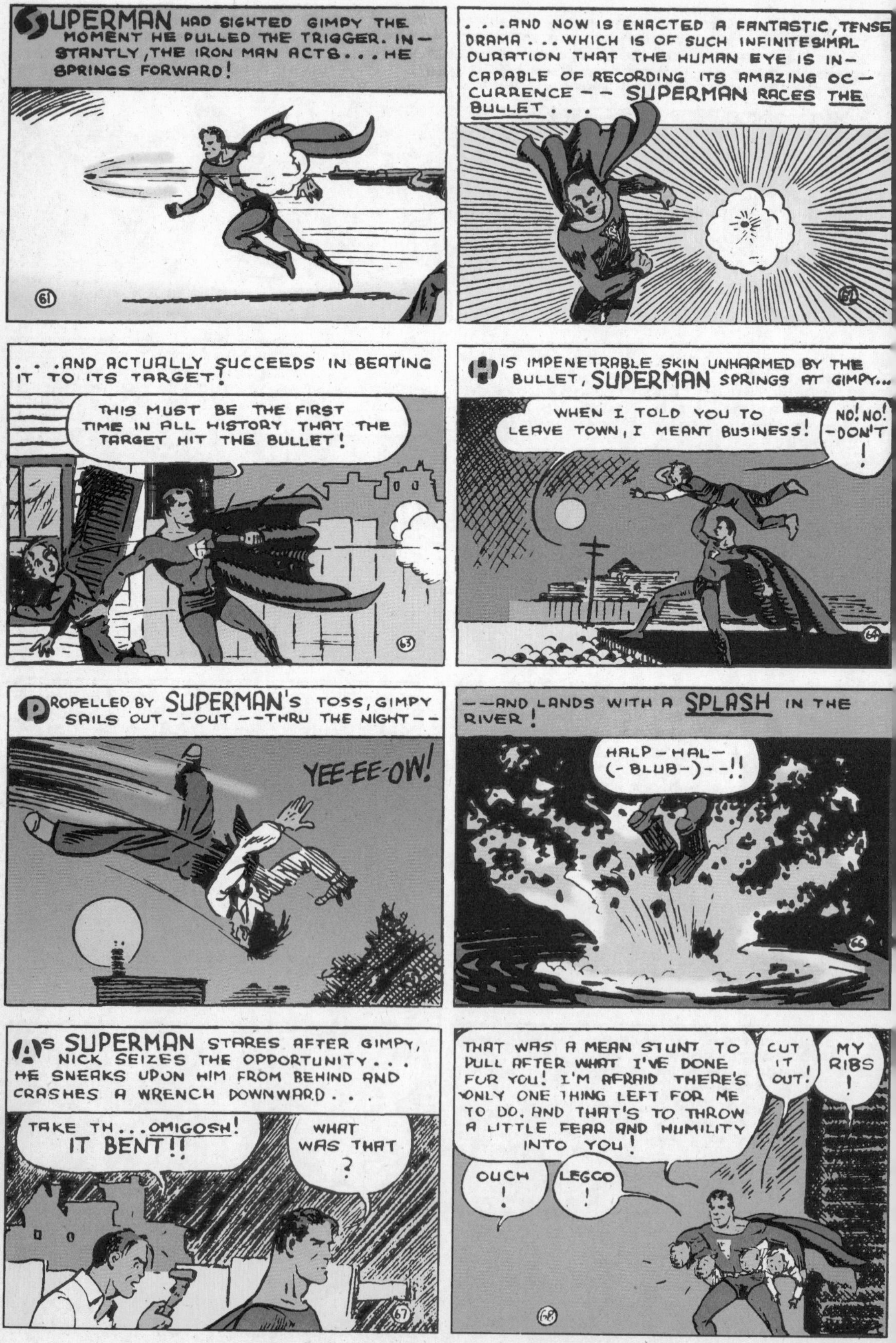
SUPERMAN HAD SIGHTED GIMPY THE MOMENT HE PULLED THE TRIGGER. IN-STANTLY, THE IRON MAN ACTS... HE SPRINGS FORWARD!
...AND NOW IS ENACTED A FANTASTIC, TENSE DRAMA...WHICH IS OF SUCH INFINITESIMAL DURATION THAT THE HUMAN EYE IS IN-CAPABLE OF RECORDING ITS AMAZING OC-CURRENCE -- SUPERMAN RACES THE BULLET...
...AND ACTUALLY SUCCEEDS IN BEATING IT TO ITS TARGET!
THIS MUST BE THE FIRST TIME IN ALL HISTORY THAT THE TARGET HIT THE BULLET!
HIS IMPENETRABLE SKIN UNHARMED BY THE BULLET, SUPERMAN SPRINGS AT GIMPY...
WHEN I TOLD YOU TO LEAVE TOWN, I MEANT BUSINESS!
NO! NO! -DON'T!
PROPELLED BY SUPERMAN'S TOSS, GIMPY SAILS OUT--OUT--THRU THE NIGHT--
YEE-EE-OW!
--AND LANDS WITH A SPLASH IN THE RIVER!
HALP-HAL- (-BLUB-)--!!
AS SUPERMAN STARES AFTER GIMPY, NICK SEIZES THE OPPORTUNITY... HE SNEAKS UPON HIM FROM BEHIND AND CRASHES A WRENCH DOWNWARD...
TAKE TH...OMIGOSH! IT BENT!!
WHAT WAS THAT ?
THAT WAS A MEAN STUNT TO PULL AFTER WHAT I'VE DONE FOR YOU! I'M AFRAID THERE'S ONLY ONE THING LEFT FOR ME TO DO, AND THAT'S TO THROW A LITTLE FEAR AND HUMILITY INTO YOU!
CUT IT OUT!
MY RIBS!
OUCH!
LEGGO!

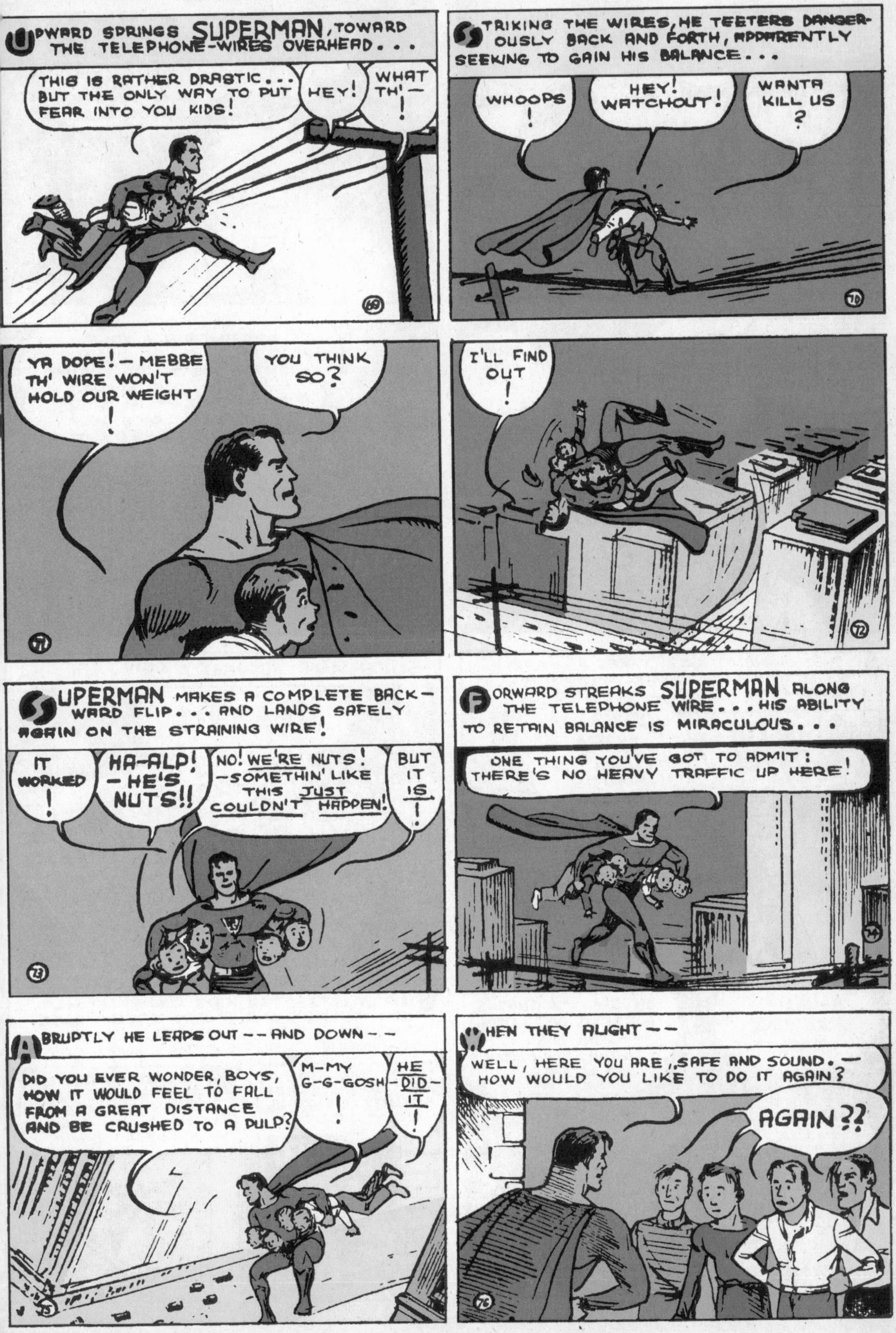
UPWARD SPRINGS SUPERMAN, TOWARD THE TELEPHONE-WIRES OVERHEAD . . .
THIS IS RATHER DRASTIC . . . BUT THE ONLY WAY TO PUT FEAR INTO YOU KIDS!
HEY!
WHAT TH'—!
STRIKING THE WIRES, HE TEETERS DANGEROUSLY BACK AND FORTH, APPARENTLY SEEKING TO GAIN HIS BALANCE . . .
WHOOPS!
HEY! WATCHOUT!
WANTA KILL US?
YA DOPE! — MEBBE TH' WIRE WON'T HOLD OUR WEIGHT!
YOU THINK SO?
I'LL FIND OUT!
SUPERMAN MAKES A COMPLETE BACKWARD FLIP . . . AND LANDS SAFELY AGAIN ON THE STRAINING WIRE!
IT WORKED!
HA-ALP! -HE'S NUTS!!
NO! WE'RE NUTS! -SOMETHIN' LIKE THIS JUST COULDN'T HAPPEN!
BUT IT IS!
FORWARD STREAKS SUPERMAN ALONG THE TELEPHONE WIRE . . . HIS ABILITY TO RETAIN BALANCE IS MIRACULOUS . . .
ONE THING YOU'VE GOT TO ADMIT: THERE'S NO HEAVY TRAFFIC UP HERE!
ABRUPTLY HE LEAPS OUT -- AND DOWN --
DID YOU EVER WONDER, BOYS, HOW IT WOULD FEEL TO FALL FROM A GREAT DISTANCE AND BE CRUSHED TO A PULP?
M-MY G-G-GOSH!
HE DID IT!
WHEN THEY ALIGHT --
WELL, HERE YOU ARE, SAFE AND SOUND. — HOW WOULD YOU LIKE TO DO IT AGAIN?
AGAIN??

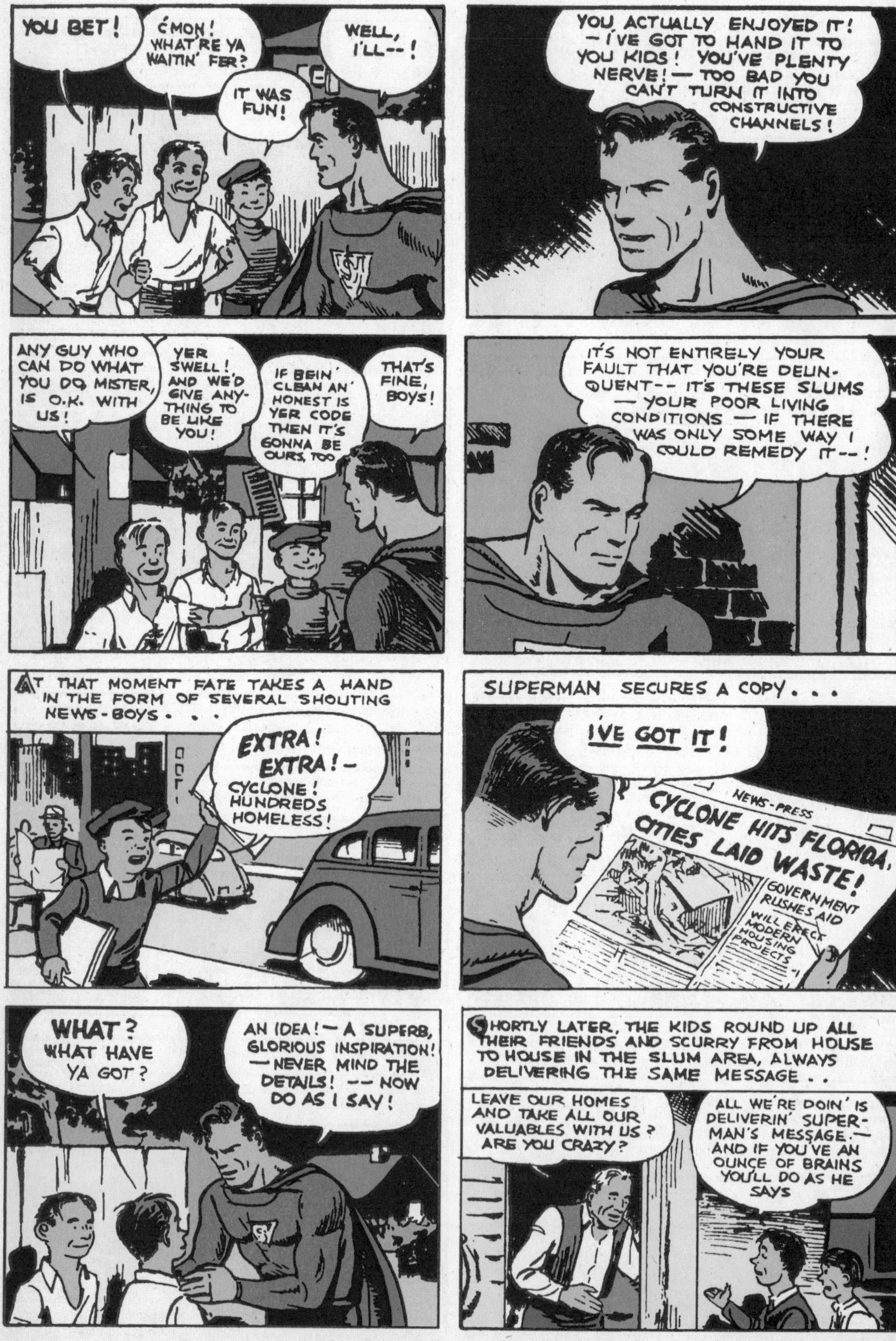

YOU BET!
C'MON! WHAT'RE YA WAITIN' FER?
IT WAS FUN!
WELL, I'LL--!
YOU ACTUALLY ENJOYED IT! -- I'VE GOT TO HAND IT TO YOU KIDS! YOU'VE PLENTY NERVE! -- TOO BAD YOU CAN'T TURN IT INTO CONSTRUCTIVE CHANNELS!
ANY GUY WHO CAN DO WHAT YOU DO, MISTER, IS O.K. WITH US!
YER SWELL! AND WE'D GIVE ANY-THING TO BE LIKE YOU!
IF BEIN' CLEAN AN' HONEST IS YER CODE THEN IT'S GONNA BE OURS, TOO
THAT'S FINE, BOYS!
IT'S NOT ENTIRELY YOUR FAULT THAT YOU'RE DELIN-QUENT-- IT'S THESE SLUMS -- YOUR POOR LIVING CONDITIONS -- IF THERE WAS ONLY SOME WAY I COULD REMEDY IT--!
AT THAT MOMENT FATE TAKES A HAND IN THE FORM OF SEVERAL SHOUTING NEWS-BOYS . . .
EXTRA! EXTRA! - CYCLONE! HUNDREDS HOMELESS!
SUPERMAN SECURES A COPY . . .
I'VE GOT IT!
NEWS-PRESS
CYCLONE HITS FLORIDA, CITIES LAID WASTE!
GOVERNMENT RUSHES AID
WILL ERECT MODERN HOUSING PROJECTS
WHAT? WHAT HAVE YA GOT?
AN IDEA! -- A SUPERB, GLORIOUS INSPIRATION! -- NEVER MIND THE DETAILS! -- NOW DO AS I SAY!
SHORTLY LATER, THE KIDS ROUND UP ALL THEIR FRIENDS AND SCURRY FROM HOUSE TO HOUSE IN THE SLUM AREA, ALWAYS DELIVERING THE SAME MESSAGE . .
LEAVE OUR HOMES AND TAKE ALL OUR VALUABLES WITH US? ARE YOU CRAZY?
ALL WE'RE DOIN' IS DELIVERIN' SUPER-MAN'S MESSAGE. -- AND IF YOU'VE AN OUNCE OF BRAINS YOU'LL DO AS HE SAYS

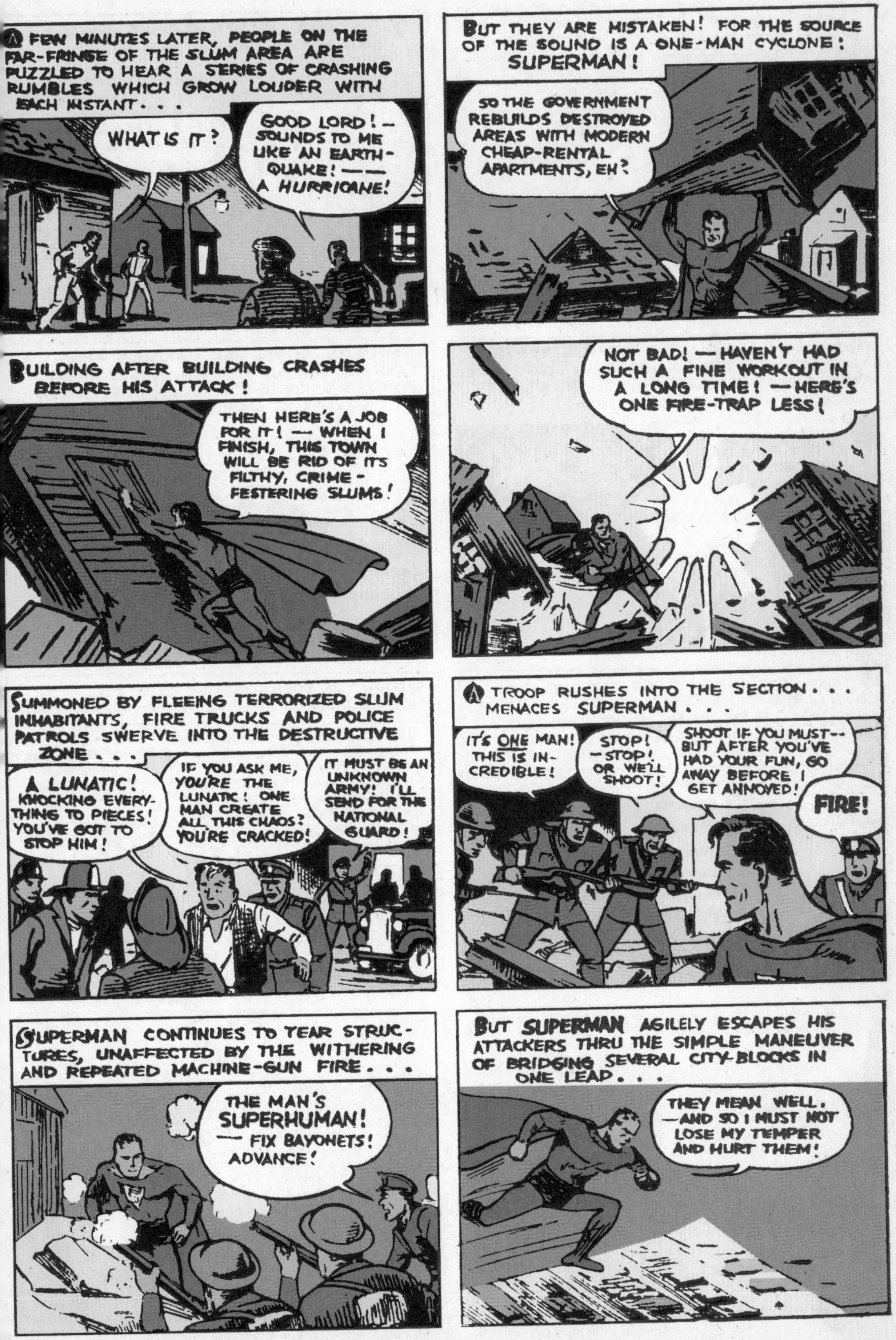
A FEW MINUTES LATER, PEOPLE ON THE FAR-FRINGE OF THE SLUM AREA ARE PUZZLED TO HEAR A SERIES OF CRASHING RUMBLES WHICH GROW LOUDER WITH EACH INSTANT . . .
WHAT IS IT?
GOOD LORD! — SOUNDS TO ME LIKE AN EARTH-QUAKE! —— A HURRICANE!
BUT THEY ARE MISTAKEN! FOR THE SOURCE OF THE SOUND IS A ONE-MAN CYCLONE: SUPERMAN!
SO THE GOVERNMENT REBUILDS DESTROYED AREAS WITH MODERN CHEAP-RENTAL APARTMENTS, EH?
BUILDING AFTER BUILDING CRASHES BEFORE HIS ATTACK!
THEN HERE'S A JOB FOR IT! — WHEN I FINISH, THIS TOWN WILL BE RID OF ITS FILTHY, CRIME-FESTERING SLUMS!
NOT BAD! — HAVEN'T HAD SUCH A FINE WORKOUT IN A LONG TIME! — HERE'S ONE FIRE-TRAP LESS!
SUMMONED BY FLEEING TERRORIZED SLUM INHABITANTS, FIRE TRUCKS AND POLICE PATROLS SWERVE INTO THE DESTRUCTIVE ZONE . . .
A LUNATIC! KNOCKING EVERY-THING TO PIECES! YOU'VE GOT TO STOP HIM!
IF YOU ASK ME, YOU'RE THE LUNATIC! ONE MAN CREATE ALL THIS CHAOS? YOU'RE CRACKED!
IT MUST BE AN UNKNOWN ARMY! I'LL SEND FOR THE NATIONAL GUARD!
A TROOP RUSHES INTO THE SECTION . . . MENACES SUPERMAN . . .
IT'S ONE MAN! THIS IS IN-CREDIBLE!
STOP! — STOP! OR WE'LL SHOOT!
SHOOT IF YOU MUST-- BUT AFTER YOU'VE HAD YOUR FUN, GO AWAY BEFORE I GET ANNOYED!
FIRE!
SUPERMAN CONTINUES TO TEAR STRUC-TURES, UNAFFECTED BY THE WITHERING AND REPEATED MACHINE-GUN FIRE . . .
THE MAN'S SUPERHUMAN! — FIX BAYONETS! ADVANCE!
BUT SUPERMAN AGILELY ESCAPES HIS ATTACKERS THRU THE SIMPLE MANEUVER OF BRIDGING SEVERAL CITY-BLOCKS IN ONE LEAP . . .
THEY MEAN WELL. — AND SO I MUST NOT LOSE MY TEMPER AND HURT THEM!

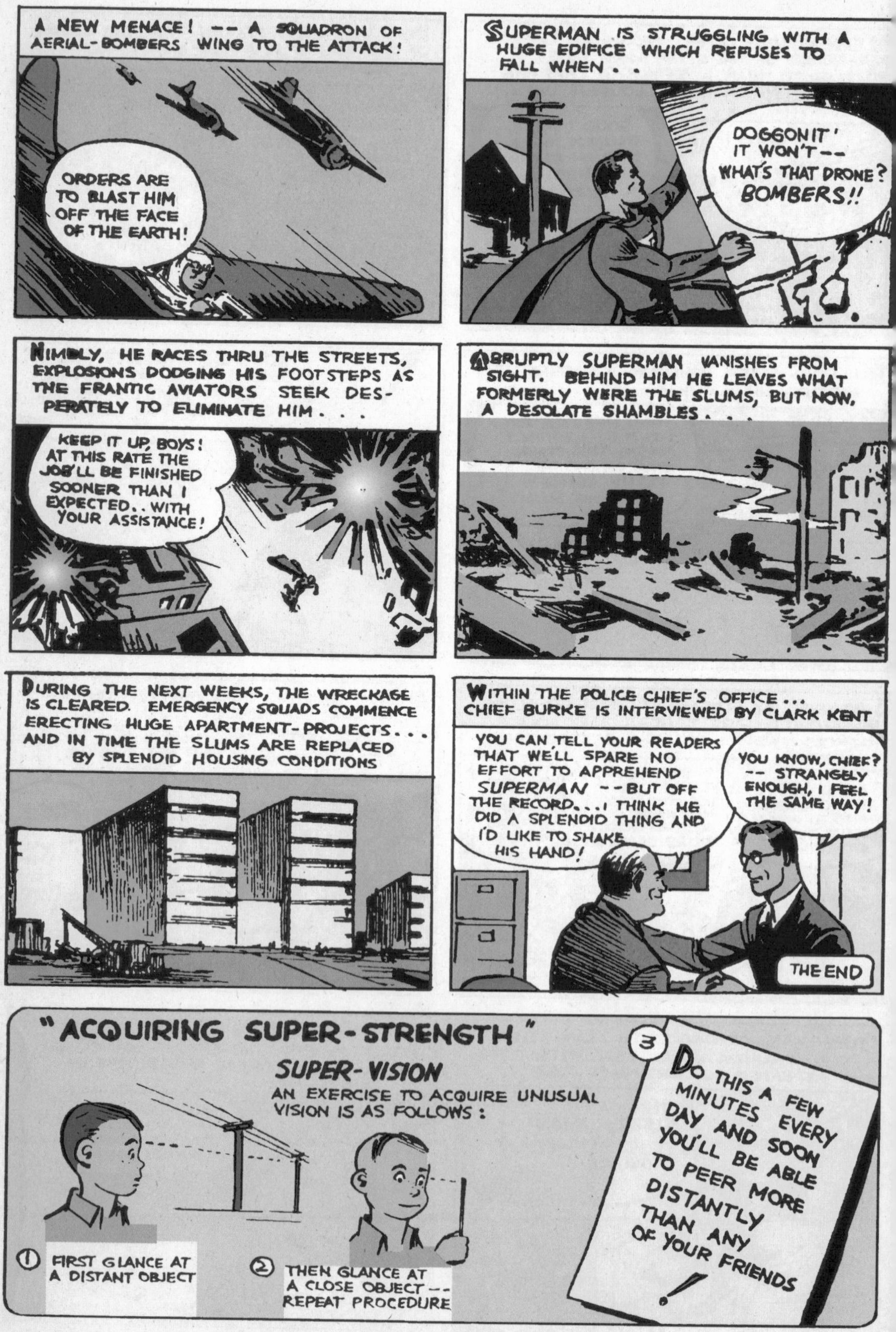

A NEW MENACE! -- A SQUADRON OF AERIAL-BOMBERS WING TO THE ATTACK!
ORDERS ARE TO BLAST HIM OFF THE FACE OF THE EARTH!
SUPERMAN IS STRUGGLING WITH A HUGE EDIFICE WHICH REFUSES TO FALL WHEN . .
DOGGONIT' IT WON'T -- WHAT'S THAT DRONE? BOMBERS!!
NIMBLY, HE RACES THRU THE STREETS, EXPLOSIONS DODGING HIS FOOTSTEPS AS THE FRANTIC AVIATORS SEEK DESPERATELY TO ELIMINATE HIM . . .
KEEP IT UP, BOYS! AT THIS RATE THE JOB'LL BE FINISHED SOONER THAN I EXPECTED.. WITH YOUR ASSISTANCE!
ABRUPTLY SUPERMAN VANISHES FROM SIGHT. BEHIND HIM HE LEAVES WHAT FORMERLY WERE THE SLUMS, BUT NOW, A DESOLATE SHAMBLES . . .
DURING THE NEXT WEEKS, THE WRECKAGE IS CLEARED. EMERGENCY SQUADS COMMENCE ERECTING HUGE APARTMENT-PROJECTS . . . AND IN TIME THE SLUMS ARE REPLACED BY SPLENDID HOUSING CONDITIONS
WITHIN THE POLICE CHIEF'S OFFICE ... CHIEF BURKE IS INTERVIEWED BY CLARK KENT
YOU CAN TELL YOUR READERS THAT WE'LL SPARE NO EFFORT TO APPREHEND SUPERMAN -- BUT OFF THE RECORD... I THINK HE DID A SPLENDID THING AND I'D LIKE TO SHAKE HIS HAND!
YOU KNOW, CHIEF? -- STRANGELY ENOUGH, I FEEL THE SAME WAY!
THE END
"ACQUIRING SUPER-STRENGTH"
SUPER-VISION
AN EXERCISE TO ACQUIRE UNUSUAL VISION IS AS FOLLOWS:
① FIRST GLANCE AT A DISTANT OBJECT
② THEN GLANCE AT A CLOSE OBJECT -- REPEAT PROCEDURE
③ DO THIS A FEW MINUTES EVERY DAY AND SOON YOU'LL BE ABLE TO PEER MORE DISTANTLY THAN ANY OF YOUR FRIENDS!

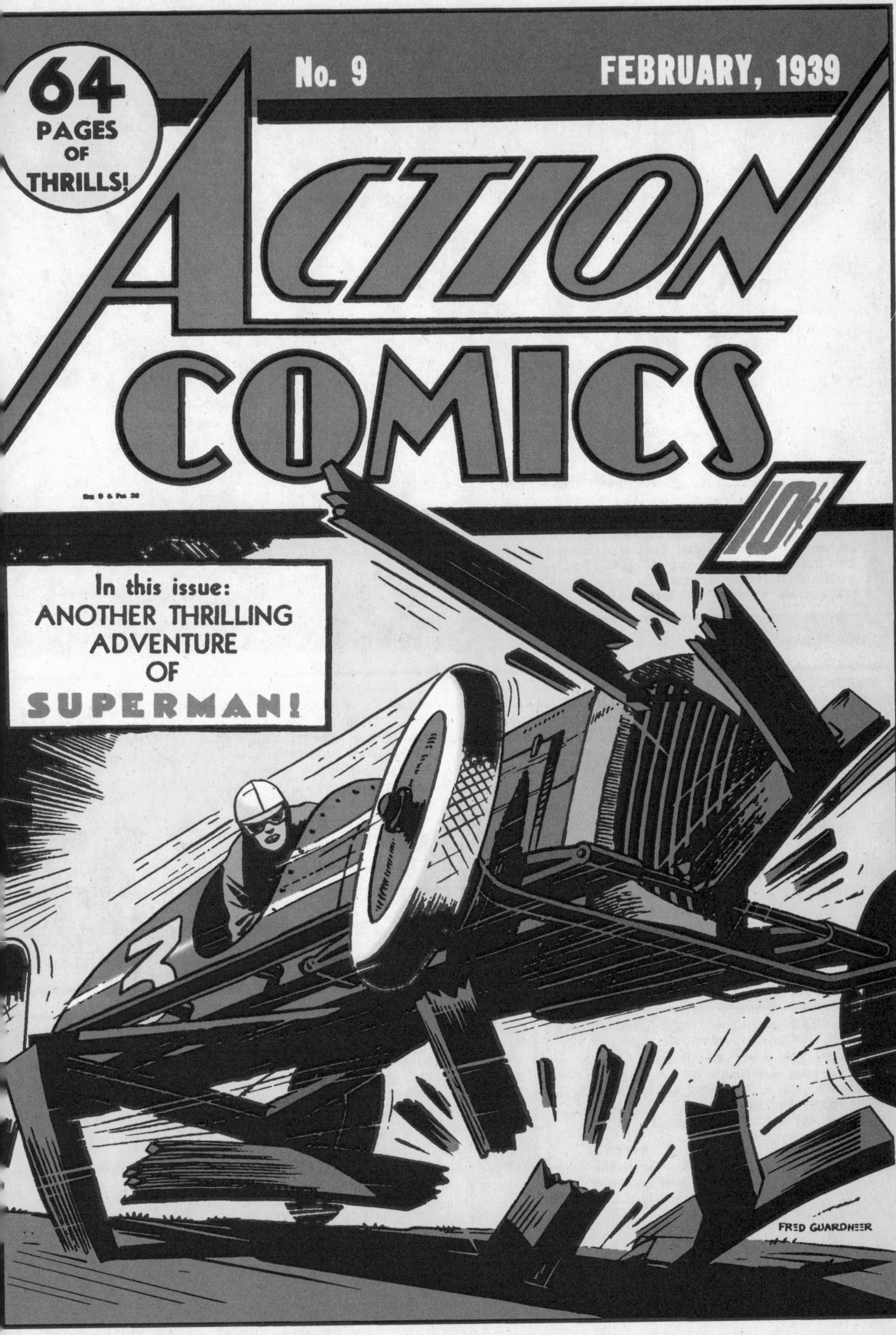
64 PAGES OF THRILLS!
No. 9
FEBRUARY, 1939
ACTION COMICS
10¢
In this issue:
ANOTHER THRILLING ADVENTURE OF SUPERMAN!
FRED GUARDNEER

SUPERMAN

JERRY SIEGEL and JOE SHUSTER

① LIFTING TREMENDOUS WEIGHTS, JUMPING STUPEN-DOUS HEIGHTS AND DISTANCES, RUNNING FASTER THAN A BULLET, RENDING STEEL WITH HIS BARE HANDS -- THESE ARE THE ASTONISHING PHYSICAL ATTRIBUTES WHICH AID **SUPERMAN**, SAVIOR OF THE HELPLESS AND OPPRESSED, IN HIS NEVER-CEASING WAR ON INJUSTICES!

② OFFICE OF THE CHIEF OF POLICE . . .

GENTLEMEN OF THE DRESS, I HAVE SUMMONED YOU HERE TO WITNESS AN ANNOUNCE-MENT OF UNUSUAL IM-PORTANCE.

STOW THE BUILD-UP, CHIEF, AND LET'S HAVE THE INFO!

YOU'RE NOT ADDRESSING A LADIES' LUNCHEON, CHIEF!

③ I'LL COME TO THE POINT AT ONCE! AS YOU KNOW, A MAN POSSESSED OF SUPER-STRENGTH NAMED **SUPER-MAN** HAS TORN DOWN OUR SLUM AREA, CAUSING MODERN APARTMENTS TO REPLACE CROWDED TENEMENTS

GOOD FOR HIM!

WHAT THE WORLD NEEDS IS A COUPLE MORE GUYS LIKE HIM!

④ REGARDLESS OF HIS MOTIVES AND OUR PERSONAL APPROVAL OF THEM, THE FACT REMAINS THAT HE HAS WANTONLY DE-STROYED PUBLIC PROPERTY AND MUST PAY THE FULL PENALTY TO THE LAW JUST LIKE ANY OTHER TRANS-GRESSOR!

AND YOU'RE GOING TO CATCH **SUPER-MAN?** --HO! HO! CHIEF, YOU'RE GETTIN' FUNNIER EVERY DAY!

⑤ WE'VE MADE EVERY EFFORT TO APPREHEND **SUPERMAN** -- AND FAILED...AND SO NOW, AS A LAST RESORT, I'VE IMPORTED DETECTIVE CAPTAIN REILLY,-- EVER HEAR OF HIM, BOYS?

EVER HEAR OF HIM?-- I SHOULD SAY SO!

WHY, HE'S THE CHICAGO DICK WHO--**WOW!** --THIS **IS** AN UNUSUAL ANNOUNCEMENT!

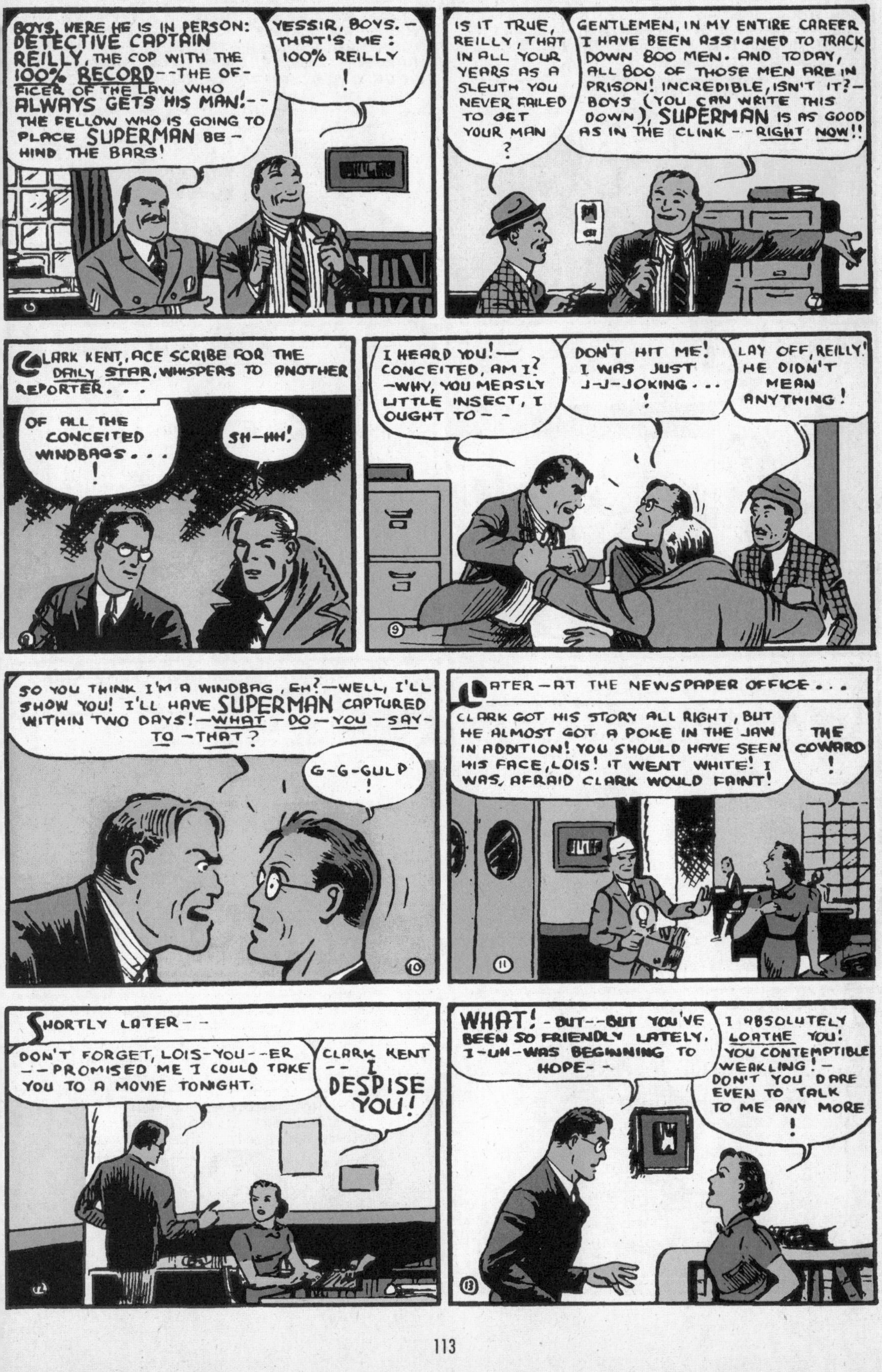
BOYS, HERE HE IS IN PERSON: DETECTIVE CAPTAIN REILLY, THE COP WITH THE 100% RECORD--THE OFFICER OF THE LAW WHO ALWAYS GETS HIS MAN!-- THE FELLOW WHO IS GOING TO PLACE SUPERMAN BEHIND THE BARS!
YESSIR, BOYS.— THAT'S ME: 100% REILLY!
IS IT TRUE, REILLY, THAT IN ALL YOUR YEARS AS A SLEUTH YOU NEVER FAILED TO GET YOUR MAN?
GENTLEMEN, IN MY ENTIRE CAREER I HAVE BEEN ASSIGNED TO TRACK DOWN 800 MEN. AND TODAY, ALL 800 OF THOSE MEN ARE IN PRISON! INCREDIBLE, ISN'T IT?— BOYS (YOU CAN WRITE THIS DOWN), SUPERMAN IS AS GOOD AS IN THE CLINK --RIGHT NOW!!
CLARK KENT, ACE SCRIBE FOR THE DAILY STAR, WHISPERS TO ANOTHER REPORTER...
OF ALL THE CONCEITED WINDBAGS...!
SH-HH!
I HEARD YOU!— CONCEITED, AM I? —WHY, YOU MEASLY LITTLE INSECT, I OUGHT TO--
DON'T HIT ME! I WAS JUST J-J-JOKING...!
LAY OFF, REILLY! HE DIDN'T MEAN ANYTHING!
SO YOU THINK I'M A WINDBAG, EH?—WELL, I'LL SHOW YOU! I'LL HAVE SUPERMAN CAPTURED WITHIN TWO DAYS!—WHAT—DO—YOU—SAY—TO—THAT?
G-G-GULP!
LATER—AT THE NEWSPAPER OFFICE...
CLARK GOT HIS STORY ALL RIGHT, BUT HE ALMOST GOT A POKE IN THE JAW IN ADDITION! YOU SHOULD HAVE SEEN HIS FACE, LOIS! IT WENT WHITE! I WAS, AFRAID CLARK WOULD FAINT!
THE COWARD!
SHORTLY LATER--
DON'T FORGET, LOIS-YOU--ER --PROMISED ME I COULD TAKE YOU TO A MOVIE TONIGHT.
CLARK KENT -- I DESPISE YOU!
WHAT! -BUT--BUT YOU'VE BEEN SO FRIENDLY LATELY. I-UH-WAS BEGINNING TO HOPE--
I ABSOLUTELY LOATHE YOU! YOU CONTEMPTIBLE WEAKLING!— DON'T YOU DARE EVEN TO TALK TO ME ANY MORE!

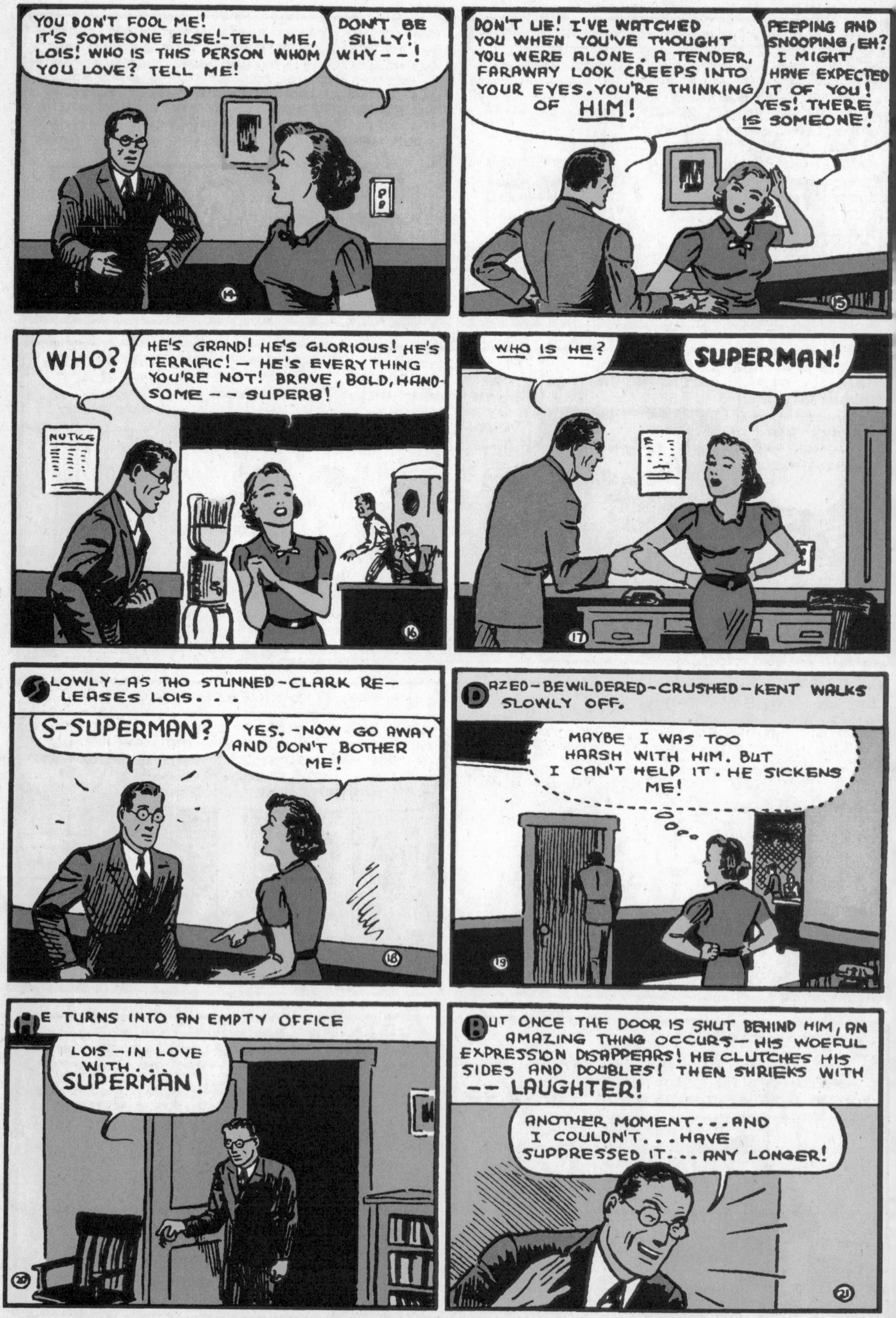
YOU DON'T FOOL ME! IT'S SOMEONE ELSE!-TELL ME, LOIS! WHO IS THIS PERSON WHOM YOU LOVE? TELL ME!
DON'T BE SILLY! WHY--!
DON'T LIE! I'VE WATCHED YOU WHEN YOU'VE THOUGHT YOU WERE ALONE. A TENDER, FARAWAY LOOK CREEPS INTO YOUR EYES. YOU'RE THINKING OF HIM!
PEEPING AND SNOOPING, EH? I MIGHT HAVE EXPECTED IT OF YOU! YES! THERE IS SOMEONE!
WHO?
HE'S GRAND! HE'S GLORIOUS! HE'S TERRIFIC! — HE'S EVERYTHING YOU'RE NOT! BRAVE, BOLD, HAND-SOME -- SUPERB!
NOTICE
WHO IS HE?
SUPERMAN!
SLOWLY-AS THO STUNNED-CLARK RE-LEASES LOIS...
S-SUPERMAN?
YES.-NOW GO AWAY AND DON'T BOTHER ME!
DAZED-BEWILDERED-CRUSHED-KENT WALKS SLOWLY OFF.
MAYBE I WAS TOO HARSH WITH HIM. BUT I CAN'T HELP IT. HE SICKENS ME!
HE TURNS INTO AN EMPTY OFFICE
LOIS-IN LOVE WITH... SUPERMAN!
BUT ONCE THE DOOR IS SHUT BEHIND HIM, AN AMAZING THING OCCURS-HIS WOEFUL EXPRESSION DISAPPEARS! HE CLUTCHES HIS SIDES AND DOUBLES! THEN SHRIEKS WITH -- LAUGHTER!
ANOTHER MOMENT...AND I COULDN'T...HAVE SUPPRESSED IT...ANY LONGER!

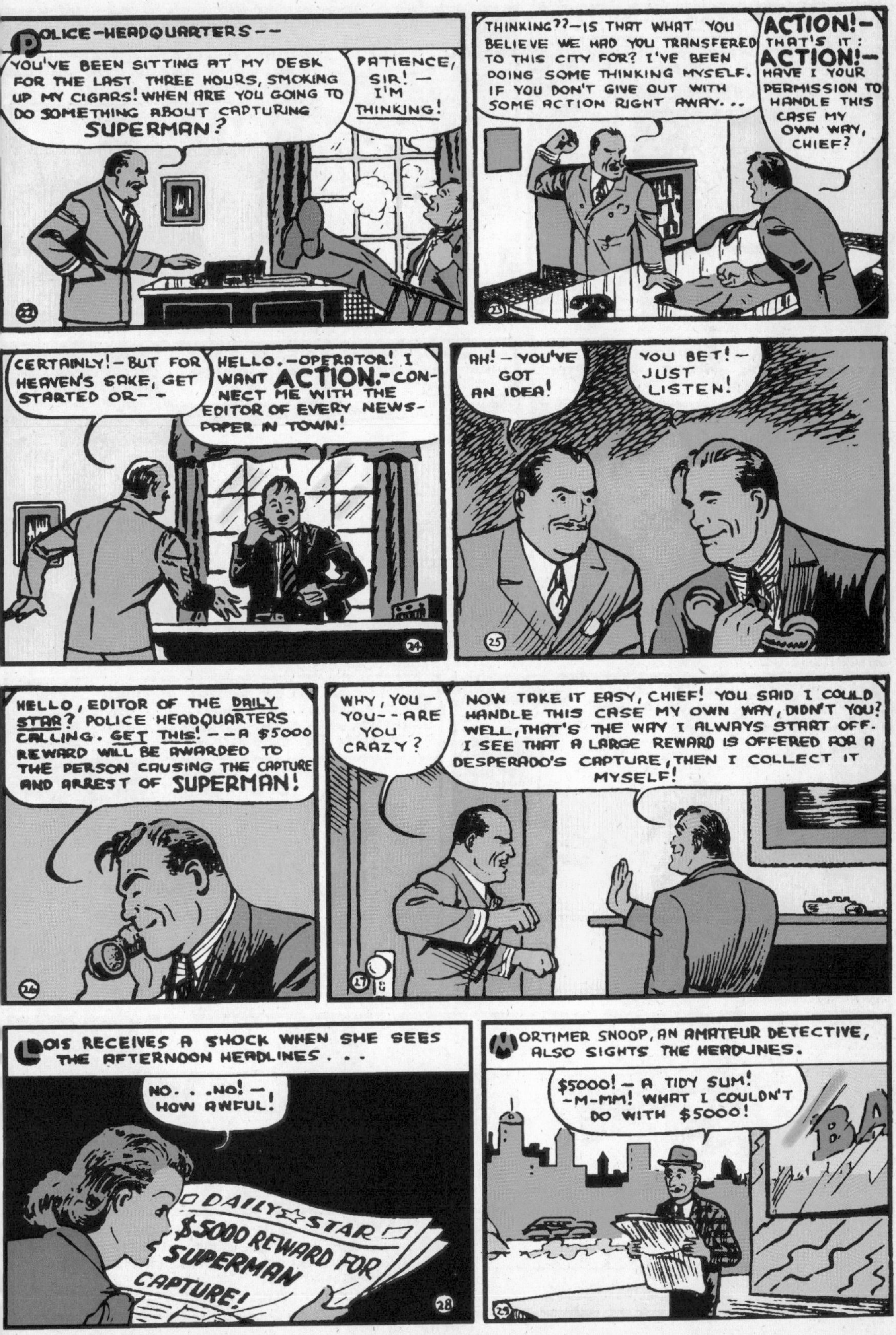
POLICE-HEADQUARTERS--
YOU'VE BEEN SITTING AT MY DESK FOR THE LAST THREE HOURS, SMOKING UP MY CIGARS! WHEN ARE YOU GOING TO DO SOMETHING ABOUT CAPTURING SUPERMAN?
PATIENCE, SIR! — I'M THINKING!
THINKING??—IS THAT WHAT YOU BELIEVE WE HAD YOU TRANSFERED TO THIS CITY FOR? I'VE BEEN DOING SOME THINKING MYSELF. IF YOU DON'T GIVE OUT WITH SOME ACTION RIGHT AWAY...
ACTION!—THAT'S IT: ACTION!—HAVE I YOUR PERMISSION TO HANDLE THIS CASE MY OWN WAY, CHIEF?
CERTAINLY!—BUT FOR HEAVEN'S SAKE, GET STARTED OR--
HELLO.—OPERATOR! I WANT ACTION.—CONNECT ME WITH THE EDITOR OF EVERY NEWSPAPER IN TOWN!
AH!—YOU'VE GOT AN IDEA!
YOU BET!—JUST LISTEN!
HELLO, EDITOR OF THE DAILY STAR? POLICE HEADQUARTERS CALLING. GET THIS!—A $5000 REWARD WILL BE AWARDED TO THE PERSON CAUSING THE CAPTURE AND ARREST OF SUPERMAN!
WHY, YOU—YOU--ARE YOU CRAZY?
NOW TAKE IT EASY, CHIEF! YOU SAID I COULD HANDLE THIS CASE MY OWN WAY, DIDN'T YOU? WELL, THAT'S THE WAY I ALWAYS START OFF. I SEE THAT A LARGE REWARD IS OFFERED FOR A DESPERADO'S CAPTURE, THEN I COLLECT IT MYSELF!
LOIS RECEIVES A SHOCK WHEN SHE SEES THE AFTERNOON HEADLINES...
NO...NO!—HOW AWFUL!
DAILY STAR
$5000 REWARD FOR SUPERMAN CAPTURE!
MORTIMER SNOOP, AN AMATEUR DETECTIVE, ALSO SIGHTS THE HEADLINES.
$5000!—A TIDY SUM! -M-MM! WHAT I COULDN'T DO WITH $5000!

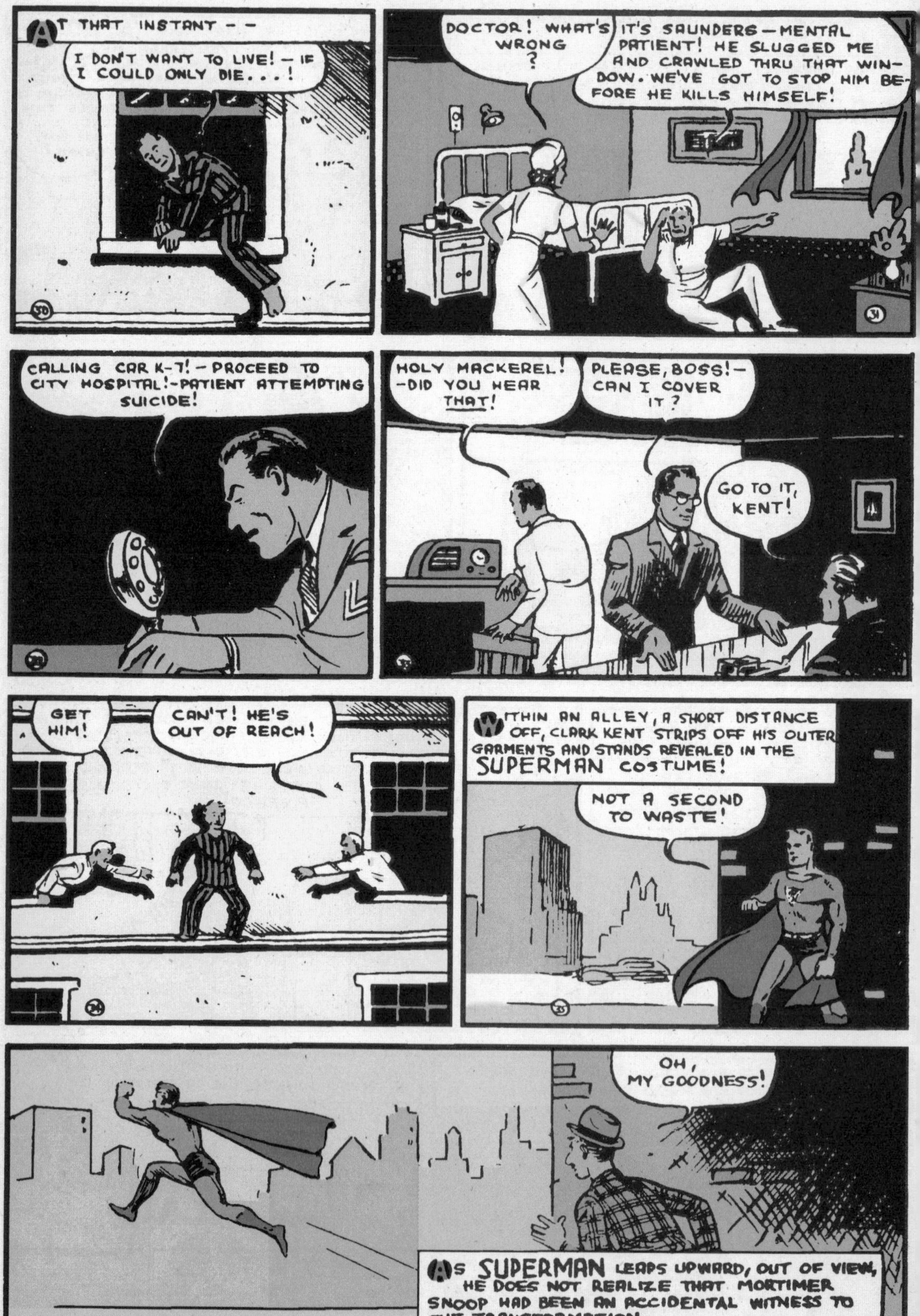
AT THAT INSTANT --
I DON'T WANT TO LIVE! — IF I COULD ONLY DIE...!
DOCTOR! WHAT'S WRONG?
IT'S SAUNDERS — MENTAL PATIENT! HE SLUGGED ME AND CRAWLED THRU THAT WINDOW. WE'VE GOT TO STOP HIM BEFORE HE KILLS HIMSELF!
CALLING CAR K-7! — PROCEED TO CITY HOSPITAL! — PATIENT ATTEMPTING SUICIDE!
HOLY MACKEREL! — DID YOU HEAR THAT!
PLEASE, BOSS! — CAN I COVER IT?
GO TO IT, KENT!
GET HIM!
CAN'T! HE'S OUT OF REACH!
WITHIN AN ALLEY, A SHORT DISTANCE OFF, CLARK KENT STRIPS OFF HIS OUTER GARMENTS AND STANDS REVEALED IN THE SUPERMAN COSTUME!
NOT A SECOND TO WASTE!
OH, MY GOODNESS!
AS SUPERMAN LEAPS UPWARD, OUT OF VIEW, HE DOES NOT REALIZE THAT MORTIMER SNOOP HAD BEEN AN ACCIDENTAL WITNESS TO THE TRANSFORMATION.

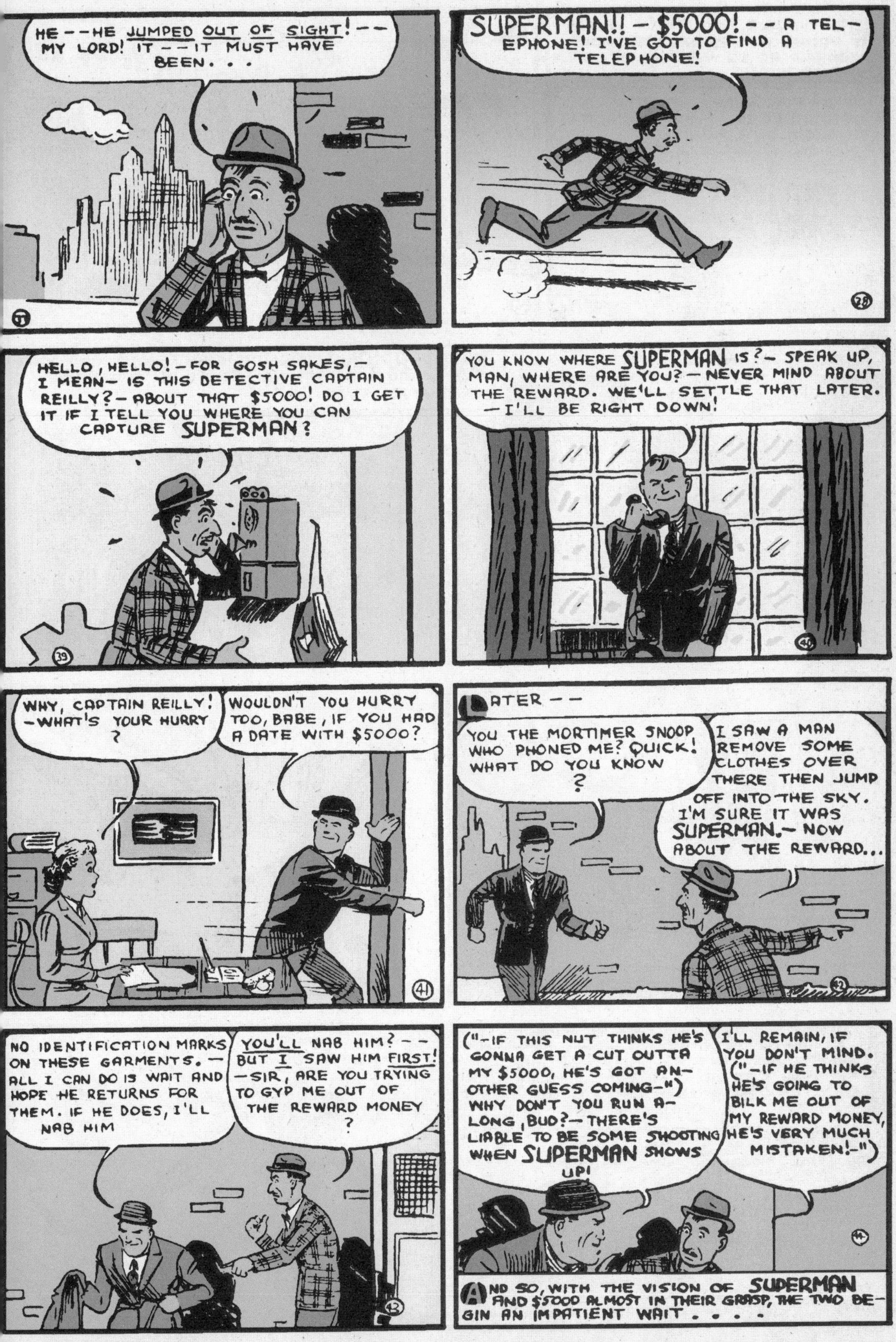
HE--HE JUMPED OUT OF SIGHT!-- MY LORD! IT--IT MUST HAVE BEEN...
SUPERMAN!! - $5000! -- A TEL-EPHONE! I'VE GOT TO FIND A TELEPHONE!
HELLO, HELLO! - FOR GOSH SAKES, - I MEAN - IS THIS DETECTIVE CAPTAIN REILLY? - ABOUT THAT $5000! DO I GET IT IF I TELL YOU WHERE YOU CAN CAPTURE SUPERMAN?
YOU KNOW WHERE SUPERMAN IS? - SPEAK UP, MAN, WHERE ARE YOU? - NEVER MIND ABOUT THE REWARD. WE'LL SETTLE THAT LATER. - I'LL BE RIGHT DOWN!
WHY, CAPTAIN REILLY! - WHAT'S YOUR HURRY?
WOULDN'T YOU HURRY TOO, BABE, IF YOU HAD A DATE WITH $5000?
LATER --
YOU THE MORTIMER SNOOP WHO PHONED ME? QUICK! WHAT DO YOU KNOW?
I SAW A MAN REMOVE SOME CLOTHES OVER THERE THEN JUMP OFF INTO THE SKY. I'M SURE IT WAS SUPERMAN. - NOW ABOUT THE REWARD...
NO IDENTIFICATION MARKS ON THESE GARMENTS. - ALL I CAN DO IS WAIT AND HOPE HE RETURNS FOR THEM. IF HE DOES, I'LL NAB HIM
YOU'LL NAB HIM? -- BUT I SAW HIM FIRST! - SIR, ARE YOU TRYING TO GYP ME OUT OF THE REWARD MONEY?
("-IF THIS NUT THINKS HE'S GONNA GET A CUT OUTTA MY $5000, HE'S GOT AN-OTHER GUESS COMING-") WHY DON'T YOU RUN A-LONG, BUD? - THERE'S LIABLE TO BE SOME SHOOTING WHEN SUPERMAN SHOWS UP!
I'LL REMAIN, IF YOU DON'T MIND. ("-IF HE THINKS HE'S GOING TO BILK ME OUT OF MY REWARD MONEY, HE'S VERY MUCH MISTAKEN!-")
AND SO, WITH THE VISION OF SUPERMAN AND $5000 ALMOST IN THEIR GRASP, THE TWO BE-GIN AN IMPATIENT WAIT . . .

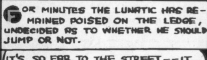
FOR MINUTES THE LUNATIC HAS REMAINED POISED ON THE LEDGE, UNDECIDED AS TO WHETHER HE SHOULD JUMP OR NOT.

IT'S SO FAR TO THE STREET--IT MIGHT HURT ME--BUT THEN, IT'LL BE OVER IN A MINUTE!

FINALLY--HE JUMPS--

YE-EE-EE!

FROM ATOP ANOTHER BUILDING . . .

HE'S LEAPT!--CAN I MAKE IT?

SUPERMAN LAUNCHES HIMSELF OUT AND DOWNWARD IN A FRANTIC EFFORT TO SAVE THE DEMENTED MAN'S LIFE!

FINGERS ALMOST TOUCHING-- PAVEMENT NEAR--

GOT HIM !

NEXT INSTANT, AS SUPERMAN STRIKES THE SIDEWALK, IT EXPLODES IN A HAIL OF STONY FRAGMENTS!--BUT THE MANIAC IS SAVED!!

WHEW!--THAT WAS A MATTER OF SECONDS!

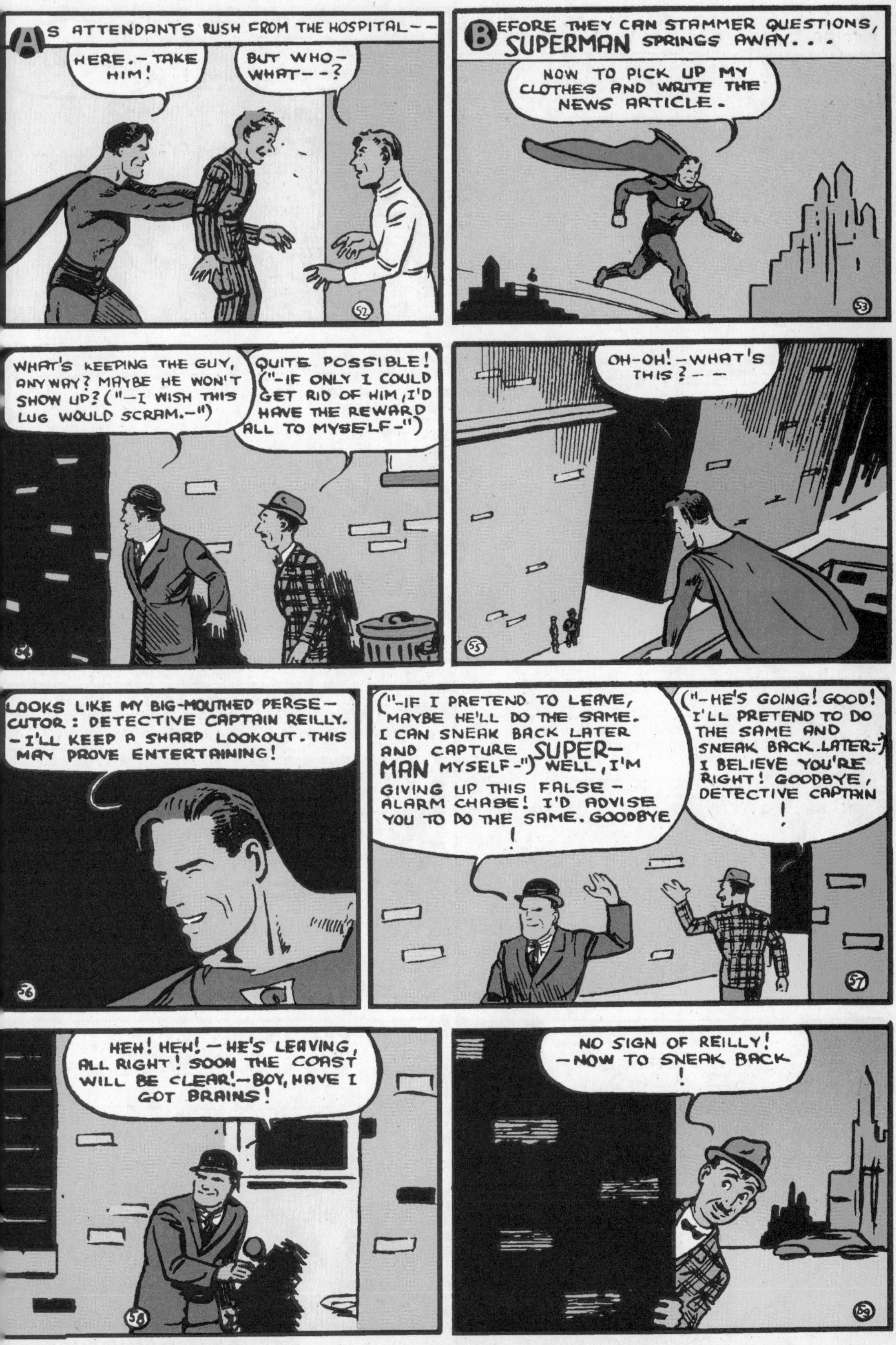
AS ATTENDANTS RUSH FROM THE HOSPITAL--
HERE.-TAKE HIM!
BUT WHO-WHAT--?
BEFORE THEY CAN STAMMER QUESTIONS, SUPERMAN SPRINGS AWAY...
NOW TO PICK UP MY CLOTHES AND WRITE THE NEWS ARTICLE.
WHAT'S KEEPING THE GUY, ANYWAY? MAYBE HE WON'T SHOW UP? ("-I WISH THIS LUG WOULD SCRAM.-")
QUITE POSSIBLE! ("-IF ONLY I COULD GET RID OF HIM, I'D HAVE THE REWARD ALL TO MYSELF-")
OH-OH!-WHAT'S THIS?--
LOOKS LIKE MY BIG-MOUTHED PERSE-CUTOR: DETECTIVE CAPTAIN REILLY. -I'LL KEEP A SHARP LOOKOUT. THIS MAY PROVE ENTERTAINING!
("-IF I PRETEND TO LEAVE, MAYBE HE'LL DO THE SAME. I CAN SNEAK BACK LATER AND CAPTURE SUPERMAN MYSELF-") WELL, I'M GIVING UP THIS FALSE-ALARM CHASE! I'D ADVISE YOU TO DO THE SAME. GOODBYE!
("-HE'S GOING! GOOD! I'LL PRETEND TO DO THE SAME AND SNEAK BACK LATER-") I BELIEVE YOU'RE RIGHT! GOODBYE, DETECTIVE CAPTAIN!
HEH! HEH!-HE'S LEAVING, ALL RIGHT! SOON THE COAST WILL BE CLEAR!-BOY, HAVE I GOT BRAINS!
NO SIGN OF REILLY! -NOW TO SNEAK BACK!

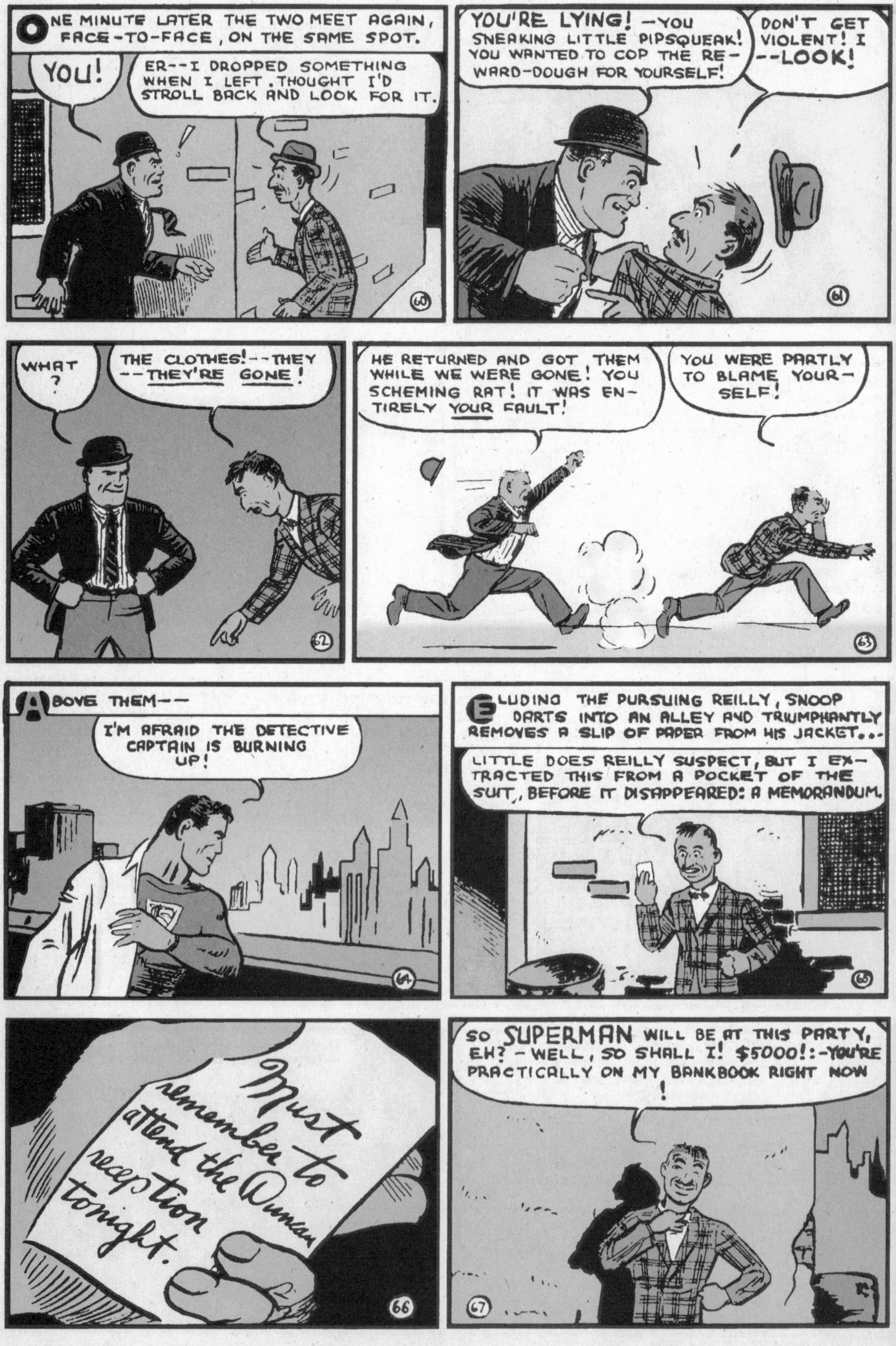

ONE MINUTE LATER THE TWO MEET AGAIN, FACE-TO-FACE, ON THE SAME SPOT.
YOU!
ER--I DROPPED SOMETHING WHEN I LEFT. THOUGHT I'D STROLL BACK AND LOOK FOR IT.
YOU'RE LYING! —YOU SNEAKING LITTLE PIPSQUEAK! YOU WANTED TO COP THE RE-WARD-DOUGH FOR YOURSELF!
DON'T GET VIOLENT! I --LOOK!
WHAT?
THE CLOTHES!--THEY --THEY'RE GONE!
HE RETURNED AND GOT THEM WHILE WE WERE GONE! YOU SCHEMING RAT! IT WAS EN-TIRELY YOUR FAULT!
YOU WERE PARTLY TO BLAME YOUR-SELF!
ABOVE THEM--
I'M AFRAID THE DETECTIVE CAPTAIN IS BURNING UP!
ELUDING THE PURSUING REILLY, SNOOP DARTS INTO AN ALLEY AND TRIUMPHANTLY REMOVES A SLIP OF PAPER FROM HIS JACKET...
LITTLE DOES REILLY SUSPECT, BUT I EX-TRACTED THIS FROM A POCKET OF THE SUIT, BEFORE IT DISAPPEARED: A MEMORANDUM.
Must remember to attend the Dunsan reception tonight.
SO SUPERMAN WILL BE AT THIS PARTY, EH? - WELL, SO SHALL I! $5000!:-YOU'RE PRACTICALLY ON MY BANKBOOK RIGHT NOW!

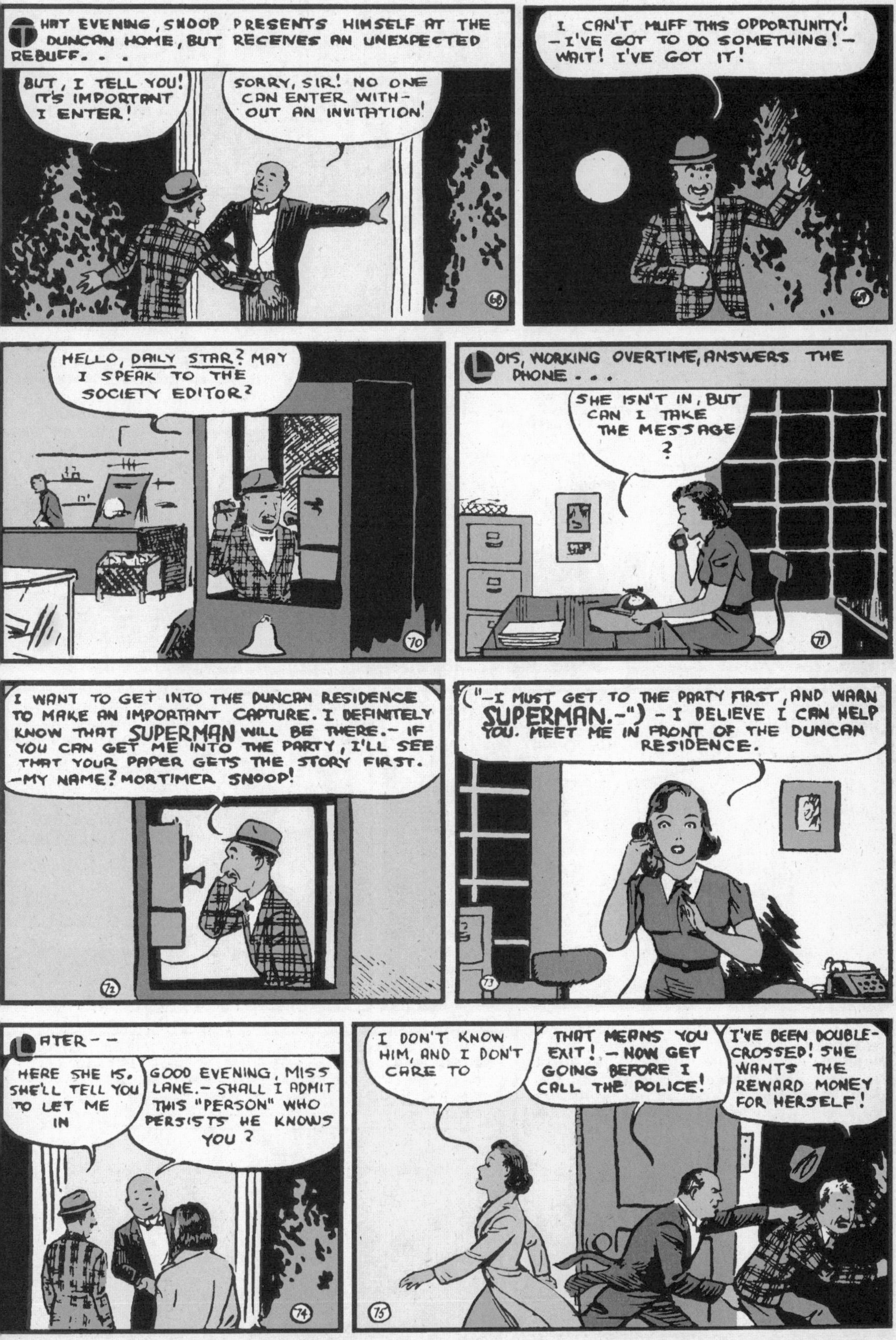
THAT EVENING, SNOOP PRESENTS HIMSELF AT THE DUNCAN HOME, BUT RECEIVES AN UNEXPECTED REBUFF. . .
BUT, I TELL YOU! IT'S IMPORTANT I ENTER!
SORRY, SIR! NO ONE CAN ENTER WITH-OUT AN INVITATION!
I CAN'T MUFF THIS OPPORTUNITY! —I'VE GOT TO DO SOMETHING!— WAIT! I'VE GOT IT!
HELLO, DAILY STAR? MAY I SPEAK TO THE SOCIETY EDITOR?
LOIS, WORKING OVERTIME, ANSWERS THE PHONE . . .
SHE ISN'T IN, BUT CAN I TAKE THE MESSAGE?
I WANT TO GET INTO THE DUNCAN RESIDENCE TO MAKE AN IMPORTANT CAPTURE. I DEFINITELY KNOW THAT SUPERMAN WILL BE THERE.— IF YOU CAN GET ME INTO THE PARTY, I'LL SEE THAT YOUR PAPER GETS THE STORY FIRST. —MY NAME? MORTIMER SNOOP!
("—I MUST GET TO THE PARTY FIRST, AND WARN SUPERMAN.—") —I BELIEVE I CAN HELP YOU. MEET ME IN FRONT OF THE DUNCAN RESIDENCE.
LATER— —
HERE SHE IS. SHE'LL TELL YOU TO LET ME IN
GOOD EVENING, MISS LANE.— SHALL I ADMIT THIS "PERSON" WHO PERSISTS HE KNOWS YOU?
I DON'T KNOW HIM, AND I DON'T CARE TO
THAT MEANS YOU EXIT! —NOW GET GOING BEFORE I CALL THE POLICE!
I'VE BEEN DOUBLE-CROSSED! SHE WANTS THE REWARD MONEY FOR HERSELF!

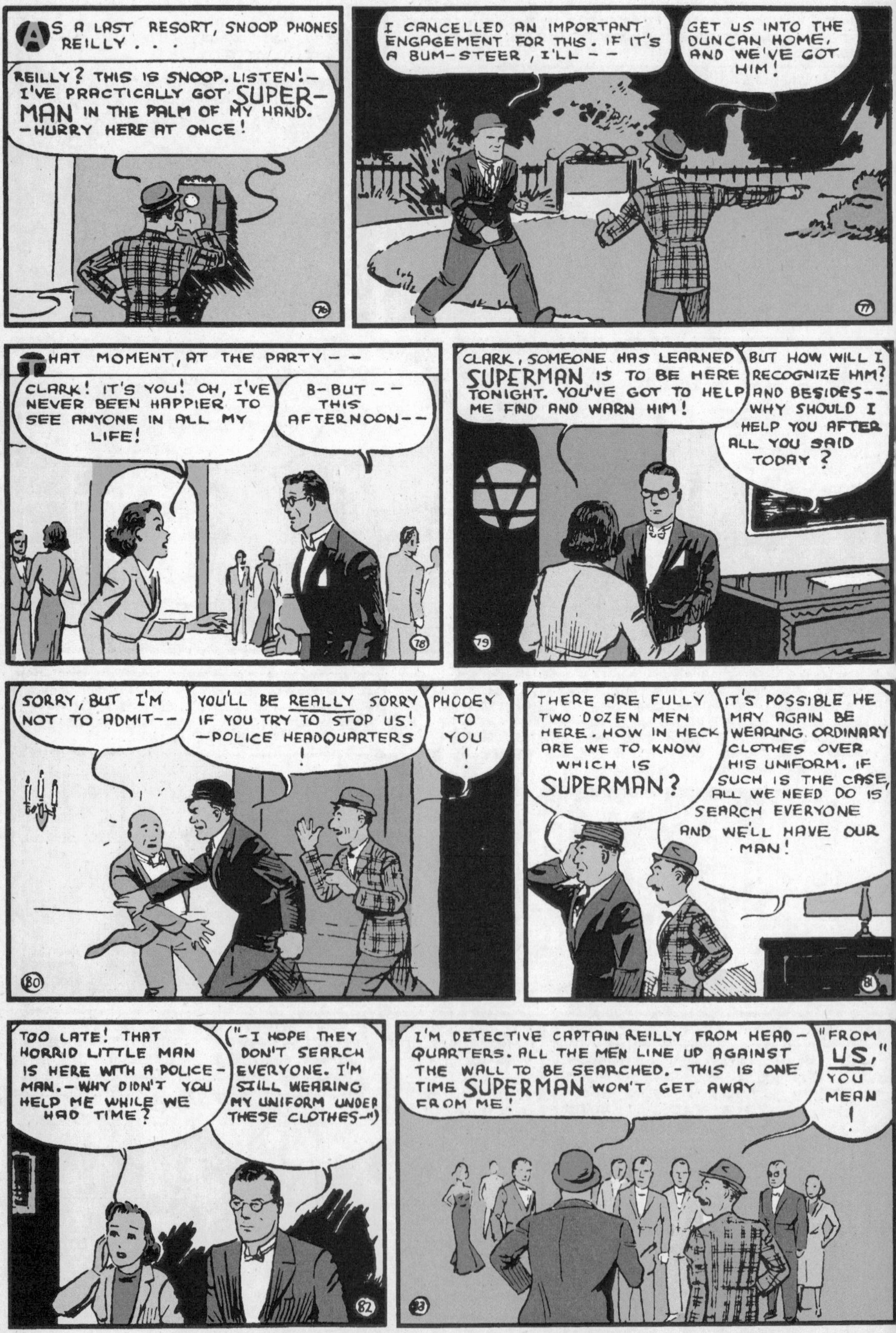
AS A LAST RESORT, SNOOP PHONES REILLY . . .
REILLY? THIS IS SNOOP. LISTEN!— I'VE PRACTICALLY GOT SUPERMAN IN THE PALM OF MY HAND. —HURRY HERE AT ONCE!
I CANCELLED AN IMPORTANT ENGAGEMENT FOR THIS. IF IT'S A BUM-STEER, I'LL — —
GET US INTO THE DUNCAN HOME, AND WE'VE GOT HIM!
THAT MOMENT, AT THE PARTY — —
CLARK! IT'S YOU! OH, I'VE NEVER BEEN HAPPIER TO SEE ANYONE IN ALL MY LIFE!
B-BUT — — THIS AFTERNOON — —
CLARK, SOMEONE HAS LEARNED SUPERMAN IS TO BE HERE TONIGHT. YOU'VE GOT TO HELP ME FIND AND WARN HIM!
BUT HOW WILL I RECOGNIZE HIM? AND BESIDES — — WHY SHOULD I HELP YOU AFTER ALL YOU SAID TODAY?
SORRY, BUT I'M NOT TO ADMIT — —
YOU'LL BE REALLY SORRY IF YOU TRY TO STOP US! —POLICE HEADQUARTERS!
PHOOEY TO YOU!
THERE ARE FULLY TWO DOZEN MEN HERE. HOW IN HECK ARE WE TO KNOW WHICH IS SUPERMAN?
IT'S POSSIBLE HE MAY AGAIN BE WEARING ORDINARY CLOTHES OVER HIS UNIFORM. IF SUCH IS THE CASE, ALL WE NEED DO IS SEARCH EVERYONE AND WE'LL HAVE OUR MAN!
TOO LATE! THAT HORRID LITTLE MAN IS HERE WITH A POLICEMAN. —WHY DIDN'T YOU HELP ME WHILE WE HAD TIME?
("—I HOPE THEY DON'T SEARCH EVERYONE. I'M STILL WEARING MY UNIFORM UNDER THESE CLOTHES—")
I'M DETECTIVE CAPTAIN REILLY FROM HEADQUARTERS. ALL THE MEN LINE UP AGAINST THE WALL TO BE SEARCHED. —THIS IS ONE TIME SUPERMAN WON'T GET AWAY FROM ME!
"FROM US," YOU MEAN!

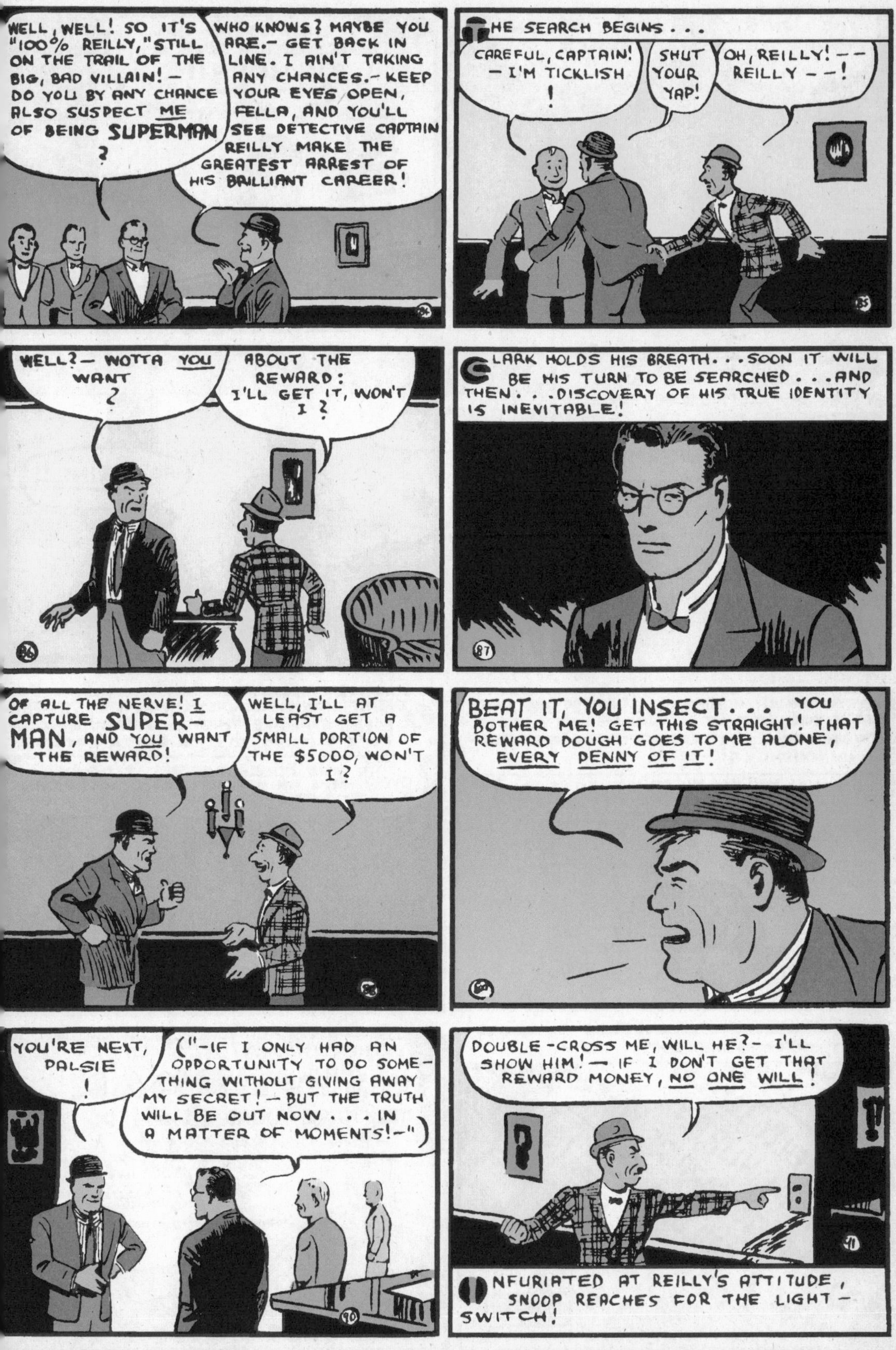
WELL, WELL! SO IT'S "100% REILLY," STILL ON THE TRAIL OF THE BIG, BAD VILLAIN! — DO YOU BY ANY CHANCE ALSO SUSPECT ME OF BEING SUPERMAN ?
WHO KNOWS? MAYBE YOU ARE.— GET BACK IN LINE. I AIN'T TAKING ANY CHANCES.— KEEP YOUR EYES OPEN, FELLA, AND YOU'LL SEE DETECTIVE CAPTAIN REILLY MAKE THE GREATEST ARREST OF HIS BRILLIANT CAREER!
84
THE SEARCH BEGINS . . .
CAREFUL, CAPTAIN! — I'M TICKLISH !
SHUT YOUR YAP!
OH, REILLY! — — REILLY — —!
85
WELL? — WOTTA YOU WANT ?
ABOUT THE REWARD: I'LL GET IT, WON'T I ?
86
CLARK HOLDS HIS BREATH . . . SOON IT WILL BE HIS TURN TO BE SEARCHED . . . AND THEN . . . DISCOVERY OF HIS TRUE IDENTITY IS INEVITABLE!
87
OF ALL THE NERVE! I CAPTURE SUPER-MAN, AND YOU WANT THE REWARD!
WELL, I'LL AT LEAST GET A SMALL PORTION OF THE $5000, WON'T I ?
BEAT IT, YOU INSECT . . . YOU BOTHER ME! GET THIS STRAIGHT! THAT REWARD DOUGH GOES TO ME ALONE, EVERY PENNY OF IT!
YOU'RE NEXT, PALSIE !
("—IF I ONLY HAD AN OPPORTUNITY TO DO SOME-THING WITHOUT GIVING AWAY MY SECRET! — BUT THE TRUTH WILL BE OUT NOW . . . IN A MATTER OF MOMENTS! —")
90
DOUBLE-CROSS ME, WILL HE? — I'LL SHOW HIM! — IF I DON'T GET THAT REWARD MONEY, NO ONE WILL!
91
INFURIATED AT REILLY'S ATTITUDE, SNOOP REACHES FOR THE LIGHT-SWITCH!

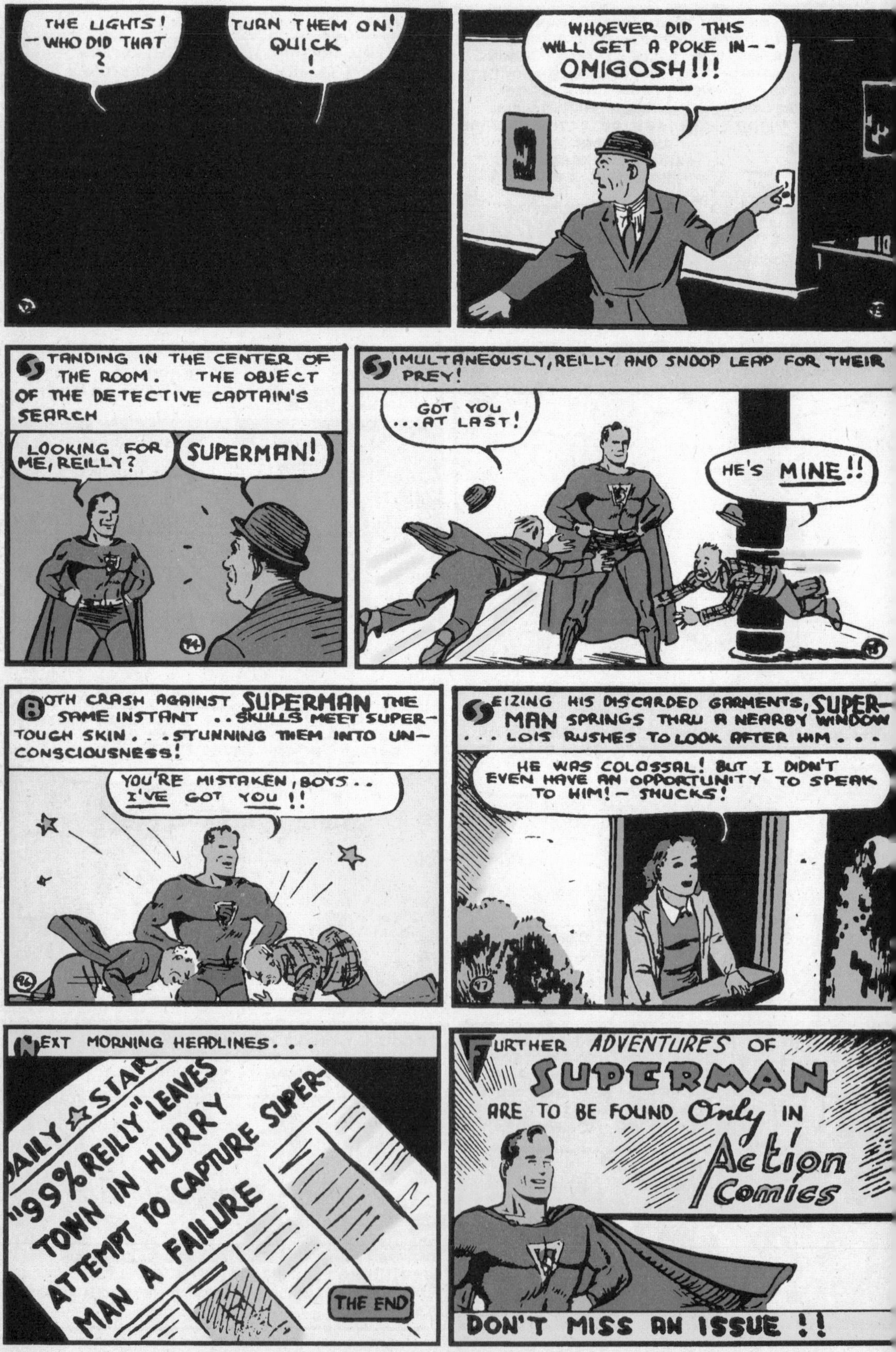
THE LIGHTS! —WHO DID THAT ?
TURN THEM ON! QUICK !
WHOEVER DID THIS WILL GET A POKE IN-- OMIGOSH!!!
STANDING IN THE CENTER OF THE ROOM. THE OBJECT OF THE DETECTIVE CAPTAIN'S SEARCH
LOOKING FOR ME, REILLY?
SUPERMAN!
SIMULTANEOUSLY, REILLY AND SNOOP LEAP FOR THEIR PREY!
GOT YOU ...AT LAST!
HE'S MINE!!
BOTH CRASH AGAINST SUPERMAN THE SAME INSTANT ..SKULLS MEET SUPER-TOUGH SKIN. . .STUNNING THEM INTO UNCONSCIOUSNESS!
YOU'RE MISTAKEN, BOYS.. I'VE GOT YOU!!
SEIZING HIS DISCARDED GARMENTS, SUPERMAN SPRINGS THRU A NEARBY WINDOW . . . LOIS RUSHES TO LOOK AFTER HIM . . .
HE WAS COLOSSAL! BUT I DIDN'T EVEN HAVE AN OPPORTUNITY TO SPEAK TO HIM! — SHUCKS!
NEXT MORNING HEADLINES. . .
DAILY STAR
"99% REILLY" LEAVES TOWN IN HURRY
ATTEMPT TO CAPTURE SUPERMAN A FAILURE
THE END
FURTHER ADVENTURES OF SUPERMAN ARE TO BE FOUND Only IN Action Comics
DON'T MISS AN ISSUE !!

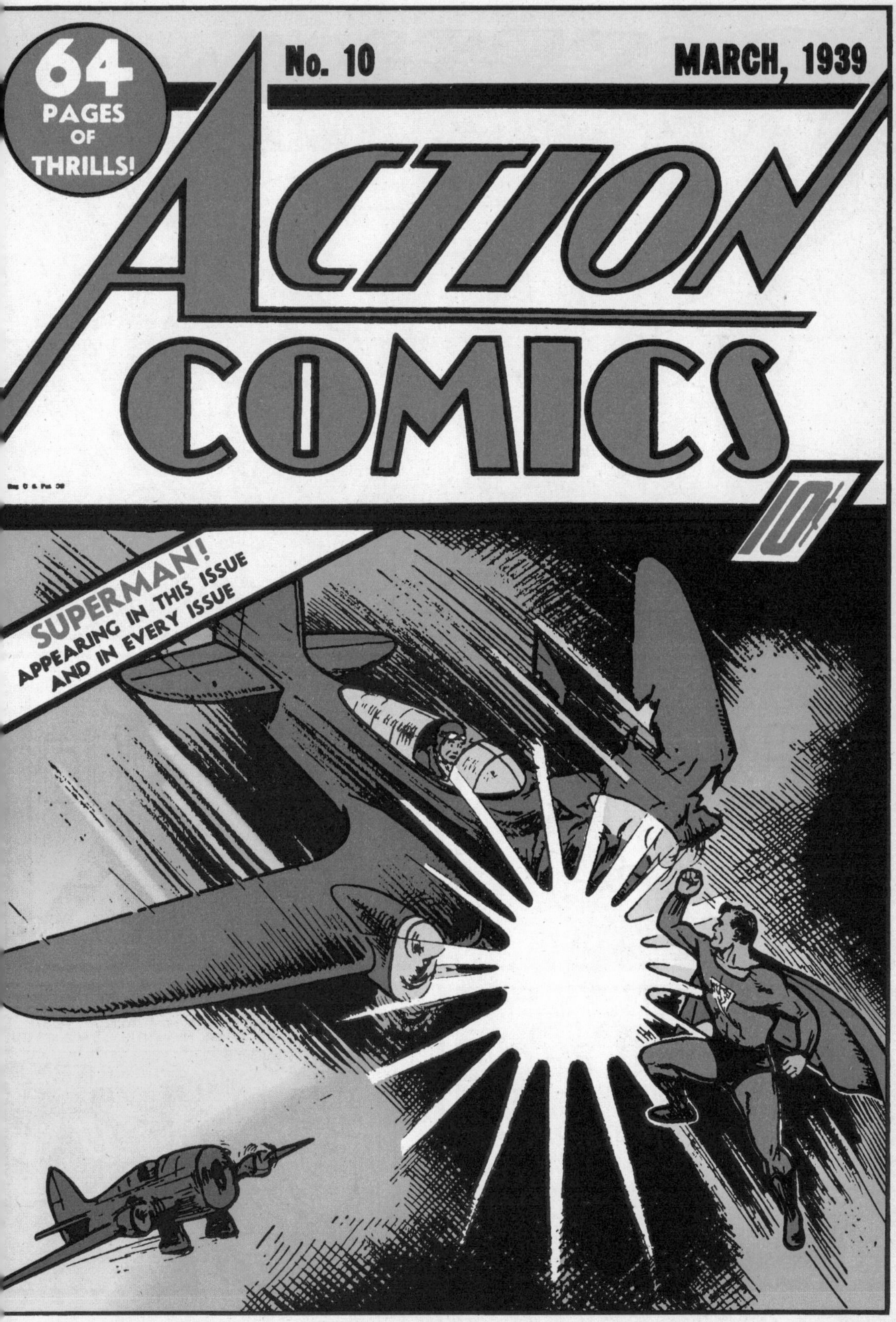
64 PAGES OF THRILLS!
No. 10
MARCH, 1939
ACTION COMICS
10¢
SUPERMAN!
APPEARING IN THIS ISSUE AND IN EVERY ISSUE

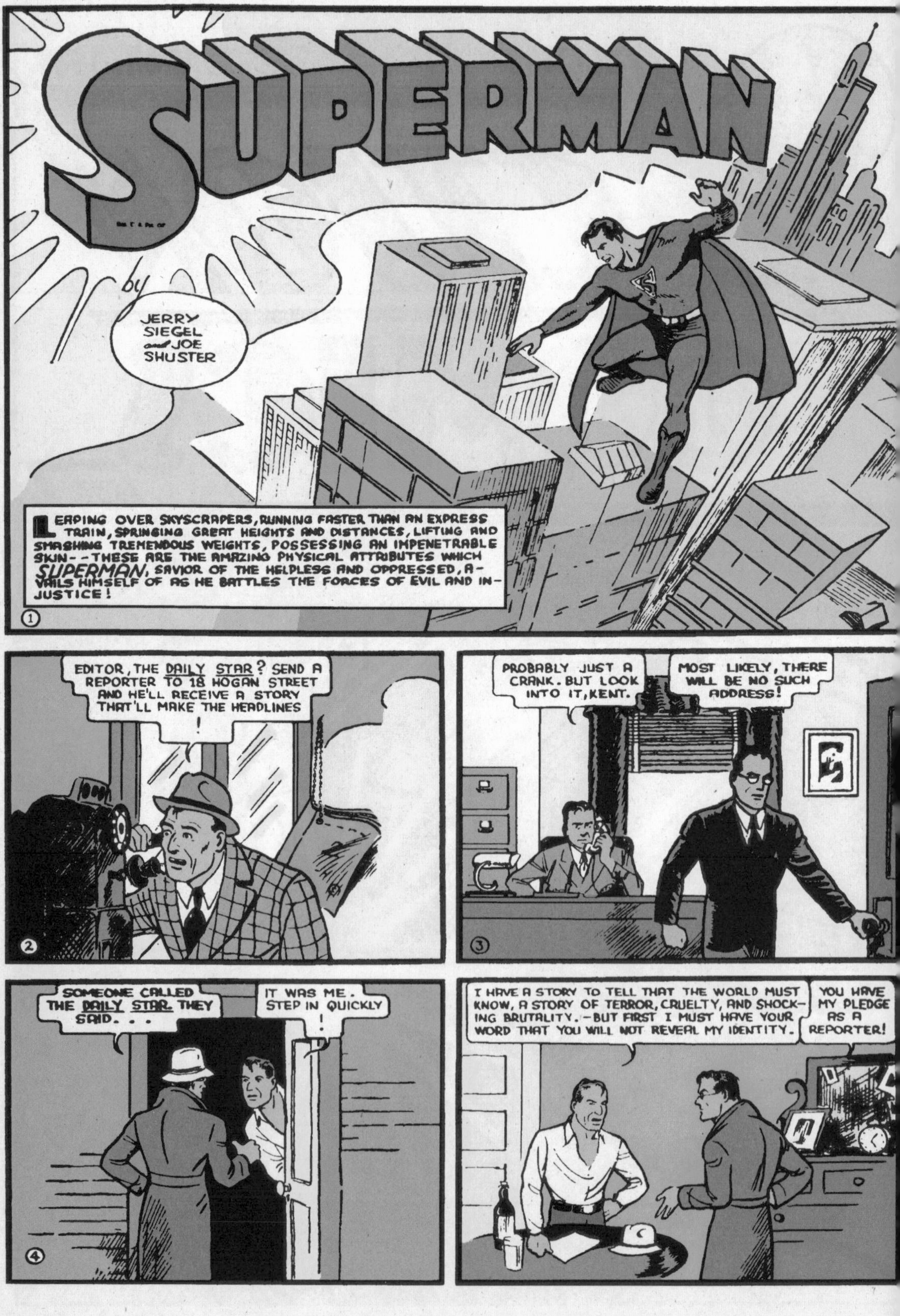
SUPERMAN
by
JERRY SIEGEL and JOE SHUSTER
LEAPING OVER SKYSCRAPERS, RUNNING FASTER THAN AN EXPRESS TRAIN, SPRINGING GREAT HEIGHTS AND DISTANCES, LIFTING AND SMASHING TREMENDOUS WEIGHTS, POSSESSING AN IMPENETRABLE SKIN--THESE ARE THE AMAZING PHYSICAL ATTRIBUTES WHICH SUPERMAN, SAVIOR OF THE HELPLESS AND OPPRESSED, A-VAILS HIMSELF OF AS HE BATTLES THE FORCES OF EVIL AND IN-JUSTICE!
1
EDITOR, THE DAILY STAR? SEND A REPORTER TO 18 HOGAN STREET AND HE'LL RECEIVE A STORY THAT'LL MAKE THE HEADLINES!
2
PROBABLY JUST A CRANK. BUT LOOK INTO IT, KENT.
MOST LIKELY, THERE WILL BE NO SUCH ADDRESS!
3
SOMEONE CALLED THE DAILY STAR, THEY SAID. . .
IT WAS ME. STEP IN QUICKLY!
4
I HAVE A STORY TO TELL THAT THE WORLD MUST KNOW, A STORY OF TERROR, CRUELTY, AND SHOCK-ING BRUTALITY.-BUT FIRST I MUST HAVE YOUR WORD THAT YOU WILL NOT REVEAL MY IDENTITY.
YOU HAVE MY PLEDGE AS A REPORTER!

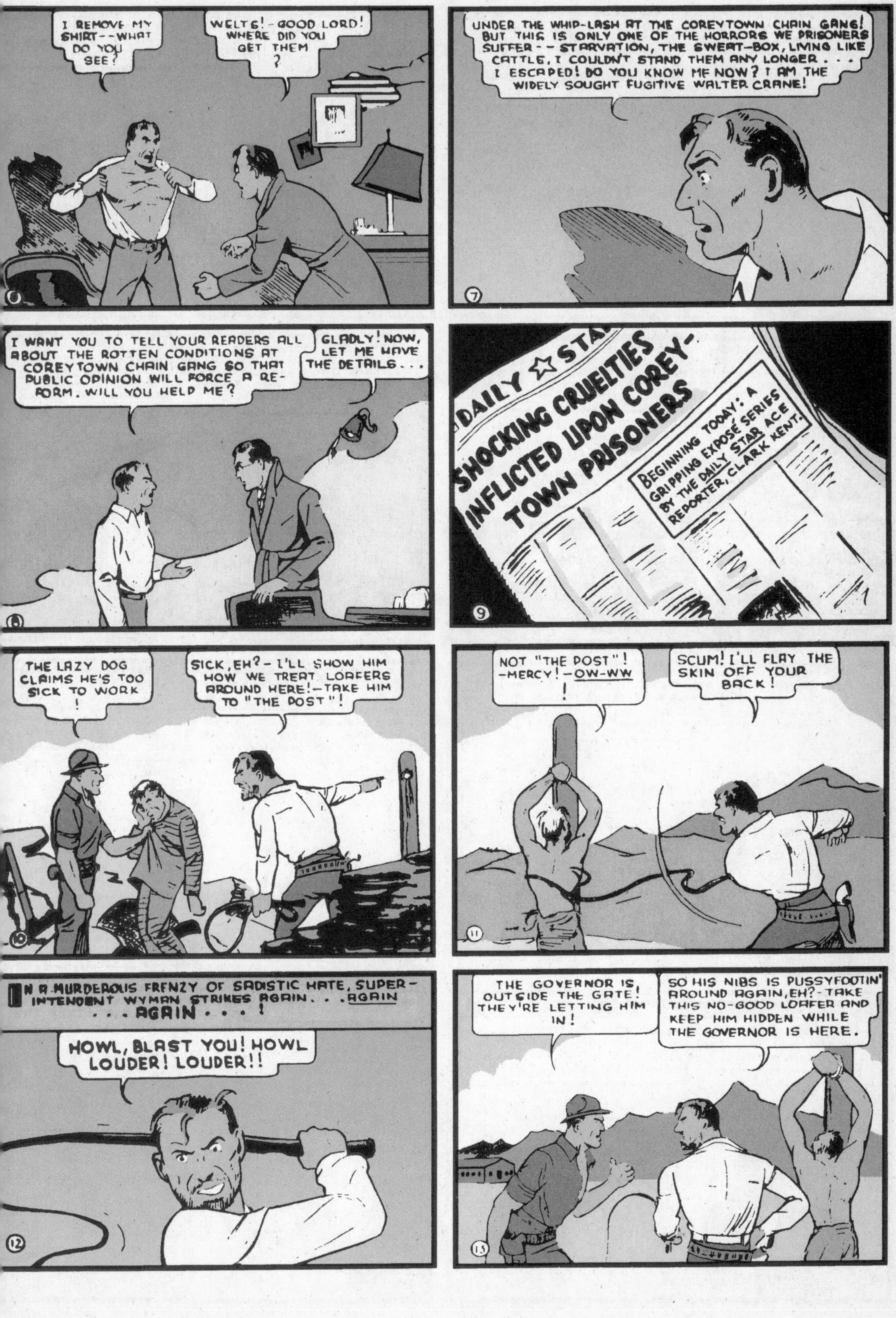
I REMOVE MY SHIRT--WHAT DO YOU SEE?
WELTS!-GOOD LORD! WHERE DID YOU GET THEM ?
UNDER THE WHIP-LASH AT THE COREYTOWN CHAIN GANG! BUT THIS IS ONLY ONE OF THE HORRORS WE PRISONERS SUFFER--STARVATION, THE SWEAT-BOX, LIVING LIKE CATTLE. I COULDN'T STAND THEM ANY LONGER... I ESCAPED! DO YOU KNOW ME NOW? I AM THE WIDELY SOUGHT FUGITIVE WALTER CRANE!
I WANT YOU TO TELL YOUR READERS ALL ABOUT THE ROTTEN CONDITIONS AT COREYTOWN CHAIN GANG SO THAT PUBLIC OPINION WILL FORCE A RE-FORM. WILL YOU HELP ME?
GLADLY! NOW, LET ME HAVE THE DETAILS...
DAILY ☆ STA
SHOCKING CRUELTIES INFLICTED UPON COREY-TOWN PRISONERS
BEGINNING TODAY: A GRIPPING EXPOSÉ SERIES BY THE DAILY STAR ACE REPORTER, CLARK KENT.
THE LAZY DOG CLAIMS HE'S TOO SICK TO WORK!
SICK, EH?-I'LL SHOW HIM HOW WE TREAT LOAFERS AROUND HERE!-TAKE HIM TO "THE POST"!
NOT "THE POST"! -MERCY!-OW-WW!
SCUM! I'LL FLAY THE SKIN OFF YOUR BACK!
IN A MURDEROUS FRENZY OF SADISTIC HATE, SUPER-INTENDENT WYMAN STRIKES AGAIN...AGAIN...AGAIN...!
HOWL, BLAST YOU! HOWL LOUDER! LOUDER!!
THE GOVERNOR IS OUTSIDE THE GATE! THEY'RE LETTING HIM IN!
SO HIS NIBS IS PUSSYFOOTIN' AROUND AGAIN, EH?-TAKE THIS NO-GOOD LOAFER AND KEEP HIM HIDDEN WHILE THE GOVERNOR IS HERE.

Panel 14:
WELL, WELL, WELL! IF IT AIN'T GOVERNOR BIXBY! GLAD YA DROPPED IN! ALWAYS GLAD TO SEE MY GOOD FRIEND, THE GOVERNOR!

I'M AFRAID YOU WON'T PARTICULARLY ENJOY MY VISIT THIS TIME, WYMAN. —LOOK AT THIS: A NEWS-PAPER SERIES DECRYING CONDITIONS HERE!

Panel 15:
IT'S A BLASTED DIRTY LIE!!

IF I BELIEVED FOR ONE SECOND THAT IT WAS TRUE, BY HEAVENS, I'D....!

Panel 16:
THERE'S NO BETTER WAY TO SATISFY YOU THAN TO HAVE YOU SPEAK DIRECTLY TO THE MEN THEMSELVES, HAVE THEM TELL YOU WHAT THEY THINK OF THEIR TREATMENT.

YOU MAY BE STRICT, SUPERINTENDENT, BUT I CAN'T BELIEVE YOU'D BE GUILTY OF DOWN-RIGHT CRUELTY!

Panel 17:
STOP WORK, MEN! —THE GOVERNOR, HERE, WANTS TO KNOW IF ANY OF YOU HAVE BEEN MIS-TREATED. NOW DON'T BE AFRAID TO TALK. IF ANYONE HAS A BEEF TO MAKE, WHY, SPEAK UP!

Panel 18:
I'M GOING TO SPEAK UP!

SHUT UP, YOU FOOL! —IF YOU DARE TO OPEN YOUR MOUTH, WYMAN WILL KILL YOU, NOT QUICKLY, BUT THRU A SLOW, LINGERING TORTURE!

Panel 19:
THE MEN STAND SILENT, WHILE GUARDS GRIP THEIR RIFLES IN READINESS, SHOULD ANY MAN DARE TO TALK.

YOU SEE, GOVERNOR, THEY'VE NOTHING TO SAY. THEY'RE CONTENTED. NOW DO YOU BELIEVE ME?

MOST ASSUREDLY! —WE MUST STOP THIS SLANDEROUS SERIES!

Panel 20:
AFTER THE GOVERNOR HAS GONE --

THE PRISONER YOU WHIPPED, SIR! HE'S DIED OF HIS INJURIES!

WHO CARES? —THAT STORY IN THE NEWSPAPER. THERE'S ONLY ONE MAN WHO COULD HAVE SUPPLIED THE DETAILS.

Panel 21:
WALTER CRANE!

RIGHT! —PACK MY THINGS! —I'M TAKING A LITTLE TRIP NORTH!

Panel 22: TWO DAYS LATER—EDITOR'S OFFICE OF THE _DAILY STAR_...

THIS STORY YOU'VE BEEN RUNNING ABOUT ME IS LIBELOUS! I DEMAND A RETRACTION AND APOLOGY!

SORRY. WE SECURED OUR INFORMATION FROM AN AUTHORITATIVE SOURCE. IF YOU WANT TO SUE, GO RIGHT AHEAD. IT WILL MAKE A GOOD STORY FOR OUR PAPER.

Panel 23: I WANT TO TALK TO THIS WISE GUY, CLARK KENT, WHO WRITES THESE LIES!

THAT CAN BE ARRANGED. --KENT, WILL YOU PLEASE STEP INTO MY OFFICE.

Panel 24: CLARK, MEET SUPERINTENDENT WYMAN WHO CLAIMS TO BE A MUCH MALIGNED MAN. --IT APPEARS HE RESENTS YOUR ARTICLE PERTAINING TO HIS CHAIN GANG.

SUPERINTENDENT WYMAN!

THAT'S RIGHT, YOU LYING SKUNK!

Panel 25: LYING? THAT'S NOT TRUE. I--

IF YOU DIDN'T MAKE UP THOSE STORIES OUT OF YOUR OWN HEAD, WHERE DID YOU GET THEM? I'VE A RIGHT TO KNOW!

Panel 26: I--UH--I--YOU SEE--WELL, I GOT THEM FROM--DASH IT, I CAN'T TELL YOU--

Panel 27: IT HAPPENS TO BE A REPORTER'S CODE NEVER TO REVEAL HIS SOURCE OF INFORMATION IF PLEDGED NOT TO DO SO.

WELL, I HAPPEN TO KNOW WHO THE STOOLIE IS: WALTER CRANE! --ANSWER ME! IT IS HIM, ISN'T IT?

I--UH--

Panel 28: MR. KENT! I DON'T LIKE TO BE CRUDE, BUT DO YOU HAPPEN TO REALIZE THAT HARBORING A FUGITIVE CRIMINAL MAKES YOU AN ACCESSORY TO THE FACT? DO YOU REALIZE THAT IF YOU DON'T REVEAL CRANE'S HIDING PLACE YOU WILL BE EQUALLY GUILTY, AND FACE A JAIL SENTENCE?

Panel 29: KEEPING TO HIS ADOPTED ATTITUDE OF COWARDLINESS, KENT FRANTICALLY BLURTS OUT--

HE'S STAYING AT 18 HOGAN STREET! --DON'T PROSECUTE ME! I'LL TELL YOU ANYTHING YOU WANT TO KNOW!

THAT'S MORE LIKE IT!

KENT!

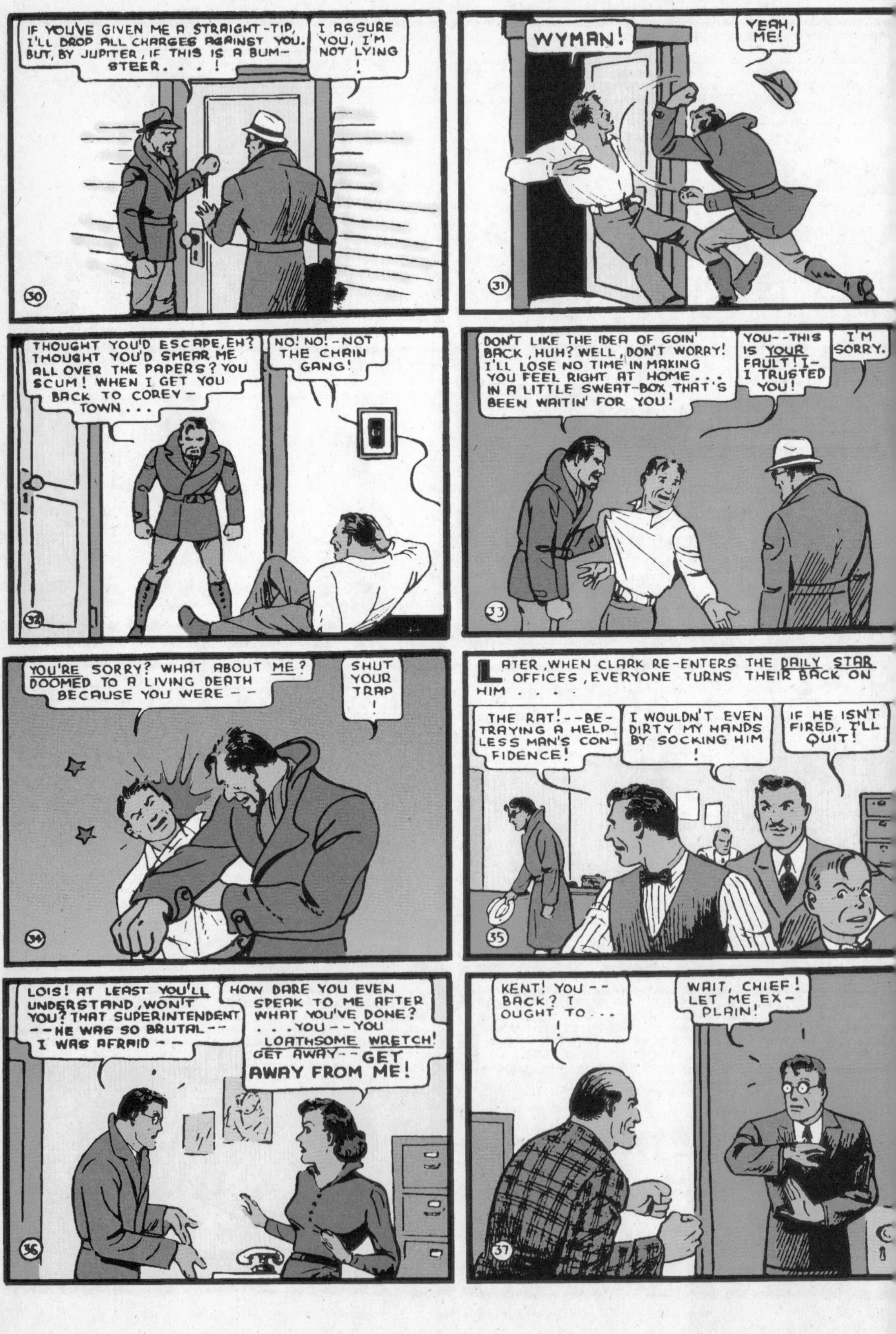

IF YOU'VE GIVEN ME A STRAIGHT-TIP, I'LL DROP ALL CHARGES AGAINST YOU. BUT, BY JUPITER, IF THIS IS A BUM-STEER . . . !
I ASSURE YOU, I'M NOT LYING !
WYMAN!
YEAH, ME!
THOUGHT YOU'D ESCAPE, EH? THOUGHT YOU'D SMEAR ME ALL OVER THE PAPERS? YOU SCUM! WHEN I GET YOU BACK TO COREY-TOWN...
NO! NO! --NOT THE CHAIN GANG!
DON'T LIKE THE IDEA OF GOIN' BACK, HUH? WELL, DON'T WORRY! I'LL LOSE NO TIME IN MAKING YOU FEEL RIGHT AT HOME . . . IN A LITTLE SWEAT-BOX THAT'S BEEN WAITIN' FOR YOU!
YOU--THIS IS YOUR FAULT! I-I TRUSTED YOU!
I'M SORRY.
YOU'RE SORRY? WHAT ABOUT ME? DOOMED TO A LIVING DEATH BECAUSE YOU WERE --
SHUT YOUR TRAP !
LATER, WHEN CLARK RE-ENTERS THE DAILY STAR OFFICES, EVERYONE TURNS THEIR BACK ON HIM . . . .
THE RAT! --BE-TRAYING A HELP-LESS MAN'S CON-FIDENCE!
I WOULDN'T EVEN DIRTY MY HANDS BY SOCKING HIM !
IF HE ISN'T FIRED, I'LL QUIT!
LOIS! AT LEAST YOU'LL UNDERSTAND, WON'T YOU? THAT SUPERINTENDENT --HE WAS SO BRUTAL-- I WAS AFRAID --
HOW DARE YOU EVEN SPEAK TO ME AFTER WHAT YOU'VE DONE? . . .YOU--YOU LOATHSOME WRETCH! GET AWAY--GET AWAY FROM ME!
KENT! YOU-- BACK? I OUGHT TO . . . !
WAIT, CHIEF! LET ME EX-PLAIN!

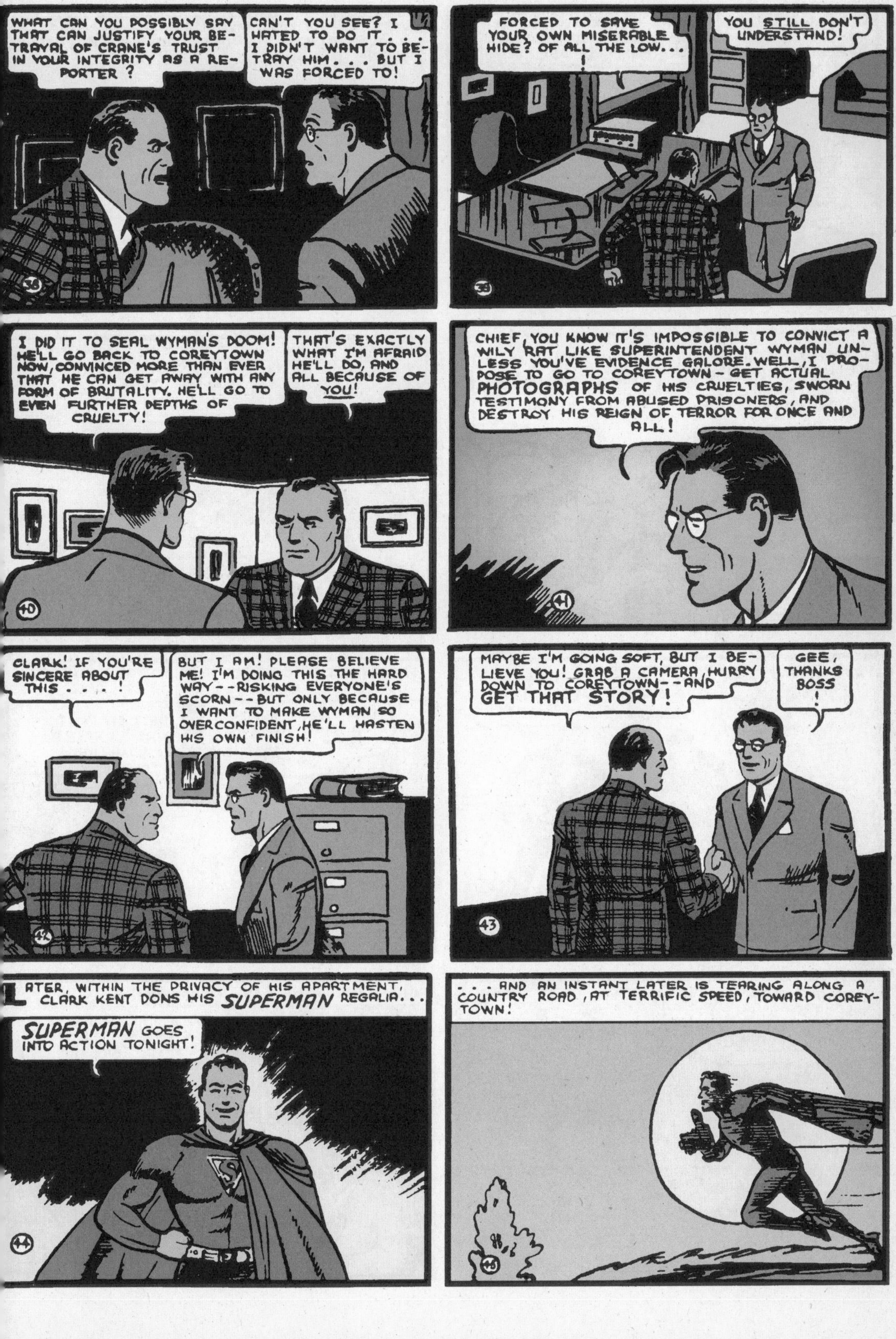
WHAT CAN YOU POSSIBLY SAY THAT CAN JUSTIFY YOUR BE-TRAYAL OF CRANE'S TRUST IN YOUR INTEGRITY AS A RE-PORTER ?
CAN'T YOU SEE? I HATED TO DO IT . . . I DIDN'T WANT TO BE-TRAY HIM . . . BUT I WAS FORCED TO!
FORCED TO SAVE YOUR OWN MISERABLE HIDE? OF ALL THE LOW... !
YOU STILL DON'T UNDERSTAND!
I DID IT TO SEAL WYMAN'S DOOM! HE'LL GO BACK TO COREYTOWN NOW, CONVINCED MORE THAN EVER THAT HE CAN GET AWAY WITH ANY FORM OF BRUTALITY. HE'LL GO TO EVEN FURTHER DEPTHS OF CRUELTY!
THAT'S EXACTLY WHAT I'M AFRAID HE'LL DO, AND ALL BECAUSE OF YOU!
CHIEF, YOU KNOW IT'S IMPOSSIBLE TO CONVICT A WILY RAT LIKE SUPERINTENDENT WYMAN UN-LESS YOU'VE EVIDENCE GALORE. WELL, I PRO-POSE TO GO TO COREYTOWN - GET ACTUAL PHOTOGRAPHS OF HIS CRUELTIES, SWORN TESTIMONY FROM ABUSED PRISONERS, AND DESTROY HIS REIGN OF TERROR FOR ONCE AND ALL!
CLARK! IF YOU'RE SINCERE ABOUT THIS . . . !
BUT I AM! PLEASE BELIEVE ME! I'M DOING THIS THE HARD WAY--RISKING EVERYONE'S SCORN--BUT ONLY BECAUSE I WANT TO MAKE WYMAN SO OVERCONFIDENT, HE'LL HASTEN HIS OWN FINISH!
MAYBE I'M GOING SOFT, BUT I BE-LIEVE YOU! GRAB A CAMERA, HURRY DOWN TO COREYTOWN--AND GET THAT STORY!
GEE, THANKS BOSS !
LATER, WITHIN THE PRIVACY OF HIS APARTMENT, CLARK KENT DONS HIS SUPERMAN REGALIA...
SUPERMAN GOES INTO ACTION TONIGHT!
. . . AND AN INSTANT LATER IS TEARING ALONG A COUNTRY ROAD, AT TERRIFIC SPEED, TOWARD COREY-TOWN!

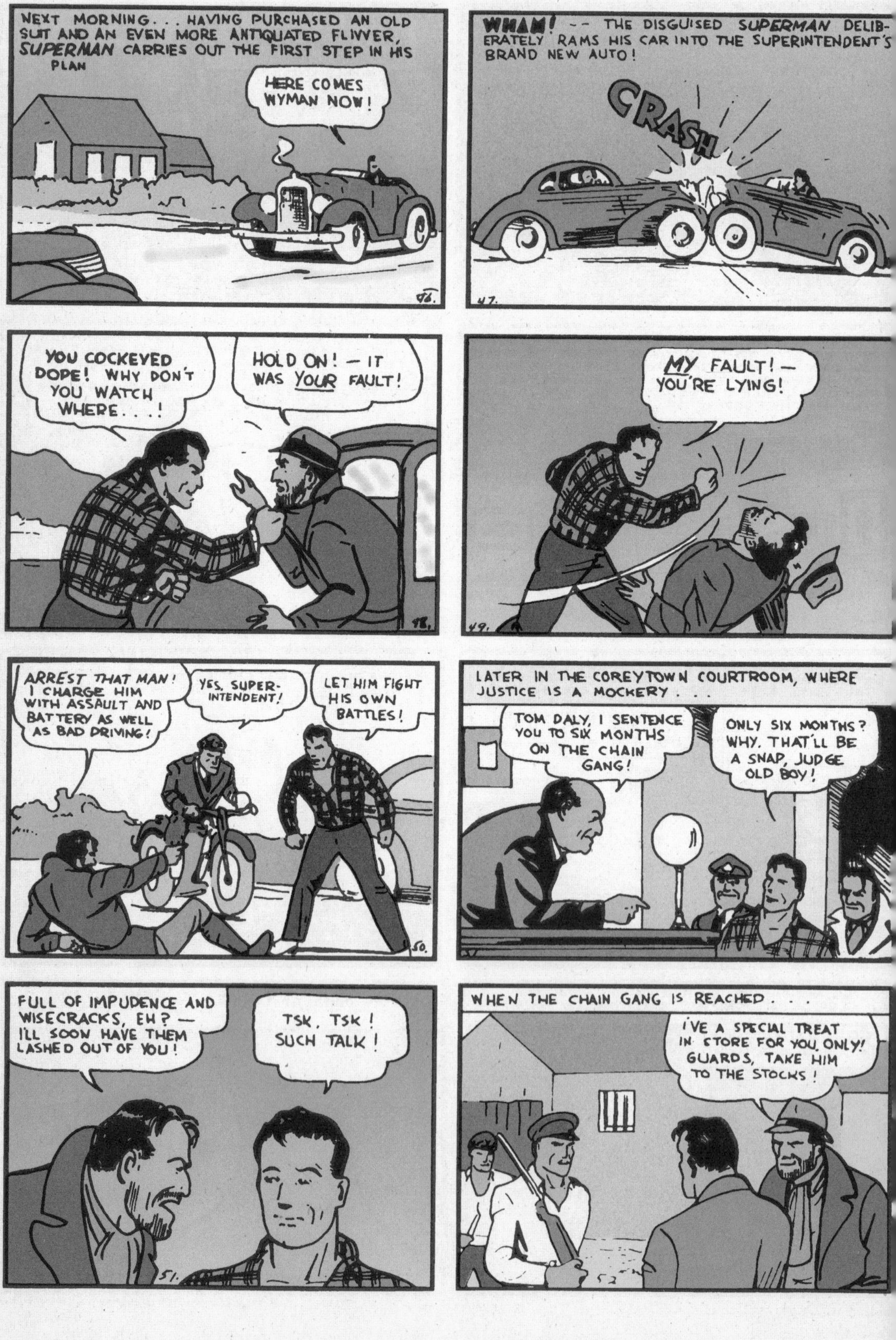
NEXT MORNING. . . HAVING PURCHASED AN OLD SUIT AND AN EVEN MORE ANTIQUATED FLIVVER, SUPERMAN CARRIES OUT THE FIRST STEP IN HIS PLAN
HERE COMES WYMAN NOW!
WHAM! -- THE DISGUISED SUPERMAN DELIBERATELY RAMS HIS CAR INTO THE SUPERINTENDENT'S BRAND NEW AUTO!
CRASH
YOU COCKEYED DOPE! WHY DON'T YOU WATCH WHERE. . .!
HOLD ON! — IT WAS YOUR FAULT!
MY FAULT! — YOU'RE LYING!
ARREST THAT MAN! I CHARGE HIM WITH ASSAULT AND BATTERY AS WELL AS BAD DRIVING!
YES, SUPER-INTENDENT!
LET HIM FIGHT HIS OWN BATTLES!
LATER IN THE COREYTOWN COURTROOM, WHERE JUSTICE IS A MOCKERY . . .
TOM DALY, I SENTENCE YOU TO SIX MONTHS ON THE CHAIN GANG!
ONLY SIX MONTHS? WHY, THAT'LL BE A SNAP, JUDGE OLD BOY!
FULL OF IMPUDENCE AND WISECRACKS, EH? — I'LL SOON HAVE THEM LASHED OUT OF YOU!
TSK, TSK! SUCH TALK!
WHEN THE CHAIN GANG IS REACHED . . .
I'VE A SPECIAL TREAT IN STORE FOR YOU, ONLY! GUARDS, TAKE HIM TO THE STOCKS!

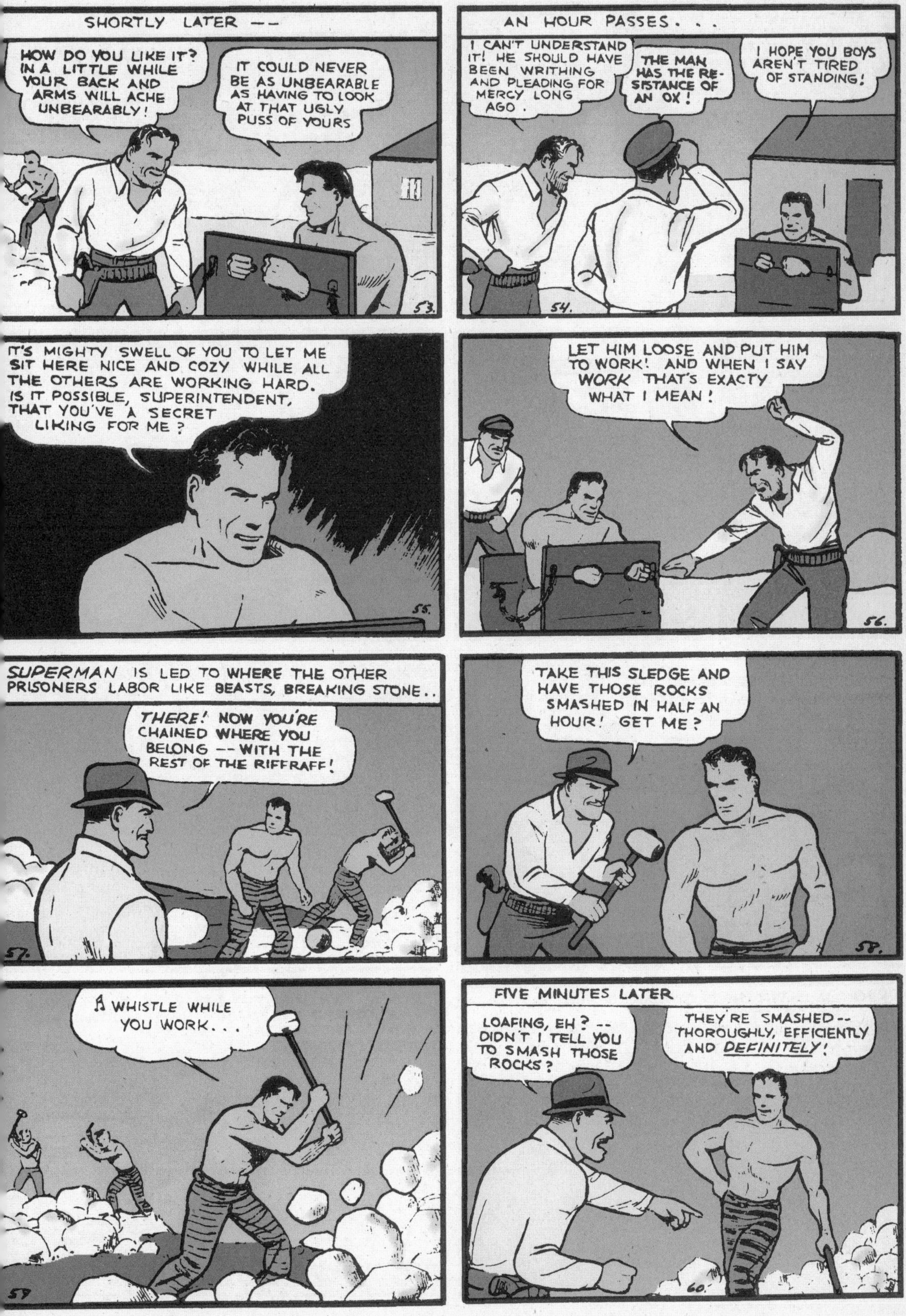
SHORTLY LATER --
HOW DO YOU LIKE IT? IN A LITTLE WHILE YOUR BACK AND ARMS WILL ACHE UNBEARABLY!
IT COULD NEVER BE AS UNBEARABLE AS HAVING TO LOOK AT THAT UGLY PUSS OF YOURS
AN HOUR PASSES. . .
I CAN'T UNDERSTAND IT! HE SHOULD HAVE BEEN WRITHING AND PLEADING FOR MERCY LONG AGO.
THE MAN HAS THE RE-SISTANCE OF AN OX!
I HOPE YOU BOYS AREN'T TIRED OF STANDING!
IT'S MIGHTY SWELL OF YOU TO LET ME SIT HERE NICE AND COZY WHILE ALL THE OTHERS ARE WORKING HARD. IS IT POSSIBLE, SUPERINTENDENT, THAT YOU'VE A SECRET LIKING FOR ME?
LET HIM LOOSE AND PUT HIM TO WORK! AND WHEN I SAY WORK THAT'S EXACTY WHAT I MEAN!
SUPERMAN IS LED TO WHERE THE OTHER PRISONERS LABOR LIKE BEASTS, BREAKING STONE..
THERE! NOW YOU'RE CHAINED WHERE YOU BELONG -- WITH THE REST OF THE RIFFRAFF!
TAKE THIS SLEDGE AND HAVE THOSE ROCKS SMASHED IN HALF AN HOUR! GET ME?
♫ WHISTLE WHILE YOU WORK. . .
FIVE MINUTES LATER
LOAFING, EH? -- DIDN'T I TELL YOU TO SMASH THOSE ROCKS?
THEY'RE SMASHED -- THOROUGHLY, EFFICIENTLY AND DEFINITELY!

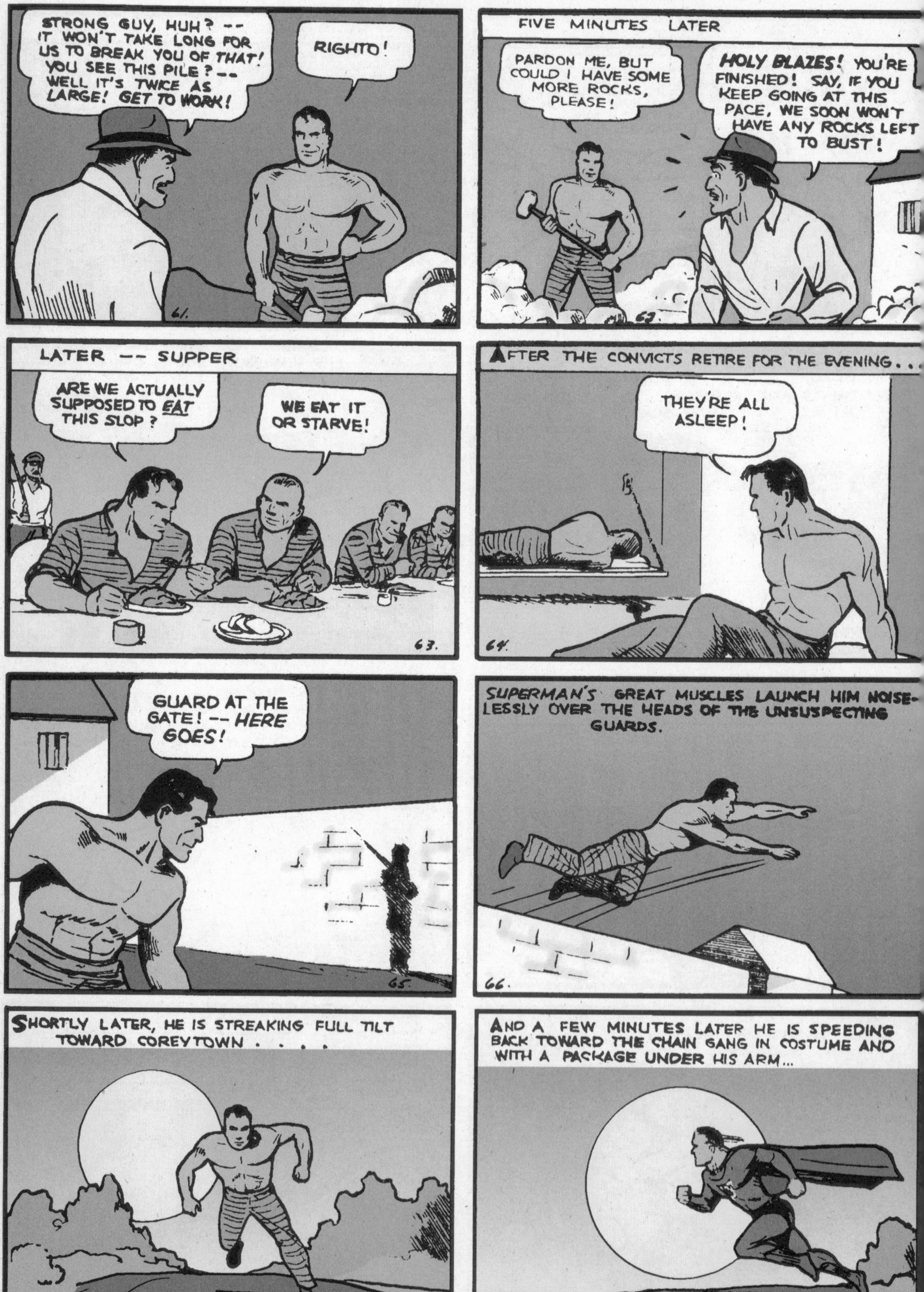

STRONG GUY, HUH? -- IT WON'T TAKE LONG FOR US TO BREAK YOU OF THAT! YOU SEE THIS PILE? -- WELL IT'S TWICE AS LARGE! GET TO WORK!
RIGHTO!
61.
FIVE MINUTES LATER
PARDON ME, BUT COULD I HAVE SOME MORE ROCKS, PLEASE!
HOLY BLAZES! YOU'RE FINISHED! SAY, IF YOU KEEP GOING AT THIS PACE, WE SOON WON'T HAVE ANY ROCKS LEFT TO BUST!
62.
LATER -- SUPPER
ARE WE ACTUALLY SUPPOSED TO EAT THIS SLOP?
WE EAT IT OR STARVE!
63.
AFTER THE CONVICTS RETIRE FOR THE EVENING...
THEY'RE ALL ASLEEP!
64.
GUARD AT THE GATE! -- HERE GOES!
65.
SUPERMAN'S GREAT MUSCLES LAUNCH HIM NOISELESSLY OVER THE HEADS OF THE UNSUSPECTING GUARDS.
66.
SHORTLY LATER, HE IS STREAKING FULL TILT TOWARD COREYTOWN . . . .
67.
AND A FEW MINUTES LATER HE IS SPEEDING BACK TOWARD THE CHAIN GANG IN COSTUME AND WITH A PACKAGE UNDER HIS ARM...
68.

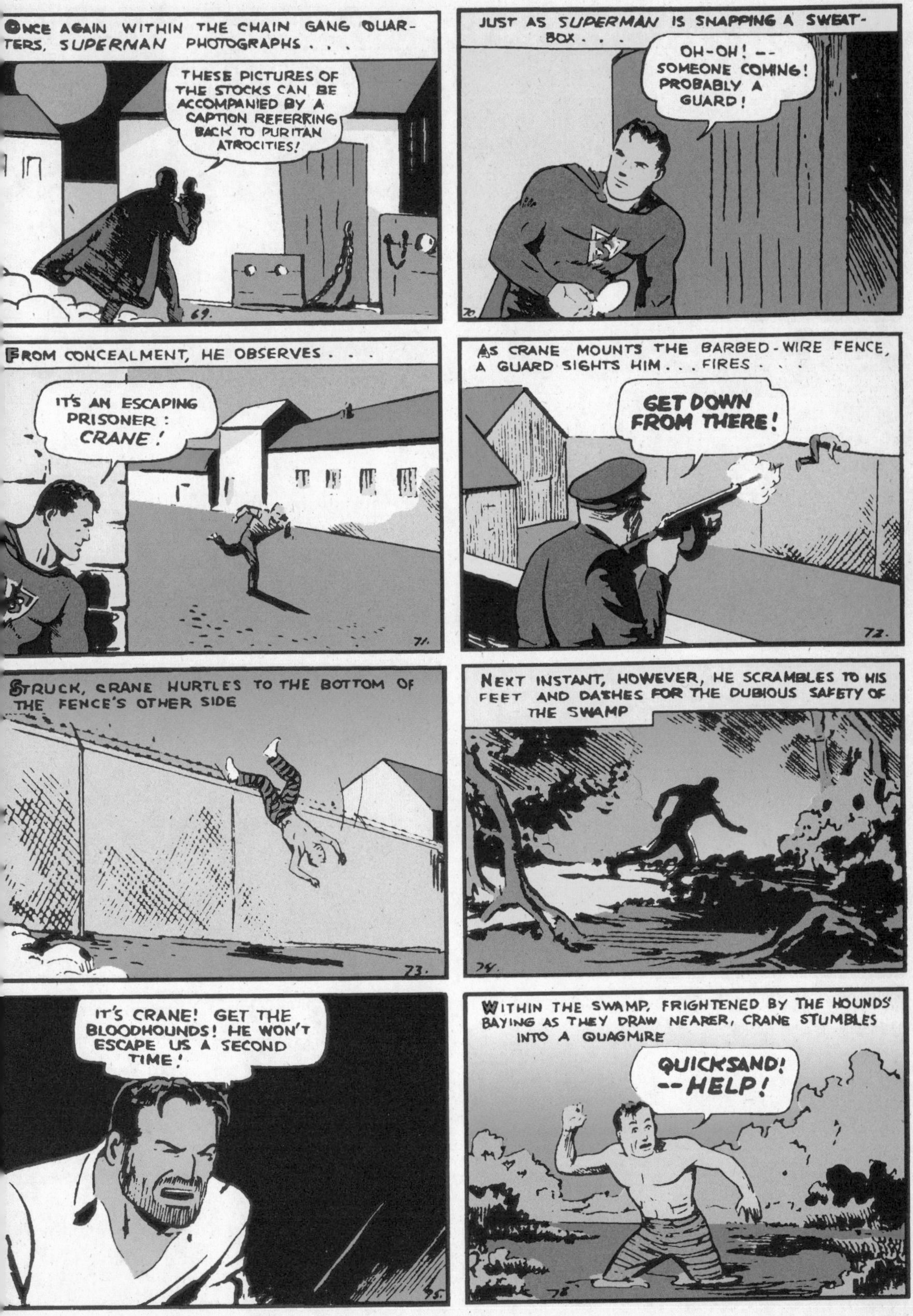

ONCE AGAIN WITHIN THE CHAIN GANG QUARTERS, SUPERMAN PHOTOGRAPHS . . .
THESE PICTURES OF THE STOCKS CAN BE ACCOMPANIED BY A CAPTION REFERRING BACK TO PURITAN ATROCITIES!
69.
JUST AS SUPERMAN IS SNAPPING A SWEAT-BOX . . .
OH-OH! -- SOMEONE COMING! PROBABLY A GUARD!
70.
FROM CONCEALMENT, HE OBSERVES . . .
IT'S AN ESCAPING PRISONER : CRANE!
71.
AS CRANE MOUNTS THE BARBED-WIRE FENCE, A GUARD SIGHTS HIM . . . FIRES . . .
GET DOWN FROM THERE!
72.
STRUCK, CRANE HURTLES TO THE BOTTOM OF THE FENCE'S OTHER SIDE
73.
NEXT INSTANT, HOWEVER, HE SCRAMBLES TO HIS FEET AND DASHES FOR THE DUBIOUS SAFETY OF THE SWAMP
74.
IT'S CRANE! GET THE BLOODHOUNDS! HE WON'T ESCAPE US A SECOND TIME!
75.
WITHIN THE SWAMP, FRIGHTENED BY THE HOUNDS' BAYING AS THEY DRAW NEARER, CRANE STUMBLES INTO A QUAGMIRE
QUICKSAND! --HELP!
76.

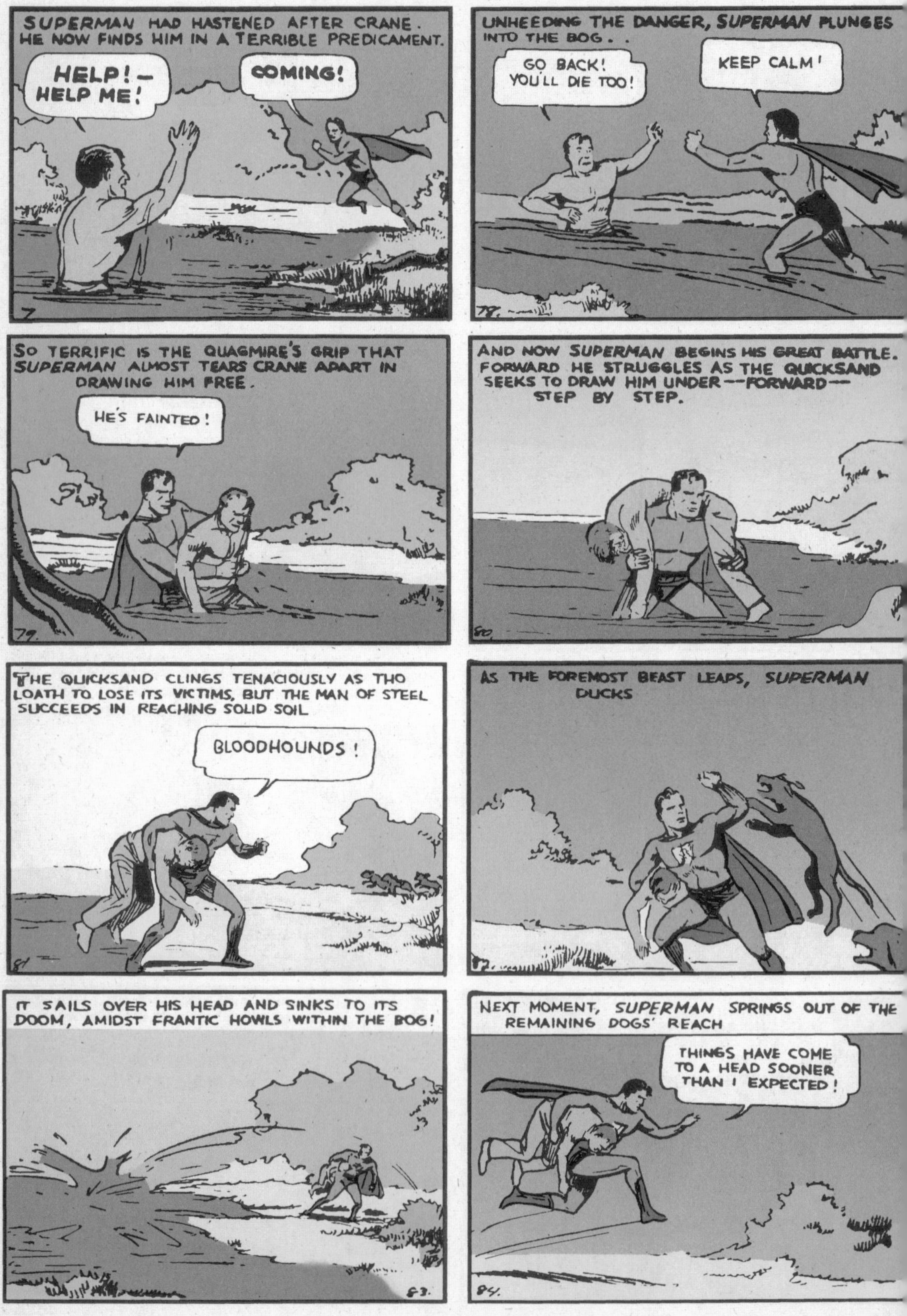
SUPERMAN HAD HASTENED AFTER CRANE. HE NOW FINDS HIM IN A TERRIBLE PREDICAMENT.
HELP!— HELP ME!
COMING!
UNHEEDING THE DANGER, SUPERMAN PLUNGES INTO THE BOG. .
GO BACK! YOU'LL DIE TOO!
KEEP CALM!
SO TERRIFIC IS THE QUAGMIRE'S GRIP THAT SUPERMAN ALMOST TEARS CRANE APART IN DRAWING HIM FREE.
HE'S FAINTED!
AND NOW SUPERMAN BEGINS HIS GREAT BATTLE. FORWARD HE STRUGGLES AS THE QUICKSAND SEEKS TO DRAW HIM UNDER--FORWARD-- STEP BY STEP.
THE QUICKSAND CLINGS TENACIOUSLY AS THO LOATH TO LOSE ITS VICTIMS, BUT THE MAN OF STEEL SUCCEEDS IN REACHING SOLID SOIL
BLOODHOUNDS!
AS THE FOREMOST BEAST LEAPS, SUPERMAN DUCKS
IT SAILS OVER HIS HEAD AND SINKS TO ITS DOOM, AMIDST FRANTIC HOWLS WITHIN THE BOG!
NEXT MOMENT, SUPERMAN SPRINGS OUT OF THE REMAINING DOGS' REACH
THINGS HAVE COME TO A HEAD SOONER THAN I EXPECTED!

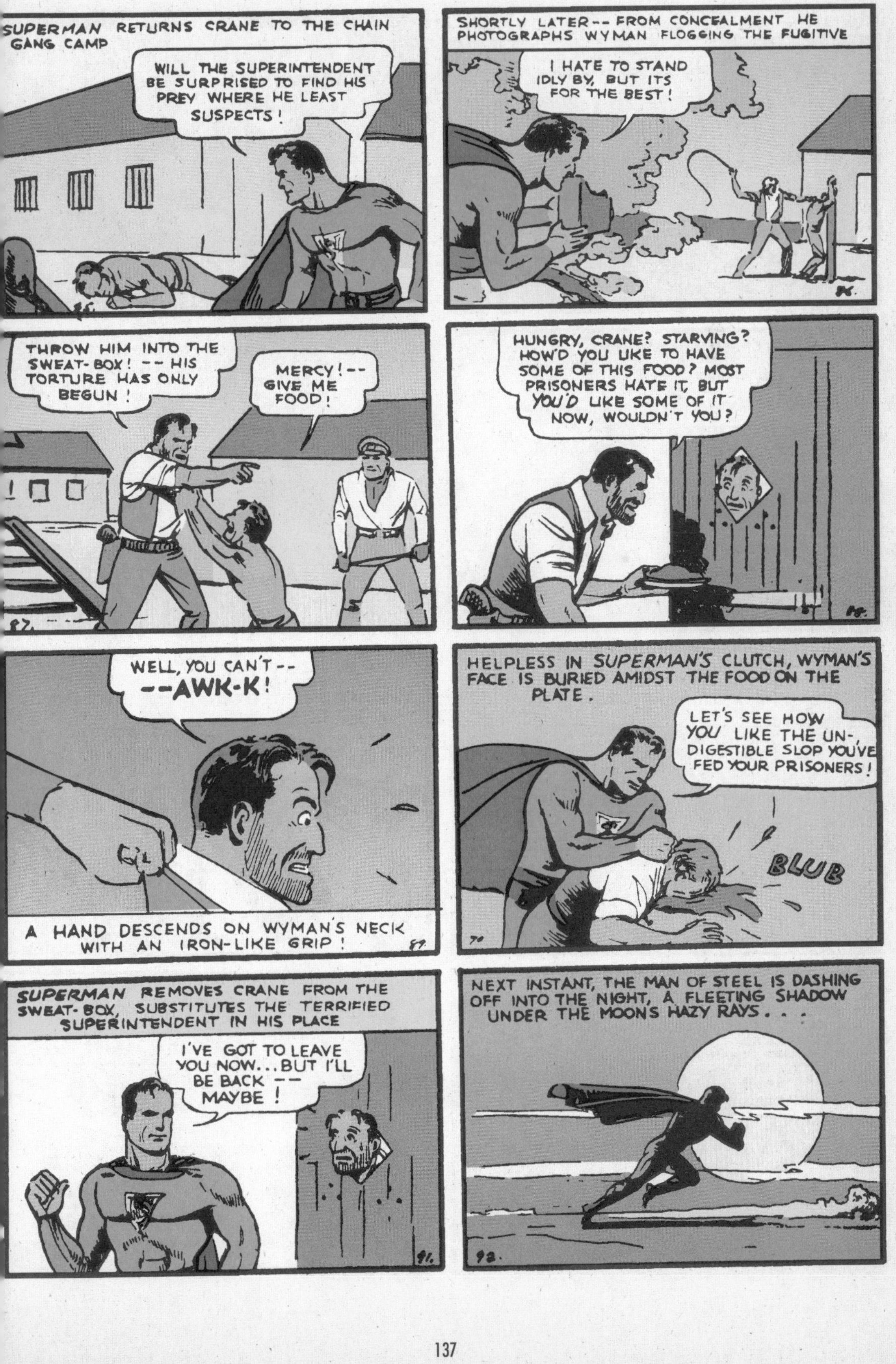
SUPERMAN RETURNS CRANE TO THE CHAIN GANG CAMP
WILL THE SUPERINTENDENT BE SURPRISED TO FIND HIS PREY WHERE HE LEAST SUSPECTS!
SHORTLY LATER-- FROM CONCEALMENT HE PHOTOGRAPHS WYMAN FLOGGING THE FUGITIVE
I HATE TO STAND IDLY BY, BUT ITS FOR THE BEST!
THROW HIM INTO THE SWEAT-BOX! -- HIS TORTURE HAS ONLY BEGUN!
MERCY!-- GIVE ME FOOD!
HUNGRY, CRANE? STARVING? HOW'D YOU LIKE TO HAVE SOME OF THIS FOOD? MOST PRISONERS HATE IT, BUT YOU'D LIKE SOME OF IT NOW, WOULDN'T YOU?
WELL, YOU CAN'T -- --AWK-K!
A HAND DESCENDS ON WYMAN'S NECK WITH AN IRON-LIKE GRIP!
HELPLESS IN SUPERMAN'S CLUTCH, WYMAN'S FACE IS BURIED AMIDST THE FOOD ON THE PLATE.
LET'S SEE HOW YOU LIKE THE UN-DIGESTIBLE SLOP YOU'VE FED YOUR PRISONERS!
BLUB
SUPERMAN REMOVES CRANE FROM THE SWEAT-BOX, SUBSTITUTES THE TERRIFIED SUPERINTENDENT IN HIS PLACE
I'VE GOT TO LEAVE YOU NOW... BUT I'LL BE BACK -- MAYBE!
NEXT INSTANT, THE MAN OF STEEL IS DASHING OFF INTO THE NIGHT, A FLEETING SHADOW UNDER THE MOON'S HAZY RAYS...

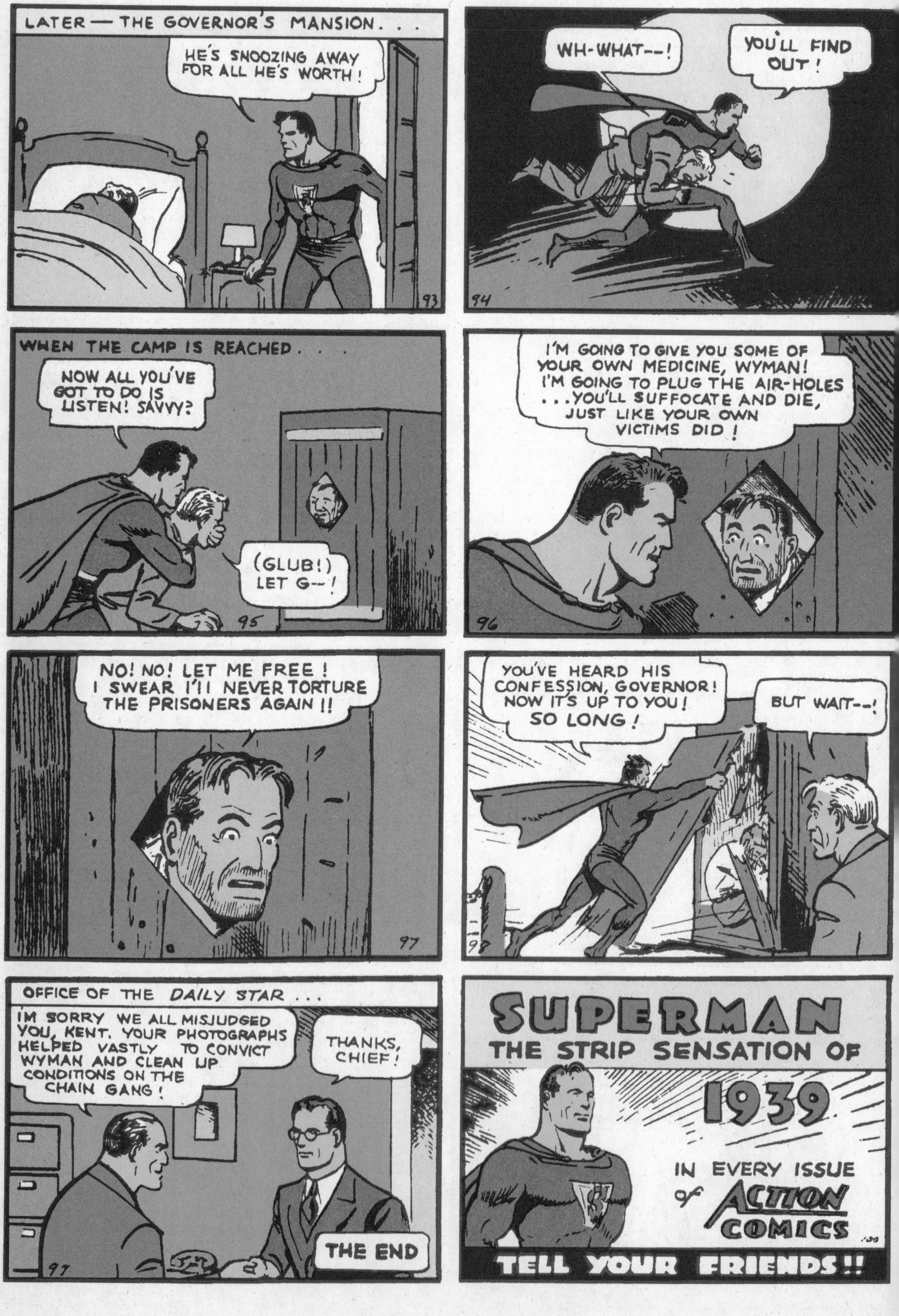

LATER — THE GOVERNOR'S MANSION. . .
HE'S SNOOZING AWAY FOR ALL HE'S WORTH!
93
WH-WHAT--!
YOU'LL FIND OUT!
94
WHEN THE CAMP IS REACHED. . .
NOW ALL YOU'VE GOT TO DO IS LISTEN! SAVVY?
(GLUB!) LET G--!
95
I'M GOING TO GIVE YOU SOME OF YOUR OWN MEDICINE, WYMAN! I'M GOING TO PLUG THE AIR-HOLES . . .YOU'LL SUFFOCATE AND DIE, JUST LIKE YOUR OWN VICTIMS DID!
96
NO! NO! LET ME FREE! I SWEAR I'LL NEVER TORTURE THE PRISONERS AGAIN!!
97
YOU'VE HEARD HIS CONFESSION, GOVERNOR! NOW IT'S UP TO YOU! SO LONG!
BUT WAIT--!
98
OFFICE OF THE DAILY STAR . . .
IM SORRY WE ALL MISJUDGED YOU, KENT. YOUR PHOTOGRAPHS HELPED VASTLY TO CONVICT WYMAN AND CLEAN UP CONDITIONS ON THE CHAIN GANG!
THANKS, CHIEF!
THE END
97
SUPERMAN
THE STRIP SENSATION OF
1939
IN EVERY ISSUE of ACTION COMICS
TELL YOUR FRIENDS!!

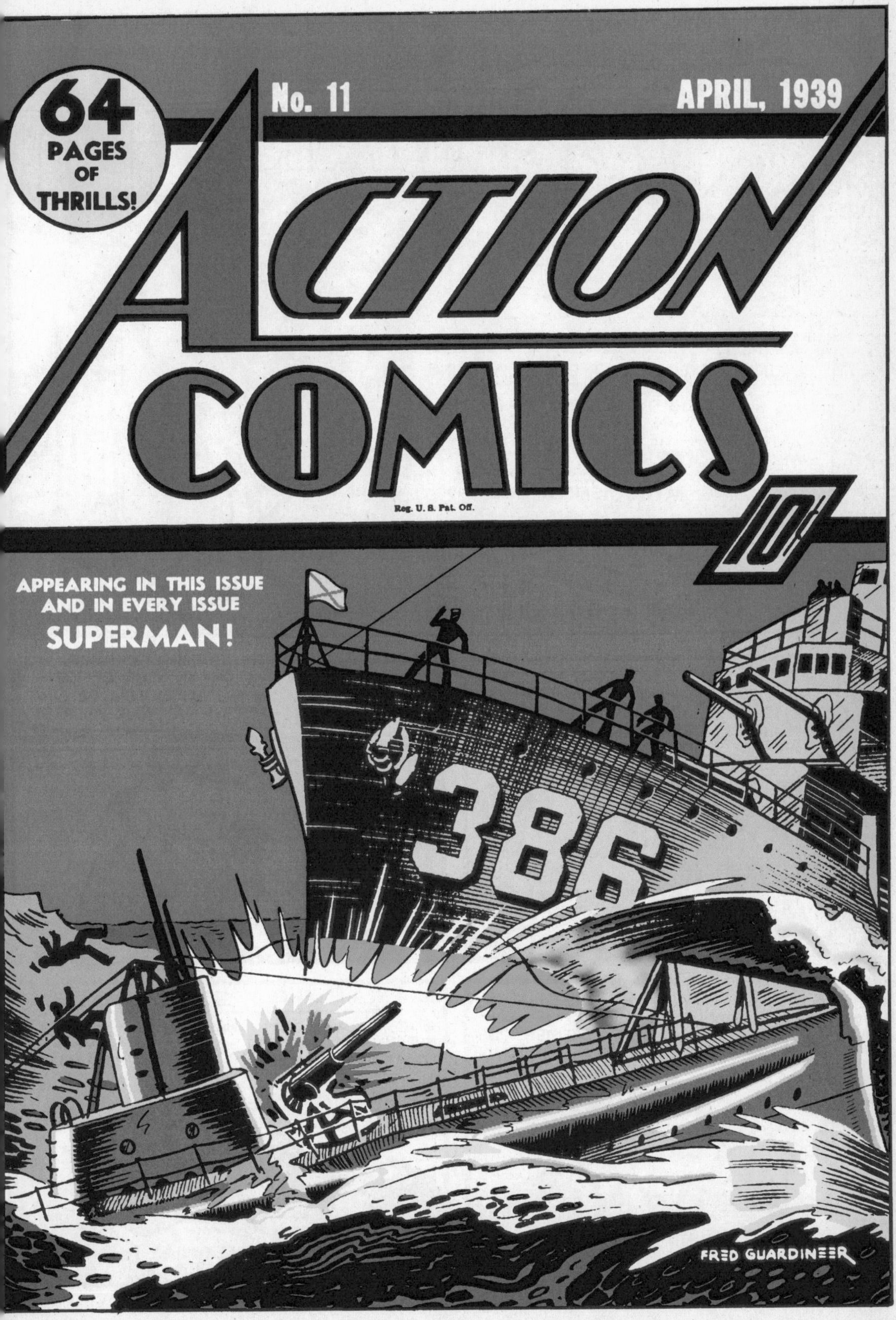
64 PAGES OF THRILLS!
No. 11
APRIL, 1939
ACTION COMICS
Reg. U. S. Pat. Off.
10¢
APPEARING IN THIS ISSUE AND IN EVERY ISSUE SUPERMAN!
386
FRED GUARDINEER

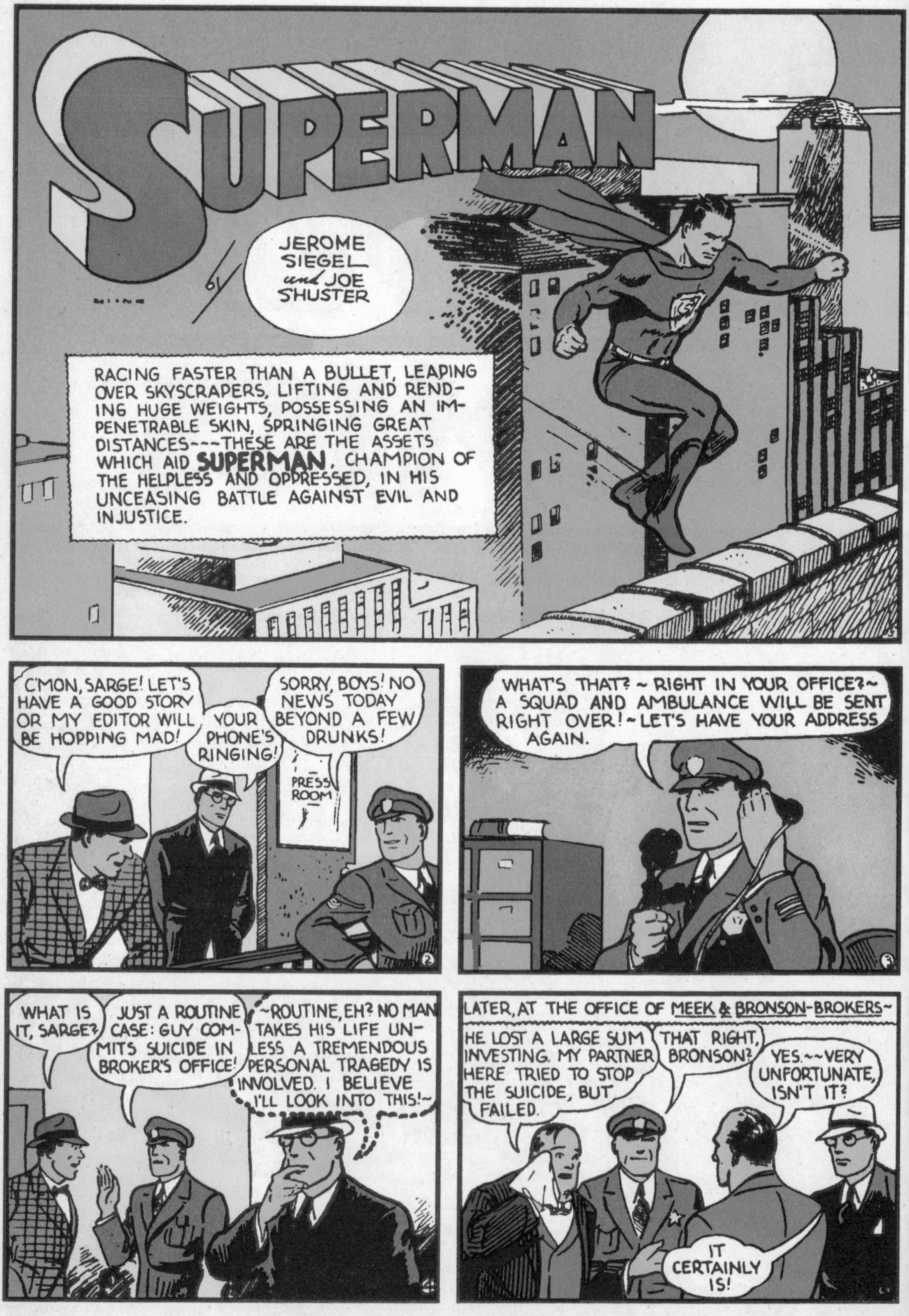

SUPERMAN
JEROME SIEGEL and JOE SHUSTER
RACING FASTER THAN A BULLET, LEAPING OVER SKYSCRAPERS, LIFTING AND RENDING HUGE WEIGHTS, POSSESSING AN IMPENETRABLE SKIN, SPRINGING GREAT DISTANCES---THESE ARE THE ASSETS WHICH AID SUPERMAN, CHAMPION OF THE HELPLESS AND OPPRESSED, IN HIS UNCEASING BATTLE AGAINST EVIL AND INJUSTICE.
C'MON, SARGE! LET'S HAVE A GOOD STORY OR MY EDITOR WILL BE HOPPING MAD!
YOUR PHONE'S RINGING!
SORRY, BOYS! NO NEWS TODAY BEYOND A FEW DRUNKS!
PRESS ROOM
WHAT'S THAT? ~ RIGHT IN YOUR OFFICE?~ A SQUAD AND AMBULANCE WILL BE SENT RIGHT OVER! ~ LET'S HAVE YOUR ADDRESS AGAIN.
WHAT IS IT, SARGE?
JUST A ROUTINE CASE: GUY COMMITS SUICIDE IN BROKER'S OFFICE!
~ROUTINE, EH? NO MAN TAKES HIS LIFE UNLESS A TREMENDOUS PERSONAL TRAGEDY IS INVOLVED. I BELIEVE I'LL LOOK INTO THIS!~
LATER, AT THE OFFICE OF MEEK & BRONSON-BROKERS~
HE LOST A LARGE SUM INVESTING. MY PARTNER HERE TRIED TO STOP THE SUICIDE, BUT FAILED.
THAT RIGHT, BRONSON?
YES.~~VERY UNFORTUNATE, ISN'T IT?
IT CERTAINLY IS!

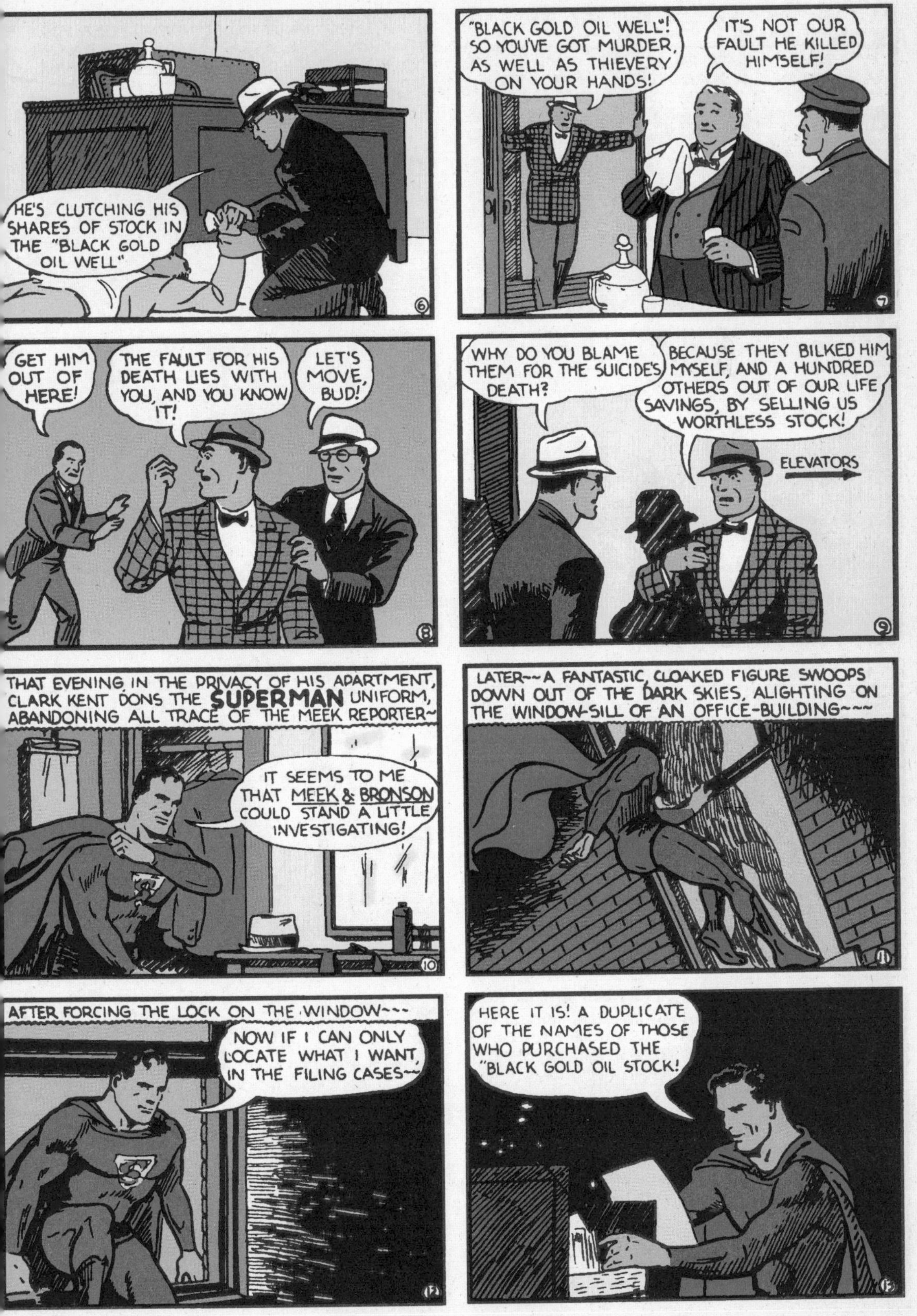
HE'S CLUTCHING HIS SHARES OF STOCK IN THE "BLACK GOLD OIL WELL"
"BLACK GOLD OIL WELL"! SO YOU'VE GOT MURDER, AS WELL AS THIEVERY ON YOUR HANDS!
IT'S NOT OUR FAULT HE KILLED HIMSELF!
GET HIM OUT OF HERE!
THE FAULT FOR HIS DEATH LIES WITH YOU, AND YOU KNOW IT!
LET'S MOVE, BUD!
WHY DO YOU BLAME THEM FOR THE SUICIDE'S DEATH?
BECAUSE THEY BILKED HIM, MYSELF, AND A HUNDRED OTHERS OUT OF OUR LIFE SAVINGS, BY SELLING US WORTHLESS STOCK!
ELEVATORS
THAT EVENING IN THE PRIVACY OF HIS APARTMENT, CLARK KENT DONS THE SUPERMAN UNIFORM, ABANDONING ALL TRACE OF THE MEEK REPORTER~
IT SEEMS TO ME THAT MEEK & BRONSON COULD STAND A LITTLE INVESTIGATING!
LATER~~A FANTASTIC, CLOAKED FIGURE SWOOPS DOWN OUT OF THE DARK SKIES, ALIGHTING ON THE WINDOW-SILL OF AN OFFICE-BUILDING~~~
AFTER FORCING THE LOCK ON THE WINDOW~~~
NOW IF I CAN ONLY LOCATE WHAT I WANT, IN THE FILING CASES~~
HERE IT IS! A DUPLICATE OF THE NAMES OF THOSE WHO PURCHASED THE "BLACK GOLD OIL STOCK!

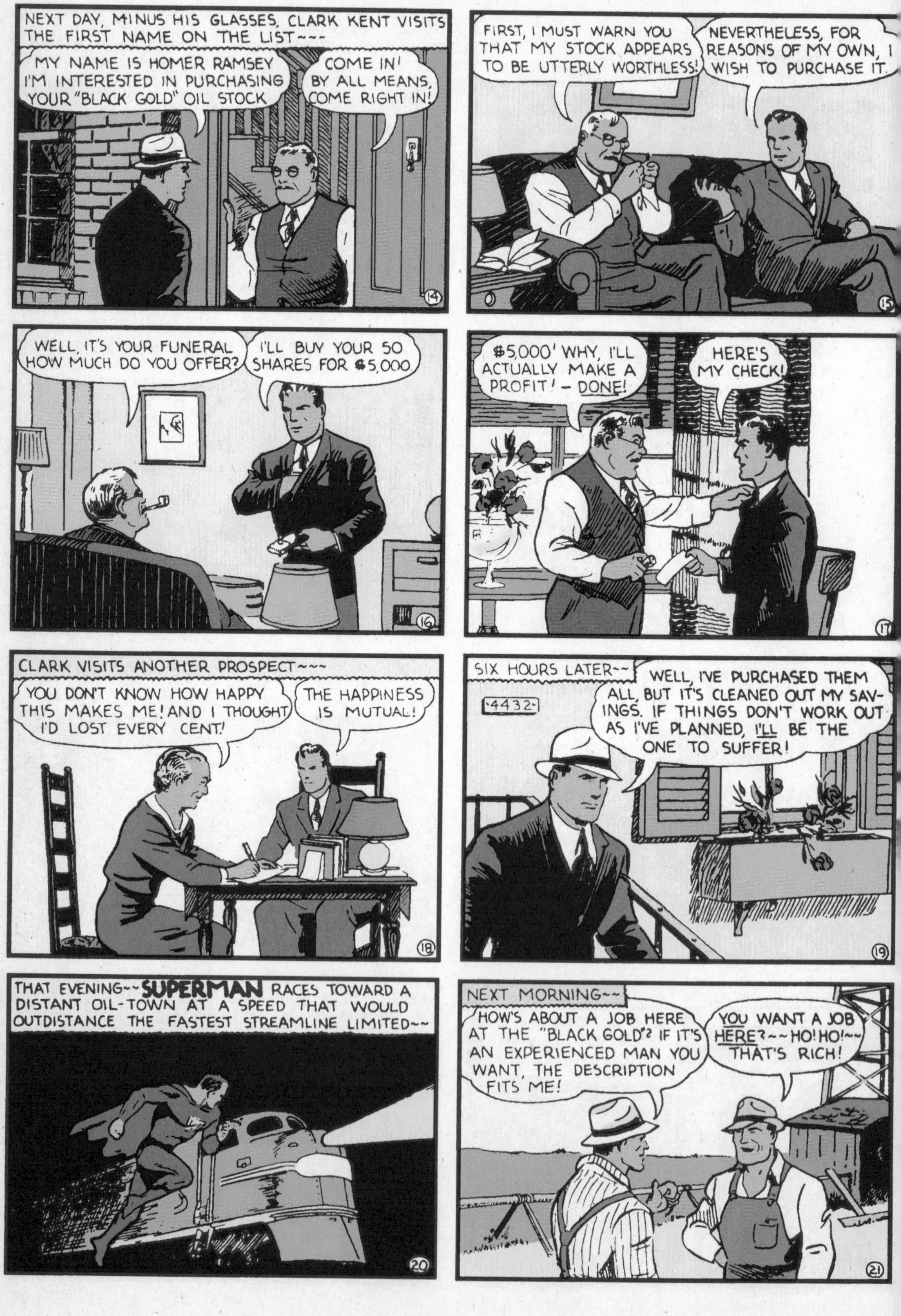
NEXT DAY, MINUS HIS GLASSES, CLARK KENT VISITS THE FIRST NAME ON THE LIST---
MY NAME IS HOMER RAMSEY I'M INTERESTED IN PURCHASING YOUR "BLACK GOLD" OIL STOCK
COME IN! BY ALL MEANS, COME RIGHT IN!
14
FIRST, I MUST WARN YOU THAT MY STOCK APPEARS TO BE UTTERLY WORTHLESS!
NEVERTHELESS, FOR REASONS OF MY OWN, I WISH TO PURCHASE IT.
15
WELL, IT'S YOUR FUNERAL HOW MUCH DO YOU OFFER?
I'LL BUY YOUR 50 SHARES FOR $5,000
16
$5,000! WHY, I'LL ACTUALLY MAKE A PROFIT! - DONE!
HERE'S MY CHECK!
17
CLARK VISITS ANOTHER PROSPECT---
YOU DON'T KNOW HOW HAPPY THIS MAKES ME! AND I THOUGHT I'D LOST EVERY CENT!
THE HAPPINESS IS MUTUAL!
18
SIX HOURS LATER--
4432
WELL, I'VE PURCHASED THEM ALL, BUT IT'S CLEANED OUT MY SAVINGS. IF THINGS DON'T WORK OUT AS I'VE PLANNED, I'LL BE THE ONE TO SUFFER!
19
THAT EVENING--SUPERMAN RACES TOWARD A DISTANT OIL-TOWN AT A SPEED THAT WOULD OUTDISTANCE THE FASTEST STREAMLINE LIMITED--
20
NEXT MORNING--
HOW'S ABOUT A JOB HERE AT THE "BLACK GOLD"? IF IT'S AN EXPERIENCED MAN YOU WANT, THE DESCRIPTION FITS ME!
YOU WANT A JOB HERE?--HO! HO!-- THAT'S RICH!
21

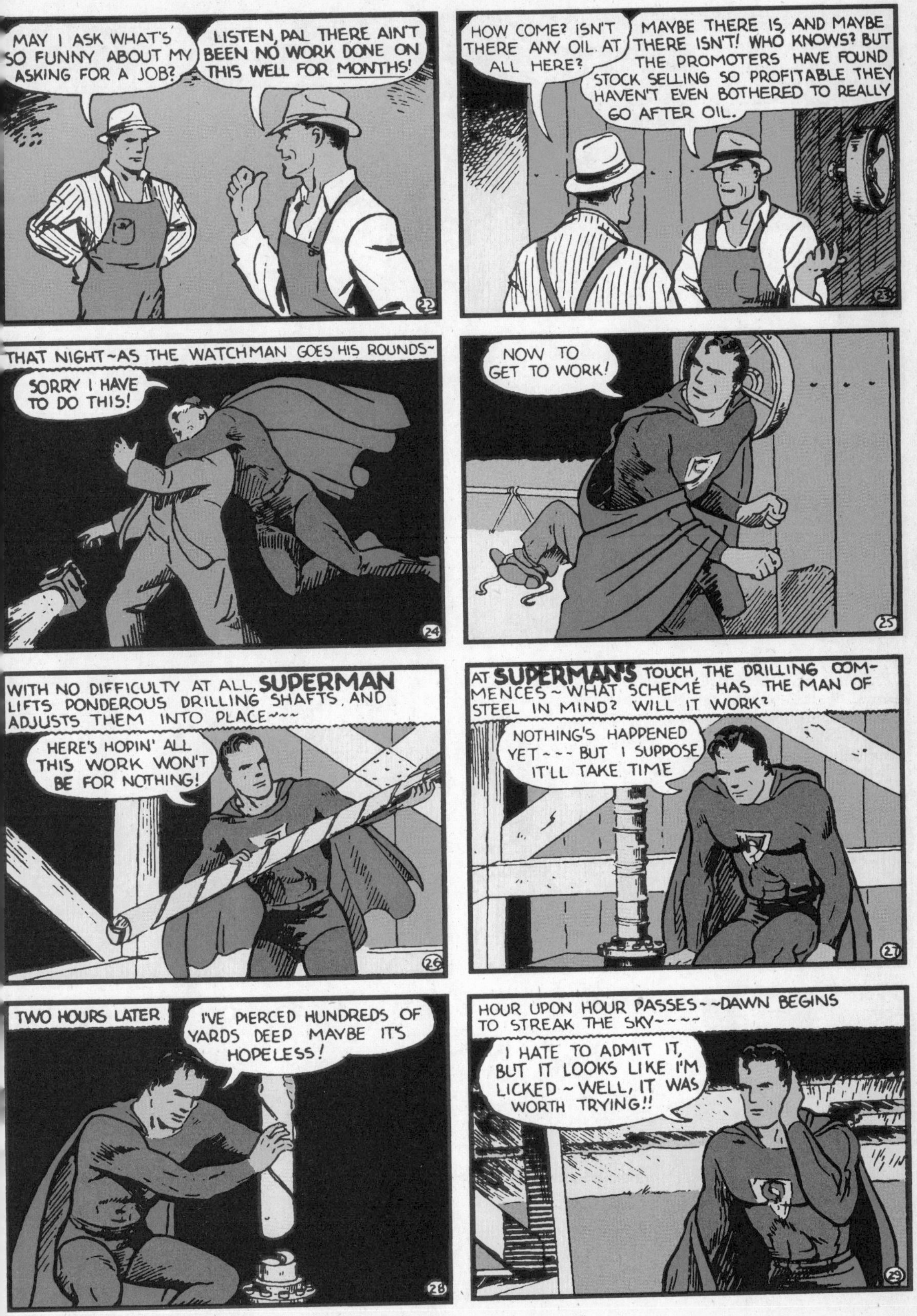

MAY I ASK WHAT'S SO FUNNY ABOUT MY ASKING FOR A JOB?
LISTEN, PAL THERE AIN'T BEEN NO WORK DONE ON THIS WELL FOR MONTHS!
22
HOW COME? ISN'T THERE ANY OIL AT ALL HERE?
MAYBE THERE IS, AND MAYBE THERE ISN'T! WHO KNOWS? BUT THE PROMOTERS HAVE FOUND STOCK SELLING SO PROFITABLE THEY HAVEN'T EVEN BOTHERED TO REALLY GO AFTER OIL.
23
THAT NIGHT~AS THE WATCHMAN GOES HIS ROUNDS~
SORRY I HAVE TO DO THIS!
24
NOW TO GET TO WORK!
25
WITH NO DIFFICULTY AT ALL, SUPERMAN LIFTS PONDEROUS DRILLING SHAFTS, AND ADJUSTS THEM INTO PLACE~~~
HERE'S HOPIN' ALL THIS WORK WON'T BE FOR NOTHING!
26
AT SUPERMAN'S TOUCH, THE DRILLING COMMENCES~WHAT SCHEME HAS THE MAN OF STEEL IN MIND? WILL IT WORK?
NOTHING'S HAPPENED YET~~~ BUT I SUPPOSE IT'LL TAKE TIME
27
TWO HOURS LATER
I'VE PIERCED HUNDREDS OF YARDS DEEP MAYBE IT'S HOPELESS!
28
HOUR UPON HOUR PASSES~~DAWN BEGINS TO STREAK THE SKY~~~~
I HATE TO ADMIT IT, BUT IT LOOKS LIKE I'M LICKED~WELL, IT WAS WORTH TRYING!!
29

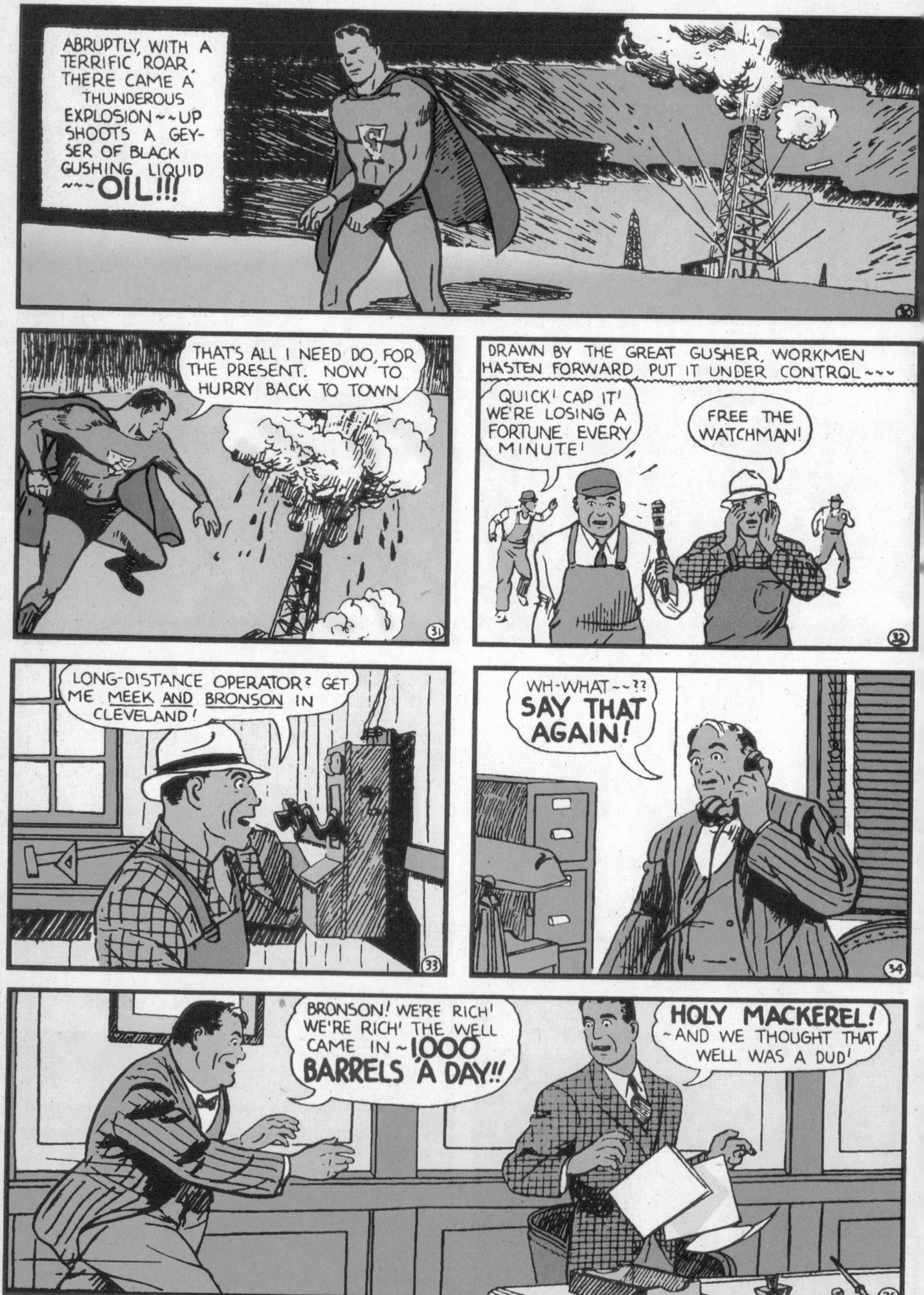
ABRUPTLY, WITH A TERRIFIC ROAR, THERE CAME A THUNDEROUS EXPLOSION~~UP SHOOTS A GEYSER OF BLACK GUSHING LIQUID ~~~OIL!!!
THAT'S ALL I NEED DO, FOR THE PRESENT. NOW TO HURRY BACK TO TOWN
DRAWN BY THE GREAT GUSHER, WORKMEN HASTEN FORWARD, PUT IT UNDER CONTROL~~~
QUICK! CAP IT! WE'RE LOSING A FORTUNE EVERY MINUTE!
FREE THE WATCHMAN!
LONG-DISTANCE OPERATOR? GET ME MEEK AND BRONSON IN CLEVELAND!
WH-WHAT~~?? SAY THAT AGAIN!
BRONSON! WE'RE RICH! WE'RE RICH! THE WELL CAME IN~1000 BARRELS A DAY!!
HOLY MACKEREL! ~AND WE THOUGHT THAT WELL WAS A DUD!

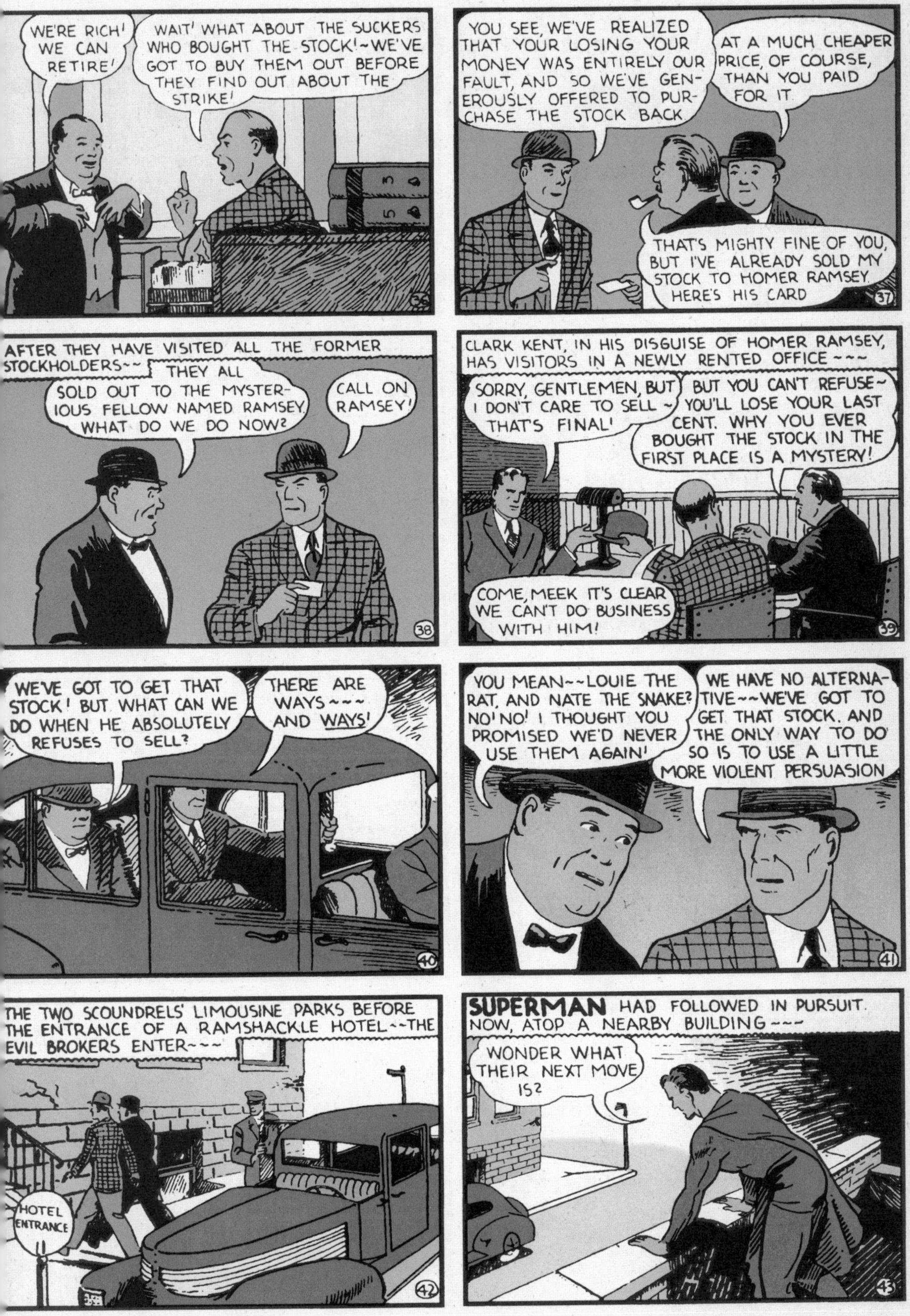
WE'RE RICH! WE CAN RETIRE!
WAIT! WHAT ABOUT THE SUCKERS WHO BOUGHT THE STOCK!~WE'VE GOT TO BUY THEM OUT BEFORE THEY FIND OUT ABOUT THE STRIKE!
36
YOU SEE, WE'VE REALIZED THAT YOUR LOSING YOUR MONEY WAS ENTIRELY OUR FAULT, AND SO WE'VE GENEROUSLY OFFERED TO PURCHASE THE STOCK BACK
AT A MUCH CHEAPER PRICE, OF COURSE, THAN YOU PAID FOR IT
THAT'S MIGHTY FINE OF YOU, BUT I'VE ALREADY SOLD MY STOCK TO HOMER RAMSEY. HERE'S HIS CARD
37
AFTER THEY HAVE VISITED ALL THE FORMER STOCKHOLDERS~~
THEY ALL SOLD OUT TO THE MYSTERIOUS FELLOW NAMED RAMSEY. WHAT DO WE DO NOW?
CALL ON RAMSEY!
38
CLARK KENT, IN HIS DISGUISE OF HOMER RAMSEY, HAS VISITORS IN A NEWLY RENTED OFFICE~~~
SORRY, GENTLEMEN, BUT I DON'T CARE TO SELL~ THAT'S FINAL!
BUT YOU CAN'T REFUSE~ YOU'LL LOSE YOUR LAST CENT. WHY YOU EVER BOUGHT THE STOCK IN THE FIRST PLACE IS A MYSTERY!
COME, MEEK IT'S CLEAR WE CAN'T DO BUSINESS WITH HIM!
39
WE'VE GOT TO GET THAT STOCK! BUT WHAT CAN WE DO WHEN HE ABSOLUTELY REFUSES TO SELL?
THERE ARE WAYS~~~ AND WAYS!
40
YOU MEAN~~LOUIE THE RAT, AND NATE THE SNAKE? NO! NO! I THOUGHT YOU PROMISED WE'D NEVER USE THEM AGAIN!
WE HAVE NO ALTERNATIVE~~WE'VE GOT TO GET THAT STOCK. AND THE ONLY WAY TO DO SO IS TO USE A LITTLE MORE VIOLENT PERSUASION
41
THE TWO SCOUNDRELS' LIMOUSINE PARKS BEFORE THE ENTRANCE OF A RAMSHACKLE HOTEL~~THE EVIL BROKERS ENTER~~~
HOTEL ENTRANCE
42
SUPERMAN HAD FOLLOWED IN PURSUIT. NOW, ATOP A NEARBY BUILDING~~~
WONDER WHAT THEIR NEXT MOVE IS?
43

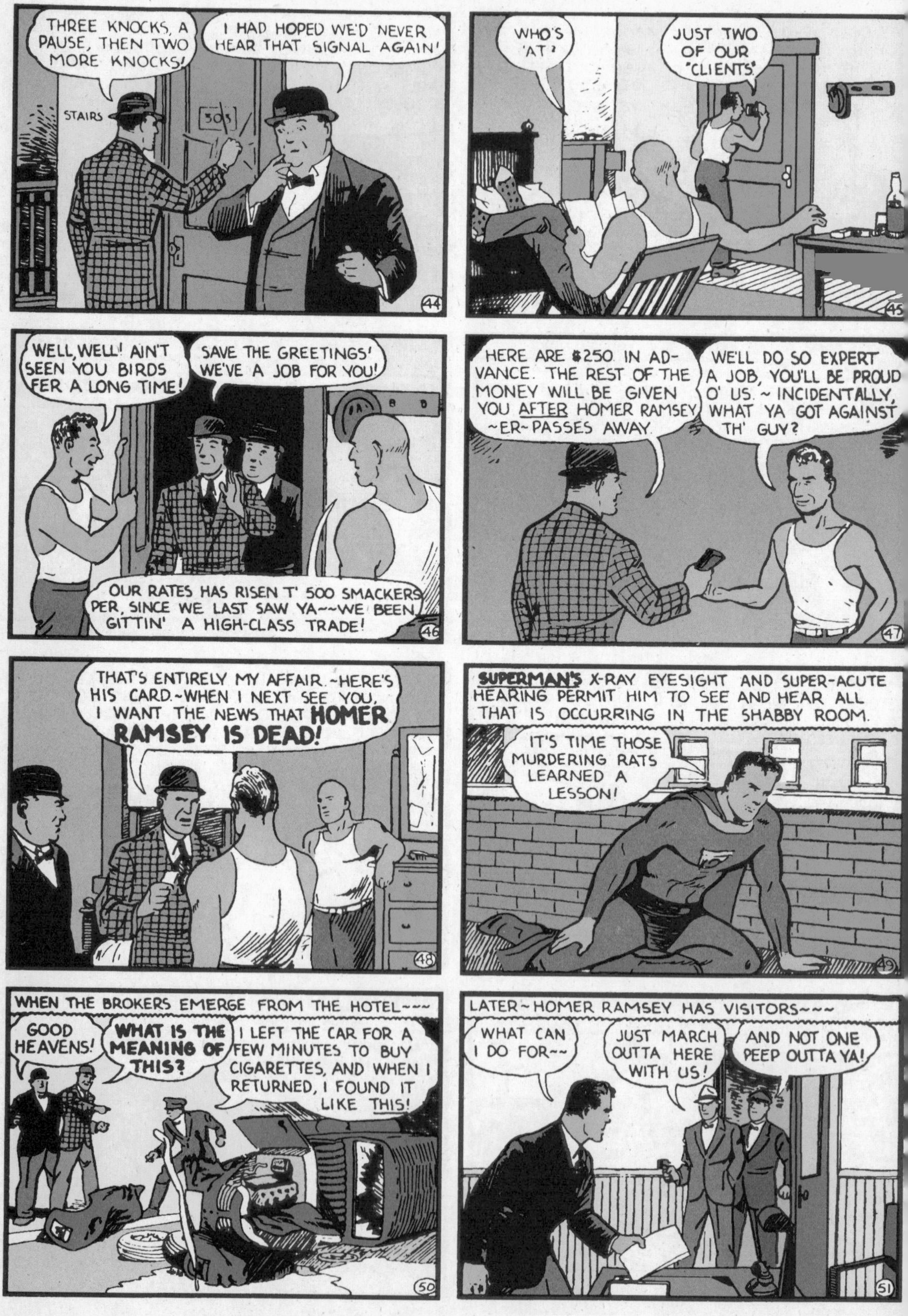
THREE KNOCKS, A PAUSE, THEN TWO MORE KNOCKS!
I HAD HOPED WE'D NEVER HEAR THAT SIGNAL AGAIN!
STAIRS
303
WHO'S 'AT?
JUST TWO OF OUR "CLIENTS"
WELL, WELL! AIN'T SEEN YOU BIRDS FER A LONG TIME!
SAVE THE GREETINGS! WE'VE A JOB FOR YOU!
OUR RATES HAS RISEN T' 500 SMACKERS PER, SINCE WE LAST SAW YA--WE BEEN GITTIN' A HIGH-CLASS TRADE!
HERE ARE $250 IN ADVANCE. THE REST OF THE MONEY WILL BE GIVEN YOU AFTER HOMER RAMSEY ~ER~ PASSES AWAY.
WE'LL DO SO EXPERT A JOB, YOU'LL BE PROUD O' US. ~ INCIDENTALLY, WHAT YA GOT AGAINST TH' GUY?
THAT'S ENTIRELY MY AFFAIR. ~HERE'S HIS CARD. ~WHEN I NEXT SEE YOU, I WANT THE NEWS THAT HOMER RAMSEY IS DEAD!
SUPERMAN'S X-RAY EYESIGHT AND SUPER-ACUTE HEARING PERMIT HIM TO SEE AND HEAR ALL THAT IS OCCURRING IN THE SHABBY ROOM.
IT'S TIME THOSE MURDERING RATS LEARNED A LESSON!
WHEN THE BROKERS EMERGE FROM THE HOTEL---
GOOD HEAVENS!
WHAT IS THE MEANING OF THIS?
I LEFT THE CAR FOR A FEW MINUTES TO BUY CIGARETTES, AND WHEN I RETURNED, I FOUND IT LIKE THIS!
LATER~ HOMER RAMSEY HAS VISITORS---
WHAT CAN I DO FOR--
JUST MARCH OUTTA HERE WITH US!
AND NOT ONE PEEP OUTTA YA!

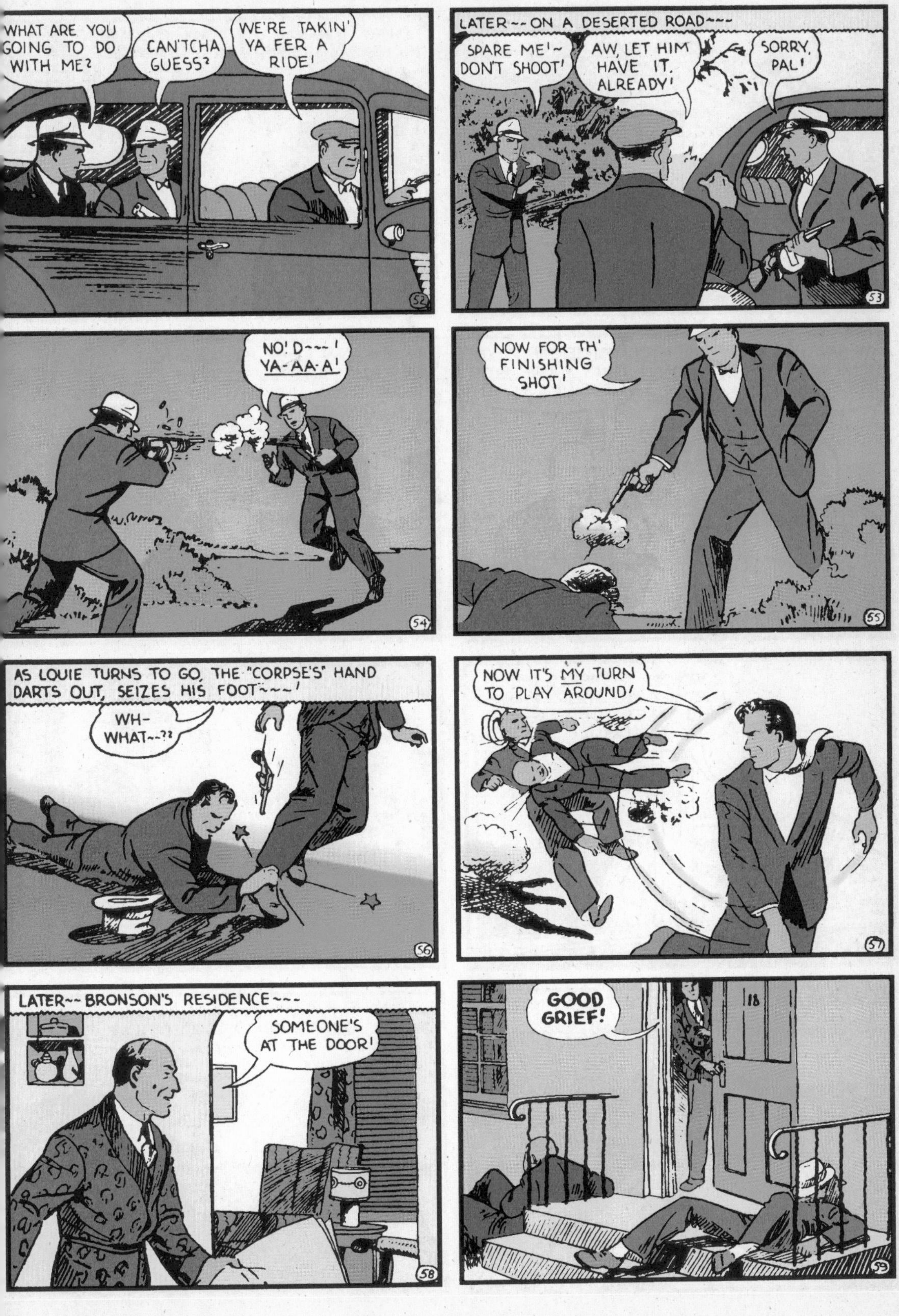
WHAT ARE YOU GOING TO DO WITH ME?
CAN'TCHA GUESS?
WE'RE TAKIN' YA FER A RIDE!
52
LATER--ON A DESERTED ROAD---
SPARE ME!-- DON'T SHOOT!
AW, LET HIM HAVE IT, ALREADY!
SORRY, PAL!
53
NO! D---! YA-AA-A!
54
NOW FOR TH' FINISHING SHOT!
55
AS LOUIE TURNS TO GO, THE "CORPSE'S" HAND DARTS OUT, SEIZES HIS FOOT---!
WH- WHAT--??
56
NOW IT'S MY TURN TO PLAY AROUND!
57
LATER--BRONSON'S RESIDENCE---
SOMEONE'S AT THE DOOR!
58
GOOD GRIEF!
18
59

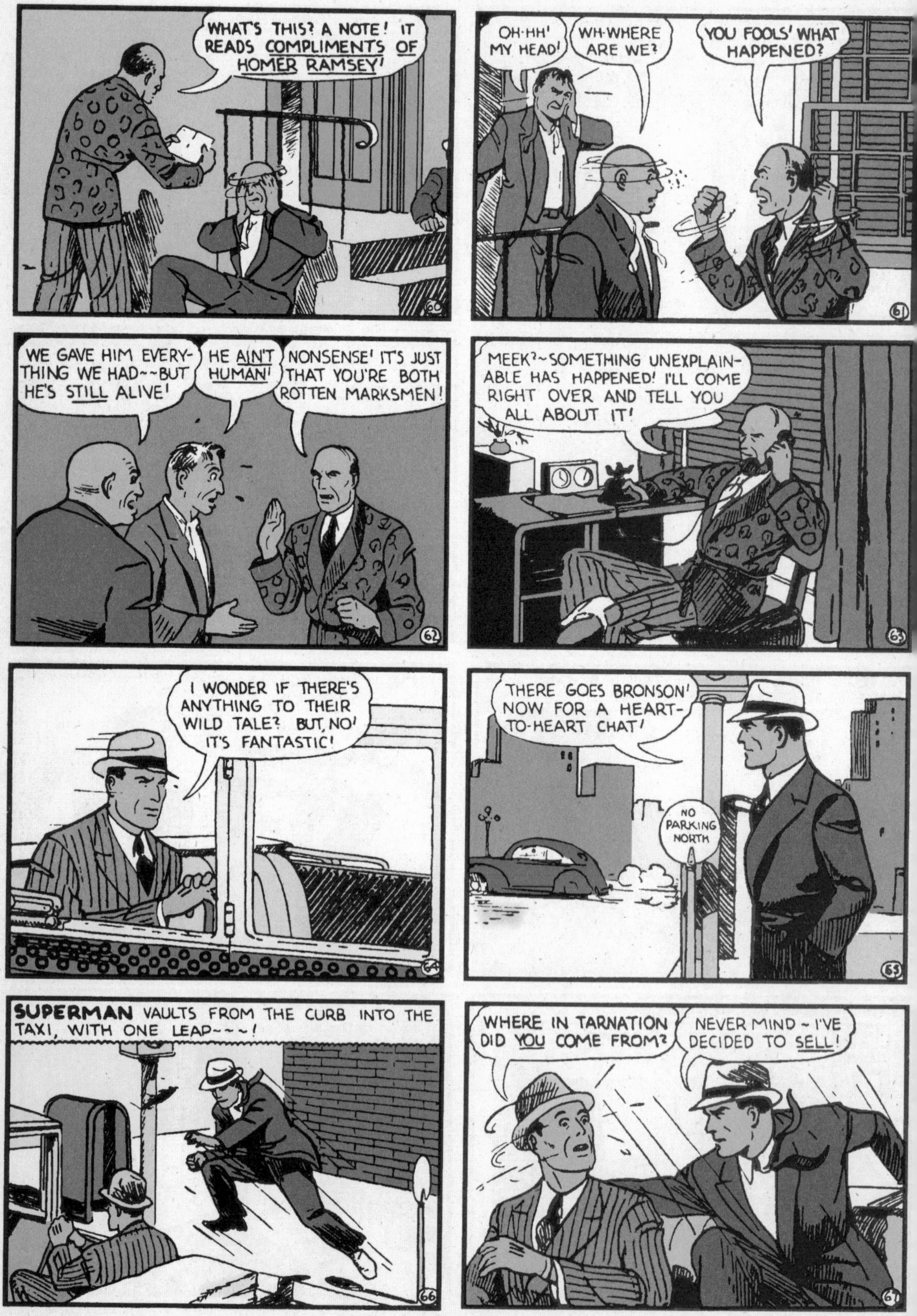
WHAT'S THIS? A NOTE! IT READS COMPLIMENTS OF HOMER RAMSEY!
OH-HH' MY HEAD!
WH-WHERE ARE WE?
YOU FOOLS! WHAT HAPPENED?
WE GAVE HIM EVERYTHING WE HAD~~BUT HE'S STILL ALIVE!
HE AIN'T HUMAN!
NONSENSE! IT'S JUST THAT YOU'RE BOTH ROTTEN MARKSMEN!
MEEK?~SOMETHING UNEXPLAINABLE HAS HAPPENED! I'LL COME RIGHT OVER AND TELL YOU ALL ABOUT IT!
I WONDER IF THERE'S ANYTHING TO THEIR WILD TALE? BUT, NO! IT'S FANTASTIC!
THERE GOES BRONSON! NOW FOR A HEART-TO-HEART CHAT!
NO PARKING NORTH
SUPERMAN VAULTS FROM THE CURB INTO THE TAXI, WITH ONE LEAP---!
WHERE IN TARNATION DID YOU COME FROM?
NEVER MIND ~ I'VE DECIDED TO SELL!

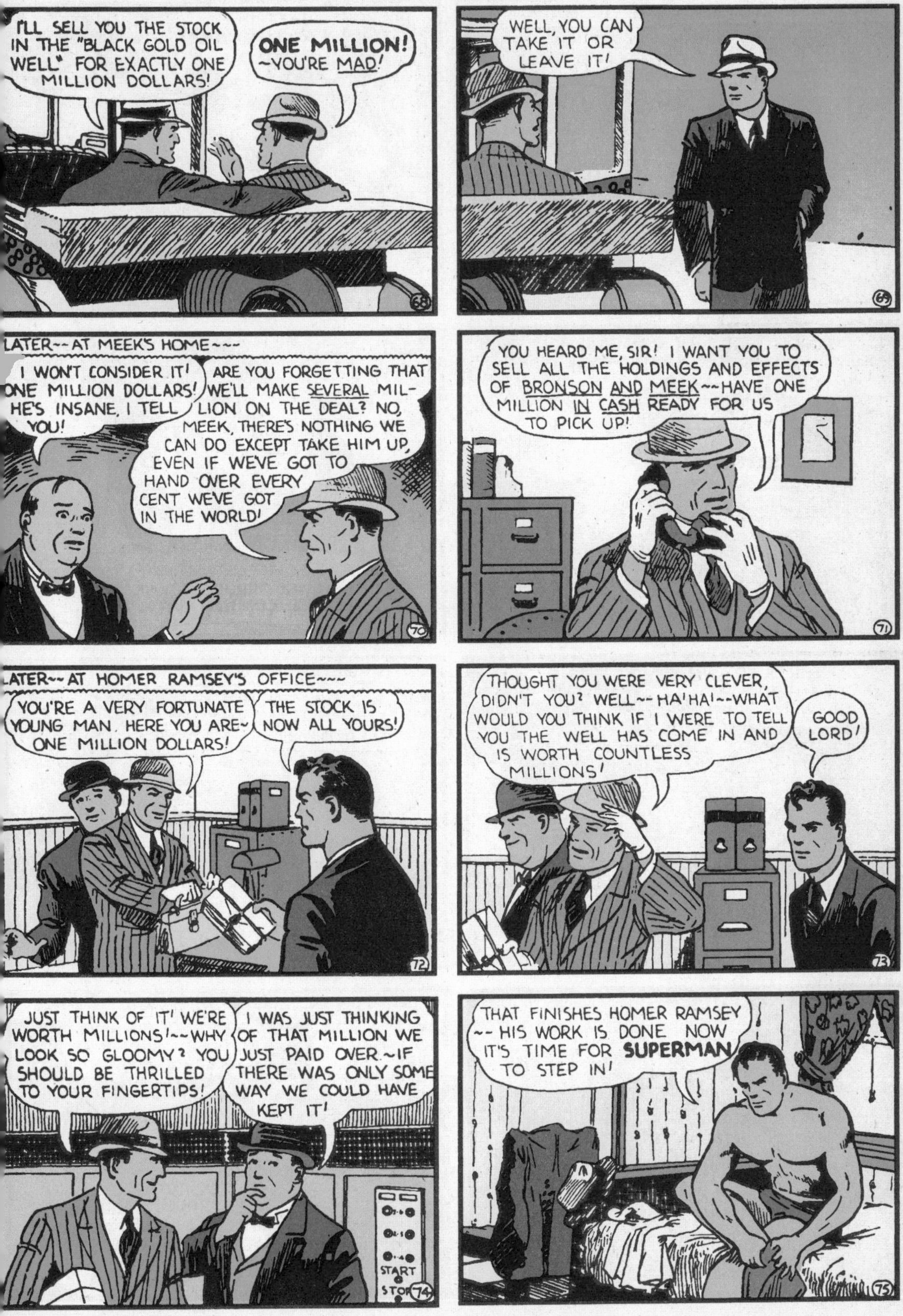
I'LL SELL YOU THE STOCK IN THE "BLACK GOLD OIL WELL" FOR EXACTLY ONE MILLION DOLLARS!
ONE MILLION! ~YOU'RE MAD!
WELL, YOU CAN TAKE IT OR LEAVE IT!
LATER-- AT MEEK'S HOME---
I WON'T CONSIDER IT! ONE MILLION DOLLARS! HE'S INSANE, I TELL YOU!
ARE YOU FORGETTING THAT WE'LL MAKE SEVERAL MILLION ON THE DEAL? NO, MEEK, THERE'S NOTHING WE CAN DO EXCEPT TAKE HIM UP, EVEN IF WE'VE GOT TO HAND OVER EVERY CENT WE'VE GOT IN THE WORLD!
YOU HEARD ME, SIR! I WANT YOU TO SELL ALL THE HOLDINGS AND EFFECTS OF BRONSON AND MEEK--HAVE ONE MILLION IN CASH READY FOR US TO PICK UP!
LATER-- AT HOMER RAMSEY'S OFFICE---
YOU'RE A VERY FORTUNATE YOUNG MAN. HERE YOU ARE~ ONE MILLION DOLLARS!
THE STOCK IS NOW ALL YOURS!
THOUGHT YOU WERE VERY CLEVER, DIDN'T YOU? WELL--HA! HA!--WHAT WOULD YOU THINK IF I WERE TO TELL YOU THE WELL HAS COME IN AND IS WORTH COUNTLESS MILLIONS!
GOOD LORD!
JUST THINK OF IT! WE'RE WORTH MILLIONS!--WHY LOOK SO GLOOMY? YOU SHOULD BE THRILLED TO YOUR FINGERTIPS!
I WAS JUST THINKING OF THAT MILLION WE JUST PAID OVER~IF THERE WAS ONLY SOME WAY WE COULD HAVE KEPT IT!
START
STOP
THAT FINISHES HOMER RAMSEY -- HIS WORK IS DONE. NOW IT'S TIME FOR SUPERMAN TO STEP IN!

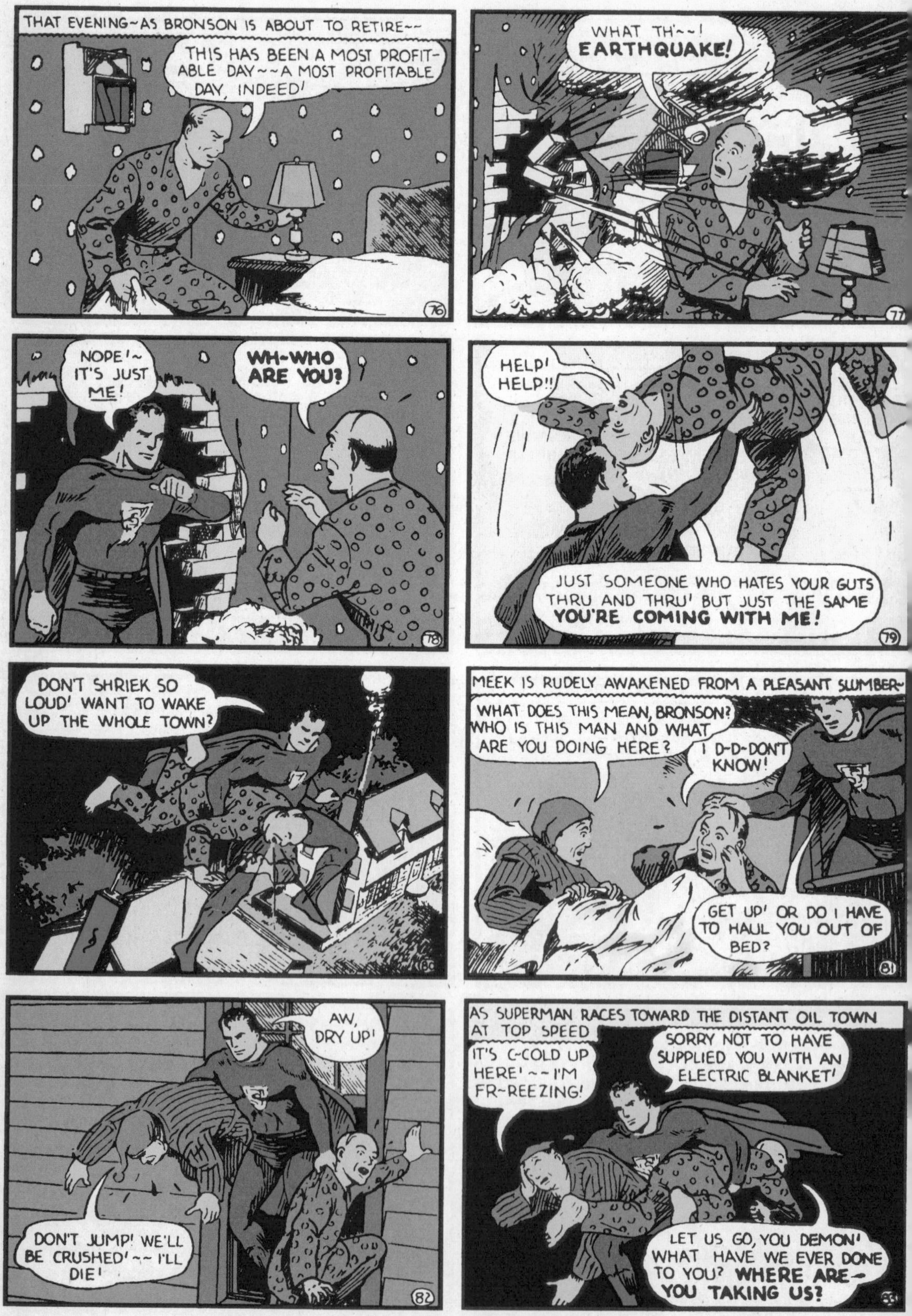
THAT EVENING~AS BRONSON IS ABOUT TO RETIRE~~
THIS HAS BEEN A MOST PROFIT-ABLE DAY~~A MOST PROFITABLE DAY, INDEED!
WHAT TH'~~! EARTHQUAKE!
NOPE!~ IT'S JUST ME!
WH-WHO ARE YOU?
HELP! HELP!!
JUST SOMEONE WHO HATES YOUR GUTS THRU AND THRU! BUT JUST THE SAME YOU'RE COMING WITH ME!
DON'T SHRIEK SO LOUD! WANT TO WAKE UP THE WHOLE TOWN?
MEEK IS RUDELY AWAKENED FROM A PLEASANT SLUMBER~
WHAT DOES THIS MEAN, BRONSON? WHO IS THIS MAN AND WHAT ARE YOU DOING HERE?
I D-D-DON'T KNOW!
GET UP! OR DO I HAVE TO HAUL YOU OUT OF BED?
AW, DRY UP!
DON'T JUMP! WE'LL BE CRUSHED!~~ I'LL DIE!
AS SUPERMAN RACES TOWARD THE DISTANT OIL TOWN AT TOP SPEED
IT'S C-COLD UP HERE!~~I'M FR~REEZING!
SORRY NOT TO HAVE SUPPLIED YOU WITH AN ELECTRIC BLANKET!
LET US GO, YOU DEMON! WHAT HAVE WE EVER DONE TO YOU? WHERE ARE-YOU TAKING US?

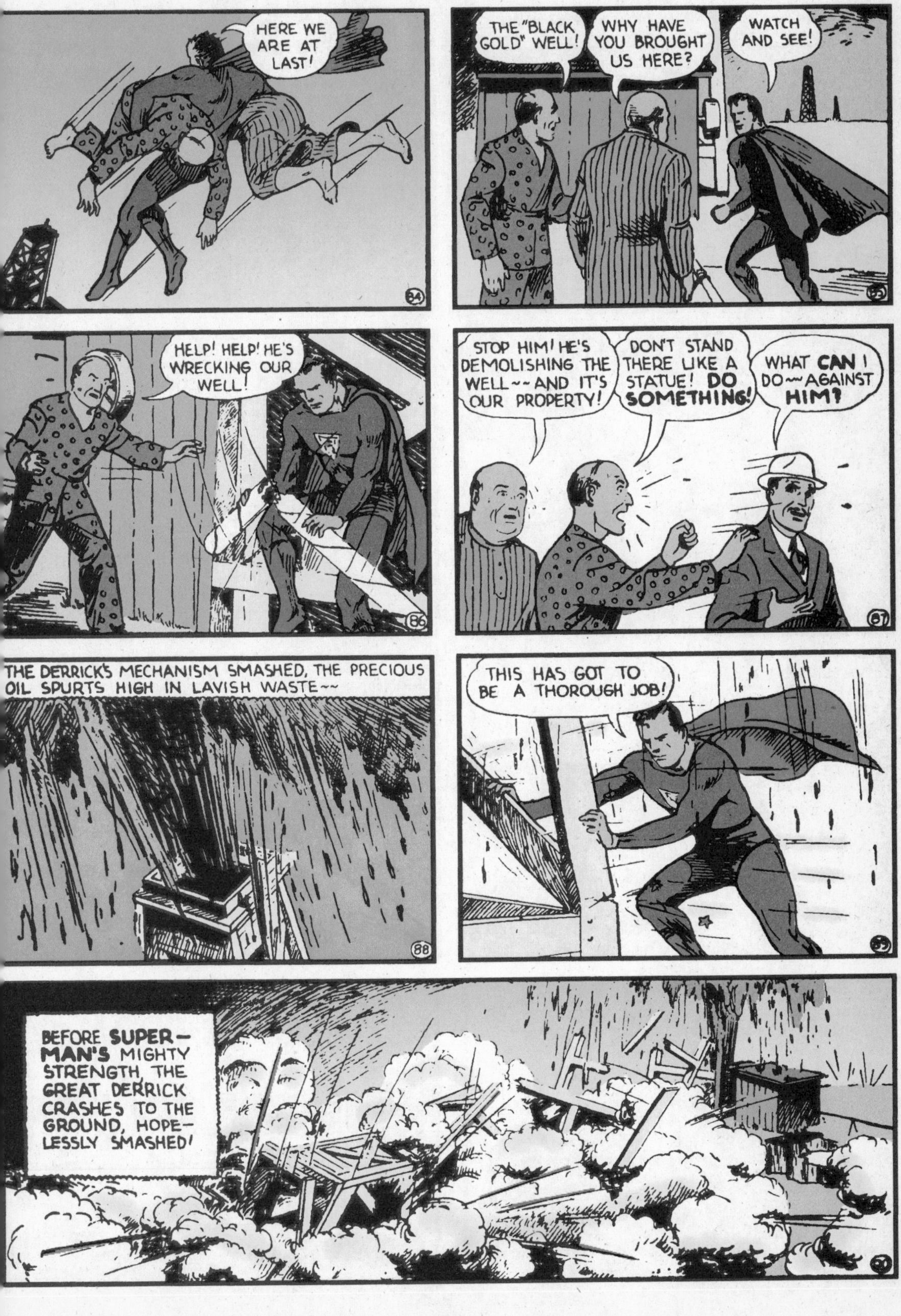
HERE WE ARE AT LAST!
THE "BLACK GOLD" WELL!
WHY HAVE YOU BROUGHT US HERE?
WATCH AND SEE!
HELP! HELP! HE'S WRECKING OUR WELL!
STOP HIM! HE'S DEMOLISHING THE WELL~~AND IT'S OUR PROPERTY!
DON'T STAND THERE LIKE A STATUE! DO SOMETHING!
WHAT CAN I DO~~AGAINST HIM?
THE DERRICK'S MECHANISM SMASHED, THE PRECIOUS OIL SPURTS HIGH IN LAVISH WASTE~~
THIS HAS GOT TO BE A THOROUGH JOB!
BEFORE SUPER-MAN'S MIGHTY STRENGTH, THE GREAT DERRICK CRASHES TO THE GROUND, HOPE-LESSLY SMASHED!

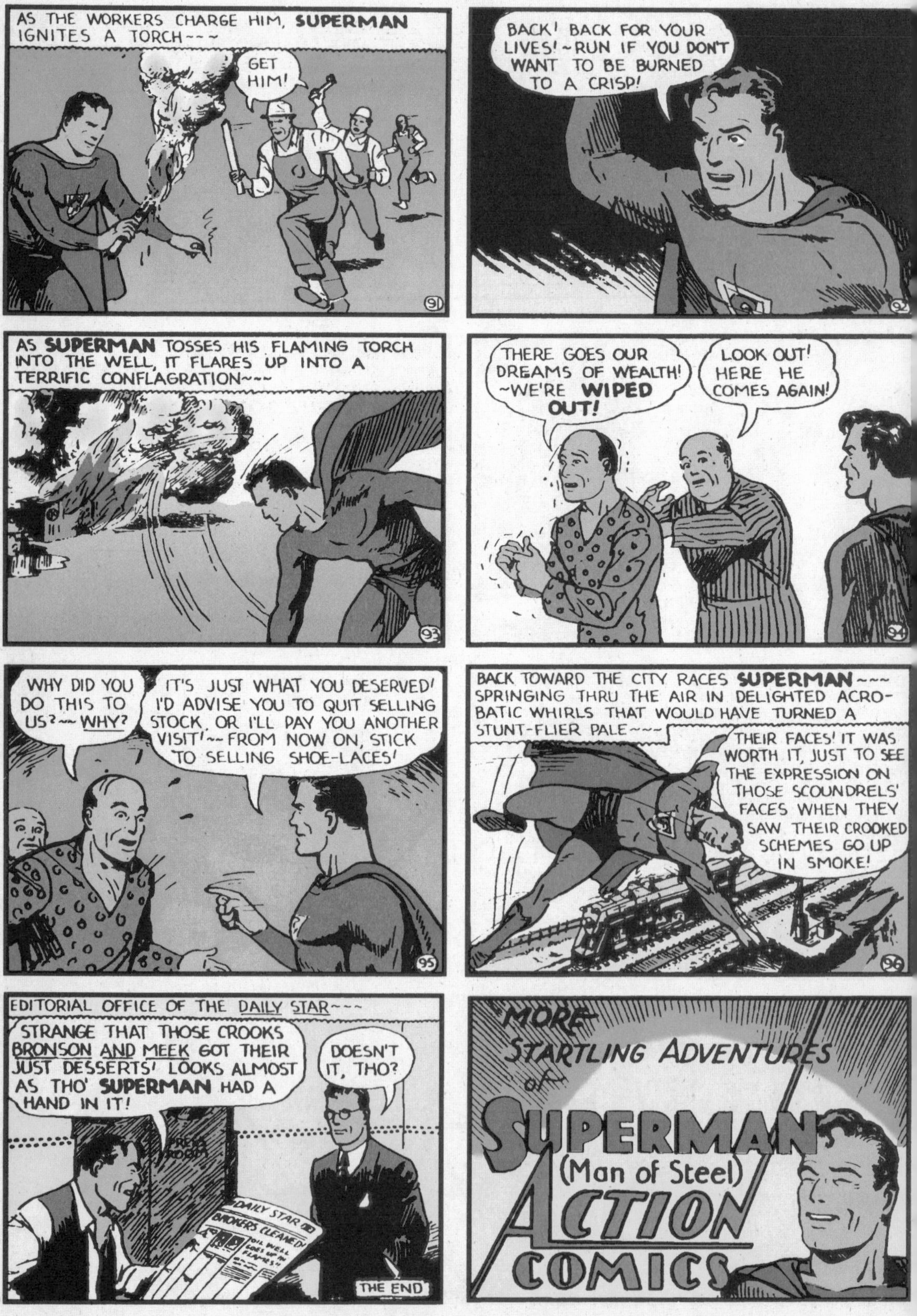
AS THE WORKERS CHARGE HIM, SUPERMAN IGNITES A TORCH---
GET HIM!
BACK! BACK FOR YOUR LIVES! ~RUN IF YOU DON'T WANT TO BE BURNED TO A CRISP!
AS SUPERMAN TOSSES HIS FLAMING TORCH INTO THE WELL, IT FLARES UP INTO A TERRIFIC CONFLAGRATION---
THERE GOES OUR DREAMS OF WEALTH! ~WE'RE WIPED OUT!
LOOK OUT! HERE HE COMES AGAIN!
WHY DID YOU DO THIS TO US?~~WHY?
IT'S JUST WHAT YOU DESERVED! I'D ADVISE YOU TO QUIT SELLING STOCK, OR I'LL PAY YOU ANOTHER VISIT!~~FROM NOW ON, STICK TO SELLING SHOE-LACES!
BACK TOWARD THE CITY RACES SUPERMAN--- SPRINGING THRU THE AIR IN DELIGHTED ACROBATIC WHIRLS THAT WOULD HAVE TURNED A STUNT-FLIER PALE---
THEIR FACES! IT WAS WORTH IT, JUST TO SEE THE EXPRESSION ON THOSE SCOUNDRELS' FACES WHEN THEY SAW THEIR CROOKED SCHEMES GO UP IN SMOKE!
EDITORIAL OFFICE OF THE DAILY STAR---
STRANGE THAT THOSE CROOKS BRONSON AND MEEK GOT THEIR JUST DESSERTS! LOOKS ALMOST AS THO' SUPERMAN HAD A HAND IN IT!
DOESN'T IT, THO?
DAILY STAR
BROKERS CLEANED!
THE END
MORE STARTLING ADVENTURES of
SUPERMAN
(Man of Steel)
ACTION COMICS

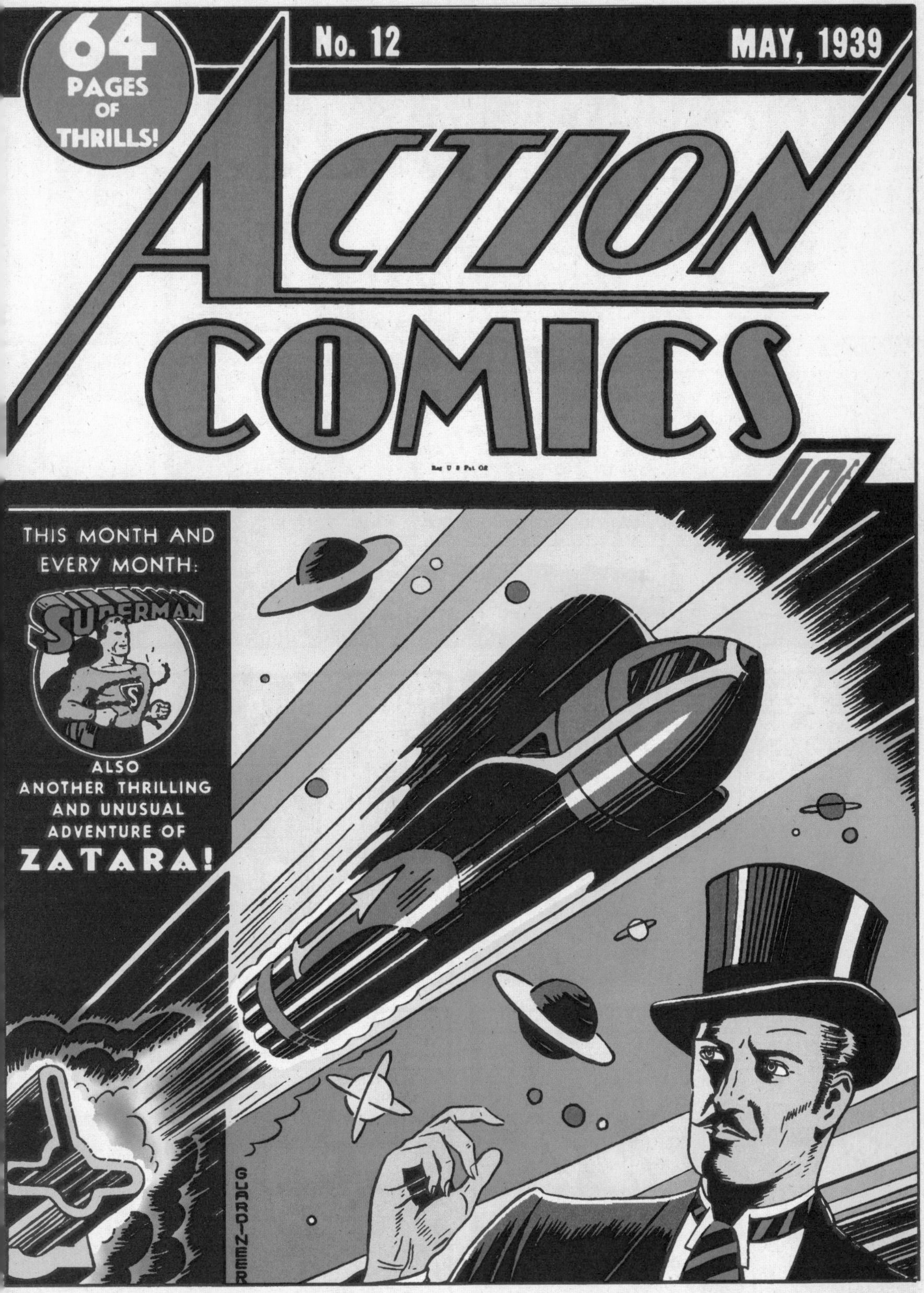
64 PAGES OF THRILLS!
No. 12
MAY, 1939
ACTION COMICS
Reg. U. S. Pat. Off.
10¢
THIS MONTH AND EVERY MONTH:
SUPERMAN
ALSO ANOTHER THRILLING AND UNUSUAL ADVENTURE OF
ZATARA!
GUARDINEER

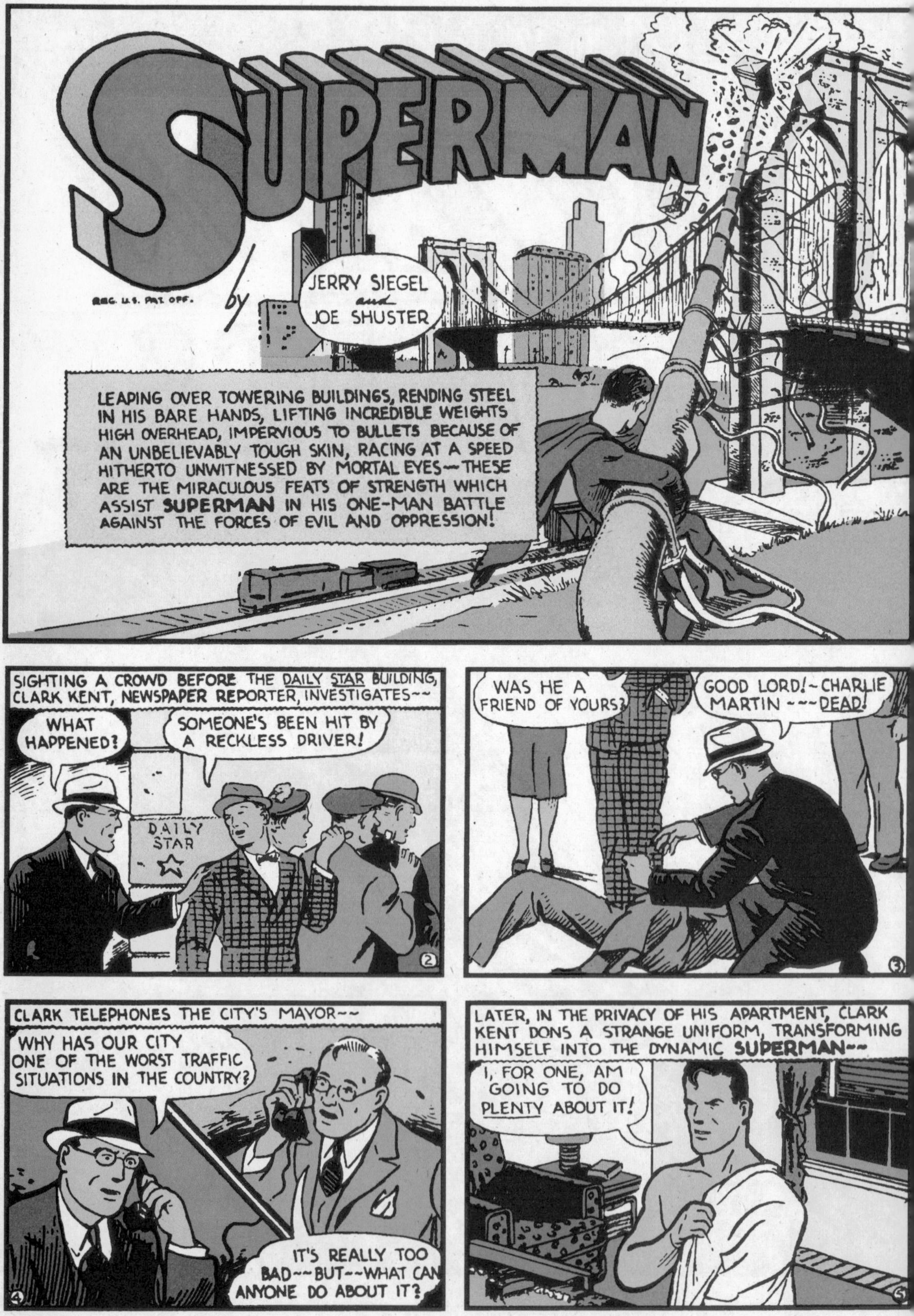
SUPERMAN
REG. U.S. PAT. OFF.
by
JERRY SIEGEL and JOE SHUSTER
LEAPING OVER TOWERING BUILDINGS, RENDING STEEL IN HIS BARE HANDS, LIFTING INCREDIBLE WEIGHTS HIGH OVERHEAD, IMPERVIOUS TO BULLETS BECAUSE OF AN UNBELIEVABLY TOUGH SKIN, RACING AT A SPEED HITHERTO UNWITNESSED BY MORTAL EYES~~THESE ARE THE MIRACULOUS FEATS OF STRENGTH WHICH ASSIST SUPERMAN IN HIS ONE-MAN BATTLE AGAINST THE FORCES OF EVIL AND OPPRESSION!
SIGHTING A CROWD BEFORE THE DAILY STAR BUILDING, CLARK KENT, NEWSPAPER REPORTER, INVESTIGATES~~
WHAT HAPPENED?
SOMEONE'S BEEN HIT BY A RECKLESS DRIVER!
DAILY STAR
2
WAS HE A FRIEND OF YOURS?
GOOD LORD!~CHARLIE MARTIN~~~DEAD!
3
CLARK TELEPHONES THE CITY'S MAYOR~~
WHY HAS OUR CITY ONE OF THE WORST TRAFFIC SITUATIONS IN THE COUNTRY?
IT'S REALLY TOO BAD~~BUT~~WHAT CAN ANYONE DO ABOUT IT?
4
LATER, IN THE PRIVACY OF HIS APARTMENT, CLARK KENT DONS A STRANGE UNIFORM, TRANSFORMING HIMSELF INTO THE DYNAMIC SUPERMAN~~
I, FOR ONE, AM GOING TO DO PLENTY ABOUT IT!
5

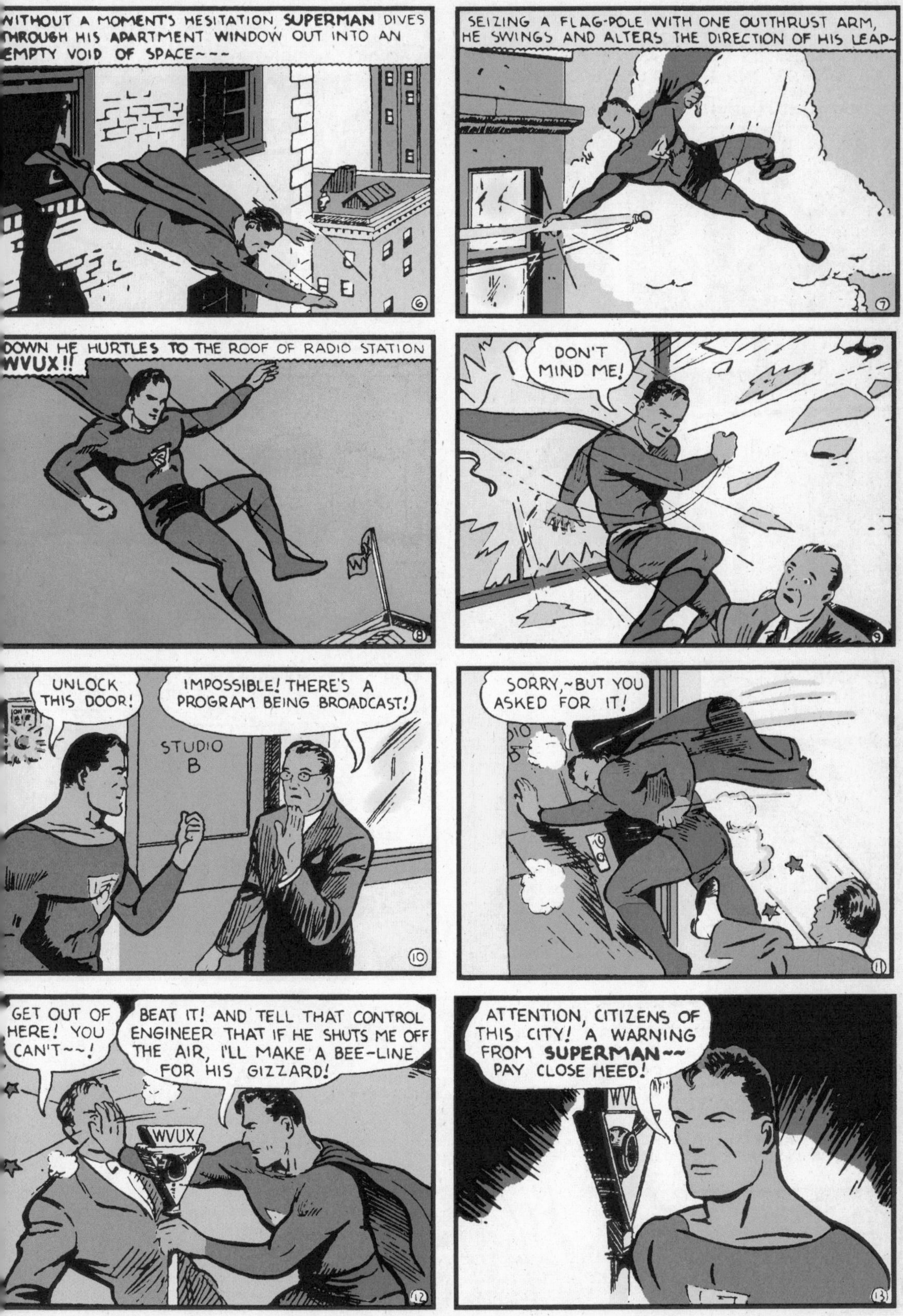
WITHOUT A MOMENT'S HESITATION, SUPERMAN DIVES THROUGH HIS APARTMENT WINDOW OUT INTO AN EMPTY VOID OF SPACE---
SEIZING A FLAG-POLE WITH ONE OUTTHRUST ARM, HE SWINGS AND ALTERS THE DIRECTION OF HIS LEAP--
DOWN HE HURTLES TO THE ROOF OF RADIO STATION WVUX!!
DON'T MIND ME!
UNLOCK THIS DOOR!
IMPOSSIBLE! THERE'S A PROGRAM BEING BROADCAST!
STUDIO B
SORRY,~BUT YOU ASKED FOR IT!
GET OUT OF HERE! YOU CAN'T~~!
BEAT IT! AND TELL THAT CONTROL ENGINEER THAT IF HE SHUTS ME OFF THE AIR, I'LL MAKE A BEE-LINE FOR HIS GIZZARD!
WVUX
ATTENTION, CITIZENS OF THIS CITY! A WARNING FROM SUPERMAN~~ PAY CLOSE HEED!

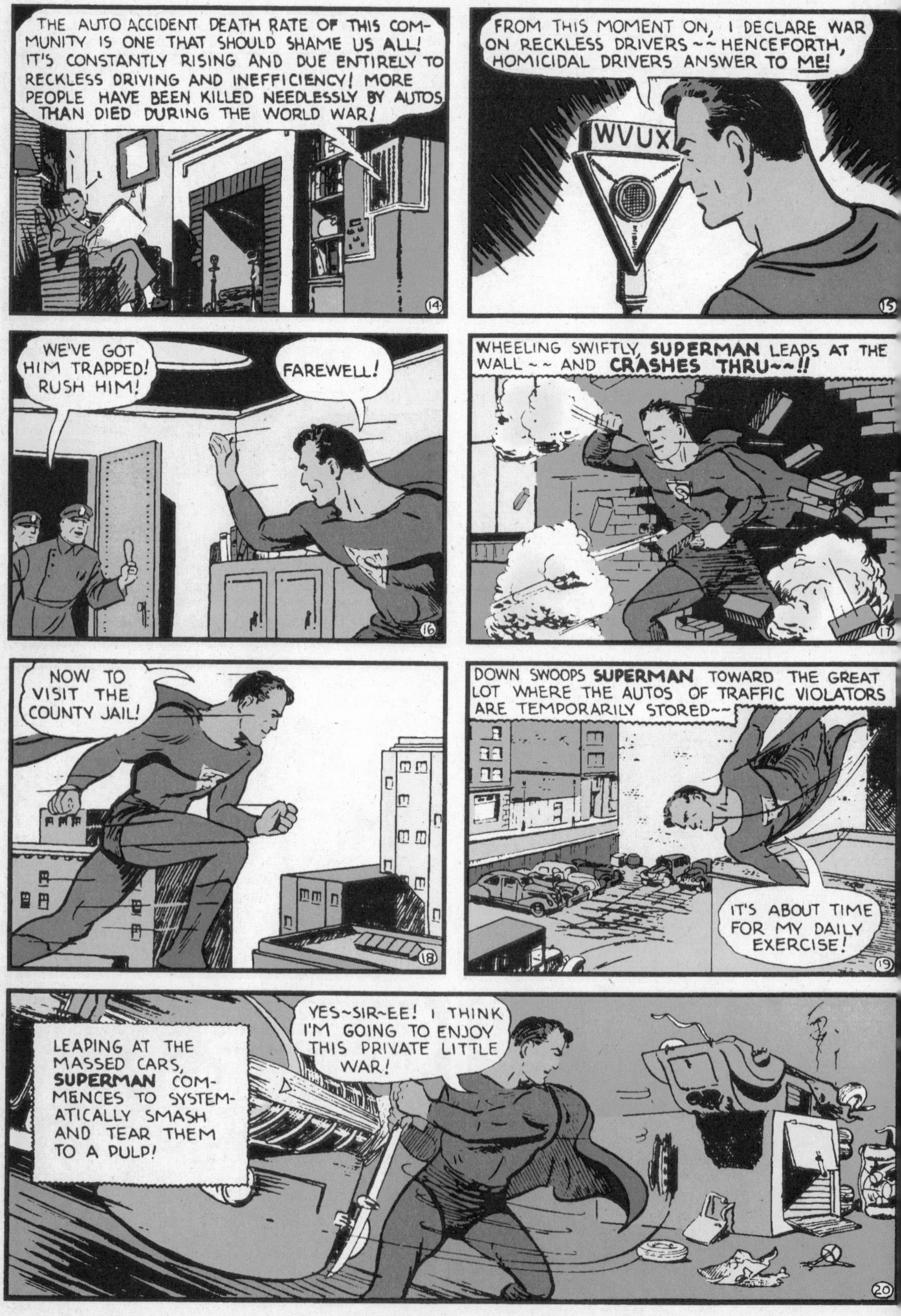
THE AUTO ACCIDENT DEATH RATE OF THIS COMMUNITY IS ONE THAT SHOULD SHAME US ALL! IT'S CONSTANTLY RISING AND DUE ENTIRELY TO RECKLESS DRIVING AND INEFFICIENCY! MORE PEOPLE HAVE BEEN KILLED NEEDLESSLY BY AUTOS THAN DIED DURING THE WORLD WAR!
FROM THIS MOMENT ON, I DECLARE WAR ON RECKLESS DRIVERS ~~ HENCEFORTH, HOMICIDAL DRIVERS ANSWER TO ME!
WVUX
WE'VE GOT HIM TRAPPED! RUSH HIM!
FAREWELL!
WHEELING SWIFTLY, SUPERMAN LEAPS AT THE WALL ~~ AND CRASHES THRU~~!!
NOW TO VISIT THE COUNTY JAIL!
DOWN SWOOPS SUPERMAN TOWARD THE GREAT LOT WHERE THE AUTOS OF TRAFFIC VIOLATORS ARE TEMPORARILY STORED~~
IT'S ABOUT TIME FOR MY DAILY EXERCISE!
LEAPING AT THE MASSED CARS, SUPERMAN COMMENCES TO SYSTEMATICALLY SMASH AND TEAR THEM TO A PULP!
YES~SIR~EE! I THINK I'M GOING TO ENJOY THIS PRIVATE LITTLE WAR!

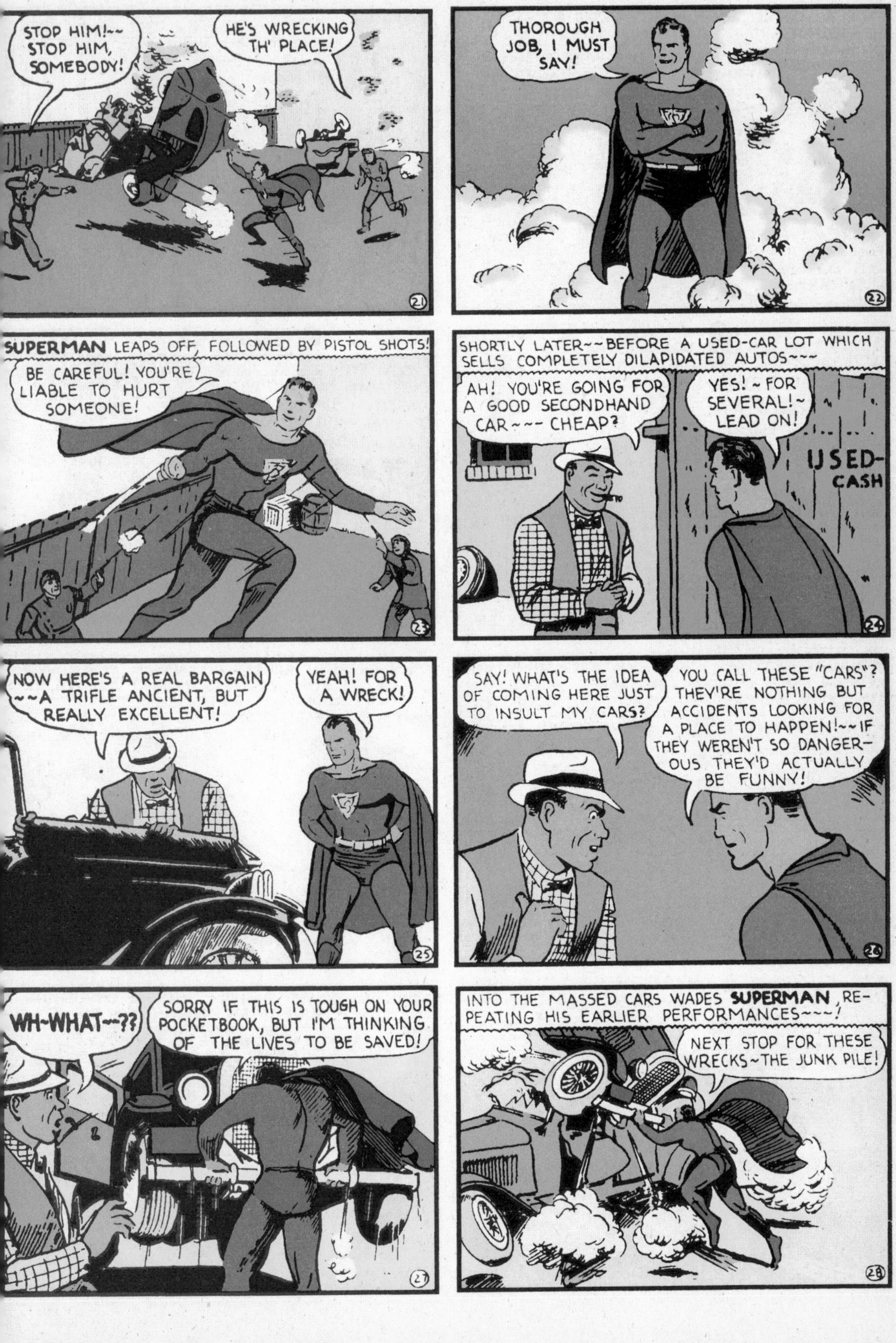
STOP HIM!~~ STOP HIM, SOMEBODY!
HE'S WRECKING TH' PLACE!
THOROUGH JOB, I MUST SAY!
SUPERMAN LEAPS OFF, FOLLOWED BY PISTOL SHOTS!
BE CAREFUL! YOU'RE LIABLE TO HURT SOMEONE!
SHORTLY LATER~~BEFORE A USED-CAR LOT WHICH SELLS COMPLETELY DILAPIDATED AUTOS~~~
AH! YOU'RE GOING FOR A GOOD SECONDHAND CAR~~~ CHEAP?
YES! ~ FOR SEVERAL!~ LEAD ON!
USED-
CASH
NOW HERE'S A REAL BARGAIN ~~A TRIFLE ANCIENT, BUT REALLY EXCELLENT!
YEAH! FOR A WRECK!
SAY! WHAT'S THE IDEA OF COMING HERE JUST TO INSULT MY CARS?
YOU CALL THESE "CARS"? THEY'RE NOTHING BUT ACCIDENTS LOOKING FOR A PLACE TO HAPPEN!~~IF THEY WEREN'T SO DANGER-OUS THEY'D ACTUALLY BE FUNNY!
WH-WHAT~~??
SORRY IF THIS IS TOUGH ON YOUR POCKETBOOK, BUT I'M THINKING OF THE LIVES TO BE SAVED!
INTO THE MASSED CARS WADES SUPERMAN, RE-PEATING HIS EARLIER PERFORMANCES~~~!
NEXT STOP FOR THESE WRECKS~THE JUNK PILE!

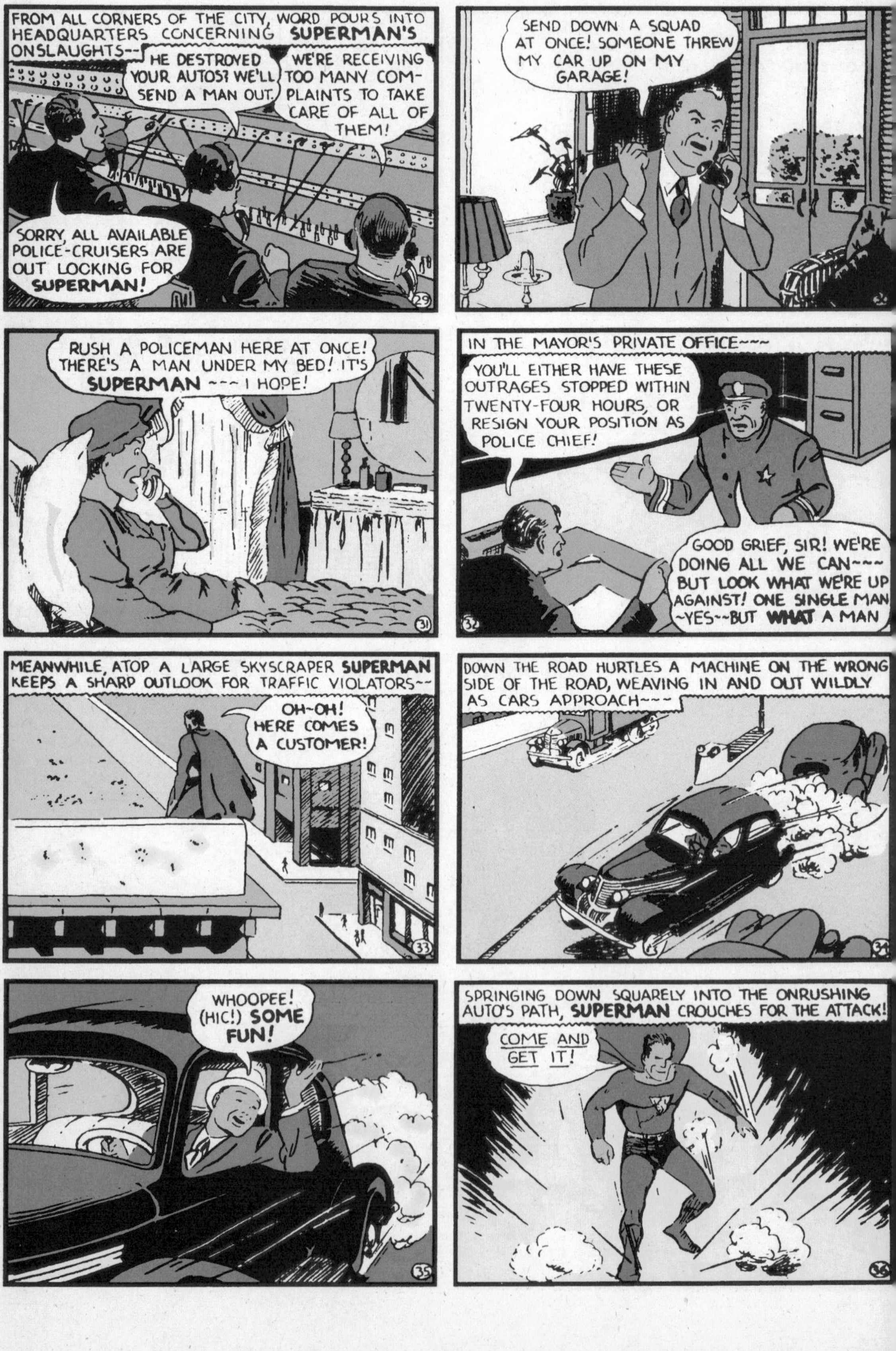
FROM ALL CORNERS OF THE CITY, WORD POURS INTO HEADQUARTERS CONCERNING SUPERMAN'S ONSLAUGHTS--
HE DESTROYED YOUR AUTOS? WE'LL SEND A MAN OUT.
WE'RE RECEIVING TOO MANY COM-PLAINTS TO TAKE CARE OF ALL OF THEM!
SORRY, ALL AVAILABLE POLICE-CRUISERS ARE OUT LOOKING FOR SUPERMAN!
29
SEND DOWN A SQUAD AT ONCE! SOMEONE THREW MY CAR UP ON MY GARAGE!
RUSH A POLICEMAN HERE AT ONCE! THERE'S A MAN UNDER MY BED! IT'S SUPERMAN --- I HOPE!
31
IN THE MAYOR'S PRIVATE OFFICE---
YOU'LL EITHER HAVE THESE OUTRAGES STOPPED WITHIN TWENTY-FOUR HOURS, OR RESIGN YOUR POSITION AS POLICE CHIEF!
GOOD GRIEF, SIR! WE'RE DOING ALL WE CAN--- BUT LOOK WHAT WE'RE UP AGAINST! ONE SINGLE MAN -YES--BUT WHAT A MAN
32
MEANWHILE, ATOP A LARGE SKYSCRAPER SUPERMAN KEEPS A SHARP OUTLOOK FOR TRAFFIC VIOLATORS--
OH-OH! HERE COMES A CUSTOMER!
33
DOWN THE ROAD HURTLES A MACHINE ON THE WRONG SIDE OF THE ROAD, WEAVING IN AND OUT WILDLY AS CARS APPROACH---
34
WHOOPEE! (HIC!) SOME FUN!
35
SPRINGING DOWN SQUARELY INTO THE ONRUSHING AUTO'S PATH, SUPERMAN CROUCHES FOR THE ATTACK!
COME AND GET IT!
36

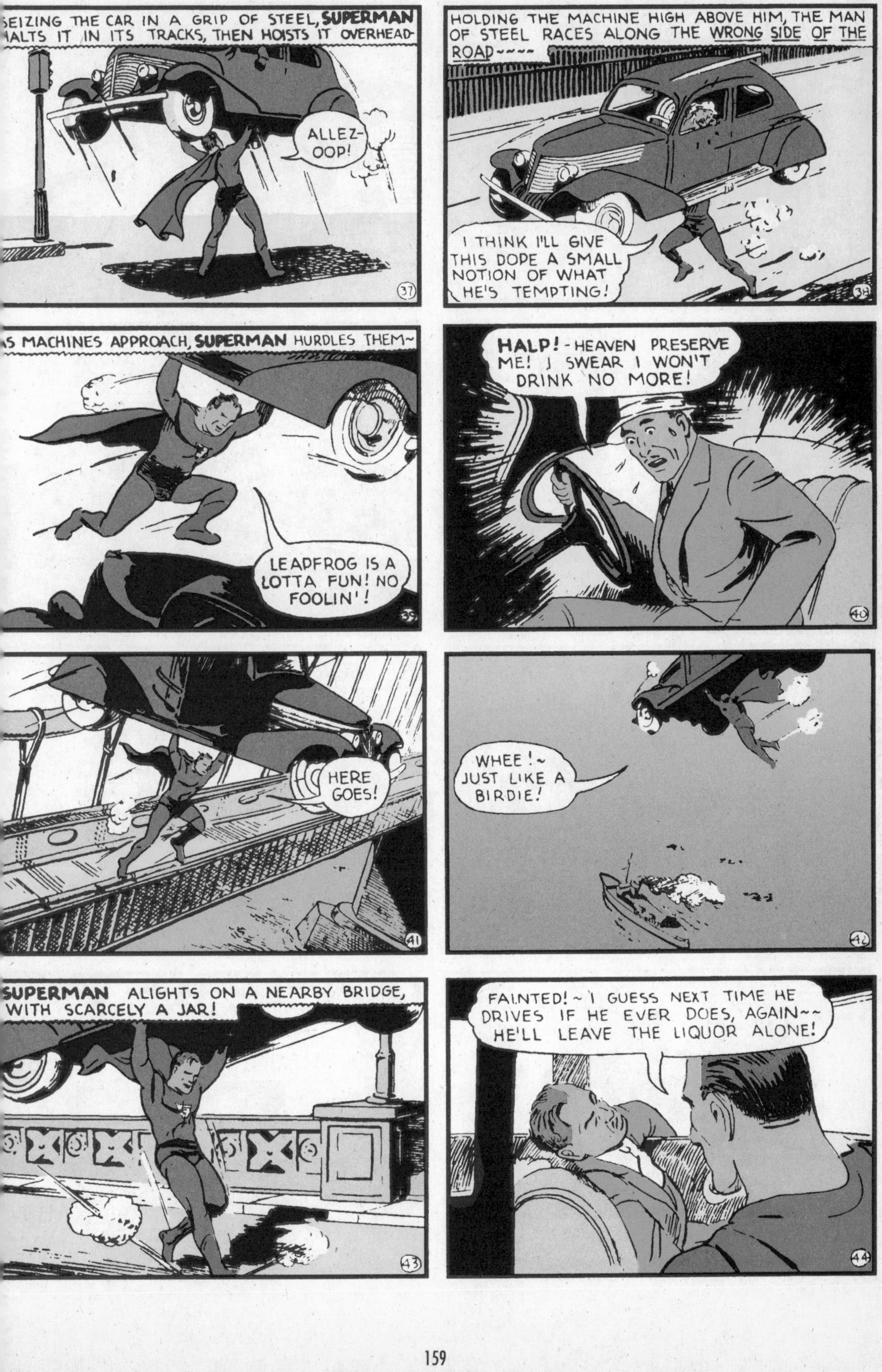
SEIZING THE CAR IN A GRIP OF STEEL, SUPERMAN HALTS IT IN ITS TRACKS, THEN HOISTS IT OVERHEAD-
ALLEZ-OOP!
HOLDING THE MACHINE HIGH ABOVE HIM, THE MAN OF STEEL RACES ALONG THE WRONG SIDE OF THE ROAD~~~~
I THINK I'LL GIVE THIS DOPE A SMALL NOTION OF WHAT HE'S TEMPTING!
AS MACHINES APPROACH, SUPERMAN HURDLES THEM~
LEAPFROG IS A LOTTA FUN! NO FOOLIN'!
HALP! - HEAVEN PRESERVE ME! I SWEAR I WON'T DRINK NO MORE!
HERE GOES!
WHEE!~ JUST LIKE A BIRDIE!
SUPERMAN ALIGHTS ON A NEARBY BRIDGE, WITH SCARCELY A JAR!
FAINTED! ~ I GUESS NEXT TIME HE DRIVES IF HE EVER DOES, AGAIN~~ HE'LL LEAVE THE LIQUOR ALONE!

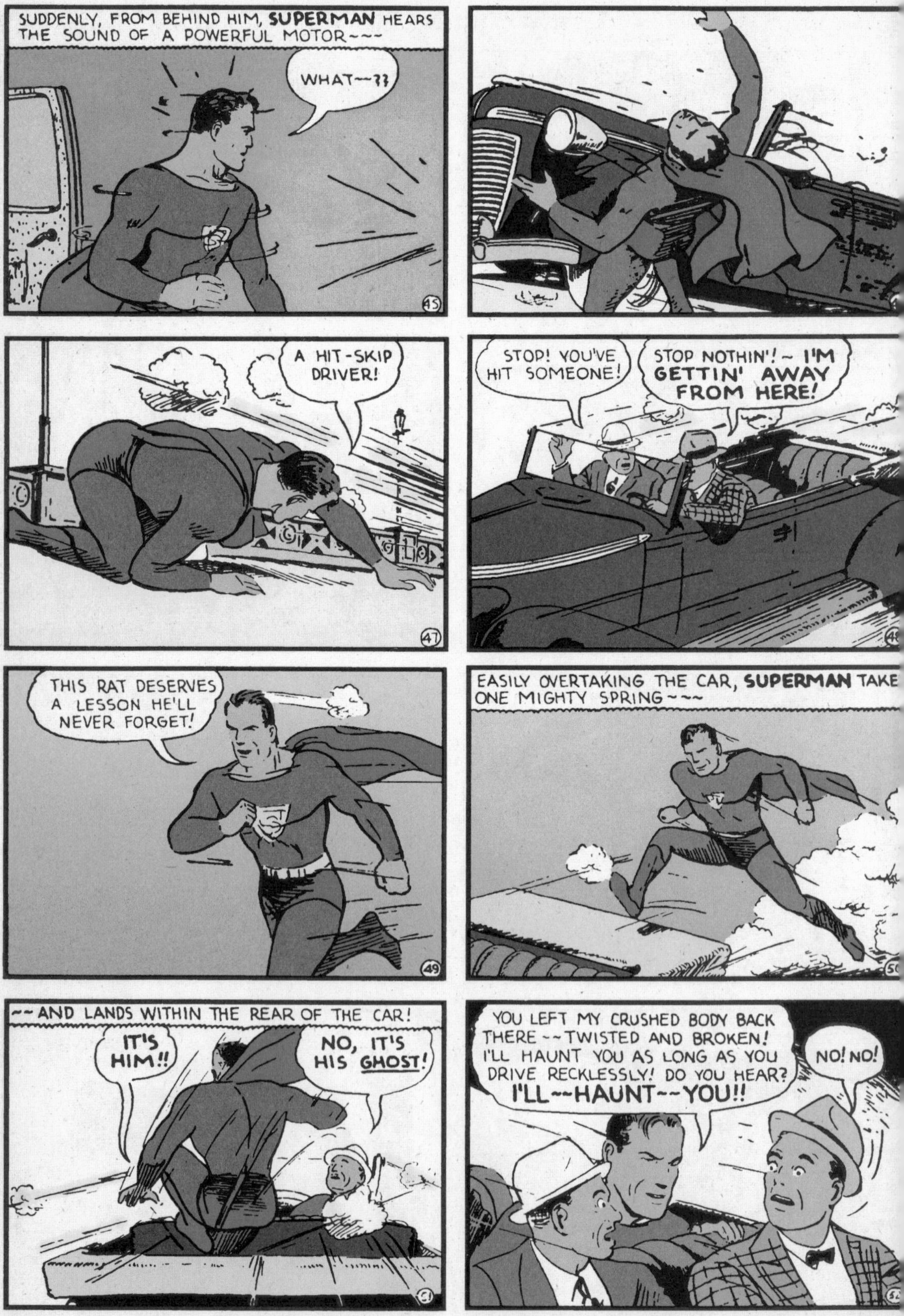
SUDDENLY, FROM BEHIND HIM, SUPERMAN HEARS THE SOUND OF A POWERFUL MOTOR~~~
WHAT~~??
A HIT-SKIP DRIVER!
STOP! YOU'VE HIT SOMEONE!
STOP NOTHIN'! ~ I'M GETTIN' AWAY FROM HERE!
THIS RAT DESERVES A LESSON HE'LL NEVER FORGET!
EASILY OVERTAKING THE CAR, SUPERMAN TAKE ONE MIGHTY SPRING~~~
~~AND LANDS WITHIN THE REAR OF THE CAR!
IT'S HIM!!
NO, IT'S HIS GHOST!
YOU LEFT MY CRUSHED BODY BACK THERE~~TWISTED AND BROKEN! I'LL HAUNT YOU AS LONG AS YOU DRIVE RECKLESSLY! DO YOU HEAR? I'LL~~HAUNT~~YOU!!
NO! NO!

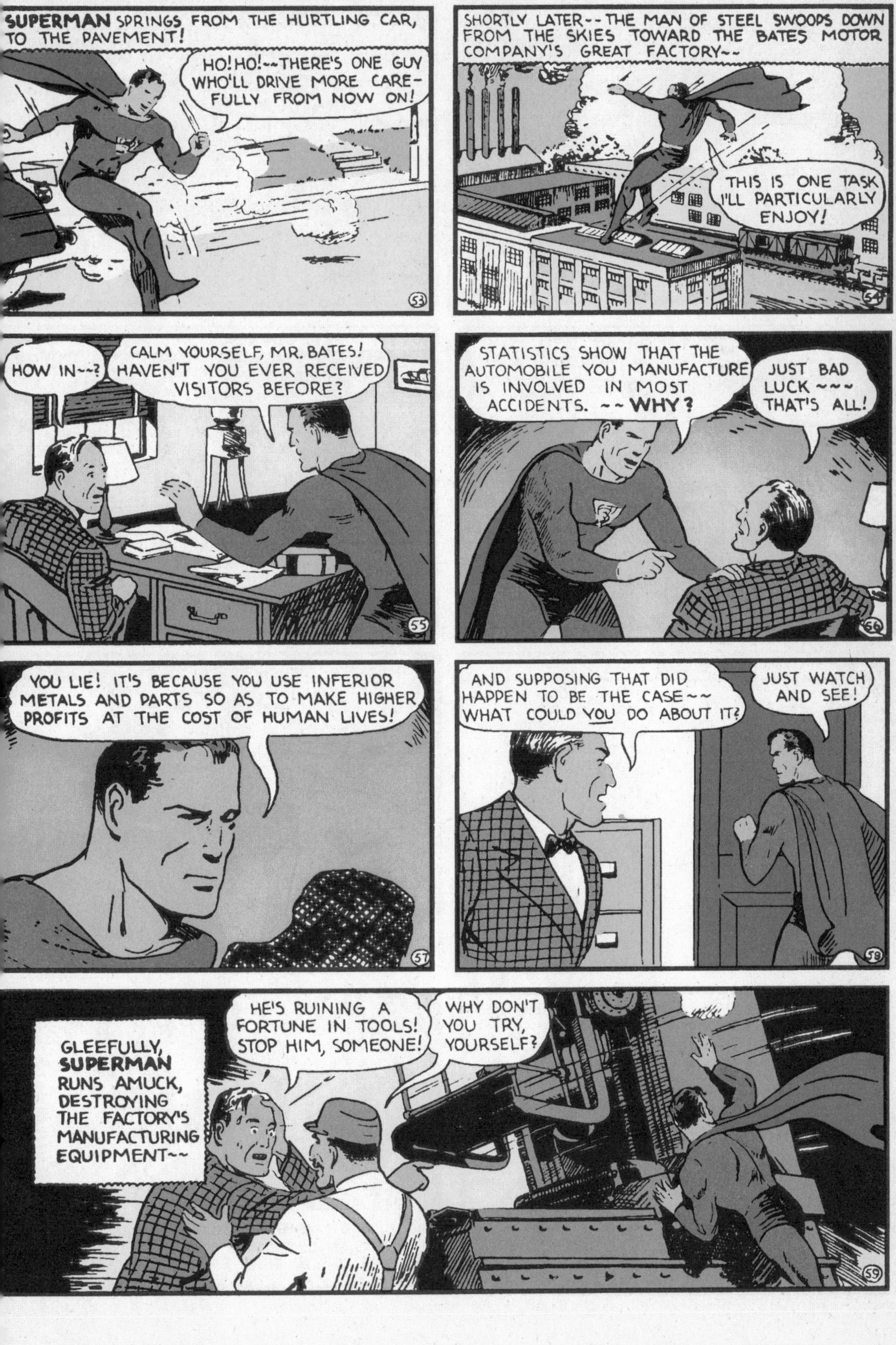

SUPERMAN SPRINGS FROM THE HURTLING CAR, TO THE PAVEMENT!
HO! HO!--THERE'S ONE GUY WHO'LL DRIVE MORE CARE-FULLY FROM NOW ON!
SHORTLY LATER--THE MAN OF STEEL SWOOPS DOWN FROM THE SKIES TOWARD THE BATES MOTOR COMPANY'S GREAT FACTORY--
THIS IS ONE TASK I'LL PARTICULARLY ENJOY!
HOW IN--?
CALM YOURSELF, MR. BATES! HAVEN'T YOU EVER RECEIVED VISITORS BEFORE?
STATISTICS SHOW THAT THE AUTOMOBILE YOU MANUFACTURE IS INVOLVED IN MOST ACCIDENTS. --WHY?
JUST BAD LUCK ~~~ THAT'S ALL!
YOU LIE! IT'S BECAUSE YOU USE INFERIOR METALS AND PARTS SO AS TO MAKE HIGHER PROFITS AT THE COST OF HUMAN LIVES!
AND SUPPOSING THAT DID HAPPEN TO BE THE CASE~~ WHAT COULD YOU DO ABOUT IT?
JUST WATCH AND SEE!
GLEEFULLY, SUPERMAN RUNS AMUCK, DESTROYING THE FACTORY'S MANUFACTURING EQUIPMENT~~
HE'S RUINING A FORTUNE IN TOOLS! STOP HIM, SOMEONE!
WHY DON'T YOU TRY, YOURSELF?

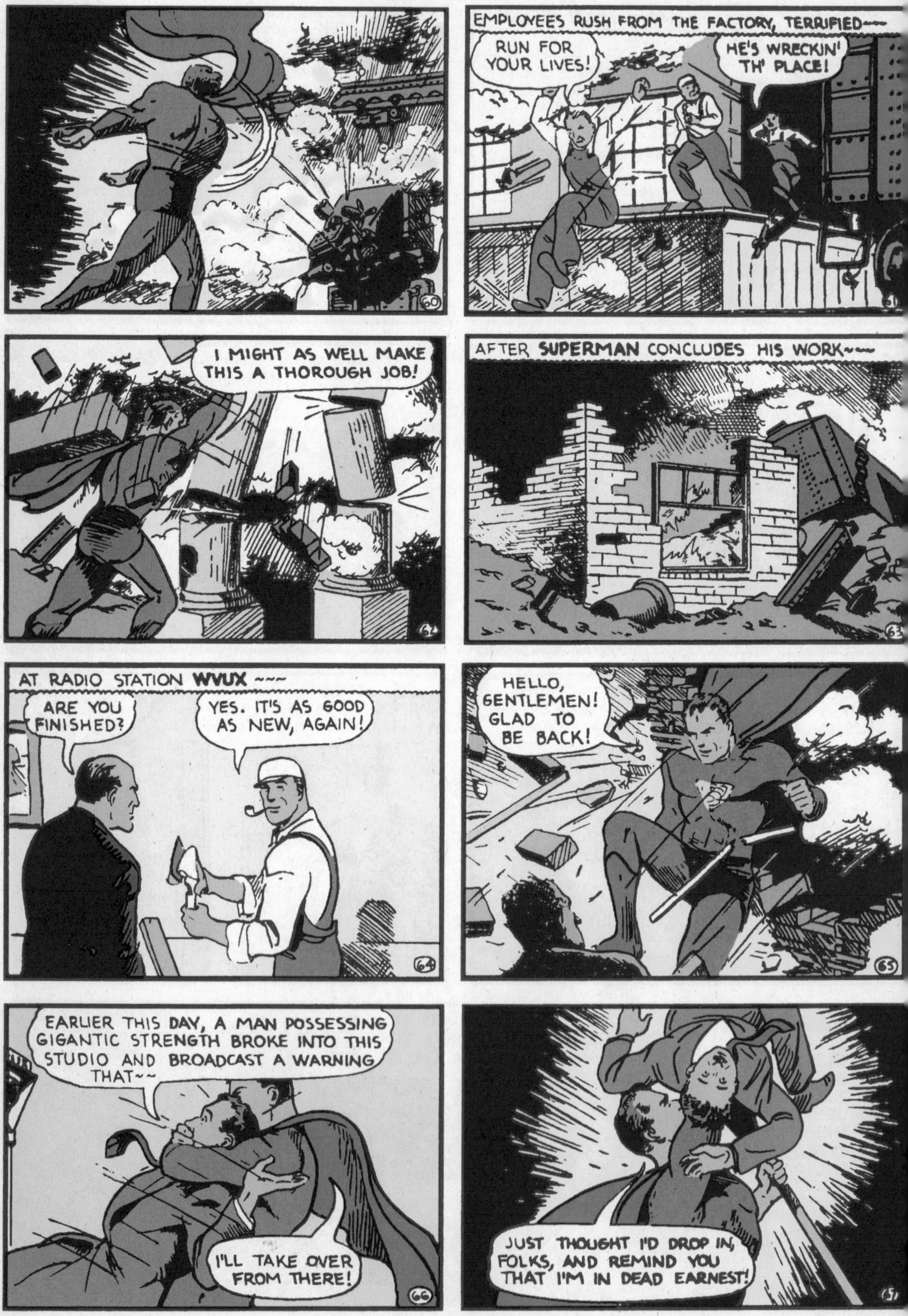
EMPLOYEES RUSH FROM THE FACTORY, TERRIFIED---
RUN FOR YOUR LIVES!
HE'S WRECKIN' TH' PLACE!
I MIGHT AS WELL MAKE THIS A THOROUGH JOB!
AFTER SUPERMAN CONCLUDES HIS WORK---
AT RADIO STATION WVUX ---
ARE YOU FINISHED?
YES. IT'S AS GOOD AS NEW, AGAIN!
HELLO, GENTLEMEN! GLAD TO BE BACK!
EARLIER THIS DAY, A MAN POSSESSING GIGANTIC STRENGTH BROKE INTO THIS STUDIO AND BROADCAST A WARNING THAT~~
I'LL TAKE OVER FROM THERE!
JUST THOUGHT I'D DROP IN, FOLKS, AND REMIND YOU THAT I'M IN DEAD EARNEST!

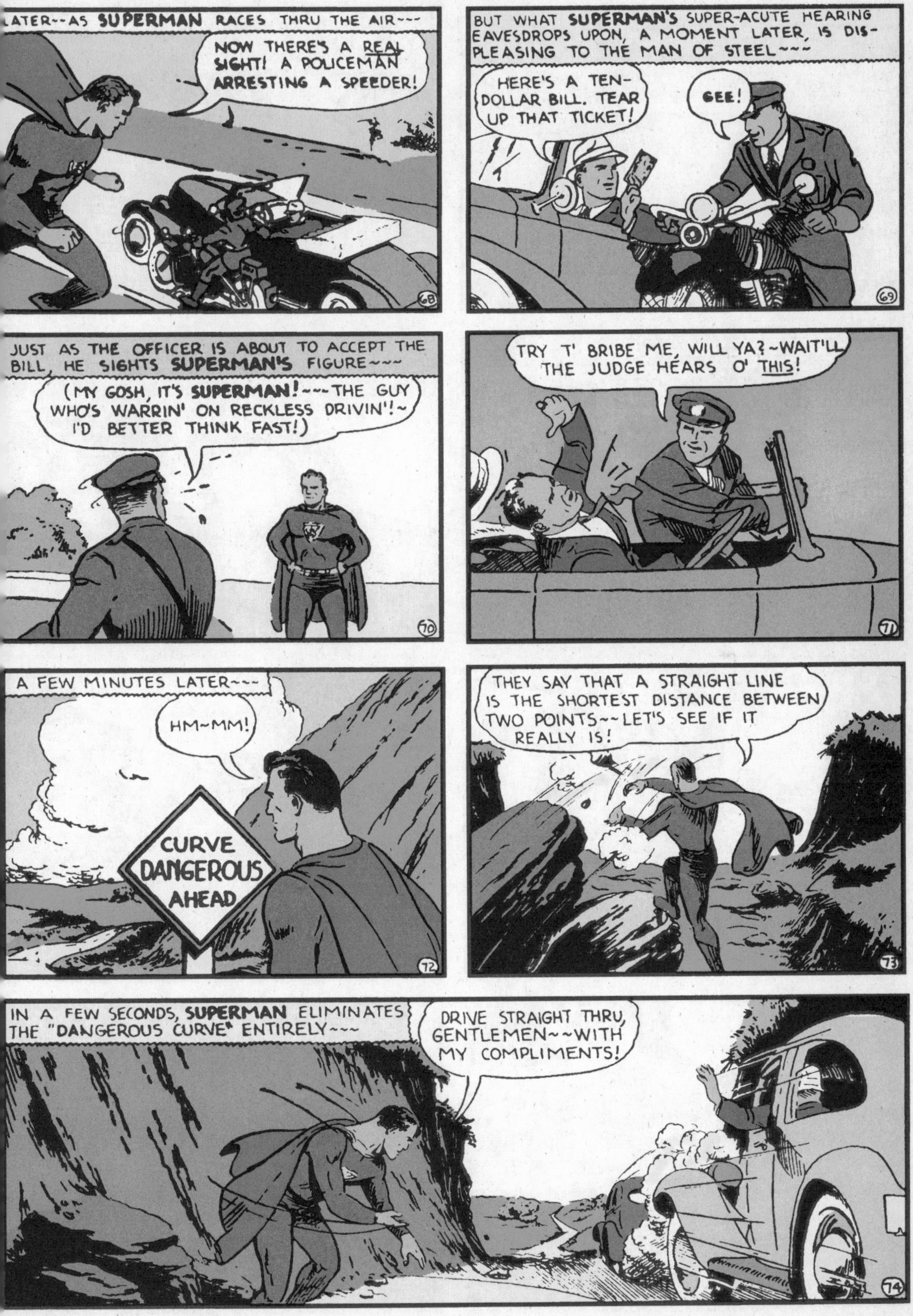

LATER--AS SUPERMAN RACES THRU THE AIR---
NOW THERE'S A REAL SIGHT! A POLICEMAN ARRESTING A SPEEDER!
BUT WHAT SUPERMAN'S SUPER-ACUTE HEARING EAVESDROPS UPON, A MOMENT LATER, IS DISPLEASING TO THE MAN OF STEEL---
HERE'S A TEN-DOLLAR BILL. TEAR UP THAT TICKET!
GEE!
JUST AS THE OFFICER IS ABOUT TO ACCEPT THE BILL, HE SIGHTS SUPERMAN'S FIGURE---
(MY GOSH, IT'S SUPERMAN!---THE GUY WHO'S WARRIN' ON RECKLESS DRIVIN'!~ I'D BETTER THINK FAST!)
TRY T' BRIBE ME, WILL YA?~WAIT'LL THE JUDGE HEARS O' THIS!
A FEW MINUTES LATER---
HM~MM!
CURVE DANGEROUS AHEAD
THEY SAY THAT A STRAIGHT LINE IS THE SHORTEST DISTANCE BETWEEN TWO POINTS~~LET'S SEE IF IT REALLY IS!
IN A FEW SECONDS, SUPERMAN ELIMINATES THE "DANGEROUS CURVE" ENTIRELY---
DRIVE STRAIGHT THRU, GENTLEMEN~~WITH MY COMPLIMENTS!

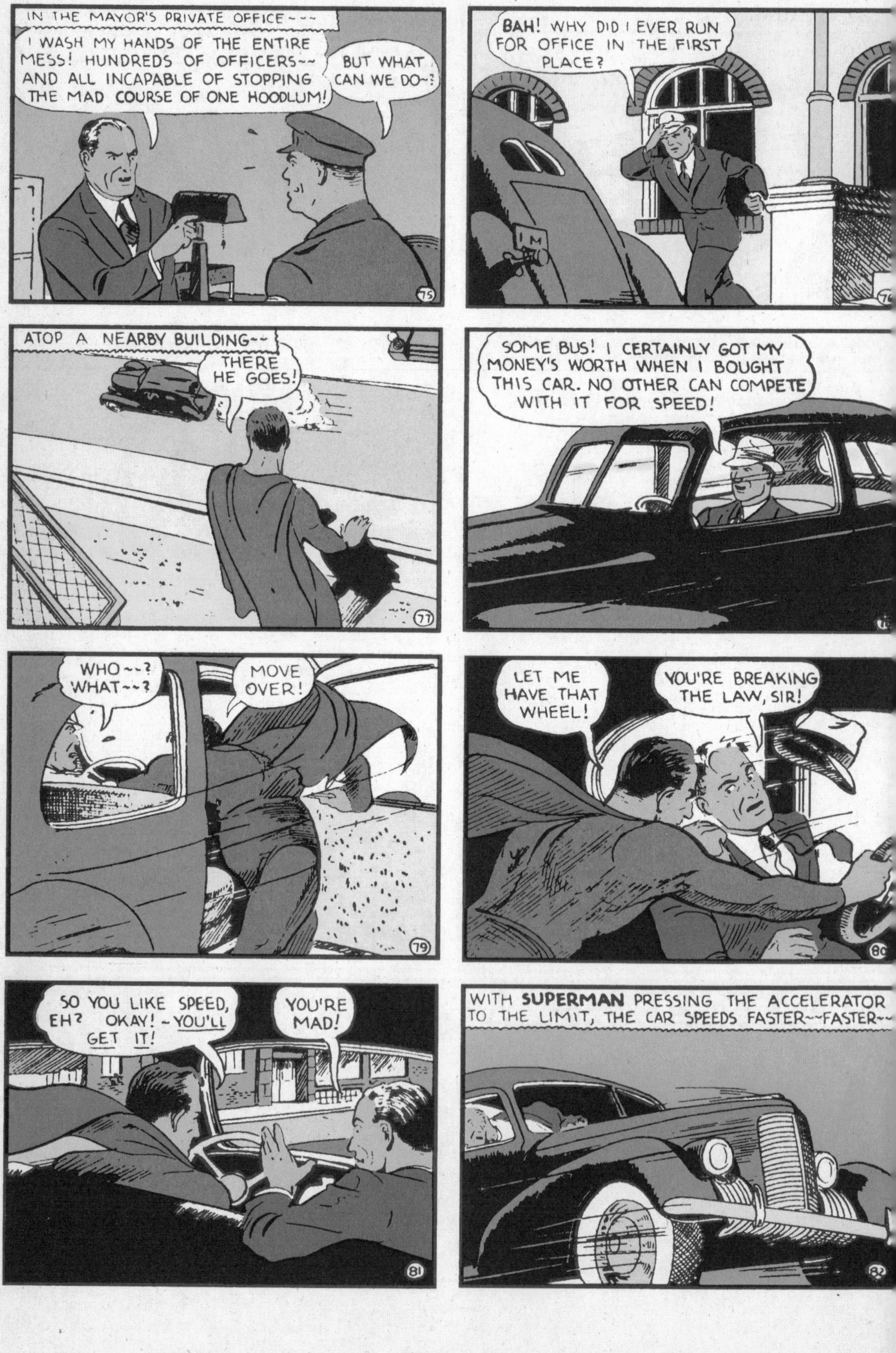
IN THE MAYOR'S PRIVATE OFFICE---
I WASH MY HANDS OF THE ENTIRE MESS! HUNDREDS OF OFFICERS-- AND ALL INCAPABLE OF STOPPING THE MAD COURSE OF ONE HOODLUM!
BUT WHAT CAN WE DO--?
75
BAH! WHY DID I EVER RUN FOR OFFICE IN THE FIRST PLACE?
ATOP A NEARBY BUILDING--
THERE HE GOES!
77
SOME BUS! I CERTAINLY GOT MY MONEY'S WORTH WHEN I BOUGHT THIS CAR. NO OTHER CAN COMPETE WITH IT FOR SPEED!
WHO--? WHAT--?
MOVE OVER!
79
LET ME HAVE THAT WHEEL!
YOU'RE BREAKING THE LAW, SIR!
SO YOU LIKE SPEED, EH? OKAY! - YOU'LL GET IT!
YOU'RE MAD!
81
WITH SUPERMAN PRESSING THE ACCELERATOR TO THE LIMIT, THE CAR SPEEDS FASTER--FASTER--

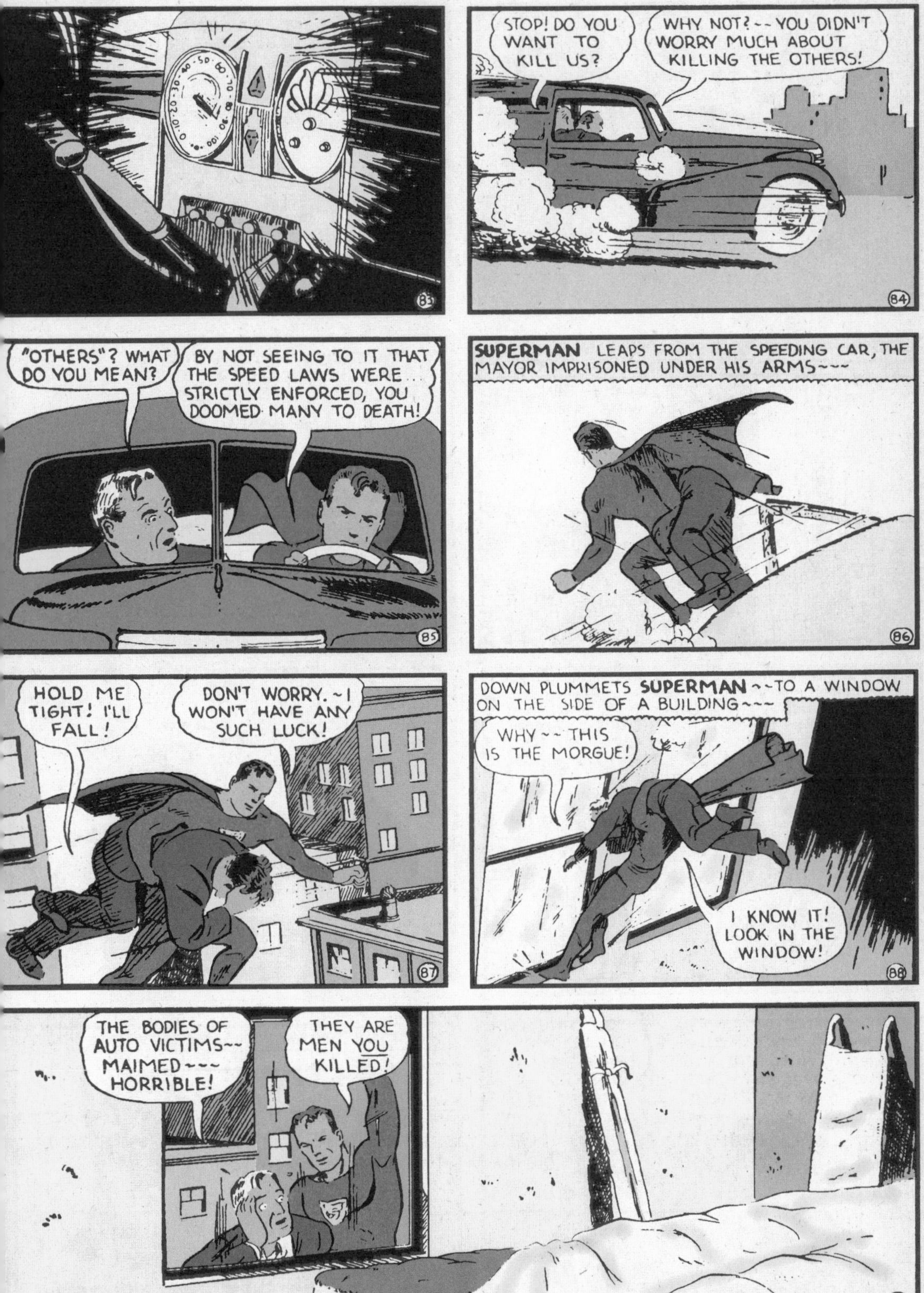

STOP! DO YOU WANT TO KILL US?
WHY NOT?-- YOU DIDN'T WORRY MUCH ABOUT KILLING THE OTHERS!
"OTHERS"? WHAT DO YOU MEAN?
BY NOT SEEING TO IT THAT THE SPEED LAWS WERE STRICTLY ENFORCED, YOU DOOMED MANY TO DEATH!
SUPERMAN LEAPS FROM THE SPEEDING CAR, THE MAYOR IMPRISONED UNDER HIS ARMS---
HOLD ME TIGHT! I'LL FALL!
DON'T WORRY.-I WON'T HAVE ANY SUCH LUCK!
DOWN PLUMMETS SUPERMAN--TO A WINDOW ON THE SIDE OF A BUILDING---
WHY--THIS IS THE MORGUE!
I KNOW IT! LOOK IN THE WINDOW!
THE BODIES OF AUTO VICTIMS--MAIMED---HORRIBLE!
THEY ARE MEN YOU KILLED!

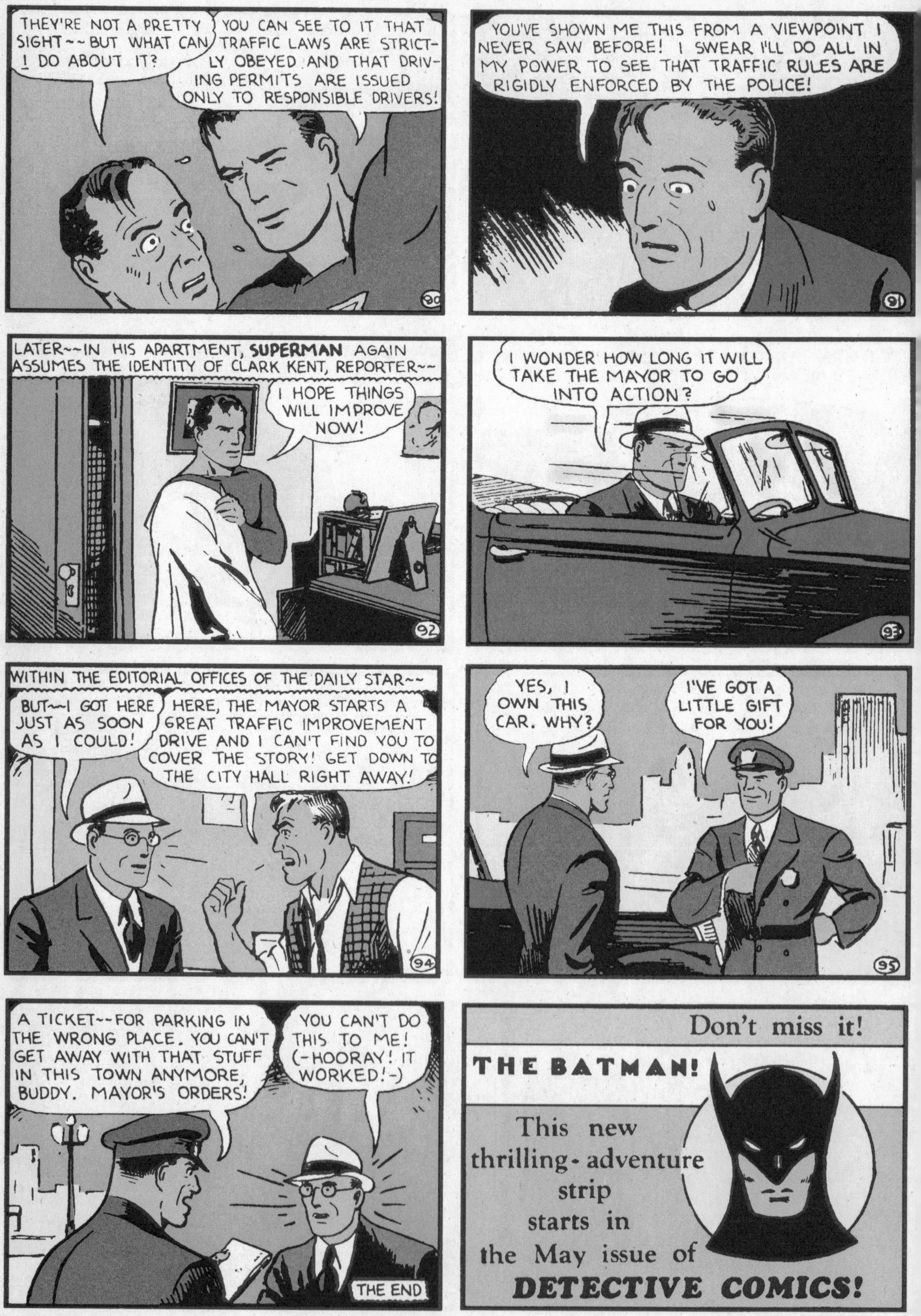
THEY'RE NOT A PRETTY SIGHT~~BUT WHAT CAN I DO ABOUT IT?
YOU CAN SEE TO IT THAT TRAFFIC LAWS ARE STRICTLY OBEYED AND THAT DRIVING PERMITS ARE ISSUED ONLY TO RESPONSIBLE DRIVERS!
YOU'VE SHOWN ME THIS FROM A VIEWPOINT I NEVER SAW BEFORE! I SWEAR I'LL DO ALL IN MY POWER TO SEE THAT TRAFFIC RULES ARE RIGIDLY ENFORCED BY THE POLICE!
LATER~~IN HIS APARTMENT, SUPERMAN AGAIN ASSUMES THE IDENTITY OF CLARK KENT, REPORTER~~
I HOPE THINGS WILL IMPROVE NOW!
I WONDER HOW LONG IT WILL TAKE THE MAYOR TO GO INTO ACTION?
WITHIN THE EDITORIAL OFFICES OF THE DAILY STAR~~
BUT~~I GOT HERE JUST AS SOON AS I COULD!
HERE, THE MAYOR STARTS A GREAT TRAFFIC IMPROVEMENT DRIVE AND I CAN'T FIND YOU TO COVER THE STORY! GET DOWN TO THE CITY HALL RIGHT AWAY!
YES, I OWN THIS CAR. WHY?
I'VE GOT A LITTLE GIFT FOR YOU!
A TICKET~~FOR PARKING IN THE WRONG PLACE. YOU CAN'T GET AWAY WITH THAT STUFF IN THIS TOWN ANYMORE, BUDDY. MAYOR'S ORDERS!
YOU CAN'T DO THIS TO ME! (-HOORAY! IT WORKED!-)
THE END
Don't miss it!
THE BATMAN!
This new thrilling-adventure strip starts in the May issue of
DETECTIVE COMICS!

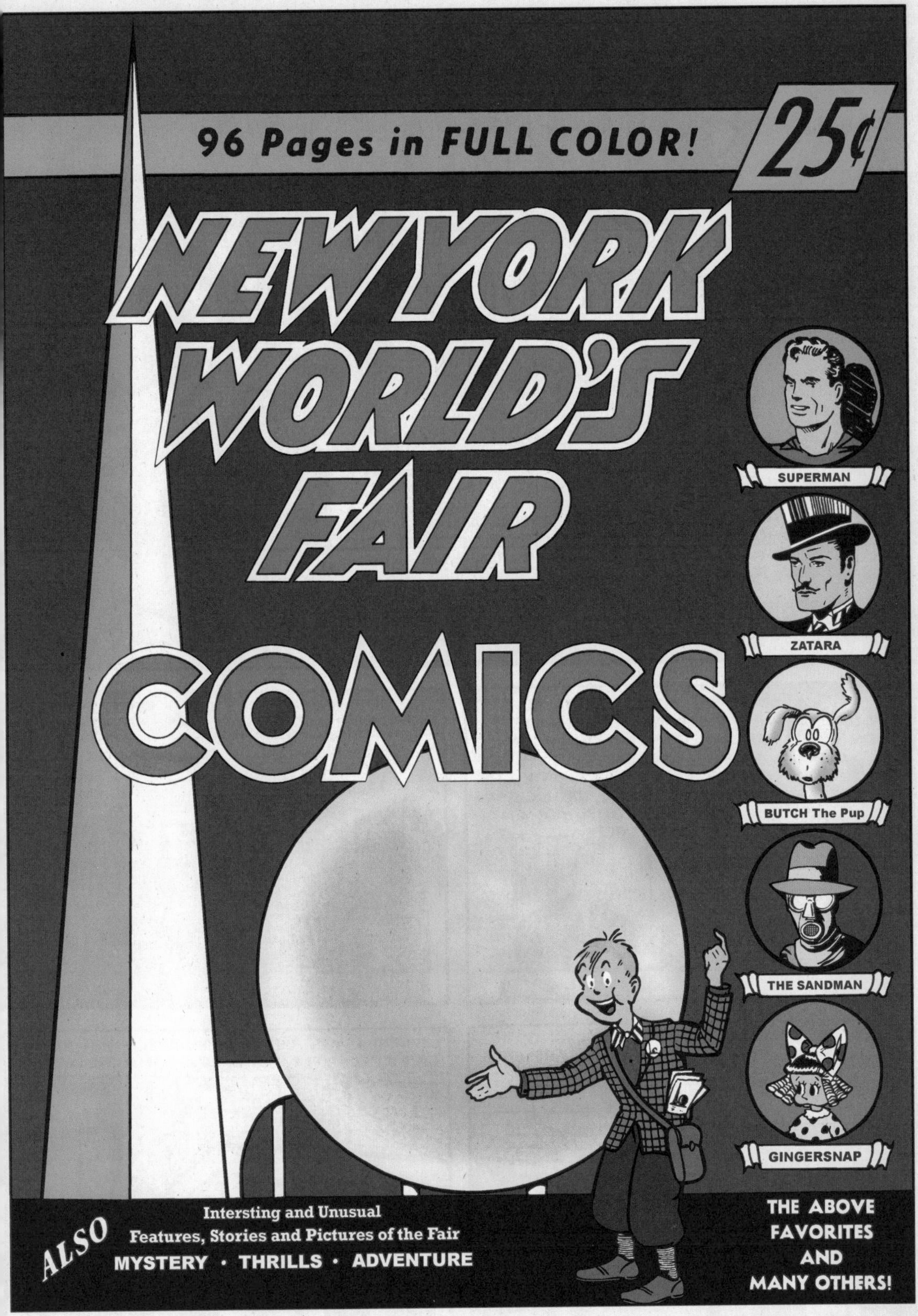
96 Pages in FULL COLOR!
25¢
NEW YORK WORLD'S FAIR
COMICS
SUPERMAN
ZATARA
BUTCH The Pup
THE SANDMAN
GINGERSNAP
ALSO
Intersting and Unusual
Features, Stories and Pictures of the Fair
MYSTERY · THRILLS · ADVENTURE
THE ABOVE
FAVORITES
AND
MANY OTHERS!

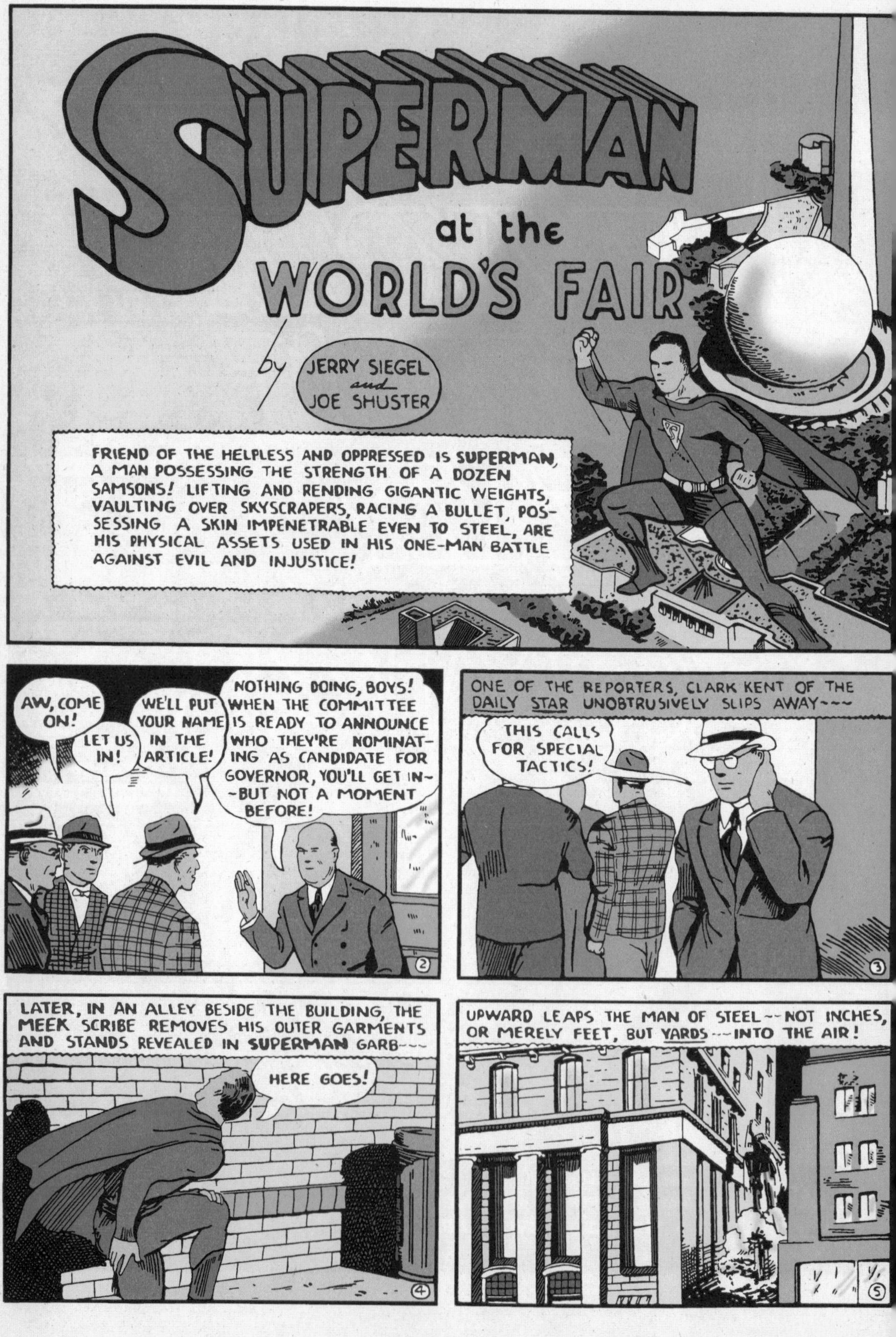
SUPERMAN
at the
WORLD'S FAIR
by JERRY SIEGEL and JOE SHUSTER
FRIEND OF THE HELPLESS AND OPPRESSED IS SUPERMAN, A MAN POSSESSING THE STRENGTH OF A DOZEN SAMSONS! LIFTING AND RENDING GIGANTIC WEIGHTS, VAULTING OVER SKYSCRAPERS, RACING A BULLET, POSSESSING A SKIN IMPENETRABLE EVEN TO STEEL, ARE HIS PHYSICAL ASSETS USED IN HIS ONE-MAN BATTLE AGAINST EVIL AND INJUSTICE!
AW, COME ON!
LET US IN!
WE'LL PUT YOUR NAME IN THE ARTICLE!
NOTHING DOING, BOYS! WHEN THE COMMITTEE IS READY TO ANNOUNCE WHO THEY'RE NOMINATING AS CANDIDATE FOR GOVERNOR, YOU'LL GET IN--BUT NOT A MOMENT BEFORE!
2
ONE OF THE REPORTERS, CLARK KENT OF THE DAILY STAR UNOBTRUSIVELY SLIPS AWAY---
THIS CALLS FOR SPECIAL TACTICS!
3
LATER, IN AN ALLEY BESIDE THE BUILDING, THE MEEK SCRIBE REMOVES HIS OUTER GARMENTS AND STANDS REVEALED IN SUPERMAN GARB---
HERE GOES!
4
UPWARD LEAPS THE MAN OF STEEL--NOT INCHES, OR MERELY FEET, BUT YARDS---INTO THE AIR!
5

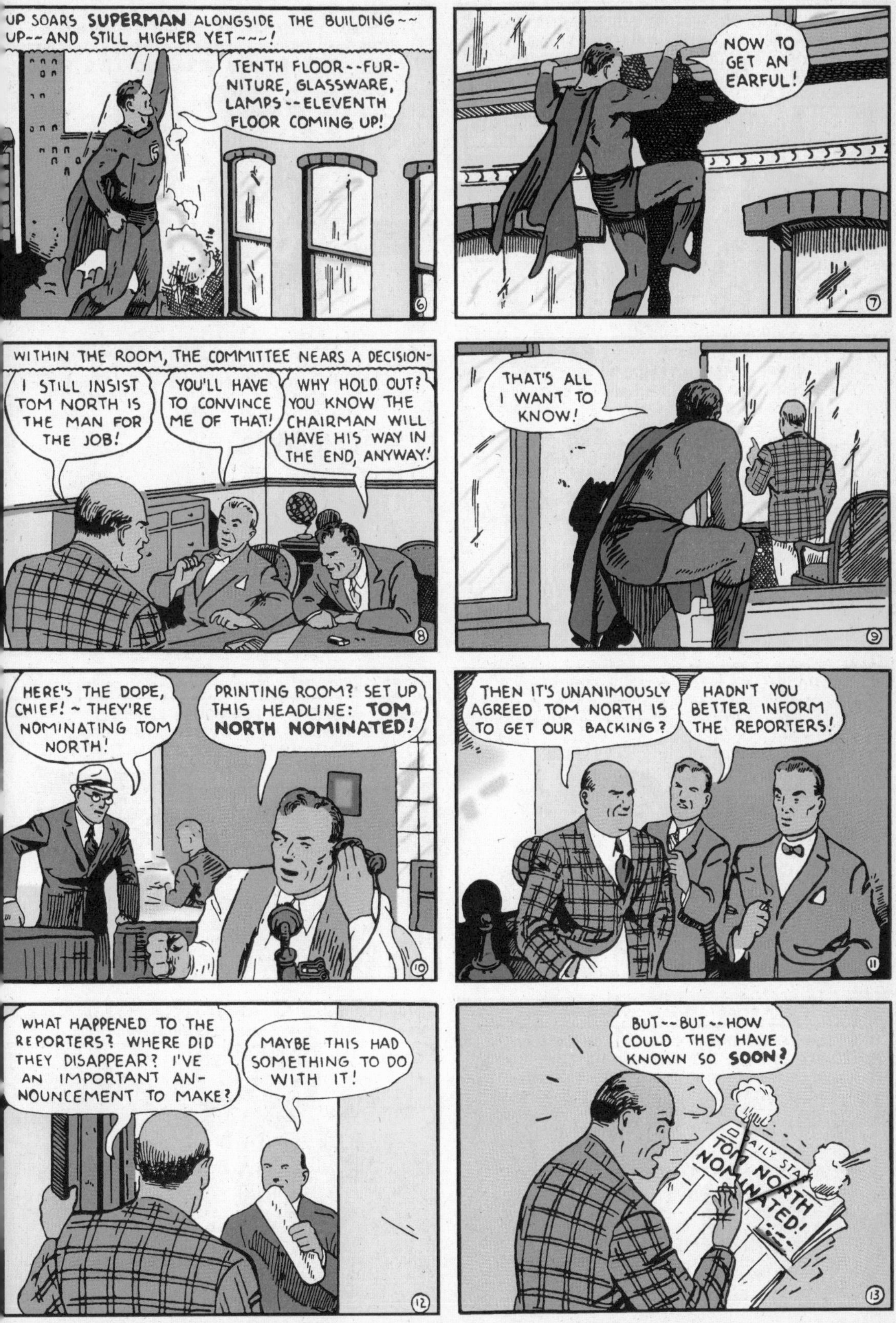
UP SOARS SUPERMAN ALONGSIDE THE BUILDING-- UP--AND STILL HIGHER YET---!
TENTH FLOOR--FURNITURE, GLASSWARE, LAMPS--ELEVENTH FLOOR COMING UP!
NOW TO GET AN EARFUL!
WITHIN THE ROOM, THE COMMITTEE NEARS A DECISION-
I STILL INSIST TOM NORTH IS THE MAN FOR THE JOB!
YOU'LL HAVE TO CONVINCE ME OF THAT!
WHY HOLD OUT? YOU KNOW THE CHAIRMAN WILL HAVE HIS WAY IN THE END, ANYWAY!
THAT'S ALL I WANT TO KNOW!
HERE'S THE DOPE, CHIEF! - THEY'RE NOMINATING TOM NORTH!
PRINTING ROOM? SET UP THIS HEADLINE: TOM NORTH NOMINATED!
THEN IT'S UNANIMOUSLY AGREED TOM NORTH IS TO GET OUR BACKING?
HADN'T YOU BETTER INFORM THE REPORTERS!
WHAT HAPPENED TO THE REPORTERS? WHERE DID THEY DISAPPEAR? I'VE AN IMPORTANT ANNOUNCEMENT TO MAKE?
MAYBE THIS HAD SOMETHING TO DO WITH IT!
BUT--BUT--HOW COULD THEY HAVE KNOWN SO SOON?
TOM NORTH NOMINATED!

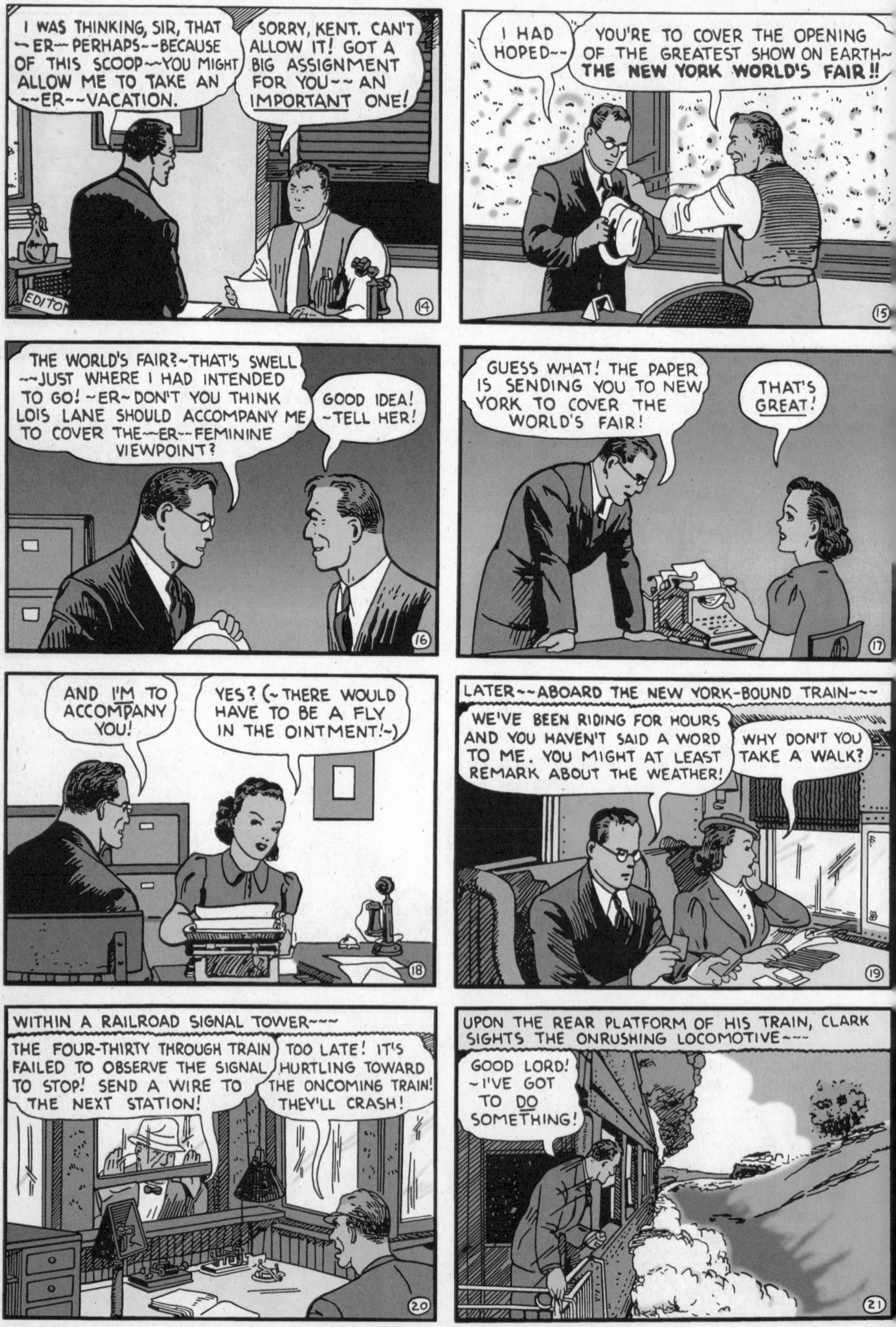
I WAS THINKING, SIR, THAT ~ER~ PERHAPS--BECAUSE OF THIS SCOOP~~YOU MIGHT ALLOW ME TO TAKE AN ~~ER~~VACATION.
SORRY, KENT. CAN'T ALLOW IT! GOT A BIG ASSIGNMENT FOR YOU~~ AN IMPORTANT ONE!
EDITOR
14
I HAD HOPED~~
YOU'RE TO COVER THE OPENING OF THE GREATEST SHOW ON EARTH~ THE NEW YORK WORLD'S FAIR!!
15
THE WORLD'S FAIR?~THAT'S SWELL ~~JUST WHERE I HAD INTENDED TO GO! ~ER~ DON'T YOU THINK LOIS LANE SHOULD ACCOMPANY ME TO COVER THE~~ER~~FEMININE VIEWPOINT?
GOOD IDEA! ~TELL HER!
16
GUESS WHAT! THE PAPER IS SENDING YOU TO NEW YORK TO COVER THE WORLD'S FAIR!
THAT'S GREAT!
17
AND I'M TO ACCOMPANY YOU!
YES? (~THERE WOULD HAVE TO BE A FLY IN THE OINTMENT!~)
18
LATER~~ABOARD THE NEW YORK-BOUND TRAIN~~~
WE'VE BEEN RIDING FOR HOURS AND YOU HAVEN'T SAID A WORD TO ME. YOU MIGHT AT LEAST REMARK ABOUT THE WEATHER!
WHY DON'T YOU TAKE A WALK?
19
WITHIN A RAILROAD SIGNAL TOWER~~~
THE FOUR-THIRTY THROUGH TRAIN FAILED TO OBSERVE THE SIGNAL TO STOP! SEND A WIRE TO THE NEXT STATION!
TOO LATE! IT'S HURTLING TOWARD THE ONCOMING TRAIN! THEY'LL CRASH!
20
UPON THE REAR PLATFORM OF HIS TRAIN, CLARK SIGHTS THE ONRUSHING LOCOMOTIVE~~~
GOOD LORD! ~I'VE GOT TO DO SOMETHING!
21

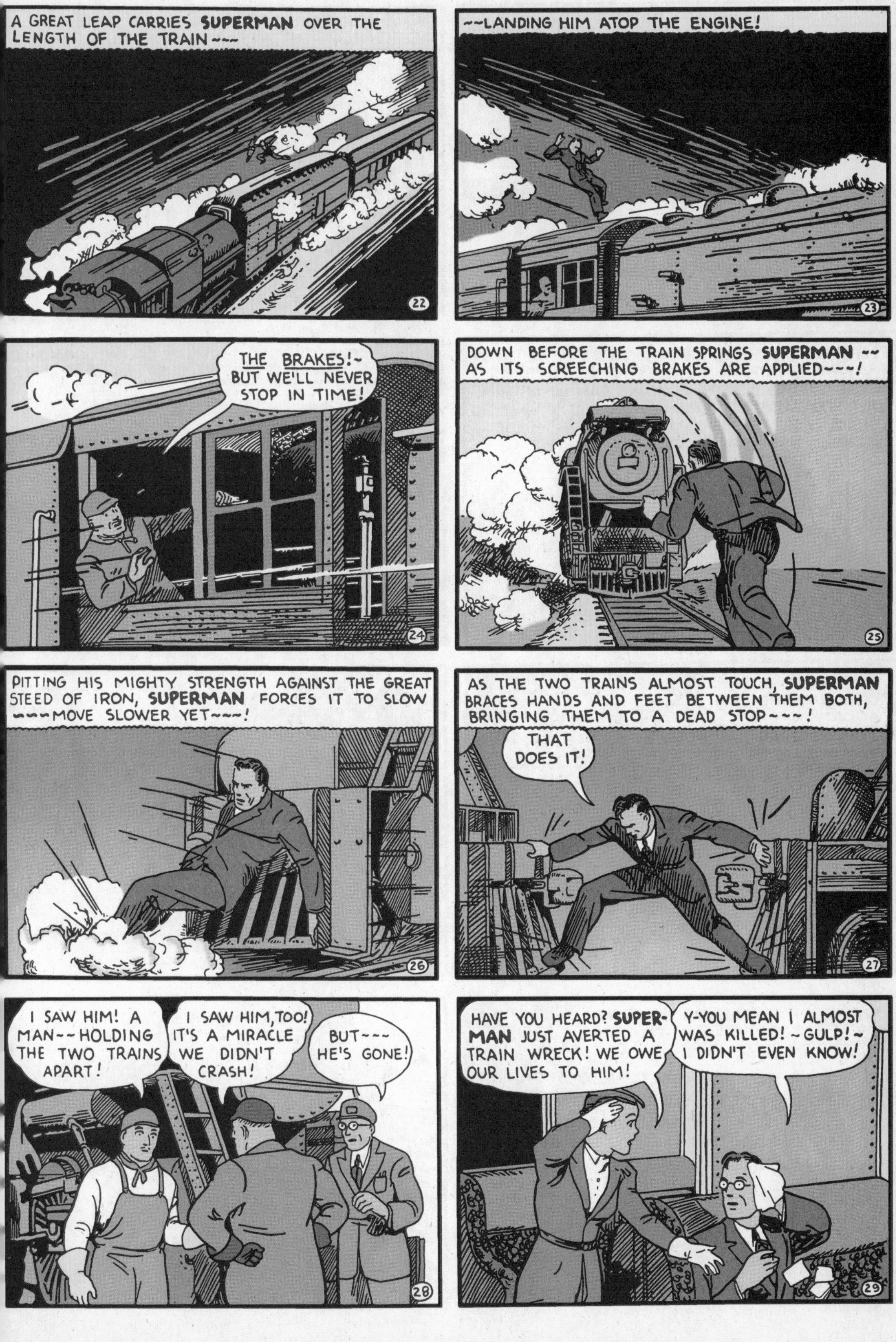
A GREAT LEAP CARRIES **SUPERMAN** OVER THE LENGTH OF THE TRAIN---
22
--LANDING HIM ATOP THE ENGINE!
23
THE BRAKES!- BUT WE'LL NEVER STOP IN TIME!
24
DOWN BEFORE THE TRAIN SPRINGS **SUPERMAN** -- AS ITS SCREECHING BRAKES ARE APPLIED---!
25
PITTING HIS MIGHTY STRENGTH AGAINST THE GREAT STEED OF IRON, **SUPERMAN** FORCES IT TO SLOW ----MOVE SLOWER YET---!
26
AS THE TWO TRAINS ALMOST TOUCH, **SUPERMAN** BRACES HANDS AND FEET BETWEEN THEM BOTH, BRINGING THEM TO A DEAD STOP---!
THAT DOES IT!
27
I SAW HIM! A MAN--HOLDING THE TWO TRAINS APART!
I SAW HIM, TOO! IT'S A MIRACLE WE DIDN'T CRASH!
BUT--- HE'S GONE!
28
HAVE YOU HEARD? **SUPERMAN** JUST AVERTED A TRAIN WRECK! WE OWE OUR LIVES TO HIM!
Y-YOU MEAN I ALMOST WAS KILLED! ~GULP!~ I DIDN'T EVEN KNOW!
29

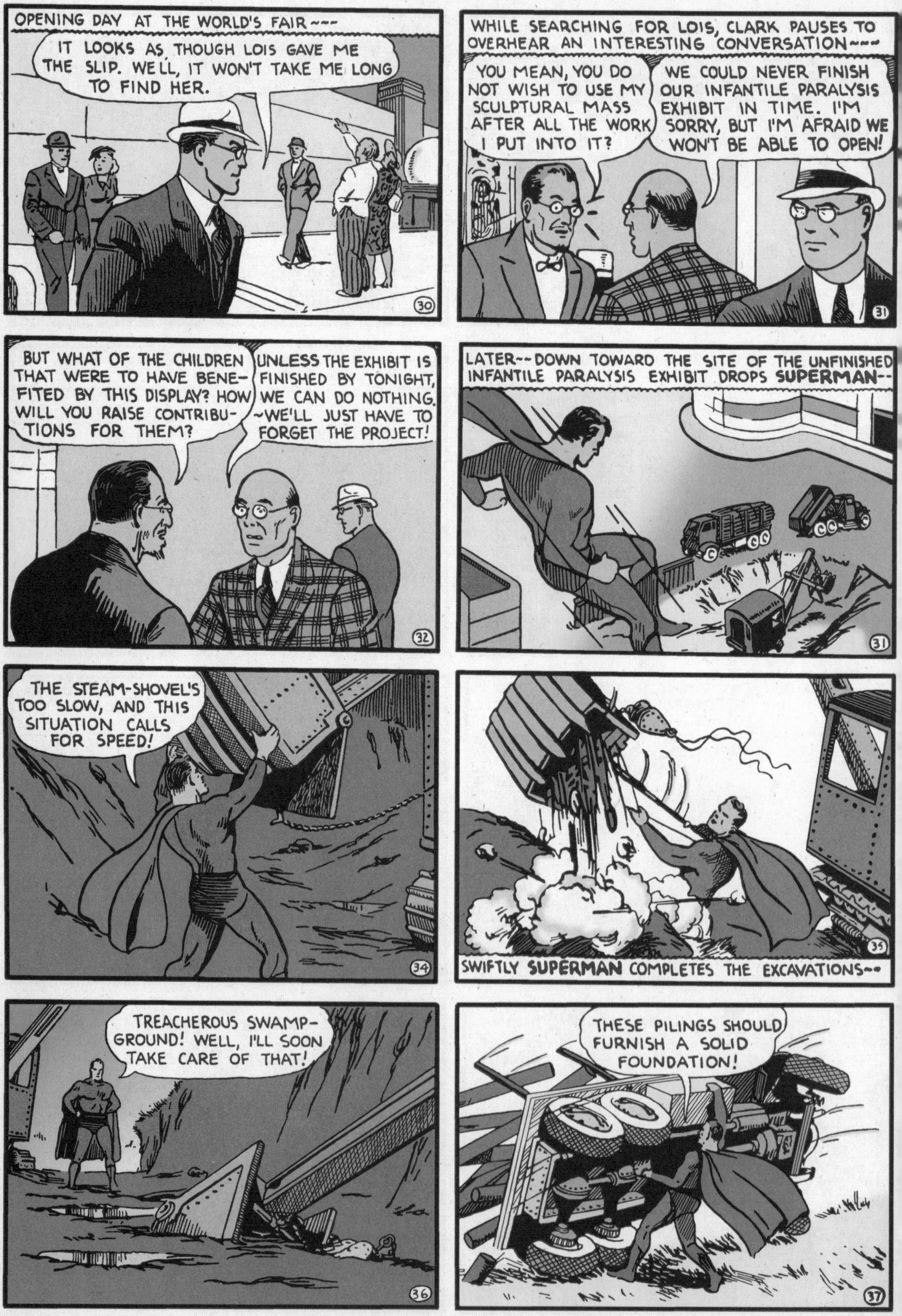
OPENING DAY AT THE WORLD'S FAIR---
IT LOOKS AS THOUGH LOIS GAVE ME THE SLIP. WELL, IT WON'T TAKE ME LONG TO FIND HER.
30
WHILE SEARCHING FOR LOIS, CLARK PAUSES TO OVERHEAR AN INTERESTING CONVERSATION---
YOU MEAN, YOU DO NOT WISH TO USE MY SCULPTURAL MASS AFTER ALL THE WORK I PUT INTO IT?
WE COULD NEVER FINISH OUR INFANTILE PARALYSIS EXHIBIT IN TIME. I'M SORRY, BUT I'M AFRAID WE WON'T BE ABLE TO OPEN!
31
BUT WHAT OF THE CHILDREN THAT WERE TO HAVE BENE-FITED BY THIS DISPLAY? HOW WILL YOU RAISE CONTRIBU-TIONS FOR THEM?
UNLESS THE EXHIBIT IS FINISHED BY TONIGHT, WE CAN DO NOTHING. -WE'LL JUST HAVE TO FORGET THE PROJECT!
32
LATER--DOWN TOWARD THE SITE OF THE UNFINISHED INFANTILE PARALYSIS EXHIBIT DROPS SUPERMAN--
31
THE STEAM-SHOVEL'S TOO SLOW, AND THIS SITUATION CALLS FOR SPEED!
34
35
SWIFTLY SUPERMAN COMPLETES THE EXCAVATIONS--
TREACHEROUS SWAMP-GROUND! WELL, I'LL SOON TAKE CARE OF THAT!
36
THESE PILINGS SHOULD FURNISH A SOLID FOUNDATION!
37

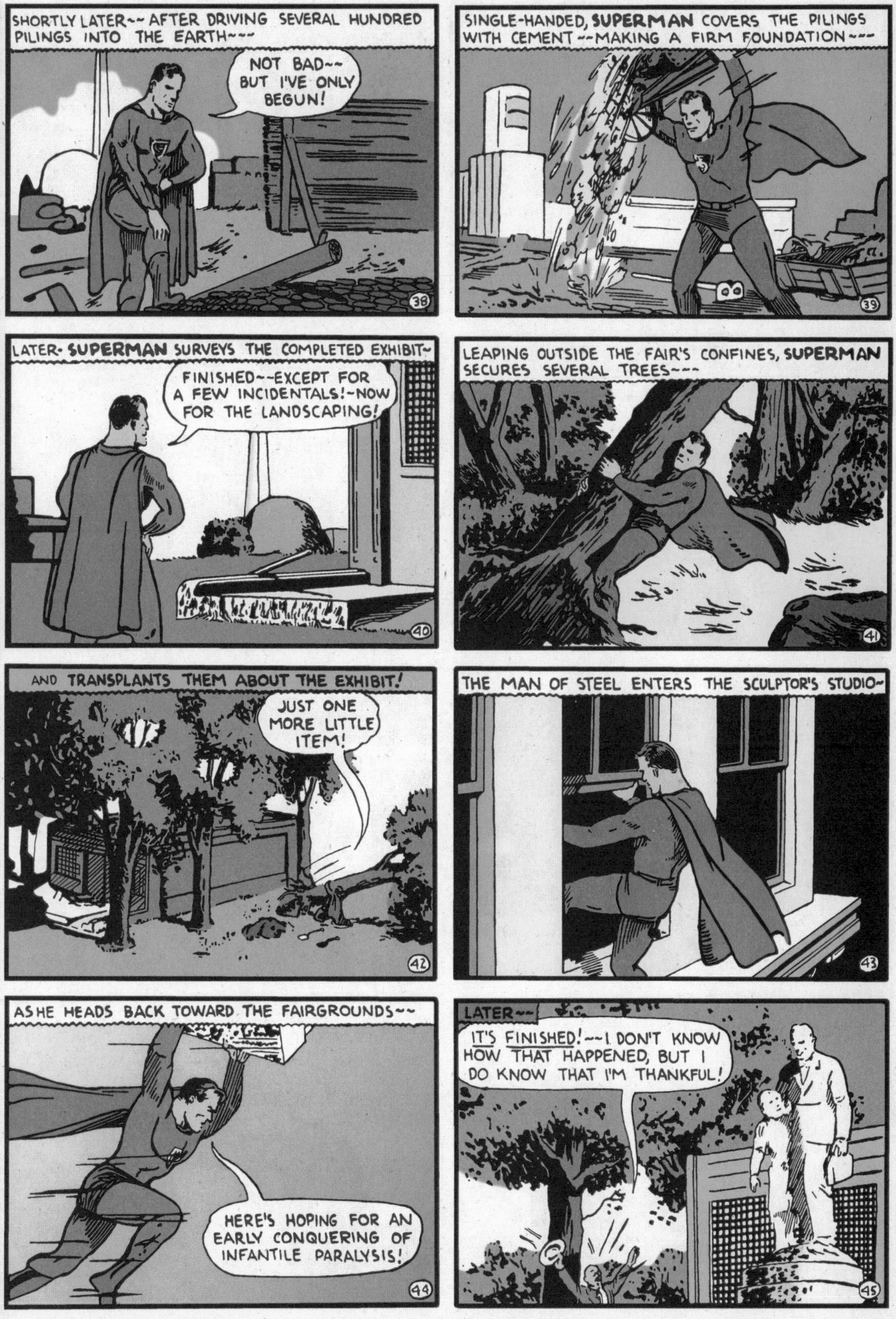
SHORTLY LATER-- AFTER DRIVING SEVERAL HUNDRED PILINGS INTO THE EARTH---
NOT BAD-- BUT I'VE ONLY BEGUN!
38
SINGLE-HANDED, SUPERMAN COVERS THE PILINGS WITH CEMENT --MAKING A FIRM FOUNDATION ---
39
LATER- SUPERMAN SURVEYS THE COMPLETED EXHIBIT-
FINISHED--EXCEPT FOR A FEW INCIDENTALS!-NOW FOR THE LANDSCAPING!
40
LEAPING OUTSIDE THE FAIR'S CONFINES, SUPERMAN SECURES SEVERAL TREES---
41
AND TRANSPLANTS THEM ABOUT THE EXHIBIT!
JUST ONE MORE LITTLE ITEM!
42
THE MAN OF STEEL ENTERS THE SCULPTOR'S STUDIO-
43
AS HE HEADS BACK TOWARD THE FAIRGROUNDS--
HERE'S HOPING FOR AN EARLY CONQUERING OF INFANTILE PARALYSIS!
44
LATER--
IT'S FINISHED!--I DON'T KNOW HOW THAT HAPPENED, BUT I DO KNOW THAT I'M THANKFUL!
45

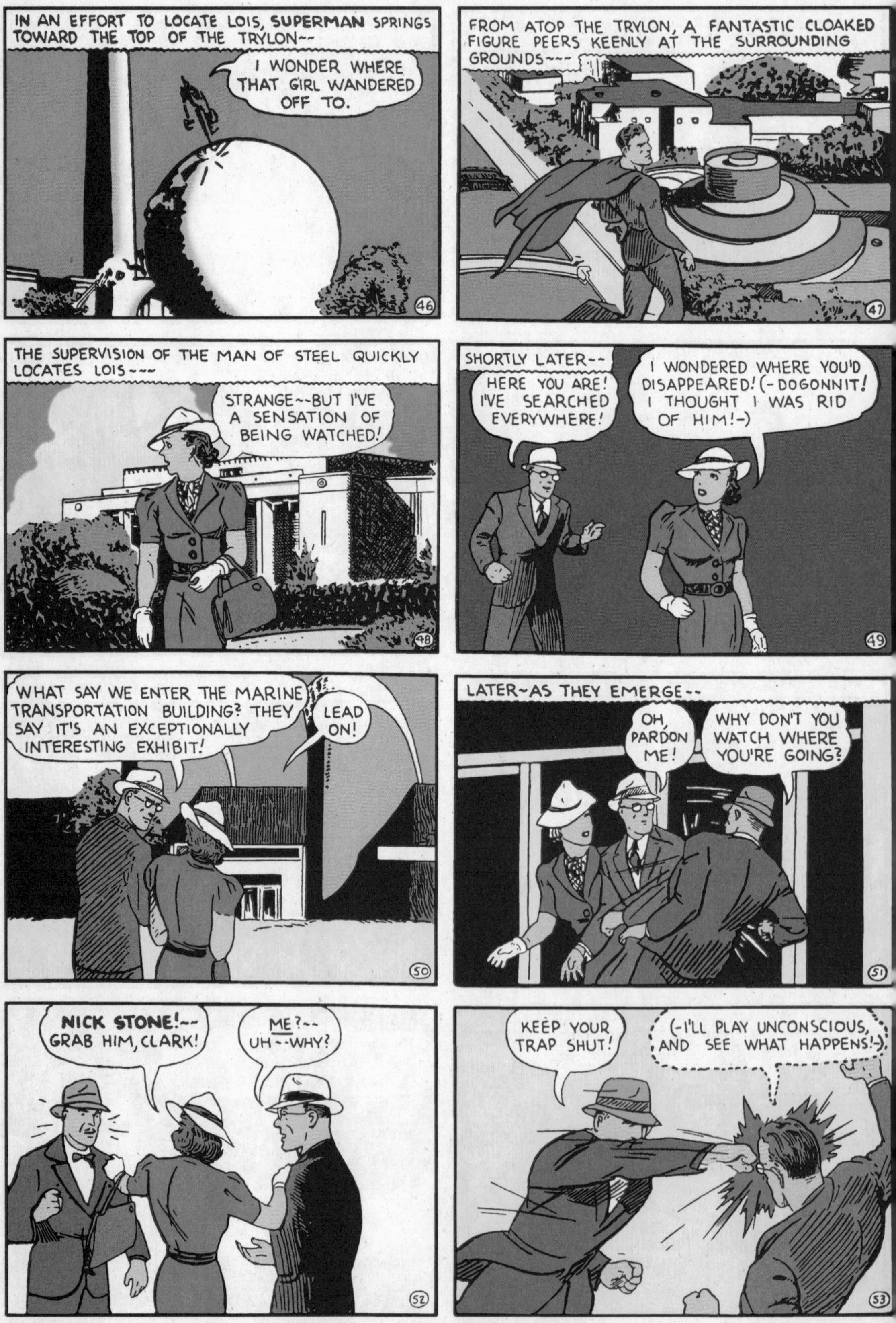
IN AN EFFORT TO LOCATE LOIS, SUPERMAN SPRINGS TOWARD THE TOP OF THE TRYLON--
I WONDER WHERE THAT GIRL WANDERED OFF TO.
46
FROM ATOP THE TRYLON, A FANTASTIC CLOAKED FIGURE PEERS KEENLY AT THE SURROUNDING GROUNDS---
47
THE SUPERVISION OF THE MAN OF STEEL QUICKLY LOCATES LOIS---
STRANGE--BUT I'VE A SENSATION OF BEING WATCHED!
48
SHORTLY LATER--
HERE YOU ARE! I'VE SEARCHED EVERYWHERE!
I WONDERED WHERE YOU'D DISAPPEARED! (-DOGONNIT! I THOUGHT I WAS RID OF HIM!-)
49
WHAT SAY WE ENTER THE MARINE TRANSPORTATION BUILDING? THEY SAY IT'S AN EXCEPTIONALLY INTERESTING EXHIBIT!
LEAD ON!
50
LATER-AS THEY EMERGE--
OH, PARDON ME!
WHY DON'T YOU WATCH WHERE YOU'RE GOING?
51
NICK STONE!-- GRAB HIM, CLARK!
ME?-- UH--WHY?
52
KEEP YOUR TRAP SHUT!
(-I'LL PLAY UNCONSCIOUS, AND SEE WHAT HAPPENS!-)
53

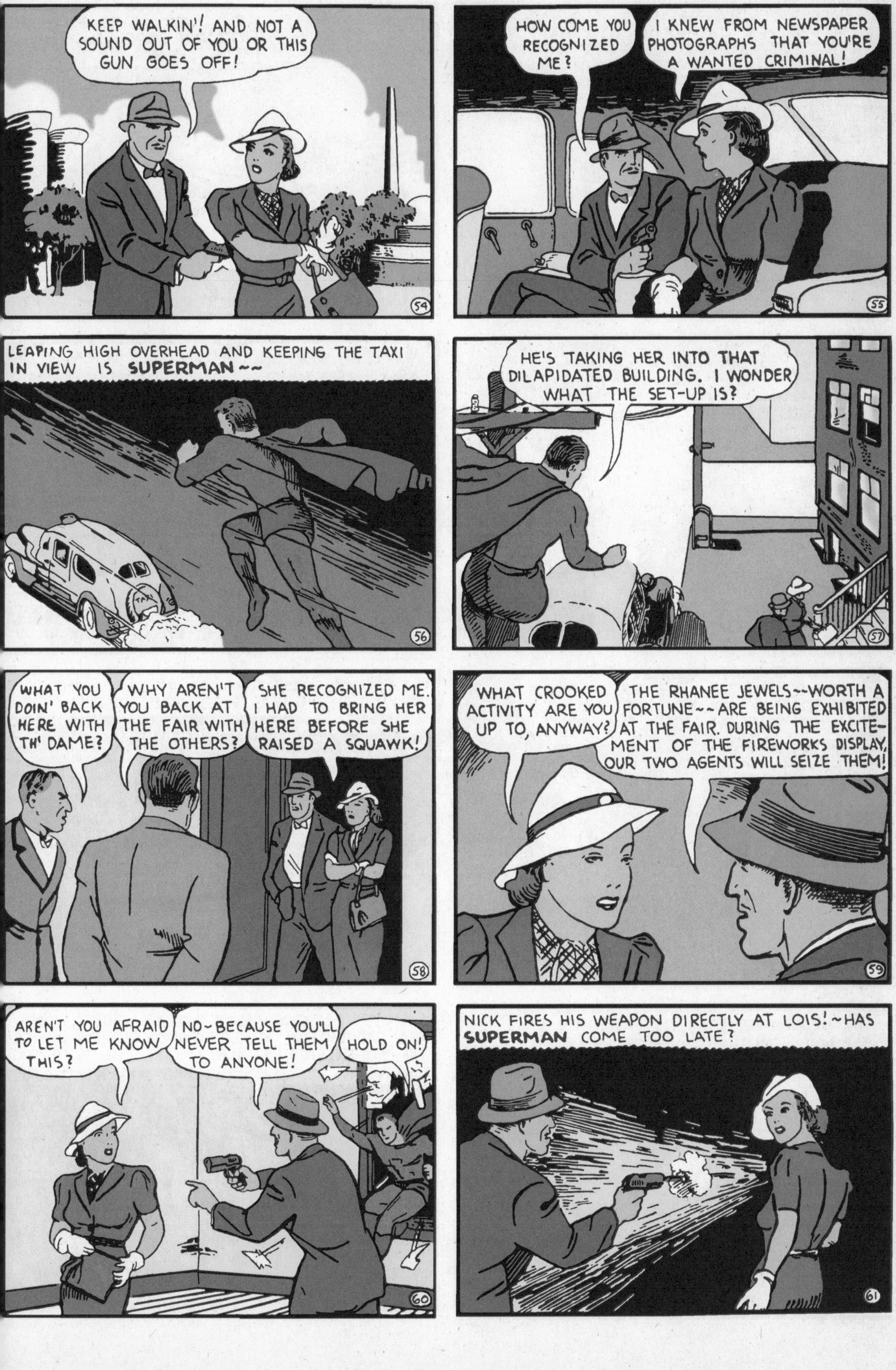
KEEP WALKIN'! AND NOT A SOUND OUT OF YOU OR THIS GUN GOES OFF!
54
HOW COME YOU RECOGNIZED ME?
I KNEW FROM NEWSPAPER PHOTOGRAPHS THAT YOU'RE A WANTED CRIMINAL!
55
LEAPING HIGH OVERHEAD AND KEEPING THE TAXI IN VIEW IS SUPERMAN~~
56
HE'S TAKING HER INTO THAT DILAPIDATED BUILDING. I WONDER WHAT THE SET-UP IS?
57
WHAT YOU DOIN' BACK HERE WITH TH' DAME?
WHY AREN'T YOU BACK AT THE FAIR WITH THE OTHERS?
SHE RECOGNIZED ME. I HAD TO BRING HER HERE BEFORE SHE RAISED A SQUAWK!
58
WHAT CROOKED ACTIVITY ARE YOU UP TO, ANYWAY?
THE RHANEE JEWELS~~WORTH A FORTUNE~~ARE BEING EXHIBITED AT THE FAIR. DURING THE EXCITEMENT OF THE FIREWORKS DISPLAY, OUR TWO AGENTS WILL SEIZE THEM!
59
AREN'T YOU AFRAID TO LET ME KNOW THIS?
NO~BECAUSE YOU'LL NEVER TELL THEM TO ANYONE!
HOLD ON!
60
NICK FIRES HIS WEAPON DIRECTLY AT LOIS! ~HAS SUPERMAN COME TOO LATE?
61

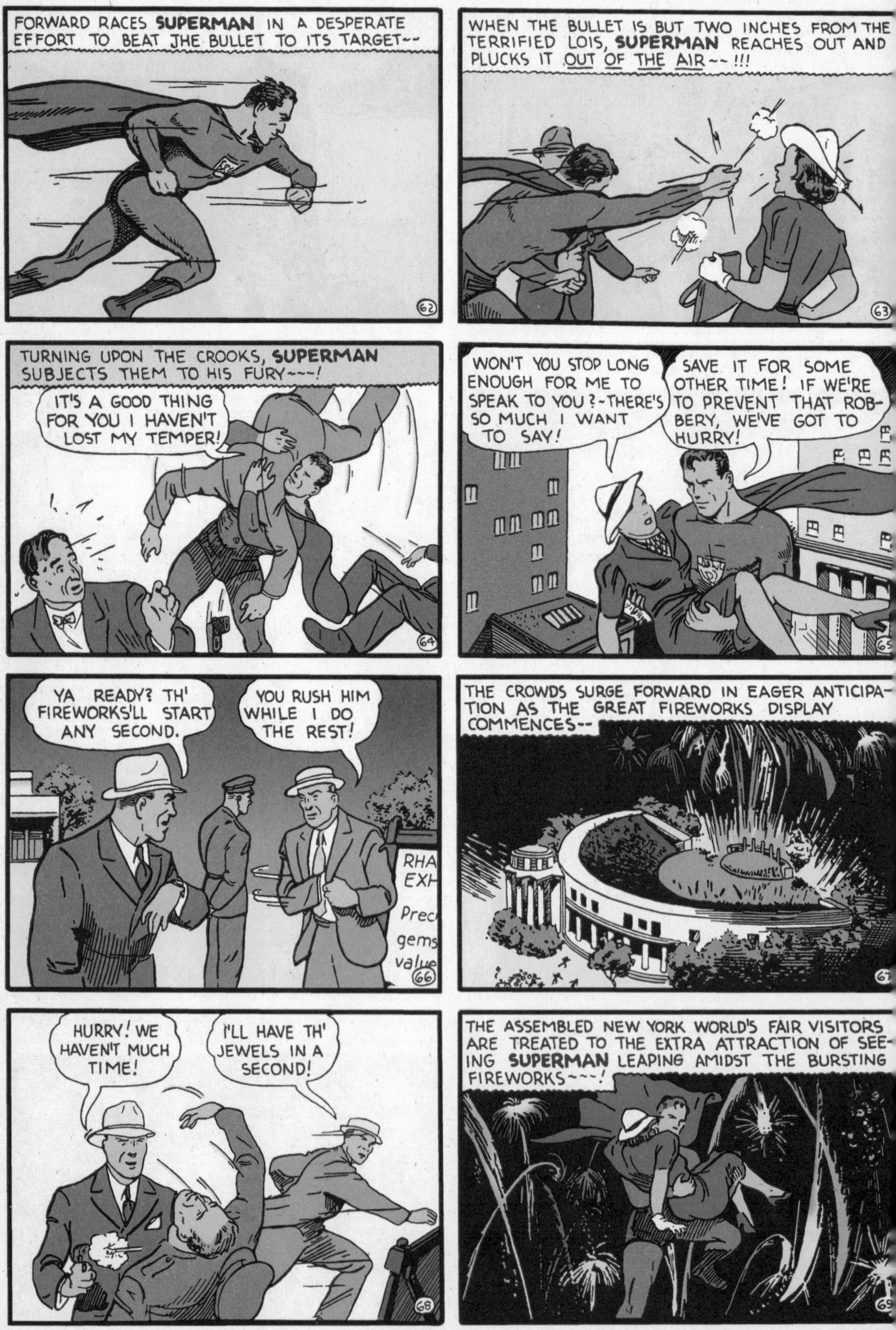

FORWARD RACES SUPERMAN IN A DESPERATE EFFORT TO BEAT THE BULLET TO ITS TARGET--
WHEN THE BULLET IS BUT TWO INCHES FROM THE TERRIFIED LOIS, SUPERMAN REACHES OUT AND PLUCKS IT OUT OF THE AIR--!!!
TURNING UPON THE CROOKS, SUPERMAN SUBJECTS THEM TO HIS FURY---!
IT'S A GOOD THING FOR YOU I HAVEN'T LOST MY TEMPER!
WON'T YOU STOP LONG ENOUGH FOR ME TO SPEAK TO YOU?-THERE'S SO MUCH I WANT TO SAY!
SAVE IT FOR SOME OTHER TIME! IF WE'RE TO PREVENT THAT ROBBERY, WE'VE GOT TO HURRY!
YA READY? TH' FIREWORKS'LL START ANY SECOND.
YOU RUSH HIM WHILE I DO THE REST!
THE CROWDS SURGE FORWARD IN EAGER ANTICIPATION AS THE GREAT FIREWORKS DISPLAY COMMENCES--
HURRY! WE HAVEN'T MUCH TIME!
I'LL HAVE TH' JEWELS IN A SECOND!
THE ASSEMBLED NEW YORK WORLD'S FAIR VISITORS ARE TREATED TO THE EXTRA ATTRACTION OF SEEING SUPERMAN LEAPING AMIDST THE BURSTING FIREWORKS---!

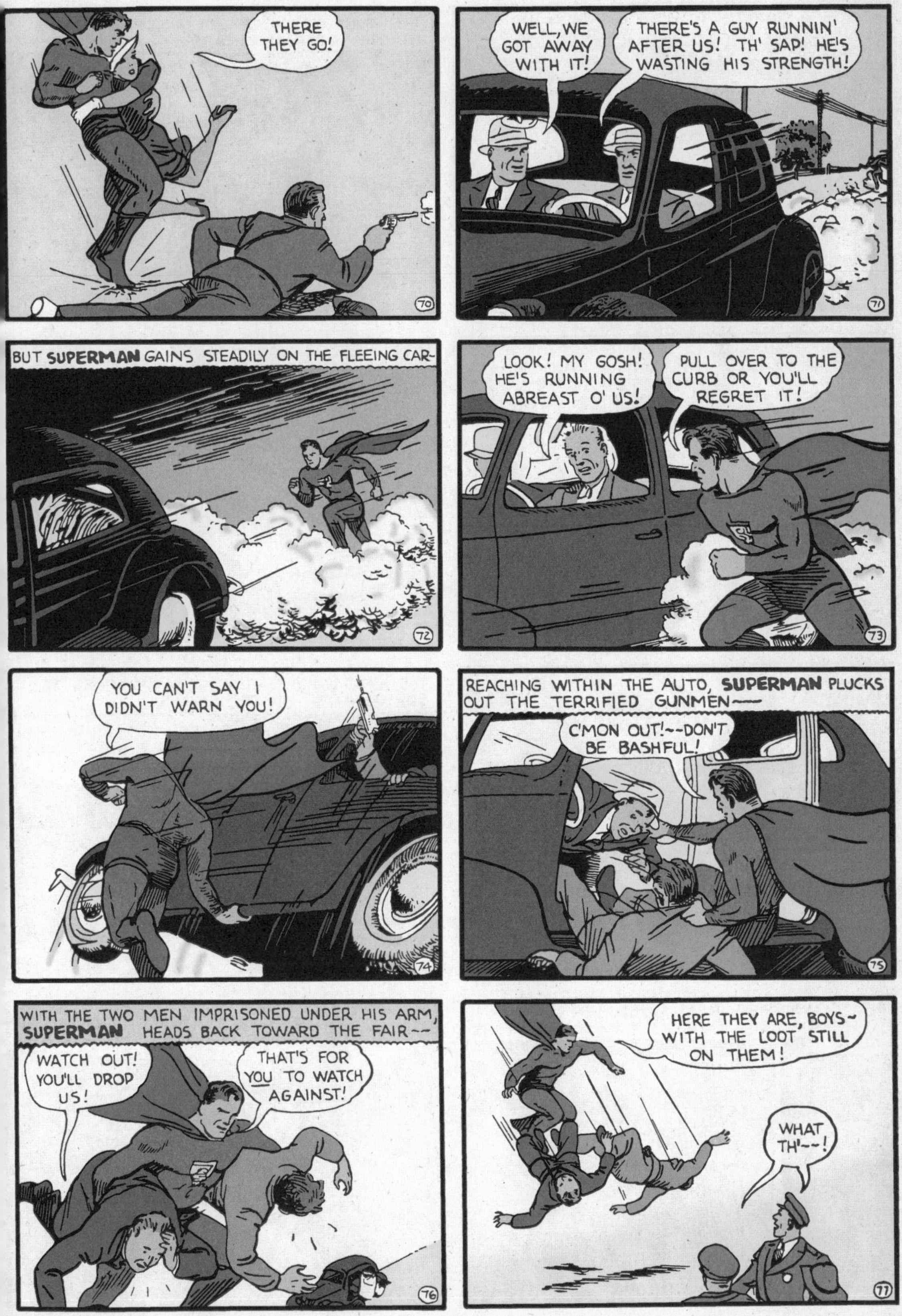
THERE THEY GO!
WELL, WE GOT AWAY WITH IT!
THERE'S A GUY RUNNIN' AFTER US! TH' SAP! HE'S WASTING HIS STRENGTH!
BUT SUPERMAN GAINS STEADILY ON THE FLEEING CAR-
LOOK! MY GOSH! HE'S RUNNING ABREAST O' US!
PULL OVER TO THE CURB OR YOU'LL REGRET IT!
YOU CAN'T SAY I DIDN'T WARN YOU!
REACHING WITHIN THE AUTO, SUPERMAN PLUCKS OUT THE TERRIFIED GUNMEN---
C'MON OUT!--DON'T BE BASHFUL!
WITH THE TWO MEN IMPRISONED UNDER HIS ARM, SUPERMAN HEADS BACK TOWARD THE FAIR--
WATCH OUT! YOU'LL DROP US!
THAT'S FOR YOU TO WATCH AGAINST!
HERE THEY ARE, BOYS-- WITH THE LOOT STILL ON THEM!
WHAT TH'--!

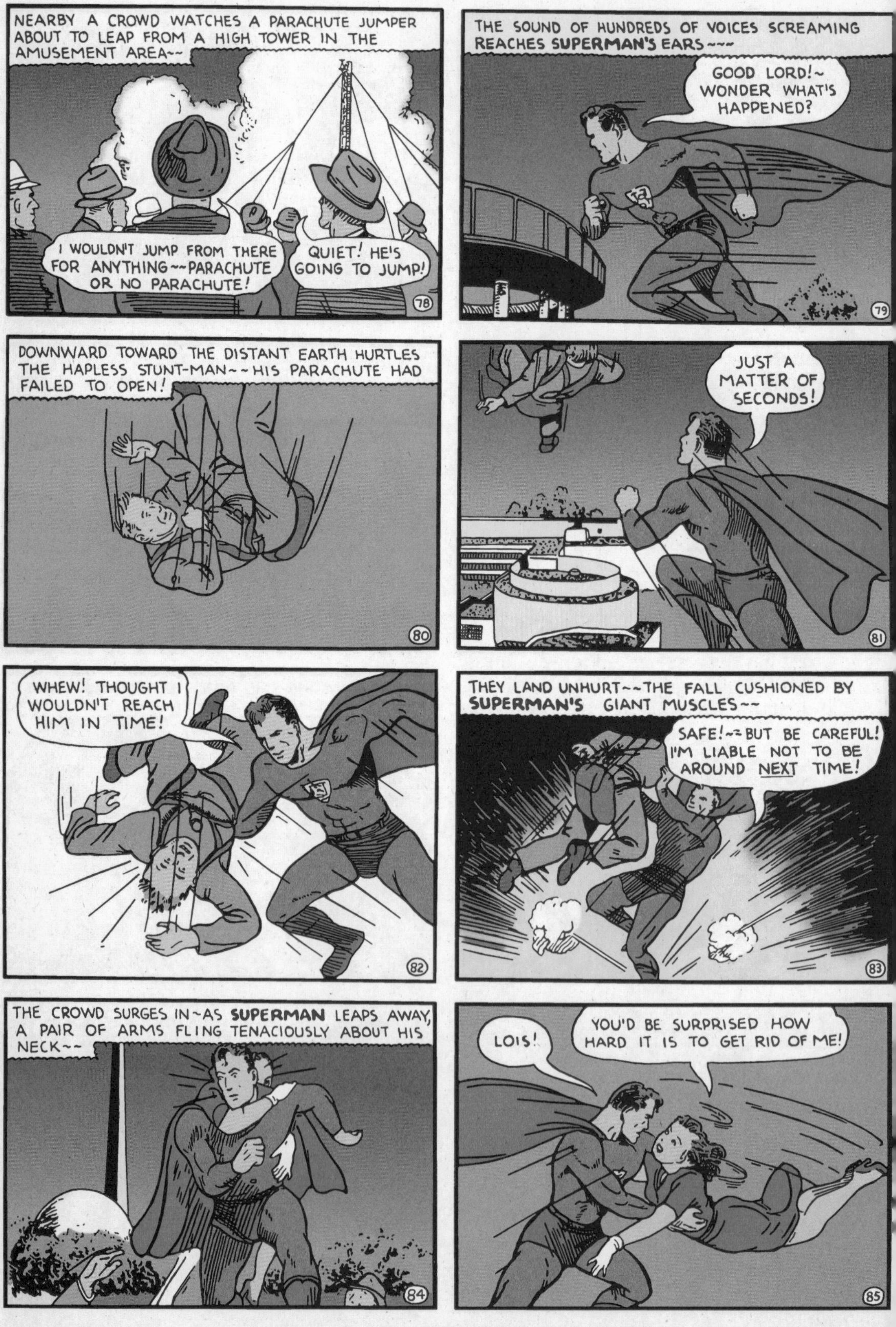
NEARBY A CROWD WATCHES A PARACHUTE JUMPER ABOUT TO LEAP FROM A HIGH TOWER IN THE AMUSEMENT AREA~~
I WOULDN'T JUMP FROM THERE FOR ANYTHING~~PARACHUTE OR NO PARACHUTE!
QUIET! HE'S GOING TO JUMP!
78
THE SOUND OF HUNDREDS OF VOICES SCREAMING REACHES SUPERMAN'S EARS~~~
GOOD LORD!~ WONDER WHAT'S HAPPENED?
79
DOWNWARD TOWARD THE DISTANT EARTH HURTLES THE HAPLESS STUNT-MAN~~HIS PARACHUTE HAD FAILED TO OPEN!
80
JUST A MATTER OF SECONDS!
81
WHEW! THOUGHT I WOULDN'T REACH HIM IN TIME!
82
THEY LAND UNHURT~~THE FALL CUSHIONED BY SUPERMAN'S GIANT MUSCLES~~
SAFE!~~BUT BE CAREFUL! I'M LIABLE NOT TO BE AROUND NEXT TIME!
83
THE CROWD SURGES IN~AS SUPERMAN LEAPS AWAY, A PAIR OF ARMS FLING TENACIOUSLY ABOUT HIS NECK~~
84
LOIS!
YOU'D BE SURPRISED HOW HARD IT IS TO GET RID OF ME!
85

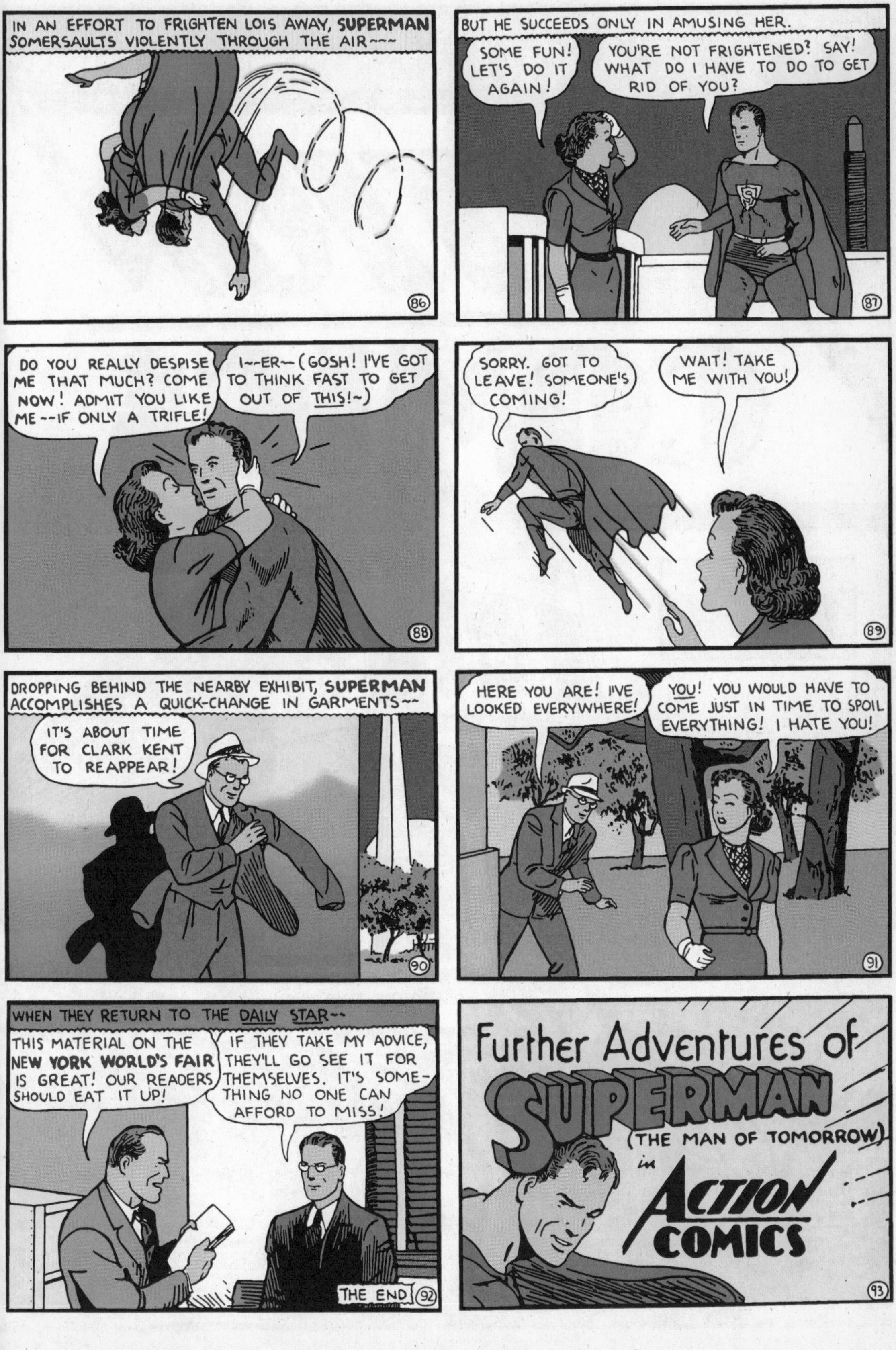
IN AN EFFORT TO FRIGHTEN LOIS AWAY, SUPERMAN SOMERSAULTS VIOLENTLY THROUGH THE AIR---
86
BUT HE SUCCEEDS ONLY IN AMUSING HER.
SOME FUN! LET'S DO IT AGAIN!
YOU'RE NOT FRIGHTENED? SAY! WHAT DO I HAVE TO DO TO GET RID OF YOU?
87
DO YOU REALLY DESPISE ME THAT MUCH? COME NOW! ADMIT YOU LIKE ME--IF ONLY A TRIFLE!
I--ER--(GOSH! I'VE GOT TO THINK FAST TO GET OUT OF THIS!-)
88
SORRY. GOT TO LEAVE! SOMEONE'S COMING!
WAIT! TAKE ME WITH YOU!
89
DROPPING BEHIND THE NEARBY EXHIBIT, SUPERMAN ACCOMPLISHES A QUICK-CHANGE IN GARMENTS--
IT'S ABOUT TIME FOR CLARK KENT TO REAPPEAR!
90
HERE YOU ARE! I'VE LOOKED EVERYWHERE!
YOU! YOU WOULD HAVE TO COME JUST IN TIME TO SPOIL EVERYTHING! I HATE YOU!
91
WHEN THEY RETURN TO THE DAILY STAR--
THIS MATERIAL ON THE NEW YORK WORLD'S FAIR IS GREAT! OUR READERS SHOULD EAT IT UP!
IF THEY TAKE MY ADVICE, THEY'LL GO SEE IT FOR THEMSELVES. IT'S SOMETHING NO ONE CAN AFFORD TO MISS!
THE END
92
Further Adventures of
SUPERMAN
(THE MAN OF TOMORROW)
in
ACTION COMICS
93

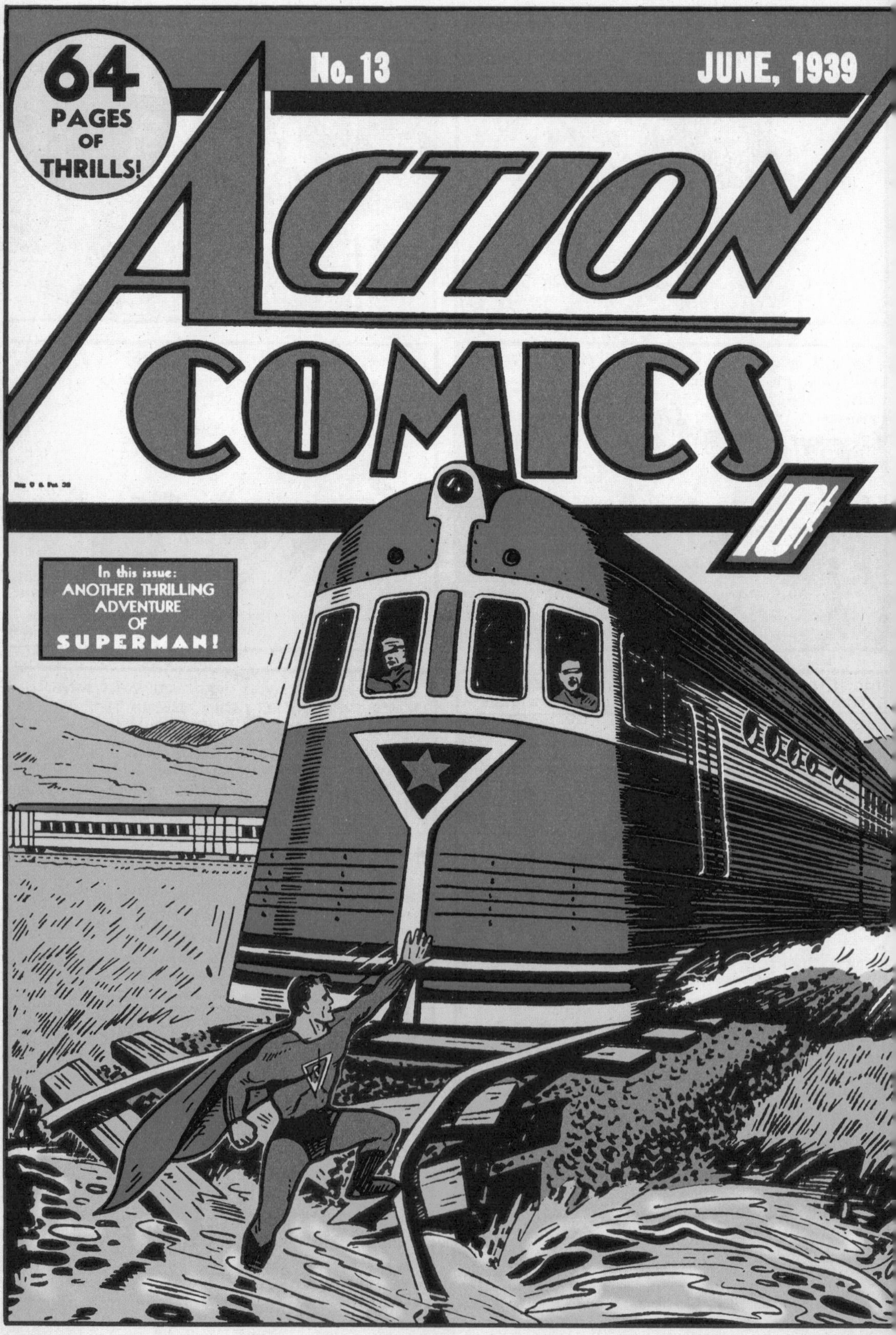

64 PAGES OF THRILLS!
No. 13
JUNE, 1939
ACTION COMICS
10¢
In this issue: ANOTHER THRILLING ADVENTURE OF SUPERMAN!

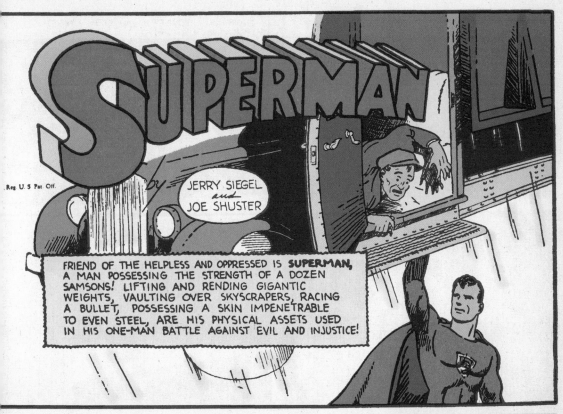

SUPERMAN

Reg U.S Pat. Off.

by JERRY SIEGEL and JOE SHUSTER

FRIEND OF THE HELPLESS AND OPPRESSED IS **SUPERMAN**, A MAN POSSESSING THE STRENGTH OF A DOZEN SAMSONS! LIFTING AND RENDING GIGANTIC WEIGHTS, VAULTING OVER SKYSCRAPERS, RACING A BULLET, POSSESSING A SKIN IMPENETRABLE TO EVEN STEEL, ARE HIS PHYSICAL ASSETS USED IN HIS ONE-MAN BATTLE AGAINST EVIL AND INJUSTICE!

THE CAB IN WHICH CLARK KENT, ACE REPORTER OF THE <u>DAILY STAR</u>, IS DRIVING TO WORK, IS DELIBERATELY RAMMED BY ANOTHER CAB!

WATCH OUT!

②

YOU DID THAT ON PURPOSE!

PROVE IT!

③

THAT WAS NO ACCIDENT! HE DELIBERATELY RAN INTO US! ~WHY?

HE BELONGS TO THE <u>CAB PROTECTIVE LEAGUE</u>, AN ORGANIZATION THAT IS TRYING TO VICTIMIZE THE INDEPENDENT COMPANIES!

④

THAT EVENING~~WITHIN THE PRIVACY OF HIS APARTMENT, CLARK KENT DISCARDS HIS FALSE ATTITUDE OF MEEKNESS AS HE DONS THE **SUPERMAN** COSTUME~~

<u>CAB PROTECTIVE LEAGUE</u>, EH? SOUNDS LIKE JUST THE SORT OF A SET-UP I LIKE TO BREAK DOWN!

⑤

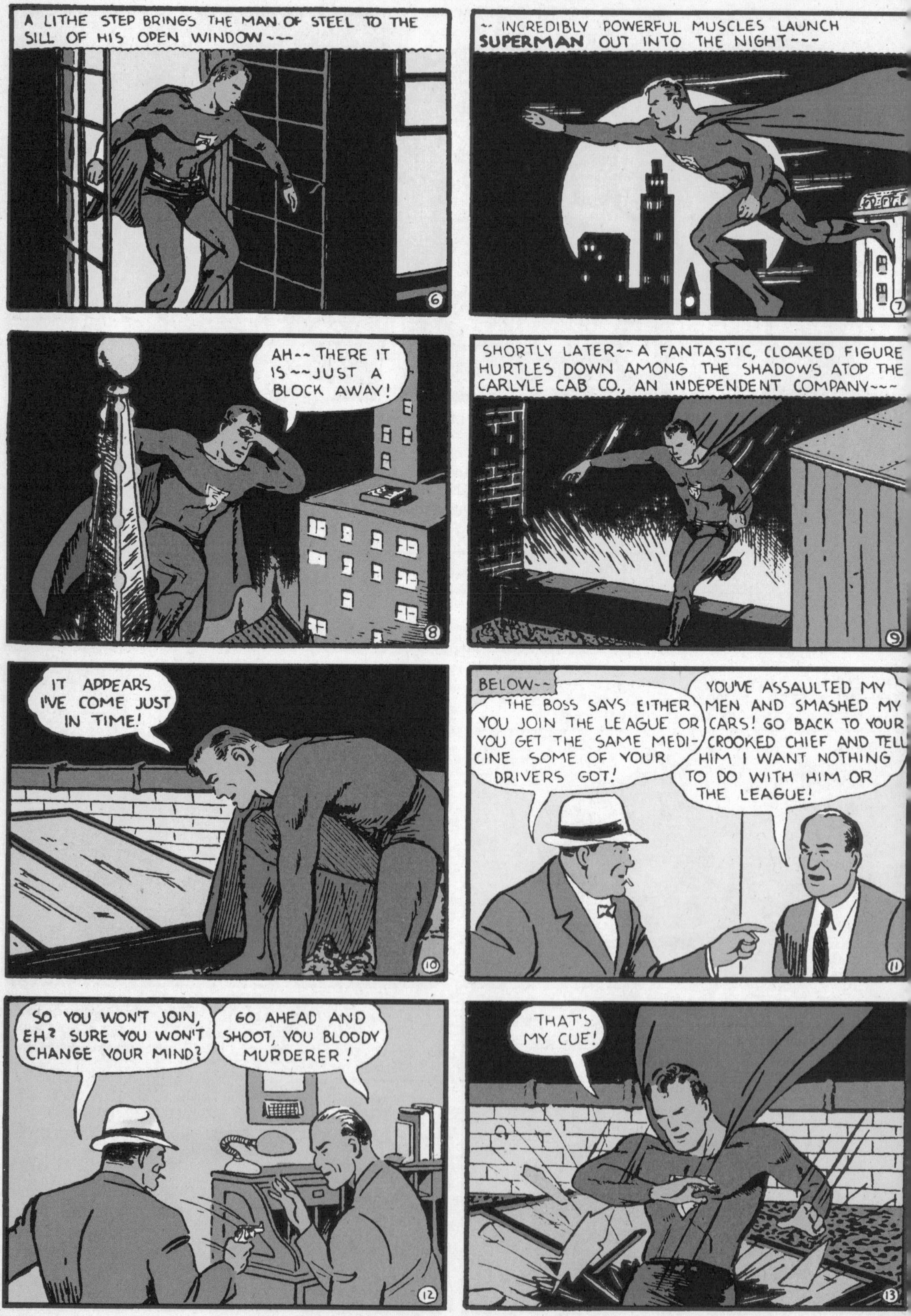
A LITHE STEP BRINGS THE MAN OF STEEL TO THE SILL OF HIS OPEN WINDOW---
6
-- INCREDIBLY POWERFUL MUSCLES LAUNCH SUPERMAN OUT INTO THE NIGHT---
7
AH-- THERE IT IS--JUST A BLOCK AWAY!
8
SHORTLY LATER-- A FANTASTIC, CLOAKED FIGURE HURTLES DOWN AMONG THE SHADOWS ATOP THE CARLYLE CAB CO., AN INDEPENDENT COMPANY---
9
IT APPEARS I'VE COME JUST IN TIME!
10
BELOW--
THE BOSS SAYS EITHER YOU JOIN THE LEAGUE OR YOU GET THE SAME MEDI-CINE SOME OF YOUR DRIVERS GOT!
YOU'VE ASSAULTED MY MEN AND SMASHED MY CARS! GO BACK TO YOUR CROOKED CHIEF AND TELL HIM I WANT NOTHING TO DO WITH HIM OR THE LEAGUE!
11
SO YOU WON'T JOIN, EH? SURE YOU WON'T CHANGE YOUR MIND?
GO AHEAD AND SHOOT, YOU BLOODY MURDERER!
12
THAT'S MY CUE!
13

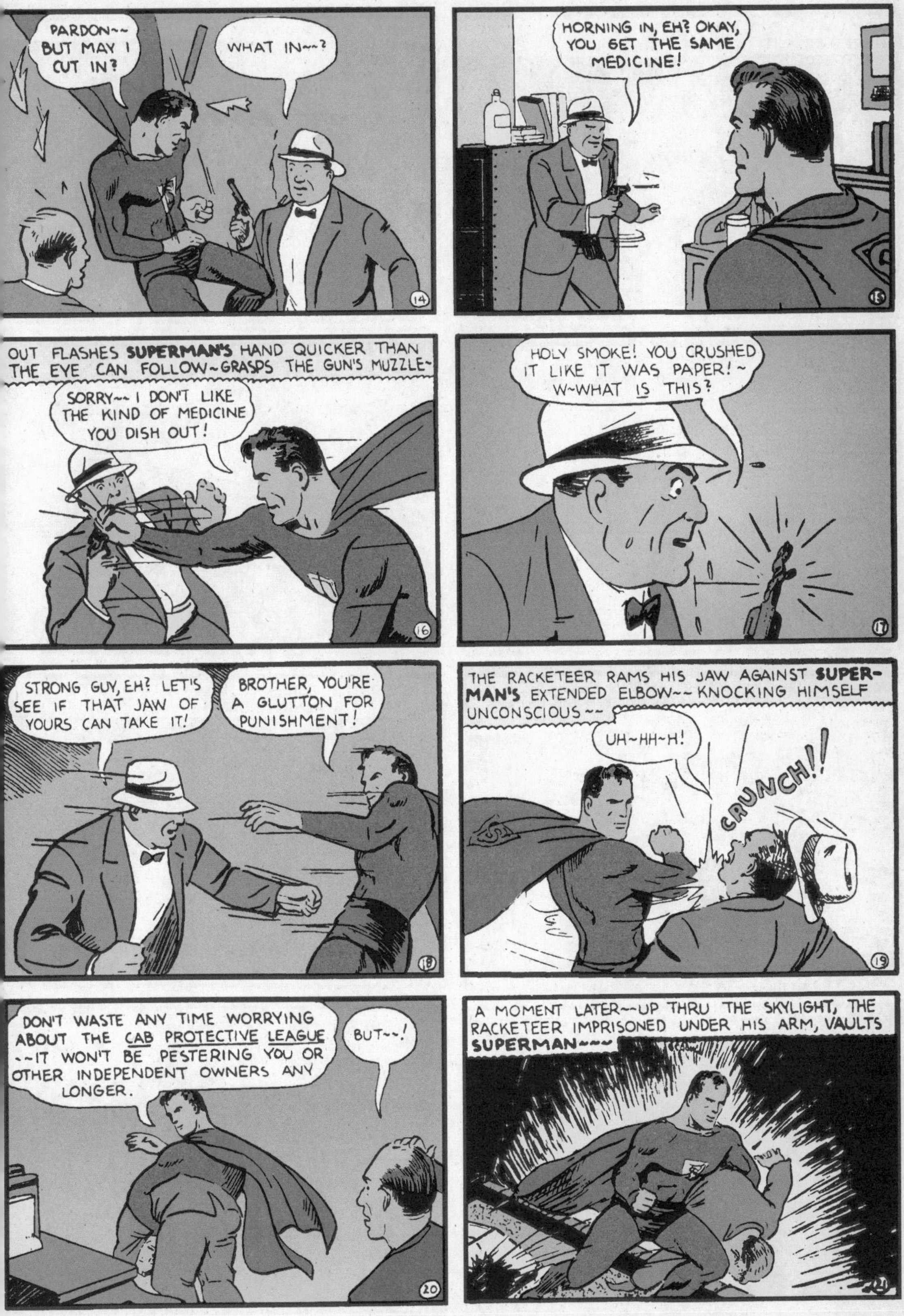

PARDON-- BUT MAY I CUT IN?
WHAT IN--?
14
HORNING IN, EH? OKAY, YOU GET THE SAME MEDICINE!
15
OUT FLASHES SUPERMAN'S HAND QUICKER THAN THE EYE CAN FOLLOW~GRASPS THE GUN'S MUZZLE~
SORRY-- I DON'T LIKE THE KIND OF MEDICINE YOU DISH OUT!
16
HOLY SMOKE! YOU CRUSHED IT LIKE IT WAS PAPER! ~ W~WHAT IS THIS?
17
STRONG GUY, EH? LET'S SEE IF THAT JAW OF YOURS CAN TAKE IT!
BROTHER, YOU'RE A GLUTTON FOR PUNISHMENT!
18
THE RACKETEER RAMS HIS JAW AGAINST SUPERMAN'S EXTENDED ELBOW-- KNOCKING HIMSELF UNCONSCIOUS--
UH~HH~H!
CRUNCH!!
19
DON'T WASTE ANY TIME WORRYING ABOUT THE CAB PROTECTIVE LEAGUE --IT WON'T BE PESTERING YOU OR OTHER INDEPENDENT OWNERS ANY LONGER.
BUT--!
20
A MOMENT LATER--UP THRU THE SKYLIGHT, THE RACKETEER IMPRISONED UNDER HIS ARM, VAULTS SUPERMAN---
21

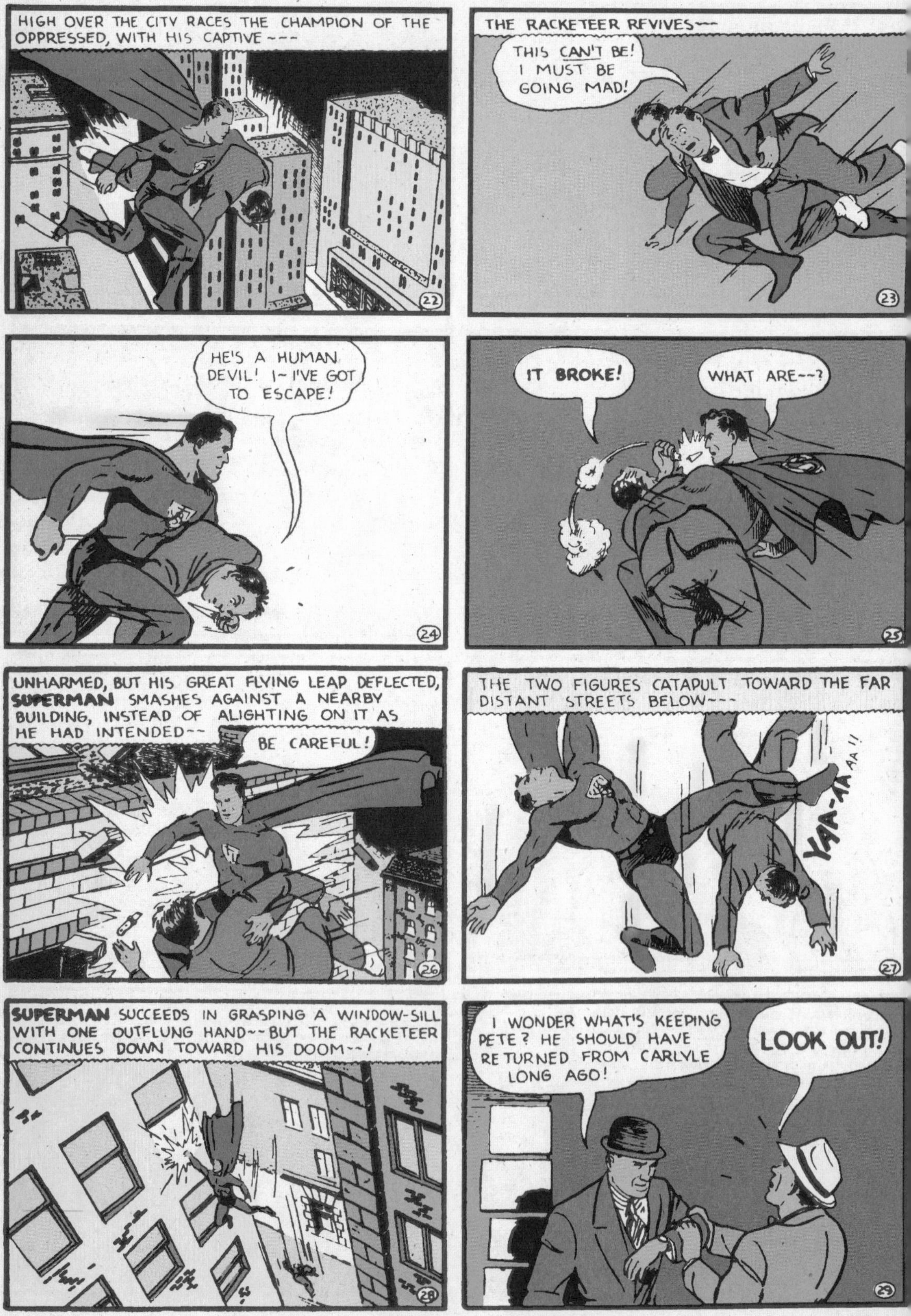
HIGH OVER THE CITY RACES THE CHAMPION OF THE OPPRESSED, WITH HIS CAPTIVE---
THE RACKETEER REVIVES---
THIS CAN'T BE! I MUST BE GOING MAD!
HE'S A HUMAN DEVIL! I-I'VE GOT TO ESCAPE!
IT BROKE!
WHAT ARE--?
UNHARMED, BUT HIS GREAT FLYING LEAP DEFLECTED, SUPERMAN SMASHES AGAINST A NEARBY BUILDING, INSTEAD OF ALIGHTING ON IT AS HE HAD INTENDED--
BE CAREFUL!
THE TWO FIGURES CATAPULT TOWARD THE FAR DISTANT STREETS BELOW---
YAA-AA AA!!
SUPERMAN SUCCEEDS IN GRASPING A WINDOW-SILL WITH ONE OUTFLUNG HAND--BUT THE RACKETEER CONTINUES DOWN TOWARD HIS DOOM--!
I WONDER WHAT'S KEEPING PETE? HE SHOULD HAVE RETURNED FROM CARLYLE LONG AGO!
LOOK OUT!

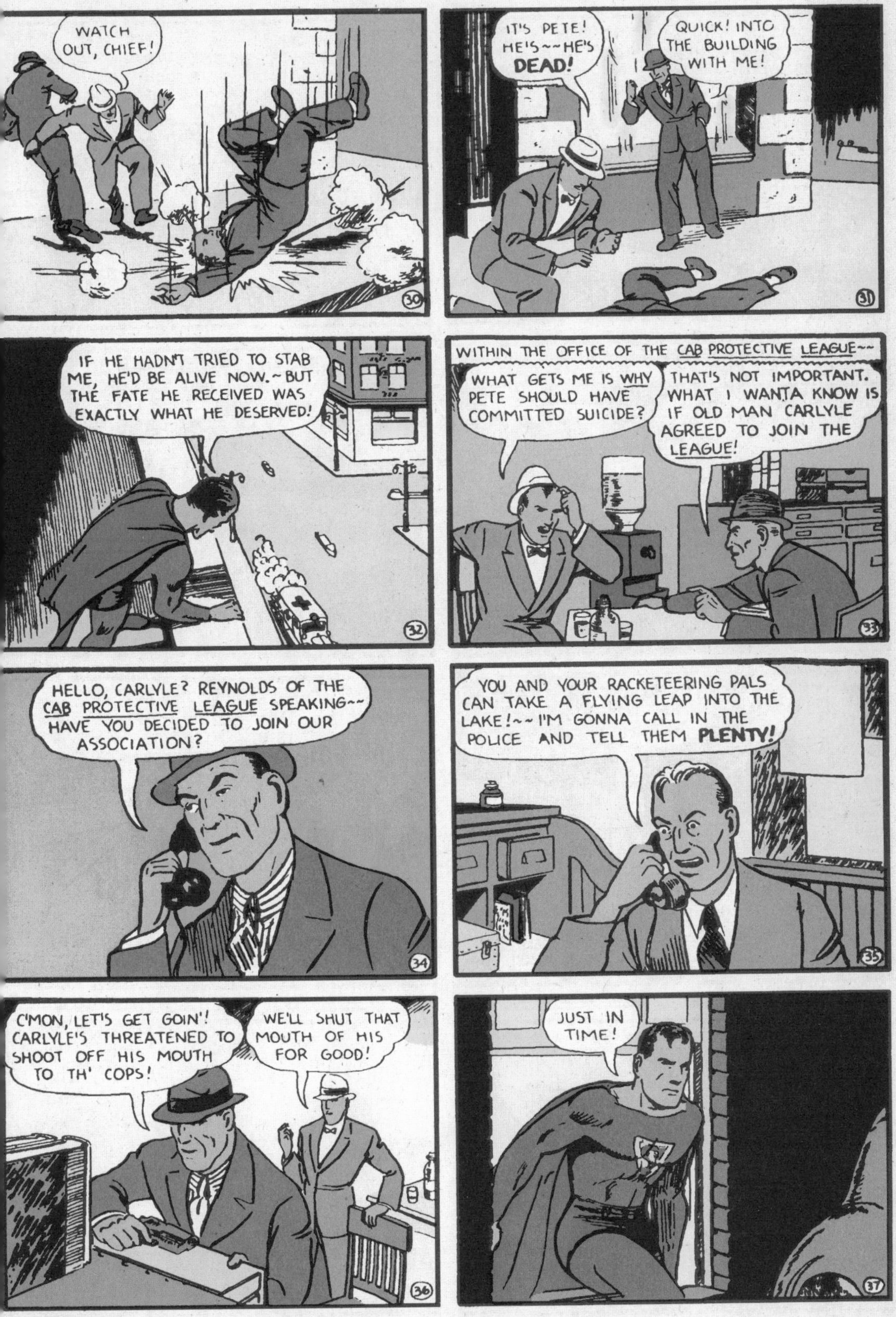
WATCH OUT, CHIEF!
IT'S PETE! HE'S~~HE'S DEAD!
QUICK! INTO THE BUILDING WITH ME!
IF HE HADN'T TRIED TO STAB ME, HE'D BE ALIVE NOW.~BUT THE FATE HE RECEIVED WAS EXACTLY WHAT HE DESERVED!
WITHIN THE OFFICE OF THE CAB PROTECTIVE LEAGUE~~
WHAT GETS ME IS WHY PETE SHOULD HAVE COMMITTED SUICIDE?
THAT'S NOT IMPORTANT. WHAT I WANTA KNOW IS IF OLD MAN CARLYLE AGREED TO JOIN THE LEAGUE!
HELLO, CARLYLE? REYNOLDS OF THE CAB PROTECTIVE LEAGUE SPEAKING~~ HAVE YOU DECIDED TO JOIN OUR ASSOCIATION?
YOU AND YOUR RACKETEERING PALS CAN TAKE A FLYING LEAP INTO THE LAKE!~~ I'M GONNA CALL IN THE POLICE AND TELL THEM PLENTY!
C'MON, LET'S GET GOIN'! CARLYLE'S THREATENED TO SHOOT OFF HIS MOUTH TO TH' COPS!
WE'LL SHUT THAT MOUTH OF HIS FOR GOOD!
JUST IN TIME!

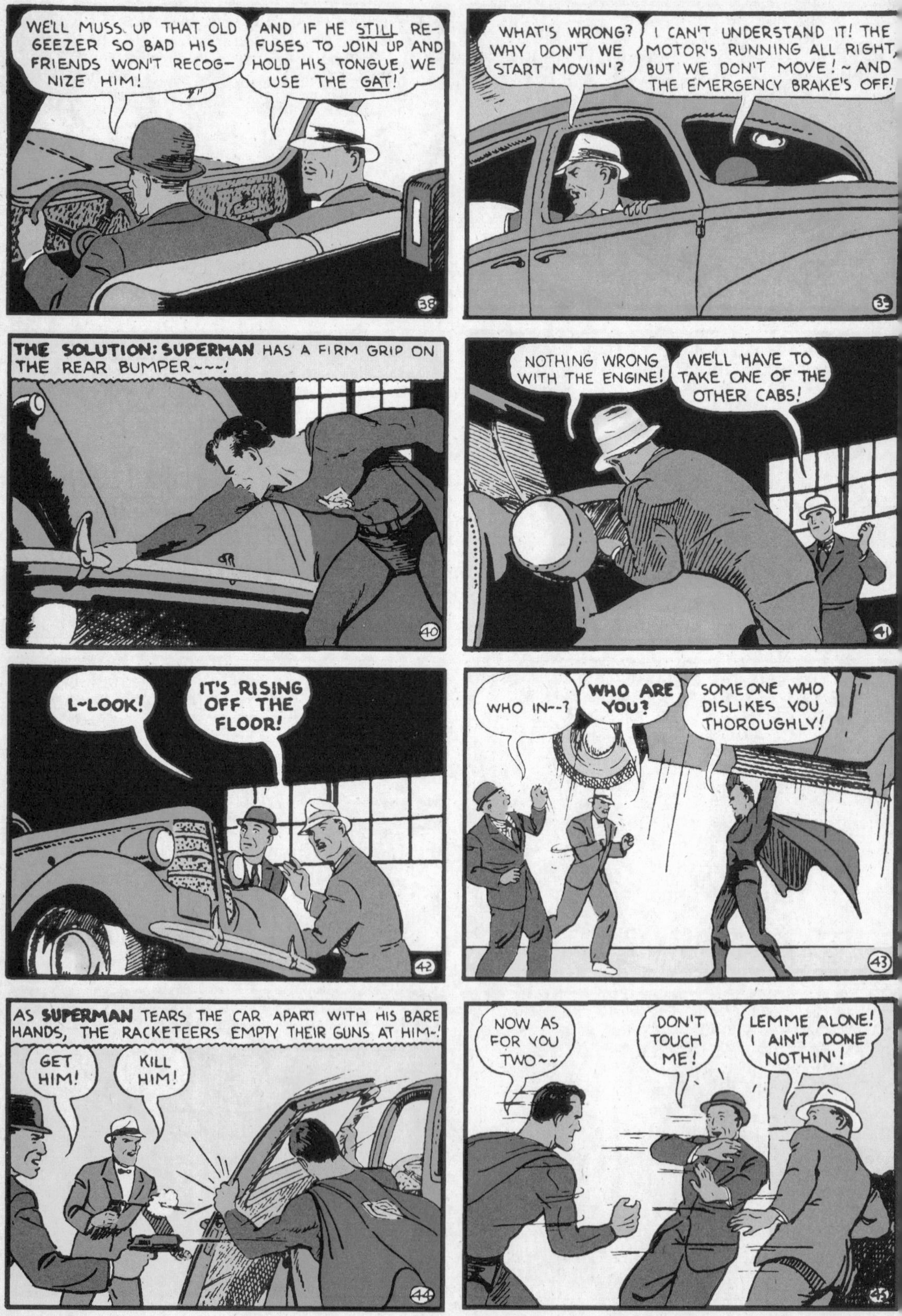
WE'LL MUSS UP THAT OLD GEEZER SO BAD HIS FRIENDS WON'T RECOG-NIZE HIM!
AND IF HE STILL RE-FUSES TO JOIN UP AND HOLD HIS TONGUE, WE USE THE GAT!
WHAT'S WRONG? WHY DON'T WE START MOVIN'?
I CAN'T UNDERSTAND IT! THE MOTOR'S RUNNING ALL RIGHT, BUT WE DON'T MOVE! ~ AND THE EMERGENCY BRAKE'S OFF!
THE SOLUTION: SUPERMAN HAS A FIRM GRIP ON THE REAR BUMPER~~~!
NOTHING WRONG WITH THE ENGINE!
WE'LL HAVE TO TAKE ONE OF THE OTHER CABS!
L~LOOK!
IT'S RISING OFF THE FLOOR!
WHO IN--?
WHO ARE YOU?
SOMEONE WHO DISLIKES YOU THOROUGHLY!
AS SUPERMAN TEARS THE CAR APART WITH HIS BARE HANDS, THE RACKETEERS EMPTY THEIR GUNS AT HIM-!
GET HIM!
KILL HIM!
NOW AS FOR YOU TWO~~
DON'T TOUCH ME!
LEMME ALONE! I AIN'T DONE NOTHIN'!

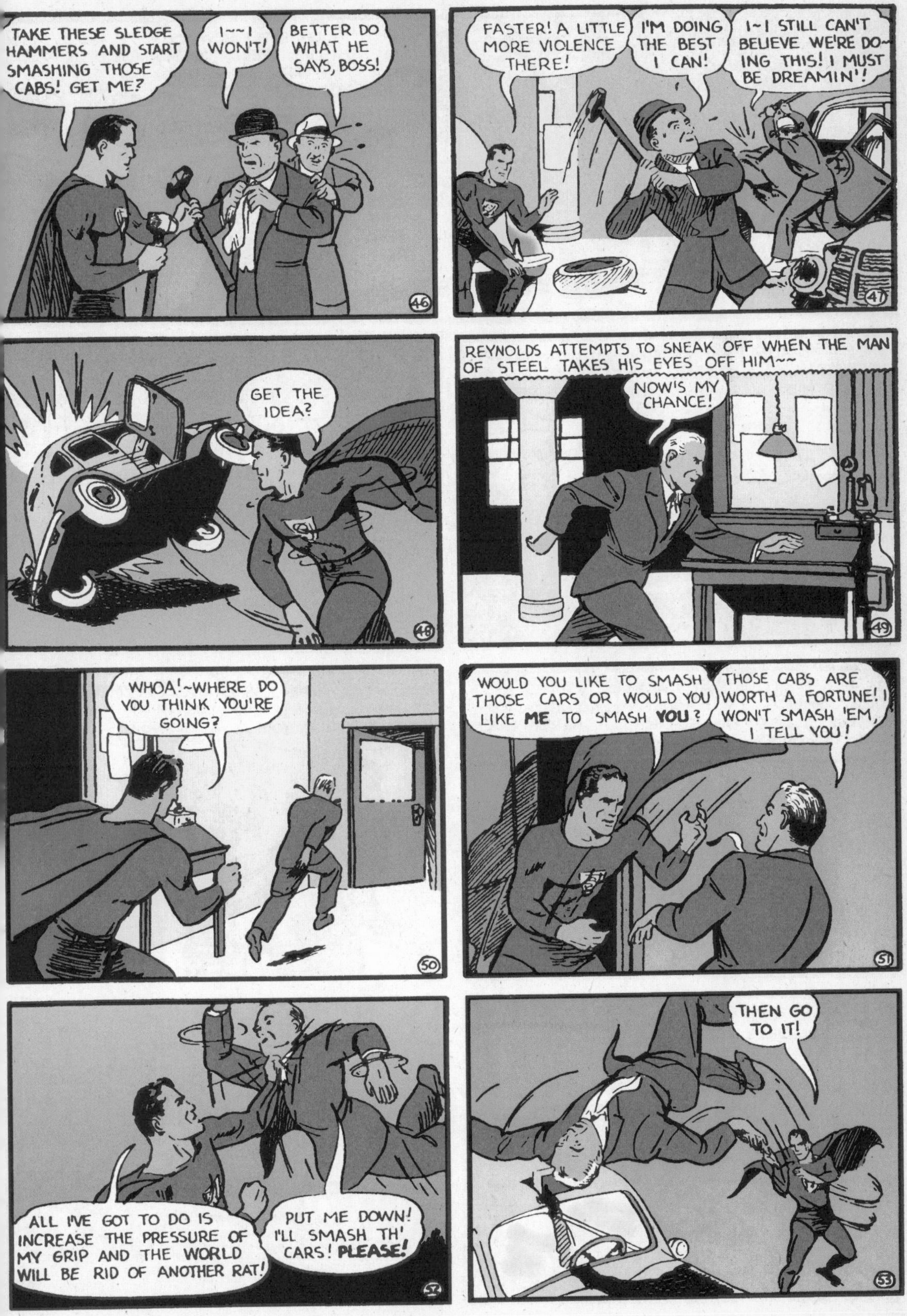
TAKE THESE SLEDGE HAMMERS AND START SMASHING THOSE CABS! GET ME?
I~~I WON'T!
BETTER DO WHAT HE SAYS, BOSS!
46
FASTER! A LITTLE MORE VIOLENCE THERE!
I'M DOING THE BEST I CAN!
I~I STILL CAN'T BELIEVE WE'RE DOING THIS! I MUST BE DREAMIN'!
47
GET THE IDEA?
48
REYNOLDS ATTEMPTS TO SNEAK OFF WHEN THE MAN OF STEEL TAKES HIS EYES OFF HIM~~
NOW'S MY CHANCE!
49
WHOA!~WHERE DO YOU THINK YOU'RE GOING?
50
WOULD YOU LIKE TO SMASH THOSE CARS OR WOULD YOU LIKE **ME** TO SMASH **YOU**?
THOSE CABS ARE WORTH A FORTUNE! I WON'T SMASH 'EM, I TELL YOU!
51
ALL I'VE GOT TO DO IS INCREASE THE PRESSURE OF MY GRIP AND THE WORLD WILL BE RID OF ANOTHER RAT!
PUT ME DOWN! I'LL SMASH TH' CARS! **PLEASE!**
52
THEN GO TO IT!
53

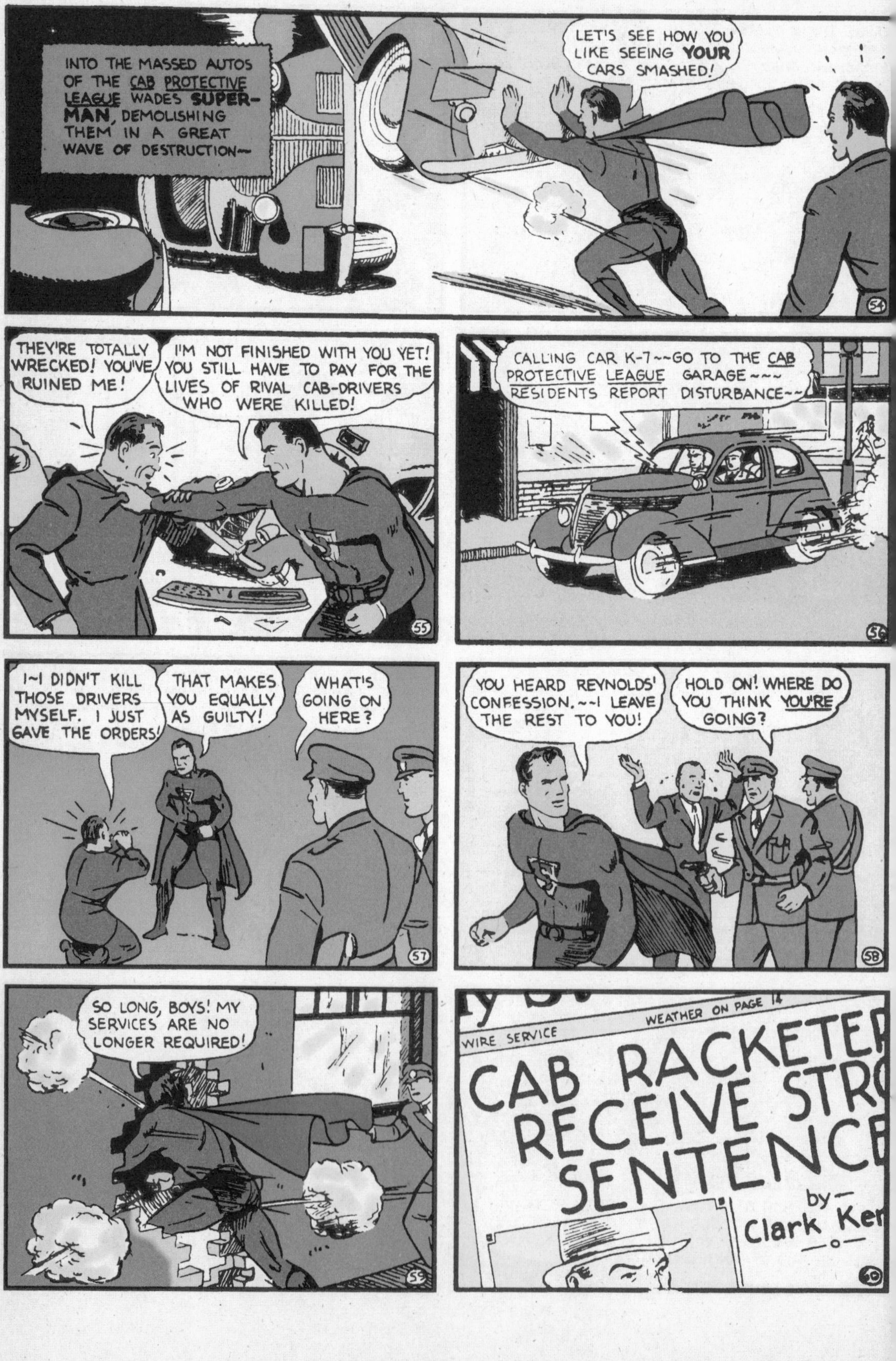
INTO THE MASSED AUTOS OF THE CAB PROTECTIVE LEAGUE WADES SUPERMAN, DEMOLISHING THEM IN A GREAT WAVE OF DESTRUCTION~~
LET'S SEE HOW YOU LIKE SEEING YOUR CARS SMASHED!
54
THEY'RE TOTALLY WRECKED! YOU'VE RUINED ME!
I'M NOT FINISHED WITH YOU YET! YOU STILL HAVE TO PAY FOR THE LIVES OF RIVAL CAB-DRIVERS WHO WERE KILLED!
55
CALLING CAR K-7~~GO TO THE CAB PROTECTIVE LEAGUE GARAGE~~~ RESIDENTS REPORT DISTURBANCE~~
56
I~I DIDN'T KILL THOSE DRIVERS MYSELF. I JUST GAVE THE ORDERS!
THAT MAKES YOU EQUALLY AS GUILTY!
WHAT'S GOING ON HERE?
57
YOU HEARD REYNOLDS' CONFESSION.~~I LEAVE THE REST TO YOU!
HOLD ON! WHERE DO YOU THINK YOU'RE GOING?
58
SO LONG, BOYS! MY SERVICES ARE NO LONGER REQUIRED!
59
WEATHER ON PAGE 14
WIRE SERVICE
CAB RACKETER
RECEIVE STR
SENTENC
by—
Clark Ke
60

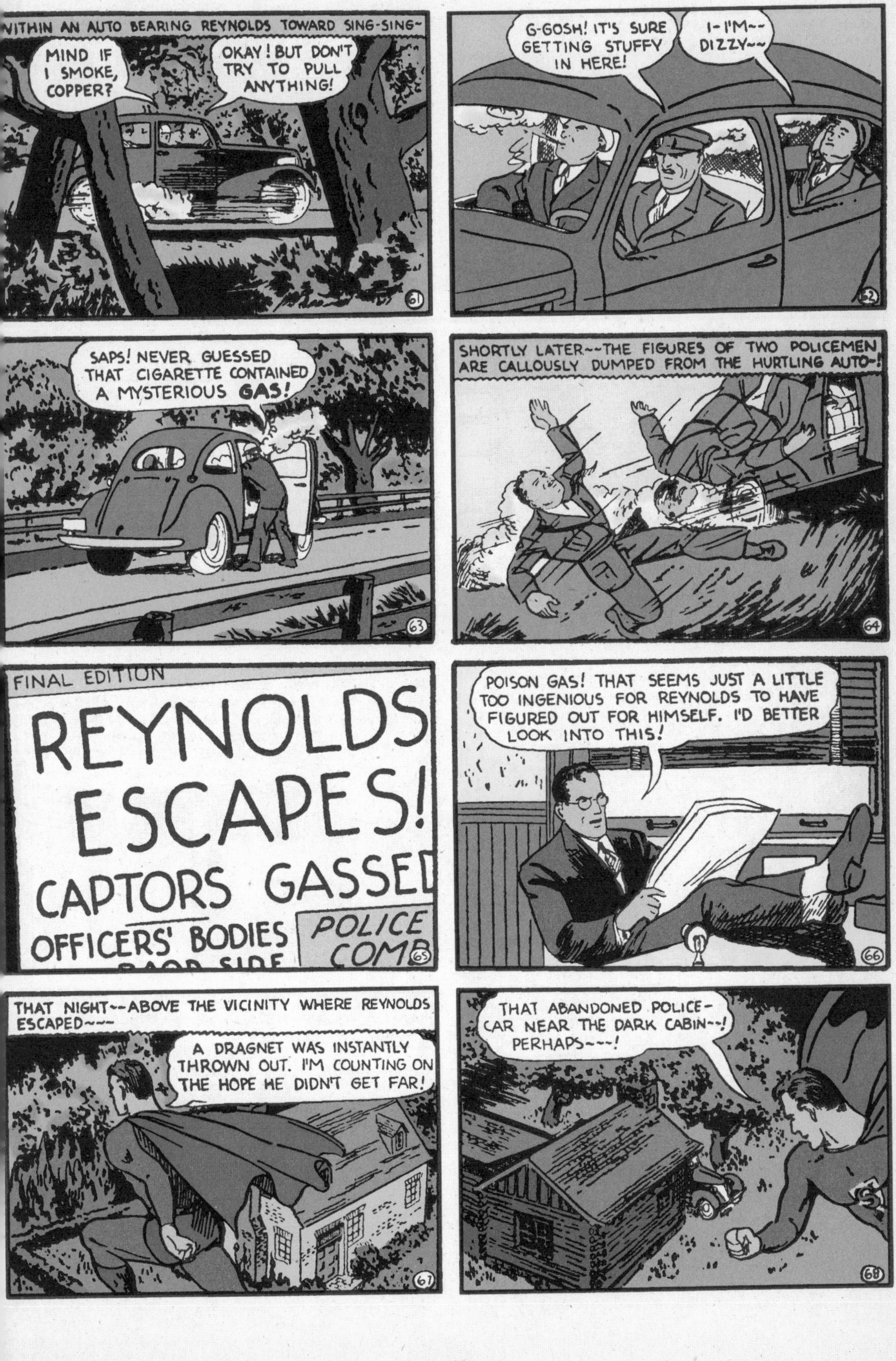
WITHIN AN AUTO BEARING REYNOLDS TOWARD SING-SING~
MIND IF I SMOKE, COPPER?
OKAY! BUT DON'T TRY TO PULL ANYTHING!
G-GOSH! IT'S SURE GETTING STUFFY IN HERE!
I-I'M-- DIZZY--
SAPS! NEVER GUESSED THAT CIGARETTE CONTAINED A MYSTERIOUS GAS!
SHORTLY LATER--THE FIGURES OF TWO POLICEMEN ARE CALLOUSLY DUMPED FROM THE HURTLING AUTO-!
FINAL EDITION
REYNOLDS ESCAPES!
CAPTORS GASSED
OFFICERS' BODIES
POLICE COMB
POISON GAS! THAT SEEMS JUST A LITTLE TOO INGENIOUS FOR REYNOLDS TO HAVE FIGURED OUT FOR HIMSELF. I'D BETTER LOOK INTO THIS!
THAT NIGHT--ABOVE THE VICINITY WHERE REYNOLDS ESCAPED---
A DRAGNET WAS INSTANTLY THROWN OUT. I'M COUNTING ON THE HOPE HE DIDN'T GET FAR!
THAT ABANDONED POLICE-CAR NEAR THE DARK CABIN--! PERHAPS---!

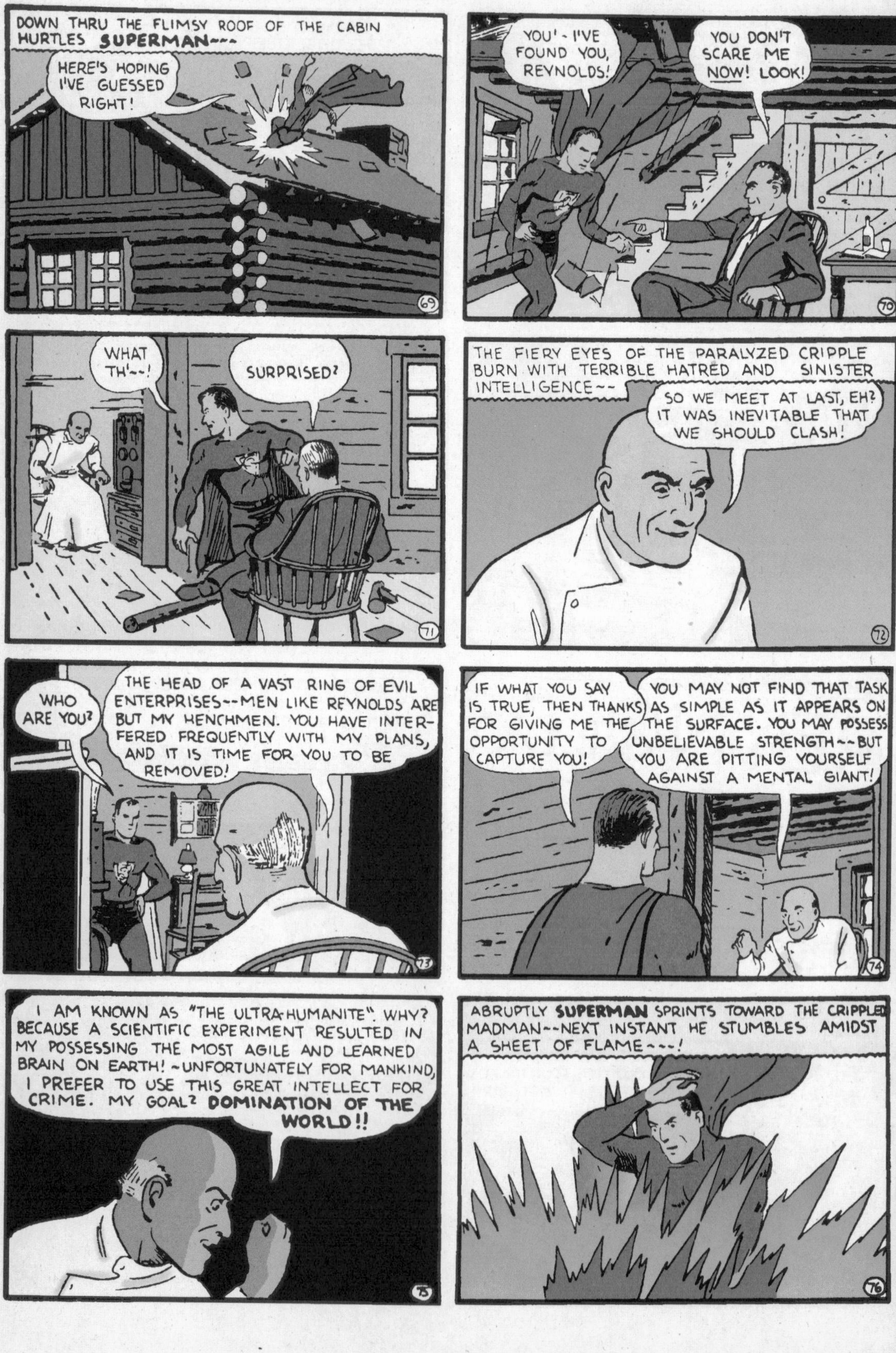
DOWN THRU THE FLIMSY ROOF OF THE CABIN HURTLES **SUPERMAN**---
HERE'S HOPING I'VE GUESSED RIGHT!
YOU! - I'VE FOUND YOU, REYNOLDS!
YOU DON'T SCARE ME NOW! LOOK!
WHAT TH'--!
SURPRISED?
THE FIERY EYES OF THE PARALYZED CRIPPLE BURN WITH TERRIBLE HATRED AND SINISTER INTELLIGENCE--
SO WE MEET AT LAST, EH? IT WAS INEVITABLE THAT WE SHOULD CLASH!
WHO ARE YOU?
THE HEAD OF A VAST RING OF EVIL ENTERPRISES--MEN LIKE REYNOLDS ARE BUT MY HENCHMEN. YOU HAVE INTERFERED FREQUENTLY WITH MY PLANS, AND IT IS TIME FOR YOU TO BE REMOVED!
IF WHAT YOU SAY IS TRUE, THEN THANKS FOR GIVING ME THE OPPORTUNITY TO CAPTURE YOU!
YOU MAY NOT FIND THAT TASK AS SIMPLE AS IT APPEARS ON THE SURFACE. YOU MAY POSSESS UNBELIEVABLE STRENGTH--BUT YOU ARE PITTING YOURSELF AGAINST A MENTAL GIANT!
I AM KNOWN AS "THE ULTRA-HUMANITE". WHY? BECAUSE A SCIENTIFIC EXPERIMENT RESULTED IN MY POSSESSING THE MOST AGILE AND LEARNED BRAIN ON EARTH! -UNFORTUNATELY FOR MANKIND, I PREFER TO USE THIS GREAT INTELLECT FOR CRIME. MY GOAL? **DOMINATION OF THE WORLD!!**
ABRUPTLY **SUPERMAN** SPRINTS TOWARD THE CRIPPLED MADMAN--NEXT INSTANT HE STUMBLES AMIDST A SHEET OF FLAME---!

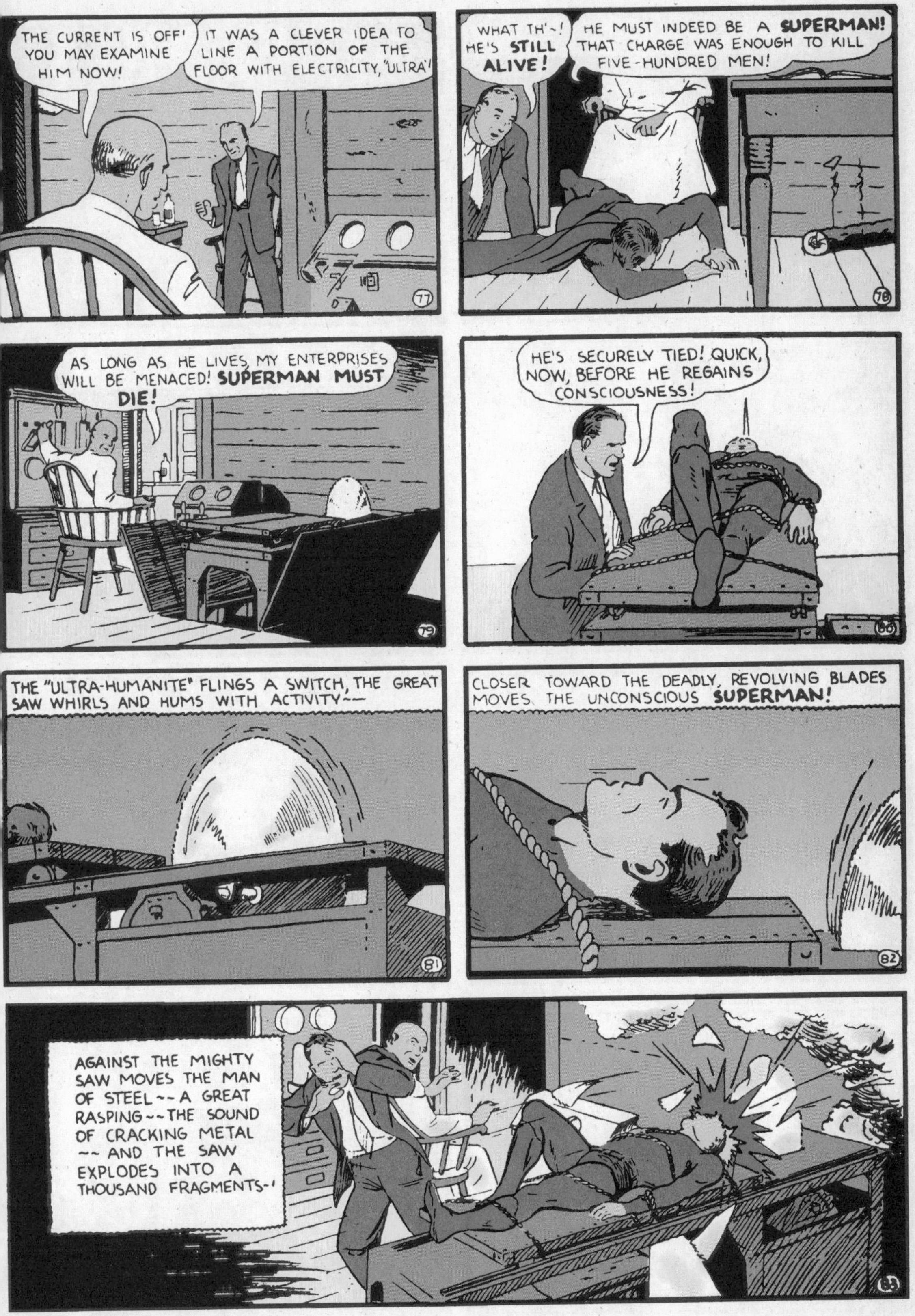
THE CURRENT IS OFF! YOU MAY EXAMINE HIM NOW!
IT WAS A CLEVER IDEA TO LINE A PORTION OF THE FLOOR WITH ELECTRICITY, "ULTRA"!
WHAT TH'-! HE'S STILL ALIVE!
HE MUST INDEED BE A SUPERMAN! THAT CHARGE WAS ENOUGH TO KILL FIVE-HUNDRED MEN!
AS LONG AS HE LIVES, MY ENTERPRISES WILL BE MENACED! SUPERMAN MUST DIE!
HE'S SECURELY TIED! QUICK, NOW, BEFORE HE REGAINS CONSCIOUSNESS!
THE "ULTRA-HUMANITE" FLINGS A SWITCH, THE GREAT SAW WHIRLS AND HUMS WITH ACTIVITY--
CLOSER TOWARD THE DEADLY, REVOLVING BLADES MOVES THE UNCONSCIOUS SUPERMAN!
AGAINST THE MIGHTY SAW MOVES THE MAN OF STEEL -- A GREAT RASPING -- THE SOUND OF CRACKING METAL -- AND THE SAW EXPLODES INTO A THOUSAND FRAGMENTS-!

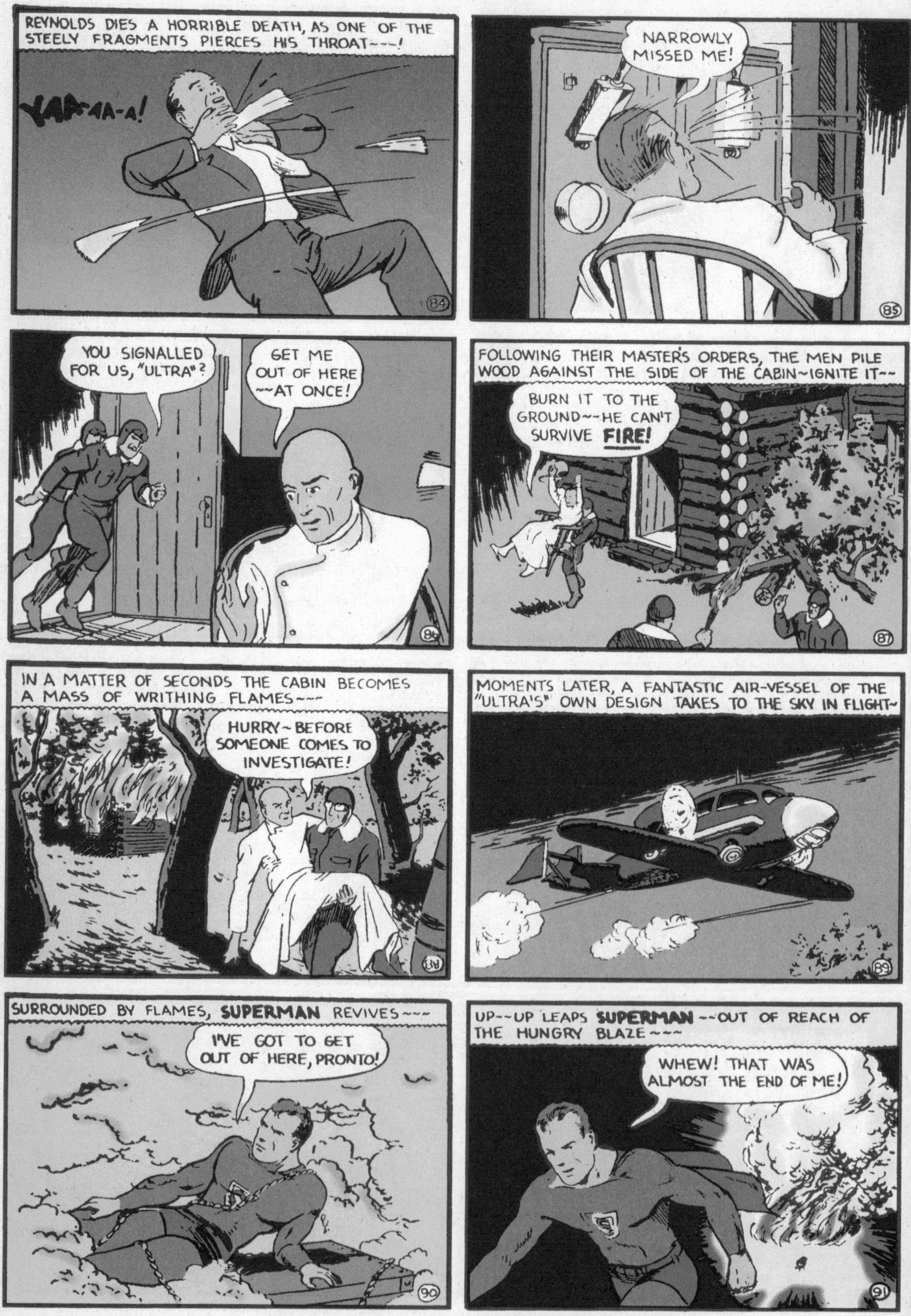
REYNOLDS DIES A HORRIBLE DEATH, AS ONE OF THE STEELY FRAGMENTS PIERCES HIS THROAT---!
YAA-AA-A!
NARROWLY MISSED ME!
YOU SIGNALLED FOR US, "ULTRA"?
GET ME OUT OF HERE --AT ONCE!
FOLLOWING THEIR MASTER'S ORDERS, THE MEN PILE WOOD AGAINST THE SIDE OF THE CABIN~IGNITE IT~~
BURN IT TO THE GROUND~~HE CAN'T SURVIVE FIRE!
IN A MATTER OF SECONDS THE CABIN BECOMES A MASS OF WRITHING FLAMES---
HURRY~BEFORE SOMEONE COMES TO INVESTIGATE!
MOMENTS LATER, A FANTASTIC AIR-VESSEL OF THE "ULTRA'S" OWN DESIGN TAKES TO THE SKY IN FLIGHT~
SURROUNDED BY FLAMES, SUPERMAN REVIVES---
I'VE GOT TO GET OUT OF HERE, PRONTO!
UP--UP LEAPS SUPERMAN --OUT OF REACH OF THE HUNGRY BLAZE---
WHEW! THAT WAS ALMOST THE END OF ME!

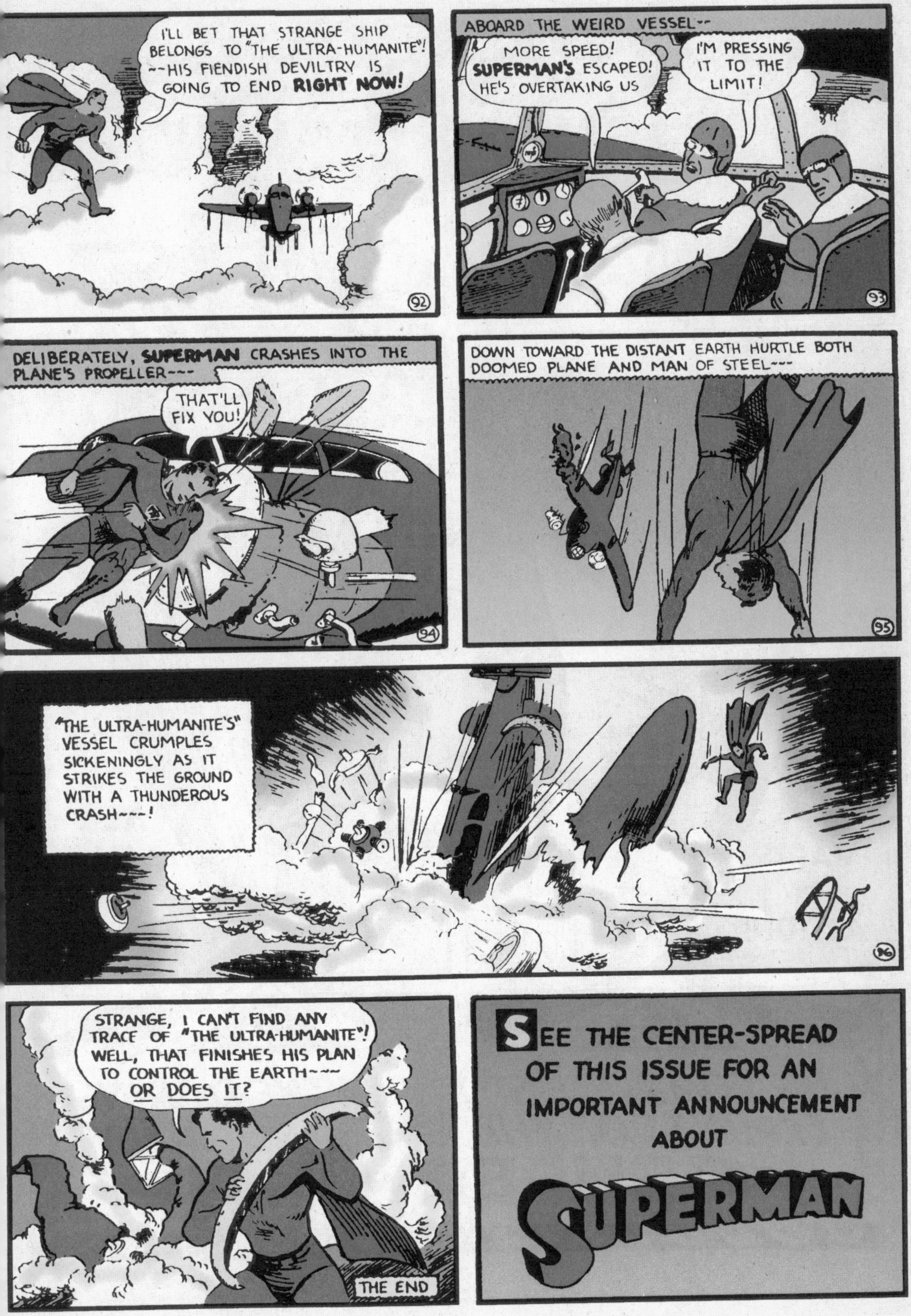
I'LL BET THAT STRANGE SHIP BELONGS TO "THE ULTRA-HUMANITE"! --HIS FIENDISH DEVILTRY IS GOING TO END RIGHT NOW!
92
ABOARD THE WEIRD VESSEL--
MORE SPEED! SUPERMAN'S ESCAPED! HE'S OVERTAKING US
I'M PRESSING IT TO THE LIMIT!
93
DELIBERATELY, SUPERMAN CRASHES INTO THE PLANE'S PROPELLER---
THAT'LL FIX YOU!
94
DOWN TOWARD THE DISTANT EARTH HURTLE BOTH DOOMED PLANE AND MAN OF STEEL---
95
"THE ULTRA-HUMANITE'S" VESSEL CRUMPLES SICKENINGLY AS IT STRIKES THE GROUND WITH A THUNDEROUS CRASH---!
96
STRANGE, I CAN'T FIND ANY TRACE OF "THE ULTRA-HUMANITE"! WELL, THAT FINISHES HIS PLAN TO CONTROL THE EARTH--- OR DOES IT?
THE END
SEE THE CENTER-SPREAD OF THIS ISSUE FOR AN IMPORTANT ANNOUNCEMENT ABOUT
SUPERMAN

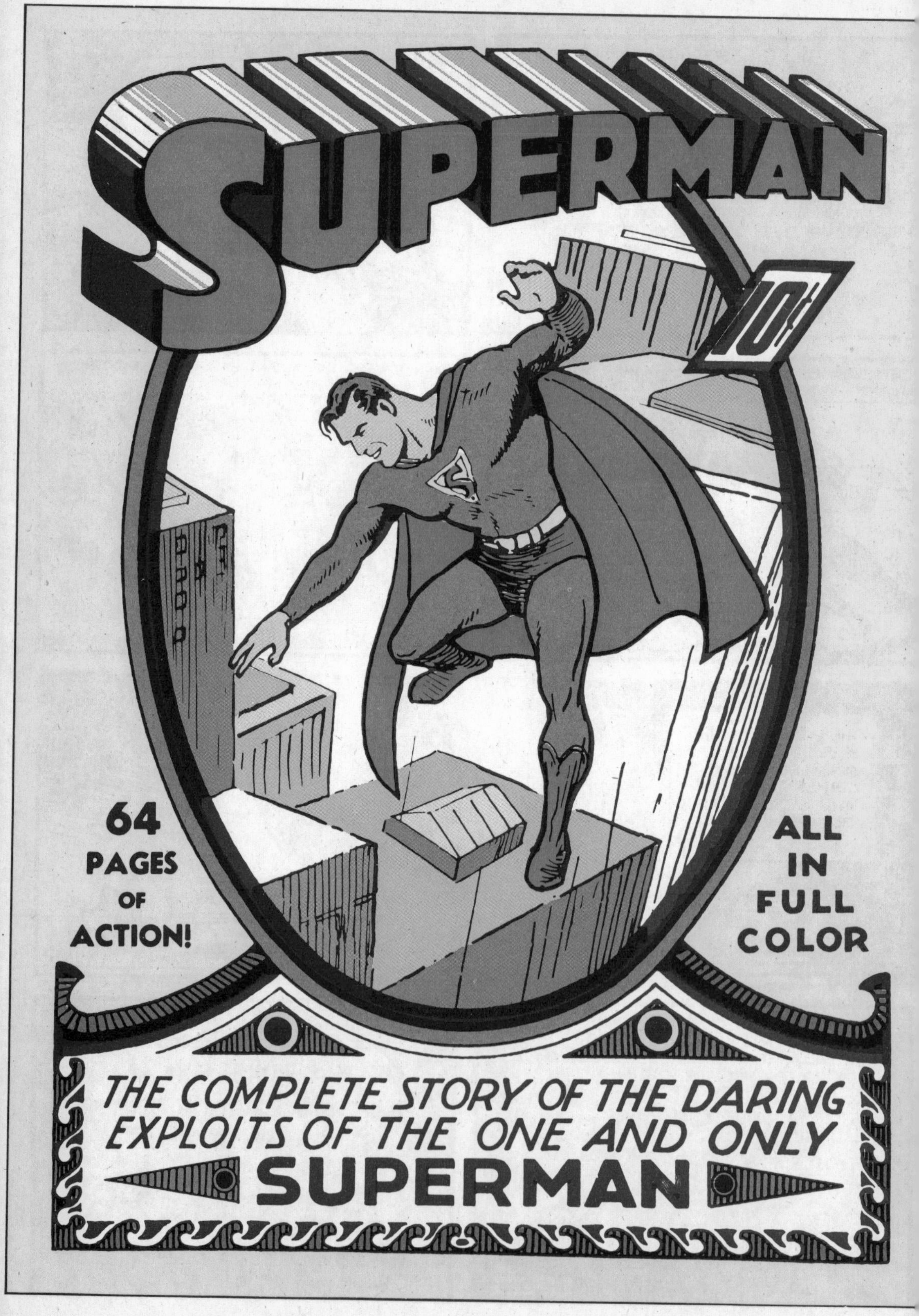
SUPERMAN
10¢
64
PAGES
OF
ACTION!
ALL
IN
FULL
COLOR
THE COMPLETE STORY OF THE DARING
EXPLOITS OF THE ONE AND ONLY
SUPERMAN

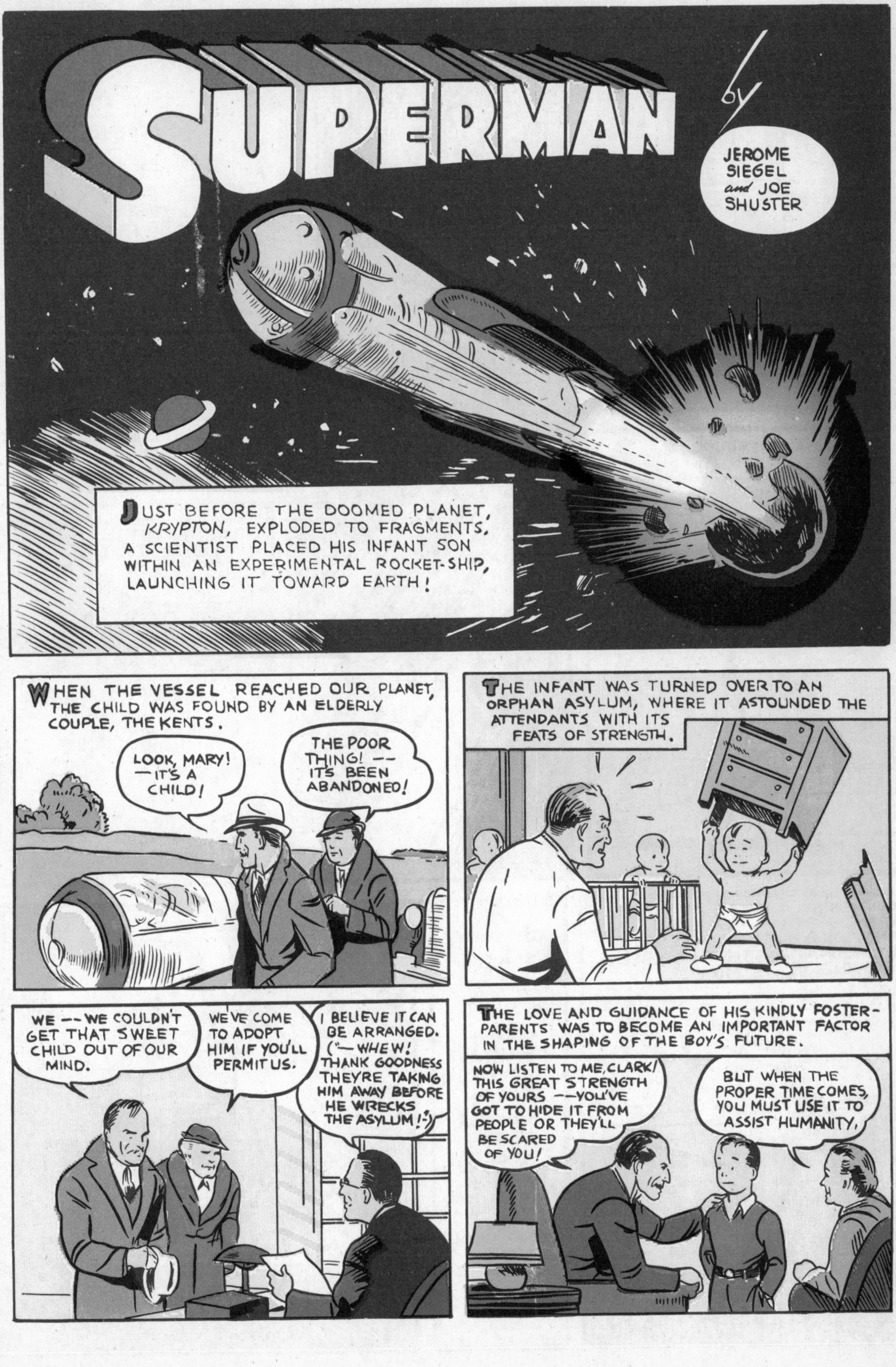
SUPERMAN
by
JEROME SIEGEL and JOE SHUSTER
JUST BEFORE THE DOOMED PLANET, KRYPTON, EXPLODED TO FRAGMENTS, A SCIENTIST PLACED HIS INFANT SON WITHIN AN EXPERIMENTAL ROCKET-SHIP, LAUNCHING IT TOWARD EARTH!
WHEN THE VESSEL REACHED OUR PLANET, THE CHILD WAS FOUND BY AN ELDERLY COUPLE, THE KENTS.
LOOK, MARY! —IT'S A CHILD!
THE POOR THING! -- IT'S BEEN ABANDONED!
THE INFANT WAS TURNED OVER TO AN ORPHAN ASYLUM, WHERE IT ASTOUNDED THE ATTENDANTS WITH ITS FEATS OF STRENGTH.
WE -- WE COULDN'T GET THAT SWEET CHILD OUT OF OUR MIND.
WE'VE COME TO ADOPT HIM IF YOU'LL PERMIT US.
I BELIEVE IT CAN BE ARRANGED. ("— WHEW! THANK GOODNESS THEY'RE TAKING HIM AWAY BEFORE HE WRECKS THE ASYLUM!")
THE LOVE AND GUIDANCE OF HIS KINDLY FOSTER-PARENTS WAS TO BECOME AN IMPORTANT FACTOR IN THE SHAPING OF THE BOY'S FUTURE.
NOW LISTEN TO ME, CLARK! THIS GREAT STRENGTH OF YOURS --YOU'VE GOT TO HIDE IT FROM PEOPLE OR THEY'LL BE SCARED OF YOU!
BUT WHEN THE PROPER TIME COMES, YOU MUST USE IT TO ASSIST HUMANITY.

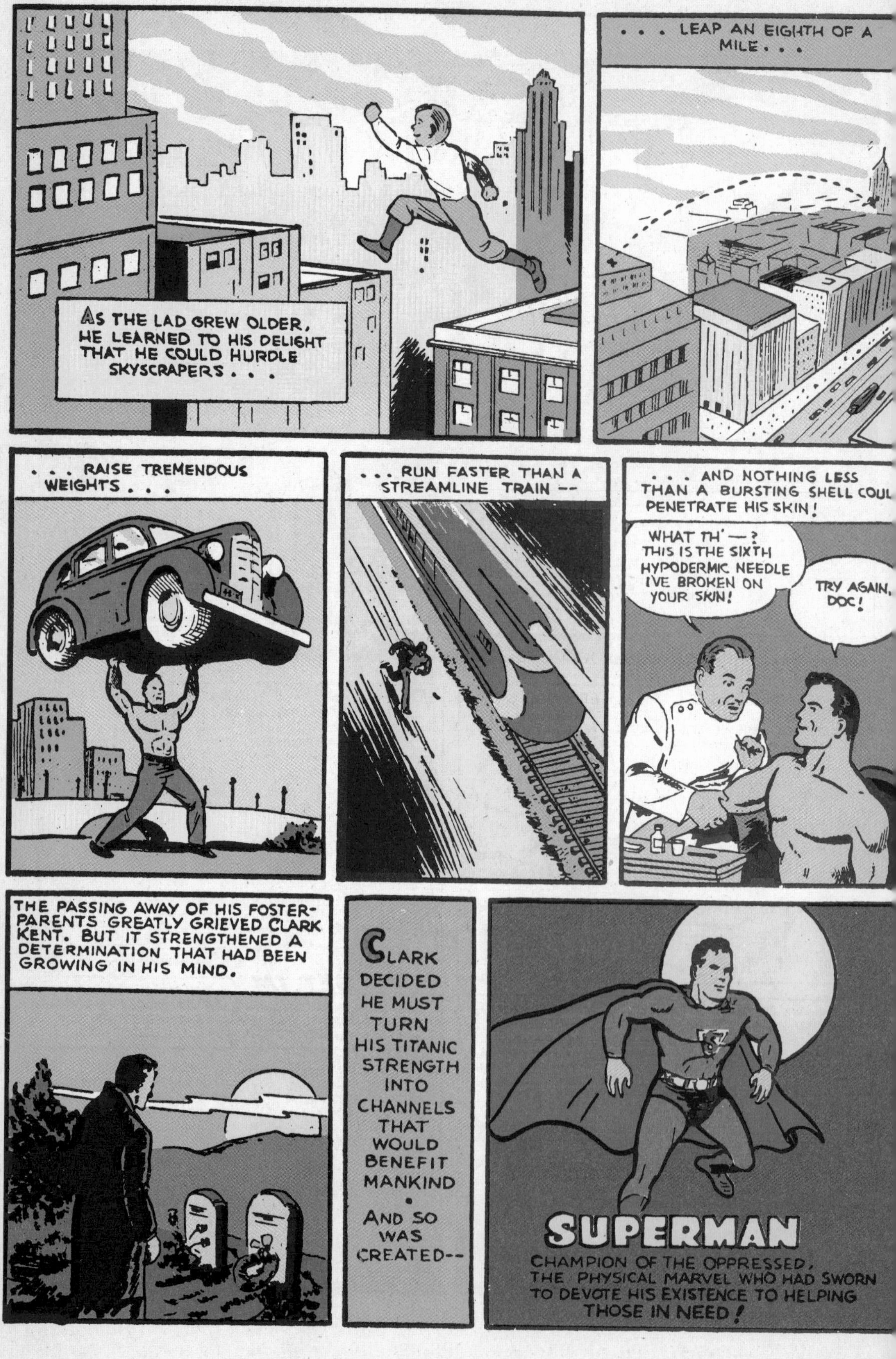

AS THE LAD GREW OLDER, HE LEARNED TO HIS DELIGHT THAT HE COULD HURDLE SKYSCRAPERS . . .
. . . LEAP AN EIGHTH OF A MILE . . .
. . . RAISE TREMENDOUS WEIGHTS . . .
. . . RUN FASTER THAN A STREAMLINE TRAIN --
. . . AND NOTHING LESS THAN A BURSTING SHELL COUL
PENETRATE HIS SKIN!
WHAT TH' — ? THIS IS THE SIXTH HYPODERMIC NEEDLE I'VE BROKEN ON YOUR SKIN!
TRY AGAIN, DOC!
THE PASSING AWAY OF HIS FOSTER-PARENTS GREATLY GRIEVED CLARK KENT. BUT IT STRENGTHENED A DETERMINATION THAT HAD BEEN GROWING IN HIS MIND.
CLARK DECIDED HE MUST TURN HIS TITANIC STRENGTH INTO CHANNELS THAT WOULD BENEFIT MANKIND
AND SO WAS CREATED--
SUPERMAN
CHAMPION OF THE OPPRESSED, THE PHYSICAL MARVEL WHO HAD SWORN TO DEVOTE HIS EXISTENCE TO HELPING THOSE IN NEED!

OUTER WAITING-ROOM OF THE *DAILY STAR*...

YOU MAY SEE THE EDITOR NOW. BUT IF YOU ASK ME, YOU'RE WASTING YOUR TIME.

THERE'S NOTHING LIKE TRYING!

I KNOW I HAVEN'T HAD ANY EXPERIENCE, SIR, BUT STILL, I THINK I'D MAKE A GOOD REPORTER.

SORRY, FELLA! CAN'T USE YOU!

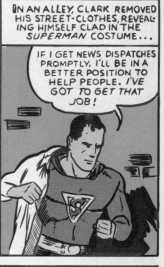

IN AN ALLEY, CLARK REMOVED HIS STREET-CLOTHES, REVEALING HIMSELF CLAD IN THE *SUPERMAN* COSTUME...

IF I GET NEWS DISPATCHES PROMPTLY, I'LL BE IN A BETTER POSITION TO HELP PEOPLE. I'VE GOT TO GET THAT JOB!

SUPERMAN LAUNCHES HIMSELF UP ALONG THE SIDE OF THE BUILDING IN A GREAT LEAP!

WITHIN THE EDITOR'S OFFICE...

WHAT'S THAT? A MOB ATTACKING THE COUNTY JAIL? *COVER THAT STORY!*

HM-M! SOUNDS LIKE MY BIG CHANCE TO IMPRESS THE EDITOR!

HERE'S HOPING I GET THERE ON TIME!

THAT VERY MOMENT...BEFORE THE COUNTY JAIL...

GET 'IM!

LYNCH TH' DIRTY DOG!

JAIL

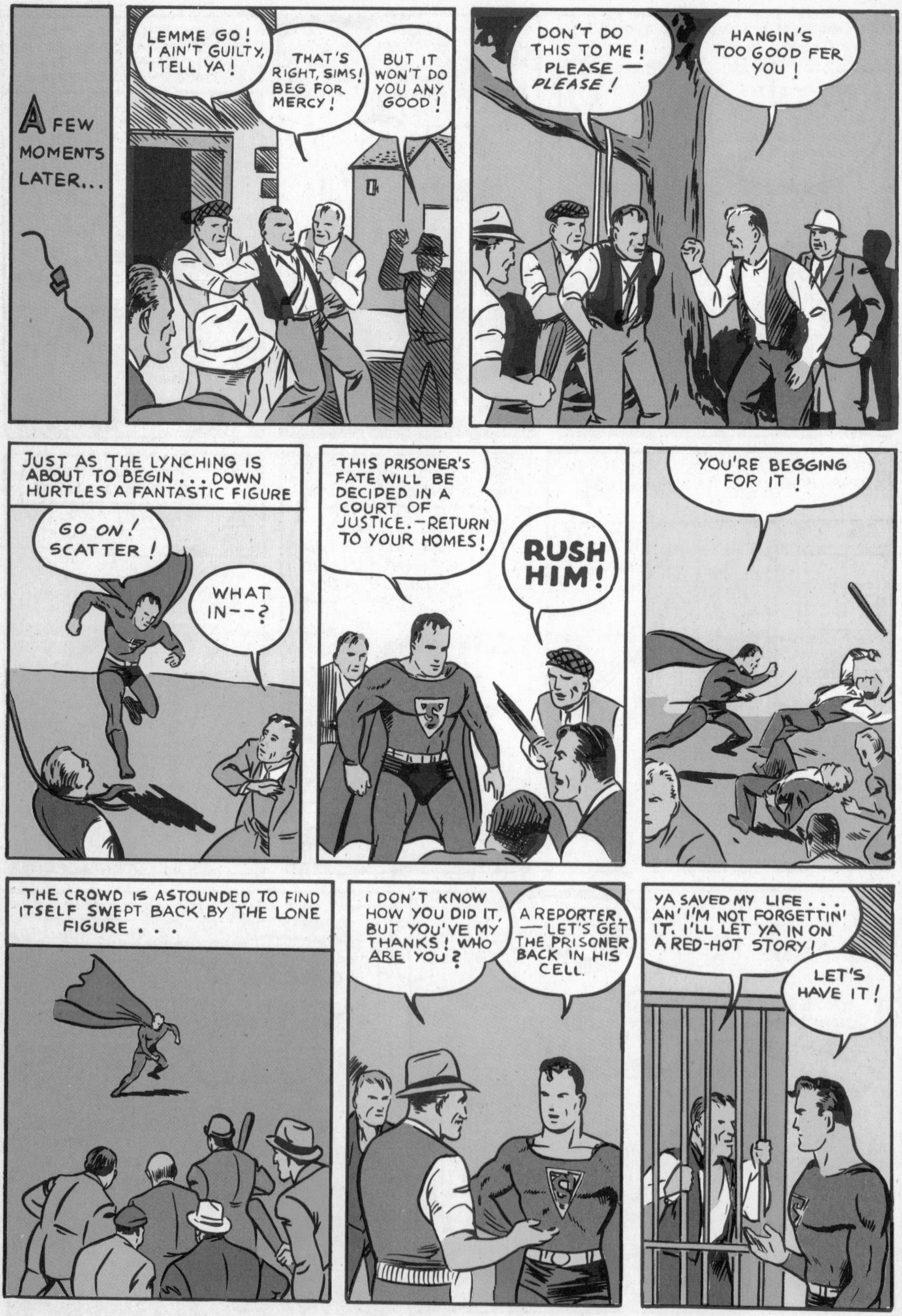

A FEW MOMENTS LATER...
LEMME GO! I AIN'T GUILTY, I TELL YA!
THAT'S RIGHT, SIMS! BEG FOR MERCY!
BUT IT WON'T DO YOU ANY GOOD!
DON'T DO THIS TO ME! PLEASE — PLEASE!
HANGIN'S TOO GOOD FER YOU!
JUST AS THE LYNCHING IS ABOUT TO BEGIN ... DOWN HURTLES A FANTASTIC FIGURE
GO ON! SCATTER!
WHAT IN--?
THIS PRISONER'S FATE WILL BE DECIDED IN A COURT OF JUSTICE.—RETURN TO YOUR HOMES!
RUSH HIM!
YOU'RE BEGGING FOR IT!
THE CROWD IS ASTOUNDED TO FIND ITSELF SWEPT BACK BY THE LONE FIGURE . . .
I DON'T KNOW HOW YOU DID IT, BUT YOU'VE MY THANKS! WHO ARE YOU?
A REPORTER. — LET'S GET THE PRISONER BACK IN HIS CELL.
YA SAVED MY LIFE . . . AN' I'M NOT FORGETTIN' IT. I'LL LET YA IN ON A RED-HOT STORY!
LET'S HAVE IT!

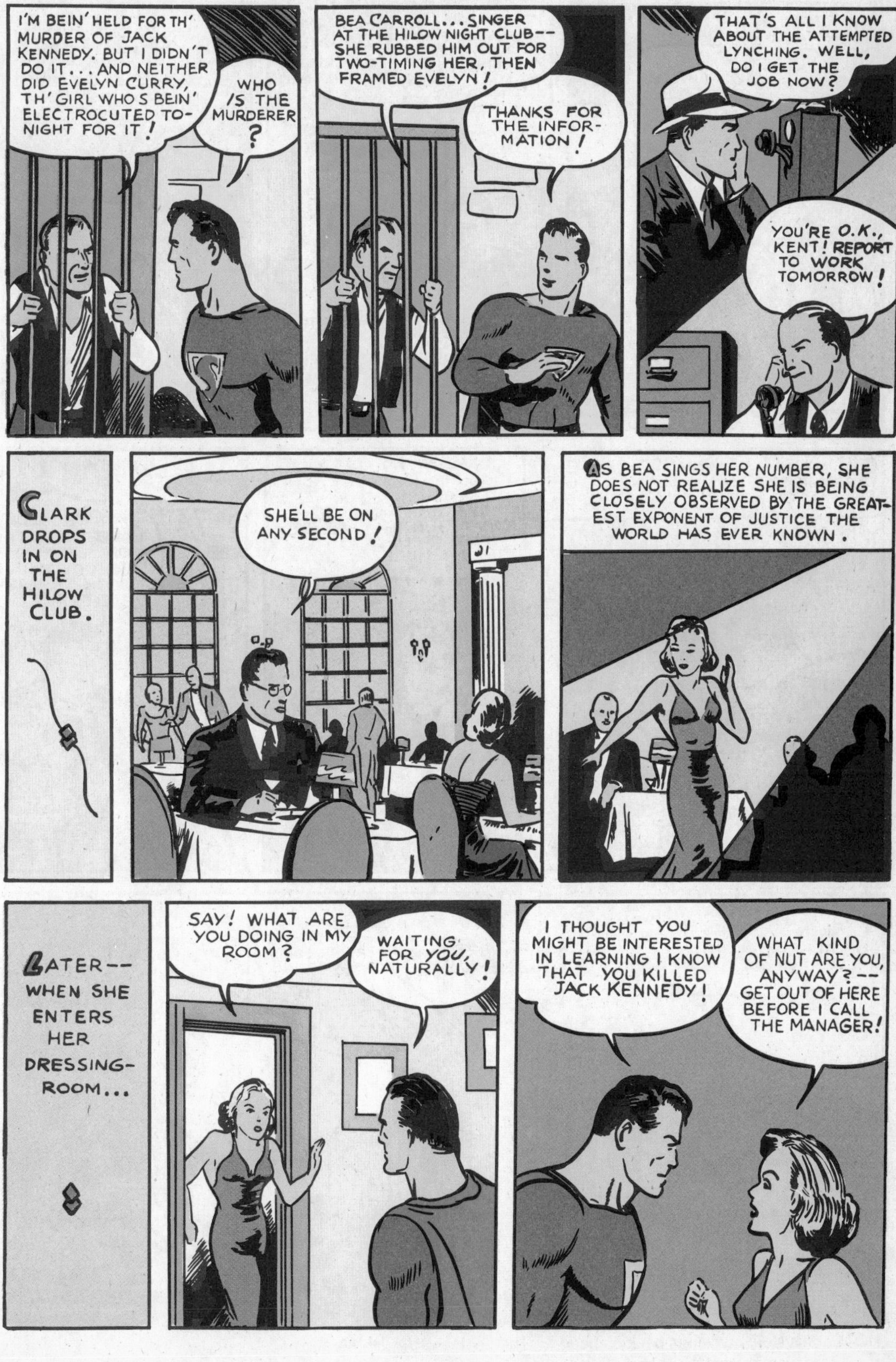
I'M BEIN' HELD FOR TH' MURDER OF JACK KENNEDY. BUT I DIDN'T DO IT... AND NEITHER DID EVELYN CURRY, TH' GIRL WHO'S BEIN' ELECTROCUTED TO-NIGHT FOR IT!
WHO IS THE MURDERER?
BEA CARROLL... SINGER AT THE HILOW NIGHT CLUB-- SHE RUBBED HIM OUT FOR TWO-TIMING HER, THEN FRAMED EVELYN!
THANKS FOR THE INFORMATION!
THAT'S ALL I KNOW ABOUT THE ATTEMPTED LYNCHING. WELL, DO I GET THE JOB NOW?
YOU'RE O.K., KENT! REPORT TO WORK TOMORROW!
CLARK DROPS IN ON THE HILOW CLUB.
SHE'LL BE ON ANY SECOND!
AS BEA SINGS HER NUMBER, SHE DOES NOT REALIZE SHE IS BEING CLOSELY OBSERVED BY THE GREATEST EXPONENT OF JUSTICE THE WORLD HAS EVER KNOWN.
LATER-- WHEN SHE ENTERS HER DRESSING-ROOM...
SAY! WHAT ARE YOU DOING IN MY ROOM?
WAITING FOR YOU, NATURALLY!
I THOUGHT YOU MIGHT BE INTERESTED IN LEARNING I KNOW THAT YOU KILLED JACK KENNEDY!
WHAT KIND OF NUT ARE YOU, ANYWAY?-- GET OUT OF HERE BEFORE I CALL THE MANAGER!

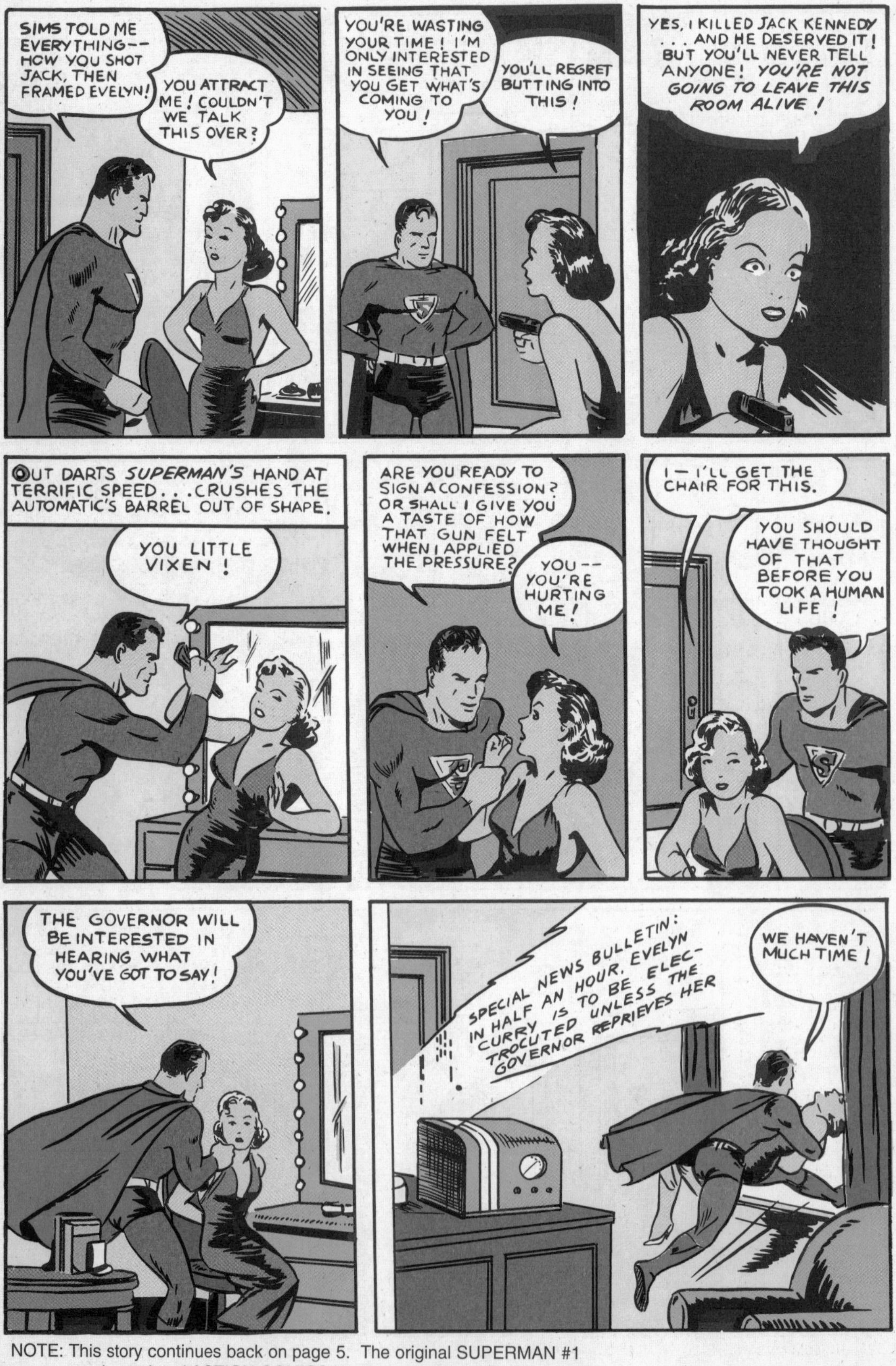
SIMS TOLD ME EVERYTHING-- HOW YOU SHOT JACK, THEN FRAMED EVELYN!
YOU ATTRACT ME! COULDN'T WE TALK THIS OVER?
YOU'RE WASTING YOUR TIME! I'M ONLY INTERESTED IN SEEING THAT YOU GET WHAT'S COMING TO YOU!
YOU'LL REGRET BUTTING INTO THIS!
YES, I KILLED JACK KENNEDY . . . AND HE DESERVED IT! BUT YOU'LL NEVER TELL ANYONE! YOU'RE NOT GOING TO LEAVE THIS ROOM ALIVE!
OUT DARTS SUPERMAN'S HAND AT TERRIFIC SPEED. . .CRUSHES THE AUTOMATIC'S BARREL OUT OF SHAPE.
YOU LITTLE VIXEN!
ARE YOU READY TO SIGN A CONFESSION? OR SHALL I GIVE YOU A TASTE OF HOW THAT GUN FELT WHEN I APPLIED THE PRESSURE?
YOU-- YOU'RE HURTING ME!
I-- I'LL GET THE CHAIR FOR THIS.
YOU SHOULD HAVE THOUGHT OF THAT BEFORE YOU TOOK A HUMAN LIFE!
THE GOVERNOR WILL BE INTERESTED IN HEARING WHAT YOU'VE GOT TO SAY!
SPECIAL NEWS BULLETIN: IN HALF AN HOUR, EVELYN CURRY IS TO BE ELECTROCUTED UNLESS THE GOVERNOR REPRIEVES HER
WE HAVEN'T MUCH TIME!

NOTE: This story continues back on page 5. The original SUPERMAN #1 comic reprinted ACTION COMICS #1-4, except for these preceding four pages which were all new.

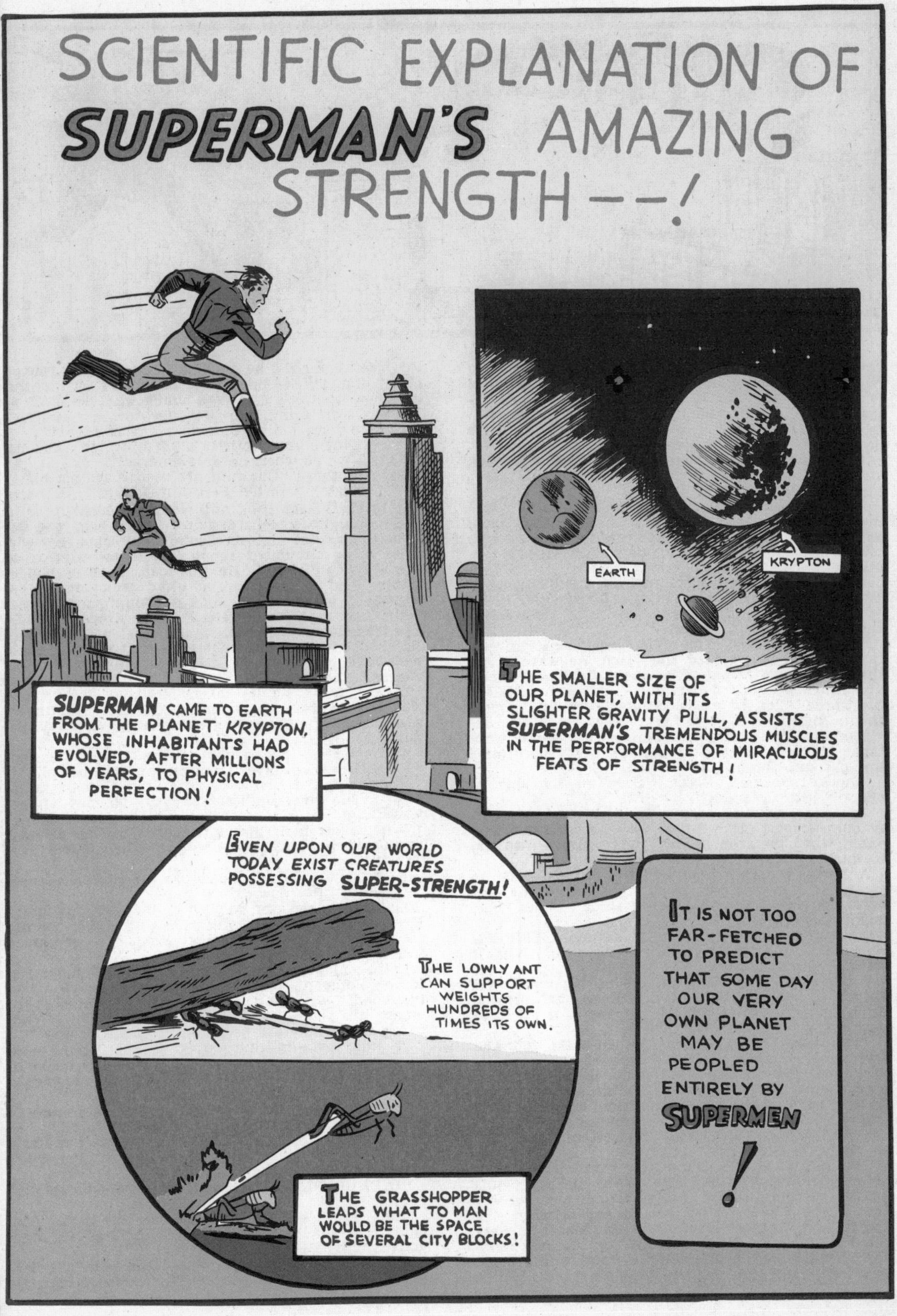

SCIENTIFIC EXPLANATION OF SUPERMAN'S AMAZING STRENGTH --!
SUPERMAN CAME TO EARTH FROM THE PLANET KRYPTON, WHOSE INHABITANTS HAD EVOLVED, AFTER MILLIONS OF YEARS, TO PHYSICAL PERFECTION!
EARTH
KRYPTON
THE SMALLER SIZE OF OUR PLANET, WITH ITS SLIGHTER GRAVITY PULL, ASSISTS SUPERMAN'S TREMENDOUS MUSCLES IN THE PERFORMANCE OF MIRACULOUS FEATS OF STRENGTH!
EVEN UPON OUR WORLD TODAY EXIST CREATURES POSSESSING SUPER-STRENGTH!
THE LOWLY ANT CAN SUPPORT WEIGHTS HUNDREDS OF TIMES ITS OWN.
THE GRASSHOPPER LEAPS WHAT TO MAN WOULD BE THE SPACE OF SEVERAL CITY BLOCKS!
IT IS NOT TOO FAR-FETCHED TO PREDICT THAT SOME DAY OUR VERY OWN PLANET MAY BE PEOPLED ENTIRELY BY SUPERMEN!

SUPERMAN

by JERRY SIEGEL AND JOE SHUSTER

SMASHED desks, overturned filing cabinets, strewn plaster, gaping holes in the walls, shining steel fixtures drooping in sad caricature of their former modernistic splendor, greeted the startled Detective Sergeant's eyes, as he swung open the office door to the firm *Harvey Brown, Patent Attorney*

A quivering wreck of a man arose from the floor, stridently shrieked, "He can't do this to me! Get him! Arrest him!"

Sergeant Blake surveyed the fellow's torn clothing, mussed hair, and blackened eyes, then once again speechlessly regarded the carnage in the room. "What in blazes has happened here?" he roared, finding his voice at last, "A cyclone?"

"Cyclone, nothing!" exclaimed the trembling man. "Worse! I've just had a visit from SUPERMAN!"

"SUPERMAN!" The word burst from Blake's lips with the force of an explosion.

"Yes! He claimed I've stolen my clients' inventions. After he wrecked the place, he warned me that if I didn't go out of business, he'd come back and finish the job! I demand . . . " Brown halted his tirade. The Detective Sergeant was no longer in the room.

The remaining members of the riot squad were taken aback to see their superior officer come hurtling out into the hall at full tilt.

"Quick!" shouted Blake. "Seen anyone since I charged into the room?"

"No one," volunteered a puzzled officer. "That is, no one except a guy wearing a strange costume who asked what the trouble was, then stepped into the elevator."

A howl of baffled rage left the Sergeant as he sprang to the wall and desperately jabbed the elevator button. "Fools!" he roared. "That was SUPERMAN!"

Concerted cries left the policemen. "SUPERMAN! . . . and he's in that elevator! . . . What'll we do?"

Blake seized the hand of one of his men, and shoved it against the button. "Keep that pressed down for a full three minutes, Mooney—or I'll have your badge.—You others, come with me!"

Toward the nearby stairway dashed Blake, followed by his men. As they clattered down at top speed, he explained, "Fortunately, the elevator is automatically operated by the push-buttons on the various floors. As long as Mooney presses the button, SUPERMAN is trapped. And when the three minutes are up, and the Man of Steel gets off at the bottom floor, we'll be ready for him!"

Two minutes later found the policemen ranged before the first floor entrance to the elevator, guns out, all eyes strained on the indicator which showed that the car was stalled somewhere between the second and the first floor. Triumph blazed in Sergeant Blake's eyes. Visions of a pat on the back from the Commissioner, a promotion in rank, and a boost in salary, dangled tantalizingly in his mind.

"Careful, men!" he warned the officers grouped about him. "We've prayed for this break for months. and now that it's come, we don't want to muff it. He was seen going into that elevator . . . and he's bound to come out of that door any moment!"

"And *that's* what bothers me," muttered someone. "What'll we do when he *does* emerge?"

Said another "Our guns are useless against him!"

"Nonsense!" retorted Sergeant Blake. "All we've got to do is keep cool, and we've got him!"

But his glib comeback didn't satisfy even the Detective Sergeant himself. There were some very wild tales being circulated about this fellow who called himself SUPERMAN. He was said to be a modern Robin Hood . . . a person who had dedicated his existence to assisting the weak and oppressed. It was whispered that he possessed super-strength, could lift tremendous weights, smash steel with his bare hands, jump over buildings, and that nothing could penetrate his amazingly super-tough skin. But, of course, pondered the Sergeant, these were mere rumors, fantastic fairy tales. Probably SUPERMAN was just an ordinary person whose better than average strength had been immensely exaggerated Without a doubt!

Nevertheless, the hardboiled cop couldn't prevent an apprehensive shiver from creeping up his spine!

Suddenly, the arrow on the indicator began to move. The three minutes were up! Mooney had released the button, and the elevator was descending!

With a clash of metal the door to the elevator swung open. Fingers tensed on gun-triggers . . . Then . . .

A hesitant, alarmed voice broke the electric silence: "My word! Put down those guns!"

Out of the elevator stepped a slim, nervous figure. Meek eyes blinked fearfully behind thick-rimmed glasses. No SUPERMAN, this! Rather, a very much frightened young man.

From somewhere behind him, the dumbfounded Detective Sergeant heard a smothered titter. His face reddened. "Where's SUPERMAN?" he shouted at the mouse-like young man who stood before him. "What in all that's holy are *you* doing in that elevator?"

"I was just—er—descending to the lobby, when something apparently went wrong with the mechanism. I'll admit I was terrified for a few moments, but . . . "

"Answer me!" thundered Blake. "Did you see a man in a strange uniform in that elevator?"

"No one at all . . . that is, except myself. I'm afraid there must be some mistake, Sergeant. I'm Clark Kent, reporter on the *Daily Star*."

"But SUPERMAN was seen to enter the elevator by one of my men How do you explain that?"

Clark shrugged. "It's beyond me," he said. "Possibly your man was high-strung, or had an over-active imagination"

A loud laugh went up at this. The Detective Sergeant whirled to face his men, his features registering keen disappointment. "I guess it was just a false alarm, at that! Let's head back for headquarters, to turn in a report."

"I say, that's odd!" interrupted Kent. "I was just about to go to Police Headquarters myself, in search of a story. Do you mind if I accompany you?"

Later, as they sped through the streets with the squad car, Clark learned that people adjoining Brown's office had telephoned for a police car, complaining of a terrific rumpus going on in the Patent Attorney's office . . . and how Blake had expected SUPERMAN to emerge from the elevator.

"Very amusing," chuckled Clark. "It'll make a good feature article for the *Daily Star*."

"Hold on!" bellowed Blake in protest. "You can't print that. It would make me look like a sap!—Don't print it! And maybe some day I'll return the favor!"

The reporter shrugged. "Well, if you feel that strongly about it, I'll forget the yarn . . . temporarily."

The conversation was cut short as they parked before the police station. As they emerged from the car, an officer rushed up and exclaimed to Blake. "Have you heard? 'Biff' Dugan has just been captured!"

A happy grin quickly chased the glum expression from the Detective Sergeant's face. "'Biff' was a long-sought murderer who had been eluding the law for months. "I knew we'd catch up with that rat," Blake chuckled.

Swift strides hurried Blake and Kent into the station. A few moments later the prisoner, an ugly hulking brute who sullenly refused to talk, stood before them.

"Thought you could evade the law, did you?" demanded the Sergeant. "Well, maybe you know better now!"

Clark tugged at Blake's sleeve. "Remember, Sergeant? You offered to do me a favor. I'd like to take you up, now!"

Suspiciously, Blake inquired: "What?"

"Allow me to interview the prisoner in private."

"And what," asked Blake, "is wrong with interviewing him right here in front of me?"

"You can see he's in no mood to talk. Perhaps if I could speak to him alone . . . "

"Are you looney? It's against regulations. It's . . . "

Clark smiled tauntingly. "If I can't have this interview, I'll have to write up a certain other story One about a dumb Detective Sergeant who had his men surround an elevator in the hope . . . "

"Wait!" cried Blake. "You can have that interview!" He added ominously. "But if anything happens to the prisoner, you'll be held personally responsible."

Shortly later, within an adjoining room, Clark was occupied with the task of prying replies from a glum prisoner when there came a knocking at the room's door.

Bart turned from the prisoner. Opened the door slightly.

It was Blake. He demanded: "Is the prisoner still there?"

"Naturally," replied Clark, exasperated. "See for yours . . . " Abruptly Kent's words were choked off in a gasp of astonishment. Alarmed, the Sergeant burst into the room. In one glance he saw the reporter's hand pointing toward an open window . . . and no sight of Dugan anywhere.

"He's escaped!" exclaimed Clark.

Sergeant Blake roared with rage, seized the frail reporter, and shook him angrily. "You—!" he choked. "It's *your* fault! This makes you an accessory to the fact!"

The Detective Sergeant will never completely remember what happened just then. One moment he was shaking a fear-struck reporter, and the next instant he was whirling up into the air, as though caught in the grip of a hurricane. Next instant, he struck the wall, uttered a groan, and lapsed into unconsciousness.

Clark Kent looked at the Sergeant's recumbent figure, muttered, "Sorry, but I haven't time to use

kid gloves," then, with amazing rapidity he stripped off his glasses and outer garments, revealing himself clad in a weird close-fitting costume, and flaring cape. In this apparel, it was apparent that he really possessed a fine physique of breathtaking symmetry.

One lithe leap brought him to the window-sill. There he poised momentarily, while his keen telescopic vision surveyed the vicinity. And then, as he sighted the figure of "Biff" scrambling into a parked auto, he dived out into space.

Out—out—sped the fantastic figure . . . its mighty muscles launching it across an incredible distance. The auto was a full three hundred yards away, but SUPERMAN smashed down into the gravel before it, just as the car's gears clashed and it leapt ahead.

Within the car, Dugan snarled. This solitary figure which had hurtled down from nowhere . . . it alone stood between him and escape. He pressed the accelerator down to the limit, with the intention of smashing into the body, crushing it beneath his auto's wheels.

He struck the figure with a *crash!* But then, the impossible happened! Instead of being flung beneath the wheels, SUPERMAN held his ground . . . actually kept the roaring machine from moving!

Astounded by this miracle, "Biff" threw the clutch into reverse, but again he was treated to an exhibition of super-strength. Having seized the front bumper, the Man of Steel prevented the automobile from backing up!

A shriek of sheer horror tore from Dugan's throat. Frenziedly, he flung open the door of the automobile, sprang out . . . and looked up to find himself faced by SUPERMAN'S grim figure!

Half mad with fright he leapt at the Man of Tomorrow, seeking to fight his way past. But it was like bucking against a stone wall. His fists encountered flesh as hard as metal, fracturing his knuckles!

Suddenly "Biff" was possessed with but one desire. To flee . . . to get away from this indestructible demon of wrath! He whirled, raced off with all his might, screeching at the top of his lungs. Next instant, arms of steel encircled him from behind. There was a pressure at the back of his neck. Then . . . unconsciousness. . .

———◆———

SERGEANT Blake revived to find Clark Kent kneeling beside him. He felt his forehead groggily, then suddenly remembering what had occurred, seized the reporter. "You're under arrest!" he shouted.

"What for?" inquired Kent.

"For aiding 'Biff' Dugan to escape, that's why! And . . . "

Clark pointed to a figure huddled on the floor nearby. "Before you say any more, look over there!"

Blake looked, blinked uncomprehendingly, then exclaimed: "Dugan!—But how . . . ?"

"All I know," replied Clark, "is that a man wearing a strange costume jumped to the window-sill, tossed 'Biff' in, then leapt away."

The Detective Sergeant sprang erect. "Do you realize who that must have been! SUPERMAN!"

Clark's eyes widened. "Gosh! I guess you're right!"

"You know," grudgingly admitted Sergeant Blake, "sometimes I think SUPERMAN isn't such a bad guy, at that. But," he hastily amended, "don't think that doesn't mean I won't arrest him the minute I get my hands on him!"

"Let's hope you get within reaching distance," said Clark Kent.

Detective Sergeant Blake cast a quick suspicious glance at the reporter. For a moment he'd fancied he had detected a trace of mockery in Kent's voice. But Clark's visage was completely solemn.

THE END

Boys and Girls: *Meet the creators of the one and only* **SUPERMAN**—*America's Greatest Adventure Strip!*

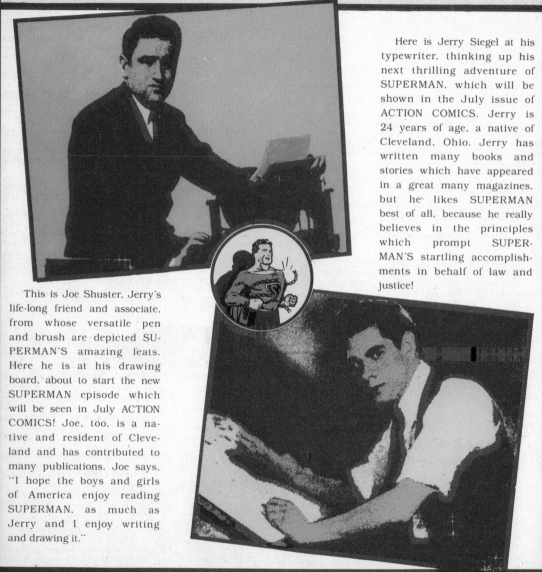

Here is Jerry Siegel at his typewriter, thinking up his next thrilling adventure of SUPERMAN, which will be shown in the July issue of ACTION COMICS. Jerry is 24 years of age, a native of Cleveland, Ohio. Jerry has written many books and stories which have appeared in a great many magazines, but he likes SUPERMAN best of all, because he really believes in the principles which prompt SUPERMAN'S startling accomplishments in behalf of law and justice!

This is Joe Shuster, Jerry's life-long friend and associate, from whose versatile pen and brush are depicted SUPERMAN'S amazing feats. Here he is at his drawing board, about to start the new SUPERMAN episode which will be seen in July ACTION COMICS! Joe, too, is a native and resident of Cleveland and has contributed to many publications. Joe says, "I hope the boys and girls of America enjoy reading SUPERMAN, as much as Jerry and I enjoy writing and drawing it."

JERRY SIEGEL *and* **JOE SHUSTER** *are also the creators of* "*Slam Bradley*" *and* "*Spy*" *which appear in* DETECTIVE COMICS; "*Radio Squad*" *which appears in* MORE FUN COMICS; *and* "*Federal Men*" *which appears monthly in* ADVENTURE COMICS.

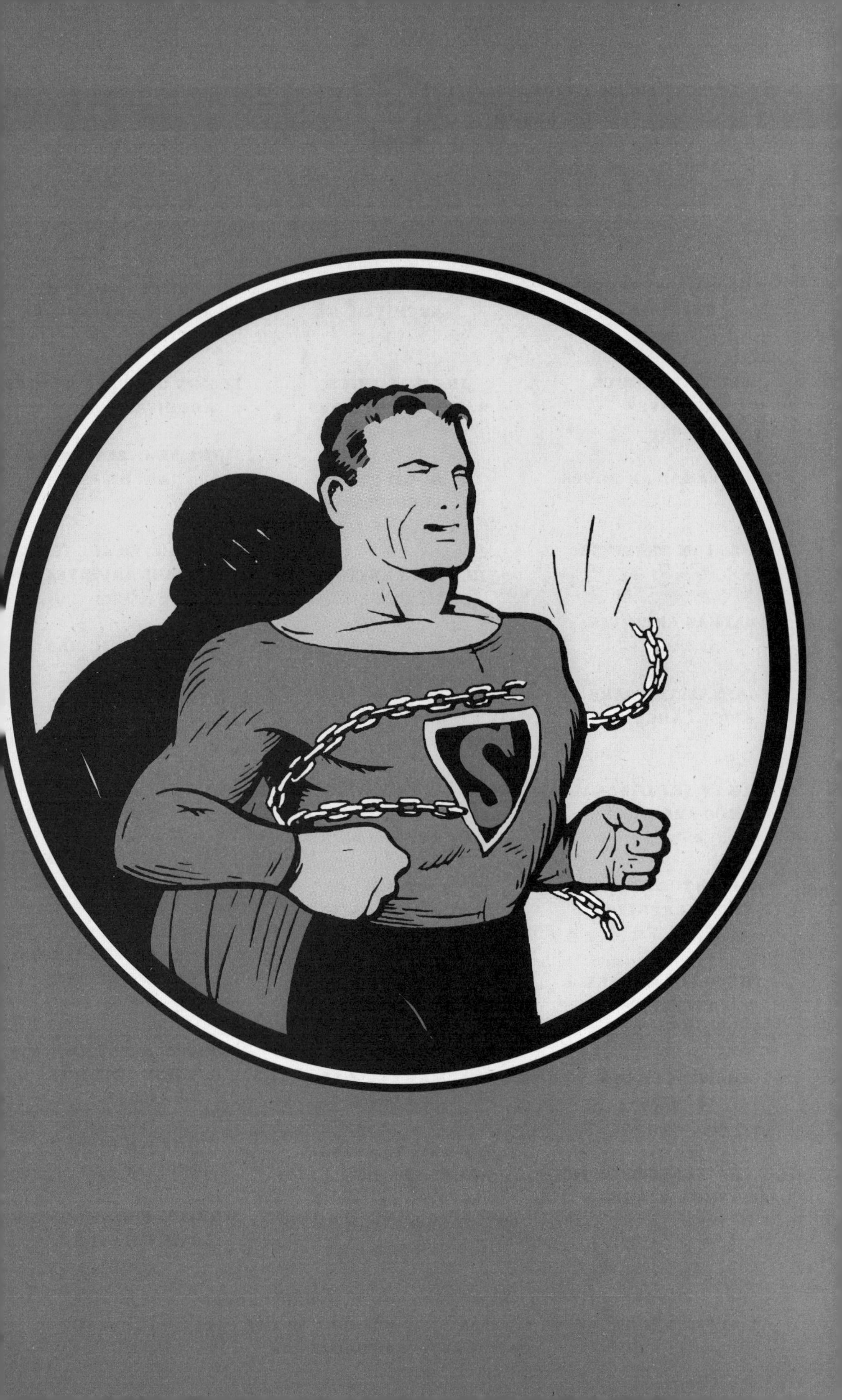

MORE CLASSIC TALES OF THE MAN OF STEEL

SUPERMAN:
THE MAN OF STEEL
VOLS. 1 - 6

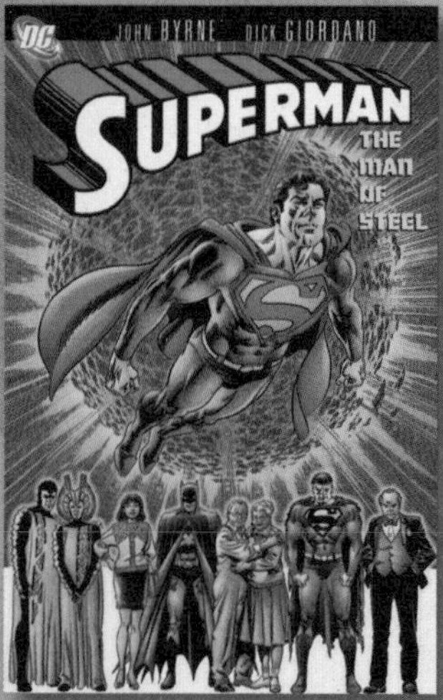
JOHN BYRNE · DICK GIORDANO
SUPERMAN
THE man OF STEEL

JOHN BYRNE

SUPERMAN:
BIRTHRIGHT

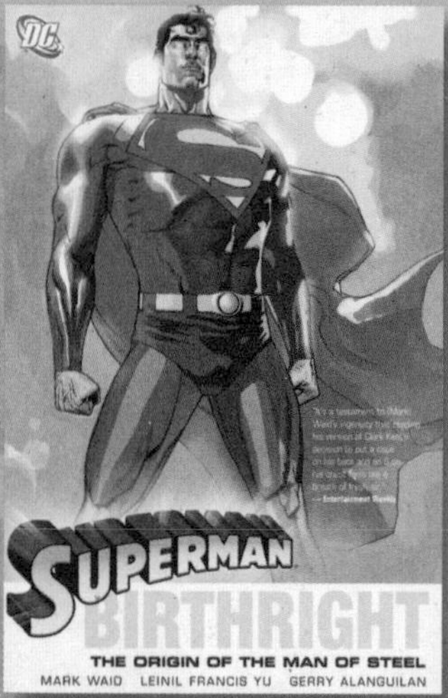
SUPERMAN
BIRTHRIGHT
THE ORIGIN OF THE MAN OF STEEL
MARK WAID LEINIL FRANCIS YU GERRY ALANGUILAN

MARK WAID
LEINIL YU

SUPERMAN:
CAMELOT FALLS
VOLS. 1 - 2

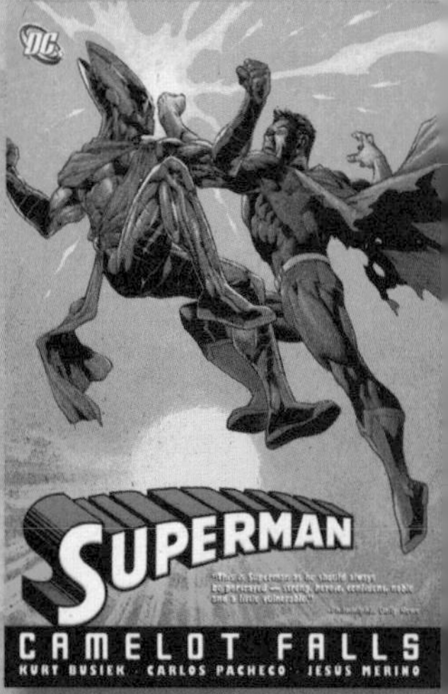
SUPERMAN
CAMELOT FALLS
KURT BUSIEK · CARLOS PACHECO · JESUS MERINO

KURT BUSIEK
CARLOS PACHECO

SUPERMAN:
OUR WORLDS AT WAR

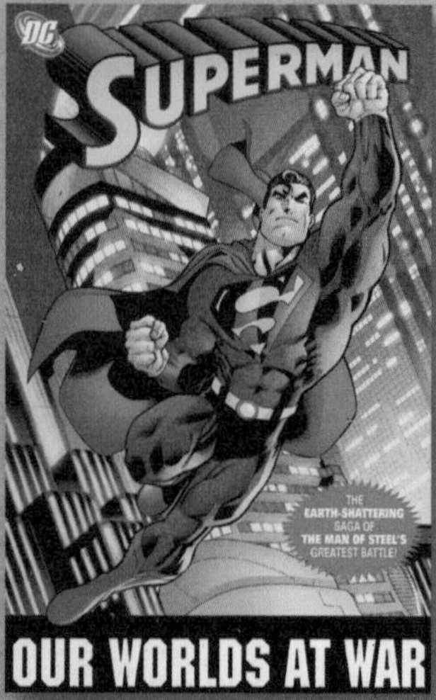
SUPERMAN
THE EARTH-SHATTERING SAGA OF THE MAN OF STEEL'S GREATEST BATTLE!
OUR WORLDS AT WAR

VARIOUS
WRITERS & ARTISTS

SUPERMAN:
RED SON

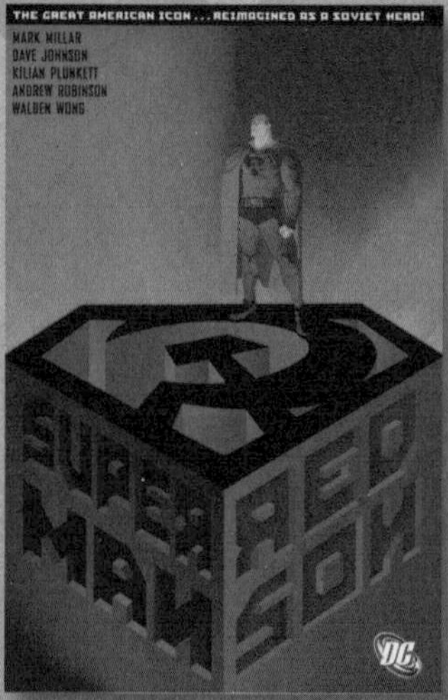
THE GREAT AMERICAN ICON... REIMAGINED AS A SOVIET HERO!
MARK MILLAR
DAVE JOHNSON
KILIAN PLUNKETT
ANDREW ROBINSON
WALDEN WONG

MARK MILLAR
DAVE JOHNSON
KILLIAN PLUNKETT

SUPERMAN:
SECRET IDENTITY

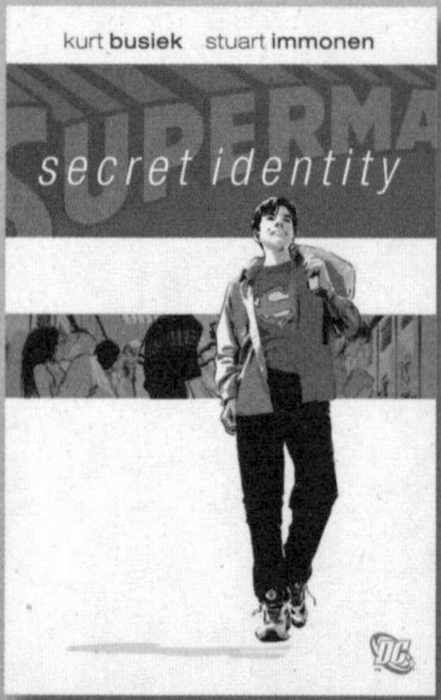
kurt busiek stuart immonen
secret identity

KURT BUSIEK
STUART IMMONEN

SEARCH THE GRAPHIC NOVELS SECTION OF
DCCOMICS.COM
FOR ART AND INFORMATION ON ALL OF OUR BOOKS!